FORMER PEOPLE

ALSO BY DOUGLAS SMITH

Working the Rough Stone
Love and Conquest
The Pearl

Douglas Smith

FORMER PEOPLE

The Last Days of the Russian Aristocracy

MACMILLAN

First published 2012 by Farrar, Straus & Giroux, New York

First published in Great Britain 2012 by Macmillan
an imprint of Pan Macmillan, a division of Macmillan Publishers Limited
Pan Macmillan, 20 New Wharf Road, London N1 9RR
Basingstoke and Oxford
Associated companies throughout the world
www.panmacmillan.com

ISBN 978-0-230-74906-1

1 3 5 7 9 8 6 4 2

A CIP catalogue record for this book is available from
the British Library.

Printed and bound by CPI Group (UK) Ltd, Croydon, CR0 4YY

Visit **www.panmacmillan.com** to read more about all our books
and to buy them. You will also find features, author interviews and
news of any author events, and you can sign up for e-newsletters
so that you're always first to hear about our new releases.

TO EMMA AND ANDREW

There is no more Russian nobility. There is no more Russian aristocracy . . . A future historian will describe in precise detail how this class died. You will read this account, and you will experience madness and horror . . .

—*The Red Newspaper* (Petrograd),
No. 10, January 14, 1922

CONTENTS

NOTE ON DATES AND SPELLING

Before February 1918, Russia followed the Julian (Old Style) calendar that in the twentieth century was thirteen days behind the Gregorian (New Style) calendar used in the West. In January, the Bolshevik government decreed that Russia would adopt the Gregorian calendar at the end of the month; thus January 31, 1918, was followed the next day by February 14. I have chosen to give Old Style dates for events in Russia before January 31, 1918, and New Style after that; wherever there is a chance for any confusion, I have added the notations "O.S." or "N.S." A number of documents used in *Former People* are impossible to date with precision since some Russians continued to use the Julian calendar for years after 1918, and it is not always possible to know which system of dating has been used.

There is no universal standard for transliterating Russian names into English. For the sake of simplicity I have chosen the masculine ending for all surnames (Dolgoruky, not Dolgorukaya), except when the feminine form is well established in English. Difficulty is presented by the various ways members of the same family anglicize their names. "Голицын" appears with equal validity as "Golitsyn," "Galitzine," "Golitsin," "Galitsin," and "Golitzin." In such instances I have opted to use the Library of Congress transliteration format but have not silently changed spellings used in quotations. Although such an approach assures the greatest fidelity to the documents upon which *Former People* draws, it makes for some inconsistency.

PRINCIPAL FIGURES

THE SHEREMETEVS

Count Sergei Dmitrievich Sheremetev—"Count Sergei," "The count"
Countess Yekaterina Pavlovna Sheremetev (b. Vyazemsky), his wife—
 "Countess Yekaterina"

Their Children

Count Dmitry Sheremetev—"Dmitry"
 Countess Irina Sheremetev (b. Vorontsov-Dashkov), his wife—"Ira"
Count Pavel Sheremetev—"Pavel"
 Countess Praskovya Sheremetev (b. Obolensky), his wife—"Praskovya"
Count Boris Sheremetev—"Boris"
Countess Anna Sheremetev (m. Saburov)—"Anna"
 Alexander Saburov, her husband—"Alik"
Count Pyotr Sheremetev—"Pyotr"
 Countess Yelena Sheremetev (b. Meiendorff), his wife—"Lilya"
Count Sergei Sheremetev—"Sergei"
Countess Maria Sheremetev (m. Gudovich)—"Maria"
 Count Alexander Gudovich, her husband—"Alexander"

Their Grandchildren

Children of Dmitry and Irina Sheremetev

Countess Yelizaveta Sheremetev (m. Vyazemsky)—"Lili"
 Prince Boris Vyazemsky, her husband
Countess Irina—"Irina"
Count Sergei Sheremetev—"Sergei"
Countess Praskovya—"Praskovya"
Count Nikolai Sheremetev—"Nikolai"
Count Vasily Sheremetev—"Vasily"

Child of Pavel and Praskovya Sheremetev

Count Vasily Sheremetev—"Vasilik," "Vasily"

Children of Anna and Alexander Saburov

Boris Saburov—"Boris"
Xenia Saburov—"Xenia"
Georgy Saburov—"Yuri"

Children of Pyotr and Yelena Sheremetev

Count Boris Sheremetev—"Boris"
Count Nikolai Sheremetev—"Nikolai"
 Cecilia Mansurov, his wife—"Cecilia"
Countess Yelena Sheremetev (m. Golitsyn)—"Yelena"
 Prince Vladimir Golitsyn, her husband—"Vladimir"
Countess Natalya Sheremetev—"Natalya"
Count Pyotr Sheremetev—"Pyotr"
Countess Maria Sheremetev—"Maria"
Count Pavel Sheremetev—"Pavel"

Children of Maria and Alexander Gudovich

Countess Varvara Gudovich (m. Obolensky)—"Varvara," "Varenka"
 Prince Vladimir Obolensky, her husband—"Vladimir"
Count Dmitry Gudovich—"Dmitry"
Countess Maria Gudovich (m. Istomin, Lvov)—"Merinka"
 Pyotr Istomin, her first husband—"Pyotr"
 Sergei Lvov, her second husband—"Sergei"
Count Andrei Gudovich—"Andrei"

Count Alexander Dmitrievich Sheremetev—"Count Alexander"
    Countess Maria Fyodorovna Sheremetev (b. Geiden), his wife—
        "Countess Maria"

Their Children
Countess Yelizaveta Sheremetev—"Yelizaveta"
Count Dmitry Sheremetev—"Dmitry"
Countess Alexandra Sheremetev—"Alexandra"
Count Georgy Sheremetev—"Georgy"

THE GOLITSYNS

Prince Vladimir Mikhailovich Golitsyn—"The mayor"
Princess Sofia Nikolaevna Golitsyn (b. Delianov), his wife—"Sofia"

Their Children

Prince Mikhail Golitsyn—"Mikhail"
    Princess Anna Golitsyn (b. Lopukhin), his wife—"Anna"
Prince Nikolai Golitsyn—"Nikolai"
    Princess Maria Golitsyn (b. Sverbeev), his wife
Princess Sofia Golitsyn (m. Lvov)—"Sonya"
    Konstantin Lvov, her husband
Prince Alexander Golitsyn—"Alexander"
    Princess Lyubov Golitsyn (b. Glebov), his wife—"Lyubov"
Princess Vera Golitsyn (m. Bobrinsky)—"Vera"
    Count Lev Bobrinsky, her husband—"Lev"
Prince Vladimir Golitsyn—"Vladimir Vladimirovich"
    Princess Tatiana Golitsyn (b. Govorov), his wife—"Tatiana"
Princess Yelizaveta Golitsyn (m. Trubetskoy)—"Yelizaveta," "Eli"
    Prince Vladimir Trubetskoy, her husband—"Vladimir"
Princess Tatiana Golitsyn—"Tatiana"
    Pyotr Lopukhin, her husband

Their Grandchildren

Children of Mikhail and Anna Golitsyn
Princess Alexandra Golitsyn (m. Osorgin)—"Lina"
 Georgy Osorgin, her husband—"Georgy"
Prince Vladimir Golitsyn—"Vladimir"
 Countess Yelena Sheremetev, his wife—"Yelena"
Princess Sofia Golitsyn (m. Meyen)—"Sonya"
 Viktor Meyen, her husband—"Viktor"
Prince Sergei Golitsyn—"Sergei"
 Klavdia Bavykin, his wife—"Klavdia"
Princess Maria Golitsyn (m. Veselovsky)—"Masha"
 Vsevolod Veselovsky, her husband—"Vsevolod"
Princess Yekaterina Golitsyn—"Katya"

Child of Nikolai and Maria Golitsyn
Prince Kirill Golitsyn—"Kirill"
 Natalya Volkov, his wife—"Natalya"

Children of Alexander and Lyubov Golitsyn
Princess Olga Golitsyn—"Olga"
Princess Marina Golitsyn—"Marina"
Princess Natalya Golitsyn—"Natalya"
Prince Alexander Golitsyn—"Alexander"
Prince George Golitsyn—"George"

Children of Vera and Lev Bobrinsky
Countess Alexandra Bobrinsky (m. Baldwin)— "Alka"
 Philip Baldwin, her husband
Countess Sofia Bobrinsky (m. Witter)—"Sonya"
 Reginald Witter, her husband
Count Alexei Bobrinsky—"Alexei"
Countess Yelena Bobrinsky

Children of Vladimir Vladimirovich and Tatiana Golitsyn
Prince Alexander Golitsyn—"Alexander"
 Darya Krotov, his wife—"Darya"
Princess Yelena Golitsyn—"Yelena"

Princess Olga Golitsyn (m. Urusov)—"Olga"
    Prince Pyotr Urusov, her husband—"Pyotr"

Children of Yelizaveta (Eli) and Vladimir Trubetskoy
Prince Grigory Trubetskoy—"Grisha"
Princess Varvara Trubetskoy—"Varya"
Princess Alexandra Trubetskoy—"Tatya"
Prince Andrei Trubetskoy—"Andrei"
Princess Irina Trubetskoy—"Irina"
Prince Vladimir Trubetskoy—"Volodya"
Prince Sergei Trubetskoy—"Sergei"
Prince Georgy Trubetskoy—"Georgy"

Their Great-grandchildren

Children of Vladimir and Yelena Golitsyn (b. Sheremetev)
Yelena Golitsyn (m. Trubetskoy)—"Yelena"
    Andrei Trubetskoy, her husband
Mikhail Golitsyn—"Mishka"
Illarion Golitsyn—"Lariusha"

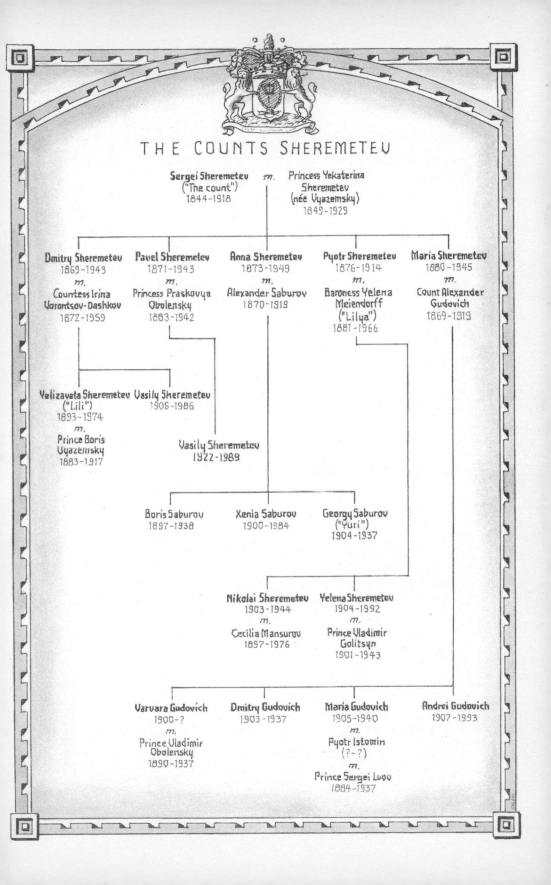

THE COUNTS SHEREMETEV

Sergei Sheremetev
("The count")
1844–1918

m.

Princess Yekaterina
Sheremetev
(née Vyazemsky)
1849–1929

Dmitry Sheremetev
1869–1943
m.
Countess Irina
Vorontsov-Dashkov
1872–1959

Pavel Sheremetev
1871–1943
m.
Princess Praskovya
Obolensky
1883–1942

Anna Sheremetev
1873–1949
m.
Alexander Saburov
1870–1919

Pyotr Sheremetev
1876–1914
m.
Baroness Yelena
Meiendorff
("Lilya")
1881–1966

Maria Sheremetev
1880–1945
m.
Count Alexander
Gudovich
1869–1919

Yelizaveta Sheremetev
("Lili")
1893–1974
m.
Prince Boris
Vyazemsky
1883–1917

Vasily Sheremetev
1906–1986

Vasily Sheremetev
1922–1989

Boris Saburov
1897–1938

Xenia Saburov
1900–1984

Georgy Saburov
("Yuri")
1904–1937

Nikolai Sheremetev
1903–1944
m.
Cecilia Mansurov
1897–1976

Yelena Sheremetev
1904–1992
m.
Prince Vladimir
Golitsyn
1901–1943

Varvara Gudovich
1900–?
m.
Prince Vladimir
Obolensky
1890–1937

Dmitry Gudovich
1903–1937

Maria Gudovich
1905–1940
m.
Pyotr Istomin
(?–?)
m.
Prince Sergei Lvov
1884–1937

Andrei Gudovich
1907–1993

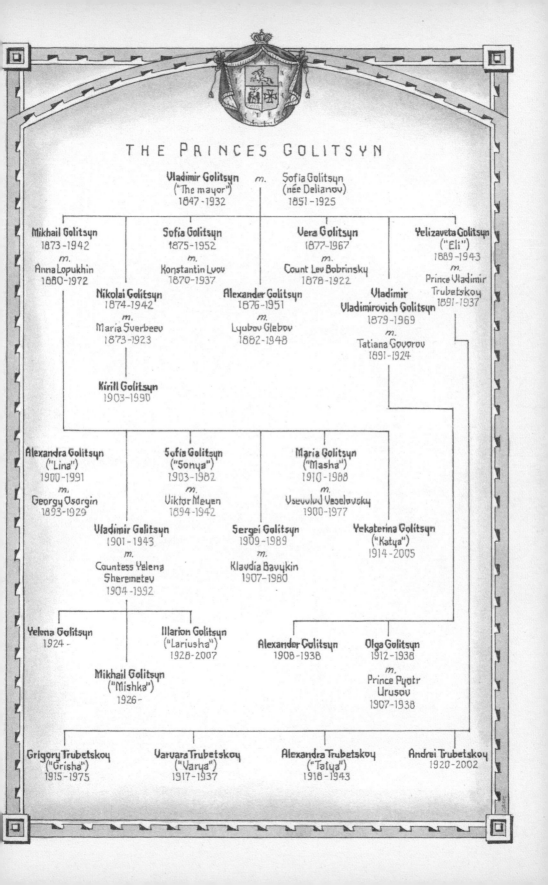

THE PRINCES GOLITSYN

Vladimir Golitsyn ("The mayor") 1847-1932 — m. — **Sofia Golitsyn** (née Delianov) 1851-1925

Mikhail Golitsyn 1873-1942
m.
Anna Lopukhin 1880-1972

Sofia Golitsyn 1875-1952
m.
Konstantin Lvov 1870-1937

Vera Golitsyn 1877-1967
m.
Count Lev Bobrinsky 1878-1922

Yelizaveta Golitsyn ("Eli") 1889-1943
m.
Prince Vladimir Trubetskoy 1891-1937

Nikolai Golitsyn 1874-1942
m.
Maria Sverbeev 1873-1923

Alexander Golitsyn 1876-1951
m.
Lyubov Glebov 1882-1948

Vladimir Vladimirovich Golitsyn 1879-1969
m.
Tatiana Govorov 1891-1924

Kirill Golitsyn 1903-1990

Alexandra Golitsyn ("Lina") 1900-1991
m.
Georgy Osorgin 1893-1929

Sofia Golitsyn ("Sonya") 1903-1982
m.
Viktor Meyen 1894-1942

Maria Golitsyn ("Masha") 1910-1988
m.
Vsevolod Veselovsky 1900-1977

Vladimir Golitsyn 1901-1943
m.
Countess Yelena Sheremetev 1904-1992

Sergei Golitsyn 1909-1989
m.
Klavdia Bavykin 1907-1980

Yekaterina Golitsyn ("Katya") 1914-2005

Yelena Golitsyn 1924-

Illarion Golitsyn ("Lariusha") 1928-2007

Alexander Golitsyn 1908-1938

Olga Golitsyn 1912-1938
m.
Prince Pyotr Urusov 1907-1938

Mikhail Golitsyn ("Mishka") 1926-

Grigory Trubetskoy ("Grisha") 1915-1975

Varvara Trubetskoy ("Varya") 1917-1937

Alexandra Trubetskoy ("Tatya") 1918-1943

Andrei Trubetskoy 1920-2002

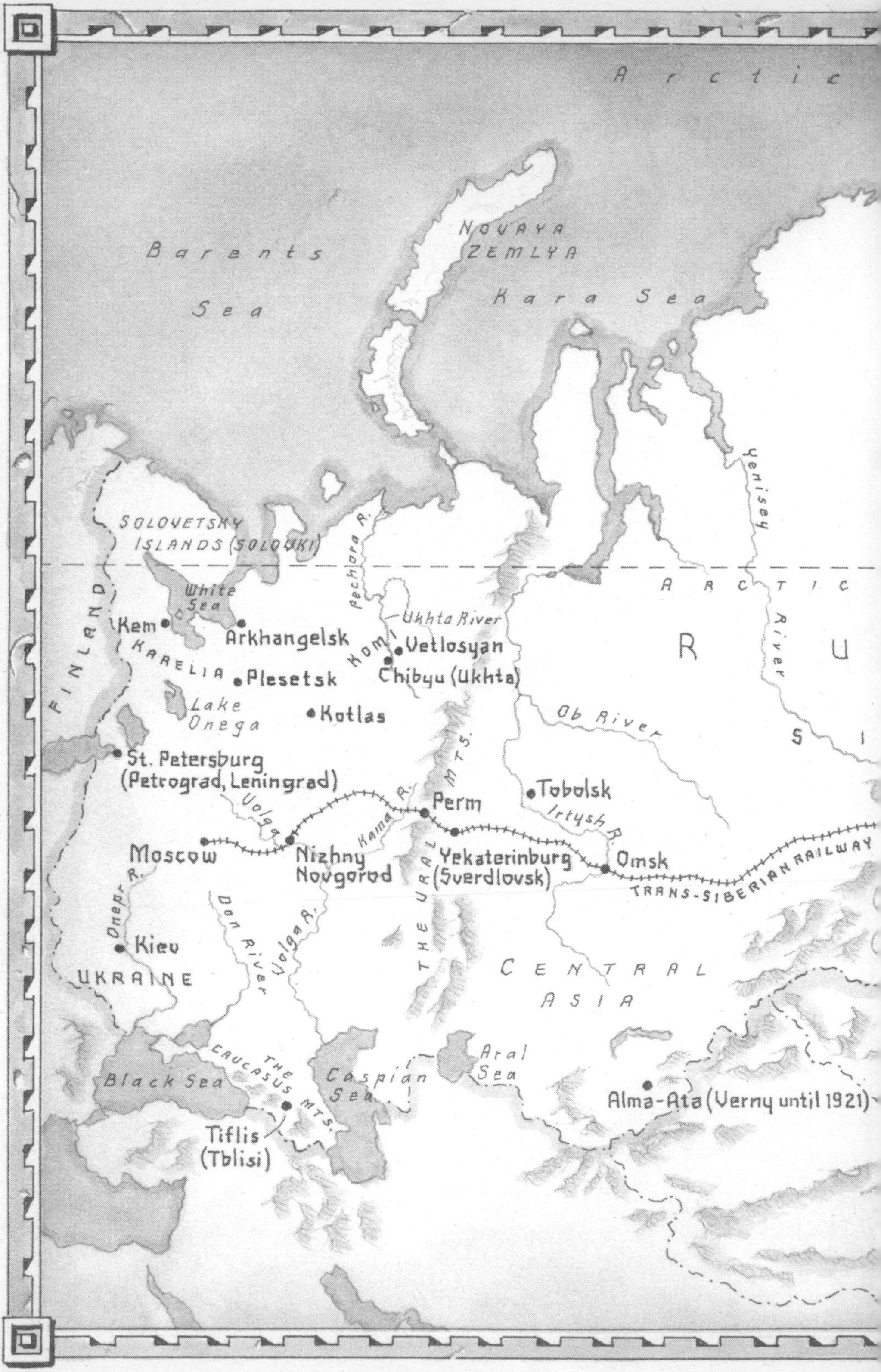

Arctic
Barents Sea
NOVAYA ZEMLYA
Kara Sea
SOLOVETSKY ISLANDS (SOLOVKI)
White Sea
FINLAND
Kem
Arkhangelsk
KARELIA
Plesetsk
Lake Onega
Kotlas
Pechora R.
Ukhta River
Komi
Vetlosyan
Chibyu (Ukhta)
Yenisey
ARCTIC
River
R
U
S
Ob River
St. Petersburg
(Petrograd, Leningrad)
Volga
Kama R.
Perm
Tobolsk
Irtysh R.
Moscow
Nizhny Novgorod
Yekaterinburg
(Sverdlovsk)
Omsk
TRANS-SIBERIAN RAILWAY
THE URAL MTS.
Dnepr R.
Don River
Volga R.
Kiev
UKRAINE
CENTRAL ASIA
THE CAUCASUS MTS.
Black Sea
Caspian Sea
Aral Sea
Alma-Ata (Verny until 1921)
Tiflis
(Tblisi)

RUSSIA
c. 1920

0   Miles   500

Ocean

YAKUTIA

CIRCLE

S   S   I   A

KOLYMA

B E R I A   Lena R.

Magadan
(from 1929)

Bering
Sea

Sea of
Okhotsk

Lake
Baikal

Irkutsk

SAKHALIN

(OUTER)
MONGOLIA

MANCHURIA

Harbin

Vladivostok

Pacific

Ocean

CHINA

JAPAN

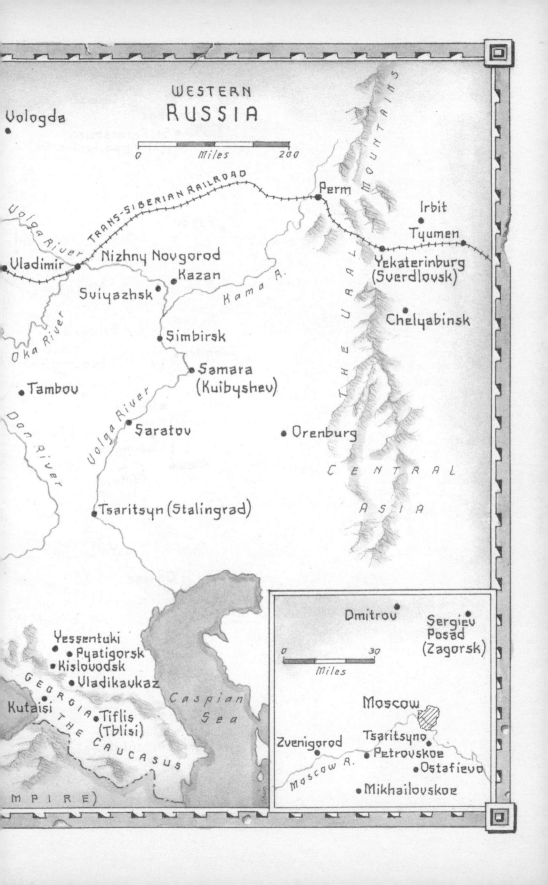

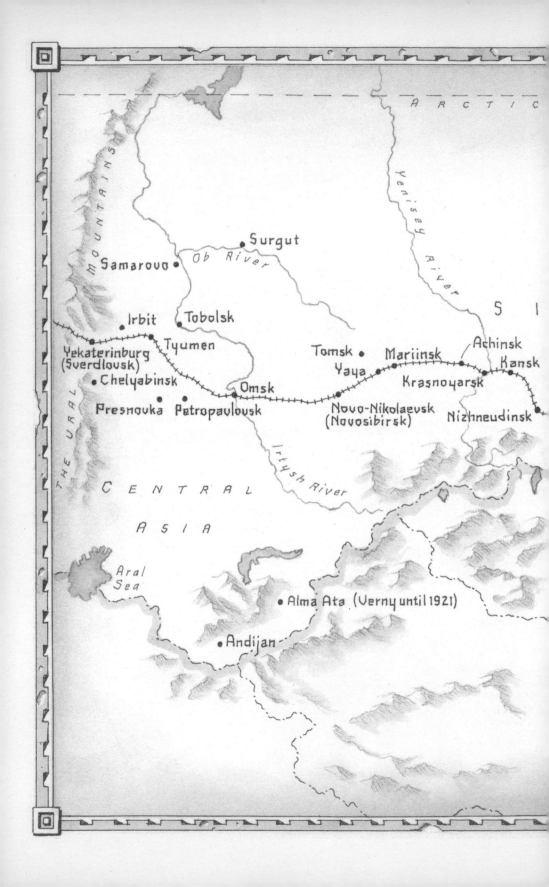

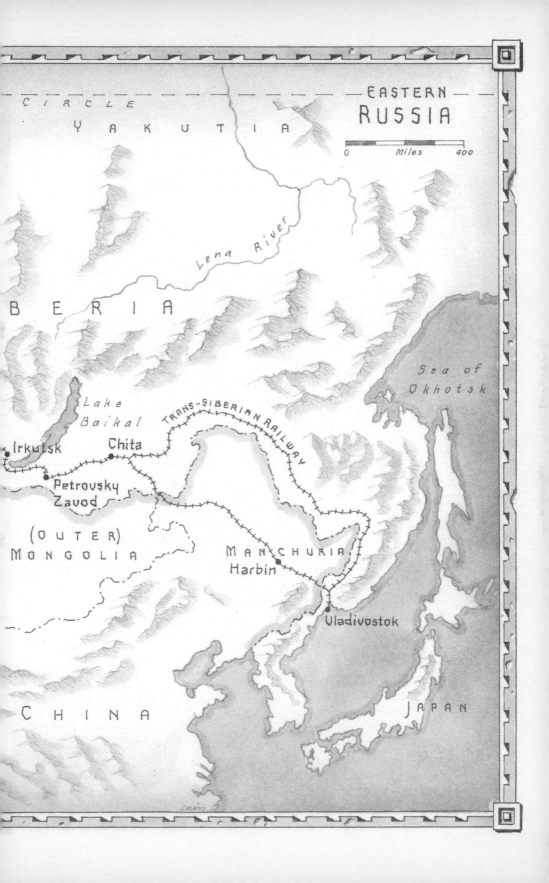

FORMER PEOPLE

PROLOGUE

THE CORNER HOUSE, MOSCOW, NOVEMBER 23, 1918, LATE EVENING

The nurse was preparing a fresh bandage when the men from the Cheka, the feared Bolshevik political police, burst into the room. "Can't you see there's a man dying in here?" she asked, and turned, stopping them in their tracks.[1] There before them in the half-light lay Count Sergei Dmitrievich Sheremetev, aged seventy-three, aide-de-camp to the late emperor Alexander III, member of the Imperial State Council, chief master of the hunt, and scion of one of Russia's great aristocratic families. In poor health for years, Count Sergei was near death, the gangrene in his legs spreading toward his torso and requiring the doctors to make one last attempt to save his life by radical amputation. The unexpected visitors, all except one, filed out of the room. The leader of the group, Yakov Peters, an intense man with thick dark hair and a prominent forehead, stayed to observe the operation and see whether the man he had come to arrest would survive.

They had arrived without warning, driving up Vozdvizhenka Street in several cars from the direction of the Kremlin. After turning into the courtyard of the Corner House, the grand Sheremetev home, they parked and locked the gate behind them to keep anyone from escaping. Panic gripped the servants on the main floor of the Corner House. At first it was not clear what was happening; ever since the abdication of Tsar Nicholas II the previous year and the collapse of the old regime the country had descended into chaos and lawlessness. Armed gangs roamed the streets at night, robbing, looting, and killing at will. Once powerful and still enormously rich families like the Sheremetevs were their preferred victims. Yet as the men in their dark leather jackets barged into the house, it became clear these were not mere bandits, but members of the All-Russian Extraordinary Commission for Combating Counterrevolution and Sabotage, the so-called Cheka.

After mounting the main staircase, they charged into the dining room, where they found the Sheremetev family seated at the table. "Hands up!" shouted Peters, leveling his Nagant revolver at them. Stunned, they all remained seated and raised their hands. Even the old butler, Dmitry Fyodorovich, just then serving Countess Yekaterina Sheremetev, Count Sergei's wife, laid the food platter on the floor and put his hands in the air. Not seeing Count Sergei at the table, Peters and a few of the other Chekists went to find him. The adults were locked in the dining room for the night, while the Sheremetev grandchildren were permitted to go to their nanny in another part of the house. Among the children were Yelena Sheremetev, in a gold silk skirt, her long hair tied up with a big white bow, and her older brother, Nikolai. When the children told their nanny what was happening, she took the family jewels that had been sewn to a long piece of velvet and dropped them into a water tank, just as she had been instructed to do in such an event.

Many in the family had sensed this day was coming; there had been numerous signs during the past months that the Bolsheviks had placed the Sheremetevs in their sights. That summer two of Count Sergei's sons-in-law had been briefly arrested: Alexander Saburov, a former officer of the Chevaliers Gardes and civil governor of Petrograd, and Count Alexander Gudovich, a gentleman of the bedchamber at the court of Nicholas II. Shortly thereafter, a Red Army soldier had come to the house and arrested Baron Joseph de Baye, a French citizen and old friend of Count Sergei's, who had lived with the family for many years. When the count asked on whose orders his friend the baron was being arrested, the soldier pointed at the Kremlin, saying, "Theirs." In September, the count's son, also named Sergei, was arrested at the family estate of Ostafievo, the Cheka agents mistaking him for his father. A group of worried scholars wrote to Anatoly Lunacharsky, the Bolshevik commissar of enlightenment, requesting that he extend "special protective measures" to the count and his son Pavel at their Vozdvizhenka home.

Lunacharsky replied that "all Revolutionary powers" would be used for their protection.[2] The commissar evidently had little power to offer protection.

The importance the Bolsheviks attached to Count Sheremetev, one of the most prominent representatives of old Russia, the Russia now being swept away by the whirlwind of the revolution, was evident by the presence of Yakov Peters that night at the Corner House. Born to the family of a poor Latvian farmer, Peters had been a committed revolutionary since the beginning of the century. He had been arrested by the tsarist police for taking part in labor strikes and tortured after the Revolution of 1905. For the rest of his life he had the mangled fingernails to prove his commitment to the cause. After his release he fled to London in 1908. Peters returned to Russia in the spring of 1917 and played an active role in the Bolsheviks' seizure of power in October. Together with Felix Dzerzhinsky, he established the Cheka and for years served as one of its leaders, notorious for his cruelty.[3]

Peters was among the authors of the Red Terror unleashed in September 1918 after the murder of Moisei Uritsky, head of the Petrograd Cheka, and the failed assassination attempt on the life of Lenin by Fanya Kaplan in late August. The goal of the Cheka's terror was to unleash a campaign of class warfare against "counterrevolutionaries" and so-called enemies of the people. In September, the Communist leader Grigory Zinoviev pronounced: "To overcome our enemies we must have our own socialist militarism. We must carry along with us 90 million out of the 100 million of Soviet Russia's population. As for the rest, we have nothing to say to them. They must be annihilated."[4] Peters's Cheka colleague Martin Latsis let there be little doubt where these unfortunate ten million were to be found: "Do not look in the file of incriminating evidence to see whether or not the accused rose up against the Soviets with arms or words. Ask him instead to which class he belongs, what is his background, his education, his profession. These are the questions that will determine the fate of the accused. That is the meaning and essence of the Red Terror."[5] Peters himself had expounded on the role of terror: "Anyone daring to agitate against the Soviet government will immediately be arrested and placed in a concentration camp." The enemies of the working class will meet with "mass terror [. . .] and will be destroyed and crushed by the heavy hammer of the revolutionary proletariat."[6]

The hammer of the Red Terror had now been lowered on the Corner House. Yakov Peters and Sergei Sheremetev embodied the epochal struggle facing Russia in 1918: on one side stood Peters, young, strong, and armed with the righteous conviction of the Bolshevik cause; on the other lay Sheremetev, sick, weak, defeated, and dying. In Count Sergei's room that night, two Russias stood face to face—that of the future and that of the past.

History, we are told, is written by the victors. What is less often stated, though no less important, is that history is usually written *about* the victors; winners get more attention in the history books than losers. The literature on the Russian Revolution proves the point. The biographies of Lenin vastly outnumber those of Nicholas II, as do the books on the Bolsheviks compared with those on the Mensheviks. Yet losers are no less worthy of being remembered than winners, if only to help us to appreciate the full richness of what came before and to preserve the memory of those unjustly forgotten by history.

I came across this forgotten history while writing a book on Count Sergei's grandfather Count Nikolai Sheremetev, an eccentric and fabulously rich aristocrat famous for his private serf opera company and his scandalous marriage to its prima donna, a singer named Praskovya Kovalyova, who performed as "The Pearl."[7] Through my research I came to know several of Nicholas and Praskovya's descendants, and hearing their stories about what had happened to the family during the revolution, I was drawn to the larger history of the fate of the nobility during these tumultuous years. While on a visit to Moscow in the spring of 2006 I searched the many drawers of the card catalog devoted to the "Great October Socialist Revolution" at the Russian State Library (the former Lenin Library, not fully online at the time) but could not find anything on the nobility. Surprised, I asked a librarian why there was nothing in the catalog. The look she gave me was one of disbelief, as if I had asked who was buried in the Lenin mausoleum. "*Shto?* What?" she stuttered. "The revolution and the nobility? Of course not, because the revolution had nothing to do with the nobles, and they had nothing to do with the revolution," she instructed this clueless American historian.[8] While researching this book, I have received similarly dismissive comments from people in the West. Of course, the nobility was destroyed, I have been told, and rightly so. There is a belief among some people that the nobility got what was coming to it, and so we need not be surprised or even care. Both points of view—that the revolution had nothing to do with the nobility or that it did but need not concern us—are wrong, historically and morally.

As one of the overlooked stories of the Russian Revolution, the fate of the nobility warrants being told. The destruction of an entire class cannot help eliciting our interest. But there are other reasons as well. The destruction of the nobility was one of the tragedies of Russian history. For nearly a millennium, the nobility, what the Russians called *bélaya kost'*, literally "white bone" (our "blue blood"), had supplied Russia's political, military, cultural, and artistic leaders. The nobility had served as the tsars' counselors and officials, as their generals and officers; the nobility had produced generations of writers, artists, and thinkers, of scholars and scientists, of reformers and revolutionaries. In a society that was slow to develop a middle class, the nobility played a preponderant role in the political, social, and artistic life of the country disproportionate to its relative size. The end of the nobility in Russia marked the end of a long and deservedly proud tradition that created much of what we still think of today as quintessentially Russian, from the grand palaces of St. Petersburg to the country estates surrounding Moscow, from the poetry of Pushkin to the novels of Tolstoy and the music of Rachmaninov.

The story of the Russian nobility also warrants telling since its fate foreshadowed that of other groups in the coming decades. The Bolsheviks' decision to single out the nobility for political persecution, for the expropriation of its property, for imprisonment, execution, and its designation as "former people" signaled a ruthless, Manichaean mentality that condemned entire collectives of people to harsh repression and even death. What is more, the tactics used against the nobility would be adopted against all of the regime's supposed class enemies. Lenin saw such enemies everywhere, whether among the more moderate socialists who refused to endorse his radical vision or the Russian peasant slightly better off than his neighbors. He insisted such enemies had to be crushed, and they were. Yet in one of the strange dynamics of the revolution, defeating one's class enemies was no guarantee of safety, for as the old enemies were defeated, new ones had to be found to justify the continuing struggle for the bright future of the Communist tomorrow. And so just as Stalin later destroyed the Old Bolsheviks, including Yakov Peters, who was arrested and killed in the Great Terror, so too would the entire peasantry be brutally subjugated. A revolution made in the name of the poor would destroy their lives in even greater numbers than those of the rich, the revolution's original targets.

On a larger scale, the tragedy of the nobles' fate also foreshadowed future atrocities of the bloody twentieth century when race, class, ethnicity, and religion were used both to incite and to justify oppression and mass killing, from Hitler's Germany to Pol Pot's Cambodia and Kambanda's Rwanda. Chased from their homes and their property expropriated, forced to clean the streets as a form of public humiliation, sent to labor camps, killed with a bullet to the back of the head for the crime of their social origin, Russian nobles were one of the first groups subjected to a brand of political violence that became a hallmark of the past century.

Former People tells the story of how the Russian elite was dispossessed and destroyed between the revolutions of 1917 and the Second World War. It is filled with tales of looted palaces and burning estates, of flights in the night from marauding peasants and Red Army soldiers, of imprisonment, exile, and execution. Yet it is also a story of survival and accommodation, of how many of the tsarist ruling class— abandoned, displaced, and repressed—overcame the psychic wounds inflicted by the loss of their world and struggled to find a place for themselves in the new, hostile order of the Soviet Union. It reveals how even at the darkest depths of the terror, daily life went on: men and women fell in love; children were born; friends gathered; simple pleasures were cherished. Ultimately, *Former People* is a testament to humans' remarkable ability to find happiness even amid the most harrowing of circumstances.

How does one begin to describe the destruction of an entire class? It is a process so vast as to defy comprehension. The scale is too large, the point of observation required to encompass it all too remote to make individual lives intelligible. Appreciating the fate of nearly two million people strains the imagination, and we as humans seem somehow constructed to better apprehend, and empathize with, much smaller numbers. Over the past six years I have been fortunate to meet and correspond with many individuals whose families are the subjects of *Former People*. Their generosity and willingness to share their experiences and collections of family documents have been the most pleasant part of writing this book. Reading dozens of personal accounts and listening to even more stories in homes, archives, and libraries in Russia and the West, I found myself drawn to the experiences of two families in particular—the Sheremetevs and the Golitsyns. Both belonged to the highest level of the nobility, the aristocracy; both had esteemed and ancient histories; both suffered horribly during the revolution and after; both were torn apart, some family members leaving Russia forever; and both left behind a wealth of letters, diaries, memoirs, and photographs that provide the kinds of sources required to write this history in a full, accurate, and convincing manner.

The Golitsyns formed an extensive clan—unlike the titled Sheremetevs—with more than a dozen separate branches at the time of the revolution. One of these descended from Prince Fyodor Golitsyn, a gentleman of the bedchamber in the reign of Catherine the Great and later trustee of Moscow University. Prince Vladimir Golitsyn, Fyodor's grandson and the long-serving mayor of Moscow, was a contemporary of Count Sergei Sheremetev's. Whereas the Sheremetevs maintained connections with the court and particularly with the royal family in St. Petersburg, the Golitsyns were a true Moscow family that had little to do with the imperial capital. Nevertheless, the families knew each other—nothing unusual in the small world of the Russian aristocracy— and even though Vladimir (liberal Westernizer) and Sergei (conservative monarchist) could barely tolerate each other, some of their children socialized and worked together. Two of their grandchildren—Yelena Sheremetev and Vladimir Golitsyn, named after his grandfather—fell in love at the Corner House in the early 1920s and married. Thanks to their large numbers, the princely line of the Golitsyns managed to survive in Russia; the Sheremetevs, however, did not.

The lives of several generations of the Sheremetevs and Golitsyns form the unifying thread that runs through *Former People*. While every noble experienced the revolution and the transition to the new Soviet order in his own way, what happened to the Sheremetevs and Golitsyns, and how they reacted to these events, were true for the majority of the nobility. Their lives were simultaneously exceptional, as is the case for every individual, and ordinary for the members of their class in Russia in those years.*

In late September 1917, a month before the Bolsheviks seized power, Lenin wrote: "A revolution, a real, profound, a 'people's' revolution to use Marx's expression, is the incredibly complicated and painful process of the death of the old order and the birth of the new social order, of the mode of life of tens of millions of people. Revolution is a most intense, furious, desperate class struggle and civil war."[9] The Bolshevik Revolution was seen by its creators as a Promethean leap into a new era of human history that would leave the past behind forever, and it is largely this half of the story, Lenin's "birth of the new social order," that historians have been most intent on exploring. Less well known, though no less important, is the other half: "the death of the old order."

In 1920, while riding on a train from Siberia to Moscow, Dmitry Fedotoff-White, a former tsarist naval officer, fell into conversation with a group of Red soldiers. He was reading *The ABC of Communism*, the new popular primer on bolshevism by Nikolai Bukharin and Yevgeny Preobrazhensky, which prompted a discussion on Marxism and the revolution. What struck Fedotoff-White in talking with the men was the large gap between the lofty ideals espoused by the leaders of the revolution and the goals that motivated its foot soldiers. These men had no understanding or even interest in Marxist theory, nor were they concerned with what the new Russian society would look like. Rather, they were motivated by one thing: the desire to destroy the old order. "To all of them, the Bolshevik revolution meant the destruction of monarchy, aristocracy, bureaucracy, and the officer class," he wrote. "They were all rebels against the old order of things, but that was about all there was to their political feelings."[10]

The role of ideology in the revolution and subsequent civil war is a complex one (more than this one interaction implies), but Fedotoff-White makes a crucial point in understanding the sheer ferocity of

---

*Although *Former People* explores the fate of the entire nobility (*dvoriánstvo*, in Russian), since so much of the book follows the aristocratic Sheremetev and Golitsyn families, I have chosen "aristocracy" for my subtitle.

these years—namely, that the will to destroy was stronger than the will to create and that it was the major force directing the course of events. From the beginning of the revolution, Lenin and the Bolsheviks feared the restoration of the old order; the surest way to prevent this was to rip it out by the roots and kill it. To destroy every vestige of the tsarist past was to deny their enemies any chance to revive it. The Bolsheviks soon realized, however, that they could not survive without the knowledge, skills, and education of the old elite. The workers and peasants, in whose name the Bolsheviks claimed to rule, were simply not qualified to run a vast state. And so began an uneasy collaboration between the old and new masters of Russia that was to last for more than two decades.

The persistence of the former educated elite, many of whom were nobles, stoked frustration and anger amid the classes in whose name the revolution had been made. If the Great October Socialist Revolution signaled a new dawn in human history, why then, many asked, were former counts and princesses, former landowners and tsarist officials still in positions of authority, still living in their homes or on their estates; indeed, why were they even still alive if they belonged to a world that had been buried long ago? Reliance on the former elite posed a threat to the Soviet regime. But it also presented it with a convenient excuse for why the reality of life did not measure up to the regime's grand promises. If socialism had yet to be achieved, if workers were not living better, if life was still a struggle, then this was not the fault of the leaders or a sign of the flaws within Marxist ideology; rather, it could be explained by the existence of class enemies—of saboteurs, wreckers, White Guards, and monarchists—waging a secret war from within to destroy the Soviet Union. Like other despised minorities, these former people became an easy scapegoat upon which to lay the blame for the Bolsheviks' failures and a target at which popular anger could be directed without fear of reprisal.

For many Russian nobles the revolution came as no surprise. Even as early as the eighteenth century some far-seeing noblemen could imagine the day when they would be swept away by the masses. At the height of the French Revolution in 1792, Count Semyon Vorontsov, Russia's ambassador to Great Britain, wrote to his brother back home:

France will not calm down until its vile principles have established themselves in Russia. As I have already told you, this will not be a war for life, but a war till death between those who have nothing and those who own property, and since the latter are few in number so must they inevitably perish. This infection shall become universal. Our distance from this turmoil will protect us for a time; we shall be the last ones, yet nonetheless we shall be victims of this worldwide plague. We shan't witness it; not you or I, but my son will.[11]

Vorontsov erred about the revolution's timing, but he was right that it would be a war to the death between the haves and the have-nots and that the former would lose. For centuries the Russian nobility had lived off the numbing toil of the peasant serfs. Noble landowners, whether cruel tyrants or benevolent masters, enjoyed equally the fruits of this favored status. Their wealth, culture, indeed their entire manner of life were made possible by a harsh system of forced servitude that by the eighteenth century hardly differed from American slavery. The emancipation of the serfs in 1861 did little to change the subservient relationship of the peasant to his former owner. The chasm that separated the world of the masses from the thin layer of the powerful and the privileged lasted right up until 1917.

The peasants had little choice but to tolerate their condition. At times they did rise up, and the results were inevitably violent and bloody. The great rebellions of Stenka Razin and Yemelian Pugachev in the seventeenth and eighteenth centuries, which scorched much of Russia and left tens of thousands dead, inspired hope in the downtrodden and instilled fear in the upper classes. The Russian countryside erupted again in the summer of 1917. This time, however, it would be different, and the peasants would not be subdued. For the nobles on the land it was like waking up and finding oneself trapped behind enemy lines. "It seems we have suffered a shipwreck," Zenaide Bashkiroff's grandmother informed her at their estate of Kourbatika. "We are in the position of the Swiss Family Robinson. [. . .] We shall live in perpetual fear of attacks from the wild tribes outside."[12] The "wild tribes" had become even wilder after three years of war. The pointless slaughter of World War I had inured the peasant-soldier to the most horrific violence, and he returned to his village from the front brutalized and shorn of restraint.

Not long after Princess Vera Urusov fled her estate of Kotovka in southern Russia, deserters and peasants tore it apart board by board, stone by stone, before burning what was left to the ground. When they finished, they defiled her father's grave. Two servants tried to stop them, but they were grabbed by the mob and beheaded; the peasants fed one of the heads to the dogs. Later, when asked to account for the viciousness of their attack on the Urusovs' property, they replied, "Because they sucked our blood." A few nobles, Vera among them, were able to see beyond their own personal loss and acknowledge in the tide of violence sweeping across Russia a moment of historical reckoning. She, and her generation of the nobility, would be the ones to pay for the injustice of serfdom. It seems that even at a young age Vera sensed this day would come. One of her favorite childhood games had been pretending she was an aristocrat caught in the French Revolution trying to escape the fury of the mob.[13]

In many ways the fate of the Russian nobility mirrored that of the French a little more than a century before. In the early 1790s, French nobles became targets of repression and violence as the forces of revolution rallied behind the slogan of "War on the castles, peace to the cottages!" The nobility was stripped of its titles, its ancient privileges, and much of its wealth. At the height of the Terror châteaus were ransacked and plundered, thousands of nobles were imprisoned and killed, and hundreds lost their heads to the guillotine in Paris.[14] Nobles who fled the country were branded traitors and enemies; their property was confiscated, and in extreme cases their family members in France were taken hostage. Nobles who remained became known as ci-devants, the first instance of former people. And following a strange dynamic that would be repeated in Russia, as the revolution progressed and the counterrevolutionary threat retreated, the perceived danger the nobles represented and the repressive measures against them increased. When the revolution did not develop as its leaders had promised, they pointed to the nobles as the reason, as would happen in Russia too. Attacking the old elite became an easy way to gain popularity and prove one's commitment to the cause and to the people.[15]

But there were important differences as well. Despite the great violence and bloodshed of the French Revolution, what happened in the first few decades of the twentieth century in Russia was on an incomparable scale. Of the 16,594 persons condemned to death by extraordinary courts during the Terror in France, 1,158 of them were nobles, less than 1 percent of the entire noble estate. And when the total number of the Terror's victims is taken into account, fewer than 9 percent of the victims were nobles.[16] The numbers killed in Russia were of an entirely different magnitude. Between 1917 and 1941, the nobility faced several successive waves of terror that likely killed tens of thousands, if not more; given the chaotic manner in which so much of the violence was carried out, accurate records were not kept, and so the exact number will likely never be known. The fate of the Golitsyns offers stark proof of the extent of the terror. Of its many branches extant in 1917, only one survived in Russia; all the others were killed off or forced into exile. Dozens of Golitsyns were arrested by the Bolsheviks and then shot or died in prison; dozens more simply vanished in the storm of the revolution, and their fate remains unknown. Today there are more Golitsyns in North America than in Russia.[17]

It was not just the scale of the killing either. When Napoleon, himself a ci-devant, seized power in 1799, he began to bring back the old nobility and to merge it with a new titled elite of his own making. Repressive legislation was abolished, and nobles of the ancien régime slowly began to return to positions of authority. With the final defeat of Napoleon and the restoration of the Bourbons in 1814, the process of revival was complete.[18] But in Russia there would be no restoration, neither of the monarchy nor of the nobility. Stalin, unlike Napoleon, was no ci-devant; far from retreating from the revolution's early extremes, he would reinvigorate them and unleash a new, final war against the state's class enemies.

By the 1940s, the nobility had been annihilated. For those persons who had somehow survived, there was little left to remind them of life before 1917. They had lost their homes and sold off their belongings over the years at outdoor markets or commission stores for a pittance; their letters and photographs had been destroyed or hidden away. Families had been decimated and separated one from another by exile and imprisonment. Most former nobles hid as best they could in the shadows. One's past was poison, and the stories told of the ancestors were purposely forgotten or spoken of in a whisper. Some changed their names to avoid notice; some lied or gave evasive answers to questions about their past and family history. Survival typically required self-imposed amnesia, the repression of memory. Those who refused to do this often suffered the harshest punishment.[19] Yet, paradoxically, through its unceasing repression of former people the state made it impossible for them to forget who they were and where they came from.[20]

The children of the old nobility born in the 1930s and 1940s had no personal knowledge of life before the revolution, nor were they exposed to the horrors of the civil war. Still, they too learned of the need for silence. Learning to keep quiet about one's private life was part of every Soviet person's experience, but it was even more so for former people and their children.[21] They grew up in a world that acted as if there had been no life before 1917. Yelena Shuvalov, born in 1930 into an old family of Russian counts whose ancestors had included prominent courtiers, diplomats, and generals, recalled how as a child she soon understood that self-preservation necessitated silence:

> We did not take any interest in the past. That just wasn't done. It wasn't even a consideration. I remember from my early childhood, when I'd ask something, I was told, and it always amazed me, "The less you know, the better." I heard this either from my uncle or from mama or papa. I was grade-school age, it was the end of the 1930s, and that was the way back then, no one said anything.[22]

It was only after the Second World War, and particularly with the death of Stalin in 1953 followed by Khrushchev's Thaw, that the silence began to fade. A few former nobles began to talk and write openly about their forefathers, and then in the 1960s some began to return, surreptitiously, to the places where their ancestral country homes had once stood. In the 1980s under Mikhail Gorbachev's new policies of glasnost and perestroika, local historians, teachers, and folklorists began to seek out the children and grandchildren of provincial nobles for information on the life and culture of these small corners of Russia. After seventy years, a few thin bonds between the locals and the heirs of the old landlords were reestablished.[23] The past two decades have witnessed an explosion of interest in reclaiming Russia's lost history, and this process has extended to the fate of Russia's noble families. No longer afraid to speak, noble descendants are publishing their family archives, organizing conferences, studying their genealogies, and trying to recover a sense of connection to their families and their past.[24]

Olga Sheremetev was in her apartment across the courtyard from the Corner House that November night the Cheka came. She and the rest of her family cowered while the men ransacked the house. No one could sleep, and they sneaked glances out their windows to see what was happening. Throughout the night and early morning cars came and went. Men could be seen in the darkness going in and out and hauling things to the cars. Peters and his men did not leave until seven in the morning. Olga's husband, Boris, himself only recently freed from a Bolshevik prison, went next door as soon as they had left. He found Count Sergei utterly crushed. The men had taken his personal correspondence, his diaries, and gold and silver worth around ten million rubles. Maria Gudovich, the count's younger daughter, was forced to watch as the Cheka agents stuffed their pockets with her jewelry. One Chekist took Countess Yekaterina Sheremetev's pincushion in his hand, and as he plucked from it every last jewel-headed pin, he told her, "This is how we take everything."[25] But worst of all, they had arrested nine men. Six of them were family members: the Sheremetevs' sons Pavel, Boris, and Sergei, their sons-in-law Gudovich and Saburov, and their grandson Boris Saburov. Anna Saburov, the elder Sheremetev daughter, was beside herself with worry over her husband and son and kept trying to calm herself by repeating words about the inescapability of fate and God's will. Everyone was anxious the Cheka would return. No one had any idea what had become of the men. "We're completely in the dark," confided Olga to her diary.[26] Both Gudovich and Saburov père would be shot in prison the following year.

Four days later Count Sergei turned seventy-four. He was in a dreadful state that morning, drifting in and out of consciousness, but as the day wore on, he revived. He spent his birthday in the company of his wife and a few family members. At one point his old friend Vladimir Dzhunkovsky, an adjutant to Grand Duke Sergei Alexandrovich and governor-general of Moscow, stopped by to pay his respects. His visit unleashed a flood of memories for the count of his days at the court of Alexander III. Count Sergei lived a few more weeks, dying in his bed on December 17. His body was laid out on a table and dressed in a black suit. They buried him two days later at a new cemetery across from the Novospassky Monastery. He could not be buried there in the family crypt, where Sheremetevs had lain for centuries, since the Bolsheviks had run off all the monks and turned it into a prison.

The revolution and everything it wrought almost destroyed Count Sergei, a man committed to tsarism and all it represented. In letters to friends he wrote of the tragedy that had descended upon their home-land; they were living through "a modern-day Mongol yoke" and un-der "the sword of Damocles." "I have the feeling," he wrote, "that I'm riding on a train that has just left the tracks." Still, he tried to keep faith in Russia and its future. He busied himself reading histories of the French Revolution and Napoleon and sought comfort in the thought that Russia too would emerge from the dark night of anarchy into the light of a better future with order and peace restored. He continued to profess his faith in God and quoted the words of Alexander Pushkin: "I gaze forward without fear."[27]

PART I

Before the Deluge

Were we all, the whole upper crust of Russian society, so totally insensitive, so horribly obtuse, as not to feel that the charmed life we were leading was in itself an injustice and hence could not possibly last?
—Nicolas Nabokov,
Bagázh: Memoirs of a Russian Cosmopolitan

1

RUSSIA, 1900

At the dawn of the twentieth century, Russia was hurtling into the modern age. In the two decades before the First World War, the country experienced exceptional rates of industrial growth, outpacing those of the United States, Germany, and Great Britain. Under Minister of Finance Sergei Witte massive domestic and foreign investment was made in Russian industry, mining, and railroads. Between 1850 and 1905, Russia went from 850 miles of railroads to nearly 40,000. The oil industry grew to match that of the United States, and Russia surpassed France in steel production. In the early 1880s, St. Petersburg and Moscow were connected by the longest telephone line in the world. The first cinemas appeared in Russia in 1903, the same year the number of electric streetlights in St. Petersburg reached three thousand. By 1914, Russia had become the fifth-largest industrial power in the world.[1] The pace and future promise of economic growth and power made the other powers view Russia with a combination of wonder, envy, and fear.[2]

Yet despite rapid industrialization, the explosive growth of Russia's urban centers, and unprecedented foreign investment, Russia in 1900 was still a feudal society. Its social makeup resembled a pyramid with a large base extending gradually to a narrow tip. At the bottom was the great mass of peasants, 80 percent of the entire population. At the top was the emperor, the autocratic ruler of a vast, multiethnic empire of almost 130 million people in 1897. In between lay several social groups defined by laws and customs that went back hundreds of years: the clergy, the townsmen, the so-called distinguished or honored citizens, the merchants, and the nobility.[3] Unlike Western Europe or the United States, there was no large urban middle class or bourgeoisie. In the late 1890s, just over 13 percent of the population lived in cities, compared with 72 percent in England, 47 in Germany, and 38 in the United States. Russia's cities were home to the vast majority of the country's small educated elite, while in the rural areas less than a quarter of the population was literate.[4]

Not only was Russia still a traditional peasant society, but it remained politically mired in the past. Russia was ruled not by laws or institutions but by one man, the emperor. According to the Fundamental Laws of 1832, "The Russian Empire is ruled on the firm basis of positive laws and statutes which emanate from the Autocratic Power." The Russian emperor's power was understood as unlimited; imperial decrees, as well as verbal instructions and commands, had the force of law. This is not to say there were no laws or no sense of legality, rather, that the emperor had the freedom and power to decide whether he cared to recognize them.[5]

By the latter decades of the nineteenth century Russia's educated classes were growing increasingly concerned by the dichotomy of a modernizing society and an old-fashioned and rigid political system. While the country was moving into the modern era, the state seemed impervious to change. Tsar Alexander II had of course taken steps to modernize Russia during the era of the Great Reforms. In 1861, the serfs were freed, ending a horrific system of human bondage stretching back hundreds of years that, by the eighteenth century, had descended to a level of inhumanity akin to American slavery.[6] In 1864, the legal system was reformed to create an independent judiciary in which all Russians, except peasants, the vast majority of the population, were to be equal before the law. The same year local society was granted greater authority over managing its affairs, chiefly in the areas of public education, health, and roadways, with the creation of zemstvos, elected institutions of local self-government separate from the central government. The "tsar-liberator" had approved a plan to consult with a small number of representatives of society to consider further reforms (the so-called Loris-Melikov Constitution) when he was blown up by a bomb thrown by members of the terrorist organization The People's Will on March 1, 1881.

Upon coming to the throne, Alexander III tore up the Loris-Melikov Constitution and issued an imperial manifesto reasserting undiluted and absolute autocratic power. Minister of the Interior Count Dmitry Tolstoy baldly stated the new program of the government with a single word, "Order."[7] Counterreforms were instituted to undo or limit the reforms of the 1860s. In the summer of 1881, the government issued new Temporary Regulations intended to keep the peace and protect public order. The regulations invested the government with ever-greater power to monitor, arrest, and exile its subjects without recourse. Houses could be searched; businesses and schools closed; any sort of gathering, whether public or private, prohibited. The regulations even gave the government power to deny town councils and zemstvos the right to meet and to dismiss from such bodies anyone considered politically unreliable. Intended to last only three years, the Temporary Regulations were repeatedly renewed by Alexander III and later by Nicholas II, creating a state of near-martial law.[8]

Alexander III brought renewed repression, but little else. If some could see in Alexander the revived spirit of Peter the Great with his cudgel, others just saw the cudgel.[9] He had no need of society, even its most conservative, pro-autocratic members. In March 1881, a group of aristocratic conservatives founded the Holy Company to safeguard the life of the new tsar and take the fight to the revolutionaries. When its members, who included Count Sergei Sheremetev, dared suggest that repressive measures alone might not be enough to defeat the regime's enemies and some sort of changes to the government ought to be considered, the emperor's ministers denounced the Holy Company and forced it to disband. According to Minister Dmitry Tolstoy, the Holy Company was infected with "noxious liberalism."[10]

Alexander III's son and heir Nicholas was at Livadia, in the Crimea, when, in October 1894, he got the news that his father was dead. According to Grand Duke Alexander Mikhailovich, his brother-in-law, a stunned Nicholas took him by the arm and said, "What am I going to do, what is going to happen to me, to you, [. . .] to mother, to all of Russia? I am not prepared to be a Czar. I never wanted to become one. I know nothing of the business of ruling." The grand duke, and history, would confirm the truth of Nicholas's words. Alexander Mikhailovich wrote that Nicholas's personal qualities, while "praiseworthy in a simple citizen," were "fatal in a Czar."[11] Weak, indecisive, overwhelmed by the responsibilities of rule, and mindlessly beholden to "fate," Nicholas did prove to be fatal to himself, fatal to his family, and fatal to Russia.

From the start of his reign, Nicholas pledged to continue to rule in the spirit of his late father. Nicholas maintained tight censorship of the press, furthered the policy of limiting the power of the zemstvos, restricted the autonomy of Russia's universities, and renewed the Temporary Regulations. When, in January 1895, a delegation of zemstvo representatives wished him a long and successful reign and dared mention their desire to play a role in communicating to the government the wishes of the people, Nicholas stopped them by calling their desire a "senseless dream." "Let all know," he told them, "that in devoting all my strength to the people's well-being, I shall safeguard the principles of autocracy as firmly and as unswervingly as did my late, unforgettable father."[12]

But he could not, and he did not. Where the father had known what he wanted, the son was never sure; where the father had been resolute, the son had trouble making and sticking to a decision. Intent on showing that his hand was firmly on the rudder of state, Nicholas insisted on overseeing nearly every decision that attended administering a great empire. It did not take long for the ill-equipped emperor to become overwhelmed and then paralyzed by indecision. When confronted with difficult problems, Nicholas was apt to go pale, light a cigarette, and fall silent.[13] Society wits quipped that "Russia did not need a constitution to limit the monarchy since she already had a limited monarch." Confusion, incoherence, stasis, and a sense of aimless drift began to emanate from the office of the emperor and infect the government.[14]

Nonetheless, there was one aspect of Russian political culture that survived the reign of Alexander III. The Russians call it *proizvól*, a word that lacks any clear English equivalent but is most often translated as "arbitrary rule." Proizvol was evident in the workings of the Okhrana, the secret police, an organization that was charged with combating terrorists but that seemed to suspect everyone, even the emperor's loyal subjects, of subversion. Proizvol was evident in the sweeping authority of the provincial governors, who often ruled over vast regions of the empire as venal satraps. The educated classes, particularly the men in the zemstvos whose work the governors obstructed and whose authority they tried to thwart, resented their power the most. The state's interference in the zemstvos proved to have far-reaching consequences: by 1900, the zemstvos were dominated by the nobility, and in cracking down on them, the government turned its most important ally into an opponent.[15]

At the end of the nineteenth century, the nobility comprised almost 1.9 million people, about 1.5 percent of the entire population of the Russian Empire. The nobility was a diverse group, divided by nationality (Russians, Poles, Georgians, Baltic Germans), religion (Russian Orthodoxy, Catholicism, Lutheranism), education and wealth (from a great deal of both to little of either), and political outlook (from reactionaries to revolutionaries). There were hereditary nobles, whose privileged status passed to their offspring, and personal nobles, whose did not. So great was the diversity among the empire's nobility that historians continue to debate whether it even deserves to be considered a distinct social class.[16] If there was one thing that defined a noble, it was, as a commentator wrote in "The Tasks of the Nobility" in 1895, a certain quality "of being among the chosen, of being privileged, of not being the same as all other people."[17] The Russian nobility was never, however, a class of idle rich. Rather, it had always been a service class that initially derived its privileges and then increasingly its own identity from serving the grand princes of Muscovy and later the tsars of imperial Russia whether at court, in the military, or in the administration.

At the top of the nobility was the aristocratic elite, roughly a hundred or so families with great landed wealth dating back to at least the eighteenth century. These nobles often held high positions at court or in the government.[18] The aristocracy was typically old, titled, and rich. It intermarried and had a sense of itself as a self-defined group. Aristocrats belonged to the same clubs and salons, and the young men served in the elite imperial guards regiments like the Chevaliers Gardes, the Horse Guard, and the Emperor's Life Guard Hussars. Part of the aristocracy (including the Golitsyns, Gagarins, Dolgorukys, and Volkonskys) descended from the ancient princely dynasties of Riurik and Gedymin; others came from nontitled boyar families of the Muscovite court, most notably the Naryshkins and the Sheremetevs, a branch of which acquired the title of count under Peter the Great; or from other old noble families that had served in the cavalry units, such as the Shuvalovs, Vorontsovs, and Orlovs.[19]

Princess Sophy Dolgoruky, born into the aristocracy in the final decade of the tsarist empire, recalled how "[i]n the old days any lesser mortal who had not been born into the privileged caste was considered not 'born.' *'Elle n'est pas née'* was a phrase to which my youthful ears were quite accustomed, if my grandmother referred to one who had married into the select club of European aristocracy, but was unable to claim a title in her own right." (Nevertheless, as Sophy points out in her memoir, Grandmother chose to remain silent about the fact that her great-grandmother had been bought at a slave market in Constantinople by an Austrian prince and then handed over to the Polish count Potocki as the winnings in a card game.) While the members of this tiny elite held different interests and attitudes, they all, according to Sophy, prized education, possessed unimaginable wealth (though this was never mentioned, for to do so showed an utter lack of breeding), and lived in "a luxury that was a natural part of existence."

So, for instance, sheets and pillow-cases were changed daily. All were of very fine cool linen with the personal initial and crown (to indicate the title) embroidered on every item. Underclothes naturally would never be worn twice and towels were changed immediately after use. The tablecloths covering the long tables and the napkins intricately folded at each place would have the family coat of arms actually woven into the centre. Obviously each big house had its own laundry on the premises, together with a plethora of servants who, with their families, lived, feudal fashion, in two sides of the house round the courtyard, above the stables and garages. Thinking back to the Dolgorouky household it [*sic*] seems incredible that such a number of people were needed to care for the physical comfort of one family.

In the large marble-floored front hall sat the *svetzar* whose only duty was to open the door and lay down the strip of red carpet to car or carriage, so that the shoes of those arriving or departing should not be sullied by contact with the pavement. To keep him company in the hall were the couple of liveried footmen on duty that day—or when my uncle was in residence—a couple of Cossacks in full uniform.[20]

Below the aristocracy lay the great mass of nobles who filled the ranks of the officer corps and the civil administration or had gone into the so-called free professions as lawyers, doctors, teachers, or scientists. About half of all urban nobles were either in state service or in these professions around the turn of the century; the next largest category was rentiers.[21] The nobility had traditionally been the landowning class, and this remained true right up to 1917. Until the emancipation in 1861, the nobility had for centuries lived off the labor of millions of serfs, labor that made some nobles fabulously rich. If there is one image of the prerevolutionary landed nobility that has stuck in the popular imagination, it is that of the Ranevskys in Anton Chekhov's *The Cherry Orchard*. Impecunious, trapped by tradition, doomed to oblivion by the forces of modernity, Lyubov Ranevskaya cannot bring herself to cut down the orchard and rent out the land for summer vacationers ("Summer cottages, summer residents—I'm sorry, it's all too vulgar," she says with a sigh) and loses her estate and everything she holds dear.[22]

It is tempting to take Chekhov's play for sociology and to see in the story of the Ranevskys the plight of the entire Russian nobility, an ancient class inescapably shuffling toward extinction. But the reality was never quite so bleak. The lower rungs of the rural nobility were indeed becoming more impoverished, and many were forced to sell their lands; between 1861 and 1905, the rural nobility lost an average of 1 percent of its land a year through either sale or foreclosure. Nonetheless, as late as 1915, the nobility still owned more land than any other group.[23] Moreover, for wealthier nobles selling land was not a necessity but a smart economic move; nobles across Europe were then taking advantage of the steep rise in land values to sell off land at a great profit and invest in stocks and bonds. Indeed, by 1910, nearly one-half of the nobles in St. Petersburg were living on income from such investments. Count Sergei Sheremetev and his half brother Alexander owned more than forty-six commercial properties in St. Petersburg and Moscow from which they earned solid returns. Count Alexander also sold land to invest in banks and stock corporations that proved quite profitable. In 1914, Count Sergei Sheremetev built one of St. Petersburg's first shopping centers, the so-called Sheremetev Passage. And in 1910, in contrast with Chekhov's Madame Ranevskaya, Count Sergei saw nothing vulgar at all in leasing a good deal of the land at his ancestral home of Kuskovo to Muscovites looking for summer dacha plots.[24]

For hundreds of years the Russian tsars had relied on the nobility to maintain order over the countryside. Even after the emancipation of the serfs in 1861, the nobility continued to serve as the de facto rulers of rural Russia until 1917 as a result of the dearth of state administrators at the local level.[25] The thirty thousand or so noble families that remained on their estates in the early years of the twentieth century represented small, isolated islands of privilege and authority amid a vast peasant sea of poverty and resentment, for even forty years after emancipation, the legacy of serfdom remained profound.[26] The peasants were still angry that upon receiving their freedom they had not been given land, which they had traditionally considered theirs since they were the ones who worked it; rather, to compensate the nobility, the peasants had been forced to purchase land through redemption payments to the state. Landownership had become an increasing source of anger as the rural population exploded, creating a serious land shortage. Peasants were forced to rent noble lands, often at high rates, leaving them with little to show for their hard work at the end of the season. The peasantry sank deeper into poverty and eyed the local nobleman's lands with ever-greater hunger. Most peasants in the black-soil Russian provinces subsisted on bread, pickled cabbage, and onion. So hard was life in the countryside that more than three-quarters of peasant army recruits called up in 1891 were declared unfit for service because of poor health.[27]

Even after winning their freedom, Russia's peasants had been kept in a servile status and lived in a separate world from that of their former masters and other privileged segments of society. Peasants alone lived according to the customary law of the village; they were not entitled to freely sell their land as individuals; they paid proportionally higher taxes than the nobles; and until 1889, just to leave their villages, they were required to obtain passports, which were granted only if they had paid all their redemption payments, taxes, and debts to the commune.[28] Nobles and peasants were divided not just by an economic barrier but by an even more important cultural barrier. The nobles, by and large, were Europeanized; they were children of the reforms of Peter the Great. The peasants were not; they lived in a different cultural and psychological world of tradition, habit, and religion that had changed little since the days of early Muscovy and one in which the nobles were viewed wearily as fallen Christians and, at times, forces of evil.[29]

Nobles and peasants continued to behave as masters and subjects well after 1861. As late as 1910, when Princess Barbara Dolgoruky rode out among the peasant women near her family estate, the peasants would drop to their knees in respect. The princess found the age-old habit distasteful and so strictly forbade them from doing it in the future. Henceforth, they remained standing, for the peasants were used to doing as their masters instructed, at least when they were present.[30] Alexander Davydoff, born into a prominent noble family in 1881, was stunned by what he saw after leaving the city to return to run the family estate of Sably in 1905. Both the landowners and peasants seemed to be content to play hypocritical, dishonest roles with each other. The former typically adopted an aloof, superior, and sententious attitude (or, what he found even worse, one of treacly sentimentality), while the latter adopted a pose of false ignorance and "voluntary humiliation" and then tried to cheat the master behind his back. "It is evident that each side tried to cheat the other," he wrote, "but whereas the peasants guessed perfectly well the thoughts of the landowners, the latter were incapable of piercing the stone wall of the dissembling character of the peasant." This legacy of serfdom, in Davydoff's estimation, pervaded all such relations. The peasants excelled at "trickery," what he called "the usual weapon of the weak against the strong."[31]

Land hunger and the rise of industrialization forced many peasants to leave the countryside to seek work in the new factories, and by 1900, the working class numbered roughly 1.7 million, about 200,000 fewer than the number of Russia's nobles. Working conditions in the factories were horrible, and workers had almost no way of protesting their condition. Not only were workers denied the right to organize, but they were even prohibited from assembling merely to discuss common problems.[32] One female worker recalled later: "My family was technically free, but the spirit of serfdom and slavery still lived on." Men, women, and children worked long days, sometimes as much as eighteen hours, and their small pay could rarely keep up with the rise in the price of goods. Many went hungry for long stretches; life was brutish and crushing and without hope.[33] The influx of peasants to the cities created terrible housing shortages. Workers were housed in barracks, tenements, and dank cellars; some workers slept in the factories under their machines. There was massive overcrowding, filth, and disease. Typhus, cholera, and tuberculosis were rampant. By the 1870s, St. Petersburg had the highest mortality rate of any major city in Europe. There were no protective labor laws, but few dared complain out of fear of being fired.

For as bad as being a worker was, it was better than the existence of the urban poor and unemployed. The slums that sprang up in Russia's major cities were dark, hostile places rife with banditry, prostitution, murder, and lawlessness. Some slums were so bad the police did not dare enter. Girls and boys as young as ten sold themselves on the streets for a few kopecks. The people of this shadow world survived by theft or begging or they died of starvation.[34]

Recalling the early years of his life in Russia, Vladimir Nabokov wrote: "The old and the new, the liberal touch and the patriarchal one, fatal poverty and fatalistic wealth got fantastically interwoven in that strange first decade of our century."[35]

Nabokov was born in the last year of the nineteenth century into a wealthy noble family. His grandfather Dmitry Nabokov had served as minister of justice under Alexander II and III, and his father, also Vladimir Dmitrievich, was a prominent liberal Westernizer and, after the Revolution of 1905, a leader of the Constitutional Democratic Party (the Kadets). Vladimir Dmitrievich's political views confounded his mother, and she simply could not understand her son's liberal notions and his commitment to fundamental change. How was it, Nabokov writes in *Speak, Memory*, that "my father, who, she knew, thoroughly appreciated all the pleasures of great wealth, could jeopardize its enjoyment by becoming a liberal, thus helping to bring a revolution that would in the long run, as she correctly foresaw, leave him a pauper."[36]

The Nabokovs' great wealth included a fine home in St. Petersburg, the estate of Vyra, and a domestic staff of fifty-five. At Vyra the peasants looked to Nabokov's father as the *bárin*, the master, and would come to the manor house for help settling their local disagreements or for special favors and subsidies. Inclined to be generous, Nabokov père typically acquiesced to their requests, at which point they would raise him up and toss him in the sky three times, higher and higher with each throw. The custom made the Nabokovs' old governess uneasy. "One day they'll let him fall," she observed prophetically.[37]

It is one of history's tragic ironies that the origins of the revolution that would destroy the Russian nobility were in fact laid by the nobility itself. Throughout the late 1780s and early 1790s, as the revolution raged in France, Russia's polite society followed with nervous agitation in the pages of the Moscow and St. Petersburg *Gazette* the news of the burning and looting of the châteaus and the executions of Louis XVI and Marie Antoinette.[38] The tales of violence coming out of France brought to mind the attack on the nobility that had swept over Russia in the 1770s, when a Don Cossack army deserter named Yemelian Pugachev led a mass rebellion of the poor and dispossessed against the established order. Proclaiming the end of serfdom, taxation, and military service, Pugachev set out to exterminate all landlords and tsarist officials and unleashed a paroxysm of bloodshed and terror across an enormous swath of territory. By the time the *Pugachyóvshchina* was put down, tens of thousands of Russians had been killed and raped, and their homes looted and burned. There had been other peasant revolts before, but nothing of such magnitude, and the name of Pugachev seared itself into the memory of noble Russia, never to be forgotten.[39] Alexander Pushkin immortalized the Pugachyovshchina in his novel *The Captain's Daughter,* famous for its oft-quoted line "God save us from a Russian revolt, senseless and merciless."

The specter of another Pugachyovshchina forced Russia to consider reform from above or face revolt from below. In 1790, Alexander Radishchev published *A Journey from St. Petersburg to Moscow,* a burning indictment of serfdom and the oppression of Russia's poor at the hands of the rich and a thinly disguised call to overthrow the monarchy. Catherine the Great ordered all copies of the book confiscated and destroyed (it remained banned until 1868) and its author sentenced to death (she commuted the sentence to Siberian exile). A noble, Radishchev as a young man had studied in Europe, where he had fallen under the influence of the French philosophes and the ideas of the Enlightenment that instilled in him a profound hatred of tyranny. Radishchev is often considered the founding father of the Russian intelligentsia from whom descends a long line of men and women committed to reforming, or even destroying, the Russian political and social order.[40]

That the first critic of Russian autocracy was a nobleman is not surprising considering that for most of the eighteenth and early years of the nineteenth century, the nobility formed the core of the small educated elite. At the beginning of the eighteenth century, Peter the Great set out to modernize Russia, and to do so, he forced his noblemen to adopt the ways of their Western European peers. An unintended consequence of Peter's embrace of Europe was that the nobility learned not only the latest technology and forms of polite behavior (shipbuilding from the Dutch, manners from the French) but also to think for themselves and to compare life at home with the more advanced and open societies of Western Europe. State service was obligatory for Russian noblemen until 1762. By then the ethos of service had become deeply ingrained in the nobleman's self-identity, so much so that even after the emancipation from state service, most noblemen continued to serve. By the end of the eighteenth century, however, the nobleman's understanding of service had begun to change, and increasingly the object of service shifted from that of the state to the Russian people or nation.[41]

If by the time of Radishchev at least one nobleman dared call for radical change, thirty-five years later some even dared act. On December 14, 1825, a group of officers and members of the guards regiments, many of them from high aristocratic families, rebelled on St. Petersburg's Senate Square. The Decembrists, as the rebels came to be called, advocated the end of serfdom, a constitution, and basic liberties. Their revolt was quickly put down and its leaders were executed or exiled to Siberia by order of Tsar Nicholas I. These noble sons became martyrs to future revolutionaries, who, though forced underground, nurtured their dream of radical change. "Our sorrowful task will not be for nothing," the poet Prince Alexander Odoevsky averred following the revolt. "The spark will kindle a flame."[42]

The middle years of the nineteenth century produced a new generation of noble revolutionaries, such as radical populists Alexander Herzen, the "father of Russian socialism," and Mikhail Bakunin, the anarchist and theorist of peasant revolution. This new generation of Russian revolutionaries went abroad to escape tsarist censorship and prisons. In London, Paris, and Geneva, Bakunin mingled with revolutionaries and communists and wrote on the Russian peasants' propensity for violence as a tool for revolution and the overthrow of the tsarist state and the noble landlords. Bakunin's ideas influenced the other great Russian anarchist, Prince Pyotr Kropotkin.[43] Radical nobles did more than just theorize revolution. Nikolai Sablin was born into a hereditary noble family in the Vologda province in 1849. A poet, populist, and member of The People's Will, he committed suicide just as police were about to arrest him in 1881 in connection with the assassination of Alexander II. Before putting the gun to his own head, he fired off three shots to warn his comrades.[44]

By the latter decades of the nineteenth century, the revolutionary intelligentsia had become a much more socially diverse group and had largely shed its noble origins. Still, it should perhaps not be too surprising that Russia's greatest revolutionary was himself a nobleman. Vladimir Ulyanov, better known as Lenin, was the son of a hereditary nobleman and actual state counselor, whose title brought with it the right to be addressed as "Your Excellency." After his father's death, Vladimir lived with his mother and siblings at their mother's family estate near Kazan. Just like other young noble boys, he loved to hunt, swim, and sail. His mother's family money allowed Lenin to spend his time reading and studying Marx; later the family money helped subsidize Lenin after he devoted himself full time to the revolution. Lenin was neither the family's only nor its first revolutionary. In 1887, his older brother Alexander was arrested and hanged for taking part in a plot to kill Alexander III.

Exiled to Siberia in 1897 for his political activity, Lenin claimed noble status in order to soften the harshness of his punishment. During his many years in Western Europe before the revolution, Lenin and his wife, Nadezhda Krupskaya, hired domestics to help with the cooking and cleaning. When it suited him, Lenin had no qualms about admitting his noble background. In 1904, in Geneva, he registered at a private library as "W. Oulianoff, gentilhomme russe."[45] Lenin never fully shed his noble origins. When Nicolas Nabokov, a cousin of the writer, went with his tutor in the spring of 1917 to hear Lenin speak from the balcony of the Kschessinska mansion, what he noticed first was that he spoke in "the manner of upper-class salon snobs." How odd, young Nicolas found it, for someone whose manner of speech reflected Nicolas's own class to stand up there and say such hateful, unpatriotic things about Russia.[46]

2

THE SHEREMETEVS

Since the 1500s, the Sheremetevs occupied high positions at the court of the Muscovite grand princes and were members of the Boyar Duma. Several Sheremetevs displayed skill in Muscovy's military campaigns against the Tatars and in the Livonian Wars of Ivan the Terrible. (According to one account, "Sheremet" once meant "a man with the courage of a lion.") The powerful boyar Fyodor Sheremetev played a key role in the election of Mikhail Romanov to the throne in 1613, thus establishing the ruling dynasty for the next three hundred years. Fyodor, who was related to the Romanovs through marriage, reportedly endorsed Mikhail's candidacy with the words "Let's pick Misha Romanov, he's young and stupid." Foreigners claimed that the tsar's wife was Fyodor Sheremetev's maid.[1]

Count Boris Sheremetev was Peter the Great's much-decorated field marshal, and his grandson Count Nikolai Sheremetev was one of the richest grandees in the reign of Catherine the Great. Something of an eccentric, Nikolai devoted his life and fortune to building the finest opera company in all Russia, composed of his personal serfs. He scandalized society by falling in love with his brilliant leading soprano, a serf named Praskovya Kovalyova, who performed as "The Pearl." They wed, secretly, in 1801, but only after Nikolai had concocted a fanciful genealogy for Praskovya that claimed she was the long-lost descendant of a Polish nobleman. She died two years later, soon after giving birth to their son, Dmitry. Praskovya's death left Nikolai heartbroken.[2] Although famous for his charity, which became one of the family's finest traits and the source of the popular expression "to live on the Shereme-tev account," Dmitry achieved little of note, other than to amass even more wealth and serfs, creating what may well have been the largest fortune in nineteenth-century Russia, consisting of some three hundred thousand serfs and more than 1.9 million acres (763,000 hectares) of land.[3] When he died in 1871, Dmitry's fortune was divided between his two sons and his half brothers Sergei, born in 1844, and Alexander, born in 1859.

As befitted a Sheremetev, Alexander attended the Corps des Pages before joining a guards regiment and then being named aide-de-camp to Nicholas II in 1902. Like his grandfather Count Nikolai Sheremetev, Alexander had a passionate love of music. In the 1880s, he established his own symphony orchestra and enjoyed giving free concerts in St. Petersburg. He was himself a fine pianist and head of the Imperial Court Choir, where he worked alongside the composer Mily Bala-kirev.[4] Alexander's other love was firefighting. At his Ulyanka estate he organized the Peter the Great Firefighting Brigade, six hundred men strong and outfitted with the latest firefighting technology. Tsar Nicholas granted Alexander special permission to quit receptions at the Winter Palace when there was a fire in the city so he could don his firefighter's uniform and ride off with his brigade to battle the flames.[5]

Alexander inherited from his father more than five hundred thousand acres in thirteen provinces, one home in St. Petersburg, and ten houses in Moscow, including the extraordinary palace-estate of Ostankino. He lived with his wife, Countess Maria Geiden, and their four children (Yelizaveta, Dmitry, Alexandra, and Georgy) in a sumptuous St. Petersburg mansion on the fashionable French Embankment. The family lived grandly. Alexander never traveled without a large retinue of servants and domestics, his musicians and choristers, and even cows from his villages to assure a ready supply of fresh milk.[6]

Like his younger half brother, Count Sergei Sheremetev grew up in luxury and privilege. Educated at the Corps des Pages, he joined the Chevaliers Gardes and was then named an adjutant to Grand Duke Alexander in 1868. When the grand duke ascended the throne in 1881 as Alexander III, he named Sergei his aide-de-camp; other posts, distinctions, medals, and honorific titles followed. Alexander and Sergei were as near to friends as the gulf between autocrat and subject might allow, and for the rest of Alexander's reign, Sergei remained one of the closest men to him, with whom the emperor spoke regularly and whose opinions he valued.[7]

Sergei's passions were Russian history and culture, to which he devoted his time, energy, and enormous fortune. He was a diligent amateur historian and a patron of a number of scholarly societies and organizations; he established libraries across Russia open to the public, funded the dying art of icon painting, and patronized artists. His great love was the Russian country estate. Although he had inherited vast property from his father and three houses in St. Petersburg and two in Moscow, Sergei purchased a number of estates as a way of preserving them for future generations. Among them were Mikhailovskoe and Ostafievo.[8] Ostafievo had been a favored meeting place for the poet Pushkin, who dubbed it "the Russian Parnassus," Vasily Zhukovsky, and Adam Mickiewicz, and it was here that the great nineteenth-century historian Nikolai Karamzin wrote his monumental history of Russia. Sergei lavished money and attention on these estates.[9] As part of his daughters' dowries, Sergei purchased for Anna the estate of Voronovo with a manor house of sixty rooms and for Maria the estate of Vvedenskoe, where in the second half of the nineteenth century artists like Mikhail Vrubel, Isaac Levitan, and Valentin Serov often gathered.[10]

Conservative, devout, and patriotic, Sergei followed in the path of the Slavophiles, who believed that Russia was neither European nor Asian, but something unique, a land and people apart with their own traditions, culture, and history. He stood firmly opposed to those Russians who argued for the need to adopt Western European political and legal institutions and remained an unbending believer in autocracy as the only true form of government for Russia. *Samobýtnyi*—original, native, distinct—was the word he used to describe Russia's church, its monarchy, its nobility, and its history. His love of Russia came with a darker side. He was an anti-Semite who bemoaned the "Jew-Masonry" spreading over Russia, destroying "our age-old foundations." He was a foe of cosmopolitanism, Art Moderne, and the decadents.[11] Minister of Finance Count Sergei Witte, a Westernizer who clashed with him on several occasions, described Count Sergei as "an honorable but odd man [. . .] a pillar of mindless Russian conservatism."[12]

Sergei was a true patriarch, and his interests dominated the life of the Sheremetev family. Everyone and everything revolved around him, his projects, whims, and travels. His wife, born Princess Yekaterina Vyazemsky, was the granddaughter of Prince Pyotr Vyazemsky, a poet and friend of Pushkin's. Gentle, warm, and endearing, with large blue eyes and blond hair, Yekaterina was loved by all in the family. Her interests tended toward botany and natural history, which she studied and published on, and she was happiest at home among her family, never caring much for society or the court. Yekaterina and Sergei lived with their seven children (Dmitry, Pavel, Boris, Anna, Pyotr, Sergei, and Maria) and their spouses, nearly two dozen grandchildren, and countless relatives and hangers-on, all grateful for the Sheremetevs' unimpeachable generosity. Winters were spent in the Fountain House in St. Petersburg, summers at Mikhailovskoe, with stopovers at their Moscow home, the Corner House, what the family called "the Sheremetevs' refuge."[13] There were visits as well to other Sheremetev properties like Kuskovo, Ostafievo, Pokrovskoe, and Balanda.

Count Vladimir Musin-Pushkin, a nephew of Sergei's, recalled how entering the Sheremetev household was like stepping back into the past. The spirit of Catherine the Great's Russia seemed to still be alive at Kuskovo and Mikhailovskoe. Sergei rarely dressed before noon, preferring to remain in his sumptuous brown silk dressing gown and Louis XVI frilled nightshirt. Getting dressed required the help of three valets, the chief among them having the honor of washing the count's face with a sponge.[14] The Sheremetevs, like other aristocrats, lived with scores of domestics, servants, governesses, and tutors. Life without them was unimaginable. The Sheremetev children grew up with the children of the emperor and empress. Dmitry and Anna were especially close to Tsarevich Nicholas (the future last tsar) and his sister Grand Duchess Xenia, while Pyotr, Sergei, and Maria spent much time with the young children, Grand Duke Mikhail and Grand Duchess Olga. In 1892, Dmitry married Countess Irina "Ira" Vorontsov-Dashkov, daughter of the governor-general of the Caucasus Count Illarion Vorontsov-Dashkov, in the social event of the season attended by more than six hundred guests, including the entire royal family. It took a whole train car just to ship in the fresh flowers for the ceremony.[15]

Dmitry served in the Chevaliers Gardes, and in March 1896, after Nicholas had ascended the throne, Dmitry became one of his aides-de-camp. He began a public, official life and spent much of his time near the tsar at court or attending to all manner of official ceremonies. Dmitry loved to hunt, and he made frequent hunting trips with Nicholas to the emperor's estate of Spala or to the Sheremetev estate of Balanda, famous for its wolf hunting. Unlike his father, who could not help negatively comparing Nicholas with Alexander III, Dmitry had a strong personal attraction to and respect for the last tsar, although he too recognized Nicholas's weakness of character.[16]

Dmitry's younger brother Pyotr was also one of Nicholas's aides-de-camp. Pyotr died of tuberculosis at a sanatorium in Yalta in the spring of 1914. His daughter, Yelena Sheremetev, then a little girl, wrote in her memoirs of those sad days. The royal family was then in Yalta, and Yelena recalled seeing the grand duchesses "all dressed alike, with long white dresses, black velvet ribbons about their necks, and large straw hats." Another time she spied Tsarevich Alexei walking on the other side of the Livadia palace gates.[17] Nicholas and Alexandra visited Pyotr as he lay dying in Yalta. When Yelena turned to leave the church after her father's funeral, Nicholas and Alexandra stood before her. Stunned, she did not know what to do: Should she curtsy, as she had always been instructed? As she stood there frozen in place, they approached and kissed her on the forehead.[18] In her memoir, Yelena also recalled Easter parties at the Anichkov Palace hosted by Dowager Empress Maria Fyodorovna, the widow of Alexander III. With her cousins, Yelena, wearing her white and blue silk dress and black stockings, would ride over from the Fountain House in a carriage. Maria Fyodorovna would greet the children and invite them to hunt for Easter eggs hidden throughout the palace. The hunt was followed by a magic show and hot chocolate. All the children left with big baskets full of eggs and presents.[19] At Christmas, a large wooden slide was erected in the Fountain House's ballroom for the children and their many friends, who would slide down on small carpets and then sail across the slick parquet floor, screaming with delight the whole way.[20]

Of all the sons, Pavel, born in 1871, was the closest to his father. He shared his father's love of Russian history and culture, graduating from the University of St. Petersburg's Historical-Philological Department and then going on to research and publish on the history of the Romanov and Sheremetev families, noble country estates, and Russian monasteries. He belonged to various scholarly societies, wrote poetry and painted, and his works were shown at numerous exhibitions.[21] After university Pavel served in the Semenovsky Life Guards Regiment and was with his regiment at the coronation of Nicholas II in 1896. Pavel was deeply affected by the tragedy at Khodynka Field, where thousands of people waiting to collect souvenirs were trampled to death. The tsar refused to let the tragedy stop the coronation celebrations, a decision Pavel found abhorrent, and not long thereafter he quit the military.[22]

Pavel was a complicated man, full of contradictions and with a character given to anguishing over Russia's so-called cursed questions: What has happened? Who is to blame? What is to be done? His notebooks from the 1890s show a young man deeply concerned about the state of Russia. On a trip to Zurich in June 1898, he jotted down his thoughts on where the current workers' movement was heading and whether it might be possible to influence "the class struggle, to direct it and to avert the bloody conflicts that inevitably threaten us in the future." "What are we to do," he wondered, writing about the nobility, "where is our union, our organization in the political struggle against the autocracy? Is it the zemstvo? But what is it doing? [. . .] Autocracy cannot last much longer at home. Thanks to 'Khodynka' its significance has been undermined; it has been undermined both in the eyes of society and in the eyes of the common people."[23]

For Pavel the answer lay in trying to expand the zemstvo movement to the lowest levels of society, thereby creating greater freedom of expression and involvement in Russia's problems for as many of its subjects as possible. In 1899, he moved to the Zvenigorod district and joined the Moscow provincial zemstvo, in which he served until 1911. Pavel threw himself into zemstvo work, devoting himself to the spread of public education and writing and giving speeches. Pavel was convinced of the need to let society, in the broadest sense, be heard and to grant it greater autonomy in its affairs. The state's distrust of the people had to be overcome. Echoing his father's Slavophilism, Pavel rejected the idea that the answer lay in adopting Western parliamentary forms and institutions. Pavel equated such notions with the intelligentsia, whom he considered too deracinated and too taken with foreign forms and ideas to be effective; the intelligentsia, in his mind, was cut off from Russian reality and ignorant of how the Russian masses lived and so had no idea what they wanted and needed. He saw no contradiction between traditional Russian autocracy and allowing greater opportunity for all Russians at the local level to take part in running their own lives. The greatest danger lay in bureaucratic proizvol, arbitrariness, which was undermining the people's faith in autocracy. By refusing to listen to the voices of the people, the state was exhibiting "a distrust that will be fatal for Russia." He wrote, "By showing contempt for society, the government is teaching society how to disdain political authority." Russia, Pavel warned, cannot be held together "merely by external force," but only with all the sources of the country working in consort. "There is unrest in the air," he wrote in 1902. "There is no calm."[24]

Pavel's concern over the crisis facing Russia led him to help found a group called *Beséda*, the Symposium, in Moscow in 1899. Made up of about forty aristocrats active in the zemstvos, Beseda brought together men united by a common question: How to avoid revolution? The group was unique for its diversity of political views, which extended from Slavophile monarchists like Dmitry Shipov, on the right, to Marxist radicals like Prince Vladimir Obolensky, on the left, with room for liberals like Prince Mikhail Golitsyn in the middle. All its members were committed to an honest, open discussion of Russia's ills, especially the state's attempts to curtail the influence of the zemstvos, and of the need to secure local self-government. At its first meeting the group declared its main goal to be "the awakening of social activity and public opinion, which are so weak in Russia and have been so artificially repressed, to such an extent that it will have greater authority for Petersburg."[25] Political organizations like Beseda were illegal, and Pavel and his fellow *sobesédniki* knew this, yet given the lofty status of its members, the state was willing to turn a blind eye. For Pavel, autocracy could coexist with a law-based state that allowed society to organize itself and express its own interests. One of the speeches he gave in 1905 bore the oxymoronic title "Autocracy and Self-Government."[26] The Englishman Bernard Pares met Pavel during this period and heard him speak of Beseda and his ideas for Russia. Pares was greatly impressed, calling him "a brilliant and fascinating young noble [. . .] who must have been one of the cleverest and most convincing spokesmen of conservatism."[27]

Count Sergei recognized Pavel as his spiritual heir. In February 1907, he composed a testament to be read by Pavel upon his death. "I turn to you, knowing your love and your feelings for our native past, knowing your special care and sympathy for our familial history. Preserve these feelings together with your attachment to our holy Orthodox church and our beloved motherland."[28] For the rest of his life Pavel felt the responsibility to Russia and to the family that his father had placed upon him. It later influenced greatly the difficult decision he would have to make about whether to leave Russia.

Anna was the elder of the two Sheremetev daughters. Born at Mikhailovskoe in 1873 and named after Sergei's much adored mother, she received an excellent education and was gifted with a beautiful voice. Her parents sent Anna to study singing in Italy, and after her return Sergei loved to have Anna sing for guests of the Fountain House. She was a maid of honor at the court of Empress Maria Fyodorovna in the reign of Alexander III, and as a teenager she danced with the tsarevich Nicholas at balls at the Winter Palace.[29]

One contemporary described Anna as refined and charming and the kind of woman who moved men to spill blood and compose love songs. Aware of her power over men, she enjoyed using it and watching its effect.[30] Profoundly religious, she was drawn to mysticism and the spiritual world and believed she possessed the power of prophecy.[31] Politically, she agreed with her family's ideas about Russia's unique character and considered autocracy the only true system for Russia, although she too complained of Tsar Nicholas's weakness and lack of courage.[32] Still, she was a young woman of her day. She read the monthly *The Women's Cause*, followed the educational ideas of Montessori, and wondered in her diary whether she was a *feministka*. She often found society life in St. Petersburg suffocating and longed for a quieter, simpler life in the countryside. When the society hostess Countess Betsy Shuvalov asked Anna to join a new women's club, she wondered what benefit to society there was in a bunch of aristocratic ladies gathering to drink tea and gossip.[33] At the family estates of Mikhailovskoe and Voronovo she taught peasant orphans in the village schools how to read and write.[34]

In 1894, Anna married twenty-four-year-old Alexander "Alik" Saburov. The young groom did not impress his father-in-law. "Your taste, not mine," he informed his daughter, his words in part motivated by his belief that the Saburovs did not measure up to the Sheremetevs, even though the Saburovs were an ancient Muscovite boyar family. Aristocratic society seemed to agree. Anna had been one of the most sought-after young ladies of her day, and most seemed to think she could have made a better match.[35] Alik's father had been a prominent diplomat, and one of Saburov's grandfathers, Alexander Ivanovich Saburov, had taken part in the Decembrist movement. Alik served in the Chevaliers Gardes, which he found empty and pointless, before being made deputy governor of Moscow in 1902 and then, in 1916, civil governor of Petrograd, as well as master of ceremonies at the imperial court. He spoke German and Italian, played the piano, and was a noted dancer, a particularly popular partner of Dowager Empress Maria Fyodorovna.[36]

Anna and Alik were happy together. They had four children—Alexei (who died young), Boris, Xenia, and Georgy (called Yuri)—with whom they spent summers at Mikhailovskoe and winters on the French Riviera. Shortly before the revolution, Anna and Alik were making plans to betroth Xenia to Grand Duke Fyodor Alexandrovich, the son of Grand Duke Alexander Mikhailovich and Grand Duchess Xenia, the younger sister of Nicholas II.[37]

Anna's younger sister, Maria, born in 1880, was her father's favorite. Shy, delicate, and religious, Maria was given a fine education at home and showed artistic talent as a painter. Like her sister Anna, she was a maid of honor at court. In 1900, Maria married Count Alexander Gudovich, a former cavalry officer and gentleman of the bedchamber. Among those attending the wedding was Grand Duke Sergei Alexandrovich, governor-general of Moscow and younger brother of Alexander III.[38] The grand duke would be blown up by a terrorist bomb outside the Kremlin five years later.

3

THE GOLITSYNS

Tracing their family back to Grand Prince Gedymin, the fourteenth-century founder of Lithuania, the Golitsyns were among Russia's oldest and most esteemed noble clans. They were also its largest. Under the Muscovite grand princes, the Golitsyns counted twenty-two boyars, more than any other family, and by the end of the nineteenth century the massive family tree had grown to sixteen distinct branches.[1] For centuries the Golitsyns had distinguished themselves on the battlefield, at court, in the diplomatic service, and in the arts and sciences. Prince Nikolai Borisovich Golitsyn, a veteran of the Napoleonic Wars, was a patron of Beethoven's and the dedicatee of the so-called Golitsyn String Quartets (Opus 127, 130, 132); Prince Boris Golitsyn was one of the founders of modern seismology and the creator of the first electromagnetic seismograph; Prince Dmitry Golitsyn was the first Catholic priest ordained in the United States, in 1795, and for forty years he spread the gospel in western Pennsylvania as the "Apostle of the Alleghenies"; and Prince Nikolai Dmitrievich Golitsyn was the last prime minister of tsarist Russia in 1917.[2]

Prince Vladimir Mikhailovich Golitsyn was born in 1847 in Paris. Much of his early years were spent in France, and for the rest of his life he professed a profound love for everything French. French was his first language, and he learned to speak Russian fluently only after returning to his homeland for good in the 1860s. Growing up in France, Prince Vladimir attended the imperial balls of Napoleon III, where he once met Baron d'Anthès, notorious as the duelist who felled Alexander Pushkin in 1837. In Nice, he met Pushkin's aging widow, Natalya Goncharova (he found her still quite beautiful), and in Berlin he was introduced to Prime Minister Otto von Bismarck. As a boy he had been presented to Emperor Nicholas I, and on visits to Moscow he shared meals with ancient courtiers from the reign of Catherine the Great and the heroes of Borodino and Austerlitz.[3]

In 1865, Prince Vladimir enrolled in the faculty of natural history at Moscow University. He was swept up by the optimism during this era of the Great Reforms under Tsar Alexander II. "We all had one cherished wish, one dream," he wrote in his memoirs, "the continuation and expansion of the recently given freedom."[4] After serving several years in the Moscow City Duma, Prince Vladimir was appointed deputy governor of Moscow in 1883 and then governor of Moscow Province four years later. In 1891, however, he was suddenly and unexpectedly removed from his position by the new governor-general of Moscow, Grand Duke Sergei Alexandrovich. Although this was never publicly acknowledged, Prince Vladimir had been fired as punishment for his increasingly liberal views.[5]

His work in the provincial government had proved to him what he called "the complete vileness" of the autocracy and especially the abuse of power by its officials and the "criminal blindness of the ruling circles."[6] Completely disillusioned with the tsarist political system, Prince Vladimir railed against Russians' "civil and political ignorance," which he traced back to the reign of Tsar Paul I (1796–1801), who, in his opinion, began "to teach us to see tsarist power as a form of despotism, personal caprice and proizvol and to consider this the law of power, order, and prosperity."[7] A pacifist who abhorred violence of any kind (he would not hunt, fish, or even pick flowers), Prince Vladimir refused to equate patriotism with blind loyalty and love of the Romanovs; revolted by notions of Russians as God's chosen people, he called himself a follower of "Pantheism in the spirit of Spinoza and Goethe, whom I idolize."[8] He was ambivalent toward his own social class, preferring what he called "an aristocracy of culture and intelligence, an aristocracy of lofty souls and sensitive hearts."[9]

Prince Vladimir returned to public life in 1897, when he was elected mayor of Moscow, a post to which he was to be reelected three times and that established him as a prominent voice for liberal reform and the defense of the rule of law. As mayor he built schools and hospitals, improved the city's water supply, began the plans for a city subway system, and helped negotiate the establishment of the Tretyakov Art Gallery. In late 1904, the mayor (as Prince Vladimir will be called in this book) appealed to the government to undo its long-standing repressive measures and to introduce freedom of conscience, the press, and assembly. His appeal was seen in many conservative circles as a direct challenge to the authority of the tsar; progressives hailed him as "the bright Champion of honor and truth." Minister of the Interior Alexander Bulygin threatened the mayor with legal action, and the right-wing extremist Black Hundreds later blamed him for the revolutionary violence in Moscow that followed in 1905. The government forced the mayor from office by the end of the year. As a show of support, the city Duma voted unanimously to bestow upon him the title of honorary citizen, making him only the twelfth person ever to be accorded the distinction.[10]

Vladimir married Sofia Delianov in 1871. Sofia spoke five languages, played the piano, and patronized artists such as Isaac Levitan, Leonid Pasternak (father of the writer Boris), and Valentin Serov, as well as the more experimental World of Art and Knave of Diamonds groups. At their Moscow home the Golitsyns hosted a salon for many of the day's leading creative figures.[11] Between 1872 and 1892 Sofia bore ten children, eight of whom survived to adulthood. All the sons attended Moscow University. Mikhail, the eldest, studied law; Nikolai studied philology and later became the director of the State Archives of the Ministry of Foreign Affairs; Alexander studied medicine and became a doctor; and Vladimir Vladimirovich studied physics. The elder two daughters, Sofia and Vera, were maids of honor at court. By the outbreak of war in 1914, all the children had married and started their own families.[12]

Growing up in Moscow, Prince Mikhail Golitsyn and his younger brother Vladimir Vladimirovich were frequent guests at the Sheremetevs' Corner House, where they took dancing lessons with the children of Count Sergei and Countess Yekaterina. Under the direction of a former dancer of the Bolshoi Theater, the boys and girls learned the classical ballet poses and were taught to waltz, polka, and dance the mazurka. Each lesson ended with a large quadrille. Young Maria Sheremetev was

Vladimir Vladimirovich's favorite partner. All the grown-ups came to watch them with approving smiles. After the lessons tea and cakes were served and the children were released to play on the grand main staircase or organize games of hide-and-seek throughout the expansive house.[13]

In 1896, Mikhail left Moscow for the Golitsyn estate of Buchalki in Tula Province, where he was elected chairman of the district nobility and became active in the work of the local Epifanovsky District zemstvo. The following year in Tula Mikhail crossed paths with Count Pavel Sheremetev. The two young men shared many views about the need to expand the power of the zemstvos and to resist the encroachment of the central government in its affairs. Whereas others placed Pavel within the conservative camp, Mikhail found him to be liberal, even leftist, in his political opinions and noticed he was associating with "so-called Reds." Count Sergei Sheremetev became so upset with his son that he threatened to cut off his allowance; for a time Pavel barely had enough money to get by. In 1900, Mikhail became a member of Beseda and attended its meetings along with Pavel at the Sheremetev homes in Moscow and St. Petersburg. Mikhail remained active in Beseda for several years.[14]

Whereas Pavel was moving further to the right after 1900, Mikhail was moving further to the left. He took part in secret underground meetings with other liberal nobles to discuss the sorrowful condition of rural Russia and ways to bring equal rights to the peasants. At his Buchalki home, he and his wife hosted weekly gatherings with local teachers at which they read political literature and talked ideas. Mikhail's activities and political opinions became known to the Tula governor, who pressured him to stop the meetings and placed the Golitsyns under surveillance. By 1905, Mikhail had become convinced of the need for a constitutional order. He was once nearly arrested for meeting with a group of peasants, and the pressure of the government authorities, plus the disapproval of many of his conservative noble neighbors, who by now had come to view him as almost a revolutionary, led Mikhail to quit the zemstvo and to leave Buchalki with Anna and their children for Moscow in 1912.[15]

Mikhail's brother Vladimir Vladimirovich was considered the "Reddest" of all the Golitsyn sons. After university he left Moscow to run the family estate of Livny in Orel Province. He too served in the zemstvo, acting as the chairman of the zemstvo board, and in the local town Duma. As a young man one summer in the countryside he happened to catch sight of a peasant girl, "with big sad eyes and a charming face," tending a flock of geese. He fell in love with this "rare treasure" and knew someday they had to be married. Tatiana Govorov was a dozen years his junior, uneducated, and ignorant of Vladimir's world, but regardless they married secretly in 1907. Only after he had helped educate her did Vladimir introduce Tatiana to his family, and they all took to her at once. They settled at Livny and were still there with their three young children (Alexander, Yelena, and Olga) when the revolution broke out in 1917.[16]

Most in the family could overlook a Golitsyn's marrying a peasant, but the liberal notions of the mayor and his sons were another matter. Even the mayor's own wife found their liberalism distasteful and misguided. An unbending supporter of autocracy, she blamed her son Mikhail's politics on the pernicious influence of the other nobles in the Epifanovsky district, strangely overlooking the influence of his father. Reflecting on these years in 1918, Sofia wrote that such liberal views had been common in their circles: "In those days many liked to act the liberal and so they led us to this current terrible time when everything has been ruined." The Golitsyn household in the years leading up to 1917 was filled with heated political rows between Sofia and the mayor and their children; no one would back down or even admit that the other side had a valid point. Nevertheless, none of them, she wrote, could have imagined the coming horrors: "We hardly suspected the kind of disaster that was approaching our beloved Motherland."[17] The liberalism of Mikhail and Vladimir Vladimirovich so upset their uncle Prince Alexander Mikhailovich Golitsyn, the mayor's older, unmarried brother, that he passed them over in his will and left his large estate of Petrovskoe to their brother Alexander. Alexander and his new wife, Lyubov, settled there in 1901. He set up a small free hospital for the peasants and also began work as a surgeon in the hospital at Zvenigorod.[18]

Sofia and the mayor's daughters dutifully married into respectable noble families: Sofia (Sonya), their eldest, to Konstantin Lvov, an officer in one of the guards regiments; Vera to Count Lev Bobrinsky, a wealthy landowner; Tatiana to Pyotr Lopukhin, the brother of Anna Lopukhin, Mikhail Golitsyn's wife; and Yelizaveta ("Eli") to Prince Vladimir Sergeevich Trubetskoy. The Trubetskoys were, like the Sheremetevs and Golitsyns, another of Russia's great aristocratic clans with a distinguished, ancient lineage. Vladimir's father, Prince Sergei Nikolaevich Trubetskoy, was a noted philosopher, the rector of Moscow University, and a prominent liberal of national reputation. He was chosen by the zemstvos in 1905 to present their appeal for representative assembly and major reforms to the tsar. He spoke before Nicholas on June 6, and the tsar, moved by what he heard, seemed to agree with Trubetskoy's appeal, though in the end he failed to act. Trubetskoy died a few months later at the age of forty-three in the middle of a fight to ensure the autonomy of Moscow University from the authorities. His funeral attracted large crowds and occasioned violence in the streets of Moscow and St. Petersburg. A student speaking at his funeral captured the mood of many: "The death of Trubetskoy proves again that in Russia, great, free men can only die." Sergei Trubetskoy's family was talented and well educated. His brother Yevgeny was a religious thinker, writer, and founding member of the liberal Kadet Party, and his son Nikolai became one of the great linguists of the twentieth century.[19]

Vladimir, however, shared neither his family's intellectual interests nor its political views. From a young age, Vladimir cared little for his studies, much to his parents' displeasure. His passion was the military, and after originally flirting with the idea of a career in the navy, he enrolled in the Blue Cuirassier Life Guards Cavalry Regiment. Tall, lithe, handsome, and fearless, Vladimir excelled in the guards, becoming a model officer. He loved what he called the regiment's "primitive romance"—its tradition and discipline, its fabled history, its standard, its handsome chestnut chargers, its esprit de corps. The highlight of the year were the maneuvers and parades before Nicholas II. The first time Vladimir saw the tsar, he was overwhelmed: "My first, large parade in the summer of 1912 evoked in me a hitherto unknown feeling and ushered in a decisive change in my thinking. I felt, suddenly, that I loved the Emperor with a profound passion, although I did not really consider why. The thought struck me what a great fortune it would be for me to be taken into his brilliant suite."[20]

That same summer Vladimir, aged twenty, married Eli, two years his senior. The subject of his marrying was a concern to the other men in the Blue Cuirassiers, for none of them could choose a bride without the approval of his fellow officers. Any acceptable young lady had to be of noble background; no guards officer was permitted to marry a peasant, a merchant's daughter, or any other commoner, regardless of her wealth or education. The officers also had to be convinced of her good reputation and virtue as well as the quality of her relations.[21] For someone of Eli's background, this was not difficult, and their marriage marked the union of two illustrious families. The mayor had to admit, however, that his cherished liberalism and pacifism were utterly foreign to his new son-in-law. Vladimir and Eli went on to have nine children in their twenty-five years of marriage before dying many miles apart from each other in Stalin's dark prisons.

The Golitsyns wintered in Moscow and summered at Petrovskoe or Buchalki. Sergei Golitsyn, the younger of Mikhail and Anna's two sons, born in 1909, recalled his early years at Buchalki in his richly detailed memoir. Although his family did not have the wealth of the Sheremetevs or Yusupovs, still, Sergei grew up surrounded by servants, who were seemingly everywhere in the manor house and on the grounds. As early as the age of four Sergei knew that he was different from other children. He was a prince, a descendant of Gedymin, and so had to be brave like his ancestors. He knew this in part from what his nanny and his grandmother Golitsyn told him; Sergei secretly liked thinking he was better than the other children his age. His father, on the other hand, was chiefly concerned with his work and was rarely at home, much less tending to the children. From his rather liberal mother, little Sergei learned that the society they lived in was not perfect, that there were good and bad tsars, that resisting the bad ones, as the Decembrists had, was a good thing, and that the reigning tsar was surrounded by some wicked men, especially "Grishka" Rasputin. His mother believed in hard work and made sure her children were each assigned a small plot of the garden at Buchalki that they were responsible for tending. With regard to religion, there was no disagreement in the family: Orthodox faith and belief in God were at the foundation of life and beyond question.[22]

We belonged to the class of masters, and this order seemed natural [Sergei wrote], in accordance with centuries' old traditions. True attachment could exist between masters and their people, but at the same time there was always a high invisible glass barrier between them. Some masters were known as liberals, they tried to help the peasants, yet they would never, for example, make their own bed or empty their own chamber pot; and their children were brought up in the same spirit. Once a peasant woman came to see my mother together with her son. I took him by the hand and led him to my sandbox, hoping to play with him, but just then Auntie Sasha [Sergei's nanny] grabbed me by the arm and took me away with a hiss. Yes, the life of the masters was completely different from that of the peasants.[23]

This glass barrier was everywhere. The linden tree walk at Buchalki leading to the manor house was only for the masters; servants and others were to stick to the narrow path along the walk's far left side. Although the villagers and the Golitsyns attended the same church, the masters had their own entrance, which led to a raised and enclosed section, the so-called Princes' Spot, reserved for them. Distinguishing masters from the people was important, but not always easy. When Pyotr Raevsky appeared in Buchalki in the first automobile—a bright cherry red contraption that terrified the locals with its noise and smoke—the pressing question at lunch was where to seat his English driver. His background, attire (dark goggles, leather helmet and jacket), and obvious skill with this new device seemed to place him above the status of the servants who ate in the kitchen, yet it did not seem quite right to seat him at the table on the veranda with the family and their guests. In the end a compromise was found: the driver ate on the veranda, but by himself at his own table.[24]

Situations like this suggested the world was changing, though great effort went into denying it. Life was lived according to a set pattern of rituals and traditions that seemed to exist outside time, to have the appearance of being eternal. Life was thoroughly structured and ordered, and there was a familiar, comforting rhythm to the days, months, seasons of the year. The evening meal at the Golitsyns, for example, never varied from the routine. At three in the afternoon, tea was served from the samovar. At six-thirty, Gleb, the mayor's white-liveried servant, summoned all to dinner with a bell. Around this time, Mikhail Golitsyn, Sergei's father, returned from work and joined the other men at a small table for a little vodka (always Pyotr Smirnov, No. 21) and fish or mushrooms before taking their seats at the main table. Grandmother Sofia occupied one end; the mayor, the other. The men sat near him; the women, near her. The guest of honor always sat at the first place to Sofia's right. A bottle of French Beaujolais stood in front of the mayor; a German Riesling, in front of Sofia. The bread was always black and always sliced into perfect rectangles. Gleb would appear with a large china soup tureen and place it before Sofia, followed by Anton, Sergei's father's lackey, bringing the bowls. Sofia would fill each bowl and instruct the servants whom to give it to. The children were served last. Just serving the soup took fifteen minutes. After three courses, Sergei's father typically got up and returned to work, and the rest remained at the table while Mikhail Mironovich, the cook, stood alongside Sofia in his white cap and wrote down her wishes for the next day's dinner menu. Finally, everyone got up and retired to the drawing room for coffee, candy, and cookies.[25]

So great was the respect for tradition at Petrovskoe that nothing in the house could be moved or altered. Even the furniture stayed exactly where it had been placed decades earlier.[26]

4

THE LAST DANCE

O ver two nights in February 1903, the Winter Palace hosted the grandest costume ball in the reign of Nicholas II. The first night featured a concert in the Hermitage Theater with scenes from Modest Mussorgsky's *Boris Godunov* featuring Fyodor Chaliapin and dances from Tchaikovsky's *Swan Lake* with Anna Pavlova, followed by a lavish buffet. The second and main night of the ball highlighted the dancing of sixty-five officers of the guards regiments specially selected by the empress, a dinner service, and then more dancing until the early hours of the morning. All of aristocratic society was there: the political elite, the diplomatic corps, and the foreign ambassadors.

The Ball of 1903 was to be imperial Russia's last great ball. What made it so spectacular and unusual was in large part its special theme. Although held on the two-hundredth-year anniversary of the capital's founding by Peter the Great, Nicholas chose as the theme for the ball the reign of Peter's father, Tsar Alexei Mikhailovich, and all the guests were instructed to come in costumes from the seventeenth century. Such was the excitement that vast sums of money were spent on designers and the finest tailors to create exquisite outfits of fancy brocades, silks, and satin decorated with gold, pearls, and diamonds. The men came attired as boyars, gunners, falconers, and Cossack hetmans; the ladies, as boyarinas, peasants (elaborately costumed ones anyway), and Muscovite ladies of the court. Some dressed as concrete historical figures. Count Sergei Sheremetev, for example, came as Field Marshal Count Boris Sheremetev, his great-great-grandfather. The emperor came as Tsar Alexei Mikhailovich, and Empress Alexandra, wearing a costume estimated at a million rubles, as Tsaritsa Maria Ilinichna.[1] So enormous was its effect that the ball was repeated shortly thereafter at the home of Count Alexander Sheremetev.

Nicholas's fascination with the early Romanovs was due in no small measure to his desire to flee the troubles of the twentieth century for what Grand Duke Alexander called "the glorious past of our family." The entertainment left the grand duke with a bad feeling. He recalled an evening like it some twenty-five years earlier under Alexander II, but the times had changed. "A new and hostile Russia glared through the large windows of the palace," he wrote. "This magnificent pageant of the seventeenth-century must have made a strange impression on the foreign ambassadors: while we danced, the workers were striking and the clouds in the Far East were hanging dangerously low."[2]

The Russian Empire was being rocked by disturbances in 1902–03. National resistance movements rose up in Armenia and Finland; pogroms shook Kishinev and Gomel; noble estates were attacked and burned when peasant unrest erupted in the provinces of Kharkov and Poltava following several years of famine; workers went out on strike, and their numbers grew to nearly ninety thousand, making for the largest wave of industrial protest the country had ever seen; students marched for greater autonomy of the universities; and doctors, teachers, and zemstvo leaders increased their demands for democratic reforms.[3] In early 1904, against his own better judgment, Tsar Nicholas allowed Russia to be dragged into a war against Japan. Exaggerating popular expressions of patriotic favor for the conflict and minimizing early Russian defeats, Nicholas badly misjudged the war in the Far East, which soon lost public support and exposed the many weaknesses of both Russian military and political institutions. Defeat at the hands of the "inferior" Asians served to exacerbate domestic unrest, unrest that became so serious the tsar was forced to end the Russo-Japanese War with the Treaty of Portsmouth on September 5 (N.S.), 1905.[4]

On January 9, 1905, a peaceful demonstration of workers had marched to the Winter Palace to petition the tsar for protection against their factory owners. The police opened fire on the marchers, killing at least 150 men, women, and children and leaving several hundred more

wounded on the palace square. "Bloody Sunday," as the massacre came
to be known, outraged society, severely damaged the image of the tsar,
and added fuel to the revolutionary movement. In October, the entire
country was paralyzed by a massive general strike, organized in part
by newly formed Soviets of Workers' Deputies in cities across Russia;
in December, workers and radicals in Moscow took to the streets and
engaged in armed struggle with soldiers and the police; and the sailors
of the battleship *Potemkin* mutinied at the Black Sea port of Odessa.
Forced into a corner, Nicholas had no choice but to make concessions,
and on October 17, 1905, he issued the October Manifesto, guarantee-
ing civil liberties, the creation of a legislative parliament (the Duma),
and promising future reforms.[5]

The Revolution of 1905 did not end there, however. The October
Manifesto satisfied few people, especially when it became clear that
Nicholas had every intention of undermining it and retaining as much
power as possible. By the summer of 1906 the violence had spread to
the countryside. "Russia was on fire," wrote Grand Duke Alexander
Mikhailovich, as the peasants tried to burn the landlords out once and
for all.[6]

Vladimir Korostowetz was at his family's estate of Peresash in the
province of Chernigov that summer when two neighboring landlords
were murdered, prompting most of the others to flee their estates for
the towns of Chernigov or Kiev. The Korostowetz family chose to stay,
even though by the autumn of 1906 they were utterly isolated after the
telegraph and postal service stopped operating because of the upheavals. Estates in the area were being torched almost nightly. Soon a pattern developed. A sign naming the next estate to be pillaged would
appear in the villages; the peasants would then gather to descend on it
in the dark. Sometimes entire villages would turn out for the looting,
though according to Korostowetz, this was not how they saw it. "Sharing" is what they called it, as in the peasants went to the Burovka estate
"'in order to share Sakharovitch,' or 'the people of Petriki have gone
forty versts to-day to share Komarovsky and Svetchin.'" From Peresash, Korostowetz could see the glow of fires on the night horizon and
hear "the cries of the savage mob." It was not just the nobles who got
shared. Jews, for centuries frequent victims of peasant rage, were targeted as well. Yegor, the family's head watchman, joined the plunder of
a local Jew and returned with pride over his fine haul of jewelry. The

revolution brought with it a wave of anti-Jewish violence that left thousands injured and dead. The pogroms were largely provoked by right-wing elements like the notorious Black Hundreds, which unjustly blamed the empire's Jewish population for the crisis facing the tsarist regime. It is not clear, however, the extent to which men like Yegor were motivated by anti-Semitism or greed or some combination thereof.[7]

In the spring and summer of 1906, peasant unrest broke out at the Golitsyns' Buchalki estate. The family heard talk that the peasants were planning a raid, and so in early June with loaded guns they left in the middle of the night for the town of Epifan, where government troops had just arrived. Two dozen dragoons and officers were then sent to Buchalki to keep the peace. That summer small pogroms broke out at a few other Golitsyn estates, including Livny. A year later the Golitsyns had still not returned to Buchalki, so hostile was the mood of the peasants.[8]

Some of the Sheremetev estates witnessed pogroms and uprisings during the Revolution of 1905 as well. To Count Sergei this reflected nothing more than the degradation of the Russian peasant.[9] As appalled as he was by the peasants, however, he was even more outraged by the actions of the tsar. To a conservative like Count Sergei there was no excuse for the trouble Russia and Nicholas found themselves in. Years earlier he had written of his concerns about the new tsar and how far he had diverted from the path of his late father:

> Something is going to happen, and thinking about the current situation weighs upon me. A decisive turning point is approaching. Where does Russia's future lie, where are the current masters directing her? This is all so "artificial," and yet there will be future historians who will claim that this was all "inevitable." No, no, a thousand times, no! For after such a reign a legacy had been handed down . . . All that had to be done was to follow straight along this path.

And after the October Manifesto he wrote of more disappointment in Nicholas: "Dear God, how far we have departed from 1894, and in what direction! But then I never did have any hopes for the successor. Russia in 1894 and Russia today! I don't know whether anyone will ever read this diary, but what we are now experiencing with him, I had premonitions of long ago."[10]

Having already begun to drift to the right a few years earlier, Pavel Sheremetev was pushed even further by the revolutionary events. In March 1905, together with his brother Pyotr, he founded the Union of Russian Men (*Soiúz Rússkikh Liudeí*—not to be confused with the archreactionary Union of Russian People), which became one of the largest monarchist organizations of the time. Proclaiming that "Russia and Autocracy are Indivisible," the union tried to unite men of all classes in defense of the existing order. Pavel organized meetings with workers and was part of a small delegation that met with Nicholas on June 21, 1905, urging him to resist the demands of the zemstvo leaders, men he had once found common cause with. ("We have nothing to worry about," Nicholas assured Pavel that day. "Everything will be as in the days of old.") Dominated by aristocrats and landowners, the union espoused Slavophile nationalism and blamed the unrest on the radical intelligentsia and, to a lesser extent, the Jews, positions that became more shrill over time and that appear to have made Pavel uncomfortable, prompting him to leave the union the following year.[11]

Pavel's accommodation with the tsarist state during the revolutionary upheaval of 1905–06 reflected a larger trend within the nobility, as many former critics of autocracy, terrified by the violence they had seen directed against them and, indeed, against all of privileged Russia, now sensed that it was the regime alone that was protecting them from a boundless sea of hostility. The rapprochement, however, would never be universal, much of the nobility having lost all faith in Nicholas by now, nor would it be lasting, as the next major crisis would reveal.[12]

For those few who dared to look honestly and unflinchingly upon the revolutionary violence, it was clear that the nobility was facing a future infinitely more terrifying than what Chekhov had sketched in *The Cherry Orchard*. Ivan Bunin was one of them. Bunin has been called "the last of the great gentry writers," and even though he was the first Russian writer to win the Nobel Prize for literature, he remains little known, much less read, in the West today. The Bunins were an old and once wealthy aristocratic family that was in steep decline by the time of Ivan's birth in 1870. Bunin's father, a veteran of the Crimean War, had squandered his inheritance and that of his wife on cards, wine, and hunting. Bunin's brother, Yuly, was a noted journalist with connections to The People's Will; he had been arrested in 1884 and spent a year in prison before being released to live under police supervision on the family estate. Ivan followed his brother's career, becoming a struggling journalist and writer.[13]

Bunin welcomed the October Manifesto ("I was so excited my hands were shaking . . . Such tremendous joy."), but his hopes for Russia's future were dimmed after witnessing anti-Jewish pogroms in Odessa that autumn that left him sickened. In 1906, he saw peasant revolts near Tula and Orel, and his family had to flee their own estate, part of which was destroyed, after being threatened by the locals.[14] Any illusions he may have had about the native goodness of the common people—the *naród*—evaporated; he spoke out against what he saw as the educated classes' fantasies about the peasantry, fantasies he believed were based on complete ignorance. "In no other country is there such a striking gap between the cultured and uncultured classes as in ours," Bunin told the *Moscow News* in 1912.[15] He held the country's elite in equal disdain, referring to the "pillars of society" as "garbage," and had no time for Slavophile dreams of Russia's uniqueness or its special mission in the world.[16]

Bunin laid out his dark prophetic vision in the 1911 novella *Sukhodol* (*The Dry Valley*). It tells the story of the Khrushchevs, an ancient noble family that, not unlike Bunin's own, has come down in the world. *Sukhodol* presents the world of the Russian gentry and the peasants as one of cruel suffering and doom, in which both groups are imprisoned in a circle of inescapable misery. The once grand manor house has long since fallen into disrepair; the gold spoons are "worn as thin as maple leaves." The older generation has come unhinged. A tragic love affair has driven Aunt Tonya mad, and she has left to live in a serf hut out back, banging away all night on an old piano; no one sits down to dinner without a whip, just in case the barely suppressed hatreds erupt. The deranged patriarch, Pyotr Khrushchev, has two boys, Arkady, his legitimate son and heir, and Gervaska, an illegitimate son by a peasant woman. Knowing the day will come when Arkady will assert his birthright and beat him as his master, Gervaska strikes first, killing his father, stripping him of his gold wedding band, and then fleeing. Freed from the master's authority, the peasant Yushka rapes the servant girl. By the end of the story, every last trace of the Khrushchevs and their lives in Sukhodol has been wiped from the earth. The family portraits, the letters, and finally the manor house itself vanish from neglect, theft, and fire. Weeds overtake the family graveyard; the headstones, worn smooth and illegible from wind and rain, topple and are lost.[17]

Works, such as *Sukhodol*, that cast the peasants in such unflattering light earned Bunin condemnation from the left. Critics dubbed him "a child of *The Cherry Orchard*" and a frightened nobleman. Time, however, was to prove the basic truth of his vision.[18]

The 1906 revolts in the countryside were put down with brutal force. Yet even though order was reestablished, the problems that had sparked the violence remained; what is more, the harsh tactics fueled the peasants' desire for revenge and convinced them that the next time they would have to fight even harder to drive the masters off the land for good. The tense atmosphere that now gripped the countryside did not escape the landowners. When one nobleman returned to his estate in Samara Province, he noticed the peasants' previous "courtesy, friendliness, bows" had been replaced by "animosity" and "rudeness."[19] "The manor and the village face each other like two warring camps," a group of anxious nobles informed Prime Minister Pyotr Stolypin.[20] The trauma of 1905 haunted the Russian nobility. Countess Katia von Carlow, then a young girl, could not escape the fear. She loved the family home at Oranienbaum, but she no longer felt safe there. Once she had "a sort of terrifying vision—she saw the hall and familiar corridors full of an angry and menacing crowd with sticks and weapons, forcing their way along."[21] The vision was about to become reality.

In response to the regime's crackdown, the revolutionary terror that had plagued Russia for decades now exploded. Between January 1908 and May 1910, 19,957 terrorist attacks and revolutionary robberies were recorded; 732 government officials and 3,051 private citizens were killed, and nearly another 4,000 wounded. Shadowy groups with names like Death for Death and the Group of Terrorist-Expropriators spread fear throughout society.[22] In April 1902, a Socialist Revolutionary posing as an officer fired five shots at close range into Minister of the Interior Dmitry Sipyagin, the husband of Count Sergei Sheremetev's sister-in-law[23]; in July 1904, Minister of the Interior Vyacheslav Plehve was blown up by a terrorist bomb tossed into his carriage[24]; the following year another bomb was lobbed into the carriage of Grand

Duke Sergei Alexandrovich, reducing him to nothing but bloody scraps[25]; and in 1911, a double agent shot and killed Prime Minister Stolypin in the Kiev Opera House. The tsar was so near to Stolypin that night he heard the shots himself.[26]

A sense of doom settled over Russia. The apocalypse seemed to be approaching, and no one and nothing could stop it.[27] One May night in Paris in 1914, while sharing a drink on the terrace of the Café de Rohan, a reflective Baron Nikolai Wrangel turned and announced to Count Valentin Zubov: "We are on the verge of events, the likes of which the world has not seen since the time of the barbarian invasions. [. . .] Soon everything that constitutes our lives will strike the world as useless. A period of barbarism is about to begin and it shall last for decades."[28]

Back in Russia, aristocratic society was basking in the afterglow of a spectacular year. Nineteen fourteen would prove to be society's last season and, even if only in retrospect, its brightest. Baroness Meiendorff later recalled that she had seen many sparkling social seasons, but "the *last* one, in 1914," was by far the most "brilliant."[29] Princess Marie Gagarin remembered that last season as one of wild partying, "As if foreseeing the approach of catastrophe and striving to stifle a growing apprehension, all Petersburg nervously indulged in amusement and merrymaking." It was a time of "unprecedented luxury and eloquence"; everywhere were champagne and fresh roses, lilacs, and mimosas imported from the south of France. The highlight of the season was the black and white ball at the home of Countess Betsy Shuvalov, with the officers of the Chevaliers Gardes resplendent in their uniforms. Six months later, nearly all these young men lay dead, killed in the first battles of the First World War.[30] Grand Duke Alexander Mikhailovich cast these days in florid tones: "The gypsies cried, the glasses clinked, and the Rumanian violinists, clad in red, hypnotized inebriated men and women into a daring attempt to explore the depths of vice. Hysteria reigned supreme."[31]

On June 28 (N.S.), 1914, Gavrilo Princip assassinated the archduke Franz Ferdinand of Austria in Sarajevo, setting in motion the events leading to the outbreak of World War I a month later. News of the war was greeted in Russia with an eruption of patriotic fervor, and for a moment the entire country seemed to unite behind the Russian throne.

Prince Andrei Lobanov-Rostovsky witnessed drunken workers in St. Petersburg grab a passing officer and smother him with kisses as a crowd in the street looked on and cheered.[32] It would not be long, however, before workers and soldiers would be smothering officers with deadly blows. Indeed, the danger the war posed for the regime, and for all society, had not gone unnoticed. As early as February 1914, a member of the Council of State, certain that if the war did not go well, it would lead to anarchy and revolution, had urged Nicholas to avoid war with Germany at any cost. The reactionary Minister of the Interior Nikolai Maklakov accurately sensed that the masses would rather fight Russia's own privileged classes than German soldiers. (He himself was executed by the Bolsheviks in 1918.)[33] In July, Count Sergei Witte told Boris Tatishchev that should Russia be foolish enough to go to war, it would mean "her immediate bankruptcy."[34] And in August, the mayor wrote prophetically in his diary: "Regardless how the war ends, this is the end of our vile regime."[35]

Lenin sensed the war spelled the end of tsarism as well, and for this very reason he welcomed it. He later adopted the so-called defeatist position, hoping that the war would lead to the collapse of tsarist Russia and serve as a prelude to a new war—namely, a pan-European civil war of the proletariat against the ruling classes. Social democrats, he argued, had a duty to turn the war into a larger conflict along class lines.[36] Even after the fall of the Romanovs in 1917, Lenin continued to urge a "revolutionary war" at home, throughout Europe, and even among the subjugated peoples of India, China, and Persia.[37]

In the summer of 1914 Russia entered a period of unprecedented savagery and bloodshed from which it would not exit until 1921, following four years of world war, two revolutions, and three more years of civil war and famine that claimed the lives of more than ten million people.[38] No other country paid near the price for the folly of 1914 that Russia did. The losses were staggering. By the end of the autumn campaign, more than a million and a half men had been killed, injured, or taken prisoner. The officer corps, over half of which in 1912 were noblemen, suffered exceptional losses in the first battles against Germany.[39] Fifteen million men served in the Russian armed forces during the Great War. More than four and a half million of them were killed or wounded.[40]

In the early months of the war, the Golitsyn family followed the action closely. They hung a large map in the study at the Buchalki estate and marked the shifting front lines with little red-flagged pins. Prince Vladimir Trubetskoy, Eli's husband, was off fighting with his Blue Cuirassier Life Guards Cavalry Regiment. He received the St. George's Cross for wounds suffered at the battle of Gumbinnen in August 1914. In 1915, Trubetskoy joined the staff of General Alexei Brusilov, who was so impressed with the prince that he made him commander of the first-ever Russian Army automobile unit. A man of impeachable bravery, Vladimir was left with not just physical but emotional scars as well. Once he and his men came across a young and handsome German officer covered in blood and hopelessly entangled in barbed wire; one of Trubetskoy's comrades set upon the man and beat him to death. The killing horrified Vladimir and haunted him for the rest of his life.[41] Mikhail Golitsyn spent the war years establishing and overseeing army hospitals in Moscow; his brother Alexander, a medical doctor, inspected hospitals at the various fronts and brought the latest medical techniques for treating the wounded back from visits to London and Paris. The family set up hospitals for wounded soldiers at Buchalki and the Zubalovo estate as well as at their Moscow home.[42]

Caring for sick and wounded soldiers was a popular way for nobles behind the lines, particularly women, to do their part for the war effort. The Sheremetevs too opened hospitals at a few of their properties. Countess Yekaterina Sheremetev organized shipments of relief packages to Russian prisoners of war, and her daughter Anna Saburov became the local head of an organization called the Family Hearth, dedicated to helping war orphans.[43] Yelena Sheremetev, who turned eleven in 1915, organized a bazaar with the other Sheremetev grandchildren to sell items in order to raise money for wounded soldiers, and she also helped bandage the injured at a private infirmary.[44] Of course, the most famous nurse of the war was the empress Alexandra, and her example encouraged others to get involved. While for most of these women their motives were honest and sincere, there was some element of what Countess Kleinmichel called "vanity and rivalry" to see who could house and feed and care for the men more splendidly than the rest.[45] Vladimir Nabokov's mother, who also set up a hospital, could not help seeing all these works as little more than "the ineffectiveness of part-time compassion."[46]

Almost from the beginning of the war, Russia's lack of arms and ammunition was apparent. The shortages became so severe that soldiers were sent to the front with no guns and ordered to look for them among the dead. A full quarter of the troops did not even have boots.[47] The average Russian soldier fought bravely, but what was asked of him became more than anyone could withstand. By the summer of 1915, officers had found themselves wasting scarce artillery shells on their own troops in a desperate attempt to get them to fight. So dreadful were the conditions at the front that tens of thousands shot off their own fingers to escape the carnage; even more began to desert and head back to their villages, which had been drained of millions of men. Food shortages and the rapid increase in the price of goods fueled ever larger and more frequent strikes in the cities.[48]

In September 1915, Tsar Nicholas made the disastrous decision to replace Grand Duke Nikolai Nikolaevich and assume supreme command of Russia's armed forces. From this point on, the army's mounting failures were blamed squarely on the tsar. The expression used to describe the condition of the army under Nicholas was "order, counterorder, and disorder."[49] Count Dmitry Sheremetev was at Nicholas's side for almost the entire war. Despite their long history together, Nicholas had no interest in hearing Dmitry's honest opinion on the conduct of the war. Dmitry found the post burdensome and retreated to the capital or to his estate in Finland to fish at every opportunity.[50] With the tsar off at headquarters, Empress Alexandra, along with the mysterious holy man Grigory Rasputin, took over the government. Rasputin's murky influence and the widespread perception of the German-born empress as an enemy spy fed talk of dark forces at work behind the throne and destroyed society's waning trust in the Romanovs. Count Sergei Sheremetev was among those most vexed by Alexandra and Rasputin, and their actions, together with Nicholas's inexplicable reluctance to address this widely perceived cancer on his reign, further destroyed his faith in the throne.[51]

Society's lack of trust in the government was matched by the government's lack of trust in society. Convinced that they represented the gravest threat to the crown, the Okhrana kept up surveillance on numerous aristocratic families. Among them was Count Dmitry Sheremetev's wife, Ira. In the autumn of 1914, the forty-two-year-old countess left her children for the front to set up a mobile medical unit with her own funds. Ira often found herself close to the fighting, and Dmitry worried constantly about her. So too did Alexander Protopopov, the last minister of the interior, although for different reasons. Protopopov sent his agents to spy on this "liberal lady and opponent of the 'Old Regime.'" Countess Sheremetev was not the only aristocratic lady being spied on. Countess Ignatiev and her salon were also being monitored for subversive activity. The government feared these and other ladies were gathering officers in their salons and encouraging seditious talk that might lead to a modern-day Decembrists' revolt.[52] What the agents learned led them to see in the elite's alienation from the throne a more serious threat than the one posed by the poor and disenfranchised.[53]

Nabokov père opined: "To be for the tsar meant to be against Russia."[54] And in the final year of its life, the tsarist regime found itself in the strange position of being attacked even by self-professed monarchists, who abandoned Nicholas as weak and incapable of turning around the ship of state heading for the shoals.[55] In the autumn of 1916, at the twelfth congress of the United Nobility, deputies publicly criticized the emperor for the first time ever.[56] Even members of the Romanov family were pleading with Nicholas for change and reforms to give society a greater voice and role in governing, although it was most likely too late by then to halt the drift toward revolution.[57] During the winter of 1915–16, Prince Andrei Lobanov-Rostovsky wrote from the front to his mother in Nice, advising her not to return to Russia. "The age of debility has passed," he told her. "Cosmic events are approaching." That same winter he took leave in Petrograd (the new name given to St. Petersburg during the war), staying at the Hotel Astoria and spending his nights out at the opera, going to parties, dancing the tango, and downing champagne in fancy restaurants. "I noticed in Petrograd an undercurrent of nervousness, a feverish desire to have a good time," he wrote, "and I had the impression that people were spending money as quickly as they could because they did not know what was going to happen next."[58]

The summer of 1916 found Ivan Bunin in the countryside at a cousin's estate. "This is our Rus'," he wrote then in his diary. "The thirst for self-destruction, atavism." Being close to the narod, he sensed danger:

The rye's on fire, the seed's all dead,
But who will save it and risk his head?
The smoke wafts high,
The alarm bell shames,
But who will put out the flames?
An army of madmen has broken loose,
And like Mamai, they'll scourge all Rus' . . .[59]

With millions of peasants off at the front instead of working the fields, the threat of food shortages loomed in late 1916. In cities across Russia, labor unrest grew. Unlike in years past, the police were becoming reluctant to use violence against the protesters. Instead of firing on them, soldiers now began to join the strikers in the streets, to fall in behind banners crying "Down with the War," and to add their voices to the "Marseillaise."[60] On a dark afternoon in that last winter of the Romanov dynasty a group of boys chased the automobile of the tsar's sister Grand Duchess Xenia through the streets of Petrograd, pelting it with snowballs and yelling, "Down with the dirty bourgeoisie!"[61] When Prince Andrei Lobanov-Rostovsky returned to Petrograd at the end of 1916, the city struck him as a "lunatic asylum," filled with a "poisonous" atmosphere and "profound despondency and fear."[62]

On the night of December 16, a small group of men led by Prince Felix Yusupov murdered Rasputin in Petrograd in a desperate attempt to free Russia from his harmful influence.[63] Profoundly shaken by the murder, Nicholas and Alexandra retreated into seclusion and sought consolation in reading, music, and card games. Grand Duke Alexander Mikhailovich could not believe what he was seeing. "This cannot go on for long," he warned Nicholas. "Discontent is mounting rapidly and, the further it goes, the more the abyss deepens between you and your people." The British ambassador George Buchanan encouraged Nicholas to do whatever possible to regain the people's trust before it was too late. The emperor found the idea preposterous. "Do you mean that *I* am to regain the confidence of my people, or that they are to regain *my* confidence?" One of the grand dukes warned that Russia was living through the most dangerous moment in its history, to which Empress Alexandra replied, "You are exaggerating the danger. When you are less excited, you will admit that I knew better."[64] To nearly everyone else, however, the danger of revolution seemed real and growing.

On December 29, 1916, the overseer at Kuskovo wrote to wish Count Sergei Sheremetev and his wife in Petrograd a merry Christmas. It was cold and snowy, he noted, and all was quiet now that the soldiers billeted there for much of the year had left for the front. Everything would be "just fine," the overseer added, if only there were enough food. They all were waiting for the government in Petrograd to come together and solve this problem for good.[65] Elements within the state apparatus, however, were raising the alarm that it might already be too late. A report of the Petrograd Okhrana to the department of police that autumn marked "top secret" painted a frightening picture of Russia on the brink of catastrophe. The dire shortage of food and daily necessities combined with inflation of 300 percent made imminent a dangerous rebellion on the part of the lower classes. Talk throughout the city that "Russia is on the verge of a revolution" could no longer be discounted as the product of German agents. The country stood on the brink of a "hungry revolt," after which would follow "the most savage excesses."[66]

PART II

1917

Arise, lift yourselves up, Russian people,
Arise for battle, hungry brother,
Let the cry of the people's vengeance ring out—
Onward, onward, onward!

We've suffered insult long enough,
And submitted too long to the nobles!
Let us straighten our powerful backs
And show the enemy our strength . . .

Altogether now, mighty army,
Let's plunder the palaces of the rich!
Let's take back Mother Russia,
And be done with paying rent.

So arise, brothers, arise and be bold,
And then shall the land be ours once more,
And from the bitter aspens shall we hang
Every last lackey of that Vampire-Tsar.
                        —"The Peasant Song" (1917)

5

THE FALL OF THE ROMANOVS

On the morning of Thursday, February 23, 1917, more than seven thousand women workers from the textile plants in Petrograd's Vyborg District put down their work and walked out into the streets. The fact that it was International Women's Day had little to do with their decision. Rather, their motivation to act was summed up by the single word they cried as they marched: "Bread!" The food shortages and ever-rising prices in early 1917 had devastated the city's workers and left them hungry, cold, and desperate. The first two months of the year had seen a surge of strikes and protests in the capital and cities across the empire in response to the mounting crisis. As they marched through the streets, the women were joined by workers flooding out of the factories. By ten in the morning, twenty thousand more had fallen in; by noon more than fifty thousand were marching, and before the day was over, as many as ninety thousand had taken to the streets.

As the day wore on, the calls for bread were joined with chants and banners proclaiming "Down with the War!" and "Down with the Tsar!" Marchers started smashing the windows of bakeries and breaking into food shops. Nonetheless, the authorities managed to restore order by the end of the day, and no one seemed to take special note of this latest episode of unrest. Minister of the Interior Protopopov noted in his diary, "In general, nothing very terrible has happened," and none of Nicholas's ministers bothered to report the disturbances to him at headquarters in Mogilev. The revolution, however, had begun.[1]

Throughout the night workers planned further strikes and a march to the city center. On the morning of the twenty-fourth, tens of thousands made their way from the outlying workers' districts. They were met by several hundred Cossacks and soldiers at the Alexandrovsky Bridge. At first it seemed there might be a confrontation, but the Cossacks held back and allowed the workers to cross the Neva River and make for Nevsky Prospect and the heart of Petrograd. Along the way they encountered mounted police detachments, but the size of the crowds (as many as two hundred thousand) and the multiple directions from which they converged on the center overwhelmed the police. The numbers flooding Petrograd's fine inner-city neighborhoods doubled that of the previous day and presented a sight that had not been seen since the Revolution of 1905. As the authorities in the city met to come up with an appropriate response, strike organizers stoked the momentum building in the factories and streets. Some of the soldiers sent out from the garrison to restore order joined the protesters. By Saturday, February 25, the workers' numbers had climbed to as many as three hundred thousand, and their cries had progressed from "Down with the War!" to "Long Live the Revolution!"[2]

That evening Nicholas was finally informed of the disorder in the capital. Unaware of the severity of the crisis, he drafted a terse message to General Sergei Khabalov, commander of the Petrograd military district, ordering him to end the disturbances the following day. The order stunned Khabalov. The only possible way to settle the matter in a single day was through violent confrontation, an act of war against the Russian people itself that he was loath to carry out and that he feared might well only incite further unrest or push his forces over to the side of the protesters. If he had been granted more time, Khabalov believed the tense situation might possibly be diffused. Left with no choice, however, Khabalov issued the order to fire on large demonstrations after three warnings.

Before the dawn of the twenty-sixth, posters forbidding street gatherings and warning residents that the authorities were prepared to confront any unrest with force went up throughout the city. That morning Cossacks patrolled the city center, machine guns sat at the ready to defend key intersections, and special detachments had been positioned to keep protesters from reaching Nevsky Prospect. The capital was an armed camp. As in the previous days, the marchers poured into the city, but this time they were met with gunfire. Dozens of marchers were shot and killed. But the blood spilled in the streets caused some of the soldiers to pause, and as the day wore on, the troops' resolve wavered. Men of the Pavlovsky Guards grabbed their guns and went to battle the police, and then on Monday the twenty-seventh members of the Volynsky Regiment, no longer willing to shoot unarmed civilians, turned their rifles on their commander and shot him dead. Mutiny spread among the soldiers, who spilled out into the streets to join the insurgents.[3]

As their world dissolved around them, the Sheremetevs were preoccupied with a family crisis. In the middle of February Count Pavel Sheremetev returned to Petrograd after a visit to Grand Duchess Xenia's Crimean estate at Ai Todor. The family noticed immediately that Pavel was not well and had suffered a severe emotional collapse. Doctors were called to the Fountain House to examine Pavel, and it was determined that he was suffering from "paranoia" and a nervous disorder of a "romantic" nature.

The cause of Pavel's suffering was a woman by the name of Irina Naryshkin. He had first met Irina at Mikhailovskoe in 1899 and fallen desperately in love with her, yet Irina had refused him for Count Illarion Vorontsov-Dashkov, the brother of Count Dmitry Sheremetev's wife. They had five children before the marriage broke apart. Pavel believed he had a second chance to win Irina, and again she rejected him, this time for Prince Sergei Dolgoruky. This marriage too collapsed, and Pavel professed his love to Irina yet again at Ai Todor in early 1917. Rejected for a third time, Pavel fled for Petrograd by train together with Grand Duchess Xenia and suffered a mental breakdown along the way. Count Sergei found the entire affair humiliating ("It's a rare thing to be a child at age forty-five," he wrote his daughter Maria. "I've always found this embarrassing"), but he saw to it Pavel got help. As chaos spread in the streets of Petrograd, doctors came and went from the Fountain House, and plans were made to send Pavel to the Kryukov sanatorium for nervous disorders outside Moscow.[4]

On February 27, Count Sergei wrote Grand Duchess Xenia to thank her for the concern she had shown for Pavel. He ended his letter with mention of the recent street disturbances, observing, "Something very murky is taking place."[5] That day he wrote in his diary: "There have been gunshots along Nevsky Prospect and in other places, the crowd is growing as are the red flags. [. . .] But no one knows where our government is at the moment or who is in charge of reestablishing order."[6] He also wrote to his daughter Maria, then living in Georgia, where her husband was serving as the governor of Kutaisi, "Things are very unsettled here in the city, the dissatisfaction is growing, at first people just wanted bread, but now other less clear demands are being made. [. . .] I cannot get to the Imperial Council since Nevsky Prospect is entirely filled with people and the streetcars have all stopped and there are no cabs to be had." In closing, he expressed his fear that some sort of "provocation" could lead to even greater unrest.[7]

What happened that day, February 27, has been called "the most stupendous military revolt in recorded history."[8] Following the example of the Pavlovsky Regiment, by nightfall half of the city's 160,000-man garrison had gone over to the insurgents, while the rest chose not to take any side. Soldiers and workers marched to the city's prisons and released the inmates. They raided police stations, courthouses, the Ministry of the Interior, and the headquarters of the Okhrana, where they burned its files. And they armed themselves with guns and ammunition taken from the city's arsenals. Policemen were murdered in the streets; looters ransacked stores and private residences, mobs robbed and killed respectable-looking men in the streets. The red flag was raised over the Winter Palace.

By the end of the day, Khabalov was down to no more than two thousand loyal troops. It was over. The capital was now in the control of the mob. That evening he telegraphed Nicholas at headquarters that the situation in the capital was out of control.[9] Nicholas responded by ordering loyal troops sent to crush the rebellion; but the crisis had advanced too far, and in the end no forces were ever dispatched. Back in Petrograd, the police stripped off their uniforms, abandoned the streets, and fled for their lives. The tsar's ministers met for the last time on the evening of the twenty-seventh at the Mariinsky Palace to tender their resignations. That done, the ministers too tried to run to safety under the cover of darkness.

As the old order evaporated and anarchy spread, members of the

Duma met at the Tauride Palace to consider how to address the chaos. On the afternoon of the twenty-seventh, reluctant to overstep their authority yet cognizant that something had to be done to reestablish order and resist the growing power of the revolutionary crowd, they created a Provisional Committee of Duma Members for the Restoration of Order and for Relations with Individuals and Institutions. The name perfectly captured the bland indecisiveness of what became known as the Provisional Government.[10] Among its twelve members were Mikhail Rodzianko, the rotund Duma chairman; the Kadet leader Pavel Miliukov; the former head of the Union of Zemstvos and Towns Prince Georgy Lvov; and the lawyer and socialist Alexander Kerensky.

At the same time that the Duma men were meeting in the right wing of the Tauride Palace, a rival political power was taking shape in its left wing. The Petrograd Soviet of Workers' and Soldiers' Deputies, which met for the first time on the twenty-eighth, expressed the power of the crowds in the streets, in opposition to the Provisional Government, which from the start was seen as representing Russia's privileged classes. Soldiers outnumbered workers in the Petrograd Soviet, and its executive committee comprised socialist intellectuals—mostly Mensheviks, Bolsheviks, and Socialist Revolutionaries (SRs). The creation of the soviet marked a new state of affairs known as *dvoevlástie*, or dual power, and the Provisional Government and the soviet began a tense unofficial partnership in which each would understand the nature and ultimate goals of the revolution in fundamentally different ways.[11] To gain the conditional support of the soviet, the Provisional Government had to agree to eight conditions, including amnesty for all political prisoners; freedom of speech, press, and assembly; and the abolition of all restrictions based on class, religion, and nationality. Not without reason did Lenin call Russia now "the freest country in the world." The new government also agreed to immediately abolish the police, the Okhrana, and the Corps of Gendarmes. This step, together with the dissolution of the tsarist provincial bureaucracy, was to have fatal consequences, for without new institutions to take their place, the Provisional Government was left with no means to effectively govern the country at the very moment it was descending into ever-greater disorder.[12]

On Tuesday the twenty-eighth, Count Sergei wrote in his diary:

This morning a new revolutionary leaflet appeared informing us that a "coup" has taken place! So there now, we have lived long enough to witness this festive occasion! A festival of insanity! The abnormal power of that woman [Empress Alexandra] has led us precisely to that which many had foreseen. The government is powerless. A new power from within the Duma has been established, a new administration headed by Rodzianko that threatens the State itself. We have no news at all of what has become of the State. There are no newspapers, the mail is delayed, one cannot speak by telephone or write. Rasputin's followers, all that scum, have been arrested. There has been shooting all day long; I cannot make out who is firing at whom or on whose orders. Revolution brings with it the danger of pogroms from house to house.[13]

Earlier that day a group of soldiers came to the Fountain House demanding to see Count Sergei. He was upstairs at the time with Yekaterina and Dmitry and Ira. He went to the top of the stairs and asked what they wanted. They asked whether he had any sons and, if so, how many and where they were, to which he gave vague answers, making certain not to mention any of them by name. Next they wanted to know whether there were any weapons or ammunition in the house. Police, the hated so-called pharaohs, had reportedly been seen on the roof of the Fountain House, shooting down at the insurgents. Yes, Count Sergei told them, he had a great many, though mostly seventeenth-century poleaxes and muskets, and he sent a servant to fetch a few, though this was obviously not what the soldiers had in mind. In the meantime, another group of soldiers had made their way through the house's labyrinths to the apartments of Sergei's granddaughter Lili Vyazemsky, where, hungry and exhausted, they set upon a table laden with food and then vanished. Late that afternoon, a second group of soldiers came. These men, Sergei observed, were rougher, ruder, spouting political phrases and informing the family they had been sent to search the house and instill order. After they left, the family gathered in an upstairs sitting room behind drawn curtains. Sergei noted that the blood had drained from Ira's face, and she sat stricken with panicky fear.[14]

To little Yelena Sheremetev the revolution meant there would be no more going out to play in the garden or visiting friends. Bored, she and her brothers spent the days reading Sherlock Holmes and the detective stories of Allan Pinkerton. Given the sporadic gunfire in the streets, the children were told to stay away from the windows; as the shooting increased, they all were sent to Dmitry's rooms, which faced the inner courtyard.[15] Dmitry's last day of duty as Nicholas's aide-de-camp was on February 8, after which he returned to the Fountain House and most likely never saw the tsar again.[16] As the fighting in the streets got ever closer and the sound of gunfire kept the household awake at night, the level of fear rose within the Fountain House. On March 1, a third search party came to inspect the house. In the rooms of Yelena's mother, Lilya Sheremetev, they came across a number of hunting rifles. One of them unexpectedly went off, just missing Lilya and leaving her almost deaf in one ear. The family, however, was fortunate, and the soldiers left them unharmed.[17]

As the civil governor of Petrograd, Alik Saburov was a target of the insurgents. Concerned for the safety of Anna and their children, he tried to convince them to leave together with the servants for the Fountain House, but they all refused to abandon him. On March 1, a band of soldiers came to the governor's mansion and tried to take Alik to the Tauride Palace. Noticing that all the men were drunk and fearful that he would be killed before ever reaching the palace, Alik tried to stall them by insisting that he would not go unless they had an automobile to conduct him safely. For several tense minutes the soldiers debated among themselves what to do, while Alik waited on the main stairs surrounded by his family and servants. He was rescued when one of the soldiers, a young man with a large white bandage over one eye, managed to convince the men that they had no authority to arrest Saburov without a written mandate. This soldier most likely saved Saburov's life. The men turned and left.[18]

There was a real threat to men like Saburov as mob violence and vigilantism ruled the streets of Petrograd. The idea of the February Revolution as a "bloodless revolution" was a myth created to justify the establishment of the Provisional Government and legitimize its authority.[19] If the first blood of the revolution spilled on Petrograd's streets was that of the marchers, then the rest was mostly that of the police, officers, and other persons affiliated with the old order. Paul

Grabbe, the teenage son of General Count Alexander Grabbe, recalled looking out the window of the family apartment into the street below at a large pile of logs covered with freshly fallen snow. As he looked, the logs strangely grew arms and legs, and Grabbe realized he was staring at the frozen corpses of murdered policemen. A cook at the American Embassy arrived at work in hysterics after seeing a policeman beheaded in the street by someone wielding a saber. General Stackelberg fought back when soldiers came to search his house, shooting two of them before he himself was shot in front of his wife. The soldiers then proceeded to strip him and profane his body; according to one report, his head was cut off and stuck on a spike.[20] The number killed and wounded is estimated to have been 1,443. Mutinous sailors killed hundreds of their officers in grisly fashion in Helsingfors and Kronstadt as well.[21]

The violence of the February Revolution represented an attack of the masses on privileged Russia, those marked by the word *burzhúi*, bourgeois. In the Russian context, the word had nothing to do with the bourgeoisie in the Western European sense. Rather, it was a term of scorn used for all of privileged Russia. Extremely malleable and with a long history, the term "burzhui" could denote the cultured elite, the rich, the intelligentsia, Jews, Germans, or even the revolutionaries themselves. It had nothing to do with a specific social class but stood in the eyes of the downtrodden for "the enemy" and, particularly from 1917 on, the enemy of the revolution. The people stood in opposition to the burzhui in the sense of "us versus them" or "the masses versus the classes." In the countryside, the peasants used the term to refer to all their enemies, especially the gentry and the monarchists. All it took to classify someone as a burzhui in 1917 was a starched white shirt, smooth hands, eyeglasses, or evidence of bathing. Even the color of a woman's hair could mark her.[22]

The burzhui and the other "enemies" of the revolution were demonized as animals and parasites, thus helping legitimize violence against them. The Bolsheviks and other revolutionary parties did not manufacture the term or the hatred that made it so powerful. It had true mass appeal and reflected the lower class's hatred of their betters, the hatred that fueled the revolutionary violence not only of 1917 but on into the civil war years. Over the course of 1917 and later, Lenin and the Bolsheviks became masters at cultivating this hatred and directing it against the privileged classes for their own ends.[23]

The war against the burzhui that erupted in February 1917 fitted with how Russia's lower classes interpreted the freedom that came with the revolution. Freedom was understood as something the Russians call *vólia*, total license and the right to act as one sees fit, unrestrained from any larger authority. In the popular mind, freedom had been won not for all of Russia but for "the people," the poor and the marginalized; it had been wrested from the hands of the tsar and all burzhui, and so any attempts to limit their "freedom" justified stopping and silencing the burzhui as the enemies of the revolution and the people. This tension grew over the course of the year as the Provisional Government failed to deliver on the promises of the revolution—on food, land, and an end to the war. If the freedom they had fought for still was not fully theirs, then enemies must be keeping it from them, and they had to be vanquished for the people's freedom to rain down.[24]

The response of the nobility to the February Revolution was not unified, even in Petrograd at the height of the violence. In the first days of the revolution Paul Grabbe remembered his mother coming home terribly upset. "'Imagine!' she said to me. 'I just ran into Countess Sheremetev; and how do you suppose she greeted me? She said: 'Isn't it wonderful?' and I said, 'What's wonderful?' and she said, 'Why, the Revolution, of course!' and I said, 'Well, Countess, you're hardly the one to rejoice. It is precisely people like us who stand to lose everything.'"[25] These two feelings—joy and fear—marked the most common responses, and some nobles experienced both. For young Grabbe, the initial chaos in the streets meant a school holiday, all the more welcomed for its unexpectedness. The children of Count Pavel and Natalya Ignatiev saw the February Days as "a wild street carnival that they could not wait to get outside to see."[26]

Princess Catherine Sayn-Wittgenstein, the twenty-two-year-old daughter of an ancient German noble family in Russian service since the eighteenth century, had remained devoted to the monarchy up until the revolution (though chiefly out of "stubbornness," she admitted), even though she had long since lost all faith in Nicholas. Her uncle Nikolai Zubov was a liberal Kadet, while her brother Andrei was a committed monarchist. The family had long argued about politics and especially about Empress Alexandra. When the revolution broke out in

Petrograd, Catherine was swept up in the excitement. She, like some in the family, saw a bright future for a "Russian Republic." She wanted to be in the streets with the people to show her solidarity, so along with two friends from the lyceum Catherine went out to march with the crowds and their red banners and sing the "Marseillaise." "I had a feeling of love for that unsightly crowd, and I wanted to merge with it so that it would recognize me as part of it." But the young ladies quickly sensed that they were not welcome, and the looks the workers and soldiers gave Catherine told her to stand back. "I understood that we were not part of the crowd and that it didn't need us." The feeling of being foreign to the revolution grew in the coming months and distanced Catherine ever further from it. The ideological divide within the family deepened.[27]

House searches were common in Petrograd as soldiers sought to arrest prominent officials and military officers and to take weapons out of the hands of anyone considered a foe of the revolution. Some apartments were searched as many as three times in one day.[28] One night General Grigoriev was awoken by the sound of men pounding at his door. Realizing they had come to arrest him, Grigoriev, who happened to be alone at the time, put on his cook's apron and white toque before opening the door. Acting the part of his cook, he then proceeded to take them from room to room in a futile search for General Grigoriev.[29]

Countess Kleinmichel was at home entertaining a small party of friends. Shortly after the butler announced that dinner was served, the doors flew open, and all the servants ran through the dining room, screaming, "Run! Run! The back door has just been broken in by a band of armed men!" Without bothering to grab their coats, the countess and her guests fled down the main stairs, out into the snowy night, and across the street to the house of one of her dinner guests. From there they could see what was happening back in her home. All the lights, even the chandelier in the ballroom, which had not been lit since the start of the war, were now ablaze. Gangs, armed with rifles, axes, sticks, and bayonets, were running about from room to room, tearing down all the curtains, and dragging more tables and chairs into the dining room. The party had not been canceled, although the guest list had been changed. The men sat down, and Kleinmichel's butler appeared with more dishes and cutlery; next he brought out the soup tureens and started to cover the table with bottles of wine. The sailors and soldiers were then joined by the countess's servants, and she looked on as they all raised their glasses and started making toasts. She and her friends watched for hours, unable to look away, as the party went on late into the night and the new masters of her house emptied her wine cellar.

The countess dared go out only the next morning. She spent the next couple of nights with friends, though every night they were visited by gangs of soldiers, so she eventually sought protection at the Chinese Legation. It was there, again at dinner, that fifteen soldiers broke in the door and arrested the countess. Kleinmichel was held at the Duma for a time and then allowed to return to her home, which had been looted and turned into a sort of hostel for soldiers. Reduced to two rooms, which she shared with several of her servants, she spent two weeks listening to them making speeches, singing revolutionary songs, dancing wildly to tunes hammered out on her piano. The grand staircase was turned into a rifle range, large portraits of the Romanovs serving as the targets. They sliced a hole in the mouth of Empress Elizabeth, the daughter of Peter the Great, and stuffed it with a cigarette and cut out Catherine the Great's nose. Louis de Robien, a young Frenchman from the embassy, visited to share her last bottle of French champagne. He found the countess calm and determined to hold her ground against the soldiers. She had armed herself with a pistol and told Robien she was ready to use it on herself if necessary. At the age of seventy-five, she commented, "one must know how to die." She had sold all her possessions in order to survive, but as bad as things were, she refused to think of leaving Petrograd until the war was over because she was determined to prove that the talk of her as a German spy or sympathizer was groundless.[30]

Countess Kleinmichel was one of the fortunate ones in her family. All three of her late husband's brothers were killed during the revolution. One of them, a Hussar Guards officer of twenty-five, suffered an especially wicked fate. According to the words of his orderly, first the soldiers ripped out one of his eyes and forced him to watch as they killed several of his fellow officers; next they took the other eye, broke his hands, his feet, and then tortured him for two hours by lifting him up on their bayonets and beating him with their rifle butts until he finally expired. Two of the countess's nephews were also killed: Nicholas, a former court chamberlain, at the hands of sailors in the Crimea, and a second by the Bolsheviks in the Caucasus.[31]

On March 2, 1917, at ten minutes to midnight in the city of Pskov, Tsar Nicholas II, having been convinced by his generals that this was the only hope to stop the tide of revolution destroying the army and raging in the capital, abdicated the throne in favor of his brother Grand Duke Mikhail Alexandrovich. The fatal reign of the emperor was over. "All around me nothing but treason and cowardice and deceit," Nicholas seethed as his train left Pskov an hour later. When informed the following day in Petrograd that his brother had abdicated in his favor, the grand duke did not take long to decide to reject the crown, in part, apparently, because he doubted whether his accepting it would reverse the situation and also out of fear for his own personal safety. With this, the three-hundred-year-old Romanov dynasty came to an end. But the grand duke did not completely give up on the idea of becoming tsar. He let the leaders of the Provisional Government know that he would be willing to accept the crown, but only if it were offered to him by the Constituent Assembly, a democratically elected body that would meet at a later date to determine Russia's new form of government.[32] With the news of the fall of the Romanovs, crowds in Petrograd, Moscow, and cities across the empire showed their joy by attacking tsarist symbols and insignia, toppling statues, defacing portraits, and burning double-headed imperial eagles.[33]

Upon receiving a telegram with the news of the tsar's abdication, Court Chamberlain Skadovsky purportedly dropped dead of a heart attack.[34] If this did indeed happen, then it was likely the only such death among the nobility. Many nobles did not share Princess Cantacuzène's opinion that all levels of society greeted the news "with a thankfulness almost religious," but most agreed with Baroness Meiendorff's assessment that "[t]he old system was rotten, everyone knew that."[35] "Everyone has participated in the revolution," rejoiced the Kadet prince Yevgeny Trubetskoy in the newspaper *Speech* on March 5; "everyone has made it: the proletariat, the military, the bourgeoisie, and even the nobility."[36]

Princess Cantacuzène's mother-in-law expressed great enthusiasm that the fall of the dynasty would at last mean "the destruction of all the old traditions." The princess noted that the old lady's coachman now sported a red ribbon as a sign of her political loyalties. Such overt expressions of support for the revolution by aristocrats were in fact common. Red banners and flags hung from palaces and mansions, and luxurious carriages bedecked with red bunting and ribbons ferried elegantly dressed ladies and gentlemen through Petrograd's streets. Grand Duke Kirill Vladimirovich raised the red flag atop his house on Glinka Street. While for many these acts marked true support for the revolution, for others they functioned, in the words of Prince Andrei Lobanov-Rostovsky, as "a kind of passport" to protect them from the rage of the crowds.[37]

Countess Irina Tatishchev found the generally positive response of her fellow nobles bewildering. "I did not understand, and I still do not understand," she noted in her memoirs, "how they could not grasp that in cutting off the bough upon which they were seated they would themselves fall into the abyss."[38] Yelizaveta Issakov recalled finding members of the former Imperial Council gathered in her family's apartment on March 3. Prince Georgy Lvov, prime minister of the new government, sat slumped in a chair, his head in his hands, whispering to himself, "Our sins, oh, our heavy, heavy sins." Yelizaveta's father turned to her, gravely observing, "We are on the way to anarchy."[39]

Grand Duke Mikhail visited Count Sergei at the Fountain House soon after his decision not to accept the crown without the approval of the Constituent Assembly. The count found this wise, and he praised the grand duke for preserving the concept of the monarchy.[40] In a letter to Grand Duchess Xenia he expressed hope for the future: "May God grant happiness to a renewed Russia, one that will not stop being Russia, no matter how much her external form may change. This is a new age—an interregnum before a rebirth. There have been examples of this before in our ancient past, and may a new Hermogen, new Minin and Pozharsky, and new Mikhails be found!"*[41]

---

*Patriarch Hermogen, Kuzma Minin, and Prince Dmitry Pozharsky helped rally Russians during the so-called Time of Troubles in the early seventeenth century. "Mikhails" refers to the first Romanov ruler elected to the throne in 1613.

Yet in a letter to Count Vladimir Kokovtsov, the former minister of finance and prime minister after the assassination of Stolypin, also from the first week of March, Count Sergei was less optimistic:

> Everyone must have foreseen this dizzying speed of events after the long and truly astounding patience shown by our exhausted and tormented Russia, the victim of a fateful course of criminal influences. The disappearance of a central, national figure now marks the completion of this progress, [. . .] still, many have a clean conscience. Every effort, every noble impulse, every warning was rejected. We were governed by "abnormality"!
>
> Where will this lead? How far will this go without the help of the country's best forces? I don't wish to say aloud the thoughts that come to mind. I am ready to welcome everything that will aid and revitalize our country, but I cannot welcome base desires and the return of a "Pugachyovshchina."[42]

To his daughter Maria in Kutaisi he wrote:

> I don't have the strength to express the feelings overflowing within me concerning the suicide of Russian statehood, for no one wrestled power away, rather they just picked it up as it lay impotently on the ground. The dizzying speed of events, unheard of in similar situations, offers proof of the power of the mounting indignation and burning resentment for all the criminal inaction. And now here we sit, left to the complete proizvol of the mob and unruly troops.[43]

Maria shared her feelings with her father:

> I heard today that the emperor has abdicated the throne. It is hard to write in this moment of extreme agitation. [. . .] It is agonizing not to be in Russia at this time. Thank God nothing irreparable or terrible has happened. I thank God the emperor abdicated. Still, it torments my soul to witness the joy and the demonstrations. May the Lord help him. No emperor has done what he has, and in every similar instance they all have perished.[44]

And later that month:

> Dear Father, I cannot express to you the feeling I had today when six of your letters were delivered to me. I thank God you are well.
>
> Yes, that which was obvious and unavoidable has happened. If only from now on there will be no more bloodshed and everyone will work together bravely and harmoniously for the defense of the Motherland. Here events are unfolding as they are across all of Russia. We just recently joined the new government. Today he [Maria's husband, Alik] took the oath. The streets are calm.
>
> We truly had been stupefied by the suffocating gases in which we had lived for so long, such that now, sensing that truth has finally arrived, we are tormented with worry for it.
>
> God grant that this unity, felt by us all now that everyone has come together to support the new government, will last, for in this lies our sole salvation and all our strength. Germany will not sit quietly at this moment. One can already feel that she is concentrating all her forces against us. The most decisive moment is approaching. [. . .] And I believe that everyone, from the lowliest to the most important, must understand the gravity of the hour [. . .]
>
> If only Russia might remain strong and not debase itself by falling into anarchy. Dear Father, I want to bare my entire soul to you. May Christ in his infinite patience have mercy on our country. We were unable to escape the maelstrom into which we had been thrust by the demons of these terrible trials. May God grant us all the strength to withstand them with firmness and faith. If only the voices of love were louder now, the voices calling for forgiveness, and may they be victorious against those calling for vengeance.[45]

By the end of March, the relief Maria first experienced after being released from the "suffocating gases" had been replaced by apprehension over Russia's future. She told her father in confidence that the Lord had been sending her visions of angels and burning crosses, which she took as signs of the Apocalypse. She had experienced visions before, and they had always proved prophetic. Shaken by what she believed had been foretold to her, Maria mentioned her wish to leave Kutaisi as soon as possible and join the rest of the family, perhaps at their estate of

Mikhailovskoe. At the same time, however, Maria and Alik were being warned of the danger of unrest in the countryside, leaving her unsettled and anxious.[46]

A similar mood filled the Fountain House, now being guarded by a special police detachment. Dmitry and Ira were depressed and scared and talked of leaving Petrograd as soon as possible for the relative calm of Moscow. Count Sergei considered such fear for their personal safety a stain on the family's honor. Regardless, Dmitry and Ira, together with their children, left Petrograd by train that month.[47] Count Sergei was equally disturbed by the "disgraceful" behavior of Grand Duke Nikolai Mikhailovich.[48] The grand duke, a grandson of Tsar Nicholas I, was the lone Romanov to openly endorse the revolution. Called Nicholas Égalité and the Red Prince, the grand duke had long held republican views. When the French ambassador Maurice Paléologue visited him at his palace on Millionaya Street on March 8, the grand duke told the Frenchman with all sincerity, "The collapse of the autocracy will now mean the salvation and greatness of Russia." He tried to persuade his Romanov relatives to give up their lands to the new government and began making plans to run for a seat in the Constituent Assembly on the Union of Peasants and Landlords ticket. (The electoral commission, however, refused to allow him to run and even denied all the grand dukes the right to vote, out of fear of a restoration.) Yet when Paléologue went to pay a farewell visit to the grand duke in early May, all his optimism had gone, and he was quite candid about his worries.

"When we meet again, where will Russia have got to? . . . Shall we meet again?" he asked.

"You are in a gloomy mood, Monseigneur," the ambassador replied.

"How can you expect me to forget that I'm marked down for the gallows?" Grand Duke Nikolai had good reason to fear for his life. He was shot together with three other Romanovs—his brother Georgy and his cousins Dmitry Konstantinovich and Pavel Alexandrovich, the brother of Tsar Alexander III—in Petrograd in early 1919.[49]

The February Revolution took place in Petrograd, unbeknownst to the rest of the country. Yet as the news of the events spread, first to Moscow, then to other cities in Russia in the first days of March, the reaction was remarkable in its sameness. Joy and celebrations greeted word of the abdication everywhere; there was almost no violence and no resistance.[50] The reign of the Romanovs vanished into the air like so much steam from a boiling kettle. Yelizaveta Rodzianko, the daughter-in-law of Mikhail Rodzianko, was thrilled when the news reached her in the south. Russia, she believed, was finally pulling itself from the "muck" and heading out onto a "bright path."[51] Across Russia, many nobles shared that initial feeling of relief and optimism, followed by apprehension at what the future held. A noble schoolgirl in Ukraine, Marie Kastchenko celebrated wildly the news of the abdication with her classmates; at home, her father scoffed at their happiness: "'Bloodless Revolution,' this is only the beginning."[52] In Kazan, Olga Ilyn, born into the noted Boratynsky family, was riding in a sleigh with friends to a wedding when they came upon a crowd bearing red banners. The finely dressed Olga and her companions drew their attention. The crowd spat cries of "burzhui" and then warned, "You won't be driving around like this for much longer!"[53]

By the first of March word had reached the Davydoff estate of Sably in the Crimea that something serious had taken place in Petrograd, but no one knew what precisely. Finally, when he learned what had happened, Alexander Davydoff sat stunned at his desk for two hours, contemplating the enormity of the event and the unknown future it heralded. He wondered whether he should stay or flee to one of the towns but could not be sure what to do. "To answer this question I lacked one certainty, which was whether the peasants would, as in revolutions of the past, immediately kill the landowners, destroy their homes and loot the agricultural buildings, or would they wait and see if their old dreams could not now fail to be accomplished by legal means?" Davydoff decided it would be cowardly to flee, and so he chose to remain on the estate and, as he put it, "take part in the revolution, prevent its excesses as best he could and try, even in a minimal role, to preserve the economic strength of the nation."[54]

Most of the Golitsyns were then in Moscow. Little Sergei Golitsyn, the mayor's grandson, heard about the revolution while recovering in the hospital from an appendectomy. His mother was at his side when the surgeon burst into the room, yelling, "There's revolution in Petrograd!" Sergei could not understand why the two adults were so happy at the news. "It seemed remarkable to me. How could things like that happen—the tsar, who had all those medals, and then they just got rid of him." The change was apparent immediately. Sergei noticed on the way home that the tricolor tsarist flags that had adorned all the street-cars and houses when he had gone to the hospital had vanished and been replaced by red ones.[55] Sergei's father, Mikhail, was at work when the news of the abdication was announced. Everyone immediately burst into applause and let out cries of happiness.[56]

At home, the news split the family. While the mayor and his son Mikhail and Mikhail's wife, Anna, supported the revolution, believing that now, finally, the war could be won, Russia would become stronger, and the peasants would live better and freer, the mayor's wife, Sofia, and his brother Alexander cursed it. "My soul is troubled and worried," Sofia wrote. "I can't get used to the fact there is no more tsar and that he has been spurned and cast aside by everyone. And what will this so-called Freedom give us? The loss of our lands, destroyed estates, and all manner of violence."[57] Buoyed by a renewed sense of hope, Sergei's parents threw themselves deeper into their work, Mikhail overseeing the city's hospitals, Anna serving at the Society for the Protection of Mothers and Infants.[58]

Mikhail's brother Alexander shared this optimism. Soon after the revolution, he left Moscow for the family's Petrovskoe estate, where he spent much time talking to the peasants in the area about what the revo-lution meant and answering their questions. Alexander's meetings with the peasants deepened his optimism for Russia's future, and so he agreed to serve the new Provisional Government as the commissar re-sponsible for helping reorganize the local Zvenigorod government. Like every other nobleman who tried to work with the new government and peasants, Alexander failed. Soon he had to flee the countryside and eventually Russia itself. Looking back, he wrote, "Revolution was not unexpected by us, we knew that it was inevitable, that the old rotten bureaucratic Government was too handicapped, was incapable of meet-ing the growing needs of the nation; but we did not expect it to come during the war and did not dream that it would come in this form. We all idolized too much the Russian people, and how we were mistaken!"[59]

Not everyone idolized the Russian people too much, however. Rather, it was mostly Russian liberals, especially zemstvo men like Al-exander, his brother Mikhail, and their father, who did. It was the con-servatives among the nobility, people like Alexander's mother, less susceptible to myths of the innate goodness of the narod, who intuitively sensed the danger the fall of the old regime posed and could see most clearly the dark future before them.

The family was a bit nervous about going out to Buchalki as usual that spring but decided to go anyway in early May. Life seemed to go on as before, although there were signs of change. The no trespassing signs outside the estate garden lost their power, and young local boys and girls freely came in to play and stroll and sit on the benches. On the first visit to church the Golitsyns found villagers filling the Princes' Spot, something unthinkable only a few months earlier. There were instances of peasants cutting down their trees and hay; the overseer wanted to take action, but Anna Golitsyn decided to let it go, saying she did not want trouble with the peasants. Soon the peasants began to demand that the land be turned over to the "toilers," although their demands were placated with the promise that the question of land reform would later be taken up by the Constituent Assembly.[60]

Meanwhile, in Petrograd, the Sheremetevs welcomed back Prince Boris and Princess Lili Vyazemsky. Lili, the daughter of Dmitry and Ira, had married Boris in 1912, after which they had spent much of their time at his estate of Lotarevo in Tambov Province. Lotarevo was a model estate, well known for its stud farm, and the Vyazemskys took great pride in it. Boris had served as marshal of the nobility for Usman district and president of the Tambov zemstvo and was later elected to the national Duma as a Kadet. Boris and Lili arrived at the Fountain House excited by the recent events and optimistic about the prospect of a Russian republic, all of which greatly upset Count Sergei.[61]

Throughout March Sergei had been receiving disturbing reports from his estate managers. On the sixth, a crowd of armed peasants at Mikhailovskoe had marched to the main house and demanded that all the pictures of the tsar's family inside be destroyed. They found only one, a large portrait of Nicholas II in the dining room, which the overseer was forced to remove. Next, the crowd went to the school, pulled down portraits of Nicholas II, Alexander III, and even Alexander II— the Great Liberator—and destroyed them. That of Nicholas they tore from the frame and ripped to pieces before smashing the frame into splinters. The workers and employees at Mikhailovskoe held a meeting at which they drafted a petition demanding a ten-hour work day, "polite treatment" by their employers, and two weeks' notice before being let go.[62]

Nikolai Shtegman, the overseer at Ostafievo, described what had transpired there that same day in a letter to Count Sergei:

> The days of the revolution were much more alarming here than they were in 1905 or May 1915. On the morning of March 6 a large crowd of people appeared at the estate: two workers' delegates and four guards with rifles and revolvers and a great many local peasants. They came into my apartment and immediately demanded I hand over all weapons, threatening me with their revolvers and with arrest. They rummaged through everything—the cupboards, commodes, trunks, etc. They looked everywhere for weapons, but I didn't have any. I had given my gun to the watchman to keep the rabbits away from the apples. Then they demanded I open the main house so they could have a large meeting. I had to take out all the furnishings and close the side doors. They wanted to take all the weapons out of the dining room, but after several lengthy discussions and explanations to the effect that they were nothing but old flintlocks, and rusty ones at that, they left them in place. They searched the entire estate from eight o'clock in the morning until six o'clock in the evening, during which a great many people took part.
>
> The crowd was all agitated because the day before at a factory meeting an orator named Baskakov misled them about the meaning of the revolution, telling them that now everything is ours, that if the vegetables are ripe—go on and take them, if the oats are ripe—go on and take them, if the apples are ripe—go on and take them, firewood, brushwood—you can now take everything you want and you won't have to answer for it. Down with the teachers, don't take your children to church, and a lot of other absurd nonsense. The same sorts of things were preached here too at the meeting on the estate. [. . .]
>
> I have presented to the police a thorough report and have requested that the police be sent to guard the estate. I have been told a guard will be sent. Things are now, thank God, quiet.[63]

At the Sheremetev estate of Serebryanye Prudy (Silver Ponds), news of the abdication arrived along with "leaders of extreme left parties," who organized meetings and gave speeches to the peasants aimed at turning them against the landowners and urging them to take all the land and not to wait for the Constituent Assembly. Peasants at the Podkhozhee estate began to seize some of the Sheremetevs' land and tried to stop a shipment of oats headed for Mikhailovskoe from being taken away, claiming that it was theirs now. Disturbances like this went on for a week before matters settled down. The overseer from the Sheremetev lands in the Baltic province of Livonia wrote: "After surviving the recent events we, too, have started to worry and are nervous—indeed, who at present isn't anxious?"[64]

French Ambassador Paléologue noted the growing anxiety in Petrograd during these months. Dining one evening with several of his aristocratic friends, he encountered a mood of "the darkest pessimism." One fear terrified them most: the partition of the land. "We shall not get out of it *this* time!" one landowner said. "What will become of us without our rent-rolls?" Those gathered were not just afraid of losing their land by legal means, but of "confiscation by the high hand, wholesale looting and jacquerie." Paléologue wrote after dinner: "I am certain that the same sort of conversation can be heard in every corner of Russia at the present time." Countess Lamoyska returned from the family estate in Podolia to tell her friends that "a dangerous agitation" had reached the peasants there too; she said they were acting as if they were preparing to divide up the land for themselves and now no one in the family dared return.[65] To Paléologue, this talk came as no surprise. In the first days of the February Revolution he had witnessed the looting and occupation by a mob of the Petrograd mansion of Mathilde Kschessinska, the ballerina and former mistress of Nicholas II. For him, this seemingly trivial event masked a deeper significance. "The revolution was pursuing its logical and inevitable course," he observed.[66]

Count Alexander Sheremetev, Count Sergei's half brother, was among those aristocrats most deeply affected by the revolution. On a visit in early April to the Fountain House, Sergei was shocked by Alexander's changed manner and appearance and barely recognized him. He had shaved his mustache, lost a good deal of weight, and looked old and broken; gone were all his vaunted lively spirit and endless aplomb. He was now seeing the same specialist in nervous disorders who had treated Pavel following his breakdown in February; Sergei wryly commented in a letter to Maria that "the number of such sick persons has greatly increased." Upon his wife's insistence, Alexander had bought several acres of land in Finland should the situation in Russia get any worse.[67]

Once a resolute defender of the old order, Alexander had suddenly been transformed into a democrat and now claimed, amazingly, to have been one of the victims of tsarism. In April, he wrote to Alexander Guchkov, the Provisional Government's minister of war:

> Being in my soul a republican, I have suffered morally so much, especially during the war years, that my health has been utterly shattered. The great and important events of late February, which struck me like a blinding light after a long dark nightmare, have happily ended forever that repugnant despotism that nearly destroyed our beloved Fatherland. With this powerful and great revolution, the Provisional Government, which thanks to its moral strength is equally great, has created a miraculous and glorious monument to itself.

Alexander went on to offer the government the use of his private airplane squadron for the war effort and regretted that given his age (fifty-eight) and poor health, he was not able to do more for the new regime. No longer a "count," Alexander had become, he proudly announced, "a Russian citizen."[68]

Revolutions produce counterrevolutions. Yet it is one of the remarkable things about the February Revolution that it produced no counterrevolution seeking to restore the Romanovs. The nobility, and indeed the entire Russian elite, exactly those who stood to lose the most with the fall of tsarism, either embraced the revolution or at least begrudgingly accepted it. Despite a few isolated voices, there were no calls for a return to the past. Rather, the nobility immediately pledged itself to the new Provisional Government. The permanent council of the United Nobility and local noble associations met in early March to discuss how they might help the new government and encouraged all nobles to work with it. At the same time members of the State Council, including Count Sergei, swore an oath to the Provisional Government.[69] As a whole, the nobility rallied around the new government as the best way to restore order and to unite the country against what most considered Russia's greatest challenge—namely, the war against Germany. In their eyes, the revolution had been accomplished with the downfall of the autocratic system, and the duty of every Russian was to come together in defense of the motherland against its enemy abroad and against chaos at home. For some nobles, like the mayor and his sons Mikhail, Alexander, and Vladimir Vladimirovich, the long-held dream of building a constitutional order based on law and full civil and political rights led them to support the Provisional Government; for others, support of the new order was chiefly motivated by a sense that this was the only hope for holding back the forces of disorder threatening to engulf the country. As Count Sergei expressed in a letter to the historian Sergei Platonov, "My wish for the new government is that it grows stronger and so becomes less provisional, for so far its life has meant nothing but anarchy."[70]

For more than half a century Count Sergei and his family had celebrated Easter at the Fountain House. That year relatives in Moscow had been urging them to leave Petrograd early and join them in Moscow, where life was calmer and more settled. Count Sergei, although he too wished to leave the capital, refused to break with tradition, and so on the night of April 1 the Sheremetevs once again marked the Orthodox Church's main holy day as they had every year before.[71] Finally, on the evening of April 10, Count and Countess Sheremetev and the rest of the family left the Fountain House for the Nikolaevsky Station. Everywhere were crowds, bands of soldiers, and red flags. At half past eight, the train pulled out for the overnight trip to Moscow. "Thanks be to God," Count Sergei wrote in his diary. "We are leaving stinking, criminal Petrograd."[72]

One week before this train took the Sheremetevs from Petrograd, another had arrived at the city's Finland Station from Stockholm. After sixteen years in exile, Lenin had returned to Russia.

6

A COUNTRY OF MUTINOUS SLAVES

Lenin was given a hero's welcome by the members of the Bolshevik Party when his train pulled into the Finland Station shortly after 11:00 p.m. on April 3. After a few short remarks delivered from atop an armored car, Lenin left for the Bolshevik headquarters in the former Kschessinska mansion. His speech to his fellow Bolsheviks there in the early hours of April 4 struck them like a thunderbolt and threw the gathering into frenzied confusion. Lenin attacked any support of the Provisional Government, insisting that the overthrow of the Romanovs was but the first phase of the revolution, not its end. Rejecting the view of fellow Marxists that Russia had just entered the bourgeois-capitalist stage of development that was to last for some indefinite time, Lenin insisted on the idea that had preoccupied him since the outbreak of World War I—namely, that the only path to peace lay in transforming the "bourgeois" war of nation against nation into a "class" war of the proletariat against the bourgeoisie, and the time for such a civil war was now.

Lenin laid out his ideas in the so-called April Theses. He advocated an immediate end to the "imperialist" war; no collaboration with the new government; a move to the next "socialist" phase of the revolution; the transfer of all power to the Soviets; the confiscation of landlords' estates and the nationalization of all land; the abolition of the police and army, the latter to be replaced by a people's militia; and the creation of a single national bank under Soviet control as well as Soviet control over the means of production and distribution. His fellow Bolsheviks, and indeed the entire left, found his ideas absurd. The Bolshevik newspaper *Pravda* called Lenin's plan "unacceptable," and it was denounced in various left-wing circles as "claptrap" and "the ravings of a madman." Lenin's program was rejected by the Petrograd Bolsheviks, as well as their branches in other cities. The general consensus was that after so many years in exile, Lenin was out of touch with the realities of Russia.[1]

Prime Minister Prince Georgy Lvov, the blind optimist of 1917, would have agreed. "The great Russian revolution is truly miraculous in its majestic, quiet progress," he stated early that spring; "every day that passes renews the belief in the inexhaustible creative power of the Russian people." Others drew different conclusions from what they saw happening around them. Ambassador Paléologue saw "anarchy spreading through all of Russia," and his British counterpart, George Buchanan, opined that "Russia is not ripe for a purely democratic form of government" and predicted "a series of revolutions and counterrevolutions."[2]

The Provisional Government was proving helpless in stopping the country's descent into disorder as the lawlessness and contempt for established authority that had brought down the autocracy continued to grow and spread. In the first days of May, Kerensky replaced Minister of War Guchkov, who had become convinced that Russia was ungovernable. "Is it really possible that Free Russia is only a country of mutinous slaves?" Kerensky asked as he launched his campaign to reinvigorate Russia's army. "Our army under the monarchy accomplished heroic deeds. Will it be a flock of sheep under the republic?"[3] Russia's soldiers had no desire to be sheep, but neither did they desire to go on fighting and dying for a cause they did not believe in. According to General Alexei Brusilov, "The soldiers wanted only one thing—peace, so that they could go home, rob the landowners, and live freely without paying any taxes or recognizing any authority."[4]

Given the vastness of the Russian Empire and the isolation of the village, it was not until mid-April that news of the fall of the Romanovs had reached all of the peasant masses. The news rarely produced sudden changes, and for a time life in the countryside largely went on as before. Gradually, however, as the significance of the events sank in, many peasants began to believe that the local nobles had purposely tried to keep them ignorant of what had happened and to distort the meaning of the revolution for their own benefit.[5] Even before the end of March, voices of concern about the situation in the countryside could be heard. On March 26, *New Times* quoted Prince Yevgeny Trubetskoy from Kaluga: "The danger in the countryside is quite real. The villages now have no courts, no government administration, mercy be to St. Nicholas. It is being said that the deep snows and the muddy season will save us. But for how long? Soon evil elements will realize the advantages to be had out of this disorder."[6]

Evil elements, however, had already begun to realize the advantages. On March 17, the newspaper *Day* reported peasants near Bezhetsk had locked the local landlord inside his manor and then burned it down with him inside.[7] Before the end of April, reports of pogroms and violence were coming in from a number of provinces.[8] On May 3, *New Times* printed a story on the terror that had gripped the town of Mtsensk in Orlovsk Province. For three days straight as many as five thousand peasants and soldiers went on a drunken rampage, torching several nearby estates. The rampage had erupted when a group of soldiers, looking for weapons at an estate of the Sheremetevs, came across a large wine cellar. After getting drunk, they ransacked the manor, and when word got out what was going on, the local peasants and garrison joined in. Troops, even some of the officers, sent in to restore order went over to the side of the looters. Mysterious individuals appeared in officers' uniforms and began handing out liquor and inciting the masses to further destruction. The town's residents did not dare go out at night as the crowds, armed with rifles and knives, shouted and sang and caroused.[9]

"It was during the summer of 1917," Ivan Bunin later wrote, "that the Satan of Cain's anger, of bloodlust, and of the most savage cruelty wafted over Russia while its people were extolling brotherhood, equality, and freedom."[10] Freedom for the peasants meant *vólia*, license. Anton Kazakov, a peasant from Chernigov, said freedom was "Doing whatever you want." And what the peasants, together with the returning army deserters, wanted was to destroy the landlords and take their property.[11] It was not enough to plunder them; they had to be physically annihilated and driven off the land for good. In June, a landowner near the village of Buerak in Saratov Province was shot at his estate and his servants were strangled. The entire contents of the manor were carted off.[12] The next month, the eighty-year-old son of Ivan Kireevsky, one of the founders of Slavophilism, was murdered together with his wife at his estate in Moscow Province by a group of deserters looking to steal their collection of rare books and antiques.[13] At the Kamenka estate of Countess Edith Sollohub, mutinous soldiers turned a large library into rolling papers.[14]

At the estate of Popelyova, where Tatiana Aksakov-Sivers went to join her mother in the spring, things at first seemed normal. Yet as the months wore on, outside agitators appeared and warned the local peasants to be wary of "wolves in sheep's clothing," meaning the local masters.[15] At the Rodzianko estate of Otrada in the southern province of Yekaterinoslav, Yelizaveta Rodzianko noticed that well into the summer the peasants seemed unusually quiet. "The people are silent," she thought, recalling the famous line from Pushkin's historical drama *Boris Godunov*. This was the quiet before the storm. At a church holiday the Rodziankos were joined by all the villagers for an outdoor feast. A handsome young stranger appeared and began to speak to the crowd of the achievements of the revolution, eventually coming to the subject of the landlords. "Don't touch your landowner. This land will be yours regardless. All this," he said with a grand gesture sweeping the entire horizon, "will be yours!" Yelizaveta rode home with a strange feeling. Within months the family were forced to flee Otrada for good.[16] The countryside that spring and summer was full of "strolling players," outside agitators, often deserting soldiers and sailors. They, according not just to the accounts of dispossessed nobles but to Soviet authorities as well, played a pivotal role in getting the peasants to act against the landlords.[17]

At the Kastchenkos' estate of Vesyolaya in Ukraine life seemed the same as always, at least outwardly. But then things began to change in small ways. "The change was indefinable, hard to pin down, yet grimly unmistakable," Marie Kastchenko remembered. The two old coachmen "kissed our hands with the usual respectful cordiality, but seemed uneasy and looked around, as though they were afraid somebody was watching them." In the house, things began to disappear—a scarf, a blouse, a bottle of eau de Cologne; the servants began to whisper in groups and would "then lapse into sullen silence if any of us appeared." On her walks, the peasants no longer stepped off the path to let Marie pass as before; now she had to give way to them.[18]

Alexei Tatishchev noticed that at the family estate of Tashan in the Poltava province the servants that summer "seemed reticent and at times surly" and reluctant to do their work. One day a peasant delegation came to the house to speak to his aunt. They waited on the marble terrace outside, some spitting on it in defiance. Later, one peasant, when asked to stop herding her cows in the yard, walked onto the terrace, hiked up her skirt, and then defecated in front of Tatishchev's aunt. When the woman had finished, she told the mistress to herd them herself if she was not happy. Not long thereafter, the family packed up and left for Kiev.[19]

Bunin had left Petrograd for the family estate of Glotovo in May 1917. One night soon after his arrival, the barn was torched, and then the peasants burned down the neighbor's barn. They blamed the fire on the landowner, beat him mercilessly, and hauled him off to the local town hall. Bunin went to intercede on his behalf. The crowed yelled at Bunin as speaking "for the 'old regime'" and refused to listen; one woman called Bunin and his ilk "sons of bitches" who "should be thrown into the fire. "It is disgusting to live in the country now," Bunin complained. "The village men are true children, just vile. There is 'anarchy' here and throughout the district, willfulness, confusion, and the most idiotic misunderstanding of all these 'slogans' as well as the most basic human words—it's astounding."[20] In June, Bunin was forced to submit to a humiliating inspection at the local rail station. "There are no laws," he cried. "Everyone has power except us of course. In 'free' Russia only soldiers, peasants, and workers have a voice."[21] Yet despite the horrors, Bunin, like most of the gentry, could not help feeling a deep connection to the family estate; its sense of history and simplicity and seeming timelessness was a balm amid all the upheavals. But by the middle of October, the situation had become too dangerous for the Bunins to remain in the country. During the last week of the month, they loaded up their things and left in the dark. On the way a group of women tried to block their path; Bunin pulled out his Browning and threatened to shoot, and the women stepped aside.[22]

The Golitsyns spent the summer at their Buchalki estate. In the papers they read with horror about the violence sweeping the countryside. Their servant Anton, who had never dared speak while working, now began to talk. He told them about rumors in the village that deserters had begun to arrive and were stirring up the people and inciting them to seize the land.[23]

One day Anna Golitsyn went out with her children to gather mushrooms in the woods, where they came across a fresh dugout and fire pit. They saw no one but assumed there must be brigands or deserters in the area. Anna signaled the children to be quiet and join hands, and they turned and hurried back to the manor. They never again ventured out into the woods.[24] One day a group of twenty peasants came to talk to Mikhail about their desire for some of the estate lands. He informed the men that the land was not his but his uncle's, though he promised to write to him and present their request. He urged them to be patient, however, and to wait for the Constituent Assembly that autumn, when the land question would be addressed. A soldier in the group tried to stir them up against Mikhail, but they resisted, saying as they left that they trusted their "masters" to do the right thing by them. The Golitsyns were among the fortunate landowners who managed to spend the entire summer at their estate before heading back to Moscow in the autumn. Like so many nobles, they had spent their last summer at the family estate. Buchalki was later destroyed by the waves of violence that swept over it beginning with the revolution and ending with the German invasion in 1941.[25]

That summer the nobility learned to live with the upheaval of revolution as if it were as normal and uncontrollable as the weather. During the abortive Bolshevik coup in Petrograd in July, the nighttime shooting in the streets woke up the young children of Princess Cantacuzène. She stroked them, reassuring her little ones it was nothing to worry about. "It's just the revolution," she whispered, and they turned over and "went blissfully back to sleep."[26] This attitude became widespread. That summer in Odessa Yelena Lakier started to carry a revolver and was often awoken at night by gunshots, though they stopped causing her to lose any sleep. She and her family came to think little of it. "Man has a pleasant characteristic," she observed. "He can get used to anything very fast."[27] At the height of the chaos in late November performances at Petrograd's theaters were typically sold out.[28]

Upon arriving in Moscow from Petrograd on April 11, 1917, Count and Countess Sheremetev settled at their Kuskovo estate on the edge of the city. They were joined there by several of their children, including Dmitry and Ira and their children, the Saburovs (Alik had been removed from office in early April), and other members of the extended family. They all had initially hoped to go to their estate of Mikhailovskoe, but reports from their overseer suggested they not come because the situation there was too uncertain. Before heading to Kuskovo, the Saburovs had wanted to leave for their Voronovo estate, but a local teacher had warned them not to come because of rioting in nearby villages.[29] Maria Gudovich and her children left Kutaisi in April to join her husband, Alexander, in Tiflis, and from there they set out for Russia in May to be with the rest of the family.[30]

As summer approached and the general disorder penetrated deeper into the Russian countryside, nobles started to pack up and head south to the Crimea and Caucasus.[31] In early May, Ira's mother left Moscow for the spa towns of the northern Caucasus. Dmitry and Ira stayed behind, but by the end of the month they too had had enough. One night a local man was murdered outside their house next to Kuskovo's pleasure garden; the body lay there unclaimed for several days as the authorities slowly investigated. The murder terrified Ira; her sister-in-law Lilya Sheremetev was convinced she was having a nervous breakdown.[32] In June, Dmitry and Ira left for Kislovodsk, a popular resort in the northern Caucasus. Life there went on as if nothing had happened. The weather was delightful, there was plenty of food, Ira took the cure, and the local Cossacks showed no signs of aggression. They decided to spend the winter there and rented a dacha for the family. The town was full of friends and acquaintances from up north, and more were arriving daily, so Dmitry wrote his mother that if things looked as if they were getting worse in Russia, she and the rest of the family should come join them soon before all the good houses had been taken.[33]

Among the aristocrats in Kislovodsk were several of Dmitry's Sheremetev cousins: Georgy, Yelizaveta, Alexandra, and Dmitry.[34] Their parents (Alexander and Maria Sheremetev) had chosen to stay in Petrograd, although as life in the capital became increasingly unsettled, they left for their estate in Russian Finland. Alexander invited his half brother Sergei to join them, but he refused to leave Russia. They were there when Finland declared its independence from Russia on December 6 (N.S.), 1917, and thus quite suddenly found themselves exiles. They lived well for a time, but then the money ran out. Alexander and Maria sold their Finnish lands and moved to Belgium and then to France; they lived in poverty in Paris before being taken in by a charity set up to help Russian émigrés in Ste.-Geneviève-des-Bois. Both Alexander and Maria died there and were buried in the Russian cemetery in the 1930s. Neither ever returned to Russia. All their property was nationalized, including their magnificent Petrograd home; its contents were dispersed among various museums, and its archive was pulped. In the 1930s, their home became the House of Writers, and decades later, following the collapse of the Soviet Union, a luxury hotel.[35]

Alexander and Maria's four children had all left Russia by the end of the civil war, settling in Western Europe. Georgy fought with the Whites and then fled southern Russia for Europe with his wife and their young children. He later worked as a secretary for Grand Duke Nikolai Nikolaevich, the last tsar's uncle, and oversaw a farm in Normandy. A fellow Russian émigré by the name of Alexandrov met Georgy in the 1920s at Choigny, the home of the grand duke outside Paris. Alexandrov was amazed at Georgy's attitude toward the revolution, which he saw as rare among the Russian aristocracy. He noted that Georgy bore no ill will for his fate and interpreted the revolution and his family's terrible loss as "God's proper punishment for all the sins, injustices, and lawlessness that his privileged class had committed against their 'lesser brethren' and that Christianity obliged him to devote the rest of his life atoning for these sins."[36] This obligation led Georgy to become a Russian Orthodox priest in London, where he lived out his last years.

The Sheremetevs' financial situation began to unravel within two months of the February Revolution. In late April, the controller of the family's main office in Petrograd warned Count Sergei that income from the estates had stopped coming in and he had no idea where they would find adequate funds to maintain the family's monthly expenses of seventy-five thousand rubles. Count Sergei ordered their remaining liquid capital transferred from Petrograd to Moscow, which seemed a safer haven at the time, but this was only a stopgap measure that would

not help them in the long term.[37] The question of income and investments is an interesting one. Most Russian nobles were patriots, and
they tended to invest their money at home. With the outbreak of the
First World War, many pulled their money out of Western Europe and
brought it back to Russia as a sign of their commitment to the war effort and support for the country. During the war, it was considered
disloyal to transfer capital abroad. This meant that when the revolution
erupted, few nobles had any funds outside Russia they could fall back
on. Their wealth, like their lives, was bound up with the fate of the
country.

In the spring, peasants, unwilling to wait for the promised Constituent Assembly to address the land question, began taking matters
into their own hands and seizing the Sheremetevs' estates. In April, the
Sheremetevs were forced to hand over almost two thousand acres to
the peasants in Volsky District.[38] In May, poor peasants in Novo-Pebalg
in the Baltics seized a large Sheremetev estate.[39] In July, riotous crowds
attacked and severely damaged their extensive properties in Ivanovo-
Voznesensk.[40] By October, Sheremetev estates were being plundered
and destroyed in Tambov Province.[41] In December, the peasants of the
village of Ozerki in Saratov Province met to approve the immediate
confiscation of the lands of the "former Count Sheremetev."[42] These
disturbances, while important, were at least far away. Problems nearer
to home made inescapable the economic troubles they were facing. By
late June the head of the Sheremetevs' Moscow family office reported
increasing difficulty in buying food. Yessentuki mineral water had disappeared, as had all chocolate; Dutch cheese was available, but only one
pound per person, and Count Sergei's favorite French wine was nowhere to be had.[43] Count Sergei's French chef quit and left Russia for
home. In May, members of his Moscow domestic staff went out on
strike.[44]

Back in Petrograd, figures from the Soviet of Workers' and Soldiers'
Deputies came by the Fountain House looking for additional offices
and meeting space. Count Sergei had already handed over part of the
house to the Red Cross (its flags had been hung at every entrance in an
attempt to safeguard the property), and the overseer lied to the men,
telling them the organization had taken over the entire premises and
so there were no available rooms. The Fountain House and neighboring Sheremetev properties were still under special guard, but this did

not stop frequent break-ins and burglaries.[45] During the July Days in Petrograd, their large rental property on Liteiny Street was shot up, and its apartments were looted.[46]

After some trouble acquiring gasoline for their automobiles, the Sheremetevs finally left Kuskovo for Mikhailovskoe at the end of May. For decades the family had spent their summers at this beloved estate, and despite all the challenges, Count Sergei was determined not to break with tradition. Pavel, now recovered from his mental break-down, joined the family there. They had not been there a week when they learned of an entire family of neighboring landowners murdered in their home and of a group of four persons killed by a band of soldiers in the area. The Sheremetev men got out their guns and set up a night watch around the house.[47] Yelena Sheremetev had to learn how to milk the cows and bake bread; a local peasant took Yelena and her mother out into the fields to teach them how to use the scythe, but they cut their fingers so badly they had to return home. The peasant took pity on them and started supplying the family with his own buckwheat, a generous act that he carried on even during the hungry years of 1918 and 1919. Later that year, after a raid on the manor's wine cellar, a peasant woman came to say they would be smart to leave before they were driven out. The family packed up some things and quietly left.[48] No one knew at the time that it was forever.

Russia's landowners were not just victims, however, and in late 1916, a group of them revived the All-Russian Union of Landowners, created in 1905, to protect themselves and their properties against peasant violence and expropriation. By the middle of 1917 the union, whose membership had been expanded to include wealthy peasants, had established a network of local organizations across the country and was continuing to grow despite a lack of support from the government. Prince Sergei Volkonsky described their work as "the hysterical cry of a helpless impulse against elemental forces," a characterization that, while accurate about the ultimate failure of Russia's landowners, is too harsh in its judgment of their motives and efforts.[49] The challenges they confronted were enormous, and the members themselves could not always agree on how bad the situation was or just what needed to be done. While some shared the pessimistic sentiments of the speaker to a congress of landowners in Saratov in May who welcomed the delegates with "Greetings to you, the disinherited ones," others not only refused to see the situation as lost, but did not even see the need for drastic and immediate action. At the union's first national congress in Moscow in July, one delegate insisted that although land must be given to the peasants, more time was needed for this "lengthy process."[50]

To think that settling the land question would take a long time was to miss the fact that the social revolution was rapidly overtaking the political revolution. The vast majority of Russians was not content to overthrow the monarchy and then wait patiently for their concerns about land and hunger and war to be debated and voted on by a Constituent Assembly, a body that the masses had little faith in. They wanted their demands met now. The landowners and the rest of the elite were not the only ones to overlook the need for speedy action; the Provisional Government too insisted on putting off land reform until the establishment of a Constituent Assembly.

On July 3, an uprising of soldiers broke out in Petrograd that nearly toppled the Provisional Government. For three days mutinous soldiers and armed workers traded gunfire with forces loyal to the government. As during the February Revolution, much of the violence during the July Days was directed against the burzhui. Hundreds of people were killed and wounded in the streets of the capital. Historians continue to debate the Bolsheviks' role in planning and organizing the insurrection, but most agree that had they so chosen, they could have overthrown the government. Lenin, however, hesitated, allowing the government to prevail. The leaders of the Bolsheviks were arrested on charges of treason, while Lenin managed to escape in disguise to Finland.[51]

A correspondent who had just experienced the revolt wrote Count Sergei a letter from Petrograd in which she described life in the capital and the strange, unbelievable changes taking place there. With admirable humor and pluck, she informed him how "the breadth of my political horizons is expanding not by the day, but by the minute, and all thanks to our country's democratic system."

> When, during those July Days, the bullets were freely whistling along the streets, flying through the windows and thus proving all the delights of freedom in a law-based state and causing me to save myself by

crawling into my bathtub, I realized that my previous understanding of a bathtub had been nothing but a narrow cliché, but now my knowledge has grown and I realize a bathtub can also serve as a fortress.

"Permit me to wish you good health and rest at your historic estates," she added, "created in that happy time when people understood the meaning of the word 'Motherland' and when they still had the right to be called Russians, and not 'former people.'"[52] The term, "former people," sounded odd at the time, although it soon became all too familiar.

Exhausted after four grueling months in office, Prince Georgy Lvov resigned as prime minister and left the government. He was replaced by Kerensky, who moved into the former rooms of Tsar Alexander III in the Winter Palace and began to present himself as a Russian Napoleon sent to save the country and the revolution. By now, many in Russia were in search of just such a figure. Since May Count Sergei had been counting on a strongman's stepping forward as their only hope. "But where is he, amidst this universal collapse?" he wondered.[53] The outlines of a conservative movement began to take shape that summer. Small groups sprang up with names like the Union of National Defense, the Union of Officers, and the Republican Center, all calling for order, discipline, and the curbing of the Petrograd Soviet's power. Increasingly, members of the broad Russian elite were coming to the opinion that Russia needed an authoritarian government, if only to create the necessary conditions for the successful meeting of the Constituent Assembly. Some groups went even further, arguing that only a military dictator could save Russia from destruction. If to some this smelled of counterrevolution, to conservatives, moderates, and even some liberals, Lenin and the Bolsheviks were the real counterrevolutionaries. By fomenting class conflict, undermining the authority of the Provisional Government, and generally pushing Russia deeper into chaos, the Bolsheviks, many believed, were trying to undo the February Revolution in order to seize power.[54]

By August, the mayor could see a dictatorship in Russia's future. "Revolution, in its extreme development, always leads to dictatorship," he commented in his diary, "that is, to the despotism of one man and the proizvol of his stooges, and despotism and proizvol, once introduced into a system and knowing neither limits nor responsibilities, as was the case under our autocracy, inevitably lead to revolution. We know this, and we shall see this ourselves here in the future." It was an excruciating time for him. Like his fellow liberals, he looked with despair on the chaos around him and found it hard to understand how fast the profound joy over the collapse of the old order had been replaced by disgust and shame over what had followed. Regardless, he continued to believe that they had been right in their struggle to create a law-based society. "This had been the only path to save ourselves from the reckless proizvol of the first regime as well as its indivisible product—the destructive carelessness of the subsequent anarchy."

As the political polarization grew, such voices of moderation were drowned out. Even the mayor began to wonder whether he and his fellow liberals had been naive to think Russia was ready for a constitution and representative government. Maybe the Russians were only fit to be "Forever under the yoke and kept in the condition of slavery. First there was the yoke of the tsarist regime and its dark forces, and now the yoke of the mob and groups of proletarians, these fortuitous people, and then either the yoke of a dictator or a foreign people."[55]

From August 8–10, several hundred industrialists, landowners, politicians, clergy, and generals met in Moscow at the first Congress of Public Figures to unite the country's nonsocialist forces and discuss the possible role of the military in the government. The participants agreed that national goals were being sacrificed for narrow class and personal interests. Civil war threatened Russia, and something had to be done, although they did not go so far as to endorse a military dictatorship. To rally support for the government, Kerensky responded with the State Conference, also in Moscow that same month. His attempt to unite left and right proved a public failure, highlighting the collapse of any political center at the expense of growing extremism. The conference did, however, greatly enhance the profile of General Lavr Kornilov, commander in chief of the Russian armed forces, a development that many welcomed, while others interpreted as a threat to the revolution.[56]

Protests against perceived counterrevolution broke out across Russia just as Kornilov, in response to talk of a planned Bolshevik coup, began making preparations to suppress any such uprising and move against the soviet. In what became known as the Kornilov Affair, one of the most debated moments in the history of the revolution, Kerensky turned on Kornilov, convinced that Kornilov was planning to topple him and not the soviet. Kerensky had Kornilov and several other generals arrested. The sole victors in the Kornilov affair were the Bolsheviks. Kerensky had enlisted their aid in, as he saw it, "saving" the revolution from Kornilov. He freed their leaders from prison and had forty thousand guns distributed to workers in the capital. The Bolsheviks found their fortunes revived after the fiasco of the July Days, while Kerensky lost all the support of the conservatives and liberals, the military leadership, and even much of the left. As summer gave way to autumn, Russia found itself adrift with no national government to assert authority across its enormous territory.[57]

On April 11, the day the Sheremetevs arrived in Moscow from Petrograd, Boris and Lili Vyazemsky left for their estate of Lotarevo in Tambov Province. Count Sergei was relieved to see them go. He could not make peace with their liberal views, and the unending conversations about politics left him exhausted. The situation at Lotarevo was tense. That spring the Vyazemskys had buried Boris's brother Dmitry (accidentally killed by a stray bullet while riding in an automobile in Petrograd) in the family crypt against the wishes of the peasants, who hated Dmitry for the harsh methods he had used to subdue the violence in the area during the Revolution of 1905. Boris began to worry. Outside agitators arrived, and acts of vandalism against the estate grew over the summer. Boris sent appeals to the capital for help, but none came. As it became clear that their lives were in danger, Vyazemsky decided he and Lili would have to leave Lotarevo before the end of August. Tragedy struck, however, before they could make their escape.[58]

In July, a peasant committee demanded Vyazemsky hand over his land. In turn, the peasants would agree to leave him twenty-seven acres and a small number of livestock. Vyazemsky refused, telling them they would have to wait for the Constituent Assembly. The peasants repeated their demands again in August, and this time Boris did not bother to reply.

One morning in late August hundreds of peasants from the area, led by the main Bolshevik agitator in the area, a man named Moyeseev, descended on Lotarevo. Lili and the servants urged Boris to get in the wagon out back and ride off for a few hours until they had gone, but he refused. Vyazemsky had dealt with angry mobs before and had always managed to cool tempers and keep the peace, and he went out of the house that day to meet the peasants and talk to them as always. This time, however, under the goading of Moyeseev, they refused to be talked down. For a time it was not clear which side the peasants would take: some argued Vyazemsky should be killed, some that he should be arrested, and others that he should be sent off to the front. When a group of women placed a rope around Lili's neck, the menfolk shouted at them to stop, and they took it off.

As the mood shifted back and forth, Moyeseev continued to insist that the time had come for the peasants to show the Vyazemskys who was in charge. According to one peasant, Vyazemsky finally said, "My friends, just let me go unharmed and whatever you like, you may take—be it money, land, or the estate, only leave me in peace."[59] Instead, the peasants seized Boris and Lili and locked them up in the local school. Hours passed as the peasants debated what to do next. Lili's maid brought them their raincoats and cigarettes as they waited. The village women kept staring at them through the windows, so Boris covered them up with their raincoats.[60] The next day the villagers decided to take Boris to the train station and send him to Petrograd with orders he be sent straight to the front. A local peasant, Ivan Talitsky, said the villagers assumed the trenches would be Boris's grave.[61] Lili was left to the mercy of the peasants, who by now had gotten hold of the Lotarevo wine cellar. Boris was taken to the local station, but he never made it to Petrograd. When the villagers and Boris arrived, the station was overrun with deserters and glum recruits being shipped out. Soon word spread that Prince Vyazemsky was being held at the station. The deserters found Boris, dragged him out of the station master's quarters, and beat him to death with metal rods.[62]

With the help of a maid, Lili disguised herself as a peasant and escaped to the neighbors' house. She told them what had happened, and they took her to the station to look for Boris. She found his mutilated body lying in an empty freight car off on a side track. She crawled in, sat beside him, and remained there for a long time. A young girl happened by and handed Lili some flowers. Lili then took Boris's coffin on the train back to Moscow.

The Sheremetevs learned of the killing on August 25 while at

Mikhailovskoe. The following day they received further details of what had happened to Boris, including the fact that his body had been defiled as it lay dead in the dirt. Count Sergei was deeply shaken. "This is staggering. Signs of a Pugachyovshchina, requiring we be extremely cautious." His wife, Yekaterina, suffered a mild heart attack upon hearing the news.[63] Alexander Gudovich met Lili when the train reached Moscow. A requiem was held for Boris on the twenty-ninth. Lilya Sheremetev noted that Lili "continues to be brave, supported by her strong faith. She cried today after the night service."[64]

After Boris's murder, the peasants in the area waited for some sort of government response. But as the days and then weeks passed and nothing happened, they became emboldened. Four months after the murder, Lotarevo was pillaged and then razed. Boris's brother Dmitry's grave was dug up, and his corpse tossed out onto the ground. Lili later met their old estate steward in the Crimea, and he told her how the peasants had torn the estate apart. One of the peasants said to him, "We wanted to destroy everything so that the old owners could never come back."[65] The events at Lotarevo spread fear to the surrounding estates. The landowners demanded protection from the government and punishment of the Vyazemsky peasants, but still nothing happened. Violence erupted at several estates, and manor houses were set ablaze. By the end of October, 154 estates had been plundered and destroyed in Tambov Province.[66]

Despite the tragedy at Lotarevo, not everyone in the family lost hope. Princess Cantacuzène met Boris's mother in the Crimea not long after his murder. The princess was moved by his mother's forgiveness and by the fact that like most of the nobles the princess met there, she remained optimistic about Russia's future.[67]

As autumn arrived, the terror in the countryside exploded. Newspapers no longer wrote about "disturbances" and "unrest" sweeping the land but about "anarchy." *Day* reported in late September that the peasants in Tula Province were spreading word of "the total destruction of all landowners" and seizing all their land and manors without waiting for the Constituent Assembly.[68] In October, signs began appearing in the Kozlovsky district informing the peasants on which estates nobles had fled for safety and urging them to "burn these estates as well" and so drive all the landlords out of the area for good.[69] In Kursk Province in mid-October, a mysterious organization called the Black Hand came to life, urging the peasants on to violence against the landlords.[70] In some places the violence was not limited to nobles but was directed at Jews as well.[71] The greatest explosion of peasant violence was in the traditionally volatile region of the Volga River, especially the provinces of Saratov, Samara, Penza, and Simbirsk. The peasants in this region played a crucial role in determining the fate of the revolution and spelling the end of the old order in the Russian countryside.[72]

In September, the mayor, Sofia, and the rest of the Golitsyn family returned to Moscow for the beginning of the new school year. Their son Alexander was particularly upset about recent events. Since the February Revolution he had worked diligently to help reorganize the local government in Zvenigorod until he was forced out by the Bolsheviks, who were gaining support in the area. He had now lost all his earlier optimism for the revolution and was convinced that only a strong man like Kornilov could have saved the country.[73] With chaos swirling about them, their hopes for the future dying, the mayor nonetheless looked upon his family gathered around him and was filled with joy. "At the present, tragic time, it is not just our private lives, filled with their small concerns and work, that are our refuge as well as our salvation, but even more so it is the life of our family, the feeling of complete happiness that we find in our family, so beloved and so beautiful."[74]

Few nobles were able to find such happiness. That same month Princess Catherine Sayn-Wittgenstein could think of little else but the civil war she saw gathering on the horizon. Life in Russia was a tragedy, and everyone was responsible: the Bolsheviks, the soldiers, the peasants, politicians, merchants, and the nobility as well.

Can we say that everyone but us was guilty, that we suffer innocently? Of course not. We, the noble estate, that is, have been guilty before all the other estates for centuries. We do not care to recall this, however, it is only natural that this hatred for us, for our estate, hatred based on envy, would have to explode sooner or later. Now they hate us with unyielding malice, not differentiating individuals among us, and seeing only a class of "lords," "*burzhui*," "landowners," and "masters," a class that so many obliging people have been encouraging them to hate more than anything. It is understandable and it is *forgivable* that they hate us, for we in fact hate them, we hate them with the same unyielding malice and, what is more, we despise them. [. . .] We accuse them of stupidity, of cupidity, of brutish rudeness and filthiness, we accuse them of a lack of patriotism and of all humanity, save selfishness. That they are dark and backward, this is true, but are they to blame for this? [. . .] Who taught them to love the Motherland? Cupidity, rudeness, impudence, and stupidity—these are their noted traits, but can one really expect better of a people who only recently were slaves? [. . .] Both sides have always thought in terms of "us" and "them," and we now see that therein lay our ancestral error. Both sides desire not to understand each other, not to come together, not to forgive, rather to vanquish the other.

If Russia were indeed on the verge of civil war, Catherine remarked, and one day she were to find her own head under the guillotine, she would feel no self-pity or anger and would understand, for no one was blameless.[75]

7

THE BOLSHEVIK COUP

ne constantly feels oppressed by worry of a German attack and Bolshevik supremacy. If they seize power that will be the final step into the abyss. [. . .] My soul is full of sorrow. I grieve for the Motherland."[1]

Count Sergei's grief, recorded in his diary in the first days of October, was shared by many Russians at the time. In their eyes, the country was being destroyed from without by the Germans and from within by the Bolsheviks. Popular support for the Bolsheviks was growing that autumn together with the persistent rumors of an impending Bolshevik coup. While some of the Bolshevik leadership continued to resist Lenin's insistence on an immediate seizure of power, in the end Lenin managed to impose his will at a secret meeting of the Central Committee in Petrograd on October 10, when it was agreed to prepare for an armed coup d'état against the Provisional Government. Lenin refused to consider any cooperation with the other socialist parties, and even though the attack against Kerensky's government would be carried out under the banner of "All Power to the Soviets," this would be nothing but a smoke screen to hide the Bolsheviks' real plans for a complete monopoly of power.[2]

On the evening of October 25, Princess Meshchersky went to the opera in Petrograd. She noticed some trouble with the lights and a strange atmosphere in the theater, but nothing out of the ordinary. Her experiences accord with most others in the city that night, for whom life, though chaotic and unpredictable, was uneventful.[3] But as the city's residents went about their business, the Military Revolutionary Committee (MRC) of the Petrograd Soviet, together with Red Guards and Bolshevik soldiers and sailors, were at work overthrowing the government. That day the MRC took control of the electric power station, the main post office, the State Bank, and the central telegraph exchange, as well as key bridges and railway stations. So weak had the government become that no one seemed to notice what was happening. There was almost no one left to defend the government, and so it collapsed with a whimper when faced by no more than several thousand armed men. In the early-morning hours of the twenty-sixth, a group of soldiers marched into the Winter Palace to arrest the government ministers, and there was no one to stop them. The few hundred loyal troops had all but left, either for home or for one of the city's restaurants. Kerensky himself had already abandoned the capital.

The number of soldiers who captured the Winter Palace was quickly dwarfed by those that followed, as news spread that the massive wine cellar of the tsars—tens of thousands of bottles—was being handed out and sold off. A bacchanalia of unseen proportions erupted. Crowds of drunken workers, soldiers, and sailors, including the men responsible for the attack on the palace, rioted and looted. They vandalized the Winter Palace, broke into liquor stores and shops, attacked, robbed, and killed the burzhui in the streets and in their homes. Moisei Uritsky, the head of the Petrograd Cheka from 1918, dressed every bit the Jewish intelligént, barely escaped the mob with his life. The Bolsheviks tried to pump the wine from the palace cellar out into the gutter to end the chaos, but the crowds simply lowered themselves onto the street to drink it up. Martial law was declared, and the prisons were soon filled beyond capacity. Even machine guns and threats to blow up the cellar with dynamite proved ineffective in stopping the rioting. The disorder lasted for several weeks and did not end until every bottle had been drunk. Maxim Gorky moaned that what they were witnessing was not a revolution but "a pogrom of greed, hatred, and vengeance."[4]

Count Sergei spent much of October 27 overseeing the hanging of paintings brought to Moscow from the Fountain House. Looking at the large canvases depicting scenes from Russia's past amid the present crisis brought only anguish, and he went to bed early. Around four in the morning of the twenty-eighth he was awoken by the sound of heavy gunfire from the direction of the Kremlin, only a few blocks away from the Sheremetevs' Corner House on Vozdvizhenka Street. He looked out his window and saw in the light of the streetlamps young cadets at their posts across the street guarding the state revenue building. Then the shooting stopped, all was quiet once more, and Count Sergei went back to sleep. At breakfast the shooting began again, accompanied now by heavy machine-gun fire. Soon the shooting intensified and surrounded the house. No one had any idea what was going on. There were no newspapers, nothing but rumors, including one that Generals Mikhail Alexeev and Alexei Brusilov had arrived in Moscow to set up a new government separate from Petrograd.[5]

The Bolshevik insurrection in Moscow did not go as smoothly as that in Petrograd. On October 26, the Moscow Military Revolutionary Committee, with as many as fifty thousand men, seized the Kremlin. They were opposed by the Committee for Public Safety, created upon the initiative of the city's Socialist Revolutionary mayor and consisting of military cadets, a small number of elite assault troops, and volunteers. On the morning of the twenty-eighth, the troops of the committee retook the Kremlin, during which hundreds of soldiers, the majority of them Bolsheviks, were killed.[6] That night Count Sergei wrote to a relative: "The Kremlin has been taken by the cadets. Moscow, it seems, is once again destined to play the decisive role in Russia's fate."[7]

For the next two days there was sporadic gunfire near the Corner House, with bullets landing in the courtyard. The street battles between the Bolsheviks and the cadets quickly became so intense that the Sheremetevs could not leave the house. The men and the remaining servants organized a night patrol. On the morning of the twenty-ninth, a car drove by and someone tossed a hand grenade into the intersection in front of the house, setting off a big blast but causing little damage. The same day the family managed to get a copy of the newspaper *Labor*, from which they learned that Moscow had been placed under martial law and that no one was permitted out in the streets without a pass. Late on the evening of the thirtieth all the lights went out. The family fumbled around in the dark with candles and fearing that the municipal workers had gone out on strike, began filling bathtubs and samovars with water. Next the telephones went dead. On the last day of October, the Sheremetev family office, the large bureaucracy that for centuries had managed their vast wealth and properties, ceased operations for good. That night the sky over the Corner House glowed from the fires burning across the city.[8]

The fighting grew on the first and second days of November. The committee controlled the center of Moscow, while the Bolsheviks dominated in the outlying workers' districts. During the battle for Moscow, the Red Guards units slowly progressed from the suburbs into the city, making their way toward the Kremlin. On November 2, there were rumors of the Bolsheviks gaining the upper hand and of closing in on Vozdvizhenka Street. Panic overtook the household, and Countess Yekaterina alone remained calm. The family now felt as if they were trapped inside a besieged fortress. All they had left to eat was potatoes. The gunfire and explosions kept getting louder and closer. They covered the windows and moved to the interior rooms for safety.[9] And then, when they arose on November 3, it was all over. The previous evening the Red Guards had blasted their way into the Kremlin and sent the remaining cadets running for safety. The Committee for Public Safety signed an act of surrender to the Revolutionary Committee and agreed to lay down its weapons.

Count Sergei wrote on the third:

We have learned that last evening a peace was agreed to and we all arose with a sense of relief, although conscious of the victory of the Bolsheviks thanks to the inaction of the government's defenders and the unmistakably transparent treason against and betrayal of the cadets, who were supported by no one and have perished at the hands of the conspirators! We are relieved that the bloodletting and damage to the Kremlin have stopped and recognize that although power has now passed into the hands of Lenin and Company this is both unacceptable and bound to be short-lived. The changes are visible from the window. Rifles have been laid down in the street, and Vozdvizhenka has taken on that Bolshevik look of disorder. The gunfire has largely subsided. There are lots of people out walking in the streets, as if they had all just escaped, women and children . . . We'll soon learn how many have been killed and the extent of the damage. Thank God it's all quiet again, even if only for a while.[10]

As soon as the shooting stopped, Pavel Sheremetev left the house for the Kremlin, which had been terribly damaged during the fighting. He spent almost every day there for the next several weeks, gathering up the bones of the old Muscovite grand princes that had been scattered about the ground by grave robbers.[11]

The mayor and Sofia were also in Moscow. Throughout October he had been following the rumors that "extremists" were making plans to overthrow Kerensky's government and seize power in Petrograd, none of which, given how thoroughly discredited the government had become, surprised the mayor. The rumors grew during the last week. There was word that the government had indeed been overthrown and civil war had broken out, but then on the twenty-sixth he heard that Kerensky had in fact crushed the coup against him. No one could be certain what in fact was taking place.[12]

By October, peasants at Petrovskoe were warning Alexander Golitsyn that he should leave for Moscow, for there was talk in the village of having him arrested. Fearful of the old home being pillaged, he first packed up the most valuable objects (paintings by Palma Vecchio, Canaletto, and Vigée-Lebrun) and sent them to his parents in Moscow.[13] Later that month the family decided they all would be safer in Moscow with Alexander's parents. "We are going to Moscow," Alexander and Lyubov's twelve-year-old daughter Marina observed. "It is getting dangerous to live in the country. The Bolsheviks come and talk to the peasants. Some are very unfriendly."[14] The family left Petrovskoe on October 26, the day of the Bolshevik coup. Marina's older sister Olga wondered would they ever see the estate again. They arrived in Moscow in the midst of the heavy fighting. Dead bodies lay in the streets, frightening the children.[15] By then, the revolution had already claimed the first life in the family. Four-year-old Tatiana, the daughter of Vladimir and Eli Trubetskoy, had fallen ill with scarlet fever in Moscow. Her uncle Alexander Golitsyn had been to tend to her in early October, but when the shooting began, he was unable to make his way back to the Trubetskoys for several days. By the time he finally reached her, Tatiana was dead. "Poor innocent victim of the revolution," he remarked.[16]

The extended Golitsyn family now began to gather at the home of the mayor and Sofia on Georgievsky Lane. Mikhail and his family came to live, as did the families of his sisters Eli Trubetskoy and Tatiana Lopukhin. (The Lopukhins had been forced to flee their estate of Khilkovo after it had been burned to the ground.) The men set up a night watch. This did not prevent burglars from breaking in and getting away with the family's silver. The youngest members of the family found all this most exciting. The mayor's grandson and namesake, Vladimir Golitsyn, was thrilled when he was considered old enough to be given a small-caliber gun and added to the watch. The burglary and subsequent investigation were perfectly timed since Vladimir was then devouring the detective stories of Nat Pinkerton ("King of Detectives") and Nick Carter ("Master Detective"). For Vladimir's siblings Sergei and Masha the truth of the revolution's destructive power came one morning when their governess took them to buy chocolate at their beloved Viktoria shop and found in its place a large smoking crater.[17]

To the mayor it seemed as if they were experiencing Chapter 18 of the Apocalypse. Some in the household blamed the revolution on international Zionism, some on the devil; some said it was punishment from God. Sofia was not so concerned about who was responsible, just that it all would go away somehow: "I want to wake up and everything will be as it was of old." Her husband refused to hear such talk of "the good old days." Rather, it was the old days that had produced their horrific present. "In our domestic strife one cannot but see retribution for the evil done to the people, for centuries of repression," he observed.[18] The cook, Mikhail, still came out after every dinner with his pad and pencil to take Sofia's order for the next day, but now he usually had to tell her, "That is no longer possible to buy, madam." By December, they had gone through their supply of firewood. Sergei awoke one morning to find the air in his room icy, his nanny standing over him holding his fur coat and heavy felt boots.[19]

Most Russians knew nothing of what had transpired in Petrograd, and it took several days and—for a good part of the population—weeks for the news of the Bolshevik insurrection to reach them. The general reaction, as best can be judged, was not one of astonishment or outrage. The conditions across the country had deteriorated so terribly and so swiftly since the fall of the Romanovs that most Russians were too preoccupied with their own immediate problems to worry about what might or might not be happening far away in the capital. The revolution was about events not in the capital but in their own villages or towns.

When the Kastchenko family received the news of the coup on their Ukraine estate, the first thing they decided to do was drink up all the wine in the cellar, for no doubt it would not be long before it was lost to the mob. The wine was wonderful, but it did nothing to lighten their mood. The Kastchenkos left the estate after hearing of the murder of a nearby noble family. Soon thereafter, peasants plundered the estate. The family managed to return in the summer of 1918, after troops from the Austro-Hungarian Army had moved into the area. The peasants went out to welcome the Kastchenkos back, carrying with them the things taken from the manor and the estate and explaining that they had been holding on to them "for safekeeping" until their return. When the Hungarians pulled out, so too did the Kastchenkos, afraid to remain alone amid the peasants. They made their way to Poland, certain they would someday return home, although they never did.[20]

The Sayn-Wittgensteins were at their Bronitsa estate near Mogilev when they learned of the coup on the last day of October. For weeks they had been hearing rumors that the Bolsheviks were plotting to seize power and that a plan was in the works to carry out a St. Bartholomew's Day Massacre in their area against all the landowners.* Catherine Sayn-Wittgenstein and her sister began wearing men's clothing since they decided this would make it easier to get away unnoticed, and Catherine began to carry a small Clément revolver. There was talk of looting on nearby estates, so they barricaded the manor house until it looked like "a medieval castle" and waited to see what would happen next. In November, several hundred Cossacks arrived, and the Sayn-Wittgensteins received them, mistakenly, as their protectors. The Cossacks set themselves on the family and robbed them before riding off. Defenseless, the family was next attacked one night by a band of drunken men who

*The St. Bartholomew's Day Massacre refers to the mass killing of French Huguenots (Protestants) by Catholics in Paris in 1572 during the French Wars of Religion. Rumors and fear of another such massacre based not on religion but on class were common in Russia during the revolution and the later civil war. Such rumors persisted into the 1930s.

cut the phone line, besieged the manor, and demanded money. The Sayn-Wittgensteins escaped the next morning to Mogilev, a few days before a mob descended on the manor and tore it to the ground, leaving nothing left standing but the walls.[21]

"Russia jumped off the rails on February 27," Catherine wrote in her diary, "and will not stop until she has fallen to the very bottom of the slope." This was not surprising, she noted, since the rails on which Russia had been riding "were so worn out, so unreliable, that she could not have failed but to have come off them."[22]

The Second Congress of Soviets met in Petrograd on the evening of October 25. Dominated by the Bolsheviks and boycotted by peasant organizations and army committees as unauthorized, the congress erupted into violent debate almost as soon as it opened. On one side were Trotsky and the Bolsheviks (Lenin was still in hiding in the capital, awaiting word that the Winter Palace had been taken), the architects of the coup against the Provisional Government; on the other were the Mensheviks and Socialist Revolutionaries who opposed the coup and wanted to open negotiations with the government. The Mensheviks issued a declaration describing the events of the past day as a "military conspiracy [. . .] organized and carried out by the Bolshevik Party in the name of the soviets behind the backs of all the other parties and factions represented in the soviets." The Bolsheviks' opponents called their actions "insane and criminal" and certain to ignite a civil war. Trotsky stood up and denounced them as "pathetic bankrupts," vainly instructing them to "Go where you belong from now on—into the garbage heap of history!" With that, Yuly Martov, the Menshevik leader, and his supporters rose and made for the exit amid wild, derisive cheering from the Bolsheviks and their backers among the left wing of the Socialist Revolutionaries. As he left, Martov turned and spoke: "One day, you will understand the crime in which you are taking part." Trotsky, evincing a mind-set that was to come to dominate the Bolshevik Party, assured those who remained that this rupture would only make the soviets stronger "by purging them of counterrevolutionary elements" and then went on to read a resolution denouncing their opponents.[23]

Not long after word arrived that the ministers of the Provisional

Government had been arrested at the Winter Palace in the early hours of the twenty-sixth, Anatoly Lunacharsky, the future Bolshevik commissar of enlightenment, read a statement from Lenin proclaiming that the congress, "backed by the will of the vast majority of the workers, soldiers, and peasants," was taking power into its own hands and promising immediate peace to all nations, total democracy in the army, the right of self-determination for all peoples and nationalities, worker control of the factories, and the transfer of all lands held by the nobility, the bourgeoisie, the church, and the government into the hands of the peasants. "Long live the Revolution!" Lunacharsky shouted, and was met with a wave of joyous cries and wild applause. Lenin's manifesto, adopted by the congress that day, became the key document in the creation myth of the Soviet Union, according to which the Bolsheviks were swept into power on a wave of massive popular support. In truth, thanks to the breakdown of all authority, which had begun in February of that year, they had been able to seize power without hardly anyone in the country knowing about it.[24]

It was one thing to claim power; it was quite another to possess it. Now that they had toppled the government, the Bolsheviks had to scramble to win over the country. The Decree on Land, adopted by the congress late on the twenty-sixth was a crucial first step. Lenin addressed the congress that day, saying that the new government's first duty was to settle the land question. "Private ownership of land," he told them, "shall be abolished forever," adding that all privately held land "shall be confiscated without compensation and become the property of the whole people." The only exception would be land worked by peasants, which they would be allowed to keep.

Lenin realized the importance of this decisive act. By giving the peasants the right to seize the nobles' land, he correctly judged how this could help both destroy the old order in the countryside and win the support of the peasantry. Trotsky later assessed the decree as having played a vital role not only in "the foundation of the new regime, but also as a weapon of the revolution, which had still to conquer the country." Lenin told Vladimir Bonch-Bruevich, executive secretary of the new government known as the Council of People's Commissars (or *Sovnarkóm*, the Russian acronym), "Now we have only to see to it that it is widely published and publicized. Then let . . . [the bourgeoisie] try to take it back."[25]

The Decree on Land did not incite the peasants to seize the land; rather, it sanctioned and encouraged what was already taking place. The destruction of the old order had begun well before the Bolsheviks seized power and was not their making. But Lenin understood how they could use the forces of anarchy to sweep away the remaining institutions of tsarist Russia, a prerogative for the creation of the new state. In the bloody summer of 1905, Lenin had written: "Revolutions are festivals of the oppressed and exploited. [. . .] We shall be traitors to and betrayers of the revolution if we do not use this festive energy of the masses and their revolutionary ardor to wage a ruthless and self-sacrificing struggle."[26]

This was just one aspect of the civil war that Lenin had been preaching for years. Along with this came attacks on political parties, on the press, on the institutions of self-government, indeed on anything that smacked of the old order or of the fragile democracy that began to take root after the fall of the Romanovs.[27] On October 27, the government issued the Decree on the Press, banning the "counterrevolutionary press"—that is, all newspapers that did not endorse the coup. A Left Socialist Revolutionary described the decree as a "clear and determined expression of a system of political terror and incitement to civil war." Outraged, Russian journalists fought back, and the Sovnarkóm, still too weak to enforce the decree, was not able to crush the independent press until August 1918.[28] The following month the Sovnarkóm abolished all legal estates and their privileges, all court ranks, and all noble titles, creating instead one single designation for everyone: "Citizen." All property belonging to noble institutions and societies was nationalized. Since March, the newspaper Izvestiia had been calling for "the complete abolition of all classes," and where the Provisional Government had dragged its feet, the Sovnarkóm had acted.[29] At the end of November, a law abolishing all private urban property was drafted (and finally approved in August 1918); special house committees were established as a tool for monitoring the urban populace.[30]

"The Bolshevik insurrection has ended," Olga Sheremetev wrote at the Corner House in early November. "They have won, and we find ourselves under the dominion of the Bolsheviks. For long? Already rumors about various counterrevolutions are spreading."[31]

Russia's educated classes resisted the coup from the beginning. Almost immediately, the country's civil servants went out on strike in protest, and a Committee for the Salvation of the Fatherland and Revolution was established in Petrograd to coordinate the actions of the various groups committed to restoring the Provisional Government. It was a diverse alliance of city officials, postal workers, government officials, representatives of the All-Russian Congress of Peasant Soviets, and members of various socialist parties. The committee issued a proclamation to the "Citizens of the Russian Republic," calling on all workers, peasants, soldiers, and the intelligentsia not to recognize the authority of the Bolsheviks, warning that "[a] civil war, begun by the Bolsheviks, threatens to plunge the country into the indescribable horrors of anarchy and counterrevolution."[32] (For the Bolsheviks, "counterrevolutionaries" were anyone opposed to the coup, while for their opponents, the Bolsheviks were the "counterrevolutionaries" for having overthrown the government and begun to repress their enemies.)

Russia's civil servants tried to bring down the *Sovnarkóm* by shutting their offices, locking up their files, and refusing to cooperate with their self-proclaimed new bosses. The banks closed; telegraph and telephone employees stopped working; even the capital's pharmacists went out on strike. When, in mid-November, the employees of the State Bank refused to open the vault to Vyacheslav Menzhinsky, the new commissar of finance, he had its officers brought in under armed guard and forced at gunpoint to open it. He then loaded five million rubles in a velvet bag and personally delivered it to Lenin. The strikes and work stoppages spread to Moscow and from there to several provincial towns.[33] After the Union of Unions of Government Employees in Petrograd went out on strike, the Military Revolutionary Committee issued an appeal "To all Citizens" stating that "the rich classes are resisting the new Soviet government," and threatening that "the rich classes and their supporters" will be denied the right to food unless they halt their "sabotage."[34]

The resistance, however, was not just nonviolent. Kerensky, now largely deserted by the Russian army, had managed to win the support of General Pyotr Krasnov and some of his Cossacks of the Third Cavalry Corps and to convince the general to march against Petrograd. On

October 30, Krasnov's men encountered a much larger group of Red Guards, sailors, and soldiers at Pulkovo Heights outside the capital. The Cossacks were repulsed and retreated to Gatchina, Kerensky's headquarters. Two days later, fearing for their lives, the Cossacks sold out Kerensky to the Bolsheviks for the promise of safe passage to southern Russia. Half an hour before his arrest, Kerensky, disguised as a sailor, managed to escape. From Russia he made his way to Paris and then, in 1940, to the United States.[35]

On the evening of November 14, the extended Sheremetev family gathered at the Corner House to celebrate Count Sergei's seventy-first birthday. Pavel Sheremetev arrived with the news of the *Sovnarkóm*'s having abolished all ranks and estates, and they discussed the elections for the Constituent Assembly set for November 19–21 in Moscow. Olga voted on the twenty-first. The mood in the city was panicky; the Bolsheviks were openly robbing banks, and all sorts of rumors were going about: some were saying that peace had been declared with Germany, others that a St. Bartholomew's Day Massacre, when all the burzhui would be rounded up and killed, was being planned for Moscow. "No one knows where we're heading!" Olga wrote in her diary. "We're all waiting for something to happen, and preparing ourselves for anything."[36] The Socialist Revolutionaries were the big winners in the election, garnering more than 40 percent of the vote; the Bolsheviks received 24 percent. The liberal and nonsocialist parties, chiefly the Kadets, gained only 7.5 percent.[37] To Olga, the results were meaningless. They proved to her that the country was becoming ever more polarized, not boding well for any experiment in parliamentary government; moreover, she was certain the Bolsheviks had no intention of ever allowing the assembly to meet.[38]

The *Sovnarkóm* postponed the opening of the assembly once the disappointing results became known. Next, the government outlawed the Kadet Party. The editorial offices of its newspaper were broken into and trashed, its leaders declared "enemies of the people" and arrested; two of them, Andrei Shingarev and Fyodor Kokoshkin, were murdered by their Bolshevik guards. Lenin and his followers believed that the Kadets, as representatives of the bourgeoisie, belonged to a class destined to extinction by Marx's "scientific laws" of history. Thus, repressing them was justified as part of history's master plan. "There is nothing immoral in the proletariat finishing off a class that is collapsing: that is its right," Trotsky stated. To Lenin, the assembly was as much a relic of the past as the bourgeoisie and the Kadets, and he had never seen any reason to allow it to meet. "A republic of Soviets is a higher form of democracy than the usual bourgeois republic with a Constituent Assembly," he wrote in *Pravda* in December. The long-awaited assembly did finally meet in Petrograd's Tauride Palace on January 5, 1918, though only for a day. The government immediately dissolved the assembly, which it characterized as, to quote *Pravda*, a gathering of "THE HIRE-LINGS OF BANKERS, CAPITALISTS, AND LANDLORDS [. . .] SLAVES OF THE AMERICAN DOLLAR [. . .] ENEMIES OF THE PEOPLE."[39]

The closure of the Constituent Assembly marked the death of Russian democracy. Anything and anyone that stood in the way of the Bolsheviks' grasp for power were branded counterrevolutionary. Weak and barely in control, the Bolsheviks saw threats everywhere they looked, and their response was to attack their enemies, both real and perceived. "The bourgeoisie, the landowners, and all the rich classes are making desperate attempts to undermine the revolution," Lenin wrote to Felix Dzerzhinsky in December 1917. "The bourgeoisie are prepared to commit the most heinous crimes." Dzerzhinsky, the son of impoverished Polish aristocrats, called for the *Sovnarkóm* to form a special organization to combat counterrevolution. "Do not think that I seek forms of revolutionary justice," he said. "We are not now in need of justice. It is war now—war face to face, a fight to the finish. Life or death! I propose, I demand an organ for the revolutionary settlement of accounts with counterrevolutionaries." On December 7, the *Sovnarkóm* appointed Dzerzhinsky head of the All-Russian Extraordinary Commission to Combat Counterrevolution and Sabotage. The Cheka, as it was known by its Russian acronym, would become a key weapon in the coming war.[40]

The exodus out of Petrograd and Moscow that had begun earlier that year turned into a flood following the Bolshevik coup. Even with their world collapsing around them, few nobles were trying to leave the country, largely for the simple reason that almost none of them, like most Russians, could imagine the Bolsheviks remaining in power for more than a few weeks. The many who left the two capitals, often selling whatever they had to buy scarce rail tickets, headed for the south or Siberia or for other fringes of the former empire, hoping to wait things out in quieter, safer surroundings and then return home once normalcy had been restored.

Vladimir Nabokov's father, intent on sending them to the safety of the Crimea, put his family on the train in Petrograd. Instead of disguising himself, the supercilious Vladimir traveled in spats and a derby and sporting an elegant cane. Along the way Vladimir and his brother Sergei had numerous encounters with bands of Red soldiers, but remarkably they arrived unharmed. At the time Vladimir found it all one great adventure, though later he marveled at his stupidity and blind good fortune. Near Kharkhov, Vladimir left the car and strolled about the platform among the soldiers, his mere presence a challenge to the men. As the train was leaving, he dropped his cane onto the tracks and, stooping to retrieve it, found the train in motion and pulling out of the station by the time he stood up. He was saved by a "sturdy proletarian arm" reaching out of a car that pulled him up off the platform and to safety. Years later Nabokov had to marvel: "Had I been one of the tragic bums who lurked in the midst of that station platform where a brittle young fop was pacing back and forth, I would not have withstood the temptation to destroy him."[41]

Several of the Golitsyns too began leaving Moscow that autumn. In November, Sofia and the mayor's daughter Sonya Lvov and her children left for the northern Caucasus and were soon followed by her sister Tatiana Lopukhin and her family.[42] The next to leave was the family of Alexander Golitsyn.

In light of the growing food crisis and worried that his efforts as a leading anti-Bolshevik in their Moscow neighborhood put him at risk of arrest, Alexander decided they should leave the city. After talking with people recently returned from Siberia who told him that life there was still peaceful and cheap and that there was no shortage of food, Alexander decided they all would leave for the town of Tyumen. Also shaping his decision was his conviction that bolshevism would never take hold among the strong, independent Siberians.[43] Alexander, his wife, Lyubov, and their five children left Moscow on December 3 on a hired sleeping car of the Northern Railway. The train was not scheduled to leave until 8:00 p.m., but they boarded three hours early to minimize the risk of being identified by the Bolsheviks. They were part of a group of extended family and servants making the trip. Among the group was Anna Golitsyn's mother, Anna's brother Nikolai Lopukhin, his wife, Sofia (née Osorgin), and their three daughters. They were joined by Georgy Lvov, the former prime minister, and his female companion, Yevgenia Pisarev. They took with them only what they could carry: a washbasin and jug, two samovars, a box of books and photograph albums, a sewing machine, a container for milk, a copper mortar, some clothes, and a small crib. The mayor and Sofia came to the station to see them off. Marina Golitsyn noticed that as their train pulled out, tears were streaming down her grandmother Sofia's face. "How sad," the mayor wrote after they left. "How painful it is for us that our dear, wonderful family has in fact been broken." At the time, no one ever could have imagined the travails that awaited them on their journey or that they would never see their loved ones again.[44]

The patriarchs of the Golitsyn and Sheremetev families—the mayor and Count Sergei—rarely agreed on anything, but on one thing they did: they would never leave Moscow. All around them family and friends were abandoning the city. Countess Yekaterina Sheremetev's sister, Baba Ara, was contemplating leaving for the northern Caucasus; the Gudoviches were thinking of going as well. From Kislovodsk, Dmitry Sheremetev urged his parents to come south and join him and his family. But Count Sergei would have none of it. He was appalled at the notion of leaving his home for his comfort or safety. He was displeased with Dmitry and Ira for having left. "They've all gone off and joined the Cossacks," he wrote in his diary, "and will have to pay for the unacceptable fact of being Christians. Panicky Ira is trying to save her posterity among the Cossacks."[45] Count Sergei was just as upset at the former tsar upon hearing a rumor that Nicholas had taken flight from his captors in Tobolsk; were it true, he would consider it a mark of shameful cowardice.[46] Count Sergei tried to instill in his family the idea that it was ignoble "to flee a sinking ship, and that they all simply had to die on their native soil," as one frequent guest to the Corner House recalled.[47] Yelena Sheremetev's son wrote that Count Sergei forbade anyone in the family not only from leaving Russia but from even discussing it.[48]

The many rumors going about the city at the time influenced decisions about whether to stay or go. There was word that things were going well for the anti-Bolshevik forces beginning to gather in the south. General Alexei Kaledin had recently been elected ataman of the Don

Cossacks, and some in Moscow dared hope that he and his Cossack warriors would topple the Bolsheviks. When the head yardman at the Corner House heard the rumor, he made sure to inform the Sheremetevs that he was no longer a supporter of the Bolsheviks. Pavel put faith in the bizarre rumor that there was a strong monarchist faction among the Bolsheviks and that they were gaining the upper hand and would restore the tsar in January. The speed with which rumors arose and spread kept Muscovites in a frenzied state of confusion. One minute the Bolsheviks' days seemed numbered; the next it seemed they were preparing a decisive blow against their enemies. No sooner were the Sheremetevs rejoicing over the talk of Kaledin than they got word that four hundred guillotines, including one on Palace Square in Petrograd, had been set up across Russia for the immediate execution of the burzhui. Talk of an arrest warrant having been issued for Count Sergei caused the family to worry that he would be among the first executed. And then later that same day a visitor to the Corner House told them not to worry, that they had it on good authority the German army would be in Petrograd by December 12 and then Moscow soon after, saving them all from the Bolsheviks. Amid this roller coaster of fear and hope, life somehow went on. One night in late November, having had enough talk of politics, Pavel and Lilya went to a reading by the Futurist poet Igor Severyanin and laughed as they had not in a long time.[49]

Everyone had grown weary of politics. "Politics and politics. We are all tired of the decrees, strikes, acts of 'sabotage,' the crack-downs and breakups of gatherings, the discussions and theories," Olga Sheremetev complained in early December. Of one thing she, and many Russians, were certain: the Bolsheviks would soon collapse. But she did not think there would be any restoration of the monarchy, as many in her circle now believed and hoped for. Such people were living in a dreamworld, she thought, and had created in their minds an image of life before the revolution that had never existed. Their talk that the revolution had been the work of Jews and Freemasons, ideas popularized by the writings of Sergei Nilus, notorious for spreading the antiSemitic *Protocols of the Elders of Zion*, repulsed her. Olga thought it likely that the Socialist Revolutionaries would take power after the Bolsheviks. But it did not matter, for regardless of who it was, life in Russia, she was convinced, was unlikely to get any better.[50]

On December 31, Princess Catherine Sayn-Wittgenstein wrote in her diary in Mogilev: "The last day of 1917, a year that will assuredly be remembered! It's hard to imagine any country in all of history having experienced such a year. [. . .] Has it ever before happened that a people has spoiled, indeed destroyed, its native land with its own hands?"[51]

Both Count Sergei and the mayor, however, managed to strike positive notes in their diaries. "We are about to enter the New Year amidst complete anarchy, having bid farewell to the old year, one that has been so fatal to Russia! We shall maintain our good spirits, along with our faith and hope, and we shall thank the Lord for everything," wrote Count Sergei.[52] The mayor echoed these sentiments:

> I end the year with a feeling of infinite gratitude to God for my family and for my familial happiness. Nonetheless, for the fourth time now we part with a year that forms a string of years, each of which has been more nightmarish than the previous. One doesn't wish to sum up this year either, even though we have been witnesses to what someone has justly called the crisis of humanity. Now I must end the last line of my daily chronicle and express my prayerful wish—
>
> May the Lord bless the coming year![53]

PART III

Civil War

The path of history is beyond the understanding of those who have been consigned to the routine of capitalism, of those who have been deafened by the mighty crash of the old world, by the cracking, the noise, the "chaos" (or apparent chaos) of the collapse of the age-old structures of tsarism and the bourgeoisic, of those who have been cowed by class warfare taken to its most extreme, by its transformation into civil war, a true holy war—and not in some priestly sense of the word, but in its most humane understanding: a holy war of the oppressed against their oppressors, a holy war for the liberation of the workers from all oppression.　　　　　　　—Lenin, December 1917

Yes, long live civil war! Civil war for the sake of the children, the elderly, the workers and the Red Army, civil war in the name of direct and ruthless struggle against counterrevolution.
　　　　　　　　　　　　　　　—Leon Trotsky, May 1918

We are heading for a total civil war, and it seems that the war will be a savage one . . . Oh, how hard it is to live in Russia! We are all so stupid—so fantastically stupid.
　　　　　　　　　　　　　　　—Maxim Gorky, July 1918

8

EXPROPRIATING THE EXPROPRIATORS

The Bolshevik coup plunged Russia into a civil war that would consume the country for the next three years and result in possibly as many as ten million deaths, nearly all of them civilians. As the historian Evan Mawdsley commented, "The Civil War unleashed by Lenin's revolution was the greatest national catastrophe Europe had yet seen." Russia descended into savage anarchy beyond imagination. "War and strife, famine and pestilence—the Four Horsemen of the Apocalypse," Mawdsley wrote, "devastated the largest country in Europe."[1]

Almost immediately after the Bolshevik seizure of power, forces intent on undoing Lenin's coup began to gather on the fringes of the former Russian Empire. Known generally as the White movement, it was a motley group of former tsarist officers and soldiers, Cossacks, nobles, bourgeois, and intellectuals whose political beliefs ran the spectrum from reactionary monarchists to radical socialists. In the lands of the Don Cossacks, in the forests of Siberia, and in the Baltic territories, armies formed to march on the great Russian heartland, the base of the Bolsheviks' newborn state. They were led by men like Generals Anton Denikin in the south and Nikolai Yudenich in the west and Admiral Alexander Kolchak in the east. In the autumn of 1919, the White forces came close to toppling the new Bolshevik government. The White Volunteer Army marched deep into Russia, took

Orel, and appeared to be unstoppable on its drive to Moscow. The Northwestern Army came within twenty miles of Petrograd, the soldiers at its forward positions able to make out the golden dome of St. Isaac's Cathedral in the city center. By the end of October, however, the White forces had been stopped, and the Red Army had gone on the offensive. Never again would the anti-Bolshevik forces come close to winning the war.[2]

The war of the Whites and the Reds was complicated by a number of factors. The revolution brought with it the breakup of the old empire as the non-Russian lands on the empire's borders declared independence. The Transcaucasus, Finland, part of Ukraine, and the lands of the Don, Kuban, and Orenburg Cossacks freed themselves from Russian suzerainty and resisted Bolshevik control.[3] Germany was still at war with Russia, and after the Bolsheviks initially rejected an insulting German peace offer, the kaiser's armies renewed their offensive. With the mass of the Russian Army having abandoned the front for home, there was nothing to stop the German advance. To save the new government, Lenin agreed to peace with the Germans in March 1918. The Treaty of Brest-Litovsk gave the Bolsheviks a chance at survival, but it came at a tremendous price: Russia ceded more than a quarter of its population and its arable land and a third of its average crops and its manufacturing industries and burdened itself with a punishing war indemnity.[4] And there were other armed forces to contend with: the so-called Greens, bands of peasant partisans; Nestor Makhno and his anarchist Black Army of Ukraine; foreign intervention by the armies of Poland, Britain, France, Japan, and the United States; and a legion of riotous Czech soldiers. Never simply a war of Reds against Whites, the Russian civil war was a complex, titanic struggle that swept up in its vortex a variety of social and political movements, large professional armies and small bands of partisans, local grievances and world politics, shifting battle lines and unsteady alliances that shook Russia to its foundations and very nearly destroyed it.

In January 1918, the Third Congress of Soviets adopted the Declaration of the Rights of the Laboring and Exploited People, according to which the main task of the new government was "the destruction of any human exploitation by another" and the "merciless repression of the exploiters."[5] As an early step in this task, in late 1917 the Bolsheviks issued a decree requiring the obligatory registration of all "former landowners, capitalists, and persons who held positions of authority in the tsarist and bourgeois order." The decree establishing the Cheka had called for the registration of all wealthy residents, and in December 1917 Lenin had also proposed obligatory registration for "all persons belonging to the rich classes" and "employees of banks, stock corporations, state and public institutions." (The proposal was not realized until the autumn of 1919.) The approximate number of people who fitted in these categories was somewhere between four and five million, a large percentage of whom were members of the nobility. This social categorization became the basis for the notion of "former people," also designated as "socially alien elements," "remnants of the old bourgeois world," or simply "class enemies."[6] With only a bit of exaggeration, Nicolas Nabokov wrote that the Bolsheviks had another name for former people: "the yet unslaughtered."[7]

In *The State and Revolution*, from the late summer of 1917, Lenin wrote that the primary function of the proletarian state was the destruction of the bourgeoisie. "The state is a special organization of power, it is an organization of violence for the repression of one class or another. [. . .] The proletariat needs the state as a special form of organized violence *against* the bourgeoisie."[8]

Lenin did not mean this in some theoretical way, but in concrete terms. He wrote that the Paris Commune of 1871 had failed since it had not used adequate violence to crush the bourgeoisie. Even the Terror of the French Revolution eighty years earlier, Lenin argued, had been too limited in its use of violence. "The guillotine *only* frightened, it broke only *active* resistance. This is not enough for us." Lenin insisted future revolutionaries would have to go further to achieve their goals. As early as January 1918, two months after seizing power, Lenin complained that they were being too easy on their class enemies. "If we are guilty of anything," he wrote, "then it is of being too humane, too kind in regards to the monstrous, traitorous representatives of the bourgeois-imperialist order."[9] The bourgeoisie had to be controlled, put to work, monitored. After all their property had been expropriated, the bourgeoisie would be subjugated by being forced to live by ration cards; those who refused to work would starve.[10] The control was to be total (although it never was since this was beyond the Bolsheviks', indeed any government's, capabilities); the punishment for infractions, brutal. "These enemies must be placed under special monitoring by the entire populace, they must be dealt with in the most merciless fashion for the slightest infringement of the rules and laws of socialist society."[11] Class determined everything, except when it did not. Lenin ignored his own noble background, which should have placed him in the camp of the revolution's enemies, and he was ready to use violence against the working class itself when it resisted Communist authority.[12]

On October 5, 1918, the Soviet of People's Commissars passed a resolution making labor mandatory for the bourgeoisie. Every month these former people were required to record in special labor books proof of having performed specific labor on behalf of the community; persons who either failed to have a valid booklet or did not record the required amount of forced labor were denied ration cards and the right to move freely about the country. The following year these booklets became mandatory for all residents of Moscow and Petrograd over the age of sixteen.[13] In Petrograd in 1918, residents in the fashionable parts of the city were forced out of their homes to dig graves for the victims of typhus. For his day's labor, each person received one cup of tea.[14] Princess Volkonsky recalled being made to shovel snow behind a railway station with others of her class. The work had no purpose other than as a form of public humiliation, and their guards took pleasure in laughing and mocking them as they labored. Another such work project was the compulsory cleaning of toilets in communal and government buildings.[15]

The laws of the new Communist state enshrined the idea of discrimination based on social class. The first Soviet Constitution adopted in July 1918 denied the right to vote or to hold elected office to anyone who had served the Romanov family or in the tsarist police, to anyone who hired workers to make a profit or lived off rents and investments, as well as to all traders, monks, and clergy. In May 1918, the Bolsheviks instituted the so-called class ration, linking the size of one's food ration to one's social class.[16] Workers received the largest ration; the burzhui, the lowest, which, in the words of Grigory Zinoviev, was "just enough bread so as not to forget the smell of it."[17] Preference for entrance to schools was given to children of the proletariat and the poorest peasants. Living space and rent were also based on class. The Petrograd Soviet, for example, passed a decree on March 1, 1918, limiting all

LEFT Count Sergei Sheremetev and his younger half brother, Count Alexander, from the 1870s. The uniform notwithstanding, Sergei's interests ran toward Russian history and culture, while Alexander's passions were music and firefighting. (Author's collection)

BELOW The family of Count Sergei and Countess Yekaterina Sheremetev, the Fountain House, St. Petersburg, early 1880s. Front row, left to right: Pavel, Boris, Countess Yekaterina, Maria, a governess, Sergei. Back row, left to right: Dmitry, Count Sergei, Anna Sheremetev (Count Sergei's cousin), Pyotr, Anna. (Author's collection)

ABOVE Alexander Saburov, his wife, Anna, and their children Boris and Xenia, ca. 1900. Musical, deeply religious, and possessed of the kind of beauty that, according to one contemporary, moved men to spill blood and compose love songs, Anna was to know terrible loss: her husband was executed and her two sons perished in the gulag. (Author's collection)

RIGHT The younger of the two Sheremetev girls, Maria was her father's favorite. She is shown here in 1899, a year before her marriage to Count Alexander Gudovich. (Author's collection)

Count Pavel Sheremetev in seventeenth-century dress for the Ball of 1903. Historian, artist, and conflicted monarchist, Pavel was his father's spiritual heir and the only son to remain in Russia. (Author's collection)

The Sheremetevs at Mikhailovskoe, June 7, 1915
Seated on the grass, left to right: Yelena Sheremetev (second from left), Andrei Gudovich (fourth from left), Merinka Gudovich (fourth from right), Dmitry Gudovich (reclining), Nikolai Sheremetev (far right). Seated, second row, left to right: Dmitry Sheremetev (in uniform), Maria Gudovich, Lilya Sheremetev (fifth from left), Yekaterina Sheremetev, Baron de Baye, Lili Vyazemsky (far right). Standing, back row, left to right: Varvara Gudovich, Boris Vyazemsky (in hat and tie), Sergei Sheremetev (in gray suit with beard). The back row includes a number of the children's tutors and governesses, their music teacher, and the family priest. (Author's collection)

The Corner House—"the Sheremetevs' refuge"—in Moscow, early twentieth century. (Author's collection)

Princess Yekaterina Dmitrievna Golitsyn, the daughter of Prince Dmitry Golitsyn, imperial master of the hunt, in the mid-1890s. In 1910, while a maid of honor to the imperial court, she married Count Alexander Sheremetev's son Georgy. Separated from each other during much of the civil war, they escaped southern Russia for Europe with their two young children and lived out their lives in exile. (Courtesy of Russian State Archive of Ancient Acts)

Newlyweds Prince Vladimir Golitsyn and Sofia Delianov, 1871. (Courtesy of Russian State Archive of Ancient Acts)

Student days: the mayor's three youngest sons, ca. 1900. Seated: Alexander Golitsyn (second from right) and Nikolai Golitsyn (far right). Standing: Count Mikhail Tolstoy, son of Leo Tolstoy (with guitar); Vladimir Vladimirovich Golitsyn (far right). (Courtesy of Alexandre Galitzine)

The mayor's eldest son, Prince Mikhail Golitsyn, and his wife, Anna Lopukhin, from the time of their wedding, 1899. (Courtesy of Alexandre Galitzine)

Princess Yelizaveta "Eli" Golitsyn in fancy dress a few years before her marriage to Prince Vladimir Trubetskoy. (Courtesy of Mikhail Trubetskoy)

Prince Vladimir Trubetskoy, aged eight, on his way to a masquerade ball, 1900. Born into a family of scholars, Vladimir was drawn to music and the arts as a boy before going on to a military career. (Courtesy of Mikhail Trubetskoy)

ABOVE A noble picnic, July 27, 1908. Home to the Lopukhins and later the Trubetskoys, the Menshovo estate, south of Moscow, was a popular gathering place for both families and their friends. Among the party are Anna Lopukhin's brothers Alexei and Pyotr Lopukhin (reclining behind samovar and standing, right, with teacup), Prince Vladimir Trubetskoy (extreme right), his sister Maria ("Manya," in the white hat), and his brother Nikolai (standing behind Alexei). A servant hovers in the background. (Courtesy of Mikhail Trubetskoy)

BELOW Tennis, August 23, 1909. Prince Vladimir Trubetskoy and his future bride, Princess Eli Golitsyn (first and third from left), with Vladimir's siblings. At far right stands twenty-year-old Valerian Yershov from the neighboring estate of Vorobyevo. He joined the White Army during the civil war and died of typhus in 1919. (Courtesy of Mikhail Trubetskoy)

LEFT The family of the Menshovo estate manager Shutov, 1908. (Courtesy of Mikhail Trubetskoy)

RIGHT The coachman Yegor, his family, and Lukerya, the laundress (far left), Menshovo, September 1908. (Courtesy of Mikhail Trubetskoy)

Peddlers, Menshovo, May 1890. (Courtesy of Mikhail Trubetskoy)

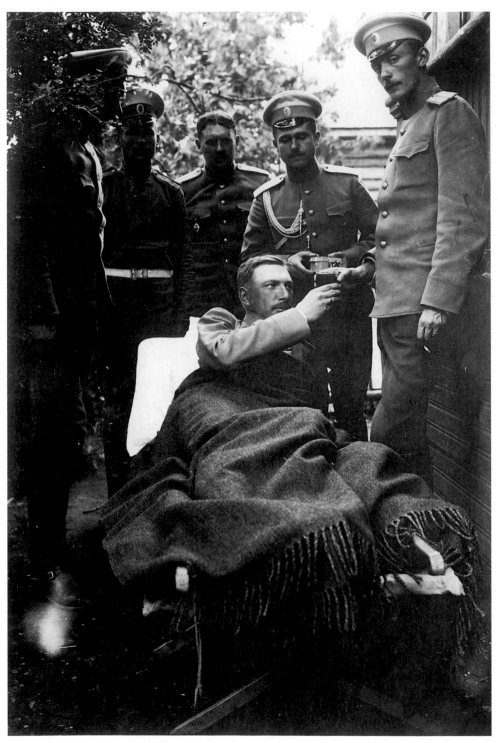

Prince Vladimir Trubetskoy (far right) in camp with his fellow officers of the Blue Cuirassiers during maneuvers in 1912, the year of his wedding to Eli. (Courtesy of Mikhail Trubetskoy)

LEFT An advocate of reform and a harsh critic of the tsarist state, Prince Vladimir Golitsyn was forced out of his position as governor of Moscow in 1891. He later returned to political life, serving several terms as the city's mayor and earning praise as "the bright Champion of honor and truth" for his liberal agenda and urban improvements. (Courtesy of Alexandre Galitzine)

BELOW Countess Catherine "Katia" von Carlow (second from left), dancing with friends in the family palace on the Fontanka River in St. Petersburg. The daughter of Duke George of Mecklenburg-Strelitz, she married Prince Vladimir Emanuelovich Golitsyn in 1913. (Courtesy of George Galitzine)

Drawn from the highest ranks of the nobility, the officers of the Imperial Chevaliers Gardes Regiment gather around Emperor Nicholas II and the tsarevich Alexei. Among the officers is Prince Vladimir Emanuelovich Golitsyn (to right of Alexei, gazing at him), aide-de-camp to Grand Duke Nikolai Nikolaevich and the husband of Countess Katia von Carlow. (Courtesy of George Galitzine)

Grand Duke Nikolai Nikolaevich, grandson of Tsar Nicholas I and commander in chief of Russian forces in the Caucasus from 1915, and Prince Vladimir Emanuelovich Golitsyn (fifth from left, with goggles, staring at the camera). Prince Vladimir took part in the Russian victory at Erzurum in February 1916 and was sent by the grand duke to report the news to the emperor at Tsarskoe Selo. (Courtesy of George Galitzine)

*Ч1. Сожженіе гербовъ
въ дни революціи*

A crowd gathers in the streets to watch the burning of the imperial coat of arms in the early days of the revolution. (Photograph © CORBIS Images)

ABOVE Members of the former elite forced to clean snow and ice from the sidewalks of Petrograd under the watch of a Soviet official. (Courtesy of Russian State Archive of Documentary Films and Photographs)

BELOW Burzhui made to shovel snow while guarded by Red Army soldiers in Petrograd, ca. 1918. (Courtesy of Russian State Archive of Documentary Films and Photographs)

A former tsarist officer selling matches on the streets of Petrograd, ca. 1918. (Courtesy of Russian State Archive of Documentary Films and Photographs)

Princess Katia Golitsyn with her sons George (left) and Nikolai during the civil war in the northern Caucasus. A Red Army soldier was so taken by George's beautiful blue eyes that he gave him a fifteen-kopeck piece and called off the search of the family home. A grateful Katia spent the money on a church candle and prayed for the man's safety. (Courtesy of George Galitzine)

The British battleship HMS *Marlborough* anchored off the Crimean coast waiting to take Dowager Empress Maria Fyodorovna and seventeen members of the imperial family into exile, April 1919. Among those present to see them off were Prince Vladimir Emanuelovich Golitsyn and his wife, Katia. Playmate of the tsarevich Alexei, Princess Sophy Dolgoruky, in hat and braids, stands staring at the camera on the right. (Courtesy of George Galitzine)

Golden wedding anniversary of Vladimir and Sofia Golitsyn, Bogoroditsk, spring 1921. Of the twenty-two pictured here, thirteen were to be arrested by the Soviet government, five died or were shot in prison, and five left the country.

Sitting, left to right: Maria "Masha" Golitsyn, Sergei Golitsyn, Grigory "Grisha" Trubetskoy, Alexei Bobrinsky, Nikolai Bobrinsky, Varvara "Varya" Trubetskoy. Middle row, left to right: Anna Golitsyn, Yekaterina "Katya" Golitsyn, Mikhail Golitsyn, Sofia Golitsyn, Vladimir Golitsyn (the mayor), Yelena Bobrinsky, Vera Bobrinsky, Alexandra "Tatya" Trubetskoy (fingers in mouth), Yelizaveta "Eli" Trubetskoy, Andrei Trubetskoy. Standing, top row, left to right: Alexandra "Lina" Golitsyn, Sofia "Sonya" Golitsyn, Vladimir Golitsyn, Vladimir Trubetskoy, Sofia "Sonya" Bobrinsky, Alexandra "Alka" Bobrinsky. (Courtesy of Alexandre Galitzine) "bourgeois" adults to one room; the remaining space and its contents were to be handed over to "proletarians" for free. Failure to follow the decree would result in expulsion from one's home and the confiscation of all property.[18]

Even the members of bourgeois families were subject to expropriation. In the spring of 1918 in Yekaterinodar, the Bolsheviks published a decree, On the Socialization of Girls and Women. According to the order, which was posted around the city, all unmarried women between the ages of sixteen and twenty-five were to be "socialized." Men wishing to participate were instructed to go to the appropriate revolutionary authority to see about acquiring up to ten females for their use. Red soldiers, acting on the decree, seized approximately sixty young women, chiefly from the local elite; some of them were grabbed from the main city park during a special raid. A few of the girls were taken to a nearby house and raped; two dozen were conducted to the local Bolshevik boss at his headquarters, and the rest were delivered to another party leader and a group of soldiers at the Hotel Bristol, where they were raped. Some of the victims were later freed, some were taken away and never seen again, and some were killed and their bodies dumped into the Kuban River. One of the girls, a fifth grader from the Yekaterinodar gymnasium, was repeatedly raped by a group of soldiers for twelve hours. When they had finished with her, they tied the girl to a tree, set her on fire, and then, mercifully, shot her.[19] A similar socialization of women was carried out in Yekaterinburg in the spring of 1918.[20]

Between November 1917 and the end of the civil war, the Bolsheviks transferred almost all of the country's public and private wealth into their own hands in what one historian has dubbed "history's greatest heist." Perhaps as much as 1.6 billion rubles (roughly $160 billion in today's dollars) was, for want of a better word, stolen.[21]

First, the Bolsheviks went after the landowners. The Decree on Land of October 26, 1917, revoked all private ownership of land without compensation for redistribution. By February 1918, on the basis of data from nineteen provinces, 75 percent of all estates in Russia had been confiscated from their owners.[22] About 10 percent of the noble landowners did manage to remain in the countryside and were given some land to work; these tended to be poorer landowners, the richer ones typically having fled or been chased off the land for good.[23] The victims were not just noble landlords. Wealthy peasants were attacked as well, their property seized and often destroyed by their poorer neighbors.[24] The attacks against the landlords in Usman county, the site of the Vyazemsky estate of Lotarevo, raged into the first months of 1918. By then at least half of all the estates there had been destroyed. When the local land committee decided to let some of the landlords stay on their estates, the peasants unleashed even greater fury, attacking the remaining estates and tearing them to the ground. Peasants in other regions acted similarly as the only way to once and for all drive off the landowners and take the land for themselves.[25] Along with the attack on individual landownership, the Bolsheviks also turned against the Orthodox Church, nationalizing church lands, including more than one thousand monasteries, in January 1918.[26]

On August 20, 1918, the All-Russian Central Executive Committee* decreed that the "homes of the bourgeoisie" were to be confiscated and handed over to city Soviets.[27] A great number of former people were either forced from their homes or subjected to what the Russians call *uplotnénie*, consolidation. The case of Prince Pavel Dolgorukov is instructive. Having recently been released from prison, Dolgorukov was living at his family's Moscow mansion in the spring of 1918. The upper floor had been taken over by a group of Red soldiers, who banged away on the family's Bechstein piano all night and sang, feasted, and drank. When the Bolsheviks moved their capital from Petrograd to Moscow in 1918, this merry band was forced out to make room for a state ministry. The ministry initially requisitioned only part of the house but then kept taking more and more rooms until it took Dolgorukov's sole room and forced him out onto the street. Dolgorukov was fortunate to have been allowed to remain in his home as long as he did. Some nobles in Moscow were given only twenty-four hours to clear out of their homes to make room for Soviet government offices.[28]

Not only was consolidation for former people physically uncomfortable (at times entire families were squeezed into a single room), but more important, it robbed them of any privacy. The fear of denuncia-

---

*Created at the Second Congress of Workers' and Peasants' Deputies on October 25, 1917, along with the *Sovnarkóm*, it functioned with the latter as the executive wing of the new state.

tion meant old family traditions (parties, Christmas celebrations, baptisms, and the like) had to be abandoned or conducted in secrecy; one no longer talked freely in one's home, but in a whisper to avoid being overheard. The mechanisms by which family memory and customs were passed from generation to generation were often severed.[29]

Through a set of policies that later came to be known as War Communism, the Bolsheviks seized control of the country's entire economy. Land, property, and private industry were nationalized; private trade was outlawed; peasants were denied the right to sell their produce and forced to turn it over to the state. The Bolsheviks began their radical transformation of economic life immediately after seizing power. Between the middle of November 1917 and early March 1918, Lenin issued approximately thirty decrees on the nationalization of private industry and manufactures.[30] On December 27, 1917, the Central Executive Committee issued decrees nationalizing the country's banks, and the same day the government sent soldiers to occupy twenty-three private banks and credit institutions in Petrograd and arrested their directors. Next the government threatened to arrest any bank directors who tried to block Bolshevik withdrawals.[31] Once in control of the banks, the Bolsheviks went after what lay in the vaults. In January, the holders of safe-deposit boxes across Russia were ordered to show up and present their keys so that their boxes could be inspected. Persons who failed to comply within three days would automatically forfeit their possessions.

Irina Skariatina was one of those who showed up at their banks that month. She wrote in her diary that everyone she knew went to open his or her box out of fear of reprisal of some sort. What met all of them at the bank was a complete surprise. The soldiers had no intention of just inspecting the boxes; rather, they confiscated the contents of every last box, not just money and jewelry, but deeds, documents, and even lockets of baby hair. It all happened so fast, and they all were so shocked by what they were witnessing, that it was only after the soldiers had marched them out of the bank and onto the street that Irina and the others realized what had happened to them. Some tried to make their way back into the bank but were stopped by the soldiers. Women broke down in tears. One woman turned and said gloomily:

"What's the use of crying? This is only the beginning—wait and see what will happen to all of us soon. Then we can cry."[32]

The Bolsheviks' timing was excellent. Following the outbreak of the Great War in 1914, wealthy Russians believed it unpatriotic to send capital and money out of Russia; some nobles apparently even sold off investments in other parts of Europe to bring their capital back home to Russia. During the war laws limiting the ability to buy foreign currency were also passed. Amid the revolutionary upheavals of 1917, when a great many nobles left Petrograd and Moscow for the south or other Russian borderlands, most left their money and valuables in the banks, never thinking for a minute they would not be safe there. The banks were thus fully loaded with money, gold, and jewelry when the Bolsheviks struck.[33] The Bolsheviks' Safes Commission, charged with cracking the country's bank vaults and safe-deposit boxes, working together with the State Treasury for the Storage of Valuables (*Gokhrán*), had taken in nearly nine hundred million rubles' worth of coin, art, antiquities, precious metals and stones by late 1921. This was added to a half ton of gold, silver, and platinum bullion; seven hundred thousand rubles in coins of various precious metals; sixty-five million tsarist rubles, and almost six hundred million rubles' worth of government and corporate bonds seized by the Bolshevik Revision Committee in Moscow banks alone in 1918.[34]

Many wealthy Russians responded to this mad hunt for precious metals and stones by hiding whatever they had left. In the spring of 1918, Countess Irina Tatishchev's grandmother packed all her pearls, rings, gold, and diamonds in a leather valise and gave it to Irina to hide. Irina took the valise to a friend's apartment, where they stashed it in a secret compartment in a bedroom wall.[35]

Such stories were legion and inspired Ilf and Petrov's novel *The Twelve Chairs*. Everyone in Russia with anything of value was trying to hide it. In 1917, Prince Felix Yusupov and his trusted servant Grigory took the family's most valuable diamonds and jewelry from Petrograd to their Moscow palace and hid them in a secret room under the stairs. After Yusupov fled Russia, the Bolsheviks captured Grigory and tortured him to tell them where they had hidden the jewels, but he never divulged the location. The Cheka set up surveillance on the palace and monitored the activities of everyone who went in and out. This went on for years, but no one was ever caught with any diamonds. The secret room was not discovered until 1925, when workmen were repairing the stairs. They found two English safes, several old trunks under heavy locks, and a large rusty metal chest, all filled with jewels and precious metals. A few years earlier Yusupov's secret fireproof rooms in the former family home on Petrograd's Moika Street had been discovered. Here the prince had hidden more jewelry, books, more than a thousand paintings, as well as musical instruments, including a rare Stradivarius artfully hidden inside a hollowed-out interior column.[36]

Alexandra Tolstoy, the daughter of the novelist, hid her jewels in the bottom of a flower pot, where they remained undetected for years. When the young Alexei Tatishchev and his cousins boarded a train in Kiev for Odessa on the last day of 1918, they noticed their scouts' uniforms felt heavier than usual but thought nothing of it. Upon their arrival, Alexei's aunt had them all immediately strip and then proceeded to rip open the linings of their pockets to retrieve the strings of pearls she had hidden. Olga Schilovsky's mother took her teddy bear and stuffed it with the diamond cipher given to her by the empress Alexandra. During a house search some soldiers threatened to rip the bear open but were stopped by little Olga's pleading sobs.[37] The Nabokovs stashed much of the family jewelry in a secret hiding place in their Petrograd mansion until their doorman, Ustin, ratted to the Reds. They fled Petrograd for Gaspra in the Crimea with their remaining jewels hidden in a container of talcum powder, which upon their arrival they buried out in the garden near an oak.[38] Princess Lydia Vasilchikov buried her pearls and rings in the woods behind the Crimean estate of Charaks. Many of her family and friends had sewn their jewels into the hems of skirts and dresses, into furs and hats.[39] The dowager empress Maria Fyodorovna had hidden her jewels in cocoa tins and buried them under some rocks at her daughter Xenia's Ai Todor estate in the Crimea; a dog's skull marked the spot.[40]

And it was not just jewels that people were frantically burying or sewing into their clothing. Galina von Meck's family buried most of their wine cellar in a flower bed behind their Moscow house. Later, when Galina grew worried the hiding place had been compromised, she began surreptitiously digging up the bottles at night with the help of some friends. They would dig while it was dark and then move the bottles during the day to a new location by disguising them under a blanket in a baby's pram.[41] The Nabokovs' chauffeur Tsiganov took apart the large Wolseley automobile piece by piece, which he then buried so well that nothing of the automobile has apparently ever been found.[42] In Petrograd, Baroness Meiendorff was so afraid of having her sugar confiscated she poured it between two sheets that she had sewn together and then laid flat on her mattress.[43]

The lust for money and valuables was boundless. In Saratov in April 1919, the town's twenty jewelers were called to a meeting at the office of the provincial auditor to answer some questions. When they realized they had been lured there as a ruse, they tried to leave but were stopped by armed guards and taken captive. One by one each jeweler was marched by Red soldiers to his store, which they robbed of all its gold and silver. Only after all the jewelers had been robbed were they let free.[44] Dentists were arrested and held hostage until they divulged where they stored the gold used to fill rotten teeth.[45]

Beginning in late 1917, members of the former privileged classes were frequently arrested and held for ransom or threatened with death unless they paid extortion money. In one such example, the Cheka arrested 105 residents of Nizhny Novgorod and held them hostage until the city's notables could come up with twenty-two million rubles. In the summer of 1918, Nicholas von Meck, the scion of a noble family that had made their fortune in the railway business, was arrested and held until his employees could raise a ransom of one hundred thousand rubles. Lenin not only knew of such practices but endorsed them.[46] The elder anarchist prince Pyotr Kropotkin was so disgusted by the Bolsheviks' policy of taking hostages that he wrote to Lenin himself to condemn it, describing it as a return to the Dark Ages.[47]

Several times during the civil war bourgeois hostages were shot en masse. In June 1919 in Kharkhov, between five hundred and one thousand men and women were shot; in August in Kiev, about eighteen hundred and some two thousand in Odessa.[48] (Workers were not exempt. In March 1919, the Bolshevik government arrested and then shot about two hundred striking metalworkers.)[49] The official policy of hostage taking soon spread to the criminal world. Bands of outlaws and Mafia-style gangs adopted the practice as their own, at times claiming to be acting as Soviet officials. The victims and their families could not always be certain who had taken away their loved ones or whether paying ransom would win them back.[50]

In urging the people to "expropriate the expropriators" and making it state policy, Lenin and the Bolsheviks unleashed a holdup of enormous proportions. Naked thievery engulfed the entire country and spread beyond anyone's control. If the Bolsheviks could simply take whatever they wanted, what was to stop everyone else? Petrograd was plagued by a rash of carjackings.[51] Even Lenin himself was a victim. Lenin had taken three luxury automobiles from the Alexander Palace's imperial garage—two Rolls-Royces and Nicholas II's Delaunay-Beleville for his personal use. He preferred to be chauffeured around in the Delaunay until his car was stopped by an armed gang in March 1918 and he was ordered out and left standing helpless on the street as the bandits got in and drove away. The expropriator in chief had been expropriated. (After that Lenin favored Grand Duke Mikhail's 1915 Rolls-Royce.)[52] An untold amount of the wealth expropriated following the revolution never reached the state but went directly into the pockets of the expropriators. So outrageous were the thefts during the work of the Safes Commission that Lenin ordered seven of the Gokhrán employees shot in November 1921 in order to send a message.[53]

Expropriating the expropriators, or looting the looters, fed a bizarre logic, for it was not always easy to tell, after all, who was who. One day a looter, the next, the looted, and so, according to the logic of the day, entitled to loot again. A joke from 1918 captures the topsy-turvy nature of life in this new world: "Question: 'Who is the proletariat?' Answer: 'An ex-bourgeois.' Question: 'And who is the bourgeois?' Answer: 'The ex-proletariat.'"[54] It was as if Russians had become trapped in a circular system of perpetual robbery. At times, however, the system did evince a strange way of distributing goods fairly. Take, for instance, the case of a man stopped at gunpoint and stripped bare on the streets of Petrograd. Moved by a sense of pity, the thieves gave their victim an old sheepskin coat so he would not freeze to death. When the man got home, he found in one of the coat pockets a collection of diamond rings and more money than he had been carrying when he was robbed.[55]

"Where are the wealthy, the fashionable ladies," the newspaper *Pravda* asked with self-satisfaction in early 1919, "the expensive restaurants and private mansions, the beautiful entrances, the lying newspapers, all the corrupt 'golden life'? All swept away. You can no longer see on the street a rich barin in a fur coat [. . .] He is exhausted and grown thin from living on a third-class ration; he no longer even has the appearance of a barin."[56]

The Frenchman Louis de Robien, then living in Russia, shook his head in disbelief:

One wonders how the "bourgeois" can live at all. All property has been confiscated in actual fact, all bank deposits seized, and all pensions and salaries stopped. It means utter destitution. A few days ago near the Cinizelli Circus I saw an old general and a priest—the old Russia itself—clearing the streets of snow in order not to die of starvation. A gang of soldiers, in the prime of life, stood and mocked them. [. . .] It is the end of a world.[57]

9

THE CORNER HOUSE

O n January 7, 1918, the Sheremetevs learned that the Bolsheviks had closed the Constituent Assembly in Petrograd. For Olga Sheremetev the news came as no surprise; days earlier she had predicted in her diary that the Bolsheviks would not permit the assembly to meet. According to Pavel, the Bolsheviks had done the right thing, for, he argued, the Socialist Revolutionaries, the largest bloc in the assembly, would be "more terrifying than the Bolsheviks." The Bolsheviks, Pavel believed, would be able to introduce "firm authority," unlike the SRs, and they would know how to deal with the Germans. Olga, however, was unconvinced.

To most at the Corner House the actions of the Bolsheviks were immaterial since the arrival of the Germans appeared imminent. By the middle of February the word was that the Germans would be in Moscow in a mere matter of days. Talk of an impending German advance into central Russia and the collapse of the Bolshevik government went on well into the summer. In late July, the Sheremetevs were discussing a rumor that a forward echelon of German soldiers had finally reached Moscow and were awaiting reinforcements before taking military action against the Bolsheviks. The German question split the Sheremetevs, just as it did the entire nobility. To some, patriotism and hatred of the Germans came first, and they preferred life—regardless of how bad—under the Bolsheviks, who were at least fellow Russians; to others, the greatest foe was internal, and the Germans represented the best hope for overthrowing the Bolsheviks, restoring order, and saving Russia. Such was the attitude of Olga. "Better the cultural yoke of the Germans than the socialist slavery of the Bolsheviks. [. . .] In the meantime, we socialize everything, we requisition, we municipalize, we—to put it in simple Russian—steal. Russia is dying now in worse fashion than it would from a German invasion."[1]

The Sheremetevs were experiencing the socialization of everything firsthand. In January 1918, Pavel traveled to Petrograd to oversee the transfer of the Fountain House to the Ministry of Enlightenment. The family hated to lose their home, but it was decided this was the best way to protect it and its collections. The following year the Fountain House opened as the Sheremetev Palace Museum, one of a number of Museums of Everyday Life then established in the former palaces of the Yusupovs, Stroganovs, and Shuvalovs in Petrograd.[2] Later that year the Sheremetev estates of Kuskovo and Ostankino were also nationalized and put in the service of the "interests of the working class."[3] Although it meant the loss of homes that had been in the family for centuries, at least these properties had a chance at survival, unlike the Voronovo estate Count Sergei had bought for his daughter Anna as a wedding present. The peasants burned Voronovo to the ground, but only after they had pulled Anna's portrait down from the wall and hacked it to pieces.[4]

The family clung to the Corner House as their last refuge. In early 1918, a section of the house was taken over by the newly created Depository of Private Archives and then the entire property was appropriated by the Socialist Academy. The Sheremetevs were permitted to remain but were reduced to living in only part of the house.[5] The idea for the Private Archives had been Pavel's, and he was put in charge of the new depository. It pained him to see so much of Russia's cultural heritage being destroyed, and so he set out to try to save whatever he could and store it in the family home.[6] In the spring of 1918, Pavel, apparently on Lenin's personal recommendation, was named custodian of the "historical and artistic treasures" at the family's former estate of Ostafievo outside Moscow, which was also nationalized and turned into a museum along the lines of the Fountain House. As its custodian, Pavel was given an apartment in the left wing of the house, where he was to remain for eleven years until being forced off the estate for good during Stalin's Cultural Revolution.[7]

On August 30, 1918, an assassin killed Moisei Uritsky, head of the Petrograd Cheka. That same day in Moscow, three shots were fired at Lenin as he was leaving a gathering of workers; two of the bullets struck Lenin, nearly killing him. Fanya Kaplan, a former anarchist turned Socialist Revolutionary who had spent years in penal servitude under the old regime, was arrested. Under questioning she insisted that she had acted alone and was not part of any larger conspiracy. In the early morning of September 3, Kaplan was taken out and shot. "Red Terror is not an empty phrase," her executioner said. "There can be no mercy for enemies of the Revolution!"

On September 1, the *Red Newspaper* called for blood: "We will kill our enemies in scores of hundreds. Let them be thousands, let them drown themselves in their own blood. For the blood of Lenin and Uritsky [. . .] let there be floods of blood of the bourgeoisie—more blood, as much as possible." The same day *Pravda* wrote: "The counter-revolution, this vicious mad dog, must be destroyed once and for all!"[8] A resolution adopted by the *Sovnarkóm* on September 5 officially endorsed the Red Terror. Maxim Gorky observed that proizvol had become state policy.[9]

"We are living under Red Terror," Olga Sheremetev wrote on September 12. "In recent days there's been nothing but executions and more executions [. . .] They're executing people because of Uritsky and Lenin, in Petrograd, in Moscow, and in the provinces [. . .] A great number of officers and former policemen and gendarmes have been killed. They say it's worse in Petrograd than here, there's famine and constant arrests [. . .] Unending Red Terror."[10] Within a week of Kaplan's attack on Lenin the Petrograd Cheka shot 512 hostages, many of them former high-ranking tsarist officials. In Kronstadt, soldiers killed 400 hostages in one night. Soon the killings spread to the provinces. No regard was made to personal guilt or responsibility; the victims were selected on the basis of their class or profession. "Never had a modern society killed its people so readily," the historian W. Bruce Lincoln observed of the Red Terror.[11] To the Bolsheviks, believers in Marx's notion that the death of the bourgeoisie was a historical inevitability, doing away with the ruling class was simply an act of euthanasia. "There is nothing immoral," Trotsky coldly affirmed, "in the proletariat finishing off a class that is collapsing: that is its right."[12]

It was amid this atmosphere of bloodlust that Yakov Peters and his men from the Cheka visited the Corner House on the night of November 23. It seems likely that when the Cheka took away six of the Sheremetev men in the early hours of the following day, many in the family feared they would never see them again. They were lucky, however, and none of them was harmed, at least immediately. The family tried to get the men released from prison. Countess Yekaterina called on Lev Kamenev, chairman of the Moscow Soviet. Although his anteroom was filled with waiting petitioners, she was ushered in directly to Kamenev, who got up, kissed her hand, and showed her to a chair. He asked what he could do for her, and the countess told him about the arrests and asked whether he might help get the men released. The matter was out of his control, Kamenev told her, but he did promise to find out what he could.[13]

On December 3, Pavel wrote his father from the Butyrki Prison:

Dear Papa,

How is your health? Life here for us is not as bad as one would think. Our cell is not cold and rather clean. We get up early, at 6:00 o'clock in the morning, and go to bed at 10:00. We are all getting along well. We sit in the corner and read the Gospels aloud. The windows open out onto the prison yard, where there is a very beautiful white church with an image of the Savior over the entrance. [. . .] The food here is much better than at the Lubyanka, where we spent the first two days. Twice a day they put out a large bowl of soup, and it's not at all bad; sometimes it's fish soup, sometimes meat with cabbage, potatoes, peas, or lentils. We sit around the bowl in a circle and eat from it with wooden spoons. There is enough bread too. Of course, we would be hungry if we didn't receive food parcels from home, which almost everyone here does. There are those unfortunate ones who go for months without anything from their families. [. . .] I shall end here, for I am out of paper. I kiss you warmly and ask for your blessing.

Your son, Pavel[14]

Count Sergei died two weeks later. "I die with a profound faith in Russia," he told the family gathered around his bed just hours before his death. "She will rise again."[15] Sergei had wanted to be buried next to his mother in the family crypt at Moscow's Novospassky Monastery, but the Bolsheviks had driven off the monks and taken over the monastery, so he was laid to rest in an adjacent cemetery instead. In the 1930s, the cemetery was bulldozed to make way for an apartment block. The graves were dug up, and the remains scattered and lost.[16]

Pavel was the first of the group to be freed. According to his niece, money Pavel had given years before to a fellow university student and revolutionary by the name of Malinovsky played a role in his release.[17] The others, except for Alik Saburov and Alexander Gudovich, were freed before the end of the year. "It was a difficult winter," Yelena Sheremetev recalled.

> We were cold and hungry, but at least we all lived together. We put in a little iron stove, and I would go for water over on Ostozhenka Street. I would freeze on the way back and duck into entranceways to try to warm up. We used whatever we could find, whatever we came across, to heat the stove. We would make tea in our communal kitchen [. . .] our chef boiled a thin potato soup or cooked up some runny millet and dished it out with one bowl for each of our three families: the Gudoviches, the Saburovs, and the Petrovichy.* And that was all.[18]

Yelena and her brother Nikolai attended a new Soviet school at the time, though the constant hunger made it nearly impossible to focus on their lessons. The high point of the day was lunch, when the children were served a bowl of watery lentil soup. Every schoolchild competed for the job of server since he could take a bit extra for himself. Yelena had to drop out of school the following year so she could stand in the food line at the League to Save the Children.[19] The famine gripping Russia in those years spared no one, except for the new elite; the Sheremetevs' remaining chef left them around this time to cook for Lenin and his comrades in the Kremlin. The family was helped by a few former peasants who brought them food from the villages. Regardless, food was scarce, and the battle against hunger was inescapable.[20]

Yelena and her family earned a bit of money by selling women's

---

*The Petrovichy (from the Russian Christian name Pyotr) were the children of the late Count Pyotr Sheremetev.

overshoes that they themselves made from old beaver-skin rugs. Like so many former nobles, they also sold their jewelry, antiques, and art for a pittance. Yelena's mother, Lilya, sold the diamond diadem she had worn to receptions at the Winter Palace for a bag of flour. They had to be wary of any such transactions since prominent families were often targeted by con men and tricksters.[21]

By 1918, life had become so hard that some at the Corner House had begun to consider leaving Russia.[22] Discussions about whether to stay or go were then taking place in noble families throughout the country. The decision was never an easy one and was shaped by a number of factors. Leaving required money, which by now many no longer had; leaving meant saying goodbye to one's family and loved ones, which many could not bear; leaving meant having a place to go and an idea of how to cross Russia's armed and dangerous borders; leaving meant giving up all hope for a life in Russia; leaving, to some, meant treason.[23] After making his escape abroad, the beloved son of Princess Meshchersky wrote to let his family know he was safe. His mother replied just once, only to say that he was now dead to her and the rest of the family. "You have forgotten about love for the Motherland—you have left your native land, so now you can forget about the mother and sister you left there."[24] Leaving also meant you felt you were in danger. Marta Almedingen, from an impoverished and obscure noble family, chose to remain since, as her mother put it, "We are so unimportant that it does not matter whether we stay or not."[25]

This was definitely not the case for members of the great aristocratic clans with prominent surnames. They found themselves before an extremely difficult decision. If they chose to leave and managed to make it abroad, they had a better chance to establish themselves than the typical Russian nobleman given their education, knowledge of foreign languages, wealth (even if only some jewels and silver stuffed in a few suitcases), and personal connections to other European noble families. But leaving could only be an act of last resort. If they could have known at the time, however, what awaited them in Communist Russia, perhaps most would have chosen this path, for only a few individuals survived from these aristocratic families. The fate of the princes Obolensky is instructive. Prince Vladimir Obolensky was killed at his estate in early 1918; later that year his older brother Alexander was shot at the Fortress of Peter and Paul in Petrograd. Prince Mikhail Obolensky was beaten to death by a mob at a railroad station in February 1918. Prince Pavel Obolensky, a cornet in the Hussars, was shot by the Bolsheviks in June 1918 and left for dead, although he somehow survived and fled to the Crimea. Princess Yelena Obolensky was killed at her estate in November 1918; her dead body was burned along with her manor house. Many more Obolenskys suffered similar horrific fates; they included seven members of the family who perished in Stalin's prisons years later.[26]

Of course, no one could foresee the future. What is more, no one had a clear idea of what was happening in Russia. A decision about whether to stay or leave could be made only on the basis of trustworthy information, and ever since the Bolshevik coup, this had become as scarce as food. Rumors became the currency of the day. "I was in no position to form any opinion as to what was happening in Petrograd, still less so in the rest of the country, let alone the outer world," wrote Marta Almedingen. "There were no papers, and even the inland post functioned erratically. For human pebbles on the national beach (and I was one of them), the only channel of information was the interchange of rumors in the food queues. [. . .] Those were the only clubs left in the city."[27] In Yekaterinoslav, Princess Vera Urusov complained of "no mail, no telephone, no trains anymore, and the rare newspaper reveals nothing. We live only by *On dit . . . On dit . . .*"[28] "We live under the power of rumors," Olga Sheremetev wrote in early 1918. "If someone said Lenin had become a Muslim or I don't know what nonsense, everyone would believe it."[29]

The idea that Lenin was a closet Muslim was not too farfetched. One popular rumor of the day held that the Bolsheviks were full of closet monarchists who planned to ride bolshevism back into power in order to restore the monarchy.[30] In the spring of 1918, in some provincial cities, there was talk that the Bolsheviks had been overthrown and Grand Duke Mikhail Alexandrovich installed in Petrograd as the new tsar; a different rumor had it that Grand Duke Nikolai Nikolaevich had established a dictatorship in Moscow.[31] There were rumors that Lenin and Trotsky had been killed and that Tsar Nicholas had escaped to England.[32] The German Army was the subject of intense gossip. Nearly every day new rumors appeared on the whereabouts of the

Germans, how they were soon to march into Petrograd and Moscow, overthrow the Bolsheviks, and save the country from ruin.[33]

While Count Sergei was alive, any talk of leaving Russia was shunned in the Sheremetev family. A Russian noble, the count believed, should be ready to die on his native soil.[34] Regardless, after his death, some in the family did leave. His sons Boris and Sergei left Moscow around 1919 and eventually settled in Western Europe. Yelena's elder brother Boris also appears to have quit Russia for Europe around this time, possibly with his uncles Boris and Sergei.[35] Life in exile was a struggle for most Russians. In France, Count Sergei's son Boris held a number of jobs, trying to make ends meet. In Geneva in 1929, his daughter Tatiana married Theodore Carl Fabergé, a fellow émigré and the grandson of Carl Fabergé, the famous founder of the family jewelry firm. The only work Theodore was able to find was repairing radios.[36] Alik Saburov and Alexander Gudovich, the count's sons-in-law, contemplated leaving for Finland for a time but then received word that matters there were no less difficult than in Russia. Moreover, as officers they felt a sense of duty to remain in Russia.[37]

For Pavel, there was never any thought of leaving Russia. First of all, he was not married and had no children to worry about. Second, unlike his brother Dmitry off in the northern Caucasus, he had never occupied any prominent official position under the old regime that put him at special risk. His mother had no intention of leaving, and it appears that Pavel felt an obligation to stay with her. Perhaps paramount in his decision to remain was his relationship to his father and their shared interest in Russian history and culture. Like his late father, Pavel believed it was his obligation to try to protect whatever he could of the family's and the country's cultural patrimony from the ravages of the revolution. Before he died, Count Sergei told his son: "You are not to sell a thing simply to fill your stomach. The Rembrandts, Raphaels, Van Dycks, Kiprenskys, and Greuzes—they all must belong to Russia, we did not collect them for ourselves, and so a museum must be established before the cold and upheavals destroy everything . . . We have no present," Sergei said, "but we have a past and we must preserve it in the name of the future."[38]

For Count Sergei's daughters Anna and Maria there could be no thought of leaving Russia or even Moscow since their husbands were still being held in the Butyrki Prison, even though no charges had ever been made against them. The Sheremetev family had been working hard to get the two men released throughout the winter of 1918–19. They even appealed to Abel Yenukidze, a longtime Bolshevik and member of the Central Executive Committee, considered a "tame Communist" with a reputation for helping nobles caught in the repressive machinery of the new Bolshevik state. Yenukidze was one of a handful of powerful Bolsheviks with such a reputation, and it was indeed earned, as some repressed nobles gladly acknowledged. But in this instance Yenukidze was unable to help.[39] The prisoners were being held as hostages, handy targets for retribution in the event of any attacks on the Bolsheviks.

Saburov and Gudovich remained at the Butyrki until July 1919, when they were moved to a concentration camp in the Andronievsky Monastery. Lenin had called for the creation of concentration camps in August 1918 (Trotsky had made a similar call two months earlier), and the idea was approved by the *Sovnarkóm* the following month. The official decree set out the rationale for the camps: "It is essential to safeguard the Soviet Republic from its class enemies by isolating them in concentration camps." The Bolsheviks were not the first to establish such camps. In 1896, General Valeriano Weyler y Nicolau, the Spanish governor of Cuba, set up the first *campos de concentración* as part of his strategy to suppress the uprisings on the island against Spain. At their height, the camps on Cuba held approximately four hundred thousand peasants; the number of people who died in them is not known. In Russia, the Cheka ran the concentration camps, which by 1922 numbered fifty-six and held roughly twenty-four thousand people. In 1919, another system of camps—forced labor camps—were also set up by the Cheka; their inmates numbered some sixty thousand by 1922. There were camps for men and women too.[40] Princess Tatiana Kurakin was arrested in Kiev and later moved to a women's camp also set up at the Andronievsky Monastery.[41]

Saburov and Gudovich joined many other nobles at the camp, including Prince Alexander Dolgoruky (the son of Countess Maria Benkendorff). The prisoners were put to work. Dolgoruky and Gudovich were regularly sent out into the city together on work details and quickly became close. Xenia Saburov would visit her father and bring him food and clothing. In August, some of the men—including Gudovich, Saburov, and Dolgoruky—were moved to a camp in the Ivanovsky Monastery. On September 21, 1919, the men were returned to the Butyrki.[42] Five days later Saburov, Gudovich, Dolgoruky, and twenty-six others were taken out and shot.[43] The reason for their murders remains a mystery. According to one story, the men were shot as the easiest way to solve the problem of overcrowding at the Butyrki. Another account has it that the men were executed in response to the northern advance of General Denikin's army, which by mid-September was approximately two hundred miles south of Moscow and appeared to be moving inexorably toward the Bolshevik capital. A third explanation posits the idea that they were shot in retaliation for an anarchist bomb attack on the Bolsheviks' Moscow Committee headquarters that killed twelve and wounded fifty-one persons that month.[44]

The family members learned of the murders only a good time later. First there were just rumors, which Yenukidze eventually confirmed. The widow of a former tsarist governor purportedly told Anna Saburov that she had seen Alik when the men were being led out to be shot. "Tell my wife that I go calmly to my death," he said to her. Neither Anna Saburov nor her sister Maria would accept that their husbands were dead. For years they clung to the belief that they were alive and being held in a secret prison. Shattered by the loss of their husbands, the sisters cut themselves off from the life of the Corner House and retreated into prayer.[45]

10

SPA TOWN HELL

Dmitry and Ira Sheremetev and their children spent the winter of 1917–18 in Kislovodsk in the northern Caucasus. The town, together with neighboring Yessentuki and Pyatigorsk, had long been a popular destination for wealthy Russians who came to escape the harsh Russian winters and enjoy the local hot springs, curative mineral waters, and mud baths. That winter Dmitry had spent much of his time in Kislovodsk's two libraries, gathering material for a book he was writing titled "Russian Nature and Hunting in the Works of Our Classics." His sons Nikolai and Vasily attended school, and his daughter Irina was being courted by a suitor, Georgy Mengden.

Much of the aristocracy was there with them in the spa towns. Life was easy and quiet and enjoyable and seemed to go on as if the revolution had never happened. In Yessentuki, the Tolstoys, Lvovs, Uvarovs, Bobrinskys, Trubetskoys, and other prominent families relaxed, strolled the wide streets, fortified their health at Dr. Zernov's sanatorium, and staged theatrical performances. The mystic George Gurdieff was there, Sergei Rachmaninov too. No one thought they would be away from Russia for long. Dr. Zernov and his family had left Moscow for Yessentuki in late November 1917 without their heavy winter clothes since they were certain they would be back home by Christmas. Dmitry was contemplating which Moscow publisher would be best for his book.[1] Count Vladimir Kokovtsov, former tsarist prime minister, found life in Kislovodsk in early November "a perfect idyll" after Petro-grad. His many old friends and acquaintances shared his view and were convinced that they were safe from the Bolsheviks thanks to the presence of the Cossacks in whose lands they now found themselves and who they were certain would never allow the Reds to gain a foot-hold.[2]

The idyll did not last long, however, and soon the civil war reached the northern Caucasus. The formerly quiet spa towns were caught in the shifting battle lines of the Reds, Whites, Cossacks, and bands of marauders. Families like the Sheremetevs went from relaxing and looking forward to their return to Russia to worrying about their own safety and even survival. By the end of 1917, the fighting had begun to disrupt rail connections in the area; then the postal service stopped, cutting the towns off from all news of the outside world. In early 1918, the Reds took Pyatigorsk, after which they began to arrest the officers in the town and close the banks. Around this time they took Kislovodsk as well. They organized public meetings to whip up the poor against the officers and bourgeoisie. They carried out house searches for money, weapons, and valuables, and all former tsarist officers were forced to register with the local authorities. In the early spring, a group of Bol-sheviks arrived from Vladikavkaz and published a list of the visiting nobles and wealthy burzhui required to appear at the Grand Hotel. Among those on the list were the ballerina Mathilde Kschessinska and, likely, Dmitry Sheremetev. The assembled group was informed it was to come up with five million rubles in two weeks as a "contribution." Should it fail, everyone on the list would be taken away to Vladikav-kaz.[3] Terror swept over the town. Many talked of trying to escape to Yessentuki, some sixteen kilometers away. They had heard that it was safer there, but no one could be certain.[4]

The Bolsheviks' main opponent in the area was the forces under the command of the Cossack general Andrei Shkuro, a brave, if reckless, veteran of World War I and, to some, a mere bandit, who later joined the army of General Denikin. Shkuro's Cossack fighters attacked sev-eral of the towns held by the Reds in the spring of 1918, including Kislovodsk. The Cossacks, usually anti-Bolshevik, were seen by the nobles as their defenders, although they could not necessarily assume the Cossacks' protection or friendship. Shkuro and his men were ex-cellent raiders, but they had trouble holding on to territory taken from the Reds. Moreover, they were at best temporary allies of the exiled nobles.[5] After Shkuro's men arrived in Kislovodsk that spring, Count Nicholas Ignatieff asked one of the fighters whether they intended to restore the monarchy once they had vanquished the Reds. "Monarchy, nothing!" the Cossack bellowed. "When we are through with these Bolshevik devils, we'll cut all the aristocrats' throats, the bloodsuckers!"[6]

In May 1918 Dmitry and Ira used Shkuro's raid to escape Kislovodsk for Yessentuki. Here they found a good many other nobles, some of them old friends and family, including Count Pyotr Vyazemsky (Dmitry's uncle), Countess Maria Musin-Pushkin (Ira's sister), and Princess Maria Trubetskoy (Anna Golitsyn's sister). In late June, Dmitry wrote his mother to wish her the best on her golden wedding anniversary. He told her that all was well and that their daughter Irina was now engaged to Georgy Mengden and looking forward to setting a wedding date. The entire family was busy spending the days working in the vegetable garden across the street from their dacha. Although he did not mention this in his letter, their gardening was no innocent hobby to while away their idle time, but necessary to ensure an adequate food supply, especially for the coming winter. Unlike in his previous letters, Dmitry no longer urged his parents to come join them.[7]

Yessentuki too had not avoided the disturbances in the area. As early as the autumn of 1917, nobles with well-known names had been subject to arrest.[8] Then, in March 1918, an old truck waving a tattered red banner and filled with soldiers arrived from Pyatigorsk. The men stopped in the local park to announce to a small group of onlookers that Yessentuki was now part of the Soviet Socialist Republic. At first, little changed. The Sheremetevs and their friends played tennis and bridge, attended church, hiked the mountains, and picked berries and gathered mushrooms. Life went on as before, although things were not easy. The money people had brought with them was running out, and they had been reduced to raising vegetables like the Sheremetevs or opening bakeries, restaurants, cafés, laundries, and other "bourgeois enterprises" to get by.[9] After a time, the Bolsheviks began to search people's homes; then some of the men were taken hostage and held for ransom. One day proclamations announcing that all the hostages had been shot as a necessary part of the policy of class warfare being introduced by the authorities were posted throughout Yessentuki. It was soon learned, however, that the signs were nothing more than a provocation.

Such confusion became the norm. No one could be certain what was happening or even who was in charge. For a time two competing Red factions fought for control of Yessentuki. Terrified, the Sheremetevs and other nobles hid what valuables they still had and tried their best to stay out of sight. In early summer a commissar by the name of Alexander Gay appeared. A leader of the Russian anarchists, Gay (born Golberg) had spent many years in exile in Switzerland before returning to Russia after the revolution. He sided with the Bolsheviks and left Moscow in May for Kislovodsk, where he became the head of the local Cheka. Joining him was his young wife, Xenia Gay, the daughter of a tsarist general and a committed Bolshevik. Alexander had something of a contradictory personality. Some sources describe him as one of the authors of the Red Terror in the northern Caucasus; others say that he could be kind and decent and did what he could to defend the nobles in the area from some of the more zealous Bolsheviks. As for Xenia, who joined her husband in the Cheka, most sources agree she was cruel and rapacious, responsible for the deaths of dozens of people. Among her schemes was a plan to socialize young bourgeois women in Kislovodsk and force them to become sex workers for the Red Army, a plan that was derailed by one of Shkuro's raids during which the women were freed from prison.[10]

One evening in late August, a car carrying a group of Bolsheviks arrived at the home of the Vorontsovs. They began to search for weapons and threatened to arrest all the men, including Dmitry Sheremetev. The men managed to send word to Gay, who came and spoke to the Bolsheviks alone. After two tense hours, the men were called before the Bolsheviks, who harangued and threatened to shoot anyone who dared set foot in the street but left without taking any of the men with them. Gay had managed to convince the Bolsheviks not to arrest the men and so in all likelihood saved their lives. Gay tried to assure them that they were in no great danger, especially with him in the area, but no one could be certain how long he could protect them, and so some of the men decided the only option was to flee Yessentuki. The plan was to escape into the mountains and to reach the Kabardin', a Muslim people of the northern Caucasus, and, with their help, to make it to the White Army. Dmitry and his sons, as well as Nikita Tatishchev and members of the Vorontsov and Pushkin families, were likely among those who decided to make their escape.

They decided to rise early in the morning and, disguised as peasants, walk to the weekly market at Pyatigorsk. There they would make contact with the Cossack women returning from market with their empty carts; for some money, they would hide on the carts under empty burlap sacks until they were safely away up in the mountains. Everything went as planned, and many of the men, including the Sheremetevs, managed to escape; only later did it become clear that their decision had saved their lives. Those who stayed behind in Yessentuki tried to make it appear as if nothing unusual were going on. If asked where their men were, the women simply said they had left for Moscow or to visit a neighboring town. At the end of August, the hostage taking began again and continued on into early September. Most of the victims were former tsarist officers, members of the government, or simply men with prominent names and titles, including the former general Nikolai Ruzsky, a sixty-four-year-old commander of the First World War; Prince Alexander Bagration-Mukhransky, another former general; and the brothers Prince Leonid and Vladimir Shakhovskoy. Hostages were also taken in Pyatigorsk and Kislovodsk.

The residents of Yessentuki placed their hopes in Shkuro and his men, and they did run the Reds out of town in mid-September, but only briefly before being forced to retreat. Shkuro's raids heightened the Reds' anger at the nobles and cemented their conviction that they were secretly fighting against them. And so, when the Reds returned, they redoubled the terror against the remaining nobles. A new round of house searches began. A group of soldiers came to the home of the Vorontsovs, searched it from top to bottom, and then looted and ransacked the place. Along with weapons, they had apparently also been searching for Dmitry Sheremetev. Ira was there, and the soldiers threatened to beat her with their rifle butts unless she told them where he was. They then marched all the women, children, and servants out of the house and had them line up as if they were about to be shot. Three of the servants were then led behind the house. The soldiers shot two of them dead and let the third go. Next, they set off with the women and children. After a ways, a maid caught up with them; she threw herself on her knees and begged them to let the prisoners go, and they did, thus likely sparing their lives. Ira and her children ran and hid in an abandoned hut, where they remained for more than a week, not even their family members knowing where they were. They were then taken in by the Lieven family and went into hiding. They dressed in simple peasant clothes, and Ira managed to acquire fake identity papers in the name of Fyodorov. The Bolsheviks carried on looking for Dmitry and Ira. During the two months Ira lived with the Lievens, the Bolsheviks captured and shot two more of the Sheremetevs' servants, possibly for refusing to reveal the family's whereabouts.[11]

On October 8, the Cheka of the northern Caucasus issued an order condemning thirty-two hostages arrested in the spa towns to immediate execution for the next counterrevolutionary uprising or attempt on the lives of "the leaders of the proletariat."[12]

Countess Varvara Bobrinsky, her twenty-year-old son, Gavril, and more than eighty other families and their servants had arrived in Yessentuki in late 1917 on a train from Moscow. Like many other noble women, she had tended to wounded soldiers and served in charitable organizations during World War I; such was her good reputation that in May 1917 the Moscow Soviet had even hired her to do educational work with soldiers being sent to the front. Gavril was among those arrested by the Bolsheviks in Yessentuki in September 1918. He was taken to Pyatigorsk, the Bolshevik center for the northern Caucasus, and locked in the cellar of the Cheka headquarters. "The hole," as the cellar was called, was filthy, rat-infested, and so crowded many slept sitting upright on the cement floor. It was overseen by a man named Skryabin, a former executioner under the tsarist regime and a sadist who liked to brag about the number of people he had tortured and executed over the years.

Varvara and her daughter followed Gavril to Pyatigorsk to see what they could do to effect his release. At first they were given no information, but then in early October they were told Gavril would be executed unless they could come up with fifty thousand rubles. Gavril was being held with approximately eighty other noblemen from Yessentuki, including the brothers Prince Nikolai and Sergei Urusov.[13] The Bolshevik bosses in Pyatigorsk tried to shake down other family members. One of them told Princess Bagration-Mukhransky that for two hundred thousand rubles she would free her father. Some did try to raise the money to free their loved ones. Varvara Bobrinsky's daughter, who had also come south, left for Yessentuki to collect enough money to save Gavril. By the time she returned it would be too late.[14]

After two weeks, thirty-two of the men, including Gavril, the Urusovs, and Prince Bagration-Mukhransky, were moved from the hole to the New Europe Hotel. The conditions there were better, and they were permitted to receive family and other visitors. Still, their future was unclear, and some of the guards delighted in tormenting them. One of them, a sailor, said in their presence, "These aren't people here, but bears and wolves, who ought to be brought up to Mashuk Mountain and dealt with just like Nicholas II was."[15] In early October, a technician was brought to the hotel to repair an electrical cable. He whispered to Gavril that he was a Cossack and part of a group planning a secret operation to free the men. Gavril believed his story and helped him scout the hotel for the best escape route. The plot, however, was soon uncovered. Gavril was sent back to the hole, and the security tightened at the hotel.

The fate of the hostages darkened. Acting upon a rumor that a local Red commander had died of wounds suffered in battle, the Cheka had several of the hostages executed early in the morning of October 6. Next, on October 13, Ivan Sorokin, a Left SR and commander of the eleventh Red Army, led a revolt against the Soviet government in the Caucasus. The revolt failed, although four high-ranking Bolsheviks were killed; Sorokin was captured in Stavropol and executed. To the local Bolshevik leaders, the revolt was an expression of counterrevolution requiring swift and harsh retribution.[16]

On the night of October 18, fifty-two hostages at the New Europe Hotel were told to gather their things and come out into the hall. Most of them thought they were about to be freed or at least moved to better accommodations. They were taken outside into a cold, wet night and marched along with thirteen other prisoners from the Pyatigorsk jail to the Cheka's headquarters. The hostages were instructed to strip down to their underwear, and their hands were tied behind their backs with thin wire. Twenty-five of them were then marched to the city cemetery. They were admitted by the cemetery's watchmen, and fifteen of the men were conducted to the edge of a large, fresh grave. Everyone was silent. They were ordered to kneel and extend their necks. Then the executioners lifted their swords.

They were inexperienced, and most of the victims were felled only after several blows. General Ruzsky was among the first killed. His executioner, the Chekist Georgy Atarbekov, later bragged of how he had finished him off. Atarbekov asked the old man as he knelt half naked in the night air whether he finally recognized the "Great Russian Revolution." Ruzsky replied, "All I see is nothing but one great robbery." With that Atarbekov plunged his Circassian dagger into Ruzsky's neck; after the fifth stabbing, the general fell dead into the pit. The killing took more than an hour. There was little noise, save the sound of the swords sinking into flesh and the breaking of bones. So gruesome was the violence, two of the executioners could not carry out the assignment and left to wait for it to end at the cemetery gates. After the fifteen had been slaughtered, the ten other hostages were chopped to death at a second pit. Before leaving, the soldiers told the watchmen not to go to bed, for they would be back soon with more victims. Before sunrise, thirty more people, including one woman, had been executed. The following night more prisoners were taken to the cemetery and butchered. The executioners received ten rubles for each victim. When the watchmen went out on the morning of the twentieth to cover the graves with sand, they discovered some of the victims were still alive. Faint moans could be heard coming up from underneath the mutilated corpses.[17]

Even though the Bolsheviks in Pyatigorsk spoke openly of the killings, and reports were published in newspapers across the northern Caucasus, many refused to believe it was true. A story began to take hold that the men had not been murdered but moved to another location. Commissar Gay himself, who likely knew the truth, tried to assure the distraught widows that their husbands were still alive. The victims' families wanted to believe him, and it seems many did. They became easy prey for soldiers offering to free their loved ones for money.

Varvara Bobrinsky, however, was not one of them. She apparently knew from the first that Gavril was dead. When she went to collect his belongings, the soldiers, who by now had come to know Gavril and his mother and sister, expressed their regret about what had happened;

some, she noticed, even had tears in their eyes. "The vast majority of them were simple, goodhearted Russian men, who sympathized with us and our beloved prisoners," she wrote in her diary. "They all said, 'We sympathize with you. Today it was them, but soon they'll arrest and then shoot us too.'" Varvara did not blame her son's jailers for having joined the Bolsheviks, for she could see how they too had been caught up in a horrible situation beyond their control. As she saw it, they could either kill or be killed. Now every Russian knew tragedy, and Varvara was certain to note that those killed were not just nobles but common folk as well.[18]

With the fighting between the Cossacks and Bolsheviks raging in the area, Varvara decided she and her daughter had to escape. They used the money they had collected to save Gavril to buy fake passports and arranged to be driven out of Kislovodsk and entrusted to guides willing to show them the path through the mountains to the Cossack village of Burgustan outside the Bolshevik zone. While on their way, a Bolshevik patrol on horseback intercepted Varvara and her daughter and forced them back to Kislovodsk. Yet just as the town was coming in to view, the patrol offered them a deal: for 4,000 rubles he would let them go. Varvara had only 3,750, which he accepted. By the light of the moon, mother and daughter retraced their steps back through the mountains. They walked all night and the next day and finally reached Burgustan on the second night. Exhausted and relieved to finally be safe, the two women were surprised to see the villagers in a panic, expecting a Bolshevik attack at any moment. Unable to stay and rest, they joined the flight from Burgustan out across the steppe in the direction of Baltapashinsk. As they walked, Varvara was struck by how empty the steppe was. Along the way they passed through a few Cossack villages, each with gallows heavy with the bodies of Red soldiers. In January 1919, Varvara and her daughter finally reached the White Army in Yekaterinodar.[19]

Soldiers had also come to arrest Prince Vladimir Emanuelovich Golitsyn in Yessentuki in the autumn of 1918. They found him sick in bed and too large and heavy to carry with them to Pyatigorsk, so they left him, saying they would be back later. His illness saved his life.

It was not the first time fate had been kind to Vladimir and his wife, Katia. Like so many other aristocrats, they had made their way to Kislovodsk after the revolution. They had not been there long when they got word Red soldiers were looking for him. As a prince, officer of the Chevaliers Gardes, and former aide-de-camp to Grand Duke Nikolai Nikolaevich, Vladimir was a prime target. Vladimir hid under the floorboards of a neighbor's house until the immediate danger had passed. He knew that he had to go into hiding. Katia rubbed his head, neck, and hands with dirt from the garden as a form of disguise, and he went off to live in a poor part of town. Katia brought him food every day, always changing her route so as not to attract attention. The soldiers came to search the house again, this time for firearms. Katia told them they did not have any in the house, thinking they had been buried out in the garden. The men told her she had better not be lying, for if they found any, they would kill her young boys in front of her and then kill her and her servants. Katia thought she had nothing to fear. Her babies' nanny, however, insisted on accompanying the men on the search. When they came to the bedroom, she quickly pulled back the bedclothes and snatched the pillow to her chest to show them there was nothing there. She managed to do it quickly enough that they did not notice the revolver that had been lying under the pillow and was now clutched against her breast. After this narrow escape, the family joined the noble exodus to Yessentuki.

Vladimir was not at home the day a group of Red soldiers came to search their house in Yessentuki. Their middle son, George, aged two, lay in his little cot, looking up at them. Upon seeing the beautiful boy with the bright blue eyes, the leader of the group stopped in his tracks. He reached into his pocket and pulled out a fifteen-kopeck coin and handed it to George, saying gently, "This is for your blue eyes." The chance encounter with the little boy threw the soldier into confusion; his demeanor changed, he called off the search and left abruptly with his men. This was the first money George had ever seen, and he was thrilled with the coin. But his mother refused to let him keep it. George broke down in tears. Katia, however, remained adamant that they could not keep the money. Instead, she took George and his brothers to the local church, where they bought a candle with the fifteen kopecks and lit it in recognition of the soldier's kindness, saying a prayer to protect his soul.

Shortly after Vladimir's narrow escape from being taken to Pyati-gorsk, a Jewish woman arrived at his doorstep. She had come from the family's Ukrainian estate of Carlowka after experiencing a premoni-tion that Vladimir's life was in danger. She had ridden a long way in a cart to reach them, bringing with her a false passport and two pillows stuffed with sable and ermine. The woman insisted Vladimir must take the passport and flee with her across the border. Eventually, he agreed to go with her, and they managed to get away to a Cossack vil-lage beyond the Bolsheviks' control. Vladimir took a small piece of paper and wrote one word on it—"Safe"—then rolled it to look like a cigarette, gave it to the woman to take back to Katia, and asked her to bring his family to him.

The woman returned for Katia and the boys, but just as they were about to drive off at dawn, Katia realized she could not find her hus-band's wedding ring. The woman said they had no time to look for it, that they had to be off before light or they were certain to be caught at the border by the Red soldiers. She pleaded, but Katia refused to go. "We must find the ring," she insisted. "No, I cannot go until the ring is found. I must have it." They went through their bundles, and then they went through them again, but the ring had vanished. Fi-nally, there it was, amazingly, in one of the bundles they had already searched but somehow overlooked in their agitation. Now Katia was ready to go, but the woman said that it was too late. The sun was up, and they had missed their chance. Again, Katia insisted, and again she got her way.

They drove and drove and finally reached the border near a remote Cossack village. The sight left them speechless: but for a shepherd and his dog, there was not a single sign of life. Everyone had been rounded up and taken away by the Red soldiers just hours before. Had they left at dawn as planned, they would have been captured along with every-one else. The lost wedding ring had saved them. They drove on to the next village, but this place had now fallen to the Reds. Unable to go farther, Katia stopped there with the boys. She claimed to be the wife of a priest who had left the family, and they stayed there for two weeks, not knowing where Vladimir had gone to or how they would ever find him. Then, as she sat one night in a restaurant, a Cossack man ap-proached and told Katia to follow him. Then he turned and left. Des-perate to get away and willing to take a chance, Katia grabbed the boys, loaded them on a small cart, and went in search of the man. They found him at the end of a street, waiting, and he took them to a small hut. Katia had expected to find Vladimir there, but it was empty. They were not there long, however, when he suddenly appeared in the early hours of the morning. After three weeks apart, the family was reunited.[20]

At the end of October, the Bolsheviks in Yessentuki celebrated the first anniversary of the revolution. The entire town was bedecked in red, and no one dared not hang a red flag on his house or go out without a red ribbon on his chest. The Bolsheviks marched through the streets, bands played, and celebratory shooting into the air went on all night. Commissar Gay had moved to Kislovodsk, and there were rumors of a new round of hostage taking to begin before the end of the month. Typhus and the Spanish influenza epidemic, which was then ravaging much of the world, hit and killed many. The town's remaining burzhui were going around without any undergarments, the Bolsheviks having expropriated them for the troops. Princess Maria Trubetskoy and the other women were selling their few remaining belongings in the street for food. The town was without electricity, and burglars took advantage of the night darkness. Families set up watches, but since all their weapons had been taken, they could do little but scream for help when attacked.

Then, in January 1919, the Whites seized all of the northern Caucasus. In the spa towns, they hunted down and killed the Red soldiers and Bolsheviks who had not managed to escape; even people guilty of no more than fraternizing with the Reds were executed. Among the victims were Alexander and Xenia Gay. The Whites found Alexander bedridden with typhus in Kislovodsk and bayoneted him to death where he lay. Xenia was arrested and sentenced to death. A large crowd came out to watch her be hanged in the hills near Kislovodsk.[21]

Varvara Bobrinsky and her daughter were on the train that brought the White Army back to Kislovodsk in January. They shared many emotional reunions with the friends they had left behind. Mother and daughter soon moved to Pyatigorsk, where the Special Commission of Inquiry into the Crimes of the Bolsheviks created by Denikin's army had begun to unearth the graves from the October murders. The commission exhumed twenty-five bodies in the first grave and handed them over to a group of doctors for autopsies. None of the bodies showed any evidence of having been shot; all were covered with wounds typical of swords, sabers, and, in one case, a bayonet. Next, they excavated the second grave in the cemetery at the base of Mashuk Mountain, not far from the spot where the poet Mikhail Lermontov had been killed in a duel in 1841. Because of the cold, dry soil, the bodies in this grave had barely decomposed; the corpses betrayed signs of maiming: some had their noses cut off, their teeth bashed in, their bellies ripped open. Finally, a third grave containing the victims of October 6 was dug up. In total, eighty-three victims were exhumed from the three graves. Among the bodies identified were General Ruzsky, the Urusov brothers, Count Alexei Kapnist, the Shakhovskoy brothers, and Prince Alexander Bagration-Mukhransky.[22]

In the second grave the investigators found the body of a tall young man with dark reddish hair dressed in a white undershirt bearing the monogram "G. B." A gold chain holding a small icon of the Chernigov Mother of God and Sergei Radonezhsky hung around his neck. His hands were tied behind his back, and his chest was covered with minor wounds. Two long gashes across his neck and the base of his head penetrating to his spinal column, most likely inflicted by a large sword, offered evidence of the cause of death. Varvara identified her son. She took his body back to Kislovodsk to be buried a second time but kept his chain and icon for herself.[23]

11

BOGORODITSK

My hopes and wishes for the beginning new year do not extend beyond the tight circle of our family," wrote the mayor on the first day of 1918. "Long may it continue to be happy, and its life full, even if, perhaps, it moves along new paths. Of other more general matters, I withhold all hope and expectation."[1] As the weeks passed, the mayor saw ever less reason to be hopeful about the coming year, and he sank into depression. He found it increasingly hard to believe what was happening around him. It was as if Russia itself had vanished. "The tsar seemed to be the personification of Russia, and Russia belonged to him, it was his property. [. . .] Everything here is being destroyed, there is no more Russia! [. . .] And we all cast about for the culprits on whom we can place all the blame. We are all just as guilty, and we all turned out to be blind, unconscious instruments of fate."[2] There were, however, a few simple things that brought him pleasure. The mayor took great joy in walking through the Moscow streets holding the hand of his grandson Vladimir or in admiring the soft light of a beautiful morning.[3]

He also took pleasure in work. He began to write his memoirs, and being active and going back over his personal history, and that of Russia, brought him renewed energy. As he worked, he came to the realization that the revolution had brought at least one benefit—namely, that now everyone had to work in order to survive and no more could members of his class be "squeamish" at having to earn a living.[4] Although he focused on his personal life in his writings, this "departure into the past," as he called it, made him think about the present crisis and its causes. Few persons of his station were able, in the thick of the events or even years later, to observe and assess the wild and tumultuous flow of history with greater perspicacity.

> April 25, 1918. One cannot help but see that we, the people of the present century, are paying for the sins of our forefathers, and particularly for the institution of serfdom with all its horrors and perversions that I was born early enough to know and to witness with my own eyes and that still disturb me now.

> June 20, 1918. Who is to blame that the Russian people, the peasant and the proletarian, proved to be barbarians? Who, if not all of us?

Their rulers were in part to blame. Alexander III's reign had amounted to nothing more than "total repression of the people's energies, of its yearning for enlightenment, freedom, and progress." As for Nicholas II, he was a "pathetic charlatan" who blindly followed his "traitorous wife."[5] Society at large was little better. The Russian muzhik was "a wild creature, almost an animal," which no one had noticed before, and beneath their "polish" the nobles were "wild in their souls . . . I don't know what's worse, what's wilder, the unruliness of the insolent, barbarian crowd or the petty tyranny of our aristocrats and grandees who consider themselves the 'salt of the earth.'"[6]

As time passed, the revolution acquired an almost mystical significance for this aging agnostic, becoming "the work of Godly Providence and righteous retribution for our sins."[7] The mayor never succumbed to the nostalgia for the tsarist past that became prevalent among many of his class. Even in the spring of 1920, after years of extreme oppression against the mayor's family, he could step back and ask himself which regime—tsarist or Soviet—was the more "absurd" and "criminal" and wonder whether the "bankruptcy" he saw all around him was "a quality of the Slavic nature or the natural fruits of the tsarist regime that had turned us into slaves."[8] As late as 1930, the mayor wrote in his diary: "Just like tsarist power, Soviet power, too, was founded on fraudulent theories—the first on Godly origin, the second on communism."[9]

That spring of 1918 the mayor and Sofia were still in Moscow, together with their son Mikhail, his wife, Anna, and their children. Mikhail had managed to find work in a bank, and although the pay was meager, not even keeping up with inflation, he did receive a small food ration of fifty grams of bread for each member of the family. As it was for all Russians then, the overriding concern was getting enough to eat. The Golitsyns were largely surviving on bread, potatoes, and dandelion greens. The mayor's little grandson Sergei hunted for willow seeds in the city's parks to try to blunt his hunger pangs. Like many others of the once wealthy, they were selling their art and jewelry to the "baggers" who smuggled food into the cities from the countryside. Sofia moaned at having to part with her paintings by the Russian masters Isaac Levitan and Vasily Polenov for a few sacks of potatoes, but there was nothing to be done. She did have to admit that the absence of rich French sauces at the family table had at least cured her perpetual indigestion and brought back a more youthful glow to her skin; she later exclaimed that thanks to the lack of food, she had finally lost more than thirty-five pounds.[10]

In May, the mayor and Sofia's daughter Vera Bobrinsky invited the family to join her at the estate of Bogoroditsk south of Moscow in Tula Province. Vera was married to Count Lev Bobrinsky, with whom she had five children. In her letter, Vera wrote that they had plenty of food and that they all were safe there, thanks to a group of local SRs protecting them from the Bolsheviks. The Bogoroditsk estate was enormous, comprising more than thirty thousand acres, a large manor house, park, and lake. The Bobrinskys, who traced their origins back to Count Alexei Bobrinsky, Catherine the Great's illegitimate son with Prince Grigory Orlov, had been one of Russia's wealthiest noble families. Following the revolution, dozens of family members and close friends moved to Bogoroditsk, including fourteen-year old Kirill Golitsyn from Petrograd and Vladimir and Eli Trubetskoy and their two children. They still had many of their servants, and they settled in to a relaxed, quiet yet sociable life, marked by regular presentations of plays and sketches starring the children and musical evenings with Grandmother Sofia on the piano, Vladimir Trubetskoy on the cello, and an Austrian prisoner of war by the name of Salzmann on the violin.[11]

Tragedy struck that summer after several members of the family had become involved in a plot to save the former tsar and his family from captivity in Tobolsk. A few of the conspirators had visited Tobolsk the previous year and established contact with Nicholas, and he had reportedly approved their operation. The plan was to rescue Nicholas and his son Alexei and spirit them away to the Orenburg Cossacks, with Nicholas shaved and traveling incognito as the French governor to Alexei, disguised as the son of wealthy parents; Alexandra and the daughters were to be taken east across Siberia to safety in Japan. One of the leaders of the conspiracy was Mikhail Lopukhin, Anna Golitsyn's youngest brother. He was responsible for recruiting trustworthy tsarist officers and was to head a select group in charge of the former tsar's safety on the journey to Orenburg. Joining him were Vladimir Trubetskoy and some of Vladimir's cousins, including Alexander and Sergei Yevgenevich Trubetskoy and Nikolai Lermontov.

Over the course of several days in early January 1918, the conspirators left Moscow in small groups, traveling along different routes so as to avoid suspicion. They quickly realized, however, that their plan had no hope of success. Every station they passed through swarmed with Red soldiers, and upon reaching Chelyabinsk, they learned that Troitsk, where they had planned to take Nicholas, had already been overrun by the Bolsheviks. Discouraged but not ready to give up, the men stayed in Chelyabinsk and hatched a new plan to hide Nicholas deep in Siberia. They sent out scouts to search for the safest route and best hiding places, but as they worked on the details of their plan, the Bolshevik presence grew ever stronger, and any chance they had of overpowering Nicholas's captors and escaping with him and his family evaporated. Fearful of being discovered, the conspirators returned to Moscow in the middle of February.

For nearly all the young officers, this was the end of the story. Their involvement in the plot remained undiscovered. Most, including Vladimir Trubetskoy, gave up their flirtation with anti-Bolshevik activities.[12] This was not the case, however, for Sergei Trubetskoy or Mikhail Lopukhin. Lopukhin now joined a new organization called the Union for the Defense of the Motherland and Freedom. Secret anti-Bolshevik cells of former tsarist officers were then forming in a few Russian cities. Between December 1918 and 1920, twenty-two underground officer groups with names such as the National Center, the Right Center, the

Tactical Center, the Sokolniky Battle Organization, the Order of the Romanovs, All for the Motherland, the Black Point, and the White Cross were uncovered and broken up by the Bolsheviks. As many as sixteen thousand men joined the anti-Bolshevik underground. Although their goals varied (from passing on information about life under the Bolsheviks to the White Army to plotting armed insurrection), nearly all the cells proved ineffective. Sergei Trubetskoy, who joined the National Center in Moscow, later wrote that although they tried to mastermind a number of conspiratorial activities, they were "completely unsuited" for such work.[13] General Denikin concurred: "With no resources, with no mutual trust among them or clear understanding of cooperation, and, mainly, with no real power, their efforts proved flabby from the beginning and did not produce any results."[14]

The Union for the Defense of the Motherland and Freedom was an exception, however. Founded by Boris Savinkov, a novelist, former leader of the SRs, and noted terrorist (he had taken part in the 1903 murder of Grand Duke Sergei Alexandrovich), the union set up cells in numerous Russian cities in 1918. Its plan to seize power in Moscow that spring with the support of German prisoners of war was uncovered by the Cheka, but the union did manage to instigate revolts in Yaroslavl, Rybinsk, and Murom, all of which were put down by the Reds. Savinkov fled the country for France, and nearly all of the union's members, including Mikhail Lopukhin, were arrested.[15]

Most of the officers arrested in the wake of the uprisings, as many as six hundred in Moscow and Kaluga alone in early July 1918, were shot.[16] Mikhail's cell had been discovered after one of its members had informed on it to the Cheka. Some of the members had enough warning to escape to the south before they could be arrested, but Mikhail was not so lucky. As soon as she learned what had happened, Anna left Bogoroditsk for Moscow to try to get Mikhail released. She went to plead before several high-ranking Bolsheviks, including Lev Kamenev, Yakov Peters, and Felix Dzerzhinsky (whose eyes burned like a "horrible fire," she noted). None of them would help. Finally, she went to see Pyotr Smidovich. A longtime Bolshevik, the chairman of the Moscow Soviet, and the son of a nobleman, Smidovich had a reputation as a good and honest man. Moreover, his brother-in-law had worked before the revolution as a tutor in the Lopukhin home and had always spoken highly of the family. Smidovich agreed to do what he could to save

Mikhail, but only if he would pledge to give up his anti-Bolshevik activities.

Anna visited Mikhail three times in prison and begged him to accept the offer; Anna's husband wrote to him as well, but he refused to cooperate. Smidovich himself went to Mikhail and asked him to reconsider, offering his protection once Mikhail was free. But he was turned down too. Mikhail said that had it been another Bolshevik he would have easily lied, but he respected Smidovich and so thought he owed it to him to be honest. Anna visited Mikhail one last time. She told him that she accepted his decision, blessed him, and left. Mikhail and forty other prisoners were driven out on the evening of August 23, 1918, to the Bratskoe Cemetery near the village of Vsekhsviatskoe; they were lined up against a brick wall and shot. After learning of Mikhail's execution, Anna went to search for his grave. She found the wall, pocked with fresh bullet holes, and the spot where he had been shot; the ground in front of it had been freshly dug up and the soil turned over. She never did find his body, however. She went to the prison and retrieved Mikhail's few personal things, including his jacket, which she gave to her son Vladimir, who wore it the rest of his life in memory of his uncle.[17]

At the prison Anna was handed a letter addressed to her from Mikhail dated August 20. On the envelope were the words: "Do not open until you have learned of my death."

Dearest Annochka,

Things have ended up so sadly and so painfully. But what are we to do? Remember my words and draw comfort from them—"Without God's will, nothing happens." Which means this is how it must be. I want to do everything in my power to comfort you and our loved ones. [. . .] I don't want you to be sad or to pity me; just remember me often and not with a sad feeling of loss, but remember everything good and joyous connected with me.

I am still alive even now, and I am certain that in the future my last minute will not be as hopelessly painful as it may seem, so don't torment yourself over me. [. . .] Thank you, dear Annochka, for your love. I was not lonely in my final moments. [. . .] Well, so it's farewell, farewell to Mama, to Zhenia, to everyone. For truth, it's nothing. Everything is in God's hands.[18]

Mikhail's execution devastated the family. Anna's younger son Sergei, then nine years old, later recalled how his uncle's death became a turning point in his life:

> I became someone different, my carefree play with the other boys all but came to an end. I would go to the park by myself, I read and thought a great deal. Since that time I began to lead a double life—one involved interaction with others, conversations, games with my sisters, hobbies, pleasures, the other, second life was secret, carried out within myself that I did not admit even to my mother. This second life, for me the more important and pleasant one, lasted throughout my childhood and youth, throughout all the subsequent years and continues to beat in my heart. [. . .] There's nothing terribly surprising about this, this is how life is in our country, for we all live a double life. What is surprising is how early, due to the tragic death of Uncle Misha, I learned to speak and act in one way, and think to myself something utterly different.[19]

By late summer conditions at Bogoroditsk had begun to deteriorate. The SRs had left, and the Bolsheviks turned their attention to the colony of nobles still living peaceably at the old family estate. An article appeared in the newspaper *The Red Voice* under the title "How Long Will We Stand for This?!," denouncing the "suspicious little countesses" and "chubby-cheeked little counts in sailor suits" at Bogoroditsk and asking when, finally, this noble nest was to be extirpated. One night in late October a group of soldiers, led by a sailor strapped with bandoliers and waving a Nagant, burst into the manor house while the family was enjoying some music. The men began searching the house, accompanied by the violin-playing Salzmann, who never put down his instrument. They found nothing other than some letters in French and German, which they held up as proof the men were spies. The next morning they loaded the mayor, Lev Bobrinsky, and Vladimir Trubetskoy into a cart and took them away; a crowd of peasants came out to watch. The other family members were given forty-eight hours to leave, and the few remaining servants were sent to live in an almshouse. Anna and her children moved into town (also called Bogoroditsk) and found shelter in a run-down inn. When it rained, the water poured through the numerous holes in the roof, cascaded down the walls, and spread out in rivulets across the floor. Anna was amazed to see how this filled her children with delight.[20]

The mayor and his two sons-in-law were freed after six weeks. They had not been home for long before being arrested a second time in early 1919. The men were first taken to Tula and from there to the Butyrki in Moscow. This time the mayor and Lev were quickly released; Kamenev, now the chairman of the Moscow Soviet, invited the mayor to come see him before he left the city. He apologized to the mayor for his arrest, telling him how well he remembered the kind treatment the mayor had given to political prisoners when he had run the city and presenting him with a letter of protection. The Golitsyns guarded Kamenev's letter with care, and it is still in their possession; it may well have saved the mayor's life, though its power did not extend to the rest of the family.[21] Vladimir Trubetskoy was eventually released as well and returned to his wife and children.[22]

Despite the arrests, searches, and horrendous living conditions, life went on for the extended Golitsyn family. Kirill Golitsyn, one of the mayor's grandchildren, who had been sent from Petrograd to live with the family at Bogoroditsk, noticed how no one gave up or even complained of his fate.

> No one was downhearted and the abnormality of life in no way showed itself in people's moods or character. Everyone adapted to the difficulties, just as every living thing adapts to the conditions of its environment. It was no doubt hardest for Grandfather and Grandmother, but the old folks didn't complain. My aunts and uncles had no time to be downhearted—they were utterly consumed by the daily struggle to find enough food for everyone.[23]

The youngest members of the family made secret nighttime raids on the apple orchard back at the former estate; the family's meat consisted of the occasional foal.[24] One of their former servants, worried that the family was starving, managed to send Anna a bit of chicken and some rusk; though they had little themselves, Anna too shared their meager larder and sent bread and coffee to those in need.[25]

The desperate search for food placed them on par with the rest of Russia. In Petrograd, people were stripping the bark from the trees and pulling up the grass from the city's parks to make soup; they descended on horses that dropped dead from starvation with knives and hatchets, lugging back to their freezing apartments whatever flesh and organs and sinew they could salvage. Prince Sergei Trubetskoy had to laugh that when his servant now announced, "Your Excellency, your horse is ready," this no longer meant it had been saddled, but cooked and served.[26]

Anna was eventually able to move her family out of the inn and into the apartment of a local schoolteacher. One of the lodgers was a young Bolshevik who fell for the charms of Anna's daughter Sonya. When Sonya rejected his advances, he denounced the family to the local authorities, and once again the family was kicked out and forced to move, this time within twenty-four hours. The harsh memory of this incident never left Sonya's brother Sergei:

> This feeling of having been insulted—they offend you, they keep you
> down, they run you out, they don't recognize you simply because you
> are your father's son—this feeling, first born in me when we were run
> out of the Bobrinskys' estate, and then compounded by this second
> eviction, which I fully comprehended and was so hard to bear, has
> been with me nearly my entire life.[27]

By late summer of 1919, as Denikin's White Army marched northward, talk had begun to spread in town that the retreating Reds had begun taking hostages and shooting them. The Golitsyns knew the risk was real. That year two of Anna's cousins had been taken hostage and shot in Orel.[28] The mayor and his son Mikhail decided to hide; the former quietly checked himself into the local hospital in a common ward, and the latter went to live with a work colleague. The danger seemed to pass after several days, however, and both returned home. On the night of October 16, the mayor was awakened to find that Vladimir Trubetskoy had been arrested after a search of his apartment in town. The Cheka had also come to arrest Mikhail, but he had managed to hide. So they arrested Anna instead, as well as their daughter Lina and Sonya Bobrinsky, their niece. As they took the women away, the Chekists told the family they would release the women if Mikhail turned himself in. The family got word to Mikhail, and he immediately presented himself to the Cheka. That evening of the sixteenth, the women were freed. A few hours later Mikhail and Vladimir and the other hostages were taken to the train station. Family members followed the two men to the station, and Mikhail's son Sergei was able to toss a few potatoes to his father before they were herded onto the train.[29]

They were taken to Tula and interned in a concentration camp. Anna said goodbye to the family and left to be near her husband. Mikhail wrote their children from the camp on November 12:

My dear ones, I write from the concentration camp, where I have been held for three days now. The camp consists of a row of wooden barracks, with all 280 of us occupying two of them and two more being readied for some new hostages. We sleep on wooden cots, and it is warm and dry inside, and the appearance is not bad. The camp is circled with barbed wire and surrounded by guards. The camp is run by a commandant [. . .], who used to work in the Bogoroditsk Cheka and questioned me about Grandfather and knows you, Vladimir.*
The commandant has a rather difficult assistant, a lawyer by training, but he's not so bad. They feed us little. Some soup during the day and mashed potatoes in the evening—sometimes they give us a bit more, sometimes very little at all. Twice daily they give us boiling water, sugar, and some bread. One cannot survive on this, and they do allow the prisoners to receive food from the outside [. . .] The last three days here I've had to do physical labor. The first day I tried to screw up my courage and walked to the Kursk railway station on the other side of town and spent the entire day loading wood and came home utterly exhausted. The next day I was deemed fit only for light work, but even this work proved to be rather difficult, and I have spent the last two days hauling around bricks, boards, and garbage. Of course, my work at an office will be arranged soon. Kalinin† will be here today to inspect the camp. After that, so they say, a commission on hostage taking will be established, and then maybe we'll be freed. I will be seeing Mama this evening [. . .] It seems to me our case is being dragged out and it's hard to count on being freed. Still, it appears the danger to our lives has passed. Nonetheless, it's boring here with nothing to do and I miss you all. I think of you often. [. . .] I hope you are all well, settled, and getting well with each other; I trust you older children are

---

*Anna and Mikhail's elder son.
†Mikhail Kalinin, titular head of the new Bolshevik state.

being nice to your younger siblings, and you younger ones are not misbehaving. Do remember me and Mama and pray for us [. . .] Your Papa.[30]

A few weeks later he wrote again:

My dear parents and children, I received today Grandmother and Grandfather's letters and we are all glad to hear that you are all well and healthy. We, too, here are all safe and well and can't wait for the amnesty process to begin. It still isn't clear whether the amnesty will apply to me and Uncle Vladimir, since we are considered titled persons, and for this reason the Cheka harbors all sorts of suspicions about us, all of which are utterly baseless. [. . .] We are indeed worried, and all this amidst the usual horrific filth. There are insects everywhere and the sinks have frozen, they feed us poorly and we survive only thanks to the food parcels from our loved ones, which they secretly give us every day or give to some good people to hand over to us, which is forbidden. [. . .] Our spirits are good, and we are well. It has been very good for me to be out in the open air so much, although it is sometimes cold at night, and I would very much like to have my felt boots or my feet get wet. It's terribly cold for so early in the season. We worked harvesting cabbage again today, which has become my specialty! We occasionally read the newspapers, though there's little in them.[31]

From Tula Anna wrote to Pyotr Smidovich, telling him what had happened and begging for help. She insisted that Mikhail represented no threat to the Bolsheviks and that he had been taken hostage only because he was "a former prince." All her efforts in Tula to gain his release had come to naught because everyone "was afraid to raise a finger 'for a former prince.'" Anna reminded Smidovich of her brother Mikhail's horrible fate the previous year and wrote that unless someone from Moscow would help, then Mikhail "will be among the first to perish."[32]

Anna and Mikhail's children suffered without their parents. Little Sergei sent his father drawings and kept asking when he would be coming home.[33] "Dear Mama, when will our torments finally end!" his sister Sonya wrote.

I simply have no more strength! How I want to see you both, to unburden my heart. It seems as though I'm losing my mind. I can't understand a thing and will soon be a complete fool. Now when I begin to say something, all of a sudden my head fills with a strange fog. It is terribly difficult for me to concentrate during my lessons, or to hear and understand the teachers. What am I to do? I really do think I shall lose my mind! [. . .] Oh God, if only this would all soon be over! I don't know what to do [. . .] Oh, mama, dearest mama, how hard this is for me! Help me, save me, pray for me.[34]

Lina Golitsyn went to Tula to be with her mother. She and Anna took turns delivering a bowl of cabbage soup every morning and evening to Mikhail and Vladimir, who were spending long days hauling bricks and digging up cabbage in the icy fields with their bare hands. The conditions at the camp were horrible, and soon all the men were infected with fleas, lice, and bedbugs; many of the hostages died from cold and hunger. Mikhail fell ill with typhus, and Vladimir began to show signs of tuberculosis. They were lucky, however, and were sent to the prison hospital to get better and were spared further outdoor work that most likely would have killed them. After three months in the camp, Mikhail was freed on January 15, 1920. An appeal to Kamenev by Mikhail's brother appears to have played a crucial role in his release.[35]

Vladimir Trubetskoy was also freed from the camp at the end of January. He returned to his family for a visit but soon had to leave. A decorated hero of the First World War, Trubetskoy was instructed to return to Moscow, where the leaders of the Red Army tried to convince him to join their ranks.

The Bolshevik coup and subsequent civil war split the Russian officer corps. Many former tsarist officers, like Vladimir, chose to sit out the war; more than forty-eight thousand officers joined the Red Army, and about double that number fought on the side of the Whites.[36] Those who fought for the Reds did so for a number of reasons. Some believed in the ideas of the Bolsheviks; some were motivated by a sense of patriotism; some were desperate for the food and money that service provided; some were coerced; some were afraid to refuse. The Bolsheviks began to call up former officers in the summer of 1918 out of dire need.

To ensure officers' loyalty, family members were sometimes taken hostage or threatened with arrest.[37] Prince Vasily Golitsyn, director of Moscow's Rumiantsev Museum, had one son serving on the Red Army general staff, while another son was off fighting for the Whites. During the civil war, Prince Vasily lived with his daughter Maria and her husband, Alexei Derevitsky, a soldier in the Red Army. Such cases of divided loyalties were not unheard of.[38]

The two best-known noblemen to join the Red Army were Mikhail Tukhachevsky and Alexei Brusilov. Tukhachevsky's motives have been the subject of considerable speculation, though it seems they were neither simple nor straightforward. Part pure ambition, part ideology, part desire to join in the forward march of history, part snobbish pleasure of being a nobleman among peasants and proletarians, Tukhachevsky, the "Red Bonaparte," joined the Bolsheviks in 1917 and was a brilliant and ruthless commander in the civil war. From 1925 to 1928, he was the chief of staff of the Red Army, and in 1935 he was named marshal of the Soviet Union. Together with eight other high-ranking military commanders, Tukhachevsky was executed on fabricated charges of treason in 1937 during Stalin's Great Terror.[39]

Born in 1853 into a noble family with a long tradition of military service, Brusilov had fought in the Russo-Turkish War of 1877–78 and, after serving as the commander in chief of the southwestern front in 1916, was made the supreme commander in chief of the Russian army in May 1917 under the Provisional Government. Brusilov was Russia's greatest living war hero, yet he refused to take sides in the civil war. In 1918, he was arrested by the Cheka and held briefly. Four of his family members were also arrested and held hostage; they were threatened with death if Brusilov joined the Whites. Brusilov's only son from his first marriage, Alexei, had also fought in World War I and was arrested by the Bolsheviks. Later freed, he joined the Red Army cavalry and was captured by the White Army and executed in the autumn of 1919. His son's death at the hands of the Whites was important in shaping Brusilov's decision to join the Reds. But perhaps just as important was his belief that whatever his own personal feelings, the Russian people had sided with the Reds and as a patriot he had to respect their wishes. In 1920, after extreme inner struggle and anguish, Brusilov joined the Red Army, an act that earned him the hatred of much of the old Russian nobility.[40]

Vladimir Trubetskoy was part of a group of officers ordered to report to Moscow for a meeting with Brusilov. The two former cavalry officers had known each other for years, and Brusilov had held Vladimir in high regard ever since his valiant exploits in the last war. After joining the Reds, Brusilov had helped free hundreds of imprisoned officers, and it is possible his efforts helped Vladimir.[41] Brusilov is purported to have played to Vladimir's patriotism, saying, "Prince, the cart has gotten stuck, and there is no one but us to pull it out. Without the army, Russia cannot be saved." Vladimir was a monarchist, and Brusilov's siding with the Bolsheviks disturbed him, yet in the end he acquiesced to his former commander's call. Vladimir was given his orders and left to join the Red Army in the south. He decided, however, to take a detour to Bogoroditsk on the way to visit his wife and children and share with them his food ration. Vladimir had only just arrived when he was denounced to the Cheka by someone suspicious of his "aristocratic appearance." Once more, Vladimir was back behind bars. Just as had happened in Tula, Vladimir soon showed the early signs of tuberculosis. As the illness grew worse, Vladimir was freed to return to his family, his military career over. In all, Vladimir was arrested three times during the five years he lived in Bogoroditsk.[42]

Mikhail Golitsyn returned to his family from Tula and found a secretarial job. Money and food were scarce. Anna took some lessons from a local cobbler and began making shoes out of the green felt carpet that had been pulled up from the floor of the mayor's study in his Moscow home. Mikhail helped in the evenings making shoe strings. Anna did not sell the shoes for money but traded them for food. They also stripped the brown suede off the old ledger books from the Bogoroditsk estate and sewed it into attractive coin purses and billfolds that they either sold or traded for necessary items back in Moscow. Their clothes they bartered at local markets for salt or sugar. The children gathered nettles and sorrel to make soup or dug potatoes. The family was too poor by now to buy horsemeat; they could afford only the head and hooves, which Anna boiled for days to create a light brown aspic. Sergei found it repugnant, but hunger was stronger than revulsion.[43]

Even though the Golitsyn children worked to help support the family, their education was not overlooked. Grandmother Sofia taught them

French, Lev Bobrinsky's sister gave them English lessons, and Anna found the children a German tutor.[44] This preoccupation with education was not unique to the Golitsyns, but generally characteristic of the nobility as a whole.[45]

Impoverished, hungry, and anxious over what future troubles lay ahead, the Golitsyns still took pleasure in life. Sonya joined the local theater and thrilled in her career as a thespian. The former princess now just played the part of nobility, acting the role of Countess Olivia in Shakespeare's *Twelfth Night*.[46] In October 1920, they finally got electricity in their home, which everyone in the family greeted as nothing short of a miracle. Instead of sitting in the dark with nothing but a few candles to break the gloom, they now had light in the evenings. One of their favorite things to do was gather around Mikhail, as he read aloud to them bathed in an electric glow.[47]

There was an empty place in the home, however. Anna and Mikhail's son Vladimir had left the family that year to join a scientific exploration of the Far North. It was a fabulous adventure for Vladimir, a budding artist who captured the icy wilds of Novaya Zemlya in his vivid watercolors and had a chance to meet fellow explorers from Norway and England, contacts that later became a factor in his arrest. Nevertheless, the family missed the humorous and creative Vladimir and pined for his return. Anna wrote her son in September, asking him to write them more often since "every letter from you is an event, a true holiday for us in our 'little peasant hut.'"[48]

12

DR. GOLITSYN

After leaving Moscow, the family of Alexander Golitsyn and their accompanying friends rode the Northern Railway for five days before arriving in Tyumen in the middle of December 1917. Along the way the train was besieged by deserting soldiers, but they managed to protect themselves by closing all the curtains, locking the doors, and stationing outside two women from the group disguised in nurses' uniforms, who frightened off any intruders with stories of patients ill with dangerous infectious diseases. Life in the Siberian town was a marked improvement over Moscow. Most of the major urban centers in Siberia, Tyumen among them, had sided with the Bolsheviks within the first months of the coup. Nonetheless, the local Bolshevik leaders were quite tame, things were quiet and comfortable, and there was plenty of food. They all found lodgings, and Alexander set up his own medical practice. He made sure to drop the title of prince from all his papers, however, and presented himself simply as Dr. Golitsyn. Prince Georgy Lvov and Nikolai Lopukhin went a step further, adopting assumed names to avoid notice.[1]

All was well until a detachment of Red Guards arrived in late January 1918. They overthrew the existing soviet and began suppressing any opposition and harassing the bourgeoisie. The new bosses forbade all gatherings, seized the homes and bank accounts of the well-to-do, and arrested potential enemies. After seeing some of their friends arrested and robbed and others flee Tyumen, the Golitsyns began to debate whether they too ought to leave. In the end they chose to remain since it appeared to them all Siberia had been lost to the Reds. They put their fate in the hands of "Providence." In March, soldiers came and arrested Georgy, Nikolai, and Alexander. When Alexander asked one of the men why he was being arrested, he was told, "Because you are a prince, a bourgeois and counterrevolutionary. We know all about you and your gang here, you are plotting something. You are not a doctor, you are a disguised officer of Kornilov's army."[2] After they had taken Alexander away, his children and the servants got down on their knees to pray.[3]

Alexander was taken to a train car at the Tyumen rail station that served as the soldiers' local headquarters. Georgy and Nikolai were held in an adjacent car; when Alexander inquired about his friends, he was informed they were due to be shot the next day, a threat that was never carried out. No charges against the men, other than the vague comments directed to Alexander upon his arrest, were ever made, and they were held prisoner for almost two weeks. Alexander was put to work treating wounded Red soldiers, which he was happy to do since he abhorred inactivity. A Red orderly with a bit of medical training was attached to Alexander to make sure this "class enemy" did not try to harm any of his patients, and Alexander quickly won over many of the men with his knowledge and care.

Alexander found most of the men to be rough and uneducated, chiefly motivated by a love of plunder and the promise of money and adventure. A few were doctrinaire Communists who truly believed they were going to build a new society in which all men would be equal. Yet even these men, Alexander noted, saw the need for blood. One young soldier told Alexander that he was ready to "unload my revolver" into the head of anyone who opposed them. When Alexander replied this would certainly require a great many bullets, he retorted: "Oh, not so many as you think, one million or so . . . Most of the people are with us." Alexander overheard the soldiers brag of their killings. He learned of soldiers going out to requisition gold and jewelry, most of which they turned over to the commissar, although some of the finest pieces they saved for themselves, which they would show to Alexander and regale him with their tales of thieving and pillaging.[4] All the while, Lyubov had been pleading, unsuccessfully, with the commissar to free her husband.

In the first week of March, the train left Tyumen. None of them knew where they were heading. Every time the train came to a stop the soldiers would pull out Georgy and parade him before the angry crowds. Lvov was certain he would never get out alive.[5] Around March 6, they arrived in Yekaterinburg on the eastern edge of the Ural Mountains. Having received word that the train was carrying several princes and ministers of the tsarist government, a mob of workmen converged on it and demanded the prisoners be handed over. "Why are you keeping those princes in safety?" they shouted at the Red soldiers. "If you can't get rid of them, we'll do it. Perish the bourgeoisie! Long live the proletariat!" Terrified the mob would get him, Alexander cowered in a dark corner of his compartment. His guard, an anarchist named Orlov, assured Alexander they would not give him up and that they would fire on the crowd if necessary. Alexander found this of little comfort, sensing that either way—sooner or later—he would be killed. The next morning he learned that the Yekaterinburg Soviet had refused to let the train leave without first handing him and his two companions over to the local revolutionary tribunal for trial. The news left Alexander distraught. He sensed his chances of surviving were slim.[6]

Revolver-wielding Chekists took the three men from the train, placed them in a truck, and drove off to the city prison. Alexander noted in his memoirs the relief he felt upon hearing the heavy prison door close behind him. "It meant complete isolation from the world, from my family and friends; but at the same time it meant a certain safety behind these thick white walls, safety from a hostile crowd or a sudden fancy of a Commissar."[7] He was placed in a solitary cell and fed some tea and dark bread. To keep his spirits up, Alexander paced back and forth from wall to wall, trying to walk what he estimated was about four miles a day; he also took comfort in the Bible and a few books by William James that he had managed to take with him. Later Georgy and Nikolai were moved in to share his cell.

About a week later, Lyubov, having left the children behind in Tyumen, arrived in Yekaterinburg. For several days she petitioned the local commissar of justice, the Left SR Nikolai Poliakov, for a chance to see her husband, and eventually he acquiesced. No formal charges had been made against the men, and their fate was unforeseeable. Fillip Goloshchekin, the hard-line Bolshevik leader in Yekaterinburg, wanted Georgy shot, although it seems the men's jailer, who took a liking to the old prince, found a way to keep them all alive. Lyubov had written to family and friends to request assistance from Moscow. News of their arrest shook the rest of the Golitsyn family.[8]

Finally, in the middle of April a lawyer from Moscow arrived to try to gain the men's freedom.[9] The men were not freed by Easter, as they had hoped, but their jailers did allow them to move to a different part of the prison so they could hear the bells of the local church. They also permitted the men a small Easter supper and quiet service, conducted by their fellow inmate Bishop Hermogen of Tobolsk. (The Reds drowned Hermogen in the Tura River two months later.)[10] In May, the men were moved to a new prison, where they met Prince Vasily Dolgoruky, the former marshal of the court. Dolgoruky informed them that the emperor and several members of the royal family had recently been brought to Yekaterinburg.[11]

Nicholas, Alexandra, their five children, and numerous servants had been sent by Kerensky in the summer of 1917 to the remote Siberian town of Tobolsk, chiefly to protect them from the increasingly radical, angry mobs in the capital. By the spring of 1918, the Soviet leaders had decided to move the Romanovs and a handful of their remaining servants to Yekaterinburg; the city was under the control of the Bolshevik Regional Soviet of the Urals, which could be relied on to guard them and was loyal to the leadership back in Moscow. Soon after the arrival of the Romanovs, Alexander, Georgy, and Nikolai were released and allowed to return to Tyumen, where they were to await trial on charges of counterrevolutionary activities. The fact that Georgy was released has never been fully explained and seems to have been either a mistake or a miracle.[12] Regardless of the reasons, had the three men stayed in Yekaterinburg, they most likely would have shared the fate of the Romanovs.

By the summer of 1918 Yekaterinburg was being threatened by an unlikely foe. During the First World War, many Czechs had refused to fight for the Austro-Hungarian Empire, even though they were its subjects, preferring instead to side with the Russians, their fellow Slavs. Fearful of being caught by the advancing Central Powers in the spring of 1918, the Czech Legion received the permission of the Bolshevik government to leave Russia via Siberia and the Trans-Siberian Railway, going almost all the way around the globe to rejoin the battle on the western front. The legion had gotten as far east as Chelyabinsk in the

Ural Mountains in late May 1918, when after the Czechs had rioted with Hungarian POWs there, the Soviet authorities ordered the legion disarmed and disbanded; those who resisted were to be shot on the spot. With that, fighting erupted in western Siberia between the legion and Red forces. The Czechs showed lightning success, and soon they controlled all Siberia and beyond to the Pacific Ocean. Mastery of Siberia depended on control of the Trans-Siberian Railway, the vital lifeline that stretched forty-nine hundred miles from Perm in the Urals to Vladivostok on the Pacific coast. More than in any other theater of the civil war, the railway was key: controlling the rail lines meant controlling the movement of men and matériel and ultimately, controlling the war. Armored trains bristling with heavy guns and cannons served as the battleships across a sea of forests and swamps.

At first wishing just to break through to Vladivostok on the coast, by early July the Czechs had decided to stay in Russia and to fight alongside the White forces and the Allies, who had begun landing troops in Vladivostok that spring. Some of the Czechs marched to Samara, west of the Urals on the Volga, and there supported the anti-Bolshevik government, the Committee of Members of the Constituent Assembly (*Komúch*). The legion's success helped lead to the creation of a Provisional Siberian Government in Omsk, made up of monarchists, SRs, and Kadets. During the spring and summer of 1918, the Czech Legion rode the Trans-Siberian from west to east and back again; by the end of May they had seized Novo-Nikolaevsk, Chelyabinsk, and Tomsk, and before the end of September they had overthrown every Soviet government in Siberia.[13]

It was the approach of the Czechs toward Yekaterinburg in July that sealed the fate of the Romanovs. The Bolsheviks had been planning to put Nicholas on trial, but there was concern, especially among the members of the Ural Regional Soviet, about Nicholas's being freed by the approaching White forces. The question of who ordered the murder of the former tsar and his family continues to divide historians. Some claim the order came from Lenin himself, while others argue the decision was made by the local leaders in Yekaterinburg, acting largely on their own initiative. The evidence suggests the latter was the case.[14]

In the early-morning hours of July 17, Nicholas, Alexandra, their five children (Olga, Tatiana, Marie, Anastasia, and Alexei), their physician,

Dr. Yevgeny Botkin, and three remaining servants (Anna Demidov, Ivan Kharitonov, and Alexei Trupp) were awakened by their captors in the Ipatiev House, told to dress, and then led downstairs to an empty room in the basement. Shortly after 2:15 a.m., Yakov Yurovsky, commandant of the Ipatiev House, entered with a group of armed men and ordered the prisoners to stand against the wall. He then read from a piece of paper: "In view of the fact that your relatives continue their offensive against Soviet Russia, the Executive Committee of the Ural Regional Soviet has decided to sentence you to death." None of the family seemed at first to realize what was happening. Yurovsky then pointed his revolver at Nicholas and fired. The murder of the Romanovs and their servants was bloody, chaotic, and savage. Not everyone died in the initial volley, and for nearly ten minutes the victims were shot and bayoneted until every last one had been killed.[15]

The bloodshed in Yekaterinburg did not begin on July 17, however. A week earlier, the Cheka had arrested Prince Vasily Dolgoruky and shot him together with Count Ilya Tatishchev. Days later Red Army soldiers shot dozens of suspected counterrevolutionaries.[16] Indeed, the killing of the Romanovs had begun a month before. On June 12, Grand Duke Mikhail (Nicholas II's youngest brother) and his British secretary, Nicholas Johnson, had been taken from the Korolev Hotel in Perm by local Cheka agents, driven out of the city, and executed.[17] The day after the massacre in the Ipatiev House, six members of the Romanov family, including Grand Duke Sergei Mikhailovich (a cousin of Nicholas II's) and Grand Duchess Elizabeth Fyodorovna (Empress Alexandra's sister), along with two others were murdered at Alapaevsk, a mining town about a hundred miles northeast of Yekaterinburg.[18] Six months later, on the night of January 27–28, 1919, Grand Duke Paul Alexandrovich (Nicholas II's uncle) and Grand Dukes Nicholas Mikhailovich, George Mikhailovich, and Dmitry Konstantinovich (all cousins of Nicholas's) were taken out of their cells in the Peter and Paul Fortress in Petrograd, lined up in front of a ditch, and shot.[19]

News of the killing of the tsar spread quickly. In Moscow, Olga Sheremetev's husband brought home a copy of the newspaper *Izvestiia* on July 19 that carried an official statement confirming the death of the "crowned executioner." According to the statement, Alexandra and Alexei had been taken to safety; no mention was made of the daughters. To Olga, the news signaled the Bolsheviks' desperation and was a sign they were losing the war. Two days later many Moscow churches held requiems for Nicholas; large crowds attended the services, and there was much weeping. Not everyone believed Nicholas was dead, however, and rumors of his fate abounded. Some said he was safe in England. Anna Saburov was among the doubters, and she told Olga that the Bolsheviks' days were numbered and the monarchy would be restored.[20] In Bogoroditsk, the Golitsyns also learned of the murder from the newspapers. Like the Sheremetevs, they attended a memorial service in the local church. Sergei later recalled that the impact of the news on the family was "enormous." That night Sergei secretly cried into his pillow.[21] Even the mayor, always a harsh critic of the tsar, called the execution "criminal and absurd"; he particularly regretted the fact that it would place upon Nicholas the mantle of martyrdom.[22]

The reaction to the murder of the tsar among the nobility was not uniform and, not surprisingly, was most deeply felt by committed monarchists.[23] Many Russians cheered the news. When the word reached a village outside Omsk, the peasants ran out into the street, dancing, singing, and shouting for joy.[24]

Back with their families in Tyumen, Alexander, Georgy, and Nikolai debated what to do next. For months, the overseer of the Golitsyns' Petrovskoe estate had been writing to beg Alexander and Lyubov to return. He described the horrific conditions there. After the poorer peasants had plundered the estate, they turned on their better-off neighbors, forcing them to come up with large sums of money as "reparations" as part of a new campaign against the "petite bourgeoisie." By the spring of 1918, all the peasants were facing starvation. Beggars roamed the land, and people had begun fighting over meager scraps of bread. Alexander and Lyubov sent food parcels to their former servants but would not think of returning. Soon they received word that the Reds were searching for the three men again, and they decided they would have to flee. The Three Musketeers, as Nikolai called themselves, set off to find the Czech Legion.[25]

On their journey the men passed through the village of Pokrovskoe, the home of Rasputin, where the villagers told them that a party of Red soldiers had come through the day before, looking for them. Convinced they needed to avoid the shifting front lines, they decided to

make a four-hundred-mile detour to the north on several hired troi-
kas. They traveled for days through fields, forests, and bogs; the mosquitoes were so thick they had to bury themselves in towels. Once they
barely had time to jump down and hide in the trees on the roadside as
a large detachment of Red soldiers came along from the opposite direction. After six days they reached the town of Ishim and a group of
Czech soldiers. They did not stay long but boarded a train for Tomsk,
farther to the east, where they hoped to be safer. Upon reaching Tomsk,
they heard that the Reds had been pushed out of Tyumen, and they
raced back to be reunited with their families after six weeks on the
road.[26] The people of Tyumen greeted the fall of the Bolsheviks with
joy. For Alexander, Georgy, and Nikolai the relief they felt was clouded
by the news that before the Bolsheviks retreated from Yekaterinburg,
they had executed most of their former prison inmates.[27]

The collapse of Soviet power across Siberia was followed by an explosion of separate, and often competing, White governments (as many
as nineteen), although the two major political centers for the anti-
Bolshevik movement were the Komuch and the Provisional Siberian
Government in Omsk. A Siberian army was organized in 1918; under
the green and white flag, symbolizing the forests and snows of Siberia,
it counted almost forty thousand troops by October. The situation was
complicated by the arrival of foreign troops in the Far East, first the
Japanese and British, followed by the French and Americans. The Japanese eventually landed nearly seventy thousand troops, although most
of them stayed on the coast; American forces numbered eight thousand. The British alone sent troops deep into Siberia—to Omsk, the
Siberian capital, in mid-October 1918, although they too did not wish
to become directly involved in the fighting.[28]

As was true of the anti-Bolshevik groups across the former empire,
those in Siberia and the Urals found it difficult to work in concert and
to organize a unified, effective structure. On the night of November
17–18, 1918, a coup of right-wing forces overthrew the government in
Omsk and set up a military dictatorship under Admiral Alexander
Kolchak, a prominent war hero, who was declared "Supreme Ruler."
Kolchak became the leader of the anti-Bolshevik forces in Siberia and
(if only in name) throughout all Russia for the next fourteen months.[29]

Despite his grand title, Kolchak's power was far from absolute, even
east of the Urals, where he was based. Power rested on control of the

Trans-Siberian Railway, and in the autumn of 1918 this was shared by various groups at different points along the route: the Czechs, the Japanese, the Americans, and also the Cossack warlords Grigory Semenov and Ivan Kalmykov. In total, these groups controlled thirty-five hundred miles of the railway, meaning Kolchak had to work with them. And although Kolchak enjoyed British support, the Americans were decidedly less convinced of his merits; the commander of the American forces, Major General William Graves, criticized what he considered the barbarity of Kolchak's army.[30]

Alexander and his family remained in Tyumen throughout the rest of 1918 and most of the following year. Prince Lvov left them for Omsk, from where he was sent by Kolchak's government on a mission to the United States to seek aid and support from President Woodrow Wilson. Georgy did meet Wilson in late November 1918, though only briefly and without winning any pledge of support from the U.S. president.[31] Lyubov and the children spent the summer of 1919 outside Tyumen at the Tatar village of Yembaevo while Alexander remained in town to work at the hospital. Their sixteen-year-old daughter Olga excitedly followed the course of the fighting. "Good news from the front," she wrote that summer in her diary.

> If I were a boy, a man, that which I so wanted, then I would certainly go to war. [. . .] Why am I not a man! I would definitely go to war, get through to the Caucasus and just be there. It is so annoying to hear that they are fighting so heroically, while our life here is petty, uninteresting (though good), and useless. If only there were a man here that I could be proud of, for whom I could pray, and whom I could send off to the heroic deeds of war! But I'm too young and silly for this, and I can only love and pray for all of Russia and all the warriors.[32]

The spring of 1919 had indeed witnessed great success for Kolchak's army. In April, his army of 110,000 men, the largest of the anti-Bolshevik armies, pushed well beyond the Urals west into the Orenburg steppes. They had driven back the Fifth and Second Red armies and retaken almost two hundred thousand square miles of territory.[33] The advance units were only fifty miles outside Kazan and close to linking up with the Russo-Allied forces in northern Russia. But this was to be the high point of Kolchak's offensive. During the late spring and summer, the Bolsheviks sent some 100,000 party workers, Communist Youth League members, and peasants to stop Kolchak's advance. The propaganda train *October Revolution* published a special appeal to rouse their fighting spirit: "Peasants! It is now your turn to defend what the Revolution has won for you. Kolchak is coming to take away your lands and to make you slaves of the landlords and village police chiefs again. Poor peasants to arms! Everyone into the battle against Kolchak!"[34]

This was effective, if less than truthful, propaganda. Indeed, it was one of Kolchak's, as well as Denikin's, weaknesses that he assumed power and led the campaign against the Bolsheviks with no clear political program. "Neither the path of reaction nor the fatal course of partisan politics," Kolchak stated. "My main objective will be to organize an effective army [and] to triumph over Bolshevism."[35] Trying to represent all the myriad forces opposed to the Bolsheviks, Kolchak and the other White leaders ended up representing no one, which was of crucial importance in their ultimate defeat. Kolchak soon faced unrest in his occupied territories, even in his capital of Omsk, where a revolt broke out that was brutally crushed by Kolchak's men; more than a thousand SRs and imprisoned workers were massacred. Behind his front lines between Omsk and Lake Baikal partisans harassed Kolchak's army.[36]

The same month Olga wrote the romantic lines in her diary the fighting had turned against the White forces in the area, and the family had to make plans to move. Lyubov, the children, and a few servants, together with the Lopukhins, packed up and took the train eastward to Omsk. They did not stay there long before securing places on a packed train heading to the town of Kansk, about sixteen hundred miles farther to the east. The train was filled with soldiers, whom the Golitsyn girls Marina and Olga found most exciting, and they flirted with the young officers nearly the entire month-long journey, much to their mother's displeasure.[37]

Throughout the summer of 1919, Kolchak's army kept retreating farther eastward. Confidence in Kolchak and his government eroded quickly, and his army began to disintegrate. Baron Budberg, a member of Kolchak's War Ministry, lamented the incompetence, disorganization, self-interest, and corruption he saw around him. Many in the government, he wrote, had "taken refuge in alcohol and cocaine"; they all had been "living beyond the law" for too long to be saved, and their cause had become, in his eyes, hopeless.[38] Before August was out, the Red forces had moved east of the Urals and retaken Yekaterinburg and Chelyabinsk. By late October they had almost reached Omsk.

Alexander had remained behind in Tyumen to help oversee the evacuation of the military hospital in advance of the Reds' march on the city. The staff loaded the wounded men into thirty freight cars filled with nothing but straw and then headed out for Krasnoyarsk. The journey took three weeks, and the rough swaying and clanking of the cars were misery for the sick and injured men. As soon as they settled the wounded in Krasnoyarsk, Alexander left to see his family in Kansk in late August. He stayed only several days but promised to return in a few months. In fact, he was not to see his family for more than a year.[39] From Kansk Alexander traveled to Omsk to work in the hospitals, then overrun with typhus. He remained until November, when the city was evacuated again. The evacuation had been announced at the end of October. Soon a mass withdrawal began; panic gripped the city, and people began to flee by whatever means possible.[40] Alexander stayed with his men and made sure that all of the sick and wounded were safely placed on trains and evacuated. Alexander and part of the staff then took off across the snow on several sleighs; they could make out advance units of Tukhachevsky's Red Fifth Army approaching on the horizon. Along with Alexander rode tens of thousands of Kolchak's soldiers. The sight of this vast movement reminded him of Napoleon's retreat from Moscow in 1812. As they rode, Alexander was comforted by the thought that they were moving closer to his family.

> I tried not to think much of the disaster, of the crash of our dreams of defeating Bolshevism and liberating Russia. A vague hope that something might befall to save the situation, some foreign interference, some new upsurge of energy of the defeated army, the change of the Commander-in-Chief—a miracle in short. In such an epoch as this, one becomes a fatalist and one begins to hope, that the strokes of fate are not always merciless.[41]

The next day caught them in a blizzard. They trudged on to the east, but the wind and snow made it hard going. Desperately cold in the open sleighs, the men climbed down to walk for stretches in an attempt to warm themselves. They journeyed through the bitter cold for a week, usually sleeping outside in the open around a fire. At times they had trouble finding enough forage for the horses. Finally, after three weeks, they reached Novo-Nikolaevsk (now Novosibirsk), more than halfway on the rail line from Omsk to Tomsk, only to find the town being evacuated as the Red advance across Siberia marched on. (It fell to the Red Fifth Army on December 14, 1919, along with as many as 31,000 White troops, 190 echelons of military supplies, and 30,000 corpses, dead from typhus.)[42] Alexander boarded a train with many of the others, but for days the train sat barely moving, and so, fearing capture, they got off and joined the men fleeing on foot. By now all discipline had broken down; the army had devolved into a band of wild, desperate men. Soldiers and Cossacks began to rob the villages they passed through, and the officers could do little to stop them. One night in the town of Mariinsk the soldiers took over a distillery and drank it dry. There was shouting and shooting all night, and the next morning many soldiers lay frozen to death in the streets.[43]

Lyubov and the rest of the family had moved from Kansk to Krasnoyarsk in the early autumn so the older children could return to school. As winter came on, the situation grew worse, and people had begun to leave the city by the beginning of December. Lyubov did not know what to do. Alexander had promised to meet up with them by December 24, yet the date had come and gone, and they had no word from him. Nikolai and his family had already left Krasnoyarsk. They were joined by Yevgenia Pisarev and the others who had left Moscow with them two years earlier; also joining them was Pierre Gilliard, a former French-language tutor to the tsar's children.

It pained them all to leave Lyubov and her children behind, but she refused to go, even after a note from Alexander arrived, begging her to take the children and leave without him.[44] Finally, as the situation became perilous and their chances of avoiding the Red Army were nearly exhausted, Lyubov decided they too would have to make their escape. They barely got away in time. In the first days of January 1920, the city fell to anti-Kolchak forces; the escape route to the east was blocked. On the eighth, the Red Fifth Army marched into Krasnoyarsk and took more than sixty thousand prisoners.[45] By now all civilian rail traffic had stopped in Siberia, and only military trains were moving. Lyubov was taken in by a Czech officer, who promised to take them as soon as the army evacuated.[46] Some of the White Army waited too long to make their escape by train and were forced to escape across the snow in sledges. For five weeks they trekked through the frozen wastes before reaching Lake Baikal.[47]

Home for many Russians caught up in the war in Siberia was a boxcar. By the time they left Krasnoyarsk in late 1919 the Golitsyns and Lopukhins had been living in such a car for many months. The boxcars were preferred over the few remaining passenger cars since these were infected by lice that carried the danger of typhus. Each car could hold up to sixty people, thirty with luggage. The occupants created their own intimate world in these rustic surroundings, with special rules and a distinctive order and even its own kind of beauty. They would fashion cozy little "nests" of rugs or shawls on the bunks and shelves that ran along both sides of the car. Refugees who had more space created whole living rooms with upholstered furniture, heavy felt and rugs on the floor, shawls decorating the walls, and kerosene lamps with shades.

The cars were so cramped that people began to learn a whole new way of inhabiting space. One made certain to keep one's arms and hands down, close to the body, to make small, contained movements so as not to get into others' personal space. The Golitsyns' servant Liza fashioned curtains out of sheets so they could have privacy to change and wash in a small basin. Since the cars were not heated, a wood-burning stove was installed in the middle with a stovepipe running up through the roof or a window. It was intensely hot near the stove, but ice cold in the corners and on the upper bunks, where the children slept. The coldest place was near the windows, which were frozen over. Fur coats were put up against the walls to try to keep out the cold, and the children would awaken in the morning under frozen blankets. One person would be in charge of tending the fire, and God forbid he let it go out, for this would bring the wrath of the entire car down upon him. Everything happened around the heat of the stove: food was cleaned, prepared, and cooked; dishes were scrubbed, clothes and bodies washed (as well as possible); firewood was chopped and coal broken up into smaller pieces. Smoke invariably hung in the air, and the faces of the passengers were dirty with soot.

The doors often had to be locked while the train was in a station to keep people from climbing in. Occasionally, the doors would be opened so the travelers could go barter for food. The diet was typically rusk with tea and a bit of milk, if it could be acquired from the peasants. Eggs and, even more rarely, boiled meat or potatoes were a luxury. Lyubov once traded clothes with villagers for a dozen geese and frozen cranberries, which they found especially delicious. The Lopukhins managed to get hold of an entire ox carcass, which they hauled up to the top of the boxcar; the Siberian winter made for the perfect freezer. At stops, they would open the door and one of them would clamber up on top and hack off some pieces of frozen meat for boiling on the stove. The Siberian winter was so bitterly cold that if the train sat too long, it would freeze to the tracks and it would take a long time to get it going again. From their car the Golitsyns often saw sleighs of refugees, all bundled up, nothing visible but their faces, blackened from frostbite, passing across the snow.[48]

Stops were also opportunities to hunt for firewood, usually acquired by ripping apart nearby fences. Fear set in whenever the fuel supply ran low; at times, the bunks had to be taken from the walls and chopped up to feed the stove. Sometimes the locomotives ran out of fuel, and then everyone had to climb out of the cars and head to the nearest stand of trees to gather wood. If there was none to be had, the train would sit motionless until another came up from behind to push it to the next village or until they were set upon by an enemy or band of partisans.[49]

Alexander Golitsyn found the communal life in the boxcars depressing.[50] Often the trains stopped for long stretches because of lack of fuel or a breakdown on the line. Alexander remembered:

The train is stopped in the steppe; a snowstorm is howling; it is warm in the box car, a kerosene lamp burns, or if there isn't one—candles; while outside a line of sleds full of soldiers of the retreating army passes. One wants to join them, even in the bitter cold. Anything not to be standing still. In the end, that was what I did (near Novo-Nikolaevsk) when during one period of ten days we travelled only 100 versts* and were almost captured by the Reds.[51]

*Ninety-six miles.

Lyubov, on the other hand, recalled her months in the boxcars as a period of rare beauty. "Everything had a special aura of love," she remembered, "and somehow torn away from reality as if it was not of this life." Although they had very little, everyone was happy to share with others and to make sacrifices, even for strangers. They could often hear the soldiers singing, and they gazed with wonderment at Lake Baikal as they rode along its frozen shores. "Sometimes in the evening, when the sun was setting, the mood was quite evocatively poetic. [. . .] It was a time of love and helpfulness to each other. And living close to nature, all around." Soon after leaving Krasnoyarsk, they stopped alongside a railcar carrying YMCA aid workers. Among them was a young American, who gave them a small Christmas tree decorated with chocolate bars and cigarettes and canned meat that allowed the Golitsyns to enjoy an unexpected Christmas feast.[52]

Kolchak fled Omsk on November 14 just hours before the Red Army, carrying with him the remains of the large imperial gold reserves (more than four hundred million gold rubles' worth of bullion and coinage) seized the previous year in Kazan by the Komuch government. The thirty-six heavily laden cars slowed his movement to a dangerously slow pace. He set out to meet the rest of his ministers, who had left earlier for Irkutsk, but the Czechs and rebellious railroad workers repeatedly stopped and diverted his train onto sidings. From behind, Red forces chased after, at times even capturing some of the trains fleeing Omsk together with Kolchak. Kolchak's train traveled for a month yet had still not reached Irkutsk, some 1,534 miles east of Omsk, where the remains of his government were awaiting him. His men began to desert his train to join the Bolsheviks.[53]

The Lopukhins and Yevgenia Pisarev managed to attach their boxcar to a train following directly behind that of Kolchak. At first it seemed like a good idea since being part of Kolchak's convoy led by his armor-plated engine bristling with cannons would provide them excellent protection. But Kolchak was also the primary target of the hostile forces all around them. The train moved slowly and stopped for long periods as Kolchak tried to determine whether it was safe to move forward. There was no good information on what was happening up ahead, though there were rumors of battles with the Reds in Irkutsk.

Gunfire could be heard close by. Apprehension and then fear spread throughout the train.

They had traveled only a few days before Kolchak's trains stopped in Nizhneudinsk, not quite halfway between Krasnoyarsk and Irkutsk. The Czechs had blocked Kolchak from moving, in part to ingratiate themselves with the new anti-Kolchak leaders in Irkutsk, whose permission the Czechs needed to continue their trek to the coast. From her car Yevgenia could see Kolchak's men leaving the train and drifting away; his personal band marched off into the nearby Bolshevik-controlled town playing the "Marseillaise." She and the others realized that if they were to keep moving east, they had to uncouple their car and try to join a different train convoy. Eventually, they convinced the Americans to attach their boxcar to their train, and after several tense days they finally left Nizhneudinsk and Kolchak behind. In the first week of 1920, Kolchak's government collapsed and the former "Supreme Leader" was taken to Irkutsk and handed over to the new Soviet government. He had had opportunities to attempt an escape but, determined to accept what fate awaited him, had refused to take them. Kolchak was interrogated and then taken out into the bitter cold morning of February 7, 1920, and shot by members of the newly established Irkutsk Military Revolutionary Committee. One of Kolchak's executioners recalled how he had bravely refused a blindfold and stood erectly, calmly waiting to be shot, "like an Englishman." They tossed his body into a hole in the ice of the Ushakovka River.[54]

At Irkutsk Yevgenia and the Lopukhins were forced to stop and once again find a new train to attach their car to. Thanks to the efforts of Pierre Gilliard, General Maurice Janin, the French commander in Siberia, agreed to take them, though only the women; Nikolai managed to talk his way onto a Red Cross train, narrowly escaping arrest as they resumed their journey. On the last day of 1919, Yevgenia wrote in her diary: "The farther we ride, the more hopeless, the murkier the future presents itself to us. Kolya* dreams of America. If we encounter SRs in Vladivostok, he won't be able to stay there and would like to try to reach America. [...] We've all decided to go to bed earlier than usual so we won't have to meet the new year."[55]

Passing Lake Baikal, they entered the territory of Ataman Semenov,

*Nikolai Lopukhin.

appointed head of the White forces in Siberia by Kolchak before his arrest. The stories told of Semenov's savagery were bloodcurdling. "They rob, they burn villages to pacify the inhabitants, and they turn everyone against them," Yevgenia wrote. "Semenov's savage division consists of Buryats and officers no less savage than the savage Buryats themselves. [. . .] I've heard soul-chilling stories of the deeds of the Semyonovtsy. They are tales straight out of the Middle Ages, with torture-chambers and not only individuals but entire groups disappearing without a trace."[56]

The stories were not exaggerations. Such was the ferocity of the civil war that victims were frequently tortured in the most grisly fashion. Mutilation of the still living was not rare. Heads and limbs were hacked off; faces bashed in, the sexual organs of men and women violated and cut off. Some people were scalped; some burned alive.[57] One witness to Semenov's atrocities claimed the ataman liked to brag that he could sleep peacefully at night only if he had killed someone that day.[58] Paul Rodzianko, a former tsarist officer, witnessed the horrors in Siberia. In his memoirs, he wrote, "The spirit of personal revenge is so deep in human nature that even military discipline cannot curb it. When our soldiers found comrades or relations mutilated they could not resist the desire to inflict suffering back. Red hate and White hate raged side by side through the beautiful wild country."[59] After the White forces entered Yekaterinburg in July 1919, they carried out a pogrom that left more than two thousand dead, most of them Jews. That same year Whites in Yalta hanged a seventeen-year-old boy for the sole reason that his surname, Bronstein, was the same as Trotsky's.[60]

Appalled and frightened by the barbarism of Semenov, Yevgenia was also saddened by the news from Russia. In early January, she learned that Denikin and his army had abandoned southern Russia and were retreating to the Crimea and Caucasus. "Our last hope has died!" she cried. "Oh, Lord, can it be that our loved ones in the Caucasus will once more fall into the hands of the Bolsheviks?" Given the confusion around them, they could not decide whether to make for Vladivostok or the city of Harbin, in Manchuria.[61] For several days they stopped in Petrovsky Zavod, a picturesque town that had been the home of the Decembrists, the first Russian revolutionaries exiled to Siberia by Tsar Nicholas I a century earlier. Being in this place filled with memories of these aristocratic exiles gave Yevgenia and Nikolai hope and strength. "One feels that their spirit is alive," Yevgenia wrote, "and thus we exiles feel better here, we find it easier to bear our cross, having such an example before our eyes."[62]

By the middle of January they had left behind the heavy forests of Siberia and come out into the barren steppe of Manchuria. Camels dotted the landscape. The local people, in long blue and black gowns and braids, came to look at the trains filled with bedraggled Russian refuges and sell them food.[63] On February 1, after six weeks' travel, Yevgenia, Nikolai, and the others finally reached Harbin.[64] Two months later, to the great surprise and delight of their friends, Lyubov and the children arrived as well.[65]

Harbin had been a small village until the turn of the twentieth century, when the Chinese granted the Russians a concession to construct a rail line to connect the Trans-Siberian Railway to Vladivostok via Manchuria, thus drastically reducing the distance of the original route. Harbin grew rapidly, and by the outbreak of the First World War it was home to more Russians than Chinese. Well into the twentieth century, it was one of the major centers of Russian émigré life, thanks largely to the stream of refugees fleeing the chaos and fighting of the civil war in Siberia.[66]

After years of deprivation, Harbin appeared like an oasis of calm, orderliness, and abundance. The Golitsyns and Lopukhins were amazed by the goods and food available in the stores and shops. "I have never in my life seen such a quantity of bread," gasped Yevgenia. But prices were high, they all were running out of money, and many did not know how they might earn a living. For some like Yevgenia, after having lived for so long in the world of the boxcars, the transition back to normal life was not easy. "In the end, despite the dark, the damp, and the cold of our boxcar," Yevgenia admitted, "nonetheless I had grown accustomed to it. In the last days our Tyumen family had lived in it so happily, so pleasantly. The walls of our boxcar did indeed protect us against all difficulties and life's hopelessness, and now we must plunge back into life."[67]

Plunging back into life meant in large part deciding whether one intended to stay in Harbin, travel on to America or Europe, or consider making peace with the revolution and returning to Russia. It was this last option that with a heavy heart Yevgenia assumed would eventually be their fate. But Yevgenia never did return to Russia. Instead, she joined

Georgy Lvov in Paris, to share his final few years with him in a house near the Bois de Boulogne.[68]

Unable to catch up with his family in December 1919, Alexander and his small party arrived at the town of Achinsk, some one hundred miles west of Krasnoyarsk, at the beginning of January. They were urged to leave immediately since the Reds were not far off, but their horses were exhausted, and so they had no choice but to stay. That night they heard shooting and several loud explosions. When they awoke the next morning, Red soldiers were entering the town. For a minute, Alexander thought of trying to run, but it was too late. They were trapped. They immediately burned all compromising papers, unharnessed the horses, unpacked their medical supplies, and hung out the Red Cross flag. Several soldiers showed up and marched them off to the commandant to register. "Prince Golitsyn?" the commandant asked Alexander. "No, Dr. Golitsyn," he replied. The commandant informed Alexander that they would be using him to help fight the new enemy, typhus, now that the Whites had been defeated, and so they were sending him to Krasnoyarsk. At the rail station he came upon a ghastly sight: a car loaded with dynamite had exploded next to a train packed with refugees days earlier. Hundreds of people had been blown to pieces, and their bodies still lay about the tracks.

On the trip to Krasnoyarsk they passed the remains of Kolchak's army and more corpses and dead horses. They heard stories of coachmen frozen stiff still gripping the reins of horses coated in ice and of a carriage with a frozen young woman clutching her dead baby in her arms. Upon reaching Krasnoyarsk, Alexander was given permission to go look for his family, but when he found the place, the people living there told him they had left two weeks earlier. He asked where they had gone, but all they could tell him was that Lyubov had spoken about going to Vladivostok. Distressed at having missed them, Alexander was glad they were at least safe.[69]

Alexander was next taken to Irkutsk and put to work in a Red Army military hospital. All the while, he plotted his escape. He fell ill with typhus after several months and could no longer work; that, paradoxically, helped save his life. He managed to obtain false documents in the name of Serebriakov and secure a place on a train carrying former

German prisoners of war and Russian nonmilitary invalids bound for Vladivostok. Emaciated, ill, and dirty, Alexander convinced the Cheka agents screening the passengers that he was indeed at death's door and of no use or danger to the Bolsheviks. He traveled for fifteen days, and past several more Cheka inspections, before arriving in Vladivostok, then under the control of Ataman Semenov. From there Alexander was able to make his way to Harbin, where he arrived in September 1920. It had been more than a year since he had last seen his wife and children.[70]

There had been another Prince Golitsyn in Irkutsk who was not so fortunate. Prince Lev Golitsyn, the last tsarist governor of Samara, had fled to Siberia with his family in the autumn of 1918. Like Alexander's family, their distant relations, Prince Lev and his family tried to stay a step ahead of the Reds in Siberia, traveling by rail, sledge, and even horseback. Lev served in Kolchak's army as a representative of the Red Cross. After Kolchak's collapse, the family ended up in Krasnoyarsk, where Lev found work in the Veterinary Department of the Red Fifth Army, charged with procuring horses for the army. The whole time Lev was under the surveillance of the Cheka and spied on by secret informers. He was arrested on May 14, 1920, as a "White Guard" and "Kolchak's Hangman," the latter a result of mistaken identity. The family saw him off to the rail station in early June 1920, when he was sent to Irkutsk. "God be with you," were his last words to them. He died that same month of typhus in the prison infirmary.[71]

Reunited with his family, Alexander set up a medical practice caring for the city's large number of refugees. Life was difficult, but nothing like what the villagers faced back at their former estate of Petrovskoe. Three years since the last Golitsyn had been forced off the estate, the overseer continued to write to Alexander and Lyubov of the dreadful conditions. All the art and furnishings had been stolen long ago and now decorated the homes of the villagers and the former estate employees. What remained in the house had been smashed and destroyed. The pages from the books in the library had been torn out to roll cigarettes, and the large archive, including maps from Napoleon's marshals, had been burned to feed the ovens and stoves. The glass had been broken out of all the windows; the woods cut down, loaded on wagons, and hauled off to Moscow for firewood.

After a year and a half fighting with the Red Army, the former butler, Ivan Kuznetsov, wrote the Golitsyns in July 1922 upon his return to Petrovskoe. He was motivated to write after so many years, he said, after attending a service in the church on St. Peter's Day. Seeing the church "lit by candles," he wrote, "reminded me of old times and of you." He went on: "The house is very spoiled and I even shed a few tears when I saw for the first time what had become of the place. In many rooms there are stoves which are heated in the winter and everything is black with soot. Outside the plaster has fallen off in places and the windows are broken and boarded up. The door handles have been pulled off and they are closed with string." He noted the people were still hungry and tea and white bread were prohibitively expensive. He asked Alexander and Lyubov to recall his former service and to find it in their hearts to send him whatever clothes they could spare, for his had been reduced to rags and he had no money to buy any new ones. "I don't know how we are going to survive," he cried.[72]

Alexander and Lyubov settled into life in Harbin. He began teaching anatomy at the Harbin Medical School and was also hired to work as a medical officer at the British consulate. Times were still hard, however. Lyubov wrote her brother-in-law Mikhail Golitsyn back in Moscow in November 1922 to tell him things had taken a turn for the worse. Once more they were facing "troubling and difficult times," and she doubted whether they would be able to remain in Harbin. They wanted to return to the family in Moscow, but none of them could imagine trying to make the trip back across Siberia after what they had been through.[73] Their salvation came in the form of the Red Cross, which engaged Alexander to find a home in Canada or the United States for the many refugees in Harbin and Manchuria. It was as a Red Cross representative that he left Manchuria for the United States, arriving in Seattle on the *President Madison* on October 7, 1923, with three hundred dollars in his pocket. A week later Alexander renounced his Russian citizenship. Lyubov and the children joined him in America the following year.[74]

13

EXODUS

In June 1918, Ivan Bunin and his wife, Vera, arrived in Odessa from Moscow. They found a nice apartment, furnished it with antiques, and hired a maid as if nothing had changed. Their home became a meeting place for politicians and intellectuals like General Baron Peter Wrangel, the writers Count Alexei Tolstoy and Konstantin Paustovsky, and Olga Knipper, the actress widow of Chekhov.[1] Despite his own material comfort and safety, Bunin was pained to be so far from his family, living under the Bolsheviks: "I send my soul over thousands of miles, into the night, the darkness, and the unknown so that I will be with my family and loved ones, and so that I can express my fear for them, my love for them, my agony for them, and my hope that God will save and protect them."[2]

Bunin would have reason to fear for himself too. In the spring of 1919, the Red Army took Odessa. His friends had urged Bunin to escape before it was too late, yet he had refused. Even though he was in danger as a nobleman and fierce critic of the new regime, Bunin would not consider going into hiding. After intervention from a friend, Lunacharsky telegraphed a protection order for posting on the Bunins' apartment door. The order did little good, and the Bunins were subjected to humiliating searches. Bunin and his wife had experienced life under the Reds before in Moscow, and they now recalled that same sense of "airlessness" they had felt earlier.[3]

The Bunins remained in Odessa for a year and a half. Bunin

watched intently what was happening around them, committing his thoughts and observations to his diary. He noted the signs and banners that appeared in the city streets: "Death to the Bourgeois," for example, and "One of Ours, Ten of Theirs." He recorded how the day before Easter decrees requiring all bourgeois under the age of forty to come out the next day to clean the streets were posted throughout the city.[4] He saw a large poster on Cathedral Square that contrasted "1918," represented by a fat bourgeois holding a worker by the collar, with "1919," that showed the same bourgeois now sweeping the street as the worker looked on; the statue of Catherine the Great was draped in a "great overcoat" with a large poster behind it reading, "The thrones are covered with the people's blood. We will cover our enemies with blood." A banner atop the London Hotel proclaimed: "Peace to the huts, War on the palaces." Bunin found it ironic that many of the posters and banners were the work of "children of the rich bourgeois," the only ones with the requisite art training and now desperate to earn some money.[5]

That spring the Military Revolutionary Tribunal ordered eighteen "counterrevolutionaries" shot; soon after, an order requiring the registration of all "bourgeois" was published. Panic struck the city, and no one was quite sure what to make of these orders. Bunin's doorman told him that the following day was to "truly be the end of the world: it will be the 'Day of Peaceful Insurrection' when every last bourgeois will be stripped of his things." The next day Bunin's friend David Shpitalnikov, a literary critic, showed up. He too had heard about the Day of Peaceful Insurrection and had furtively put on his last two pairs of trousers in case a search was made of his apartment. Later in the afternoon, the insurrection was called off after some workers had apparently revolted upon learning that they were about to be dispossessed of some goods they had just stolen themselves.[6]

Bunin reveled in pointing out the hypocrisy of Red leaders who preached "war on the palaces" and then moved into them as soon as the owners had been evicted.[7] He was revolted by this "new aristocracy": "Sailors with huge revolvers on their belts, pickpockets, criminal villains, and shaved dandies in service jackets, depraved-looking riding britches, and dandy-like shoes with the inevitable spurs. All have gold teeth and big, dark, cocaine-like eyes."[8] The Bolsheviks played to the mob's basest instincts and understood the Russians' psychology.

"Three-quarters of the people are like that: for crumbs or the right to pillage and rob, they'll give-up their conscience, soul, and God."[9] Such a way of thinking was a social, and moral, disease; moreover, as Bunin saw, it would not lift the country out of its misery: "Bolshevism is a revolution, all right, the very same revolution which forever gladdens those who do not have a present, who have a past that is always 'cursed' and a future that is always 'bright' . . . 'Seven lean cows will devour seven fat ones—but they themselves will not become fat.'"[10]

At the same time Bunin criticized the Bolsheviks and their supporters, he felt estranged from their enemies and refused to place himself in their camp. After the Whites reclaimed Odessa in the late summer of 1919, several people came to seek Bunin's support in the struggle against bolshevism. When he asked what they stood for, they told him their party had two planks: constitutional monarchy and opposition to the Jews. Bunin had long spoken out against anti-Semitism and pogroms, and he refused to join any of the White political organizations since he deemed them tainted with anti-Semitism and since he wished to remain a poet, not a party person. For Bunin, the enemies of the Bolsheviks were still blind to the narod, refusing to recognize what the people were capable of, wishing instead to blame the Jews for Russia's woe. Princess Zenaida Yusupov was a good example of this way of thinking. Her diary from 1919 is littered with references to "Jew-Masons" destroying Russia; she even called U.S. President Woodrow Wilson a Jew-Mason for being against the restoration of the Romanovs. The princess was incapable of seeing how the nobility had played any part in Russia's tragedy, which she blamed solely on the people. "Cannons alone will not help in this uneven battle!" she wrote in February 1919. "What is needed is spiritual strength, the awakening faith and the repentance of the masses. Only then can we be saved!" Bunin was repulsed by such ideas, and he denounced them publicly. In November 1919 in the newspaper the *Southern Word*, for example, Bunin strongly condemned the White anti-Jewish pogroms that had swept across Ukraine that year.[11]

The plight of Russia's Jews in the twentieth century cannot be overstated. Even before the Second World War they had been subjected to successive waves of violence that left many thousands dead and even more homeless. Pogroms erupted in the villages of Ukraine and Bessarabia (where most of the empire's Jews lived) in 1903 and again during the

Revolution of 1905. To the authorities, the Jews were themselves to blame. Tsar Nicholas told his minister of war after a particularly repugnant pogrom in Kishinev in 1903 that the attacks had been warranted, for "the Jews needed to be taught a lesson because they had been putting on airs and leading the revolutionary movement." But as bad as anti-Jewish violence had been under the tsars, it exploded with the collapse of any central authority. In the cauldron of the civil war, the Jews became defenseless scapegoats. The atrocities reached their height in 1919. Homes were destroyed, women and girls were raped and mutilated; entire families were brutally murdered. Much of the barbarity was carried out by the Whites who believed bolshevism to be a Jewish plot against Christian Russia. Nevertheless, Jews were attacked from all sides and by all social classes; neither the Whites nor the old Russian elite ever had a monopoly on anti-Semitism. Indeed, almost three hundred years earlier Cossack and peasant rebels fighting for control of Ukraine under Bogdan Khmelnitsky had massacred untold numbers of Jews, perhaps well over one hundred thousand.[12]

To Bunin, such a bloody history proved that the revolutions of 1917 and the subsequent violence did not represent a departure for Russia, rather a continuation of ancient cycles. "Russian history," he insisted, "has always been a terrible tragedy."[13] In "The Great Narcotic," published on December 7, 1919, Bunin described what he saw as an age-old Russian pattern of lurching from one extreme to another, one day carousing, robbing, and murdering and then the next being overcome with "terrible hangovers," "frenzied sentimentality," and "repentant tears."[14] No one was blameless for this tragic cycle. Everyone, including Bunin himself, had been, in his estimation, blind to the troubles in Russia, blind out of inertia and fear and self-interest. They, especially the elite, the nobility, had lived frivolously and failed to put in the hard work that might have saved the country.[15]

On February 7, 1920, as the Red Army was entering Odessa for the second and final time, Bunin and his wife boarded a ship and sailed off into exile. "This is the last time I will see the Russian shore. I burst out crying. We are on the open sea. How this trip differs from earlier ones. Before us are darkness and terror. Behind us—horror and hopelessness. I continue to worry about those who have been left behind. Did they manage to save themselves?"[16] Nevertheless, Bunin never lost faith in Russia: "I will never accept that Russia has been destroyed."[17]

By the beginning of 1920 it was increasingly clear that the Red Army was winning the war. The reasons for the Red victory were many, but perhaps most important was the fact that the Communists spoke more directly to the basic needs of the people, especially that of land, and offered a vision of the future that was more compelling than the murky promise of the Whites.[18] Prince Pavel Shcherbatov put it succinctly in early 1920 when he said, "The White army will lose since it is fighting behind an empty banner."[19] Baron Wrangel echoed this sentiment years later when he attributed the main cause for the Whites' failure to their lack of regard for "the state of feeling among the masses of the people."[20]

As the Red Army pushed back the forces of first Denikin and then Wrangel, a mass exodus from southern Russia and the Crimea began in the spring of 1919. It lasted for more than a year. After their frightening escape from the northern Caucasus, the family of Dmitry Sheremetev managed to reach the Crimea in early 1919. Dmitry and Ira and Ira's mother settled in the Vorontsov palace at Alupka; their daughter Lili Vyazemsky and her mother-in-law, Princess Maria Vyazemsky, were put up in a house on the grounds of the Yusupov estate of Koreiz, near Yalta. They told their friends of their harrowing experiences in the northern Caucasus and how they were glad to have escaped with their lives.[21] The Crimea was then home to many aristocrats and members of the Romanov family, including Dowager Empress Maria Fyodorovna, her daughter Grand Duchess Xenia, and Grand Dukes Nikolai and Pyotr Nikolaevich, who had settled at the estates of Ai Todor and Dulber. With the sound of gunfire approaching the coast on the night of April 6, the decision was made to evacuate the imperial family. The Romanovs and a few others embarked on the British battleship HMS *Marlborough* on the seventh and motored a short way to Yalta. It was from here, on the morning of April 11, that the Romanovs finally sailed into exile.[22]

The Sheremetevs left Yalta that same day. Dmitry and the boys sailed on the British destroyer *Speedy*, and Ira and the girls, on the *Princess Inna*. The family reunited in Constantinople before continuing on together to the Princes' Islands in the Sea of Marmara. (Ten years later another Russian political exile, Leon Trotsky, landed on one of the islands and spent the next four years of his life there.) Along the way they passed the *Marlborough*, and the passengers of the *Speedy* sent Dmitry to personally thank the dowager empress for her reluctance to depart Yalta until everyone wishing to leave had been evacuated.[23]

Easter 1919 found the Sheremetevs along with several hundred other Russian exiles on the SS *Bermudian* anchored in the Golden Horn off Constantinople. A candlelight vesper service was conducted on the ship's deck underneath the minarets of Hagia Sophia. A service was also held that day in the dining room of the dowager empress aboard the *Marlborough*. Princess Zenaida Yusupov recorded how they all, including Maria Fyodorovna, had tears in their eyes. "It is impossible for all of us not to cry for our dear past, which will never return," she wrote in her diary. (And it was not just her past that the princess regretted having left behind. Upon disembarking the next day at Malta, she was amazed to see how much baggage the imperial family had managed to take with them. "If I had known that they had so many trunks," the princess huffed, "I wouldn't have left so many of our own possessions behind for the Bolsheviks!")[24]

The Sheremetevs reached Malta toward the end of April and from there sailed on to the Continent. Thanks to some shares in a Baku oil company they had taken with them, Dmitry and Ira had enough money to buy a house in Cap d'Antibes. They remained there for several years until the money ran out and then moved to Rome, where their daughter Praskovya was engaged to Grand Duke Roman Petrovich of Russia, the son of Grand Duke Pyotr Nikolaevich and Grand Duchess Milica Nikolaevna (née princess of Montenegro). In 1926, Dmitry became the first chairman of the Union of the Russian Nobility in Emigration.[25] He died and was buried in Rome in 1943; Ira followed in 1959. Their son Sergei fought in the civil war before settling in Italy with his parents. Another son, Nikolai, married Princess Irina Yusupov, the only daughter of Prince Felix Yusupov, Rasputin's murderer, and went to work as a captain's assistant for a number of cruise lines. Vasily, their youngest child, found work as a chauffeur. Later he and his wife, Daria Tatishchev, purchased a farm and vineyard and ran a small inn in the Savoy region of France before moving to Paris around 1941.[26]

Few, if any, of the Russian exiles left happily, and many abhorred the thought of quitting their homeland; leaving was a last resort. Prince

Vladimir Obolensky, a longtime radical who had been arrested and exiled under the tsar, found himself in the Crimea as the Reds approached. He had never wanted to leave Russia, calling it "degrading to flee across the border just to save one's own skin." He had even refused a passport and a chance to leave earlier. But when his two sons suddenly appeared, having fought for the Whites, been captured by the Red Army, and then escaped to their father for protection, he felt it was his duty to help them out to safety. And so, reluctantly, he left Russia in November 1920. Like most of those sailing away across the Black Sea, Obolensky could not imagine that he was leaving for good.[27]

Some did sense they were parting with Russia forever. Yelizaveta Rodzianko sailed from the Crimea on the steamer *Hamburg* on February 16, 1920. As the sun faded in the cold sky, she watched the coast slip away. She found it beautiful. "I understood that I was seeing this beauty in all likelihood for the last time, that I would probably never return to Russia, that it was as if we were sailing off into space . . . I even tried to summon from within myself a feeling of grief at parting with my Motherland . . . But I could only feel one thing: happiness that we had escaped, that we were leaving, and taking our children with us."[28]

As he saw the Crimean coast shrinking away Prince Andrei Lobanov-Rostovsky listened to the men on deck around him talking about how they would be returning to Russia in triumph before two months were out. The prince disagreed. He knew then they were leaving for good.

> I had saved my life, but it was dreadful to feel at twenty-eight that one was a living dead man. The fate of belonging to a class which, to use the picturesque expression of Trotsky, was headed for the dustbin of history was too overwhelming. In my dreams I had only wanted to serve my people, however small my place might be; instead I had fought them and had been cast out. In a gale only oaks and reeds can think of resisting; leaves are blown away and go where the wind wills, I said to myself.[29]

Leaving was especially hard for those exiles with family still in Russia. As they passed Constantinople, Dmitry Sheremetev could not help thinking of his mother. She had been born in the Turkish capital, and

Dmitry wondered how she was faring back in Moscow and if he would ever see her again. Prince Vladimir Emanuelovich Golitsyn left the Crimea with his wife and children the day after the *Marlborough* had sailed. A few nights before leaving, he dreamed of his brother back in Russia.

> I saw Niki in my dream: as if he was in prison, and when I came to him he was making his toilet as usual, i.e., washing his torso, hauling down his night shirt. His cheeks were hollow, and he was absolutely pathetic and indifferent to everything around him. [. . .] I cried at his sight and was suggested to share his fate if I felt so sorry for him. But I saw dear Niki so clearly although I have not seen him in truth for almost three years now![30]

(Niki—Prince Nikolai Emanuelovich Golitsyn—was indeed imprisoned in 1919 and then again repeatedly throughout the 1920s. His brother eventually managed to help Nikolai and his family escape the Soviet Union in 1932, thanks to a personal appeal to Stalin by German President Hindenburg.[31])

The final evacuation of the Crimea took place in mid-November 1920 under General Wrangel. As they prepared to leave, Wrangel invited to join them all those who would be in danger were they to fall into the enemy's hands. In the span of a few days, 146,000 people—twice the expected number—were placed on boats and sent out over the waters of the Black Sea toward Constantinople. Wrangel embarked from Sevastopol on the cruiser *General Kornilov* on the fourteenth. "We cannot foretell our future fate," he told his fellow exiles. "May God grant us strength and wisdom to endure this period of Russian misery, and to survive it."[32]

The Russians who fled the approaching Red Army were not exaggerating the danger. Although Mikhail Frunze, the Red commander, had issued generous surrender terms, approximately fifty thousand people—most members of the former privileged classes—were shot or hanged during the final weeks of 1920. As the Red Army moved into the Crimea, the Cheka began registering the cities' inhabitants and dividing them into three categories: those to be shot; those to be sent to concentration camps; those to be spared.[33] All former White officers were ordered to appear for registration and promised safety. The several thousand who complied were arrested and then taken out over the course of several nights and murdered.[34] No one was safe. In Yalta in December 1920, the Bolsheviks even shot eighty-four-year-old Princess Nadezhda Baryatinsky, along with her daughter and son-in-law.[35]

The killing of former White officers across Russia continued until 1922, despite an amnesty of June 1920 extended to all White officers and soldiers. In Yekaterinodar, about three thousand officers were shot; in Odessa as many as two thousand; in Yekaterinburg, twenty-eight hundred. The worst, however, was in the Crimea, where as many as fifty thousand officers and officials were executed.[36] Justification, after a fashion, for the executions was made with a November 1921 modification to the June 1920 amnesty, according to which all those who had voluntarily fought with the White armies for "the goal of defending their class interests and the bourgeois order" were no longer covered by the amnesty and were henceforth to be deemed "outcasts."[37]

Around the time the White Army under Wrangel was abandoning the fight, the White forces collapsed in Siberia. Ataman Semenov was run out of his capital in Chita on October 22, 1920, and what remained of his forces fled to Manchuria. In one of the most bizarre chapters of the civil war, Baron Ungern-Sternberg, a Baltic nobleman and former lieutenant of Semenov's, set up a murderous, occultic base in Outer Mongolia for attacking Soviet Russia. He was overthrown in 1921, captured, and executed. The last White outpost was in Vladivostok, ruled by one of Kolchak's generals until his defeat by the Red Army in late October 1922. With that, the White forces had been crushed, and the civil war was truly over.[38]

No accurate figures exist for how many people had abandoned Russia by the end of the war. The estimates range from five hundred thousand to three million. The exodus included Russians from all social strata; most of them were not noble, but peasants and members of the middle class.[39] Nonetheless, the majority of the Russian nobility had left the country. According to one source, by 1921 no more than 12 percent of the prerevolutionary nobility, about ten thousand families or some fifty thousand individuals, was still in Russia.[40] The revolution and civil war had torn the nobility in two; from now on the lives of mothers

and sons, brothers and sisters would move in different directions under different circumstances. A chasm began to open between the nobles who had stayed and those who had departed that grew wider in
the coming decades and left family members strangers to one another.

By January 1921, Felix Dzerzhinsky could at last boast that the exploiters of the old regime had been vanquished: "The landowners as a
class have disappeared, the bourgeoisie has been declassed, the political masters are now nonentities."[41] The *Red Newspaper* expounded on
the victory over the nobility in an article titled "Syphilis."

> The Russian nobility has died of syphilis. Yes, yes, don't be surprised,
> of syphilis. There have been such cases before in history when entire
> classes, entire social groups, have become ill with syphilis, of course,
> in the metaphorical sense—mental syphilis, moral syphilis, ethical
> syphilis—and they died slow, tragic, harrowing, terrible deaths. [. . .]
>
> In the Crimea an entire class has died an insane death from syph-
> ilis. The Russian aristocracy, that very class upon which this syphilitic
> and mad power had been based, is dead, as is the "White Movement."
> [. . .] There is no more "White Movement," for it has died its final
> death.[42]

But not everyone of this class had died or fled. Galina von Meck was
among those who remained. She observed:

> The world we knew had died, tomorrow did not exist; there was only
> today. The future was dim and the present a chaos. Yet throughout it
> all we developed a toughness, an inner resistance, which strengthened
> with the passage of time. Although many people fled the country, oth-
> ers, the brave ones, accepted the challenge of a ravaged homeland. We
> had nothing in our purses, nothing in our stoves and nothing in our
> bellies, but we were very much alive.[43]

Some in the Soviet government agreed with von Meck's final assertion,
and they were convinced that the war against the old ruling class was
not over. Rather, only the first battle of the war had been won, and a
new one was beginning, one in which the enemy would be better hidden and harder to spot but no less dangerous. In 1921, Lenin observed
that even though the noble landlords and the capitalists had been fully

expropriated and destroyed as a political class, remnants of the enemy remained. Forced to hide their identities and driven underground, some had taken up positions within the institutions of "Soviet power."[44] For Lenin, the former people left behind after the defeat of the White armies constituted a fifth column collaborating in secret with the Communists' enemies abroad. The threat of the old order entered a new phase.[45]

PART IV

NEP

We'll drink, we'll carouse, and when death comes, we'll die.
                              —Dmitry Gudovich, Kaluga, 1927

14

SCHOOL OF LIFE

After two revolutions and seven years of war, Russia in 1921 lay in ruins. The cost in human lives was staggering. Since the autumn of 1917, approximately ten million people had perished of disease, starvation, execution, and battle wounds. Millions more, many of them Russia's best educated and most skilled, had abandoned the country. The economy and industrial infrastructure were in shambles. The total value of finished products produced in 1921 amounted to a mere 16 percent of that in 1912. According to one estimate, the national income in 1920 was only 40 percent of that of 1913. The American dollar, which had traded for two rubles in 1914, was worth twelve hundred rubles in 1920. Russia's cities and towns had been emptied out; Moscow and Petrograd had lost more than half their residents. Years of fighting, followed by back-to-back droughts in 1920 and 1921, unleashed famine along the Volga River that spread to much of central and northern Russia. Such was the extent of the hunger that some Russians were driven to cannibalism. Millions died. The entire social fabric had been shredded. Families had been torn apart, and an estimated seven million orphaned children were living on the streets, begging, stealing, and selling their bodies to survive.[1]

Although they had defeated the Whites, the Communists (the Bolsheviks' new official name from 1918) faced a restive populace. In the winter of 1920–21, labor unrest erupted in several Russian cities, including Moscow and Petrograd, the cradle of the revolution. Workers went out on strike, demanding larger food rations, greater control over the workplace, and the reintroduction of civil rights. The authorities responded with violence. In Saratov, for example, 219 workers were arrested and sentenced to death, and others were sent to prison.² In March 1921, sailors at the Kronstadt naval base rebelled, demanding an end to state control of the economy and one-party rule. This uprising too was brutally crushed. Hundreds of captured sailors, the Communists' allies during the revolutionary days of 1917, were shot, and thousands sent off to concentration camps in the Russian Far North.

The greatest threat to Soviet power, however, came from the peasants. Angered over grain requisitioning and other harsh treatment, peasants rose up in armed rebellion that stretched from Ukraine to Siberia. Such was the extent of the anger toward the Communists that in certain areas they could no longer be confident of the loyalty of their own troops. In 1920 and early 1921, some of the uprisings reached massive scale. In Tambov, Alexander Antonov led an army of fifty thousand peasants, the Greens, that overthrew Communist authority throughout a sizable portion of the province. Like the workers, Russia's peasants resented not only the state's interference in their economic lives but the repression of their political rights, and some peasants even called for the reconvening of the Constituent Assembly. The authorities trembled with the gravity of the threat. "This counter-revolution is without doubt more dangerous than Denikin, Yudenich, and Kolchak taken together," Lenin warned. At a terrible cost in human lives, Red Army troops defeated the insurgents through a brutal campaign of terror, poison gas, and mass internment in concentration camps. Their ruthless methods exacerbated the famine, thus contributing to the tremendous scale of suffering and death.³

By the spring of 1921, it was clear to Lenin that the groups in whose name the Communists had seized power had turned against them. Concessions would have to be made were the Soviet state to survive. Beginning with the Tenth Party Congress that spring, Lenin introduced a series of reforms that came to be known as the New Economic Policy, or NEP. Never intended as a permanent program, NEP was conceived as a temporary retreat to allow the country to recover and the government to maintain control before returning to the full-scale construction of a socialist society. Forced grain requisitions were replaced by a tax, and the peasants were permitted to keep their surpluses and sell them for a profit on the open market. The so-called commanding heights of the economy (large- and medium-scale industry, finance, foreign trade, wholesale commerce) were retained by the state, but retail trade and small manufacturing (fewer than twenty workers) were legalized. Reform of the financial system and the introduction of the gold-backed *chervónets* as the new monetary unit brought stability and tamed the wild inflation of the civil war years. NEP proved to be immensely successful at reviving Russia's ravaged economy. Within a few years, agriculture, industry, and trade had rebounded, and the cities came back to life. Yet with economic recovery there arose a new bourgeoisie of rich traders and entrepreneurs, the Nepmen, whose wealth and ostentatious lifestyles echoed the inequities of the old regime and caused many Russians to wonder whether the promise of the revolution had been betrayed.[4]

The British reporter Walter Duranty arrived in Moscow in 1921. Among his earliest impressions of the Soviet capital was the dreadful condition of the old aristocracy. "The countesses work as servant girls and the ex-servant girls ride in government automobiles as heads of important offices," he observed.

> Most pitiable is the lot of those aristocrats, male or female, who are devoid of any qualifications of practical value. One sees them stand patiently for hours in the open-air markets holding coats, furs, small pieces of silver, or last scraps of jewelry by sale of which they can eke out existence for a few weeks longer. The New Economic Policy has given a chance to the younger ones to open restaurants, hat stores, etc. but the position of the older ones is hopeless. However pathetic may be the sight of fortune's favorites "fallen from their high estate," there is no escape from the law of the Russian hive: "The drones must die."[5]

To another Western reporter, Edwin Hullinger, the same scene testified to the revolution's great achievement. Having stripped away the institutional foundations upon which class and caste had been built, the revolution had exposed people's true essence:

This process has resulted in many startling revelations, where every man and woman, regardless of their former social caste, has been measured up in accordance with his inherent qualities and strength. [. . .] Real nobility in the primal elements of life has been brought out and enriched, made nobler than ever, whether in prince or peasant. Feebleness and smallness, formally screened by breeding or etiquette, have been exposed. [. . .] Like a giant X-ray, the Revolution has gone through the social structure, revealing the human fiber of which it was made.[6]

As proof, Hullinger quoted the words of a former countess. "Yes, many of us can see that the Revolution was for the best," she told him. "It made us into living, real people. Many were only existing before. We have gained confidence in ourselves because we know we can do things. I like it better. I would not go back to the old. And there are many young people of our class who think as I do. But we paid a terrible price. I presume it was necessary, however." Hullinger visited the apartment of an old lady-in-waiting to the empress, her daughter, and their former servant. Below the harsh glare of the single electric lightbulb illuminating their one room, the daughter told him: "We have learned to draw happiness from the littlest of things. Before a diamond piece seldom held my delight for more than a moment. Now I am made happy—so happy—by a new pair of knitted gloves, a glimpse into a foreign newspaper, or a chance smile which fate throws my way on some kind face." Struck by her words, he told them: "You have simply grown nobler."[7]

"People who had never been near a stove learned to cook," wrote Alexandra Tolstoy. "They learned to do washing, to sweep streets; they had to hunt for food, sell, exchange, travel on the roofs of trains, on the couplings. They even learned to steal. But what was to be done?"[8] As for Alexandra, she was among the down-and-out aristocrats selling her few belongings (some old shoes and dresses, a clock, teapot, and lace) on the Moscow sidewalks.

Marta Almedingen shared Alexandra's somber assessment after arriving in Moscow from Petrograd that same year.

In Moscow the vanished aristocracy in Russia went on living out their squalid existence. In Petrograd you never heard much about them, at

least not in the world I lived in. But in Moscow they seemed everywhere, crushed, piteous, and almost forsaken. It looked as though the
same city which had once surrounded them with Oriental splendor
was now determined to hug them closer and closer to her own thin
and hungry breast, sucking their mind and blood.[9]

Marta was part of a wave of former nobles who left Petrograd for Moscow in the early 1920s. The movement out of the old capital had begun
during the revolution and picked up pace during NEP. If early on
many nobles had left to try to escape the street violence and then the
attention of the Cheka, by the early 1920s they were coming back since
life in Moscow, grim as it was, was more vibrant and exciting and offered more opportunities for work and education, even if it placed
them directly in the shadow of the central authorities. Kirill Golitsyn
was one of the former nobles who departed Petrograd for Moscow
with the introduction of NEP. Moscow struck Kirill as the center of
everything. Everyone seemed to be out having fun, in cafés, restaurants,
and theaters, at dances and house parties, and Kirill wanted to be part
of the action.[10]

Like the rest of his family, Kirill considered NEP the first intelligent
act of the new Soviet state, and he arrived in Moscow in late 1922 as a
nineteen-year-old eager to take advantage of the new conditions. His
first order of business was to make some money. After years of drab
necessity, Kirill, as was true for many young Russians in those days,
wanted to discard his old clothes for something new and stylish. Education, though important, was a secondary concern.[11] Two of Kirill's
cousins, Lina Golitsyn and Alka Bobrinsky, were by then back in
Moscow, having left Bogoroditsk in 1920 to enroll at the university.
They were soon joined by other young members of their extended
family—Lina's sister Sonya, her brothers Vladimir and Sergei, Alka's
sister Sonya, Yuri and Misha Samarin, Mikhail Olsufev, and Artemy
Raevsky. They all were young, most still teenagers, and excited to be
making their own way in the world, out from under the supervision of
their parents. They settled in the old Samarin mansion on Spiridonovka Street in the city center. The house had long since been
taken over and consolidated, but they crowded into three empty
rooms on the mezzanine, creating a sort of commune of *jeunesse
déclassée*.[12]

Yuri Samarin later recalled of this time:

Thus began the era that became known as "Spiridonovki." It was a collection of carefree youth whose lives until then had been nothing more than digging up potatoes and cutting firewood. A happy and, I would say, talented life began, although it was, thanks to our young age, rather wild. In the evenings until late into the night we played all sorts of games, including charades, and would sleep till midday, when the next trader in old clothes and things would knock on the door. Then we would head for the café by Nikitsky Gates and tuck into buns and liver sausage, not seen for a long time. Taking care of business, tending to our studies, that is, preoccupied us little. [. . .] Our life was disorganized, but friendly and harmonious, and our pranks were generally in this same spirit.[13]

They were desperately poor. Lina once wrote her mother that she could not go out since the sole had come off one of her shoes and she did not have another pair or the money to repair it.[14] They sold the Samarins' remaining possessions to get by.[15] The 1920s saw a brisk trade in art, jewelry, and antiques as the old nobility unloaded for money the last of its treasures on the new rich of Soviet Russia. A key role in this trade was played by the *mákler,* or broker acting as middleman for a commission. The brokers were often people with good connections among the former nobles, individuals such as Georgy Osorgin. The Osorgins were an old provincial noble family from Kaluga, driven off their estate of Sergievskoe by the Bolsheviks in 1918. Georgy was respected for his honesty and integrity, and so he was entrusted to arrange many of these sales.[16] It was a shady business, and the sellers, including the Golitsyns, were often taken advantage of. In the early 1920s, the Golitsyns disposed of books, jewelry, tsarist medals, paintings, and silver champagne buckets. They sold the mayor's old fur coat, though they did not get as much for it as hoped because it was rather worn and dreadfully out of fashion.[17] Of course, families like the Golitsyns were among the fortunate. Some young women of the old elite had nothing to sell but their bodies. It has been estimated that more than 40 percent of the prostitutes in Moscow in the early 1920s were from the gentry or once well-off families. The American Frank Golder was appalled at the pathetic condition of young women of the old elite in Moscow, noting that even prostitution did not pay enough to save them. As another American Golder knew at the time put it, "You can get any girl for a square meal." [18]

Although poor, this young gang on Spiridonovka was happy and overflowing with enthusiasm for life's simple pleasures. The parties, games, and dancing went on almost every night, often till dawn. They were forever playing jokes and pulling pranks, gossiping, and flirting. Georgy Osorgin fell in love with Lina Golitsyn, and they married in the autumn of 1923. Their marriage ended tragically six years later.[19]

Although it needed no help, the young Russians' social life was given a boost in the late summer of 1921 with the arrival of the Americans. In response to an appeal by the Soviet Union, the United States agreed to take on a massive famine relief program in Russia. Known as the American Relief Administration (ARA), the program was led by Herbert Hoover, the future U.S. president and the country's leading figure in organizing help for Europe's starving population after World War I. The ARA, operated in Russia by three hundred American men from August 1921 to June 1923, fed eleven million people a day at its high point at a cost of sixty million dollars. The work of the ARA saved countless lives and eased the suffering of an entire nation, making its designation as the "*beau geste* of the twentieth century" justly deserved.[20]

About fifty of the American men were stationed in Moscow. They were set up in the large houses of former nobles, each given a nickname based on its colored facade: the Pink, Blue, Brown, Green, or White House. The main administration was housed at 30 Spiridonovka Street, a large gray mansion down the street from the Samarin house. The ARA hired as local guides, interpreters, translators, and secretaries many Russians, mostly women, a great number of them from the former nobility who had the requisite education and knowledge of English. No one could have imagined then that working for the ARA could have harmful consequences. Yet later, after the Americans had left, many of these Russian employees were arrested or exiled as spies.[21]

Lina and Sonya Golitsyn and Alka Bobrinsky all got jobs with the ARA. Lina wrote her mother in Bogoroditsk how excited she was to be working for the Americans since they paid "huge wages." The Russian

employees also received food parcels, and the Americans helped process aid from relatives abroad: family members could send the ARA
ten dollars, and their relations in Russia would receive the equivalent
in foodstuffs.[22] Although modest by American standards, the parcels
evoked awe among the Russians; "the food of the gods," was how Irina
Skariatina described her ARA rations.[23] The first crate of food to reach
the Golitsyns in Bogoroditsk caused a sensation. The entire family
gathered around the wooden crate emblazoned with an American flag,
opened the lid, and then stood back in wonder at its contents of canned
condensed milk, American bacon (something no one had ever seen
before), macaroni, rice, and sugar, all of it wrapped up in bright, decorative packaging.[24] Such food was not available in Moscow stores, for
any price.

The Russians found the work fun and exciting and drew satisfac-
tion from knowing they were doing something important. Kirill Golitsyn wrote of the immense impression the "elegant and independent"
Americans made on them, how they behaved so freely and spent their
money without the slightest care. They were unlike any people the
Russians had ever known.[25] Irina Tatishchev was hired as a bookkeeper
for the ARA and then promoted to secretary. She liked working with
the Americans: "They were so merry, not like all those gloomy Soviet
officials who were dominated by fear."[26] Sonya Bobrinsky worked as
the secretary to the American William Reswick. His interpreter was a
"Princess Irina," whom he described as "a girl of rare beauty from one
of Russia's great aristocratic clans whose entire family had apparently
been murdered by the peasants during the revolution." Reswick was
amazed by Irina's energy and boundless compassion for the poor and
suffering.[27]

Not all the former nobles were so enamored of their American employers, however. Yelizaveta Fen worked in Moscow for the ARA and
then for the Quakers, one of the other Western groups involved in the
aid program. Like her peers, she got the job because of her knowledge
of English and general education, and she too was happy to be receiving the food rations in addition to free medical care and imported
medicines. But Yelizaveta did not like most of the Americans and En-
glishmen she met. She was especially upset with one American woman
she met while working for the Quakers. The woman came in wearing
an evening dress with a fine fur and rings and started to talk like a Red

commissar. When Yelizaveta tried to open the woman's eyes to the famine and despotic violence around them, the American woman looked at her with pity, Yelizaveta later recalled, as if to say: "Poor girl! Her family must have lost all their privileges in the Revolution; no wonder she's against the Soviet government!"[28]

Fen believed the Westerners then visiting Russia came with ideological blinders. No one cared to hear about the plight of people like her. She later recalled how she used to love to visit the museums at the former Yusupov estate of Arkhangelskoe and the Sheremetevs' Ostankino. She would stroll about under the stare of dour attendants and admire the art, paintings, photographs, and antiques that made it seem as if the owners had just stepped out for a moment. At Ostankino she was transfixed by the story of forbidden love between Count Nikolai Sheremetev and his serf-mistress and secret wife, Praskovya "The Pearl" Kovalyova. When she came across foreign visitors, Fen tried to tell them this remarkable story, but no one wanted to listen to her, preferring the guides' officially sanctioned explanations of the former gentry as "tyrants" and "retrogrades."[29]

Fen's reaction was not the norm, however, and it was not long before the Russians and Americans at the ARA were not just working together but socializing. The Americans threw big parties at their rented mansions, and the Russians reciprocated in their dim, cramped apartments. There were also parties at the home of John Speed Elliott, an ARA man and the chief representative of Averell Harriman's interests in Russia. His secretary, Alexandra Meiendorff, a former noble related to the Sheremetevs, was a frequent guest at his place, as were Vladimir Golitsyn and Yelena and Nikolai Sheremetev.[30] The American reporter Hullinger attended many of these parties, including one thrown by the Bobrinskys. He remarked on the contrast between the grim living conditions and lack of food and the infectious happiness of his Russian hosts. Everyone was laughing, flirting, and dancing. It made him wonder if the revolution had freed these young people to a lifestyle unknown and impossible to their parents. "Over it all hung an atmosphere of free camaraderie which would not have been possible under the gilded chandeliers and in the stately drawing-rooms of their ancestors. There was an unaffected, frank jolliness that reminded me of our own American Far West." The young women in their "pre-war dress" looked "as charming and pretty as if just home from college." One of these noble daughters told Hullinger, "I am trying to live on the surface of life. I have been in the depths for five years. Now I am going to be superficial. It hurts less."[31]

The Americans offered an escape from life's dark depths, and the Russians were grateful. They were fascinated by the Americans and their culture, especially jazz and the fox-trot. Young Russians, and not just the former nobles working for the ARA, wanted to have fun, to be frivolous and silly; they rejected the dour puritanism of official Communist culture that deemed fun to be bourgeois. The Russians and Americans danced through the night, the latest records from America spinning on their gramophones, and then raced through the empty streets in the ARA's automobiles as the sun rose over Moscow.[32] The American men were besotted by these exotic "Madame Butterflies," and their advances were frequently returned.[33] In 1923, Alka Bobrinsky married her ARA boss, Philip Baldwin, and not long thereafter left Russia for Italy to live with his mother. Her younger sister Sonya married the Englishman Reginald Witter the following year, and they left for his homeland. Not all these unions ended happily. Irina Tatishchev heard of one Russian girl from the ARA who had left Russia with an Englishman, only to learn that he had no intention of marrying her but set her up as his mistress. Devastated at his betrayal, she committed suicide.[34]

From the start, Lenin and the Communist leadership had been suspicious of the ARA and had accepted it into the country with great reluctance. It seemed to represent a beachhead of bourgeois influence. The Cheka closely monitored the ARA as well as the Russians who worked for it.[35] Many of these Russians were later singled out for repression. The Communist leadership saw the West not just as a political threat but as a more insidious source of cultural contamination. Both Maxim Gorky and Anatoly Lunacharsky were shrill critics of the fox-trot, which they considered decadent and lacking in class consciousness, a dance that was too individualistic and improvisational. The Communists wanted dancing that was only collective and planned. Gorky was convinced the fox-trot fostered moral degeneracy and led inexorably to homosexuality; Lunacharsky wanted to ban all syncopated music in the entire country. Even Vladimir Mayakovsky, the Futurist poet turned Soviet propagandist, denounced the fox-trot as "bourgeois masturbation." Foreign jazz was eventually outlawed, and playing American jazz records was punishable by a fine of one hundred rubles and six months' jail time. No one would be getting hot in the Workers' Paradise.[36]

Back in Bogoroditsk, Anna Golitsyn worried about her children living on their own in Moscow. She sent Lev Bobrinsky's sister to check on them at Spiridonovka. After going around and visiting, she wrote back to Anna that they were doing fine and she was not to worry since this was proving to be a good "school of life for our young folk." This did not put Anna at ease, and later she had Lilya Sheremetev check in on the young people as well. Her report to Anna was equally positive.[37]

Heartsick at their lengthy separation, Anna wrote a letter in the winter of 1922:

> My dear, sweet older children, if only you could know, feel, or understand how much I think of you and how my soul aches for each of you, how I pray for you, and how I pine for you.
>
> You used to say about me: Mama always says—"Pray," and all of her conversations always lead back to this. You still do not understand this. You are young, you think you are strong, and you have not yet felt just how weak we are. How difficult it is, impossible in fact, to perfect ourselves without help from on high, to live well without help from on high. Prayer strengthens one's desire to live a new life, it is what animates and inspires us. God cannot but answer if you ask Him to help you live a good life. Remember this always, believe this, and then the impossible will become possible.
>
> Maybe someday, perhaps, you will recall my words and they will help you.[38]

They all would need a strong faith in the years ahead.

15

NOBLE REMAINS

everal blocks from the old Samarin mansion on Spiridonovka in the direction of the Kremlin, the remaining members of the Sheremetev family continued to hold out at the Corner House. In August 1921, the Socialist Academy, in control of the building since 1918, gave the family one week to move out of the third floor to make way for fifty students from the Institute of Marx and Engels. The family packed up their things and moved to the top floor, where twenty-eight people now had to share ten rooms. Other family members were scattered about other parts of the house, making for a chaotic situation. The house was stuffed and overcrowded. Bookcases, old portraits in large gilt frames, all manner of trunks, chests, and boxes with the Sheremetevs' possessions crammed the Corner House's many corridors, staircases, and storerooms; despite the previous requisitioning by the Cheka, the walls were still covered with Gobelins, and the floors with heavy old rugs; dark mahogany furniture filled the rooms.[1]

The Corner House was home to three branches of the family, those of the widows Lilya Sheremetev, Anna Saburov, and Maria Gudovich and their fourteen children, as well as a number of other relations. Lilya, aged forty, had become the mistress of the house. She made a strong impression on young Sergei Golitsyn when he saw her for the first time since returning to Moscow from Bogoroditsk. This was no regular woman, he thought, but "a Lady." "Her entire appearance and proud carriage were so regal and so beautiful that in my mind I called her a queen." Lilya held out her hand to Sergei, not for him to shake but to kiss. Born too late to have learned the etiquette of his parents' generation, a nervous Sergei was not sure quite how to proceed, but he somehow managed to awkwardly put his lips to the ends of her fingers.[2]

Anna and Maria shared a room on the house's top floor. Astral specters, they were almost never seen, leaving their room mostly to go to church to pray for their missing husbands, whose deaths they refused to accept. Sergei Golitsyn had been visiting the house for two years before seeing them for the first time. He found the two sisters "majestic" yet "pale, their skin like porcelain. They were silent, sad, and having left the vanities of the world behind them, they rarely ventured out into the corridors, and when they did, everyone stepped aside to make way for them."[3] Olga Sheremetev found herself drawn to Maria. "It's strange," she wrote in her diary, "but whenever I see Maria I want to write. She is an unusual person, an unusually good person, who believes like a child and without any doubts. [. . .] Still, she is not a fanatic or pedant, and whenever I see her, my soul is warmed."[4] The presence of these widows, as well as the sad recent history of the house, created an atmosphere markedly different from that which reigned on Spiridonovka. The Corner House was not a lively place; rather, "a certain etiquette was followed here combined with a premonition of the fragility and ephemerality of the merriment that recalled 'the feast during the plague.'"[5]*

This was not to say that no fun was had there, however, for the many younger Sheremetevs, Saburovs, and Gudoviches liked to have a good time. Yelena Sheremetev, who turned seventeen in 1921, was now living in the room where her grandfather Count Sergei had died three years earlier. Like her cousins, she studied rather haphazardly when she had the time and money and inclination, though it seems her main goal was keeping up an active social life. She loved going to the cinema with her friends to see the reigning stars—especially the beautiful Vera Kholodnaya ("The Queen of the Screen")—or to marvel at the latest silent film featuring the suave thief Arsène Lupin.[6] Yelena's young

*A reference to Alexander Pushkin's dramatic work "A Feast During the Plague" (1830), later the basis for César Cui's 1900 opera of the same name.

cousin Grisha Trubetskoy shared her passion and collected photo-graphs of his favorite actors—Buster Keaton, Mary Pickford, Douglas Fairbanks, and Charlie Chaplin.[7] Yelena and her cousins also liked to go hear Fyodor Chaliapin at the Moscow Conservatory and to *Boris Godu-nov* and *Demon* at the Bolshoi.[8] Yelena, her sister Natalya (then fifteen), and their cousin Merinka Gudovich (sixteen) were never apart and made up their own "merry young pack," to quote one admiring male visitor. They all were pretty and just on the threshold of womanhood, ready to trade their girlish braids for the latest stylish cuts. They made a bit of money by selling pies in the coffeehouses then springing up around Moscow.[9]

Yelena's brother Nikolai was a gifted violinist, and in 1920 he started playing in the orchestra of the Herzen Club on Novinsky Boulevard. Over the next few years he played for a number of groups, including the Dmitrovsky Dramatic Theater and the Stanislavsky Studio. In 1924, Nikolai was hired as the concertmaster, as well as composer and vio-linist, at the Moscow Art Theater's Third Studio, later renamed after its founder, Yevgeny Vakhtangov. He remained at the Vakhtangov The-ater for the rest of his life.[10]

Tatiana Aksakov-Sivers frequented the Corner House in those days, and she was impressed by this young generation, which she de-scribed as "talented and beautiful." Of all of them, she was most im-pressed by Boris Saburov.[11] Here is how Yuri Samarin remembered him years later:

> Boris Saburov was an attractive personality in many ways. At first glance he seemed dry and vain, but once he opened up, one saw in him a very unique nature. A gifted artist, and subtle poet, he brought art and culture to our lives in distinctive, special ways. On his own initiative, he began publishing a hand-made journal at Vozdvizhenka under the name "Pens for Dreams." He was both its editor and the author of its contents, and in a real sense he did it all himself. [. . .]
>
> We would await with interest every Saturday when a new issue of "Pens" would appear. It would always have colorful illustrations in a vaguely abstract style, short novellas, verse, and caricatures poking fun at each of us. Boris was the first to introduce us to Esenin. It was his reading of Esenin that taught us to love this magnificent, unique lyric.[12]

Another of the talented and beautiful young creatures was Alexander Golitsyn. Sergei Golitsyn described his cousin as a natural leader, "handsome, confident, brave." Alexander's family had been run off their estate of Livny in the summer of 1918. One day in July, a group of peasants came in secret to see Alexander's father, Vladimir Vladimirovich. "Tomorrow your home is to be burned down," they told him before slipping away. Their warning likely saved the lives of Vladimir, his wife, Tatiana, and their three young children, Alexander, Yelena, and Olga. They immediately sent the children to Tatiana's parents in another village, and then Vladimir took off on horseback in the middle of the night to the rail station and caught the first train for Moscow. Tatiana and a servant packed up the house and with the help of friendly peasants carted off what they could take. The next morning a gang of peasants arrived to find the house deserted. They took everything that had been left and then burned it to the ground. Because of the fighting around Livny, the family was separated for two years, and it was not until the spring of 1920 that Vladimir finally managed to locate Tatiana and the children and bring them all back to Moscow.[13] Alexander frequented the Corner House in those years as a teenager. He loved to organize amateur theatricals, *The Inspector General*, *Woe from Wit*, and *Boris Godunov* being his favorites. An excellent actor, he was always given the starring role.[14]

The three widows of the Corner House personified old Russia and provided a link to the past for the younger generation, many of whom had been born too late to have known tsarist Russia as adults. They tried to inculcate in their children an appreciation for life before the revolution, for the traditions of the nobility, for the customs of their families and their vanished world. Although their children naturally had their own tastes in music, dance, and literature and lived according to a different code shaped by recent experience, still they did not reject the lost world of their parents. Rather, they remained open to the past, even curious, and sought to hold on to what could be salvaged and incorporated into this new, radically altered society.

It was this spirit that made possible the surprising rebirth of one of the defining features of noble life: the ball. Sergei Golitsyn accompanied his mother to the first of these Soviet-era balls at the Corner

House. It was held in a brightly lit hall on the top floor, with a piano, chairs, and couches placed along the walls. Around the room were tables with cheese and sausage sandwiches and apples; one of the young men would invariably spike the bowl of cranberry punch with some moonshine. All the ladies held lorgnettes and watched from the sides. Groups of young people told jokes and stories, laughed, and went out to smoke. When a young lady entered, the men would go over and kiss her hand; if she was an "old maid," they would bow. Since none of the men had tailcoats or dinner jackets, they agreed in advance to come in their everyday wear, be it an old officer's uniform, a velvet jacket, or *tolstóvka*, a type of long, belted blouse. Vladimir Golitsyn wore his sailor's suit. The ladies were in long white dresses. Many had put in a great deal of time preparing: Lina Golitsyn and the other young ladies collected fabric and lace to make their dresses for the occasion. Everyone agreed that the "merry young pack" of Yelena, Natalya, and Merinka were the beauties of the ball. The pianist and master of ceremonies was Vladimir Gadon. A small, ruddy-faced old man with a white beard and tsarist officer's jacket, the shoulders now marked with dark patches where his epaulets had once sat, Gadon had been an adjutant to Grand Duke Sergei Alexandrovich and the longtime director of the governor-general's balls in Moscow. Everyone in prerevolutionary Moscow aristocratic society had danced under his direction. Gadon would wait for Lilya Sheremetev to make a sign with her handkerchief before beginning the festivities. Every ball began with a quadrille, followed by a waltz, and then another quadrille, and so on. Although then all the rage, the fox-trot was never danced at these balls since the older ladies found it corrupt and decadent.[15]

All the dancers were former people. For many, their futures would be tragic. Sergei Golitsyn recalled decades later:

> And what of the fates of the participants of this ball? I started to compose a mournful list, read it over and stopped in horror: it was too terrifying to look at. The majority of those young gentlemen and ladies, especially the men, who so lightheartedly amused themselves at the ball later perished in the camps, others, having suffered the torments of Hell, returned, others emigrated, and others were arrested simply for their title.[16]

It was at the Corner House balls that Vladimir Golitsyn and Yelena Sheremetev fell in love. They had first met in the summer of 1920. Yelena, her mother, and a young friend by the name of Vanka Spizharny were walking to the Corner House from the Kazan railway station when they came upon Vanka's friend Vladimir. They all were introduced, and Vladimir joined them as they walked along, Yelena and Lilya in front, the two young men following behind. Vladimir made note of her red cap, her thick braids, and the long lashes framing her large gray eyes. Vladimir left for another Arctic expedition soon thereafter, however, and forgot the pretty young girl. On his visits to Moscow, Vladimir went to see Yelena's brother Nikolai at the Corner House, where he saw Yelena again. He was soon smitten. It was a difficult position for Vladimir. Yelena had many suitors, and he was still committed to several more long trips exploring the Arctic and was not certain when he would be free to return to Moscow for good. The situation filled him with jealousy. What is more, having lived with sailors in the frozen wilderness for years now, far from newly fashionable Moscow, he felt awkward and out of place in his dingy clothes.[17]

At the time his jealousy and insecurity got the better of him. None of the men was worthy of being in her very presence or that of the other young ladies. "So many new faces! But they're all just animals!" he fumed in his diary.

> Some are trying to pass themselves off as real aristocrats, but they're not succeeding. And the others, the aristocrats, have become animals themselves, just like the former, so degraded and so empty. [. . .] Can it be that even at Vozdvizhenka the strong spirit of the old family traditions is wavering, can it be that even here these vulgar provincial games are flourishing, the kissing, and the men with dirty thoughts reaching out to embrace these trusting, pure girls? My God! How did this happen? Did the revolution so utterly undermine the very root of the Russian aristocracy, forcing it to forget its old traditions![18]

To Vladimir, the balls at the Corner House offered hope that not all the old noble traditions had died and gave him a chance to be close to Yelena.

Oh, these balls are good, as are those quadrilles, one moment calmly majestic and then headlong the next, when you feel her there beside you and lovingly hold her trusting hand, which gently squeezes yours. How intoxicating are those fleeting moments during the dances, her timid hands in mine, or those conversations, brief, fragmentary, filled with hesitation and gazes during the *pas de quatre*, and you forget that you are dancing, your legs moving by themselves, like machines, in time with the music.[19]

They went boating at the former Samarin estate of Izmalkovo one summer day. As Vladimir rowed, Yelena's hand drifted in the water. She picked some water lilies and put them in her hair, making Vladimir love her even more.[20] Vladimir's love for Yelena was chivalrous, almost mystical. During an Easter church service she exuded a sublime, religious aura:

And when I, looking directly into her eyes, quietly said: "Christ is risen!" she started to glow as if from some inner light! With such sincerity and confidence she said: "He is risen indeed!" which I understood to mean that Christ had arisen again in our souls . . . Conveying a sense of trust, she leaned toward me, but I felt so beneath her that I could not imagine myself worthy of even kissing her.

In the spring of 1922, he exclaimed, "It's as if we were born for one another! There's no way I cannot love her!"[21] By late summer, however, Vladimir was gone once more, this time on a three-month expedition aboard the icebreaker *Malygin* bound for Novaya Zemlya. While he was away, Lina wrote to tell him, "Yelena loves you madly." Vladimir was back in Moscow for good before year's end.[22] By now they were engaged to be married. Both families were thrilled at the match. Vladimir's mother told her son that they all found Yelena "beautiful and charming." The fact that she was a Sheremetev added to the family's joy; the union of these two great clans was, despite everything the nobility had been through, still an occasion for celebration.[23]

Yelena and Vladimir married on April 30, 1923 in Moscow's Great Ascension Church, where ninety-two years earlier Alexander Pushkin had wed Natalya Goncharova. Their families were there, as well as about a hundred guests. Afterward they dined on fish and cabbage pies back at the Corner House. Boris Saburov read a poem he had written for the occasion. The guests toasted the couple and then smashed their crystal glasses on the parquet. After the party, they conducted Vladimir and Yelena to the station and placed them on a train for their honeymoon in Petrograd.[24]

On their return the newlyweds moved into the Golitsyn apartment at 16 Yeropkinsky Lane. The Golitsyns had left Bogoroditsk for Moscow the previous year and managed to buy the apartment thanks to an unexpected inheritance of jewelry from a recently deceased relation. The apartment was small and barely heated; baths were conducted in a porcelain basin filled with water from a pitcher. It was crowded. The mayor and Sofia were there; Mikhail and Anna, their children Sergei, Masha, and Katya; Lina and her husband, Georgy Osorgin; Vladimir Vladimirovich, Tatiana, and their three children; and for a time, the family of Eli and Vladimir Trubetskoy. Space was so limited that Sergei had to sleep in a wardrobe under the women's dresses. With the money left over after the purchase of the apartment, Vladimir Vladimirovich was able to buy an apartment on Khlebny Lane, and his family moved out after a few months.[25]

In September 1923, Vladimir and Eli Trubetskoy and their children left for the town of Sergiev Posad, some fifty miles northeast of Moscow. Home to the fourteenth-century Holy Trinity Monastery of St. Sergius, Sergiev Posad (known for most of the Soviet period as Zagorsk) was one of the most sacred places in Russia. Former nobles began moving to Sergiev Posad soon after the revolution. Among the first to come were Count Yuri Olsufev and his deeply religious wife, Sofia. St. Sergius is said to have appeared before Sofia in a dream, instructing her to move to Sergiev Posad and live close to his grave. They were joined by other noble families—the Istomins, Naryshkins, Meshcherskys, Lopukhins, as well as the polymath priest and philosopher Pavel Florensky and his family.[26] The holiness of Sergiev Posad offered spiritual consolation after the trauma of the revolution and civil war and encouraged humble acceptance of an inscrutable and unpredictable future.

Vladimir Trubetskoy managed to find work as a pianist accompanying silent movies in the local cinema during the day and playing the cello in the orchestra of the town's main restaurant at night. Not only a fine musician, Vladimir had even composed an operetta based on one of the novellas in Boccaccio's *Decameron* that was staged to considerable success in 1922. It was a relatively good time. The Trubetskoys rented the upper floor of a house with a kitchen garden out back and had enough money to hire a nanny and a cook. Vladimir enjoyed his work and approached it seriously, even watching the movies in advance so he could select the most appropriate numbers to play for each scene. Vladimir became friends with the writer Mikhail Prishvin, and the pair lost themselves for days hunting in the nearby forests.[27]

Yelena and Vladimir Golitsyn were frequent visitors to Sergiev Posad, and they summered in the village of Glinkova with the extended Golitsyn family. For the first several years of their marriage they lived at the apartment on Yeropkinsky Lane. It was a happy, if busy, time. Their first child, Yelena, was born in 1924, followed by Mikhail ("Mishka") two years later and then Illarion ("Lariusha") in 1928. Vladimir worked hard to support his growing family. A jack-of-all-trades, he wore a number of hats over the course of his life: sailor, shipbuilder, writer, graphic designer, set constructer, and even creator of children's board games. His greatest talent, however, was as an artist, and his submissions to an international exhibition of decorative arts in Paris in 1925 won him two gold and one silver medal. Most of his time was spent as an illustrator for books and popular magazines like *Pioneer, Knowledge Is Power, World Pathfinder*, and *Around the World*. He was forever hustling for commissions, and the work had to be turned around quickly on tight schedules, but it afforded the best opportunity for earning money from his craft. Vladimir Trubetskoy collaborated with Vladimir Golitsyn on these publications, contributing stories of comic misadventure and gentle satire featuring his alter ego, the déclassé nobleman Vladimir Sergeevich Khvoshch. After a while Vladimir Golitsyn was making enough money to hire a nanny for the children. Despite the exhausting demands of work, Vladimir loved to have fun, and friends were forever stopping by in the evening to drink, play charades, and dance the fox-trot. They had a small gramophone and two records, one an old recording of selections from the operas *Faust* and *Aida* and the other, a collection of 1920s dance music that they fox-trotted to so much it eventually wore out.[28]

Vladimir took great pride in his family name and the role of the Golitsyns in Russia's past. This pride took physical expression in the many portraits of generations of Golitsyns that Vladimir lovingly looked after his entire life. They had long hung in the Petrovskoe manor house but were taken for safe keeping to a storeroom in Moscow during the revolution. After moving to Yeropkinsky Lane, Vladimir retrieved the portraits and carefully hung them in the new Golitsyn home. These portraits remained with Vladimir through ten subsequent moves over the next two decades. Vladimir and the rest of the family seemed to derive a certain security and inner strength from the presence of their ancestors. Vladimir handled the portraits with an almost superstitious care, always making certain to hang them in the exact same arrangement each time they moved.[29]

The mood at the Golitsyns was welcoming, friendly, relaxed. While the younger generation enjoyed themselves, the mayor, undisturbed by the noise, sat quietly over a game of solitaire. On Saturdays a dancer from the ballet came to give lessons to the Golitsyn children and their friends; on Sundays the whole family went to church. One frequent guest remembered:

> The Golitsyn family was special . . . and I cannot compare it with any other family. In a rather small apartment four generations of this family lived in complete harmony. Everyone was given a bit of space, no one bothered anyone else, and no one complained about his fate. The Golitsyns were true aristocrats in the very best sense of the word. They never made visitors to their home from other circles feel unwelcome, as long as they did not disturb the family's established order. Anyone who happened to find himself in the Golitsyns' home felt this atmosphere and easily adapted to it. I can only recall one instance when a young man who by mere chance found himself in their company went beyond the accepted bounds of behavior. They immediately let him know that his comportment was inappropriate. Embarrassed, he excused himself and never again visited Yeropkinsky Lane.[30]

Despite the loss of their wealth and property, of their privileged legal and social status, and of so many family members from imprisonment, exile, emigration, and death, the Golitsyns remained "true aristocrats." And curiously, despite the war that had been waged against it for years, the aristocracy still possessed considerable allure. There were some Russians in the early 1920s who sought to claim the identity for themselves even when they had no right to. Moscow had a number of sham aristocrats with fanciful and wholly made-up titles such as the princes of Tversky and Macedonia. A Baron Palmbach proudly went about sporting a monocle and earring until it was discovered he was actually the son of a carpenter. Merinka Gudovich's brother Dmitry attended a ball at the home of one "Princess Zasetsky." There he came across a large portrait of his hostess as a young woman. It struck him as odd that the clothes on the portrait were not of paint, but of silk, as if they had been cut from old drapes and then affixed to the canvas. Curious, he gently lifted a corner to get a better look. Suddenly, the fabric fell to the floor, and Dmitry was shocked to be standing before "Princess Zasetsky" utterly naked in the pose of a courtesan.[31]

Identity was problematic in the early years of the Soviet Union. Just who was who? And how could one tell since the old markers of status, rank, and wealth had been destroyed? In the summer of 1922, Nikolai Sheremetev visited Vladimir Golitsyn near the northern city of Arkhangelsk. One evening they were invited to the home of an Estonian man and his family. They drank and sang and played music, enjoying themselves immensely. Over tea Vladimir asked his host how long he had been in the area. He told them he had arrived in 1914 from the Estonian village of Pebalg. With this, Nikolai sat up. "Really?" he asked. "That's our family's estate."

"Excuse me," the man said, offended, "but that estate belongs to the Counts Sheremetev."

"Yes, of course!" exclaimed Nikolai.

"So, you're saying that you're Count Sheremetev?"

"Yes."

"Hmm, and then who's this with you?"

"This is Golitsyn."

"There are princes by that name," the man said.

"He *is* a prince," said Nikolai.

"Ah, come on now, don't take me for a fool!" the man hollered.

An awkward silence followed. Nikolai and Vladimir wanted to show the man their documents to prove they were telling the truth but then thought better of it. Would he believe them, and did it really matter anyway? The atmosphere had been ruined. The two men stood up, thanked their host, and left.[32]

Of course, people who had known one another since before the revolution could tell who was who. In the early 1920s, Yelizaveta Fen visited her former school friend Katya Kozlovsky, an orphan who had been left the large estate of Dedlovo at the age of fourteen. After many years apart, Yelizaveta was stunned by her friend's transformation. The former wealthy noble girl had shed her past life and gone native. She dressed and talked like a peasant and was making house with a scruffy villager by the name of Vanya. Katya told Yelizaveta that despite her poor appearance, she had never been happier, thanks largely to Vanya. It was true, she confessed, he could be rough, but the sex with him was better than anything she had ever experienced and for the first time in her life she felt fully alive. The villagers, however, did not care much for their sex lives and were particularly upset to see their former mistress acting the peasant. Soon after Yelizaveta's visit they ran Katya and Vanya out of the village.[33]

Katya's story highlights an important paradox concerning notions of class in the Soviet Union. If, following Marx, class was a function of one's relationship to the means of production and a person's social being determined his consciousness, how was one to make sense of the class system in 1920s Soviet Russia? In light of the radical transformation of the past several years that witnessed the wholesale dismantling of the old order, and its social classes as well, were there any classes left, and if so, what were they? Part of the problem was that the class the Bolsheviks had claimed to represent, the proletariat, had largely disappeared during the fighting and industrial collapse of the civil war years. The workers who manned the factories in 1917 had vanished, for either the countryside or the Red Army, and the country's urban centers had emptied out. It would be several years before a working class of any size developed again in Russia. As for the political and economic elite, it had been destroyed as a distinct social group. And so the Communists, who had made a revolution and established a state based on the idea of class warfare, faced an awkward situation: classes in Russia had disappeared.

The state's response to this was to manufacture new classes to meet its needs. Throughout the 1920s legislation was put into place to continue the older notion of a proletarian class, which now included the poor peasantry, and a bourgeoisie, fashioned out of former nobles and aristocrats, tsarist officials, clergy, nepmen, and kulaks. (Kulaks were in theory well-to-do peasants, though the term was so vague and used so indiscriminately as to mean little more than one's enemy.) "Former people" was another manufactured class or caste made by lumping together groups that had had little or no shared identity before 1917. A related group, whose ranks overlapped with that of the former people, were the so-called outcasts or disenfranchised (*lishéntsy*), persons who had been stripped by the Soviet state of their voting rights. Of course, losing the right to vote in the Soviet Union was no great loss. Nevertheless, what made this designation so damning was the fact that with the loss of voting rights (indeed of all civil rights) came a whole series of restrictions, all crucial for survival: the denial of access to housing, ration cards, employment, higher education, and medical care.

Outcasts were denied access to public cafeterias or institutional dining halls where most average Soviets took their meals. What services outcasts were still entitled to, they had to pay higher rates for than the rest of the populace. In effect, outcasts were expelled from society and turned into pariahs, the Soviet Union's own untouchables. The names of outcasts were often posted on signs or published in newspapers as a form of public humiliation. The first outcasts had been created by the Soviet Constitution of 1918 as a way to create a class of enemies within the new order. As the 1920s progressed, restrictions against the outcasts expanded, and their numbers swelled to as many as four million. Although a great many outcasts were from the former elite, the majority had never belonged to Russia's wealthy or privileged. In predominantly Jewish towns of Ukraine, for example, nearly 40 percent of the population were outcasts in the late 1920s.[34]

The ambiguity of social class was made worse by the confusion over how one's class was to be determined. Standard questionnaires required of anyone seeking housing, education, or employment capture this confusion. In an attempt to define class, respondents were asked to give either their "social origin" or "social position." The two were obviously not the same thing, and not surprisingly, members of repressed social groups tended to ignore the former in favor of the latter. They did not write "former prince" or "son of a count" but gave their current positions. In a sense, they were trying to "pass" not unlike the way some fair-skinned American blacks tried to pass for white before the 1960s to escape the United States' system of racial apartheid. In the 1920s such deception was not usually dangerous, but it became so during the Stalin years. Efforts to hide one's past, to create what became known as a good biography, placed one in the dangerous position of being outed or discovered as an impostor. According to the logic of the time, hiding one's past in this way was proof of being a class enemy hostile to Soviet power.[35]

The Soviet Union was a country founded on the idea of struggle against internal enemies, and it is fair to say that regardless of how former people responded to questions about their social origin or position, they would have continued to face persecution. History, so the Marxists claimed, moved forward by class struggle, and the Soviet Union would be no exception. Once its rulers had invented new classes, it logically followed that there would be struggle between them. Unlike during the revolution and civil war, however, the struggle had changed. The class enemy had gone underground, and so the need for vigilance, for an ever-watchful eye, became a pervasive aspect of Soviet life. This despite the fact that the OGPU (the acronym for the Unified State Political Administration, successor to the Cheka from late 1922) in its top secret internal reports for the party leadership in the 1920s reported that the monarchists had been utterly destroyed and represented no threat.[36] The sense of being watched by others strengthened the process of masking and internal vigilance that had begun after the revolution. Galina von Meck described this as "the years when all of us in Russia lived a double life, wearing a mask when outside our homes, taking it off only when we knew it was safe to do so."[37]

Humiliation of former people figured in the class struggle and became a conscious policy of the state. The policy was motivated in part by the leadership's anxiety about its degree of control over society. Although their enemies had been defeated, still the party leaders obsessed over what they saw as the precariousness of their authority, a feeling that far from diminishing actually grew throughout the decade. The sense of vulnerability was exacerbated by the continuing reliance on the old "bourgeois specialists." Approximately 20 percent of all Soviet bureaucrats and technical experts were from the old elite; 35 percent of the leadership of the People's Commissariat of Agriculture, for example, were former nobles, and many more nobles filled the lower rungs of the ministry.[38] Even as late as 1938, former people could not be replaced. That year Mikhail Shreider, an assistant NKVD commissar and head of the Kazakhstan police, carried out an aggressive campaign to expel "socially harmful elements" from Alma Ata but had to take many of the former people off the list because the city simply could not function without their skills as doctors, engineers, and educators.

The dependence on "class enemies" not only fed a sense of insecurity among the authorities, but also fostered disillusionment among the working and lower classes, in whose name the revolution had been made. Periodic campaigns against former people, harsh critiques, and calls to "unmask the enemy" functioned as safety valves to let off social tension. Encouraging denunciations of former people that led to their firing and loss of living space allowed for upward social mobility without the state's having to actually improve living standards. The hostility of the poorer, less educated classes toward the old elite was real, however, and not a manufactured phenomenon. Even a decade after the revolution, the ability to destroy members of the old elite filled a great many with fervid pleasure. The "promotees" from the lower rungs, often made painfully aware of their lack of education, training, and sophistication when moved up to work alongside former people, delighted in seeing them brought down.[39]

The same people also felt anger toward the new political and social elites. As the twenties progressed, Russia's workers were forced to make ever more concessions and to improve their productivity for the same pay. They lost much of their autonomy and control over their labor. At the same time, the new bosses were wrapping themselves in privilege that dredged up memories of the old elite. Strikes broke out, as did demonstrations by the unemployed, anti-Communist rallies, and even attacks on officials. An OGPU agent secretly monitoring a rally of unemployed metalists in late 1926 recorded the words of one speaker: "There are two classes today: the working class and Communists who have replaced the nobles and dukes."[40] To deflect this anger, the party channeled it against the old bourgeoisie, former people, and outcasts, pinning the blame for any problems on them and other hidden enemies. The ever-increasing preoccupation with these groups paralleled a shift in the notion of class itself.

No longer a social construction, malleable and dependent upon specific economic and political relationships, class came to be understood in quasi-biological terms. It became almost a racial category, a mark of inheritance that a person was born with and was powerless to change. What mattered most was not one's life at the moment (read "social position") but one's family's status before 1917 (read "social origin"). The stain of one's ancestors could never be washed clean. It ought to be noted, however, that this biological notion of class was not unique to the Soviets but was (and still is) embraced by some nobles themselves. Consider the tale of Vladimir Vladimirovich Trubetskoy, who while on a visit to Paris in the 1960s introduced himself to Count Musin-Pushkin as "a former prince from Moscow." "Come now, you can't be serious," retorted a disbelieving Musin-Pushkin. "Has one ever heard of 'a former poodle'?"[41]

16

THE FOX-TROT AFFAIR

With the end of the civil war and the advent of NEP, a certain normalcy returned to Russia. Life seemed easier, unremarkable, although only in contrast with the barbarism that had preceded it and, though no one knew it at the time, the barbarism to follow. NEP was a contradictory period. There was relative openness in cultural and artistic life, considerable debate within the Communist Party itself, concessions to private property, and a market economy. Yet at the same time the Cheka remained vigilant, ideological control over society increased, and centralized state planning of industry and the economy expanded. What is more, no truce was ever declared with the revolution's enemies, real or imagined. The struggle went on against former people, but to quote one historian, the 1920s constituted not a frontal assault like the civil war but "low-intensity warfare."[1] The new stage of the war was fought on several fronts. Restrictive legislation was enacted. New laws aimed at so-called socially dangerous elements (SDE) were passed throughout the early 1920s. The criminal code of the RSFSR for 1922 fixed the notion of SDE in its Article 7, which established punishment for those whose activity showed them to be dangerous or harmful to society. The Central Executive Committee of the USSR further solidified the class principle in law in 1924 by stipulating greater legal protection for persons from formerly exploited groups and less for those from formerly exploiting groups. Former people and other SDE received harsher treatment by the courts, in both conviction rates and sentencing.[2]

The political police continued to hound and arrest supposed enemies, and they also resorted to more elaborate schemes to entrap their prey. Kirill Golitsyn fell into just such a trap in 1923. The bizarre episode happened in this way. In 1922, Kirill and his family, then living in Petrograd, were introduced to Mikhail Burkhanovsky, purportedly the adopted son of a former tsarist general, and his recently deceased wife. Over the course of the year, Burkhanovsky visited the family often and slowly won their trust. After many months and then only with great hesitance, he let them in on his secret life. He told the Golitsyns that he was part of a large and powerful underground monarchist organization with connections to people in high places. They were putting together a major operation against the Soviet Union and at any minute were preparing to set it in motion. Burkhanovsky confessed he was in danger of being uncovered by the OGPU. One day he arrived at the Golitsyns with a stack of monarchist proclamations and asked Kirill to hold on to them until he returned.

But Burkhanovsky never did return, and the Golitsyns never saw him again, for he was not a monarchist spy, but an agent provocateur of the OGPU. Burkhanovsky was not even his real name; the real Mikhail Burkhanovsky had been captured and killed by the Cheka before this impostor even appeared on the Golitsyns' doorstep. Burkhanovsky figured in a large deception operation code-named Operation Trust (as in "corporation"), directed against foreign and domestic monarchists potentially plotting against the Soviet Union. Active from 1921 to 1925, Operation Trust has been called the most successful Soviet intelligence operation of the 1920s, and a great many Russian exiles were lured back to the USSR and to their deaths by its agents. At the heart of Operation Trust was the Monarchist Union of Central Russia, a phony organization created by the Soviet secret police to smoke out and entrap anti-Bolsheviks, closet monarchists, and White Russian émigré groups in Berlin and Paris. Another operation known as the Syndicate, like Operation Trust the brainchild of Felix Dzerzhinsky, was created to capture Boris Savinkov, the erstwhile SR terrorist turned ardent anti-Bolshevik, then living abroad. Savinkov was lured back into the Soviet Union in 1924 by OGPU agents posing as members of the counterrevolutionary underground. He was arrested and later died under mysterious circumstances.[3]

Burkhanovsky's main target had been Kirill's mother, Maria, a former lady-in-waiting to Empress Alexandra. Maria maintained friendships with members of old St. Petersburg's high society, many of whom continued to visit her at the Golitsyn apartment, thus making it, in the eyes of the OGPU, a monarchist cell. Maria's death in June 1923 saved her from arrest. On October 23, the OGPU picked up Kirill and charged him with membership in a counterrevolutionary organization by the name of Young Russia. As proof, they pointed to the monarchist pamphlets and $150 found during a search of the family apartment. In an admirable, if naive, attempt to pass along to his son information on the case against him, Nikolai Golitsyn inserted a handwritten note into a small pie and sent it to Kirill, who was imprisoned at the Home of Preliminary Detention, the notorious Shpalerka Prison, which had once held Lenin. The jailers, not surprisingly, discovered the note. On November 14, Nikolai was arrested (for the third time since the revolution) as a member of Young Russia. Fifteen persons in all were arrested in the case. The investigation dragged on until the spring of 1924. On the first day of March, a sentence of death was recommended for Kirill and eight of the others. Miraculously, Kirill's name was taken off the list for execution, and his life was spared; later that month the OGPU sentenced him to five years' confinement in a labor camp. His father was given a sentence of three years, which he would serve in a cell together with Kirill in Moscow's Butyrki Prison.[4]

Upon learning of his son's and grandson's arrests, the mayor sent a letter in their defense to Commissar of Justice Dmitry Kursky, telling him that if Kirill was guilty of anything, it could be "only of frivolity and stupidity." As for Nikolai, he had been "apolitical" his whole life, so there was no way the charges against him could be true. Others in the extended family sprang into action. Sonya Bobrinsky paid a visit to Abel Yenukidze, Anna Golitsyn went to see Pyotr Smidovich, and her husband, Mikhail, called on Yekaterina Peshkov.

Peshkov was one of Russia's great, though little-known, heroes of the twentieth century. The daughter of an impoverished nobleman and a committed revolutionary herself, she met the writer Maxim Gorky while working as his proofreader in the 1890s and the two soon married. She bore him two children before they separated in 1903, although they remained close for the rest of their lives. During the First World War Peshkov worked in aid relief for the children of war victims, and after the February Revolution she founded the Moscow branch of the Society for the Aid of Freed Political Prisoners to assist the mass of tsarist political prisoners then being released. In May 1918, she helped found the Moscow branch of the Political Red Cross (MPRC) dedicated to easing the plight of political prisoners. Peshkov and the MPRC provided a range of support to political prisoners and their families, including free legal counsel, evidence collection, food, medicine, clothing, and books. Peshkov was a fearless and committed defender of political prisoners, and she used her connections to the new leadership, thanks to her marriage to Gorky, to free hundreds of them and to lighten the sentences of many more.[5]

In August 1922, the police raided the offices of the MPRC. Following an investigation into its activities, the offices were sealed and the organization closed. Not one to be deterred, Peshkov managed to convince the police to let her establish a new organization in the same offices under the name Aid to Political Prisoners, which came to be known by its Russian acronym, POMPOLIT. The new organization was forbidden from defending people legally and now had to rely solely on Peshkov's ability to plead their cases with the powerful. Its chief function became the material support of prisoners. To thousands of Russians in the 1920s and early 1930s, Peshkov was an angel in the darkness. She fought for everyone—socialists, anarchists, clergy, former nobles, and tsarist officers—regardless of his politics or past. Over the years she was inundated by an avalanche of appeals, nearly all of which she did her best to answer and investigate. She was granted access to prisons to check on inmates, offer moral support, and deliver letters and gifts from home. She could often find out the fate of imprisoned loved ones when their families could not get any information from the authorities. A note from POMPOLIT let a prisoner know he had not been forgotten and was often enough encouragement to give him the strength to go on living. In the mid-1930s ever-greater restrictions were placed on POMPOLIT's operations. In 1937, Peshkov's chief assistant was arrested and sent to the gulag; the following year, POMPOLIT was closed for good.[6]

The POMPOLIT offices were located at 16 Kuznetsky Most in a nondescript building at the end of a long corridor next door to a Berlitz language school. In the front room sat two secretaries and usually a large crowd of visitors waiting their turn to see Peshkov. When Mikhail Golitsyn appeared at the POMPOLIT offices in 1923, he was shown directly in to see Peshkov. He had known Yekaterina since 1917, when they had worked together at the Society for the Protection of Mothers and Infants.[7] Mikhail pleaded the case for his brother Nikolai and nephew Kirill. Peshkov was not able to get the men freed, but she did manage to keep them from being shipped north to the prison camps on the Solovetsky Islands, known as Solovkí. Thanks to her intervention, father and son were permitted to serve their sentences at Moscow's Butyrki Prison; it possibly saved their lives.[8]

On January 21, 1924, Lenin died. He had been ill since May 1922, when he suffered the first of several strokes, and he had not been involved in the running of the country for months. For four days his body lay in state in Moscow's House of Unions, formerly the home of the Noble Assembly, and hundreds of thousands came out for one final look at the leader of October. One of them was Sergei Golitsyn. He did not notice a great outpouring of sadness with Lenin's death; rather, the people had fallen silent. He went to the House of Unions with a friend and did not get home till late. Not knowing where he had disappeared to, his family was worried, and when he told them he had gone to see Lenin, they were surprised and angry. "What is it you wanted to see?" his brother-in-law Georgy Osorgin barked. "If your uncle Misha were alive he'd box your ears!"[9]

One morning two months later Lilya Sheremetev showed up in tears at the Golitsyns' apartment. She told them that the OGPU had been at the Corner House the night before and arrested her son Nikolai and her nephews Boris Saburov and Dmitry Gudovich. When Nikolai asked why they were being arrested, one of the agents snapped, "You ought to know."[10]

The arrests marked the beginning of what became known as the Fox-trot Affair. Many others, including nearly everyone who had danced the fox-trot at Spiridonovka or attended the balls at the Corner House, were soon to be arrested. Even the aged Vladimir Gadon, master of the ball, was arrested. The one family untouched by the affair were the Golitsyns, for reasons that cannot be explained and attest to the often random nature of Soviet repression. Kirill Golitsyn, already sitting in the Butyrki when the affair erupted, noted that "the régime had looked upon the parties of young people as part of some perfidious scheme" and thus "arrested all dancers of both sexes."[11] According to Galina von Meck, not only were the security organs monitoring many of these fox-trot parties, but they were even organizing some of them to set up people for arrest. Galina's sister Lucy went with a young poet to a fox-trot party in Moscow that was raided by the OGPU; all the men were arrested, and many of them were sent to Solovki.[12] The daughter of General Danilov was also arrested. Imprisoned in Tyumen, she committed her plight to light verse that belied the seriousness of her situation:

> Though legend it may be, there was a scandal on Ostozhenka,
>   you see.
> An entire bunch, each but a child, to the Urals was exiled.
>
> The Kadets and SRs forgotten, so fox-trotters, some twelve dozen,
> Were arrested by the G-P-U . . . And why? No one knew!
>
> And we, careless and gay, danced to jail without a fuss.
> Yes, let's admit with sad heart, the fox-trotters—that's us!
>
> Two hundred we were, from ten years to twenty, such a sinister age.
> We loved and laughed, we sang and dance, 'twas all the rage.
>
> We hardly knew each other, to them this was no bother.
> Here we each came, and for each the charge was the same!
>
> Oh, fox-trot, fox-trot, everyone ought to curse you. For you
> Are the cause of our imprisonment. For you we danced
> Into a damp prison, fallen under the most terrifying suspicion.
>
> Oh, fox-trot, fox-trot, stronghold of dark forces, cover of fierce
>   reaction!
> You're the nest of the Counter Rev. in the Russian Soviet Socialist
>   Fed.,
> You're its hope, you're its foundation!

Let our sad fate be a lesson to all—if you're invited to fox-trot, by
  chance,
Be sure to say, "Pardonne, but I don't dance!"[13]

Nikolai Sheremetev was released within a few days and returned to the
Corner House. Not long thereafter the OGPU returned yet again,
though this time not to make any arrests but to inform the family that
they had three days to vacate the house. With nowhere to go and no
hope of moving all their possessions in so short a time, Nikolai, Yuri
Saburov, and Andrei Gudovich hauled dozens of trunks, cases, boxes,
and crates filled with art, antiques, and furnishings out into the street
and sold them off to passersby for a pittance. Sheremetevs had lived at
the Corner House for three centuries. Within three days they all were
gone.[14]

For Lilya this was more than she could take. She had been considering trying to leave Russia for some time and chose to escape through a
fictitious marriage to a friend of her late husband, a Latvian diplomat
by the name of Baron Budberg. Budberg, Lilya, and her four youngest
children—Natalya, Pyotr, Maria, and Pavel—left Moscow's Belorus-
sian Station for Riga, seen off by fifty family members and friends and
watched the entire time by two undercover agents. Upon reaching the
Latvian capital, Budberg proposed a real marriage, but Lilya declined,
and he returned to Moscow. Lilya took the children to her parents'
Baltic estate for a time, before the family packed up once more for
Paris and then finally Rome. Sergei Golitsyn was sad yet relieved to see
his cousins go. He was certain that were they to stay, neither Pyotr nor
Pavel would survive.[15]

The family was now broken in two. It had been an agonizing decision for Lilya's daughter Yelena, but in the end she chose not to leave
with her mother and siblings. Her husband, Vladimir, would not consider leaving leave Russia and his family, and they were just starting a
family of their own. Yelena saw her mother just once more, forty-two
years later in Rome for a brief visit. A few weeks after Yelena returned
to Moscow, her mother died at the age of eighty-five.[16]

Nikolai too chose not to leave, also for reasons of the heart. Cecilia
Mansurov was twenty-seven and beautiful, with penetrating brown
eyes and lush hair. She was the new star of the Vakhtangov Theater,
where Nikolai had just landed a job. Though she was already married

and six years his senior, Nikolai could not resist her, and he began to woo Cecilia, quietly, determinedly. She did not hold out for long. A gifted musician, charming, and handsome, Nikolai won Cecilia over, and soon they were living together in a room in the former stables off the theater's courtyard. They were there but a short time before moving to an apartment at the new Vakhtangov Cooperative House on Bolshoi Levshinsky Lane. Stealing Cecilia from her husband was no great scandal; her being a Jew, however, was. Sergei Golitsyn wrote: "Many found it incomprehensible—Count Sheremetev, married to a Jew!" It was Mansurov who was responsible for getting Nikolai out of prison so quickly. She herself pleaded his case before someone with the right connections, and her beauty and acting skills did the job. She would have to do it again on her lover's behalf in the coming years, appearing before the likes of Lev Kamenev, Nikolai Bukharin, and Mikhail Kalinin. According to one of Nikolai's fellow musicians, when his mother and siblings were leaving on the train from Moscow, Nikolai took out his passport and ripped it up in front of Cecilia as proof of his commitment to her. They spent the rest of their lives together, bound by a profound, if tempestuous, love and a shared passion for music and the stage.[17]

The arrests of the Fox-trot Affair continued. Anna Saburov, Maria Gudovich, and nearly all their children—Boris and Yuri Saburov, Dmitry, Andrei, Varvara, and Merinka Gudovich—were taken to the Butyrki in the spring of 1924. The OGPU began their interrogations by asking prisoners their political views. The correct answer, regardless what one really thought, was: "I am loyal to Soviet power." During NEP such a response typically guaranteed one either a quick release from prison or internal exile. Many prisoners received the sentence known as Minus Six, banishment from the six largest cities in the USSR—Moscow, Petrograd, Kiev, Kharkov, Sverdlovsk, Tbilisi—as well as from any territories near the Soviet border. Prisoners who answered the loyalty question with "I am a monarchist" usually got sent to the camps for several years. Anna Saburov was exiled to the provincial city of Kaluga for three years, and her daughter Xenia followed her there; Boris and Yuri were given Minus Six and exiled for three years to the town of Irbit in the Urals. After serving their sentence, the brothers were sentenced to Minus Six again and moved to Kaluga in 1927. Maria Gudovich and her children Merinka, Andrei, and Dmitry

were exiled from Moscow and also ended up in Kaluga and then Tsaritsyno.[18] Having thrown the Sheremetevs out of the Corner House, the
OGPU was now removing them from the capital as well.

The Butyrskaya Prison, known as the Butyrki, had been built during
the reign of Catherine the Great. The notorious Cossack rebel Yemelian Pugachev was held in the cellar of the original stockade before his
execution in 1775, and his name was subsequently given to one of the
prison's four towers. Future rebels, revolutionaries, and assorted trou-
blemakers under the tsars and then commissars, including Nestor
Makhno, Felix Dzerzhinsky, Varlam Shalamov, and Alexander Solzhenitsyn, were held there. Even Harry Houdini spent time inside its
walls, performing a dramatic escape for the prisoners in 1908. After the
revolution, Russia's new leaders began locking up their enemies there.
In 1924, the Butyrki became the home of a new wave of enemies, several of whom landed in Cell 8 together with Nikolai and Kirill Golitsyn in what the latter called "our noble collective farm." Here Kirill
had the opportunity that had never presented itself outside in the free
world to make the acquaintance of a number of older noblemen and
to become close friends with younger nobles like Dmitry Gudovich
and Sergei Lvov. Vladimir Trubetskoy spent two months at the Butyrki
following his arrest with a number of other former nobles in Sergiev
Posad in December 1924.[19]

Kirill recorded the varied fates of the inmates of Cell 8. One of the
stranger and sadder stories belonged to Avenir Vadbolsky. A graduate
of the Corps des Pages and a former officer, Vadbolsky had danced at
the Sheremetev balls until the OGPU arrested him, thinking he was a
certain Prince Vadbolsky from the White Army of General Baron
Peter Wrangel. The OGPU interrogated Vadbolsky at the Butyrki, after
which he migrated from prison to Solovki, then back to the Butyrki,
then to exile in Berezov on the Ob River, and finally back to Moscow.
In 1929, he was taken to the Lubyanka, where his life came to an end.
In the Butyrki's women's section, Kirill met the young and fetching
Varenka Turkestanov, another victim of the Fox-trot Affair. Varenka
was later released from prison, but only after having been subjected to
strange sleep experiments (more likely, sleep deprivation). She went
back to her mother an utterly destroyed person: withdrawn, uncom-

municative, cut off from everyone and everything around her. Eventually, she roused herself to one decisive and final act and threw herself out a window.[20]

Georgy Osorgin landed in Cell 8 in March 1925. He had been arrested at the apartment of Sandra Meiendorff, Lilya Sheremetev's sister, in a so-called mousetrap. A technique borrowed from the Okhrana, the tsarist secret police, the mousetrap (*zasáda*) involved placing agents in the apartment of a person under suspicion and then detaining everyone who bothered to knock on the door. The mousetraps could go on for days until either the main target or enough possible enemies had been gathered. Sometimes the hostages were released, though not always; guilt by association was a widespread mode of operation. That Meiendorff had worked for John Speed Elliott, a representative of Averell Harriman, had attracted the attention of the OGPU.

Shortly before his arrest Osorgin wrote Grigory Trubetskoy in Paris of the worsening climate, stressing that "they have begun 'cleansing Moscow of harmful elements.'" In one night, thirty of Osorgin's friends had been arrested. So many people were being arrested a joke was born: "Question on a Soviet questionnaire: 'Have you ever been arrested, and if not, then why?'"[21] For former people like Osorgin, the humor might have been hard to find. "Yes, Uncle Grisha, life has become bleak," he wrote to Trubetskoy, "not because of the constantly poised sword of Damocles, but because it seems there is no sign of any change." Osorgin had been arrested for the first time in September 1921 in a raid of his aunt Olga Trubetskoy's home. Before they took him away, he had managed to leave his wife, Lina, a short note: "So now your turn has come, my darling, to be tested. May God help you. Pray also for me, and be completely calm: I don't worry about myself for a minute."[22]

The Golitsyns sprang into action to get Georgy released, appealing as in times past to Yenukidze, Smidovich, and Peshkov. When asked the standard question about his loyalty to the Soviet regime, Osorgin refused to lie, telling his interrogators that he was a monarchist. Genrikh Yagoda, then the de facto head of the OGPU, stated that Osorgin had acted "provocatively" during his interrogation. On October 12, 1925, Georgy was sentenced to be shot, but Peshkov intervened and won a reduced sentence of ten years in prison, saving his life for a time. Georgy remained at the Butyrki for three years. At times, he felt guilty at the suffering his arrest had caused Lina. "If it is my fate to die in prison," he wrote on a handkerchief smuggled out of prison to his mother-in-law, Anna Golitsyn, "I would like that Lina and my family would know that I die peacefully, praying that Lina might still find happiness and that her life on earth will not be limited to that chain of suffering and grief that bound her on marrying me; poor, poor Lina, why did you let her marry me?" Georgy was supported while in prison by an unshakable religious faith and memories of family and the life they had shared before the revolution at their estate of Sergievskoe, what he called "that spiritual cradle in which everything by which each of us lives and breathes was born and raised."[23]

A month after Georgy's arrest, the OGPU arrived one night during Holy Week at the Golitsyns' with arrest warrants for Mikhail and his son Vladimir. Led by a man named Chernyavy, the agents blocked the door so no one could get out and searched the apartment all night, going through their books, the children's notebooks, their photographs and letters. The Golitsyns, who had been preparing for bed when the agents arrived, sat about in their nightclothes and watched. The samovar was lit, and they offered the uninvited guests some tea; Chernyavy refused, saying it was against regulations. In the early morning, the men finally found something: two large photographs of Nicholas II and Empress Alexandra inside a trunk left for safekeeping by a cousin now living abroad. The family told the men that the trunk was not theirs and that they knew nothing about its contents, but Chernyavy did not believe them. Mikhail and Vladimir were led downstairs. The rest of the family followed and pushed into their hands a bedroll, spoon, mug, and bowl, the necessities of prison life. A paddy wagon, the feared Black Raven, sat waiting. When the raven's back doors opened, the Golitsyns could make out in the dark the faces of others arrested that night. Mikhail and Vladimir climbed in and took their places. Along with the two men, the OGPU agents confiscated all the family's personal correspondence.[24]

The family was devastated. "We, those who remained, suffered greatly the arrest of our loved ones," Sergei wrote. "I went to school and told none of my friends of my woe. I was not the only one in this situation. Andrei Kiselev, making me promise not to tell, whispered to me that Alyosha Nesterov's father had been arrested. It was horrifying just to look at Alyosha. His face had gone all black and his eyes nervously flittered about."[25] Peshkov and Smidovich immediately set to getting the men released. Peshkov met with Yagoda, who was considering letting them go had it not been for the portraits, which he was convinced the family knew about and were just waiting for the day when they could hang them again. In prison, Mikhail insisted he supported the Soviet government, particularly the efforts it was making on the behalf of the peasantry; Vladimir told them he was no monarchist, and in turn his interrogators told him to spend less time in the company of foreigners. Within three weeks, both men were freed.[26]

Mikhail and Vladimir had been struck by how much the secret police knew about them and their family's private life. The family assumed someone close to them had to be an informant. Their suspicions landed on Mikhail's nephew Alexei Bobrinsky. Alexei had been arrested along with Georgy Osorgin and then released almost immediately. Everyone in the family now made certain to be careful what they said around Alexei, although no one confronted him with their suspicions. His cousin Sergei Golitsyn, who had so looked up to him during their years in Bogoroditsk after the revolution, now fantasized about killing him as a traitor to his family and to the nobility.[27]

On the night of April 2, 1926, almost exactly a year to the day from his first arrest, Vladimir was arrested a second time and charged with espionage. Again, the agents spent an entire night searching the Golitsyn apartment for foreign literature and papers and letters from abroad. His grandfather was crushed. Yelena wrote to Peshkov, insisting Vladimir was loyal to the Soviet government and had nothing to do with any counterrevolutionary activities.

As before, the case against Vladimir was dropped, and after a few weeks he was home from the Butyrki.[28] There would be more incarcerations in the years ahead, however, from which Vladimir drew an important moral:

> When they put you in prison, at first it seems to you that you're having a terrible nightmare and that real life is the one they took you out of. Then (after 2–3 months) you get used to it and it seems to you that your cell is the real life, a nightmarish one, and freedom is a beautiful dream in which even life's difficulties and annoyances are pleasant. Don't take daily life's petty unpleasantries too close to heart—remember prison.[29]

In late July, two months after Vladimir's release, a prison guard opened the door of Cell 8 and called out Nikolai Golitsyn's name, bellowing, "With your things!" These three words brought joy to a prisoner's ears, for they meant he was being freed.[30] Kirill, Nikolai's son, had to wait two more years to hear the same.

Kirill spent fifteen years of his life behind bars, yet he refused to consider this time simply lost, unlike many people in his situation.

I, for one, am not so generous that I might easily cross off fifteen years. This was no fifteen minutes. During these years I acquired many different skills and considerable diverse knowledge; I lived with interesting people; I observed the enormous variety of human characters and types; experienced both good and bad minutes and, of course, found like-minded people and made friends, whom I remember to this very day. No, simply cross out so many years, I cannot agree to this![31]

17

VIRTUE IN RAGS

n 1921, Countess Yekaterina Sheremetev turned seventy-two. Like must Russians, she had lost much during the past four years. The world she had lived in for more than six decades had vanished nearly overnight. Her husband was dead, two of her sons-in-law had been executed, and three of her four sons, including her eldest, Dmitry, and his entire family, had fled the country. More family members had been killed during the carnage of the civil war or succumbed to hunger and disease or simply disappeared. Nevertheless, despite such hardship, Countess Yekaterina was feeling well, cheerful even, as Christmas approached.

She was living now at the old family estate of Ostafievo in an apartment in one of the manor's wings with her son Pavel and his wife. The year before, Pavel, the old bachelor whose heart had been broken in such dramatic fashion three years earlier, surprised his family by marrying Praskovya Obolensky. The daughter of Prince Vasily and Princess Maria Obolensky (née Dolgoruky), Pashenka, as she was called, sprang from the same lofty aristocratic background as her groom. Pavel's aunt described Praskovya as the perfect match for Pavel, being "very simple and serious" and "pretty," and everyone agreed they were a happy couple.[1] Pavel had been living at Ostafievo since 1918, when he was made custodian, and subsequently director, of the Museum of Everyday Life at the estate; he was kept busy making inventories of all the art and antiques, writing short guides to the collections, and leading tour groups.² Praskovya did not have permission to live at Ostafievo, even as Pavel's wife, so he successfully petitioned to have her added to the museum staff.³

In comparison with the plight of so many former nobles, life for the three Sheremetevs at Ostafievo was pleasant. They remained on at their beloved estate, enjoyed meaningful work, and were left in peace. Russian history and culture had always been Pavel's great passion, and he derived immense fulfillment from living at and caring for Ostafievo.⁴

The serenity of Ostafievo, and the inescapable history of the place personified by the aged countess Yekaterina, touched everyone who visited. In the spring of 1921, the young folk from the Corner House came out for the day. "It was a beautiful May day," Yuri Samarin wrote, "and there in the park, seated in a chair beneath a blossoming lilac, grandmother, in a violet dress, her hair a beautiful silver, received us in all her old world, majestic beauty."⁵ On August 7, the family held what would be its final celebration at Ostafievo with the wedding of Varvara Gudovich and Vladimir Obolensky, Pavel's brother-in-law. A photograph from the event has survived; it shows all the family gathered around the table—Sheremetevs, Saburovs, Gudoviches, Obolenskys—as well as more distant relations, friends, and members of the local clergy. It was a happy occasion, and everyone was glad for the young couple, but the strains of recent years show on their faces. They stare out at the camera, trying, somehow, to smile. The reception table is almost devoid of food and drink.⁶

In a letter dated December 20, 1921, to his niece Lili, now living in Paris, Pavel wrote of life at home. Things at Ostafievo were "not so bad," and he was finding special joy in watching the small winter birds pecking at breadcrumbs on his windowsill. Grandmother was doing well; she was up and walking about with the help of a cane. When two former Sheremetev peasants heard she was living at Ostafievo, they starting bringing fresh milk and bread. Their unsolicited kindness touched them and reaffirmed Pavel's faith in his countrymen. "When people curse the Russian people, one mustn't forget there are good people and that such abuse is an exaggeration." The trains had improved, and one no longer had to travel in boxcars packed in "like cattle." Pavel had been making trips back to Moscow to check on things at the Corner House. He told Lili how little space they had and how messy and disordered the home had become (particularly the Saburovs' rooms). Still, he was pleased to see the young people so full of life and in such good spirits. Material life had also improved. Pavel had been elected a member of the All-Russian Union of Writers that year, an honor that came with increased food rations, and they had plenty of firewood. Many stores had opened up in recent months, and meat and white flour had reappeared, although everything was extremely expensive and the stores were always crowded. Clothing, however, was still a problem. "We are not always smartly dressed, but, as they say, 'virtue can be recognized even when clothed in rags.'" Overall, Pavel had to admit that the government's new economic policies signaled "a change for the better."

The improvement in their lives set Pavel to thinking about Russia and Europe and where one lived best.

> I have long been intrigued by the question of whether life for those who must work themselves in order to survive is better there where you are or here. Based on your letters, life is not so easy there either. I have always considered that the more correct approach is to try to build a life here at home, and I think that I have not been mistaken. It is difficult to write about all this. Regardless, we two have no desire to leave, but how we wish to return as soon as possible to a normal life. Things are improving slowly, but they are improving.[7]

Pavel's words attest to the divide within the nobility, indeed within individual families, that the revolution and civil war had opened up. The division tore many families apart and created a gulf that has never been fully bridged to this very day. Olga Sheremetev touched on the division in her diary around this time: "Sofia Vasilevna received a letter today from a Russian woman living abroad. She writes that if she returns to Russia she will not shake the hand of any Russian who remained there. What did those emigrants who fled save—Russia or their own lives? We who have remained here have unquestionably suffered more. Was I not right in saying that we now speak different languages?"[8]

The nobles who stayed behind and those who had departed did indeed begin to speak different languages, not at all surprising as their lives moved in different directions, in different worlds. How could the noble exiles ever fully understand the lives of their family members struggling to survive in Soviet Russia? Indeed, how could the exiles understand the Russia in which their families lived? Just as the early departed loved one never ages, remaining forever young in fading photographs, so too did the Russia in the minds of the exiles remain frozen in time, lost but unchanging, growing more beautiful with each passing year of its absence.

The nostalgia for a lost Russia that existed now only in memory filled the letters Dmitry Sheremetev wrote to his mother from Europe.

> We are living on memories, on old Russian books and magazines (which, thank God, there is an abundance of here), and I have given myself the goal of completing my hunting reminiscences and have already written most of it. This has been terribly absorbing. I have relived my entire life for a second time. [. . .] I wrote about our trips with Papa across Russia, the Volga, the Caucasus, and Crimea. Village life, mushroom gathering, songbirds and flowers, all of this, as well as your museum and library, filled my heart with joyful trembling and I wanted to pour it all into the most captivating picture. All of these years just flowed from my pen [. . .] So far I have 19 large notebooks and it is still far from complete [. . .] I have also put together a Russian calendar for each day with notes, proverbs, and the like.

Dmitry wrote his mother that he so desperately wished she could read his reminiscences since "they have been written with the blood of my heart, and I have poured my entire soul into them."

Like Proust's madeleine, the taste of homemade borscht sent Dmitry back in time to his old life in Russia, unleashing the ache of loss. "We recall our dear Gavrontsy.* What a dream that was! And when you recall the Volga with her broad expanse, it simply makes you want to cry. [. . .] Even the nightingales here are not the same, they make a sort of hoarse, smacking sound without any song or melody."⁹

The difficulty of their lives as émigrés made the memory of Russia sweeter. Dmitry, Ira, and their children arrived in Europe with little

---

*A village in Poltava Province.

and from the beginning had to scramble to make ends meet.[10] Dmitry wrote his mother that the entire family was spending most of their time working in the small garden growing vegetables—cucumbers, dill, radishes, and beets for their borscht. Dmitry and Ira's daughter Irina lived with her husband, Georgy Mengden, and their little daughter at his parents' in the first years of emigration. Irina wrote Grandmother Sheremetev that "at first life was very hard and, to tell the truth, simply terrible." They managed to get by raising a few chickens and rabbits and tending the garden; Georgy took up beekeeping. Money was always short—at times there was not even enough for a pack of cigarettes—but Irina was grateful to at least have a roof over their heads.[11]

Hard as émigré life was, some Russians were willing to accept its challenges. Baba Ara, Countess Sheremetev's sister, was one of them. "Life here has become intolerable in every possible way," she wrote Lili from Moscow in February 1921. By June she had had enough and was preparing to leave and trying to convince her sister to come with her. "Let's go! Make up your mind, think of the bliss you'll feel being in Cannes,* God grant you make up your mind to come. The journey won't be hard, only the trip from Moscow to Reval will be uncomfortable, but from there it will be smooth sailing [. . .] Do think it over well." Countess Yekaterina did make up her mind—to stay, that is—and Baba Ara left without her, eventually settling in Berlin, where she continued to write to "my sweet Katya." His mother's decision not to leave Russia left Dmitry "in terrible grief."[12] Countess Yekaterina could not imagine leaving Russia. For one thing, her family still needed her. She earned a bit of money to help support her daughters Anna and Maria, and she assisted Pavel in his work at the museum.[13]

In 1923, Pavel was promoted from custodian to manager of the museum, which he ran with the help of Praskovya and his mother. The previous year Praskovya had given birth to their first, and only, child, a boy they named Vasily. Pavel instilled in Vasily a love of art and culture and taught him the history of the Sheremetevs. He liked to tell Vasily, "To spit on the past is the same thing as to spit into the well we drink from," and he always counseled his little boy: "Remember, you are Count Sheremetev."[14] Vasily never did forget, even when it would

*Dmitry, Ira, and their younger children were then in Cannes.

have been better to. Throughout the 1920s various Soviet bosses came out to Ostafievo to visit Lunacharsky and his wife, who used the manor as their personal summer home. In the summer of 1925, Lunacharsky, Maxim Litvinov, a Soviet diplomat and future commissar for foreign affairs, and Pavel were strolling in the park when Vasily came running up. Litvinov gently stroked the boy's head and asked, "What's your name?" "Count Vasily Sheremetev!" he proudly announced to the men's astonishment.[15]

Pavel cooperated with the Soviet establishment since he had little choice. Nonetheless, he harbored no illusions about the sort of people he was dealing with. Russia's new rulers, Pavel knew, had nothing but contempt for the Russia of old, the Russia he loved and whose legacy he committed himself to preserving. That same year of Litvinov's visit he wrote of his anguish:

Why should anyone care for
The shadows that have hurried off afar?
Penury and trouble loom over us all,
The days full of despicable malice;
And who has come to the throne,
Strengthening from on high their grip on power,
They care for nothing,
And strive to eradicate every trace
Of Russia's former glory . . .[16]

Museums, libraries, and archives became a refuge for many nobles. These outposts of culture were safe places where former people gathered out of the glare of the more politicized state offices and agencies. No one had to explain himself, for they all typically came from the same social milieu and had shared similar fates since the revolution. Surrounding themselves with books, manuscripts, and art from old Russia allowed them to escape, if only for a while, the hostile world of the present for the comforting familiarity of the past. Moreover, with so much of the country's cultural patrimony destroyed—palaces and estates looted and burned, entire libraries torn to pieces for cigarette paper, paintings slashed, statues pulled down and smashed to pieces, graves robbed, churches stripped of their holy relics—former people felt a profound sense of mission in their work as the keepers of Russia's cultural heritage.

They were the logical ones to undertake this. First of all, they knew intimately many of the items being gathered in the new state museums and libraries since they had once owned them or known well those who had, and second, not many other Russians had the requisite education and training. If, to paraphrase Lenin, the government administration was to become so orderly and well organized that even a cook could run the state, this did not necessarily mean she could work with old Slavic manuscripts. Nikolai Ilin of Moscow's Rumiantsev Museum made this very point: "While a cook, if necessary, could run the state, she was as yet not able to catalog books in every European language."[17]

Olga Sheremetev, on the other hand, was able, and she did. She bound books, worked as a translator, compiled bibliographic information for a number of Moscow libraries, gave lectures, and taught foreign languages. In the 1930s, she also worked at the Literary Museum in Moscow, which became a nest of former people. There, laboring together with the former noble Dmitry Shakhovskoy, she reconstructed the personal library of the nineteenth-century writer-philosopher Pyotr Chaadaev and wrote commentary on his marginalia. The literary scholar Emma Gershtein frequented the museum at the time to consult with Olga, who was helping Gershtein in her work on a biography of Mikhail Lermontov. As a Jew, Gershtein was an outsider in this gentry nest, which she found fascinating, if strange. She was surprised by the number of nobles working there, including members of the Turgenev, Bakunin, and Davydov families. The elderly Davydov, who she thought "personified the culture of the country estate," liked to sing Gypsy romances, and Kirill Pigaryov, curator of the Muranovo estate museum (another nest of former people) and the great-grandson of the poet Fyodor Tyutchev, would stop by for friendly contests with the staff on noble genealogies.

Olga loved the museum and the people there. "It is pleasant to see the people I work with," she wrote in her diary. "The air with its smell of books and archival dust is pleasant. The conversations are pleasant. It must be this is something I was born with." Gershtein held Olga Sheremetev in the highest regard: "Modest, poor and educated," she wrote in her memoirs, "with a profound glowing gaze and abundant grey hair, she was a true pioneer." As for the others, Gershtein was less impressed. "Oh, those gentry types! They were themselves particularly scared and always cautious." Gershtein might have been correct in her assessment, though her inability to see the reasons for their behavior is difficult to understand.[18]

Many Soviet citizens viewed these museums and the people working there not as oddly curious but darkly sinister. Nikolai Ilin observed that the Rumiantsev Museum, where he worked, was considered a place where "the double-dyed vermin of the old regime had comfortably ensconced themselves and so had to be destroyed for the benefit of society."[19] Attitudes like this, encouraged by the state's leaders, grew over the course of the 1920s and 1930s until finally action was taken against most centers of old Russian culture.

The director of the Rumiantsev Museum was Prince Vasily Dmitrievich Golitsyn. A former officer in the Cossack Guards Regiment, court equerry, painter, and wealthy landowner, Golitsyn had been the museum director since 1910. Following the revolution he continued in his post, laboring tirelessly to safeguard and add to the museum's exquisite collections and to wring more money, food rations, and firewood out of the new government for the museum's staff, winning him their loyalty and admiration. For years after the revolution the staff continued to call him Prince out of respect. His assistant, the historian and librarian Yuri Gotye, wrote in 1920:

> Last Tuesday we quietly and modestly celebrated the tenth anniversary of Prince V. D. Golitsyn's directorship of the Museum. [. . .] We had a warm and heartfelt talk after expressing our best wishes to the prince. Many of us in the museum still don't understand his true significance: the fact is that this irreproachably decent lord and gentleman is truly the living conscience of the museum—for ten years he has prevented us from quarrelling, playing dirty tricks, and intriguing. That sort of thing could have especially flourished "in the revolution," but this was impossible precisely because of his presence. God grant him strength and health for many years, until he carries us to some shore and we can rest from life's storms.

Golitsyn, however, would not be able to carry them to the other shore. He was arrested on March 10, 1921, just as Lenin was announcing NEP, and removed from his position as director. Although no formal charges were made, there was talk of Golitsyn's running a secret "bourgeois society" at the museum.[20]

Unlike Pavel Sheremetev, a historian by education, most of the nobles working as curators, translators, and archivists had no special training. After being freed from the Butyrki, Nikolai Golitsyn landed a job as a translator at the Institute of Marx and Engels in Moscow, and his brother Mikhail earned money translating the writings of Zola, work that brought him immense pleasure.[21] Their father, the mayor, had received a commission to translate Balzac's *Droll Stories* and Goethe's *Faust* and was paid to give lectures for groups like the Friends of Old Moscow, the Society for Friends of the Book, and the Salon TsEKUBU.*[22] The work fed the mayor's body and soul at an especially difficult time. On November 10, 1925, Sofia, his wife of fifty-four years, died in Sergiev Posad at the age of seventy-four. Her death left him disconsolate. "It was inexpressibly painful to find myself in our room," he wrote in his diary upon returning to Moscow, "now so painfully empty for me. I got settled in my cell and wrote letters all morning. Oh, but how heavy is my soul . . . now that she is no longer. I keep hearing all around me her final words—'Quel beau moment!' " The pain of losing Sofia never lessened, and for the rest of his life he wrote of his longing for the day when they would be together again forever, "THERE."[23]

The mayor's grandson Sergei dreamed of becoming a writer as a young man, but his parents pushed him to get a practical education, so he took courses in accounting and bookkeeping. Still, he refused to forsake his love of literature and hoped one day to be able to study it at university. By the mid-1920s, his chances of being admitted to a university were shrinking. Purges against the children of former people at institutes of higher learning had begun; Sergei's sister Sonya was expelled from the university, and no intervention from noted scholars could get her reinstated.[24]

Sonya's expulsion reflected a larger wave of increased repression beginning to sweep over former people. In February 1927, for example, a modification to the law on outcasts extended this status to the chil-

*TsEKUBU—the Central Commission for the Improvement of Scholars' Life—had been created by the *Sovnarkóm* in 1921 to help the country's educated elite, barely alive following the civil war, by providing food rations, small monetary grants, firewood, clothing, pen and ink, and lightbulbs. It was closed in 1931.

dren of all former landowners. Official policy, however, was far from consistent. That same month, former gendarmes, police, and prison guards were removed from the ranks of the disenfranchised, and their rights reinstated.[25] Sergei noticed the increased politicization as an eighth grader; the teachers began to single out for praise the children of workers and the children in the Pioneers and Komsomol, Communist youth organizations. A new subject called *politgràmota*, or political literacy, was introduced, and his entire school was forced to march about Red Square with Soviet flags on Revolution Day. Sergei's parents were against his taking part and had him stay home; they sent a note to his teacher saying he was ill, and when he returned to school, there were no negative repercussions.[26]

In the autumn of 1927, Sergei took the entrance examination to the VGLK (Higher State Literary Courses or Higher School of Literature) in Moscow. The most nerve-racking question on the examination had nothing to do with literature, but with his class: "What is your social position?" Sergei gave the safest possible answer: "Father: office worker, Mother: homemaker." It worked, and Sergei was accepted. The atmosphere at the VGLK deteriorated not long after Sergei's matriculation. The school newspaper bemoaned the lack of students of peasant and worker origin and denounced the large presence of "socially alien elements." CLEAN OUR RANKS OF THE ALIEN ELEMENT! urged one headline. At meetings, students spoke out against the "various princes and counts" at the school. Once Sergei stood up to one of these activists, insisting that his father had worked his entire life and that his family's only crime was "the title of prince."

There was a call to purge the school's teaching staff, and a meeting was held at which everyone was instructed to be on the watch for "hidden enemies." Each student had to submit to a special interview with the school director, the head of the student committee, and the chairman of the Communist Party's district committee. Sergei awaited the meeting with apprehension that made him physically ill. The party chairman was the one to ask the question he knew was coming: "Are you related to Prince Golitsyn?" Sergei gave the answer he had prepared in advance. Yes, he admitted, his grandfather's brother had been a rich man; but his great-grandfather had been a Decembrist, and his father had never owned any land and had worked every day of his life. Sergei's sister Masha, also attending the VGLK, had to submit to a similar interview. For three days they awaited the committee's decision. In the end, they both were allowed to stay.

Not all former nobles survived the interview. Princess Kira Zhukovsky was expelled from the school, and her father was arrested soon after; a Prince Gagarin was forced out as well. Sergei's favorite teacher, the philosopher Gustav Shpet, was later arrested as a monarchist; he was shot in Tomsk in 1937. Regardless of his luck, Sergei did not have a chance to complete his education since the VGLK was closed as a den of idealists, former people, and fox-trotters in the upheavals of Stalin's Cultural Revolution.[27]

In 1927, Yuri Saburov was released from his term of exile in Irbit and came to stay with the Golitsyns in Moscow. Unable to find work, Yuri was invited by Vladimir Golitsyn to contribute sketches and drawings to the various magazines at which he had connections. Sergei Golitsyn remembered him as a hard worker, shy and quiet, who gave what little money he earned to his mother. Sergei's sister Masha was smitten with Yuri and flirted with him shamelessly. The family learned the depth of her feelings for Yuri only when years later she broke down in tears upon hearing of his arrest.[28]

Anna Saburov was then living with her daughter Xenia in Kaluga, southwest of Moscow, where many of the former people arrested in 1924 and given a sentence of Minus Six had gone. Yuri joined his mother and sister later that year, as did his brother, Boris. After completing his three-year sentence in the Butyrki, Dmitry Gudovich went to Kaluga as well to live with his mother and siblings.[29] Tatiana Aksakov-Sivers was also there, and she spent much of her time with both families. She noticed that Anna was no longer "that gorgeous woman in the white lace dress and black hat with feathers" that she remembered from years ago, although even at the age of fifty-four and after so many hardships she was still striking and capable of having a strong effect on people. The Saburovs lived in a small house on Gorshechny Street. Two gilded chairs salvaged from the Corner House highlighted the poverty into which they had fallen. Xenia had sold off the family's few other pieces of their former wealth on her trips to Moscow to raise money for food. Boris earned a miserly income designing political posters. The once elegant Saburov had greatly changed: "He appeared worn out and went around in unusually tattered clothes."[30] The Gudoviches struggled to get by as well. Maria gave French and English lessons while Dmitry looked for work. In the meantime, his uncle Pavel Sheremetev sent him what money he could spare.[31]

Among the fox-trotters in Kaluga were Pyotr Istomin and the three Lvov brothers—Yuri, Vladimir, and Sergei. Yuri and Sergei had shared Cell 8 in the Butyrki with Dmitry Gudovich, while their brother Vladimir had escaped prison by jumping out a back window as the OGPU was coming in the front door of his apartment. They all were reunited in Kaluga. Istomin fell in love with Merinka, Dmitry's sister, and the two married in 1926. It proved a short marriage; Pyotr was arrested only months later and sent to Solovki. His arrest reminded everyone, if anyone had ever forgotten, that danger remained and even though they had served their sentences, no one could be certain of tomorrow. It was with this terrible knowledge that these young men and women gathered in the evenings to dance and drink to the sounds of Yuri Lvov's fine voice and guitar. As they laughed and sang, Tatiana Aksakov-Sivers could not help thinking of the what the future held. "At the height of the merrymaking I was at times seized by an aching sensation. I understood that all of these youths were doomed, that this was nothing more than a brief respite. I recall how sad I became when sweet Dmitry Gudovich suddenly jumped up from the table, singing the gypsy refrain: 'We'll drink, we'll carouse, and when death comes, we'll die.'"[32]

Within ten years nearly every one of them would be dead.

PART V

Stalin's Russia

In our days tears and blood flow like two big rivers and apparently, for some unknown reason, this is as it must be. They must keep running until the end, and should the springs of tears and blood run dry, then a knee will be placed down hard into the living—much more can be squeezed out.

—Mikhail Prishvin,
diary entry, July 1930

18

THE GREAT BREAK

The struggle among the Communist leadership to replace Lenin began well before his death in 1924. Confined to a wheelchair, unable to speak, Lenin by late 1923 was little more than an empty shell, feeble, powerless, obsolete. A year earlier, he had begun dictating to a secretary his opinions on the state of the party and its chief personalities in what became known as his Testament. Here he addressed the rivalry between Leon Trotsky and Joseph Stalin. Lenin never came out unequivocally in favor of either man, although in his final pronouncements he gave an increasingly negative assessment of Stalin. To many in the party, Trotsky, the man of supreme rhetorical skill, the brilliant, ruthless leader of the victorious Red Army in the civil war, seemed Lenin's logical successor.

Stalin, however, skillfully managed to defeat his rivals for control of the party over the next several years—first Trotsky, who was eventually expelled from the country in 1929, then Grigory Zinoviev, Lev Kamenev, and finally Nikolai Bukharin. Throughout these clashes, Stalin was masterful at changing his position on the most pressing political questions when it suited him in the pursuit of power. Like Lenin, Stalin knew how to be fluid, open, to adjust one's policies, or steal an opponent's, to achieve one's goals. Following Bukharin, he rejected the idea of world revolution in favor of "building socialism in one country"; following Trotsky, he embraced the need for a renewed, radical assault on Russian backwardness and an end to the gradualism of

NEP. Socialism, Stalin declared, would be built in Soviet Russia with or without the rest of the world, and it would be built now.

Stalin's beliefs were shared by many in the party who had been uncomfortable with NEP from the beginning. Even as early as 1922, the Eleventh Party Congress had affirmed that there would be no further "retreat" from the revolution than the concessions already made. Two years later laws restricting the activities of the Nepmen were adopted, and in 1927, measures against the kulaks were enacted as well. Parts of Soviet society, including workers and the young, together with much of the party membership had long been frustrated with NEP's slow approach to achieving socialism and the persistence of the old order, signs of which they saw all around them. Had the sacrifices of the revolution and civil war been made, many Russians asked, so that a new generation of traders and petty bourgeoisie could get rich at their expense and dance to the sounds of American jazz in the night spots of Moscow while they remained mired in poverty?

The pervasive disquiet was captured in *Cement*, Fyodor Gladkov's popular novel of 1925. In a section titled "The Nightmare," the young Communist Polia Mekhova feels as if she has strayed into a "strange land" as she walks the city streets. All the women in the shops are now wearing smart clothes—"flower-trimmed hats, transparent muslin, fashionable French heels. The men had also changed: cuffs and ties and patent leather boots." Cigarette smoke, tinged with ladies' perfume, wafted from the cafés where men gambled, music played, and women laughed.

Later, at a meeting of party members, Polia breaks down under the strain of the contradiction between the new world they thought they had been fighting for and the one they ended up with. In a shaky voice she cries:

> I can't endure it, because I can neither understand nor justify it . . . We fought and we suffered . . . A sea of blood and hunger . . . And suddenly—the past arises again with joyful sound . . . And I don't know which is the nightmare: those years of struggle, blood, misery, and sacrifice or this bacchanalia of rich shop windows and drunken cafés! What were the mountains of corpses for then? Were they to make the workers' dens, their poverty and their death, more dreadful? So that scoundrels and vampires should again enjoy all the good

things in life, and get fat by robbery? I cannot accept this, and I cannot live with it!

Leaving the meeting, Polia is approached by some of the rank-and-file: "Just so Comrade. [. . .] We always get the same, nothing . . . the bastards must be smashed . . . smashed . . ."[1]

The party was supposed to lead society, not just govern it, but as the twenties progressed, it increasingly seemed as though society were heading in its own direction with little regard for the party. The party leadership feared it was losing control; secret internal reports depicted a growing number of problems: worker anger, peasant resistance, alienated youth, drunkenness, and rampant corruption. By the end of the decade, the party was poised to strike back.[2]

Stalin's "revolution from above," begun in 1928, has come to be known as the Great Break. In October of that year the First Five-Year Plan was launched. Its chief goal was to turn what was still a largely rural, peasant society into a major industrial power virtually overnight. The audacity of the plan reflected Stalin's gargantuan vision and the party's belief in its own infinite powers: "There are no fortresses the Bolsheviks cannot storm," a popular slogan of the day put it. Such was the frenzied tempo of the First Five-Year Plan that it was completed in just four years and three months. Entire industries, from chemicals to automobiles, from aviation to machine building, were created out of nothing, and new cities, home to sprawling industrial complexes, sprang up in Siberia and the Urals.

The capital to pay for industrialization came from the peasants. Tens of thousands of enthusiastic Communists and workers went out into the countryside during the First Five-Year Plan to force the collectivization of agriculture. Through a campaign of encouragement, propaganda, intimidation, and deadly violence, Russia's peasants were forced to give up their land and move onto large, state-administered agricultural collectives. Their labor, and profits, would henceforth be under the direct control of the state, which would use them for its own ends. Everything was diverted to the plan, and every aspect of economic life was to be under the control of the state. All private trade, even, for a time, the sale of personal property between individuals, was banned; farmers' markets were shut down. Food and other basics disappeared from the stores; rationing had to be reintroduced, first on bread and then on nearly all staple goods. Hunger became a widespread and permanent feature of Soviet life.

The achievements of Stalin's revolution cannot be denied. In a few years the Soviet Union did indeed transform itself into one of the world's industrial powers. But the costs, in human suffering and environmental devastation, render these achievements hollow. The figures on collectivization and its fallout alone beggar comprehension. Before the program of mass collectivization ended in 1933, likely more than two million people had been deported as class enemies to Siberia, the Urals, and Central Asia. Hundreds of thousand had been killed or died from starvation and exposure. The peasants not deported did not necessarily have it any better. Collectivization brought a massive famine across Ukraine, central Russia, and the northern Caucasus that left more than five million dead by 1934. Most of the deportees were placed in special settlements and put to work clearing forests and digging mines. Beginning in 1929, the existing system of prisons was replaced with a vast new network of self-supporting corrective labor camps— the gulag. Eighteen million inmates passed through the camps between 1929 and 1953, the year of Stalin's death. These inmates formed a nation of slave laborers without whose work Stalin's plans never could have been realized.[3]

Stalin's revolution was conceived as a war. Industrialization and collectivization were two of its main fronts. Culture was the third. This front was to figure as the battle line against the Soviet Union's class enemies, and it was fought to the death. Class warfare was not only renewed but whipped into a frenzy against the usual suspects: former people, outcasts, intellectuals, Nepmen, bourgeois specialists, and kulaks.[4] In late 1926, the All-Russian Central Executive Committee had toyed with the idea of reinstating the rights of the country's outcasts if they had engaged in socially useful work and been loyal to Soviet power over the past few years. The change, however, was never made. Now new laws were being passed against socially alien groups. In 1929, for example, a new crime was added to Article 31 of the criminal code of the USSR making it illegal to attempt to reestablish the power of the bourgeoisie. Widespread purges at offices, factories, and schools left many of these people without any clear means of survival.[5]

The threat posed by former people seemed to be mounting. Internal secret OGPU documents from the early 1930s claimed that "the anti-Soviet activity of former people at the present time has grown in strength." There was concern that former people were coming together and plotting to mix counterrevolutionary actions with terrorism. *Komsomolskaia Pravda* talked of saboteurs with "grenades in their pockets" and the remnants of the old elite harboring "dreams of avenging the revolution."[6]

Around this time, former people became linked with a broader notion of "socially harmful elements," which included the unemployed, orphans, beggars, and petty criminals (both real and imagined). The Soviet leadership saw these elements as one of the most serious threats to the state, and it tried to address the threat through the introduction of internal, domestic passports in 1932. The chaos of collectivization and industrialization unleashed a modern-day *Völkerwanderung*, during which more than twenty million people flooded into Soviet cities and towns in the first years of the 1930s. By making passports obligatory for all citizens, the OGPU hoped to flush out all former people and other undesirables trying to hide and then either arrest or exile them from the major urban centers. Although there were no formal restrictions on denying former people passports, verbal instructions were given to deny passports to all "class enemies" and "former people."[7]

Eugene Lyons was a radical American journalist and political activist who went to the Soviet Union in 1928 as the chief correspondent for the United Press just as the Great Break was getting under way. He arrived a radical, but what he saw over the next six years destroyed his illusions about the Workers' Paradise. Among the many things that shook his beliefs was the treatment of former people. He was stunned at the intensity with which they were being "pried out into the open and stepped on without pity." He could not conceive of how these people being thrown out of work and denied any means to make a living were to survive; what made it even worse was that to show any concern for these unfortunate souls was denounced as "bourgeois sentimentality." When he asked officials about the plight of the former people and what was to become of them, no one could give him an answer, except to comment on the "amazing tenacity of the human animal in clinging somehow to life."

Lyons, however, was convinced many did not survive; the rest "hung on to existence somehow with bleeding fingers."[8]

"The living dead," Walter Duranty called former people in 1931, "phantoms of the past in the Soviet present."[9]

With the beginning of the Great Break, former people found there was almost nowhere now left to hide. Not only were they being hounded in the cities, but the few who had managed to survive in the country-side were being driven off the land for good. By the mid-1920s, about 11 percent of prerevolutionary landowners (some 10,756 landlords, not including their families) were still living in the countryside. Most of these had never been great landlords like the Sheremetevs, but much smaller landowners. Some had managed to hold out by setting up communes or model farms and working alongside their former peasants. Regardless, all had seen their landholdings whittled away over time and by now had only meager plots. Nonetheless, their very presence represented a problem for the Soviet state, and throughout the decade efforts had been made to remove them, not without success. In March 1925, the Soviet government issued a decree evicting all former landlords from their properties by the beginning of 1926. (The order was later amended from January 1 to August 1, 1926.) In early 1927, Tula Province, to cite one region, was still home to 371 former landlords; by the end of the year, only 138 remained. With the arrival of collectivization, they all were pushed off the land, along with every other landlord all across Russia prior to 1930. Most of these people made their way to the cities and joined the ranks of outcasts in desperate search for lodging, work, and food.[10]

Alexandra Tolstoy was among the landowners then chased off the land. In November 1917, Alexandra had left the front where she had been running a field hospital to return to her parents' famous estate of Yasnaya Polyana. Despite its connection to Leo Tolstoy, Yasnaya Polyana was in danger of the same threats of angry peasants, rebellious deserting troops, hunger, and anarchy that were besieging all of noble Russia in the countryside. Alexandra had long been a sympathizer of revolutionary ideas. Years earlier she had bought part of the estate and given it over to the local peasant community; before the war she established a dairy farm and agricultural cooperative to benefit the peasants at her own estate of Novaya Polyana.

Soon after the revolution Alexandra was run off Novaya Polyana and went to live with her mother at Yasnaya Polyana, where, in 1918, the family established the Yasnaya Polyana Society and turned the estate into a Tolstoyan commune. For protection Alexandra turned to Lunacharsky, who conferred upon her the title commissar of Yasnaya Polyana and promised his support. Despite her title and famous father, Alexandra was arrested six times, once in connection with the anti-Bolshevik underground organization known as the Tactical Center. A born organizer, Alexandra put together in prison a morning calisthenics program and a school for illiterate inmates. Although Alexandra seems to have earned the respect of many of the prisoners, she was not the most powerful. This honor belonged to "a clever swindler and thief" who went by the name "Baroness von Stein," aka "Sonka of the Golden Hand." Noble titles, it seems, had not completely disappeared in the new Russia, though they were now largely limited to the criminal world.

Throughout the twenties Alexandra waged a struggle to maintain the estate's independence and to run it along Tolstoyan lines of her late father's teachings. She established a model commune and farm, a museum, and a school. For a time the estate ran a cooperative and hospital for the peasants. All these undertakings were at odds with official Communist ideology, but Alexandra defended them by quoting Lenin: "Soviet power can permit itself the luxury of having a Tolstoy nook in the USSR." As early as 1924, the local authorities in Tula began attacking Yasnaya Polyana. The fact that the Tolstoys were still living in the manor house seven years after the revolution raised the ire of many. Moreover, Alexandra continued to teach the children religion at her school and refused to permit the state's atheist propaganda. A local newspaper denounced her school as "one of these bourgeois schools that must be destroyed without the slightest pity. All the teachers in the school are bourgeois and counterrevolutionaries. "Comrades!" it asked. "When will this damned aristocracy be choked? When shall we clear the way for building up our socialist country?"

Alexandra used her ties to powerful men in Moscow—Lunacharsky, Kalinin, Yenukidze, and even Lenin—to protect Yasnaya Polyana from the local authorities. But slowly, she began to lose control. First, she was forced to submit to inspections; then, in 1925–26, the Komsomol (Communist Youth League) established a cell in her school, and in 1928 a Communist Party cell was set up at Yasnaya Polyana, and soon the party began to take over the village institutions, the school, the cooperative, and even the social club. Eventually, Moscow also turned against Alexandra. "Secluding themselves on the estate," ran an article in *Pravda*, "these bourgeois are holding to their old practices. They have orgies, they make the museum janitors serve them and keep the samovars lit all night long; and as a reward for a night's work, they throw them crumbs from their table."

To mark the centenary of Tolstoy's birth in 1928, Alexandra asked Stalin to fund a celebration. Stalin approved her request, though he gave her only a fraction of the money she had requested. As the tensions between Alexandra and the authorities grew, she realized she would never be allowed to maintain her independence and decided the only thing for her to do was leave. In 1929, Alexandra left the Soviet Union. She never returned.[11]

19

THE DEATH OF PARNASSUS

At the end of January 1929, several hundred of the Shereme-tevs' family and friends made their way to Ostafievo. They had come to bury Countess Yekaterina Sheremetev, who had died of tuberculosis at the age of seventy-eight. She had been in declining health for several months, and the end came peacefully. The family had been expecting it. On the first day of the year, Olga Shereme-tev wrote in her diary that although it was sad the countess was dying, this was perhaps for the best since "life now is hard and meaningless."[1]

Pavel wrote his brother Dmitry that their mother "looked inde-scribably beautiful in her coffin." The family carried her coffin to the church cemetery and buried the countess near a lilac bush where gen-erations of Vyazemskys lay. Many local men and women came out to pay their respects. The family returned to the manor house. Nearly everyone was there: Pavel, Praskovya, Vasily, Anna Saburov, Maria Gu-dovich, her children Dmitry, Andrei, and Merinka, Nikolai Sheremetev, his sister Yelena and her husband, Vladimir Golitsyn, and others.[2] For centuries Sheremetevs had gathered to commemorate important fam-ily occasions. This was to be the last time. In the coming years, mar-riages, births, and deaths would be small, quiet affairs, marked so as to attract as little notice as possible. For this large gathering of former people to celebrate and bury the old countess Sheremetev did not go unnoticed by the authorities, and they were prepared to take decisive action and finally destroy this noble nest.

Since 1925, there had been talk of closing the museum and turning it into a rest home for workers. Serious pressure began two years later, when Pavel and Praskovya were stripped of their rights and declared outcasts; at the same time, Pavel lost his position as director of the museum, although he was permitted to remain as a docent. The new director was a fierce Communist by the name of Kereshi. He hated Pavel and immediately began to complain to the local authorities in Podolsk that Pavel had been wasting money and lording over everyone at the museum as its former owner. On June 16, 1928, Kereshi ordered Pavel and his family out of the museum by the first of the month and then fired him for good measure. Pavel immediately wrote to TsEKUBU and Yenukidze for help, and the latter did urge the authorities in Podolsk to ignore Kereshi's order.[3] Kereshi was sacked, and for a time things quieted down.

Then, on March 10, 1929, an article titled "The Count and 'His Servants'" appeared in *Komsomolskaia Pravda*.[4] It was an all-out attack on Pavel, apparently motivated by the recent funeral of his mother.

> The workers of the Ryazan Spinning Mill can no longer put up with their neighbor—the Ostafievo Museum. They speak about it with an anger, a hatred, and feeling of offense that cannot be hidden. Do not try to tell them of the estate's literary and artistic significance, do not arm yourself with the names of Pushkin, Zhukovsky, or Gogol in your efforts. They will interrupt your lengthy speech at the most convincing point and, suspiciously screwing up their eyes, will unexpectedly ask:
>
> "Do you think that these treasures belong to the state? Nothing of the sort! They belong to the Sheremetevs!"
>
> And nodding in the direction of the English park, through whose trees sparkles a white house built in an old architectural style, they will add:
>
> "There, do you see the house's right wing? Sheremetev is living there even now this very day."

Dmitry Ankudinov, the museum's new director, reinvigorated the campaign against Pavel. He seized Pavel's personal library and notified the Podolsk authorities that Pavel owed the museum several hundred rubles for room and board. In July, Pavel was brought before the Podolsk People's Court and asked to explain how it was, exactly, he had been managing to feed and clothe himself and his family for a year without being legally employed. Pavel told them that he had been earning a bit of money translating articles from American scientific journals and selling some of his watercolors; he told the court he had also tried to register for work with the Moscow Labor Board, but had had no luck because he was an outcast. Pavel's case eventually made it all the way to the Presidium of the All-Russian Central Executive Committee, which decided to reinstate his legal rights (and to have his library returned) but on October 22, 1929, also ordered him and his family evicted. One week later, on the twenty-ninth, Pavel, Praskovya, and Vasily left Ostafievo for good.[5]

Difficult as it must have been for Pavel to leave, at least this saved him from having to witness what happened to his beloved Ostafievo.

There is more than one story about how the Russian Parnassus met its end. According to one account, the final act in Ostafievo's destruction began in the summer of 1929. Nikolai Ilin, an employee of the Lenin Library, recalled how the library's director summoned him unexpectedly back from vacation and ordered him to go to Ostafievo and remove all the books (roughly fifty thousand) as quickly as possible. Ilin noted that several agencies had had their eyes set on Ostafievo for quite some time and had been working to have the museum evicted. He was told that the estate was needed for putting up about three thousand Pioneers (the Communist Party's children's organization). Time was of the essence. Within days Ilin was to remove the books, regardless of how or in what condition, even just throwing them into sacks if necessary, and see that they made it back to the Lenin Library. When Ilin and his small team arrived at Ostafievo, they were received like gravediggers. "We had a big job to do," he remembered.

> We worked from seven in the morning until dusk. At the same time a much larger and louder group from another organization was working to liquidate the museum. They hurriedly packed the smaller museum items in crates and stripped all the candelabra, mirrors, paintings, panels, Gobelin tapestries, and other decorations from the walls. In front of my very eyes an eighty-two kg. bronze chandelier was dropped

from the ceiling onto a billiard table on which Pushkin perhaps once played, an exquisite marble statue depicting a satyr chasing a nymph was knocked off its pedestal, crashing to the floor and shattering to pieces, and other such things. [. . .]

Our packing was almost done, so I went back to Moscow the evening before we had finished to find people to accompany the carts the next day. In the meantime, during my absence from Ostafievo, major events were about to happen. The organization charged with preparing the building for the Pioneers was led by a powerful, fat woman, a former laundress, it seems to me, who despite all her efforts was unable to get the job done on time with her crew. So the decision was made to call for the help of the local militia, who were stationed in the area. A group of ten to twelve militia men was put together, each of whom was given what was good pay for the times, and charged with cleaning out the building in just one night so that the next morning cots for the Pioneers could be set up.

I returned to Ostafievo the next morning [. . .] and upon opening the door onto the veranda I froze from shock. There, spread out over the entire veranda under the open sky, lay in one large formless mass all the remaining furniture and property from the museum. The militia men had completed their task, and on time, but to do this they had acted as if they were unloading firewood, simply throwing things on top of each other in careless fashion. About a third of the contents of the museum were lost and destroyed: part of the period furniture and fragile objects were broken in two, the paintings were ripped, smudged and stained, and what remained was left to the whim of the elements [. . .]

It was going on four in the afternoon, after the book-laden carts had barely managed to disappear around the bend in the road behind the trees and I was preparing to make my way to the train station, when the museum director, just returned from one last trip to Moscow the day before to save the museum, came panting up to the side of the building. "Tell everyone right now that the order to liquidate the museum has been rescinded!" she joyously informed us. But it was too late—the museum no longer existed.[6]

According to a different account of events, Ostafievo was closed by order of the Moscow Soviet with the intention of turning it into a rest home for members of the All-Russian Central Executive Committee. What both versions agree on is that by the end of 1929 nothing of the old estate and its collection remained. Its entire history had been erased. Much of Ostafievo's riches, including a priceless collection of the Decembrists' correspondence, were apparently stolen and never reached the libraries and archives where they were to be sent.[7]

The willful destruction of Ostafievo was but one minor skirmish on the cultural front of the Great Break. There were many more like it, and most of the other palace and estate museums in Soviet Russia met a similarly tragic fate during these years. Throughout the 1920s pressure had been mounting against the Museum of Everyday Life in the Fountain House, the former Sheremetev palace in Leningrad. City authorities argued that showing off the fabulous lifestyle of aristocrats like the Sheremetevs did not fit the requirements of the new proletarian society. The museum staff tried to skirt the issue by staging more ideologically appropriate exhibitions, such as "The Labor and Lifestyle of the Serfs" in 1927. In April 1929, however, the *Sovnarkóm* voted to close the museum and turn the building into a student dormitory or an Atheists' House, a center for antireligious propaganda sponsored by the Union of Militant Atheists. The vast collection was packed and then dispersed among a number of museums across the Soviet Union. Objects deemed not museum-worthy ended up furnishing the offices of Soviet officials and filling hotel lobbies. Subsequently, the interiors would be disfigured beyond recognition to make room for a string of organizations, including the House of Diverting Science (a popular children's museum), the Astronomical Institute, and the Arctic and Antarctic Scientific Research Institute, which dug up the entire ground floor to build a large pool for testing models of the first Soviet nuclear icebreakers.[8]

Seven OGPU agents paid a visit to the Kuskovo Estate Museum about the time Ostafievo was being destroyed. They did not at all like what they saw, and their subsequent report drips with disdain for the museum and its employees. "The palace-museum of former Count Sheremetev [. . .] is of doubtful historical value since there already are quite a number of such lairs of former satraps outside Moscow [. . .] now populated by persons with suspicious pasts."[9] They noted that the money spent on the museum could not be justified and recommended the museum be liquidated and the buildings turned into a hospital or school. The Moscow Department of Education fought to save Kuskovo. Key to the department's strategy was to rethink the ideological message of the estate. No longer intended to showcase the life of the nobility, it was now presented as a monument to Russia's serfs, exploited for the decadent whims of their masters. While Kuskovo may have been built to order by Count Sheremetev, the labor had been that of his serfs, and this, so went the new message, was what the museum was meant to celebrate and showcase. The serf masters were henceforth presented in the worst possible light. The official script intended for museum guides from the mid-1930s included lines about "how extremely boorish the Counts Sheremetev were" and instructed visitors to gaze upon the sumptuous halls and galleries of the palace in order to "better know our enemy, and consequently develop a deeper and more conscious hatred of him."[10]

By the end of the Second World War, a staggering 95 percent of Russia's country estates had disappeared. Some had been targeted for destruction; most, however, were simply abandoned, plundered, and then forgotten, left to rot and decay and finally fall to ruin.[11] An entire cultural legacy had been wiped from the face of the earth.

Expelled from Ostafievo, Pavel and his family were sent to live in Moscow's Novodevichy Monastery. Boris Sadovskoy, the Silver Age poet and critic, recorded their arrival in his diary:

> At the right wing of the monastery, two carts; wretched, pitiful jades in foul harnesses, the carts worn-out, two degenerates, one in a hat, the other a peaked cap—descendants of the once steady drays of the Russian *bogatýri*.*
>
> "What is this?"
> "Count Sheremetev has arrived."
> "Which Sheremetev?"
> "Pavel Sergeevich. They've brought his books."
> A little while later a decrepit man of medium height appeared

---

*The great warriors of the medieval Russian epic poems.

with a thin woman. "Pavel Sergeevich." He came over. He was dressed like some pauper—a torn jacket, a dirty cap, puttees on his legs. I greet him. [. . .] He replies as if we've been acquainted for ages. [. . .] Upon learning that I am Boris Sadovskoy, he displays a keen sympathy in me and introduces me to his wife, an old-fashioned and most unattractive woman in an old green dress. I kissed her sunburned, brittle hand, a wedding ring on one finger. Then the count and the countess walked out of the monastery gates. I have the impression the count has nothing to pay the draymen, and he's gone off to look for some money. The most moving thing is that he's brought his books with him or, rather, the pathetic remains of the enormous Sheremetev library, his last comfort. The draymen stood around waiting for several hours. They and the Sheremetevs—two poles of degeneration, the remnants of our two main classes: the former count and the former peasants, former owners, former masters, former people, former Russia.[12]

Sadovskoy, himself a nobleman's son, welcomed the Sheremetevs to the monastery with a dinner in his basement room.

Founded in the early sixteenth century by Vasily III, grand prince of Muscovy and father of Ivan the Terrible, the Novodevichy Monastery had for centuries served as fortress, cloister for Orthodox nuns, and quasi prison for Russian royal women forced to take the veil. In 1922, the Communists closed the monastery and turned it into a Museum of Women's Emancipation. With the beginning of the Great Break, the ancient Cathedral of the Virgin of Smolensk was shuttered, and the refectories and former cells of the sisters were converted into housing for students, factory workers, and new state employees now streaming into Moscow. One of these students, Olga Gorlushkin, became friendly with the Sheremetevs. "They were very good people," she remembered, "very simple."

Pavel Sergeevich and Praskovya Vasilevna and their nanny were all good people. They would visit me and always gave me money when I was short, even though they barely had enough for their own food and clothing. Pavel Sergeevich would go off somewhere every morning and come back in the evening. He was pensive, not very talkative, even a bit withdrawn. But their nanny and Praskovya Vasilevna always had a good word for everyone.

The Sheremetevs were given a large and bright room, but their neighbors soon objected to former people having such nice accommodations, and they were moved to a smaller, darker room in the monastery's Naprudny Tower.[13] The tower had a special place in Russian history. It was here that Sophia, the older half sister of Peter the Great and regent of Russia in the 1680s, lived out the remaining years of her life as a prisoner after Peter seized the throne. When a group of musketeers (*strél'tsy*) tried to put her back on the throne in 1698, Peter had several hundred of them hanged below her tower window to remind Sophia who was in charge. The bodies were left hanging for five months.[14]

The tower room was round and small, about fifty-five square meters. It felt even smaller since it was crammed with books, paintings, icons, and the remains of the ancient Sheremetev archive. Most of this family legacy was heaped in a pile in the center of the room and covered with a tarpaulin; bookshelves ringed the walls. Word soon spread about the new residents and their possessions, and their room was repeatedly burgled. There was no toilet, sink, or stove, all located elsewhere in the monastery. In winter the tea would freeze in their cups.[15]

Pavel scrambled to earn a bit of money to support the family. Even though he had had his rights reinstated, he still could not find work. Vladimir Bonch-Bruevich, the old Bolshevik, historian, and head of the Central Museum of Fiction, Criticism, and Journalism (part of the basis for the State Literary Museum, the haven for former people, which he also headed from 1934), came to Pavel's aid and remained a reliable ally. It was apparently thanks to Bonch-Bruevich that Pavel was hired in late 1930 as an employee of the People's Commissariat of Enlightenment and given the room in the Naprudny Tower, technically listed as his "office," or the family might have been turned out into the street.[16] Thanks to Bonch-Bruevich, Pavel received a number of small scholarly projects (writing articles, doing translations), but these still did not provide enough money to live on, and so Pavel had to hustle to find work elsewhere. He wrangled small commissions at various museums, constructing dioramas, illustrating guidebooks, writing wall text, compiling inventories, and giving tours. A scion of Russia's greatest serf-holding family, Pavel earned a few rubles making paintings depicting the harsh cruelties of serfdom. For the Ostankino museum, Pavel painted portraits of his great-grandmother, the serf opera singer Praskovya, as well as her father, an illiterate serf blacksmith, and her closest friend, Tatiana Shlykova, a brilliant serf ballerina.[17]

Pavel had always favored the company of scholars and artists. Some, such as the painter, art historian, and conservationist Igor Grabar and the painter and art restorer Pavel Korin, helped Pavel find work and were frequent visitors to the Naprudny Tower. Pavel cherished these relationships as much for the comfort and stimulation of being with persons who shared his passions as for the lifeline these friends extended him. The artistic atmosphere impressed itself on little Vasily. Pavel taught him about Russian history, culture, and religion and how to draw and paint, for which he showed talent from an early age. "One force opposing another never produced anything, other than destruction and barbarism," he told Vasily. "Only good, peaceful actions produce results, and our country must be governed with the help of good deeds." A cousin remembered Vasily as a good-looking, well-mannered boy. The two cousins acted together and loved to dance the waltz and tango.[18]

By the 1930s, the Sheremetev clan had been reduced to almost nothing. Of the counts Sheremetev, only Pavel remained. Family gatherings had become small, intimate affairs, either in the tower or in Tsaritsyno, on Moscow's southern edge, where Praskovya's brother Vladimir Obolensky lived with his family. In January 1935, the family gathered to bury one of its oldest members, Yekaterina Sergeevna Sheremetev, aged seventy-two, part of the untitled line of Moscow Sheremetevs. Led by a priest and a young relative bearing an icon, the mourners followed the funeral carriage through the Moscow streets to the Dorogomilovsky Cemetery. As they walked, passersby stopped to stare. Some hurled insults; some pelted them with snowballs. After the funeral, they returned to the tower. The priest joined them to conduct a brief service for the soul of the deceased. It happened to be Vasily's name day as well, so they shared a cake to mark the occasion. Despite everything, Olga Sheremetev had to admit it had been a fine day. "The mood was very good, and we shared very warm memories of Katya, and one could feel the love we had for her."[19]

Two years later, on January 14, 1937, they gathered again in the tower to celebrate Vasily's name day. A photograph records the occasion. Vasily, aged seventeen, stands behind his father, his mother and aunt Maria Gudovich to either side of him. Maria's daughter Varvara is there, along with Varvara's husband, Vladimir, their children, and Vladimir's sisters. A few manage a weak smile; others look blankly at the camera. It was most likely the last time they all were together. Before the snows had melted, Varvara was arrested; a few months later they came for Vladimir. Both disappeared into the abyss of Stalin's Great Terror, never to be seen again.[20]

20

OUTCASTS

The Golitsyn family found themselves relatively comfortable at the beginning of 1929. The mayor, in good health for his seventy-five years, was receiving monthly money transfers from his son Alexander, now settled and working in Los Angeles. His son Nikolai had a job as a translator at the Institute of Marx and Engels, and Vladimir Vladimirovich was working at the Bank for Foreign Trade, where he had been employed since 1923. Son Mikhail was an economist in the chemicals division at Gosplan, the state planning agency, earning a respectable two hundred rubles a month, and his wife was helping run a small business called The Embroidered Cushion. Mikhail and Anna's children were also getting on well with their own lives. Vladimir and Yelena were busy raising their three children on the money he earned as an illustrator; Sergei was studying literature at school and making some money on the side as a draftsman. Three of the girls were also studying: Masha at the Higher School of Literature, Katya at a regular state school, and Sonya at an institute for social health.

And then the troubles started.

One day in March Sergei came home to find a large sign had been hung on the gates outside their apartment block on Yeropkinsky Lane. On it were the names of nine of the building's residents who had recently been stripped of their rights and declared outcasts. Seven of them were members of his family. Indeed, everyone in his family was on it, except, that is, the two youngest—Masha and Katya—both minors. Even Alexandra Rosset, the Golitsyns' longtime domestic, still living with them a decade after the revolution, was on the list. Each was identified by the status he or she had held before the revolution: "former head of the nobility," "former prince," "former landowner," "former princess." Next to most of their names was also written "currently not working," the suggestion being they were parasites, living off the labor of others, just as in the days of old. Sergei looked for his name and saw the words "Son of a former prince, currently not working."[1]

The men were then fired from their jobs—Nikolai from the institute and Vladimir Vladimirovich from the bank. Mikhail was warned he was about to be let go, and so he resigned, thinking this would be less of a blemish on his record. Large-scale purges of former people were under way throughout the country. Not everyone, of course, lost his job. Sergei noted that it was not necessary to fire everyone; rather, it was enough to go after one or two individuals to terrify everyone else and cower all of them into submission. Some, like Prince Kirill Urusov, fought to keep their jobs. A young geologist in Moscow, Urusov was one of the few not willing to go away quietly. He publicly defended himself as a productive, loyal worker, and somehow he managed to keep his job.

Nikolai Golitsyn was the most fortunate in the family, quickly landing a new job as a translator for the French newspaper *Journal de Moscou*, where he remained until his death in 1942. Vladimir Vladimirovich was hired and fired from six different positions within three years. He managed to get by on the little money he earned from assignments at the Literary Museum, compiling a catalog of its folklore section, for example, and doing the occasional translation. (He knew five foreign languages.)[2] Vladimir Vladimirovich was fortunate to have his rights soon reinstated, some thought because his late wife, Tatiana, had been a peasant. (This is possible, though it did not help her own brother, repressed as a kulak in the 1930s.) Mikhail had it the hardest of the brothers. He was turned away everywhere he looked for work. "What are you sticking your nose in here for? We'll build socialism just fine without you," he was told. He fought to have the family's rights restored. He gathered all the documents from their past employers and petitioned to have the decision rescinded. His son Vladimir, who never did put faith in the Soviet system to right its wrongs or listen to law or reason, refused to have anything to do with this, telling his father he did not care one way or another, for he knew that he was working, and this was all that mattered. The mayor also asked Mikhail not to fight for his rights. "Just leave me in peace," were his words.[3]

Mikhail turned to Peshkov and Gorky for help. As proof of the injustice of being declared an outcast, he pointed out the fact that he was the descendant of a Decembrist, that he had been under surveillance by the tsarist police as a subversive liberal, and that he had had an excellent work record since the revolution. Neither Peshkov nor Gorky, however, was able to help. It aggrieved Mikhail to be without work. The forced inactivity and lack of purpose soon took a toll on his emotional well-being; he became despondent and lost hope for his own life and that of the family. He began to have heart trouble and could not sleep. He would lie in bed at night, repeating in the dark, "How are we all going to survive?" On the advice of his lawyer, Mikhail agreed to undergo tests at a mental asylum; the idea was if a doctor would be willing to testify to his being unable to work, this might give him some legal basis for fighting his case against the state. Upon arriving at the asylum, Mikhail felt as if he had just entered a novel by Ilf and Petrov. The place was full of completely sane people, all in hiding because of their questionable biographies or fleeing a purge or prison sentence. One of the patients would sing "God Save the Tsar!" at the top of his lungs every morning. Mikhail finally asked him, "Are you crazy?" No, the perfectly sane man answered, but "this is the only place in the entire country that I can sing whatever I want without fear of being punished." Mikhail was soon sent home, although without a doctor's certificate of mental illness and so no closer to finding a way out of his plight.[4]

When not comforting her husband, Anna was dealing with her own struggles. Together with a number of former noblewomen and a group of villagers from Buchalki, Anna had founded a workshop called The Embroidered Cushion a few years earlier. The village women made embroidered linens and pillows that Anna and her colleagues marketed and sold. The venture took off, and soon everyone at The Embroidered Cushion was making good money. When the tax inspectorate noticed the presence of several former people at the workshop, they shut it down, citing class exploitation. Anna was arrested and held for two weeks. Twice she was tried in a criminal court as a parasite on the backs of the peasant class, and both times she was acquitted. Her lawyer argued that the state should be calling her a hero and awarding her a medal for her hard work. The state, however, did not agree. Thus ended Anna's career as an entrepreneur.[5]

The repression continued. In the late hours of June 12, 1929, an OGPU agent along with several soldiers arrived at the Golitsyn apartment armed with an arrest warrant for Sergei. The usual scene followed: they searched the apartment into the early morning as the family sat dumb in their nightclothes and prepared tea and things for Sergei. Before they took him away, his parents made the sign of the cross over him and his sisters Sonya and Masha whispered to him to only answer their questions and not to say another word. He was placed in a Black Raven and driven to the Lubyanka. Part of Sergei was proud to be taken; he saw it as a sort of rite of passage marking his transition to manhood.

The following night he was awoken from his sleep and led through a warren of corridors to a small room with a writing desk, some papers, and a lamp with a green shade. A thin young man in uniform sat on the other side. He told Sergei to sit down. He offered him a cigarette, paused, and then lit into him with a volley of invective and threats and foul language. He said they knew all about Sergei, that he was a strident monarchist and a fascist, and he called him "Prince Riurik, a class enemy, a foe of Soviet power." (Here Sergei, unwisely, pointed out that the Golitsyns were in fact not descendants of Riurik, the mythic founder of the first Russian state, but of Gedymin, a fourteenth-century grand prince of Lithuania. The stunned interrogator found this elucidation neither helpful nor to the point.) He told Sergei they were well aware of what he and his friends were up to: the fox-trotting, the parties, the anti-Soviet talk. (Sergei's suspicions fell on his cousin Alexei Bobrinsky, suspected by some in the family of being an informer ever since the Fox-trot Affair of 1924.) The agent put a piece of paper in front of Sergei and asked him to write a report about his friends' anti-Soviet behavior, but Sergei refused, even after being threatened. The next day Sergei was moved to the Butyrki, where he was questioned day and night. Now his interrogators informed him it was no longer enough to prove his loyalty by telling them what he knew; now they wanted him to inform on his friends. Again, Sergei refused, and again, they let him off, though he did agree to sign a paper promising not to tell anyone about his interrogation, which they said was a "state secret." The next day the guard opened his cell: "Golitsyn! With your things." He was free.[6]

That autumn the Golitsyns were ordered to leave Moscow within two weeks. The order hit the mayor especially hard. Moscow had been his home for most of his life. His entire career had been devoted to Russia's ancient capital, and he loved the city as if it were a member of his own family. It was a part of him, and exile at his age meant he was likely to die without ever seeing it again. He was beside himself with grief when the day to leave arrived. He told his family he would not go; he simply could not leave. They did their best to calm him down. Everyone was anxious and exhausted. The previous two weeks had been busy. They had given away most of their furniture and also a great deal of their remaining books. In the courtyard they burned several generations' worth of family letters. There was only so much they could pack up and take with them. Finally, one Sunday morning in October several horse-drawn drays arrived, and they started to load up their belongings—a bit of furniture, a few cases, trunks, and boxes. Only after all the heavy things had been loaded did Vladimir bring out the family portraits, lay them on top, cover and then secure them for the journey. As they rode off, the neighbors watched in silence. Sergei wondered what they must have been thinking. The Golitsyns had lived on Yeropkinsky Lane for seven years. Here they had celebrated four weddings and three births. And here five family members had been arrested. As they were making their exit from Moscow, the wind kicked up, and it started to rain. Vladimir fussed with the tarps and ropes, trying to make certain the portraits were safe and dry. That evening they arrived at their new home, a small dacha in the village of Kotovo on the Savelovsky rail line.[7]

The mayor did not go with them to Kotovo, choosing instead to live with his daughter Eli's family in Sergiev Posad. Things were not good there either for former people. In January 1926, Eli, her husband, Vladimir, and many other former people, including the Istomins, Shakhovskoys, and Olsufevs, were stripped of their rights and declared outcasts.

In all, about three thousand individuals, or some 10 percent of the town's population, lost their rights, and it was not just nobles, but clergymen, traders, small business owners, and even tailors, metalworkers, and craftsmen. According to official documents from the time, persons were singled out if they had hired labor to make a profit, if they lived off rents or any unearned income, if they engaged in trade, if they had served in the tsarist police force, or if they happened to be dependents of outcasts over the age of eighteen. A final category comprised all "lunatics."[8]

In May 1928, *Komsomolskaia Pravda* and other newspapers began running articles complaining that Sergiev Posad was "sheltering an unbroken gang of nobles, Black Hundreds, and various other 'Excellencies.'" The press demanded to know how a group of former people could live so openly and work without fear in a number of Soviet institutions. Vladimir Trubetskoy was personally singled out.[9] "ALL THE BARONS AND PRINCES MUST BE FIRED IMMEDIATELY AND RUN OUT OF SOVIET PLACES OF WORK," screamed one headline.[10] The *Workers' Newspaper* attacked the Museum of the Holy Trinity of St. Sergius Monastery for the large number of former people on its staff. The same month the newspaper *Working Moscow* described the museum's former people as "two-legged rats." That month eighty people were arrested, including fourteen monks who worked at the museum and many former people.[11]

The Trubetskoys were now living on the edge of starvation. Beginning in late 1928, bread was rationed, but as outcasts Vladimir and his family were not entitled to any ration cards. Then, in the spring of 1929, Vladimir lost his jobs in the restaurant orchestra and the movie theater. "We are threatened with hunger," the mayor wrote; "there's no more bread." They tried to raise rabbits, but the animals died. Their few remaining personal things of value the family sold to Torgsin, a network of state stores where food and other rationed goods could be purchased for hard currency or gold, silver, jewelry, antiques, and art.[12]

In 1930, Anna Golitsyn sent a letter to her daughter:

The Trubetskoys' situation is bad. Vladimir's income is not nearly enough to support them. I went to see them, and found they had no firewood, and almost no potatoes, not to mention even the least bit of fat in their diet. They had just a simple soup—water with a few potatoes, followed by a few more potatoes sprinkled with salt. [. . .] I came with 20 rubles for grandfather from Vovik,* but I gave it to the Trubetskoys instead. They bought a load of firewood, some more potatoes, and some horsemeat. When I left Vladimir was expecting to receive some sort of pay, which will be scattered here and there, for they are 300 rubles in debt. The children's boots are all worn out, and they can't be mended, and the children are freezing, especially Varya, whose feet have frozen and become all swollen and hurt terribly whenever she walks. We are now trying to sell a red bedspread with old needlework on it to raise some money for them.[13]

If such state-enforced poverty was not humiliation enough, Vladimir had to live with the defamation of his ancestors when in June 1929 the head of the St. Sergius Holy Trinity Museum dug up the grave of Vladimir's great-grandfather. As soon as he heard of this, an outraged Vladimir went to complain, asking how he dared disturb someone's final resting place. The director, however, was utterly unfazed by Vladimir's complaint, insisting rather on sharing with him the marvelous things he had found there, such as the deceased's epaulets (still in excellent condition, he noted) and his skull, which he was keeping in his office but was willing to part with if Vladimir really wanted it. The grave robbers had also pried the leather boots off the dead man's feet. One of Vladimir's sons later saw a man strutting the streets of Sergiev Posad in them, immensely proud of his fine footwear.[14]

"Given what's happened to me this year, there's a grievous thought I cannot get out of my head . . . We've all been crushed, utterly crushed," Vladimir said to his friend Mikhail Prishvin one day returning from hunting in the woods. The destruction and brutality made Vladimir feel so despondent for Russia that at times he was physically ill.[15] Prishvin shared Vladimir's grief. "The Russian people have spoiled their light, they have thrown down their cross and pledged an oath to the prince of darkness," he wrote.[16]

Amazingly, the Trubetskoy children found ways to have fun amid these struggles. With empty stomachs they would go out into the snow to slide and ski in the nearby woods. Every year there would be a Christmas tree and Easter eggs. In the summer they loved to play in

*The mayor and his son Vladimir Vladimirovich.

the rain. When they had time, Eli and Vladimir were sure to take the children on outings to historical places. Through it all, Eli and Vladimir tried to give them a true childhood by hiding the stresses they were under and by distracting the children with games, music, and laughter from the growing danger outside the door.[17]

On April 14, 1928, the mayor's son-in-law Georgy Osorgin was sent from Butyrki to the prison camp at Solovki. When his wife, Lina, learned that he was being transferred, she went with her sister Masha to search for him at the Nikolaev train station. They caught sight of his face, now covered by a long beard, sticking out a window. Lina and Masha got close enough to speak to him but were told to move off by a guard. Among the prisoners at Solovki was Dmitry Likhachev. Likhachev, who became a great literary scholar and one of the country's most respected moral voices, was taken by Georgy. Osorgin, he recalled later, was "of average height, with blond hair and a beard and mustache, and always held himself erect in military fashion; he had a beautiful bearing. [. . .] He was always lively, happy, and witty." Likhachev saw in Georgy a humanitarian nature, infused with a profound religious faith. He was the kind of man who looked out for others. As head clerk of the infirmary Georgy always tried to help the weaker prisoners, especially the intellectuals, by finagling to get them released from hard labor.

In *The Gulag Archipelago*, Alexander Solzhenitsyn singled out Georgy as one of the "genuine aristocrats" in the camps, together with the philosophers, career military men, artists, and scholars: "Because of their upbringing, their traditions, they were too proud to show depression or fear, to whine and complain about their fate even to friends. It was a sign of good manners to take everything with a smile, even while being marched out to be shot. Just as if all this Arctic prison in a roaring sea were simply a minor misunderstanding at a picnic." Solzhenitsyn writes how Osorgin and these other inmates would laugh and be witty and ready to make light of the absurdity of their situation, all of which was lost on the camp guards. "Georgi Mikhailovich Osorgin used to walk around and mock: 'Comment vous portez-vouz on this island?' 'A lager comme a lager.' (And these jokes, this stressed and emphasized independence of the aristocratic spirit—these more than anything else irritated the half-beast Solovetsky jailers.)"

With the help of Peshkov, Lina was able to visit Georgy that August, sharing a cabin on a boat anchored along the island shore. When she left, Lina was pregnant. She managed to make a second visit a little more than a year later in October 1929, around the time her family was being expelled from Moscow. Georgy's situation was extremely tenuous at the time, and what transpired over the subsequent days remains unclear, although the end result is beyond doubt. According to Lina's brother Sergei, shortly before Lina's arrival Georgy had been confined to a small cell for the crime of giving a dying priest a bit of bread and wine for one final communion. The camp officials agreed to let Georgy out of the cell during Lina's visit, but on one condition: that he not mention to her that he had just been sentenced to death. Sergei wrote that these few days together were among the happiest of Lina's life. Fellow prisoner Dmitry Likhachev saw them walking arm in arm, she a beautiful, elegant brunette, he happy, with a mildly ironic expression. Georgy, according to Likhachev, kept his word and never did tell his wife. Lina left confident they would make it through his six-year sentence and then finally be together for good, even if that meant exile in some remote part of the country.

Here is how Solzhenitsyn recounts this final visit:

One time Osorgin was scheduled to be shot. And that very day his young wife (and he himself was not yet forty*) disembarked on the wharf there. And Osorgin begged the jailers not to spoil his wife's visit for her. He promised that he would not let her stay more than three days and that they could shoot him as soon as she left. And here is the kind of self-control this meant, the sort of thing we have forgotten because of the anathema we have heaped on the aristocracy, we who whine at every petty misfortune and every petty pain. For three days he never left his wife's side, and he had to keep her from guessing the situation! He must not hint at it even in one single phrase! He must not allow his spirits to quaver. He must not allow his eyes to darken. Just once (his wife is alive and she remembers it now), when they were

* Georgy was thirty-six; Lina, twenty-nine.

walking along the Holy Lake, she turned and saw that her husband had clutched his head in torment. "What's wrong?" "Nothing," he answered instantly. She could have stayed still longer, but he begged her to leave. As the steamer pulled away from the wharf, he was already undressing to be shot.

This last part appears to be artistic embellishment, for we do not know for certain when Georgy was shot. The sources disagree on the exact date, ranging from October 16 to 29. We do know that on one of those nights, Georgy and some of the other prisoners were called out of their barracks and marched out to the local cemetery and shot. Some accounts cite forty prisoners killed; others, four hundred. The stated reason for the executions was the inmates' failure to inform the camp bosses of a planned escape attempt. As he walked to his death, Georgy sang "Christ Is Risen" and prayed aloud with the other men alongside him. The bodies were dumped in a common grave; a few of the victims were still alive when the dirt was shoveled over them. The head of the execution squad, Dmitry Uspensky, was drunk at the time and had fired wildly at the men with his Nagant. Likhachev saw him the next morning washing the blood from his boots. In 1988, Likhachev returned to Solovki and found the site of the execution. A small house had been built upon it. Digging in the dirt around the foundation, he came across bone fragments. He met the residents, who told him that when they harvested the potatoes in their kitchen garden, they sometimes pulled up human skulls.[18]

Lina learned of Georgy's murder soon after. She found a priest willing to conduct a secret service for Georgy in a Moscow church, but when they got there, they noticed a number of other people and turned back out of fear. The impossibility of properly mourning for her husband compounded Lina's grief. About this time the Osorgin family received permission to leave the Soviet Union for France. Lina said goodbye to her family and went with them.[19]

21

THE MOUSE, THE KEROSENE,
AND THE MATCH

In 1931, two years after being exiled from Moscow, the Golitsyns moved from Kotovo to Dmitrov, an ancient Russian town sixty-five kilometers north of the capital on River Yakhroma. Dmitrov was a pleasant place with old stone houses and several fine churches, and its proximity to Moscow made it convenient for families like the Golitsyns who needed to visit but could no longer legally reside there. The quiet life of the town was about to be swept away, however, when in a few years Dmitrov became the center of the largest slave labor project in the Soviet Union.

Two hundred years earlier, Peter the Great had envisioned constructing a canal to link the Moscow and Volga rivers. It was a hydrological scheme of pharaonic scale that, not surprisingly, was never realized. But such gargantuan projects captured the spirit of the First Five-Year Plan, and in June 1931 the Central Executive Committee approved the construction of the Moscow-Volga Canal. It was initially put under the direction of the People's Commissariat of Water, but given the slow speed of the work, largely because of the lack of manpower, it was transferred to the OGPU the following year. In September 1932, Dmitlag was established to provide the necessary workforce for the Moscow-Volga Canal. Dmitlag, short for Dmitrov Corrective Labor Camp, became the largest branch of the entire gulag system over the next few years as prisoners from camps across the country were transferred there to meet the enormous demand for labor. Its size (covering a good portion of the entire Moscow region) and population grew so quickly that the camp administration lost control over its numbers. How many men and women labored at Dmitlag is still not known, although the writer, poet, and gulag survivor Varlam Shalamov estimated the camp was home to 1.2 million people in 1933. When it was finished in 1937, the Stalin Moscow-Volga Canal stretched almost eighty miles, connecting the capital to the mighty Volga and so providing the land-locked city access to five seas: the White and Baltic to the north, the Black, Caspian, and Azov to the south. Moscow, it was said, had become the "Port of the Five Seas."[1]

For the first several years work on the canal was largely done without the use of heavy machinery. The canal and its many locks, reservoirs, and hydropower stations were almost entirely built with shovels, pickaxes, wheelbarrows, and human sweat. Like some vast ant colony, armies of prison laborers swarmed over the land, digging, drilling, hauling, and dumping. The best workers received six hundred grams of bread a day; most were given only four hundred, while those being punished had to survive on three hundred. Countless thousands died. Some starved to death; some drowned or were accidentally buried in concrete, their bodies never recovered. Some were taken out at night after their shifts and shot in the woods. One of the camp bosses liked to strip recalcitrant prisoners bare in the winter and leave them to freeze in the snow.[2]

The canal project was run by Lazar Kogan, head of Moscow-Volga Construction, and Semyon Firin, head of Dmitlag (from September 1933). Dmitlag's offices were in a former monastery, which had been converted into a museum after the revolution. The staff had dared protest the closure of the museum, and so the OGPU arrested them. For Firin, previously the boss of Belbaltlag (the White Sea–Baltic Sea Camp), Dmitlag was not just about canal building but was part of a larger project of remaking Soviet man, what was known at the time as reforging. The canal was meant to change not only the country but also the people who built it: through the process of labor the prisoners would shed their flawed selves and be reborn—reforged—as new men worthy of their Soviet homeland. Firin saw himself as more than a jailer (even if on a mass scale): he was a maker of men, an arbiter of culture. Like some minor potentate, he created his own court. In the evenings he hosted a salon at his dacha for poets, writers, and other talented prisoners. He set up a Cultural-Educational Division at the camp and a theater and an orchestra staffed with prisoners; he searched the entire gulag for the most accomplished singers, musicians, and performers and had them transferred to Dmitlag. Artists were kept busy making posters and banners, and Dmitlag published more than fifty newspapers with titles like *Reforging* and *Moscow-Volga* that carried articles with instructive headlines such as "Learn to Relax" and "Drown Your Past on the Bottom of the Canal." Social and political leaders, artists, and journalists came from all over the USSR and abroad to behold the miracle taking place at Dmitlag and wonder at "Bolshevik power's infinite ability to remake man." Stalin himself visited Dmitlag three times.[3]

In the bizarre world of Dmitlag, freedom and captivity were not always distinct, however. Consider the case of Professor Nikolai Nekrasov, the last governor-general of Finland before the revolution and a former minister in the Provisional Government. An excellent engineer, he had been arrested several times, most recently in 1930, when he was sentenced to ten years. He was brought to Dmitlag as an inmate specialist, yet was given his own newly constructed house in the "the free sector" along with a car and driver. He was released in 1935 but chose to stay on and worked at Dmitlag until the project was finished. In 1940, he was arrested for a final time and then shot.

Nekrasov's story was not unique. In the mid-1930s, after spending several years in the camps, Galina von Meck and her husband, Dmitry Orlovsky (she had remarried after her first husband, Nicholas, had been shot as an enemy of the people during the Great Break), found themselves unemployed, and unemployable. Desperate, Dmitry accepted a job working for the OGPU as a statistician on the canal works near Rybinsk. One of the perquisites of the job was personal servants drawn from the inmate population. Called slaves, they were assigned to families to do manual labor about the house. "We, who had been prisoners like these poor people a year or two before," Galina observed, "enjoyed the privilege of being served by those who were our former comrades." Despite their shared experiences, the two sides were not permitted to socialize or even be friendly with each other, and people watched to make certain this rule was followed. The comfortable life at Dmitlag did not last long, however. After being let go from his position in 1938, Dmitry was arrested again and disappeared. "Farewell and forgive me" were his last words to Galina.[4]

Many former people came to work at Dmitlag, some voluntarily, some having been sent there from other camps. The need for specialists was so great that engineers and others with the required technical skills were purposely arrested, charged with Article 58, and then sent to Dmitlag to work. (Article 58, divided into fourteen separate sections, referred to part of the criminal code of 1926, and its subsequent iterations, that outlined all counterrevolutionary crimes against the state. Its widespread use in the repression of the Stalin years made it notorious.[5])

Vladimir Golitsyn was one of the artists who found work at Dmitlag. In the autumn of 1932, he was hired to decorate the hall in a local school for a ball marking the fifteenth anniversary of the OGPU. After he had finished, the former aristocrat who had witnessed the balls of tsarist Russia stayed to watch. The Gulag Ball kicked off with a number of long speeches in praise of the secret police and its "iron cohort," filled with fond recollections of the early days of the Cheka in the bloody aftermath of the Bolshevik Revolution. These were followed by the "Artistic Portion" of the evening, featuring a choir of Ukrainian kulaks, balalaika music, and various soloists, all of them camp prisoners. And then it was time to dance. The OGPU Brass Band roared to life, and one of the camp commandants pranced to the center of the hall, clapped loudly for silence, and cried out, "The Ladies' Waltz!" With that, he grabbed hold of a blond girl (a camp typist) and set about spinning her around the hall, stomping his spurs as he went. Vladimir watched for about an hour and then went home. "A rather wretched affair," he wrote that night in his diary. "Sadness."[6]

Depressing as this entertainment was, Vladimir was nonetheless able to find humor in the absurdity of their lives, and his diaries and letters are filled with observations on the strange world they inhabited in Dmitrov. He recorded the story of a prisoner who had the good fortune to purchase a winning lottery ticket, only to discover he could not collect the prize: a trip around the world. Vladimir copied down the various signs and banners posted about Dmitlag: "A slogan emblazoned on the archway at the entrance to the camp: 'The Moscow-Volga Canal—Creation of the Second Five-Year Plan and the Classless Society.'" He took special delight in a sign posted in one of the lavatories: "Red Army men! Learn to control your a[sses]! Make sure you sh[it] straight into the toilet!!" Once he was commissioned to create a poster titled "Socially Harmful Women in Freedom and in the Camps of the NKVD." He drew a series of women getting drunk, stealing, killing, gambling, fighting, and the like. As he worked, his children gathered around to watch. Little Lariusha pointed to a streetwalker and asked what she was doing wrong. "Can't you see?" his elder brother knowingly informed him. "She's smoking."[7]

Dmitry and Andrei Gudovich also came to Dmitrov. Dmitry had spent the past three years as a prisoner in Karelia working on the Belbalt Canal; Andrei was returning from Siberian exile. Both found work at Dmitlag, Dmitry in one of the design bureaus. They visited the Golitsyns often, and Vladimir enjoyed their company. He remembered gathering one June day to celebrate Yelena's name day. They pulled down two guitars from the wall and began singing the fox-trots they had danced to years ago in Moscow. To Vladimir's surprise, they all also knew the words to the songs of the Red Army from the civil war. Dmitry sang these better than anyone. "You have to spend a good eight years in the camps as he has," Vladimir observed, "in order to sing like that. Of course, his renditions are rather refined, but this gives them a special charm."[8]

The Golitsyn home was warm and welcoming. Vladimir and Yelena opened their doors to newcomers and helped them get settled. Though they had little money, they always treated their guests to black bread and a vegetable salad.[9] Vladimir and Yelena lived in one house with their three children (Yelena, aged eight; Mishka, six; and Lariusha, four in 1932), his parents, and grandfather, the mayor. His sisters Masha and Katya lived next door.

The family had not been in Dmitrov long when the mayor died of pneumonia on February 29, 1932, at the age of eighty-four. Mikhail and Anna read the prayers for the dying over him during the final hours of his life. He died peacefully, without pain. Mikhail noted how "the expression on his face became clear and amazingly calm . . . He lay there unusually handsome, graceful, or, rather, elegant—just as he always was." He was buried in Dmitrov, and for years the family visited his gravesite, until one day when they arrived to find it gone; canal workers had bulldozed the entire cemetery the night before without warning.

Among the mayor's papers was found a short piece titled "Prediction," completed a month before his death. In it he expressed his undying conviction in the inevitable collapse of the Soviet Union:

This regime does not possess the ability to create—it knows how to destroy, to abolish, to cast off—but it is incapable of creating, and its celebrated "achievements" amount to nothing, if not even less than nothing. And for this reason its collapse will come about as a result of the power of inertia, and not under the blows of some external threat or the outburst of some storm; it will fall all by itself, under its own weight [. . .] But that sooner or later this will happen, I do not doubt for a single moment.[10]

Mishka remembered his grandmother Anna as the "spiritual head of the Golitsyn clan." She always seemed to be there for everyone, whatever his troubles. Lariusha said that his grandmother "radiated light." She would gather her grandchildren around her after lunch and read to them—the Russian classics, Jonathan Swift, Sir Walter Scott, Jules Verne—and take them for long walks, teaching them about the local berries, mushrooms, the names of the flowers and butterflies. She gave Lariusha his first drawing lessons. Their grandfather Mikhail thought she spoiled them. He would get testy with his grandsons and had trouble coping with their pranks and boundless energy; their love of shooting spitballs especially tried his patience. Nonetheless, Mikhail took them out mushrooming and gave them French and English lessons. He loved his large, bustling family. "We now have fourteen grandchildren," he wrote to his brother Alexander in California in the late 1930s, "all growing like mushrooms, and we love them all so much we can't choose a favorite."[11]

Alexander was by then living in a world unimaginable to his family back in Dmitrov. After a few years in Seattle, he, Lyubov, and their children had moved in 1927 to Los Angeles where he set up a successful medical practice. Among his patients was Sergei Rachmaninov, whom Alexander cared for during the composer's final illness. Three of the four Golitsyn children ended up in the movies. Daughter Natalya had a brief career in silent films and hobnobbed with the likes of Rudolph Valentino and Charlie Chaplin, and son George worked as a producer at Universal and Walt Disney Studios, receiving an Academy Award nomination for Best Picture for *Freud* in 1960. Their brother, Alexander, had the most successful Hollywood career. As an art director at Universal Studios for three decades, Alexander designed many of Douglas Sirk's Technicolor masterpieces and worked with such figures as Fritz

Lang, Greta Garbo, Alfred Hitchcock, and Clint Eastwood. Nominated for fourteen Oscars, Alexander won three for his work on *The Phantom of the Opera* (1943), *Spartacus* (1960), and *To Kill a Mockingbird* (1962). He worked in every genre from noir to westerns, from action to horror, and among his long list of credits was the 1957 cult classic *The Incredible Shrinking Man*.[12]

Back in Dmitrov, their Golitsyn cousins were being raised on very different films. With his pals, Mishka went to the October cinema to be entertained by movies like *Lenin in October*, *We Are from Kronstadt*, and *Chapaev*, classic Soviet films propagandizing the Bolshevik Revolution and civil war. Like his siblings, Mishka was growing up to be a Soviet person. He loved the large parades on May Day and November 7, when they marched to the town's statues of Lenin and Stalin. He and his friends were big fans of the local soccer team and never missed an air show. Despite everything that had happened to their families, Mishka and his peers grew up Soviet patriots, proud of their country and its achievements and free of any nostalgia for the prerevolutionary past. Nonetheless, the family tried to keep the older traditions alive. Anna gave the little ones Bible lessons, and they continued to celebrate the Orthodox holidays. Every year they would go out late one December night and cut down a small tree for Christmas, even though the holiday was forbidden. They would sneak it back home and decorate it with the blinds drawn. Anna would help the children to light the candles.[13]

Some of Mishka's happiest times were visiting Nikolai Sheremetev and Cecilia Mansurov in Moscow. Mishka loved his "Uncle Kolya," and for the childless couple he was like an adopted son. They did not have a spare bed in their apartment, so Nikolai would lash two chairs together with his belt, lay down a sheet and blanket, and put Mishka to sleep every night with a kiss. Their home was always filled with music. Nikolai spent long hours rehearsing on the violin or at his old piano composing for performances at the Vakhtangov Theater. To relax, Nikolai loved nothing more than to play something by Saint-Saëns or passages from Tchaikovsky's Violin Concerto in D Major. Sometimes the great mezzo-soprano Nadezhda Obukhov came by to work on some tricky passages with Nikolai. When he was not playing, Nikolai took Mishka hunting along with his two Irish setters, Valta and Laska. Nothing made Nikolai happier, and he once told Mishka his dream was to die while out hunting. His wish came true, though not as he anticipated.

Yuri Yelagin played alongside Nikolai at the Vakhtangov for eight years. He was amazed by Nikolai as both a man and a musician. His fine musicianship, as well as his rare sound and perfect pitch, struck Yelagin, who was impressed by the fact that Nikolai was always ready to help Yelagin with his playing. He thought Nikolai exceedingly hand-some, the kind of man who would have fitted in among the dashing guards officers in the reign of Catherine the Great. Yelagin claimed never to have met someone so "changeable" and "many-sided." Nikolai could be simple and even coarse, acting and dressing just like a worker, making him popular with all the stagehands. And then he could just as easily appear elegant and polished and every inch the aristocrat. When-ever foreigners from Germany, France, or England visited, Nikolai was put forward to meet with them as the face of the theater because no one else could speak their languages or interact so naturally with them. He talked little of his family's past, and then only if he had been drinking vodka, as he did a great deal. Drink was Nikolai's way of coping with the pain from a pancreatic disease. He refused to see a doctor and did his best to hide the illness from others.

Nikolai experienced his share of insults and humiliation. When he went to collect his passport, the OGPU officer asked upon noticing his surname: "You wouldn't happen to be a relation of the counts Shereme-tev by chance?" "I am the very Count Sheremetev himself," Nikolai answered provocatively. His retort caused an impromptu meeting among the officials about what to do with this "Count Sheremetev." Apparently, they did not dare touch Nikolai given Cecilia's connec-tions to the top Soviet leadership. Disgusted, the officer flung the pass-port at Nikolai's feet, spitting, "Go on, take it, take your passport, you spawn of the aristocracy." Nikolai bent down, picked it up, and walked out under a chorus of abuse.

At least once Nikolai's identity made for some laughter. After an unusually long wait in a restaurant Nikolai asked the waiter if he could hurry up with their food. "You're no count," the waiter snapped, "you can wait," leaving Nikolai and his friends agape, barely able to keep from laughing. Yelagin rightly saw Nikolai as one of the lucky ones. Here was a former person who lived as he wished. He had a job as a musician and composer in one of the best theaters in the country, and he had the woman he loved, a woman coveted by many. Yelagin, and most likely Nikolai too, did not realize just how lucky he was. In September 1937, during the Great Terror, former Prince Sergei Pavlovich Golitsyn was arrested on charges of sabotage. During his interrogation, the NKVD tried to force Golitsyn to implicate Nikolai and Cecilia, whom Sergei had worked alongside for years in the theater. Sergei, however, refused. He was shot on January 20, 1938. Nikolai and Cecilia survived.[14]

On October 26, 1933, Vladimir Golitsyn took the train from Dmitrov to Moscow on business. Two days later he was arrested at the apartment of his cousin Alexei Bobrinsky. When he failed to return home after several days, Yelena went looking for him. She visited Vladimir's friend Pavel Korin, the artist. Korin was then painting a portrait of Genrikh Yagoda, deputy chairman of the OGPU, and he promised to mention Vladimir's case to Yagoda. While in Moscow Yelena learned that a few days after Vladimir's arrest, his cousins Alexander Golitsyn, the son of Vladimir Vladimirovich, and Pyotr Urusov, Alexander's brother-in-law, had also been arrested. All three were charged with being members of a secret cell plotting to kill Stalin.

As evidence the OGPU pointed to a revolver, found in Bobrinsky's apartment, which they claimed was the intended murder weapon. The existence of the gun led some in the Golitsyn family to believe that Vladimir and the others had been set up by none other than their cousin Alexei. Many in the family had long suspected that Alexei was a police informer. Their suspicions had been raised after previous arrests when the police seemed well informed on the family's private life, and Alexei seemed the only probable source. Moreover, Alexei had access to a gun. In late 1929, a recent graduate of Stanford University by the name of Robin Kinkead arrived in Moscow, where he met and was then hired as an assistant by the journalist Walter Duranty. Alexei made the acquaintance of Kinkead and became his personal secretary. The gun found by the OGPU belonged to Kinkead, and the Golitsyns were certain Alexei had taken the gun and used it to frame his own family. If that had indeed been his plan, it blew up in his face, for Alexei was arrested as well.

Vladimir was held for a short time in the Butyrki but soon freed, thanks to Yagoda's intervention. Alexei was sentenced to ten years in a labor camp near Vorkuta, north of the Arctic Circle. Alexander Golitsyn received three years and was sent to a camp at Yaya station in western Siberia. Pyotr Urusov was sentenced to three years' exile in Petropavlovsk, Kazakhstan. His wife, Olga, followed him there from Moscow.[15]

The Golitsyns' relatives in Sergiev Posad were also feeling the heat. In April 1933, Vladimir Trubetskoy was arrested after being denounced by a fellow musician. She had informed the OGPU that Trubetskoy had been infecting his wife and children with anti-Soviet attitudes. Vladimir was taken to Moscow and held in the Lubyanka, but then freed the following month.[16]

Several months before, in the autumn of 1932, the OGPU arrested a man by the name of Mikhail Skachkov. A former White officer who had fled to Czechoslovakia after the civil war before returning to the Soviet Union in 1926, Skachkov worked in the foreign division of Glavlit, the central censorship directorate. During one of his interrogations in December, Skachkov named a number of people as members of an underground counterrevolutionary organization; they included Vladimir and Sergei Golitsyn and their uncle Vladimir Trubetskoy. The agents, however, passed over these names, focusing their attention on Nikolai Durnovo, a noted linguist, and his son, Andrei. On the twenty-eighth, the Durnovos were arrested. Their arrests marked the beginning of what became known as the Affair of the Slavicists.

Under questioning, Andrei Durnovo admitted to being part of a fascist organization called the Russian Nationalist Party (RNP). On New Year's Eve, the police arrested Andrei's fiancée, seventeen-year-old Varya Trubetskoy. Days later, they arrested her father, Vladimir. Eventually, some seventy people, nearly all of them academics and intellectuals, many of them linguists and literary scholars, were arrested. Brothers Vladimir and Sergei Golitsyn were for some unknown reason never arrested, nor was Pavel Sheremetev, whose name was included on a list of suspected RNP members. The purported masters of the RNP were a group of Russian émigrés in Western Europe, chief among them Vladimir Trubetskoy's brother Nikolai, a professor at the University of Vienna and one of the twentieth century's great linguists, and his friend and colleague and fellow linguist Roman Jakobson. Nikolai Trubetskoy was among the founders of Eurasianism, a political movement within the émigré community that viewed the Bolshevik Revolution as a necessary step in Russia's unique historical path, a path that would eventually lead to the Communists' shedding their Marxism for Russian Orthodoxy. The men and women arrested in the Affair of the Slavicists were charged with secretly working toward this end under the guidance of their superiors in the West. Vladimir Trubetskoy, who had been permitted in 1930 to take his sick son Grisha for medical treatment in Paris, where he saw his brother and many other émigrés, was believed to be the RNP's go-between.

The affair was intended as a warning to members of the old intelligentsia: get in line with the Stalin Revolution, or else. Most of those arrested received sentences of internal exile, although their involvement in this affair meant many of them, including the Durnovos, would be shot during the Great Terror. Varya Trubetskoy was sentenced to three years' exile; her father, to five years in the gulag, a sentence that was then commuted to exile.[17] In April 1934, Vladimir and Varya, accompanied by several OGPU agents, were put on a passenger train in Moscow and sent to the town of Andijan, in Uzbekistan.

Once an important stop on the Silk Road before being destroyed by Genghis Khan, Andijan had for centuries been the capital of the Fergana Valley at the foot of the dramatic snowcapped Pamir Mountains, "the roof of the world." It was a town of seventy thousand, with green parks, theaters, cinemas, a bazaar, a cotton mill, and a large beer brewery. Most of the local Uzbek women still wore burkas of dark blue or gold velvet. It was a multiethnic town, with Uzbeks, Bukharan Jews, Russians, Ukrainians, Tatars, and Armenians.[18]

When she learned where Vladimir and Varya were being sent, Eli began making preparations to follow. She sold off most of the family's few possessions, borrowed money from some relatives, packed, and then boarded a train for the long trek in May 1934. They were quite a sight: Eli, eight months pregnant, surrounded by six children between the ages of eight and nineteen and a motley assortment of bundles and beat-up old suitcases. They found lodging in Andijan with a local Uzbek man who agreed to rent them half of his house. A month after she arrived Eli gave birth to her eighth child, Georgy.

Although still an outcast, Vladimir had little difficulty finding work in a restaurant orchestra and playing for the Uzbek State Theater. With some of his fellow musicians he set up a jazz band that played gigs in the towns around Andijan. He earned almost nothing and had to play every night until early in the morning, leaving him exhausted. Other than regular visits to the headquarters of the local NKVD (as the main administration of the secret or political police became known from mid-1934) to confirm he was still living in Andijan and to report on his travels with the jazz band, Vladimir was free to do as he pleased.

Vladimir and Eli created a new life for the family in Central Asia far from their loved ones back in Russia. Vladimir embraced aspects of the local culture: he gave up chairs in favor of squatting and donned native costume—a richly embroidered skullcap and long gown that he wore over jodhpurs and puttees. He and Eli got to know their Uzbek neighbors and would meet them in the courtyard to talk and share cigarettes. The older children worked, while the younger ones went to school. In the holidays they went fishing and hiking or visited the local Park of Culture and Rest, with its fun house, beer hall, and swimming pool. Over time Vladimir managed to save just enough money to purchase a few luxuries: a sewing machine for Eli, a bicycle for the children, a radio.

When he was not working, Vladimir wrote in the kitchen, the children running and playing around him. He wrote stories inspired by the beautiful, exotic world of Central Asia, none of which were ever published, being at odds with the dictates of Soviet literature at the time, and a memoir—"Notes of a Cuirassier"—of his life as an officer before the revolution. The lone copy of this memoir remarkably survived and was published for the first time in 1991. Vladimir also wrote often to his beloved nephew Vladimir Golitsyn about his adventures in Andijan. He regaled Vladimir with stories of life with the jazz band—about their wild pianist and his cocaine addiction, about the beautiful young women he flirted with on the road, and about the prostitutes trolling from table to table through the smoky café air.

His letters and stories and the accounts of everyone who knew him reveal a man with an unbroken and unbreakable spirit. Vladimir was full of the joy of life: humorous, playful, witty, even silly, a happy family man and father, a provider, a musician, a writer, a hunter and outdoorsman, and always an optimist, even when he had no reason to be. Despite everything, he knew no bitterness or remorse. While in Andijan he began thinking about where they would go once his sentence was over. His dream was to settle on the shores of the Black Sea.[19]

Before leaving the Butyrki in late 1933, Vladimir Golitsyn jotted down a few words carved into the wall of his cell: "Don't be sad upon entering, don't be joyful upon leaving. Everyone will spend time here, no one will ever forget it."[20]

The family rejoiced upon Vladimir's return to Dmitrov. There was one among them, however, who could not believe what had happened to Vladimir: his brother Sergei's fiancée, Klavdia Bavykin. Sergei had met her while working as a laborer draining swamps. She was a simple girl from a worker's family that had done well under the Soviet government. They had successful careers, earned well, and lived comfortably. What is more, they had faith in the system and its rulers. They believed the official line about "saboteurs" and "enemies of the state" and trusted that only the truly guilty ended up in prison. And now here was Vladimir straight from prison. Klavdia did not know what to make of it all. Masha Golitsyn held up her brother's coat to Klavdia's nose. It reeked of the carbolic acid used to disinfect prisoners' clothes. The smell had an almost magical effect on Klavdia, opening her eyes and waking her up to the truth about the government's supposed enemies.

Members of both families were against Sergei's and Klavdia's plan to marry. Sergei's family found Klavdia "uncultured," and they hoped he would find someone from "our circle" instead. Klavdia's family worried that marrying into a family of former people and outcasts would put not only her but all of them in danger. One relative even threatened to denounce Sergei unless he stopped seeing Klavdia. He told Sergei that he could make him vanish with a single phone call. For a long time Sergei was tormented about what to do. Fearful for Klavdia's safety, he had tried to talk her out of loving him, but she had refused to listen and insisted she was ready to share his fate. They wed in a small church off the Arbat Street in Moscow in the spring of 1934. Both agreed Klavdia should keep her surname, as this was safer; there was talk of Sergei's taking her name too, but he refused. "No, I will not change my name! I was born a prince and will remain a prince, no matter what!" he insisted. Only a few family members came to the wedding and the small reception at Klavdia's parents' apartment.[21]

The newlyweds settled near Sergei's family in Dmitrov. It was a particularly difficult time for the family. Masha was arrested and held for a short time. She lost her job and was expelled from school.[22] Money was short. Several of the Golitsyn children fell ill with scarlet fever. Vladimir was afflicted by a painful degenerative knee ailment. After years of suffering, he finally decided to have an operation. He nearly died from an overdose of ether while the surgeon removed most of his knee joint. His leg was now fused and an inch and a half shorter than the other, requiring Vladimir to use a cane for the rest of his life.[23]

Despite all this, Vladimir managed to find solace. One night, as he sat writing, his family having gone to bed, he reflected on how the revolution had affected them, on how the repression, arrests, and executions, the confiscations and forced moves had "created in our family a certain immunity, a philosophical relation to such things."

On the other hand, such uncertainty in tomorrow creates a devil-may-care attitude to one's apartment, to one's everyday surroundings and the like. Is it worth hanging new wallpaper, is it worth fixing anything if perhaps they'll come for you tomorrow? [. . .] On the other hand, you do feel with greater intensity the happiness of the moment when you're seated at the table, drawing something, and your wife is worried that she has done a poor job coloring Lariusha's trousers, Papa is moving some burning wood, stoking the fire, Mama is busy on her sewing machine, and the children are playing in the yard, which is drying out after the rains. For now, all's well, and I can feel this. But tomorrow?

He ended this diary entry with the words "Written at twelve midnight, too late, that is, for a search or arrest."[24]

Such moments were rare. By the spring of 1935, the atmosphere in Dmitrov was growing worse. Vladimir wrote: "Each time someone in a police uniform walks past we feel the acid in our stomachs churn. Only the children are happy and carefree." One day they heard a rumor that their house had been promised to someone else and they were to be evicted. Some in the family wanted to leave Dmitrov straight away for the town of Cheboksary, on the Volga. There, in the provinces, perhaps they might have more chance of escaping the notice of the police.[25] But in the end they chose to stay.

The wedding reception of Varvara Gudovich and Vladimir Obolensky, Ostafievo,
August 7, 1921. Among the guests at the reception table are the groom and bride
(seated middle left), flanked by Maria Obolensky (Vladimir's mother) and Pavel Sheremetev.
Across from them are Yekaterina Sheremetev (peering out at the camera) and Boris Saburov
(extreme right with cigarette, gazing downward). Standing (in back from left) are Dmitry
Gudovich, Nikolai Sheremetev, and Yuri Saburov (partially obscured). Yelena Sheremetev
stands in white at the far end of the table, just to the right of the centerpiece. (Author's collection)

The wedding party on the front steps at Ostafievo. The bride and groom are flanked by
Maria Gudovich and Pavel Sheremetev. Bottom row, left to right: Yevgeny Lvov,
Dmitry Gudovich, Boris Saburov (smoking, legs crossed), Nikolai Sheremetev
(in bow tie with head turned). Middle row, left to right: Yuri Saburov (smoking, in white),
Pyotr Sheremetev (in sailor suit), Lilya Sheremetev (behind him, in white),
Praskovya Obolensky (future wife of Pavel Sheremetev, next to Pyotr in large hat
with black bow). (Author's collection)

A photograph of Vladimir Golitsyn and Yelena Sheremetev taken around the time of their wedding in 1923. "It's as if we were born for one another!" Vladimir said of Yelena the previous year. "There's no way I cannot love her!" (Courtesy of Alexandre Galitzine)

Vladimir Trubetskoy and the writer Mikhail Prishvin hunting near Sergiev Posad, 1920s. (Courtesy of Mikhail Trubetskoy)

Vladimir and Yelena Golitsyn with Yelena's mother, Lilya, and three of her siblings (Maria, Natalya, and Pavel) shortly before they left Russia in 1924.

(Courtesy of Andrei Golitsyn)

Vasily, Pavel, and Praskovya Sheremetev at the Novodevichy Monastery, ca. 1930.
(Author's collection)

ABOVE LEFT Pavel Sheremetev in the Naprudny Tower alongside a photograph of his late mother and surrounded by the remains of the family archive and library that he fought to preserve. (Author's collection)

ABOVE RIGHT Vasily Sheremetev in the Naprudny Tower, 1936. (Courtesy of Russian State Archive of Literature and Art)

The Sheremetevs and Obolenskys at the Naprudny Tower to celebrate Vasily's name day, January 14, 1937. Seated, left to right: Yelizaveta Obolensky, Nikolai Obolensky, Vladimir Obolensky, Andrei Obolensky, Pavel Sheremetev. Standing, left to right: Varvara Obolensky (b. Gudovich), Olga Prutchenko, Maria Gudovich (b. Sheremetev), Yevfimiya Obolensky, Vasily Sheremetev, Praskovya Sheremetev. Shortly after this photograph was taken, Varvara and Vladimir Obolensky were arrested and never seen again. (Courtesy of Russian State Archive of Literature and Art)

Vladimir and Yelena Golitsyn with their children—Illarion, Mikhail, and Yelena—in Dmitrov, ca. 1930. (Courtesy of Andrei Golitsyn)

The mayor and his granddaughter
Irina Trubetskoy, late 1920s.
(Courtesy of Mikhail Trubetskoy)

Maria Golitsyn, her mother,
Anna, and her grandfather
Vladimir Golitsyn (the mayor)
in Dmitrov shortly before his
death. (Courtesy of Alexandre Galitzine)

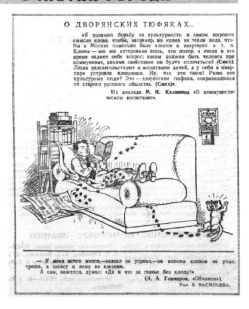

The nobility mocked in the pages of the Soviet press

TOP LEFT Count Naryshkin shown sucking up to Emperor Nicholas II and Empress Alexandra. The caption reads: "FROM THE BIOGRAPHY OF A GOLD CHASER IN HIDING . . . AND NOW UNDER THE SOVIET REGIME— WITHOUT ANY REGULAR OCCUPATION." (*Leningradskaia Pravda*, March 24, 1935)

CENTER Another cartoon from *Leningradskaia Pravda* during the Operation Former People campaign of 1935. Published together with a collection of articles under the headline WE WILL CLEAN THE CITY OF LENIN OF THE TSARS' REMAINING MEN AND THE LANDOWNING AND CAPITALIST RABBLE, the caption reads: "CLEANING UP THE CITY." (*Leningradskaia Pravda*, March 22, 1935)

BOTTOM LEFT The nobleman as dirty layabout. The caption is a play on words that means both "on noble mattresses" and "on noble layabouts." Quoting Mikhail Kalinin's "Report on Communist Education" and Ivan Goncharov's classic novel *Oblomov*, the cartoon suggests that despite their books and learning, former nobles are indolent, uncultured, and filthy, perfectly content to live in apartments swarming with bedbugs and too foul even for cats. (*Komsomolskaia Pravda*, November 2, 1940)

The Saburov children, 1935

After several years of exile and imprisonment, the Saburov family—Anna, Xenia, Boris, and Yuri—were reunited in Vladimir in 1932. Several months after these photographs were taken, Boris and Yuri were arrested for the last time. "The time of the vultures is at hand," Anna wrote. "Soon the land, every home, the waters, everything will have to give up its corpses."

Xenia, aged thirty-five. (Author's collection)

Boris, aged thirty-eight. (Author's collection)

Yuri, aged thirty-one. (Author's collection)

The actor Alexander Golitsyn was arrested in Tomsk during the Great Terror and shot on July 11, 1938. The charges against him included portraying Soviet heroes onstage in a "perverse light." (Courtesy of Alexandre Galitzine)

Alexander's sister Olga was arrested in Tomsk on New Year's Eve, 1937, a week after her husband, Pyotr Urusov. Charged with spreading "defeatist" and monarchist propaganda, she was shot on March 5, 1938. She was twenty-six. (Courtesy of Alexandre Galitzine)

The final prison photograph of Vladimir Trubetskoy. He was shot on October 30, 1937, the same day as his daughter Varvara. (Courtesy of Mikhail Trubetskoy)

Of all the Trubetskoy children, Varvara ("Varya") made the greatest effort to fit into the Soviet system. Regardless, she was arrested in July 1937 and charged with having taken part in the plot to kill the Leningrad boss Sergei Kirov. (Courtesy of Mikhail Trubetskoy)

The final photograph of Varya Trubetskoy. It was more than half a century until the surviving family members learned that she and her father had been shot in the autumn of 1937. (Courtesy of Mikhail Trubetskoy)

Arrested around the same time as her father, her sister Varya, and her brother Grigory, Alexandra "Tatya" Trubetskoy was charged with plotting to kill Stalin and sentenced to ten years in the gulag. The harsh regimen destroyed her health, and she died in 1943 at the age of twenty-four. (Courtesy of Mikhail Trubetskoy)

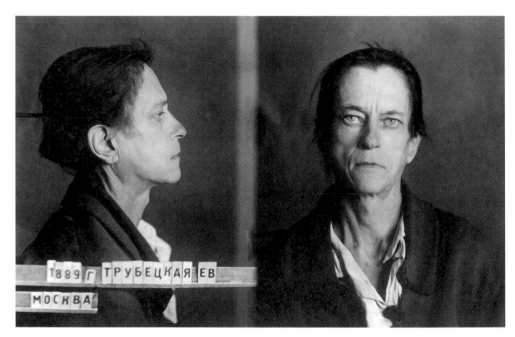

The final photographs of Eli Trubetskoy, taken shortly before her death from typhus in Moscow's Butyrki prison on February 7, 1943. (Courtesy of Mikhail Trubetskoy)

On November 25, NKVD agents came to the Golitsyn house and told Vladimir he had twenty-four hours to leave Dmitrov and move outside the one-hundred-kilometer zone around Moscow. The day before, he and Yelena had put their daughter in the hospital with scarlet fever; their two sons had been placed in isolation. There was no way they could leave. "Cruel fate has us by the throat," he complained. "Where are we to go? Why this pointless cruelty? Why are we more dangerous in Dmitrov than Mozhaisk?"[26] Vladimir sent a letter that day to Korin to ask whether he would be willing to speak to Yagoda, now the people's commissar for internal affairs—chief, that is, of the NKVD. Not wanting to put his friend in too difficult a position, he told Korin not to bother if he feared it might hurt him in any way: "It's not a catastrophe, since by our count we've already had to move ten times." Korin agreed to help and mentioned their problem to Yagoda. "So, I see you're pleading once more for your prince!" Yagoda shouted at Korin. Despite his outburst, Yagoda agreed to help. The order was rescinded, and the family was permitted to remain in Dmitrov.[27] The Golitsyns were grateful for Yagoda's intervention, but they could not count on it for much longer. The following year Yagoda was removed from his post and replaced by Nikolai Yezhov. In March 1938, during the Great Terror, Yagoda was arrested along with several thousand of his former NKVD supporters, and later shot.

Vladimir had long foreseen an equally horrifying fate for himself. A man he once met remarked how he felt "like a mouse caught in a trap who has been doused with kerosene and is just waiting for someone to come with a match.

"I see that match all the time," Vladimir added grimly.[28]

22

ANNA'S FORTUNE

n 1775, Empress Catherine the Great began building a large neo-Gothic palace south of Moscow. Work at Tsaritsyno, as it became known, went on in fits and starts for the next two decades. It was still under way in 1796, when the empress died, and was never completed. The palace soon fell into disrepair, the gardens went to seed, and in the following century the area became a popular place for Muscovites to build their summer dachas, a fact reflected in its new name, Tsaritsyno-Dachnoe. In the early years of the Soviet Union, Tsaritsyno-Dachnoe became Lenino-Dachnoe, and it was there that in 1928, having completed their three-year term of exile, Anna Saburov and her children Boris, Yuri, and Xenia settled. They were drawn to Tsaritsyno, as they never stopped calling it, largely because of its proximity to Moscow and the fact that they had family there—namely, Varvara and Vladimir Obolensky. Vladimir had found work in the area managing a state farm and later had taken a position as bookkeeper in a brick factory after having been fired for being a former prince. Around the same time the Saburovs arrived, so too did Varvara's mother, Maria Gudovich, and her siblings Dmitry, Andrei, and Merinka.[1]

The reunion was short-lived. In early 1929, Boris and Yuri were arrested; a few months later, Dmitry and Andrei were also arrested. The four cousins were charged with being members of a counterrevolutionary monarchist organization and convicted under Article 58, Section 10 of the state criminal code. Boris and Yuri were sentenced to three years of exile in Siberia, their second such sentence following the Fox-trot Affair of 1924.[2] Andrei Gudovich also received a three-year term of exile, also in Siberia, also for the second time.[3] Dmitry was given the harshest sentence: five years in a labor camp. He was sent to Belbaltlag in Kem, Karelia, near the White Sea, where he was set to work loading wood and transferred to work on building the Belbalt Canal. He remained there until 1932, when he was freed ahead of time and sent to work on the Moscow–Volga Canal in Dmitrov.[4] Amid all the misery, former Prince Sergei Lvov was courting Merinka Gudovich, and they married that same year.[5] Merinka's second marriage, like her first, would end tragically.

Boris and Yuri were moved to the Butyrki Prison to await word of their fates. At eleven o'clock on the night of August 31 they were roused from their cells and taken to the Kazan railway station. The next day the train took them into exile. Neither of them had any idea where they were heading. Xenia had gone to Moscow to check on her brothers and was there to see them off from the station. They rode as far as Sverdlovsk (the former Yekaterinburg), where they were placed in solitary confinement. It was there, on December 5, that they apparently learned they both were going to be sent to the Tobolsk district—Boris to the town of Samarovo; Yuri, to Surgut. Once he learned his destination, Boris wrote his mother asking her to send him warm things and a Bible. The brothers traveled together to Samarovo, and then Yuri went on alone to Surgut.

The brothers experienced their second Siberian exile very differently. Yuri found work doing drawings for a small reading room located in a peasant hut, and he asked his mother to send him some paints, brushes, and paper for his work. "Don't worry about me," he told his mother. "There's absolutely no need to worry. You can worry about Boris, but not about me. I am well and feel marvelous." After a few weeks Yuri was moved to Saygatino, a collection of fifteen yurts on the banks of the Ob River about thirty-five kilometers west of Surgut. Still, he was happy. He had taken a small room for himself, had enough warm clothes and plenty to eat (milk, butter, meat, fish, partridge), had learned how to make a bit of money sewing fur hats, and was gathering material for an ethnographic article he hoped to submit to a journal for publication. When he had time, he strapped on his skis and went out hunting.[6]

Boris was having a much more difficult time adjusting to exile, which he recognized in a letter to their mother. "I have given him the palm to bear some time ago and now I'm happy for him: he's full of energy and is doing so well, not at all like his brother." From Samarovo he had been moved to the village of Seliyarov, where he was living in a yurt with a family, paying them what little money he had for room and board. Food was meager, typically nothing more than some broth, fish in aspic, and tea. He was not able to find any work and instead spent most of his day reading religious works, sleeping, writing, and waiting for letters from home. He struggled with depression.[7]

Anna and Xenia were extremely worried about both of them, and they went to Moscow to see what they could do to help. They sought meetings with various tame Communists, sent appeals, and visited Peshkov. Their efforts, however, proved unsuccessful.[8]

The months passed, and little changed. The year 1930 gave way to 1931, and Boris and Yuri were still in exile. Yuri's spirits remained high, and he continued to make the most of his life in this remote corner of Siberia. Nonetheless, he too suffered periods of sadness and regret. It pained him that his fate caused his mother and sister so much grief, and he wrote to them over and over not to worry, to keep what little money and food they had for themselves and not to waste them on him. He also struggled at times with the isolation of exile. "I would so love to know what is happening in the world," he wrote on April 5, 1931, to his mother.

> Being so cut off from life is not usual in any way and does have its humorous aspects, but the main thing one feels is curiosity. [. . .] Time here neither passes nor flies, but rushes past at a gallop. There's the impression of the days flashing by, like telegraph poles seen from the window of a train. On one hand it's pleasant, but on the other it's a bit terrifying. They are vanishing, utterly wasted.[9]

If Yuri was preoccupied with a lost future, Boris was obsessed with the lost past. By the summer of 1931 he had moved back to Samarovo, where he shared a room with a stranger in the house of an old couple. Still not working, he managed to survive on the money his mother and Yuri sent; he was so poor he could not afford envelopes for the letters he was forever writing his mother, fashioning them out of old newspapers instead. The longing for his family, and especially his mother, was so intense he sought relief in comforting images of life before the revolution and in a growing religious faith of such intense mysticism that he began to experience visions and hallucinations.[10]

Boris's preoccupation with the past apparently had begun in 1926 during his first exile in Irbit. It was there that he had saved a Bible that his roommates had wanted to use to feed their stove. It was an older Bible, printed in 1883, and the date led him to wonder what his mother had been doing then. "It was long ago, isn't that right?" he asked her. "When this was printed, you were sitting somewhere in the Fountain House, what room did you live in then? Was it the one by the stairs down near Grandfather's? You once talked about how you loved this room because you had lived in it."[11] He wrote to his mother of his memories of services in the Fountain House church, of sitting and reading with Grandmother Sheremetev "in a field of rye and cornflowers," of an Easter celebration at Moscow's Uspensky Cathedral with "a crowd of people," he seated on the floor staring in wonder at the reflection of the brilliant iconostasis in an old lady's silk dress.[12] He warmed himself with the memory of a trip he took as a child before the Great War with his father through the Swiss Alps (how he had marveled at the long tunnels) and then Lombardy on their way to meet Anna in Florence. "How good it is that people have such memories, and how happy I was just now recalling you and Papa and all of us together! The fruit! The flowers! Florence! Hotel Baglioni!"[13]

Anna replied: "And I too, Borya, my dear, live in the past through my memories, especially because Papa was with us, because that life was harmonious, unbroken, and whole, and because all of our children were with us."[14] In September, she wrote how that time of the year always reminded her of the apple harvest, of happy gatherings by the samovar.

> . . . when Papa would come in around five o'clock in the afternoon from the orchard and drink white wine with peaches and then tea and he would select for himself some crusty bread or rolls. [. . .] How soothing and happy it would make me to see his calm figure again, the way he would slowly smoke his Egyptian cigarettes. [. . .] The sounds of Chopin and Schumann, or Wagner, coming from the other room, Papa swaying at the piano, losing any sense of time or place and just

living in a world of sounds, even the walls came to life, everything was filled with life. And I would go off to read in the old pink drawing-room (the one with the fireplace and bust), a fur coverlet from Albania lying across the couch. [. . .] I sat under a palm, surrounded by various old bookcases, shelves, baskets, and other small items, all very old, much from Rome.

Regardless, she counseled Boris of the need to live in the present: "Many live in the past or the future (as we do now), but one must always live in the moment—as long as you are alive, wherever you find yourself, you must fill the space all around you with yourself." Her children had been fortunate to have had such a happy childhood, "for without that nest and our little corner we would all be poorer. But the time of the vultures is at hand. Soon the land, every home, the waters, everything will have to give up its corpses." Remarkably, Anna never lost faith in tomorrow, and until her death, despite losing her husband and two of her three children to horrific deaths, she kept her faith in humanity. What is more, she had learned to live without fear; all her fear, she confessed to Boris, had died in the Corner House on Vozdvizhenka in 1918 the night the Cheka took "Papa" away.[15]

Everything of value has been preserved in us, and the traces left by the good things cannot be wiped out. I am an inveterate optimist. Neither grief nor even a pogrom, nothing at all has the power to destroy that which we hold dear and keep in our hearts.

Borya, we are sad now, we have all been separated, and each of us has his own heavy heart, and along with spiritual troubles we must struggle with physical deprivations that take much of our energies and possibly even our health. But this is nothing. The hidden meaning of my letters to you all, and most often especially to you, is my deep certainty that we must first and foremost master our own struggles and the dramas in our hearts, that is, within ourselves.[16]

Yes, Boris admitted to his mother, he still did have interests that kept him from being completely cut off from life: he loved literature and wanted to read more of Russia's great writers; he thought a good deal about art, about Futurism, about the paintings of Uncle Pavel Sheremetev.[17] His escape into the past could be explained by recent memories that "burned" and filled him with horror.[18] Boris was overcome with worry for his mother and sister and concerned that the money they sent him made their poor lives that much more difficult.

> My wish, my mad wish, that grows with every day is always for you, Xenia, and Yuri to be well, comfortable, and at peace, I'm tormented by this and can barely stand it. Sometimes it makes me crazy. [. . .] Dear Mama, do what you must for yourself! [. . .] I'm well since you support me, but who supports you? It's hard for me to even think of this, Christ Our Lord may not be far, but who's close to you?[19]

Her help unleashed awful memories of the civil war years when they were living together and she would give up her paltry share of food for him. "It's unpleasant, shameful even, to recall this. Those hungry years on Vozdvizhenka. Why is it no matter how I try I cannot stop thinking about it? I never can."[20]

The summer of 1930 found Anna and Xenia in Kaluga. Anna was offered a job teaching singing at the music school on the condition that she promise to stop attending church services and help with the school's antireligious propaganda. She refused. "I am very sorry," she told the school director, "but I simply cannot agree to this." She managed to earn a bit of money giving private English lessons. Xenia found work selling newspapers on the street. She worked a twelve-hour shift most days, and the rest of the time she helped out at the library in a technical college for some extra income.[21]

For many years Xenia had been keeping a secret from everyone in her family that finally came to light in 1931. After moving to Kaluga in 1924 following the Fox-trot Affair, Xenia had made the acquaintance of an Englishman by the name of George Daniel Page, then working as a language teacher. He was decades older than Xenia, older even than her mother. Regardless, Xenia, then twenty-four, was smitten. They became engaged but agreed not to tell anyone and kept their secret for six years before finally marrying in 1931. When Anna found out about the marriage, she was furious. The marriage, however, proved to be brief, all of one month and five days. Soon after the wedding Page began preparing to leave the Soviet Union to return to England, possibly because of pressure from the OGPU. He wanted Xenia to come with him, but though she loved him, she refused; she simply could not imagine abandoning her mother while Boris and Yuri were away in exile. On January 2, 1932, Page left the country. Xenia never saw her husband again, although she did correspond with him for many years.[22] Though the marriage was short, its consequences for Xenia would be profound.

In 1932, after three years in exile, Boris and Yuri returned home from Siberia. Anna was there in Moscow in December to meet Boris. He was a pathetic sight, weak, exhausted, bedraggled, his feet covered in worn-out galoshes stuffed with straw and held together by twine.[23] Reunited, the Saburovs settled in the provincial town of Vladimir and tried to get on with their lives. Tatiana Aksakov-Sivers visited them and could not help noticing how difficult their lives were. All had trouble finding work; they had little to eat and relied on Pavel Sheremetev's regular gifts of food and money. The four of them looked pale and weak, but at least they were all together at last.[24]

Life went on in this fashion for four years. And then tragedy befell the Saburovs once more.

In the early-morning hours of April 26, 1936, the NKVD came and arrested Boris and Yuri. "I will never forget Mother's face," Xenia recalled almost a half century later, "she came to me, stood in the door way, utterly shaken: 'Both!'" It was all Anna could say. They were sent to the commandant's office of the Ivanovo NKVD and held in the inner prison there in isolation for months. During the search of the Saburovs' apartment, the agents had found several Bibles and various books on church history. When his interrogators asked Yuri about his political beliefs, he openly stated, "I am a monarchist." Both brothers were convicted of counterrevolutionary propaganda and agitation and keeping counterrevolutionary literature—Article 58, Section 10 of the criminal code, just as in 1929. Yuri was also charged with being a member of an underground military organization. The arrests were part of a larger operation in Vladimir. A few days before the Saburovs were taken several clergymen had been arrested. One of them was Father Afanasy, bishop of Kovrov (later canonized), charged with being in contact with the Vatican and White Guards in Ukraine. The brothers were sentenced to five years in a corrective labor camp and were shipped out of Ivanovo by train sometime in September. Xenia, who had been bringing them food ever since their arrest, was at the station to see them off. Yuri claimed they were "cheerful and in good humor."[25]

The brothers traveled to Vologda and then farther eastward to the town of Kotlas. There they were separated. Yuri was sent to a group of camps known as Ukhtpechlag situated in the area of the Ukhta and Pechora rivers in the Komi region of northwestern Russia. Boris was sent to Belbaltlag in Karelia.[26] They never saw each other again. Yuri's route took him farther to the north and east, while Boris rode westerly. He stopped for a period in a transit prison in Leningrad, when he wrote Anna in the middle of October to tell her not worry, for both he and Yuri were "in good health and fine spirits." Four days later he sent another letter saying:

[I]t has been pleasant to breathe the Leningrad air again [. . .] The familiar sky grows light in the windows, a wet snow fell all day yesterday and today it's slushy. I can image the wet railings of the Fontanka, the sidewalks, the autumn days. All of this is so close to me, I've only to walk out through the prison gates. But since this is impossible, this closeness blurs into something infinitely far away and unattainable.[27]

Yuri was moved between a number of camps from late 1936 to early 1937. He wrote home on April 19, 1937, from a camp near the railway head of Vetlosyan to say that he had received a few of their postcards but none of the letters, packages, or money they had sent. He felt bad that he had been so long in writing but had been without paper or pencil for a good while. "I am not living too badly, all things considered. So far I have been in three camps, but have never been required to do any heavy labor. I've been ill with dysentery. [. . .] Lately, I've been making bast shoes—I've learned how to weave, though I don't do any of this myself, but just prepare the bast for weaving. It's not difficult, of course, and I work in a warm building." He went on to say that all his clothes had worn out, but they should not bother to send him any since he could get some through the camp authorities, though he would like some tobacco. Other than one or two fellow prisoners he could talk to, the rest were not terribly interesting, and they had few books or newspapers; but still they managed to pass the time in the evenings playing chess or reading aloud. He ended by expressing his desire to see Boris again.[28]

This was Yuri's last letter. Sometime that spring he died of dysentery. When Yuri's letters stopped coming, Anna became desperate. She began writing letters to the gulag administration, to camp directors, and to various Soviet officials, even to Lavrenty Beria, chief of the NKVD from late 1938, seeking information on Yuri's condition and whereabouts. For years Anna kept writing but could get no answers. Finally, in 1940, she received an official letter informing her that in 1938 Yuri had been sentenced to an additional ten years "without the right of correspondence" and been sent to a camp deep in Siberia. His last known location was listed as Chibyu, near the Ukhta River. Anna died never learning the truth about her son's death. He continued to haunt her dreams for the rest of her life. Once she saw him walking through a swamp heading somewhere far away. He was extremely pale and gaunt and turned to look at her with mournful eyes.[29]

After arriving in Karelia, Boris bounced between camps in Uroksa, Sennukha, and Kuzema. He fell ill in the spring of 1937 and was relieved of heavy forest work. Anna, who had been sending him food and money (the latter never reached him), wrote to Peshkov asking her to help get Boris moved to the gulag hospital at Bear Mountain (Medvezhya Gora, later changed to Medvezhegorsk). Boris had made the same request of the camp officials; failing this, he hoped that maybe he could convince them to send him to the work corridor at the Butyrki. Camp officials ignored their requests, however, and Boris's condition deteriorated. His legs were swollen from edema, and he could no longer walk. By summer, he was bedridden. He was put on a special diet, however, and his daily intake of calories and animal fats was increased.[30]

The improved diet and gentler conditions, as well as visits from a few camp doctors later that year, returned Boris to health, and by the end of 1937 he was back in the barracks at Sennukha. He spent the winter out in the deep snow and cold, felling trees in the Karelian forest. By spring his health was broken once again. The edema had returned, his legs swelled, and then his lungs began to fill with fluid, and he had trouble breathing. Anna tried to get him released—but her requests were denied. By early July 1938, Boris knew he was dying. He wrote to his mother and Uncle Pavel Sheremetev to stop sending food since it would only be wasted on him. The last letter he wrote himself was dated July 9. "As for me," Boris informed his mother, trying to shield her from the truth, "I will just say that things are as before and I am no worse, though I am getting weaker. In general, my overall condition notwithstanding, I am in good spirits and thank God for everything. I do hope to give my illness a good fight. I so terribly want to get back to you as soon as possible."[31] The swelling in Boris's arms, legs, and chest grew worse, and by the middle of July he was too ill to write. He dictated to a fellow prisoner a few more letters home. The last was from July 28. He died in his sleep two days later and was buried on August 2 in the Sennukha camp cemetery. He was less than a month away from his forty-first birthday.[32]

Unaware that Boris was dead, Anna sent him a long letter on July 31 imbued with her deep religious faith and counseling acceptance of God's will:

> If I love you, and you love me, and we both and everyone else loves Him, then we are now under the care and protection of His love. May Christ keep and protect us from everything that is unbearable, grievous, and perplexing. We do not know His will, neither our future nor how our great toil at this hour of our ordeal will be decided. But know it will only be as is best for us. You see, I am calm. [. . .] You know I love you—but God loves you even more, deeper and better, and so you and I must give up our fates to Him to decide.[33]

Several days later her letter was returned unopened. On the envelope were the words: "No longer in the camp." Her heart sank, and she expected the worse, thinking this a coded reference to his death. Anna went to Moscow to learn for certain, and there she was informed that Boris had indeed died on July 30. Anna later claimed to have experienced a vision that day. "At dawn on July 30, when Boris's soul flew away from Sennukha, my room in Vladimir filled with light and I was caressed by some spirit. [. . .] Two souls came to me in my sleep and touched both sides of my face [. . .] Without a doubt, this was all predetermined from the beginning, from the very moment of his conception."[34] Upon returning to Vladimir, Anna held a small memorial service for Boris. One night Boris appeared in her dreams. He was sitting on the road with his hands and feet tied. Anna approached and asked what had happened. He calmly told her that he could move no farther, he had no way forward, and, pointing to his tied hands and feet, said that her grief was holding him back, making it impossible for him to move on to heaven. Anna recognized she had to accept his death and let him go.

During these difficult years Anna met an old woman in Vladimir. The woman told her she was "a fortunate mother." Why, Anna asked, where is my good fortune? "Your good fortune rests in the suffering of your children, for this is a candle that forever burns before God," the woman told her.[35]

"There still are righteous people in Russia," the bishop of Kovrov once wrote, "who pray to the Lord for Her salvation. Were there no more righteous people, God would destroy us. Take for example my acquaintance Anna Saburov, the wife of the former governor of St. Petersburg. She lost her husband and father in the revolution, and in 1932 both of her sons were arrested, when she was ill herself, but never once in all her letters to me has she ever cried out to the Lord in protest."[36]

The grief over Boris's death was compounded by the fact that Anna was now alone. On the night of February 22, 1938, the NKVD returned to the Saburov apartment and arrested Xenia. They locked her up in Vladimir's former monastery for six months. She became ill. First her legs swelled, followed by her entire body, even her face. She developed terrible diarrhea; pussy sores erupted on her scalp, and she had to cut off all her hair. At the end of September, Xenia was moved to Ivanovo. There her interrogator, a man named Belekov, beat her savagely. He pummeled her face, smashing her lips and knocking out many of her teeth, and dragged her around the room by her hair. (He could be seen walking the streets of Ivanovo as a pensioner almost fifty years later.) He kept after her to confess her crimes, but she had no idea what to say since she had never been told what she had been charged with. This went on for weeks. During the beatings Xenia struggled not to lose consciousness or say something that might cast suspicion on anyone else. She only learned of the charge at her trial in early October: espionage and counterrevolutionary activities (Article 58, Section 6). As evidence the NKVD cited her marriage to Page and some German marks found in her apartment sent by an aunt living abroad. She was convicted and sentenced to ten years in a labor camp. "I did not show them that I was devastated," Xenia said. "I did not even let my lips quiver, though a flash of cold did run down my spine. They told me I could lodge an appeal. I did. I wrote on the verdict that I did not recognize the charges."[37]

On November 21, Xenia received a letter from her mother. It was marked "No. 2." (Letters were typically numbered; that way the recipient knew when a letter had not gotten through.) Letter No. 1 had contained word of Boris's death; thus this subsequent letter struck Xenia like a bolt of lightning.

> This news about Boris devastated me. You must have written about it in the first letter, which never reached me. The whole time I had a feeling that something had happened and had been having dreams. I'll write you more about this later, but for now just a few words so that you knew I am with you in heart and soul. I know better than anyone else what B. meant to you and what a loss this is for you. I am humbled by the manner in which you have received this, and am trying to accept this enormous loss in the same way, but at this moment I still cannot come to my senses.

Several days later Xenia wrote again. "Everything that concerns me now seems of secondary importance. None of it's very important, it all seems so petty." Xenia could not stop thinking about Boris; she dreamed of him every night. The loss of Boris naturally made her think of Yuri and worry even more about his well-being.[38] Both she and her mother continued to believe he was alive.

In late 1938, Xenia learned she would soon be shipped off to a camp in the north. She wrote her mother to send some shirts, undergarments, and sandals. She said was ready for anything: "I completely submit myself to fate." Xenia ended up in Plesetsk in the Arkhangelsk region. There she spent the next year and a half. It was a difficult place. The camp was full of hardened criminals, and they mocked Xenia, calling her the "Macedonian Princess." In the winter the temperature dropped to nearly minus forty degrees Fahrenheit. She was put to work moving logs for a new railroad on four hundred grams of bread a day; her feet were covered in nothing but cotton socks and bast shoes. The heavy strain and miserable conditions quickly undermined her health, and she was assigned to the Temporarily Unfit for Labor Brigade and given a larger ration. She was soon sent back out to work in the forest, but still too weak to fulfill her quota, she was put in a punishment cell, and her rations were cut; the camp officials kept for themselves the food parcels Anna sent her. After Xenia's release, some of the male prisoners took pity on her and helped her fulfill her work norm, giving her time to rest and warm herself by the fire. This cycle of forest work, illness, rest, recovery, and then return to the forest went on all winter and spring of 1939. On at least one occasion she was close to death, and it was thanks to the kindness of her fellow prisoners, food sent from her mother and Uncle Pavel (coffee, jam, milk, canned vegetables, much of which never reached Xenia), and the begrudging compassion of the camp officials that Xenia survived. She was exceedingly grateful to her mother, but, knowing how little Anna could afford these gifts and how difficult it was for her all alone back in Vladimir, it pained her to accept them. "I value your concern for my needs, both great and small, so very much. How you ease my condition. It is so true, 'There's no one like your mother!' Oh, how I feel that here. Thank you for everything!"[39]

That spring Anna was also preoccupied with her concern for Yuri. She had been sending him parcels too, but each time they came back marked "Undeliverable." It had been two years since she had had any word from him, but she refused to give up hope. She kept writing letters to the camp officials, to the gulag administration in Moscow too, begging them for information and pleading for her lost son.[40] She never received any answers.

By late May, Xenia's spirits had revived, in part because of the possibility that she might be freed. She had recently learned that some of the prisoners convicted in Ivanovo around the same time as she had been and for the same charge (Article 58, Section 6) had had their cases reviewed and their convictions overturned. Xenia was intent on writing an appeal to the NKVD and was hopeful of her chances. There was, however, one problem: all appeals had to submitted in triplicate, and there was no writing paper at the camp. And so she would have to wait until she could get paper to make her appeal.

Xenia's revived mood was also due to her good relations with the other prisoners. Throughout June and July she was out working in the forest, cutting branches and debarking felled trees. It was not easy work, but Xenia was getting on well, thanks to the men who pitched in to help her. Xenia was amazed at their compassion and sympathy. One of them in particular impressed her. He was a Turk, but she called him the Babylonian. He went out of his way to be helpful, to look after Xenia, picking up her ax when she was too tired to go on, finishing her work, and always sharing his rations. She was flattered and fell in love. When he was caught giving her money, he was sentenced to twenty-two days in an isolation cell, which made her love him all the more. "He is despotic, handsome, and smart," Xenia told her mother, "passionate and good."[41] Xenia was convinced she would have died there had it not been for the Babylonian and some of the other men she had met in the camps. She wrote to her mother:

> All these meetings, these random meetings with people, not in some ballroom, but in the middle of a forest, in the middle of the taiga, are so unusual and rare. We experienced so much together that our friendship can, of course, never be broken as if we had met in the circumstances of ordinary life. Even if we may be, so to say, people from different planets, still these relationships will remain "until the grave."

Anna, who had never been in the camps, found this difficult to understand, and despite everything that had happened to the family, she worried Xenia had let herself become too familiar with a non-Christian Turk. "But we were a hair's breadth from death!" Xenia tried to explain.

> We shared everything—joy and grief, the last crumb of bread, even clothes. Not surprisingly, given such circumstances it's hard to remain on formal terms. [. . .] Whether in the camp or in exile, everything is completely different. We had found ourselves in such conditions in which one day is equal to a year. The Babylonian and I had been acquainted for six months, yet it felt to me as if it had been an eternity! [. . .] He is so close to me, so dear to me. There is nothing at all alien about him. I understand what you are saying, and you are right, if you look at things from an older point of view, from, say, the perspective of Grandfather and Grandmother—what would they think, what would they say? But could Grandmother have ever thought, or even have imagined, that her granddaughter, with the upbringing I had and the traditions I inherited, would suddenly end up a "lumberjack" in the taiga!? And so one must measure things with a different yardstick

here. Of course, I, too, think it necessary that one remain modest, and to a certain point decorum should not be lost. [. . .] Men have shown and still do show me great respect thanks to my "modesty." I am not vulgar or forward like most modern women, so, dear Mama, you need not worry yourself about me.[42]

Throughout the late summer and into the autumn Xenia's hope of being freed grew. In August, six inmates were released; in October, thirty-six more. The promise of freedom excited Xenia's longing for home and her mother. She could see herself back in Vladimir, together again, in the kitchen baking, laughing, and rejoicing in life under the same roof. Finally, by December writing paper had become available. Her hands aching from the long days in the forest gripping her ax, Xenia sat down on December 2, 1939, and wrote, in triplicate, her appeal. And then she began to wait.[43]

23

HAPPY TIMES

ife, comrades," Stalin announced in 1935, "has become better, life has become more cheerful." His words became the defining slogan for the mid-1930s, the brief three years from 1934 to 1937 between the end of the First Five-Year Plan and the Great Terror. To millions of Soviet citizens this was quite possibly the case, if only because the massive upheavals caused by the campaigns of forced collectivization and crash industrialization had ended. Compared with the nightmare of the Great Break, life truly was better. But there was still much about life in Soviet Russia that was far from cheerful.

The same year Stalin made his famous remark, the newspaper *Komsomolskaia Pravda* ran a series of articles on "Teaching Hatred" by such luminaries as Maxim Gorky and Ilya Ehrenburg. Hatred, it turns out, was not to be condemned but instilled, encouraged, and celebrated, for persons "who cannot hate with passion are unlikely to be able to love with passion." One article printed under the headline OUR HATRED spelled out what brand of hatred was to be cultivated: "Among the noble qualities of the Soviet citizen, of the young person in the Land of the Soviets, is class hatred. We hate those principles on which the old society was founded and shall destroy them." And it was not just principles. "In our country we avail ourselves not only of amnesty, but also of a harsh and noble law: 'If the enemy does not surrender, he will be destroyed.'"[1] Happy times indeed. If the middle years of the thirties provided a moment for much of the population to catch its breath, violence's dark specter was never out of sight.

The relaxation of the Cultural Revolution was signaled by the opening of restaurants to Soviet citizens (previously only foreigners could enjoy such luxuries), the return of jazz and the nefarious fox-trot, and a boom in homegrown musical comedies. Silk stockings reappeared in the stores, and the ban on Christmas trees was lifted.[2] There was a softening in the rhetoric concerning former people and outcasts as well. In 1935, Stalin remarked, "A son does not answer for his father," words that millions of stigmatized and oppressed Soviet citizens recited in the coming years as a weapon in the struggle to regain their civil rights. The new thinking culminated in the so-called Stalin Constitution of 1936, which guaranteed full rights to all citizens "irrespective of race, nationality, religious confession, education level, way of life, social origin, property status, and past activity." Stalin himself had killed a proposed amendment that would have stripped of their rights all former people, clergymen, former White Guards, and anyone "not engaged in socially useful labor." While such restrictions had been necessary in the past, Stalin noted, they no longer were. "The distinctive thing about Soviet society at the present time," he said, "in contrast to any capitalist society, is that there are no longer any antagonistic classes. The exploiting classes have been liquidated." With the Stalin Constitution, the problem of former people seemed to disappear.[3]

The thirties also saw the abandonment of any official talk of egalitarianism and an open endorsement of privilege and favor based on one's usefulness to the state. No one enjoyed greater privilege than the party elite. Of course, there was nothing new about this. As early as the spring of 1918, Madame Lunacharsky was being driven around Petrograd in a limousine that months earlier had belonged to Grand Duke Pavel Alexandrovich, his former chauffeur Zvereff at the wheel. That same year she and her husband took up residence at the Alexander Palace in Tsarskoe Selo, just above the former rooms of the dowager empress Maria Fyodorovna. Madame Lunacharsky attended the theater dressed in brilliant evening gowns.[4] This was standard for the leaders of the revolution. But under Stalin, privilege was expanded, and the wealth made available to the ruling elite grew to mirror more fully that enjoyed by the prerevolutionary aristocracy.

Charles Ciliberti, chauffeur to U.S. Ambassador Joseph Davies, was stunned the first time he visited the dacha of Vyacheslav Molotov, chairman of the Council of People's Commissars, in 1937. He was there to deliver Mrs. Davies, born Marjorie Merriweather Post, socialite and heiress to the enormous cereal fortune of her father, C. W. Post. Molotov's property was considerably larger than Mrs. Davies's hundred-acre Long Island estate, with more and better food, and butlers who made hers look like "amateurs," in Ciliberti's estimation. In the garage, Molotov kept a sixteen-cylinder Cadillac along with several Packards and Fords. The following year Ciliberti drove Mrs. Davies to lunch at the country home of Maxim Litvinov, people's commissar for foreign affairs. So heavily laden was the serving table Ciliberti felt certain it would collapse. Like other wealthy foreigners in the Soviet Union, Mrs. Davies frequented the Torgsin stores to buy the art, antiques, and furnishings of the former nobility. She was also granted access to secret vaults filled with jewels and gold and silver, all available for purchase. When the Davieses left the country, Soviet officials presented her a pair of Chinese vases from the Sheremetevs' former palace of Ostankino.[5]

Stalin had a number of luxurious houses at his disposal. There was the dacha at Zubalovo, for example, built by a nobleman who had made a fortune in the oil business. The leader's daughter, Svetlana, loved it there, where she felt very much at home; "our Zubalovo," she liked to call it. When in the Crimea, Stalin preferred to stay at Koreiz, the former palace of Prince Felix Yusupov outside Yalta. Stalin even took the nobility's former servants; Svetlana's nanny had earlier been the governess for the children of Ulyana Samarin (née Osorgin).[6] The unashamed adoption of life's finer things extended well beyond the Kremlin court and trickled all the way down the political ladder, rung by rung, to first the provincial and then the local party bosses.

Access to special stores, cars and drivers, dachas, servants, sanatoriums on the Black Sea, elite schools and summer camps for their children: the new ruling class of Russia lived a life inconceivable to the masses. The people, however, were not entirely ignorant of their masters' lifestyle. The secret police recorded dangerous comparisons being made between the Communists and the old aristocracy: "Communists in Moscow live like lords, they go round in sables and with silver-handled canes"; "They want to get rid of equality. They want to create classes: the Communists (or former nobility) and us ordinary mortals."[7] The Soviet elite not only rejected such criticisms but refused to

acknowledge them. In their eyes, they remained revolutionaries, proletarians, Communists. They pointed out what they held to be a crucial
distinction between themselves and the former tsarist elite: they did
not *own* these things but merely had *access* to them. The English tourist
Norah Rowan-Hamilton was stunned by the lavish lifestyle of a Soviet
minister she visited. When she expressed surprise that the family ate off
china from the old tsarist mint, he defended himself: "Yes, but we do not
own these luxuries. They belong to the State. Only as servants of the
State do we use them." Pure sophism, thought Norah.[8]

Olga Sheremetev was hired to help the new elite acquire the desired
polish and sophistication. She taught French at a top military academy
to the likes of Mikhail Tukhachevsky, civil war hero and marshal of
the Soviet Union (shot in 1937), and Alexei Okulov, old Bolshevik and
commander of Red Army forces in eastern Siberia (shot in 1939). She
also gave private French lessons to the children of the Soviet diplomat
Nariman Podolsky. Getting to know these men and their families,
Olga had to admit that "among the Communists there are some surprisingly sympathetic and nice people. [. . .] They are new people, but
their interests and tastes are old; they simply bow down before different idols, though they be idols nonetheless." Be that as it may, she still
wanted as little to do with such people as possible. One winter evening
in 1935, Olga was invited to a party at the Podolskys'. The guests talked
of nothing but politics and Stalin; when someone mentioned the recent
death of Mikhail Ippolitov-Ivanov, the composer and director of the
Bolshoi Theater, no one expressed the least bit of interest. "I didn't feel
myself there at all," Olga wrote in her diary, "and left as soon as I could.
As I walked home I kept thinking that even with all their pursuit of an
educated and cultured way of life these communist families are greater
philistines than we are, although this charge is forever being thrown in
our faces."[9]

Among those granted access to this rarefied world was the American fashion photographer James Abbe, who visited the USSR in 1932.
Abbe went to the opera and sat next to Soviet officials and their wives
in fancy dress, all engaged in lots of "hand-kissing"; he went to the
Moscow racetrack, which he found nearly as "snobbish" and "fashionable" as any other in Europe; and he hung out at the bar in the swanky
Metropole Hotel. The bar was popular with diplomats and journalists
and Western tourists because of its jazz bands and the beautiful, ele-

gantly dressed barmaids and cocktail waitresses. According to Abbe, most of these women were the daughters of former aristocrats and rich bourgeois. Fluent in English, French, and German, they were forced into working in the bar as honeypots for the OGPU. It was said women who failed to get information out of the Western men disappeared. Nothing, however, could compare with the formal parties thrown by Madame Litvinov, wife of the commissar for foreign affairs. The guests would arrive in chauffeured limousines at her large prerevolutionary mansion on Moscow's Spiridonovka Street, where a decade earlier young Golitsyns and Sheremetevs had partied with their friends from the ARA. There, waiting at the top of the large staircase in a brilliant gown, Madame Litvinov welcomed her guests, a gloved hand outstretched to receive their kisses.

Perhaps the strangest experience Abbe had in the Soviet Union was his visit to a group he called "The Ex-Bomb Throwers," officially known as the Society of Former Political Prisoners and Exiles. This collection of former revolutionary terrorists lived in an urban mansion "in the atmosphere of an aristocratic club of bygone days, with a private restaurant and picture gallery containing photographs, drawings, paintings, and etchings—many of them works of art—that depict the less pleasant side of prison life under the Czars." Abbe lunched with the members in their Moscow club before being driven out to their country house, the former Sheremetev estate of Mikhailovskoe. Abbe was given a tour of the beautiful estate grounds, with its fragrant pines, clear lakes, and well-kept lawns; the old barns had been converted into a children's colony, and peasants continued to dwell in the small cottages, though now they no longer served the Sheremetevs but the members of the society. An ancient gardener left over from the days of the Sheremetevs still tended the flowers.

To Abbe, as he toured the manor, it seemed as if the previous owners had just left the day before. Everything appeared to be in excellent condition, and the house, with its elegant furnishings, lovely music room, and enormous, dark-paneled library filled with leather-bound editions of the French and English classics, exuded "the Old Régime atmosphere of culture." The members slept upstairs in canopied poster beds; a number of smaller iron cots had also been set up "for the overflow of ex-revolutionaries on summer vacation." A musical gong summoned them to dinner. "The aristocrats of Revolution were seated about the round mahogany table. As I took my place at this proletarian Round Table I observed that the Bolshevik knights and ladies were being served by peasant retainers on china which bore the coat-of-arms of the Society of Ex-Political Prisoners: a barred prison window and a chained manacle wreath!" Seated with Abbe were some of the most famous names of the Russian revolutionary movement, now old and gray and wrinkled. To one side sat Vasily Perovsky, the brother of Sofia Perovsky, who had been hanged for her role in the assassination of Alexander II. Across the table sat Mikhail Frolenko, another of the assassins and cofounder of The People's Will, who had spent twenty-four years in prison. "Throughout dinner the little group chatted, laughed, joked and recounted soft-spoken tales of bloodshed and terror of the old days of the Revolution."

As he was leaving, Abbe encountered a tiny white-haired lady sitting on the balcony. He introduced himself and was stunned to learn she was none other than Vera Figner. Figner was perhaps the most famous and notorious of Russia's revolutionaries, whose early days in the movement stretched back to the 1870s. A member of the executive committee of The People's Will, she had helped plan the assassination of Alexander II, for which she was later sentenced to death, though subsequently pardoned and given twenty-years in prison. After the revolution the publication of her memoirs brought her world fame. Abbe was stunned to meet this icon of the revolution, and he found it difficult to reconcile the image of the unbreakable terrorist-revolutionary with the sweet-looking octogenarian in her lace cap quietly picking away at her embroidery. "Here on the balcony where Old Régime nobles sunned themselves while it lasted, Vera Figner reminisced verbally with me," Abbe wrote. "The conversation veered to the present Soviet system. As Vera Figner discussed the government she had devoted her life to establishing, her comment came softly and her eyes were dull with tragedy. Her words caused me to glance sharply over my shoulder for fear she might be over-heard. 'This is not what we fought for,' she murmured."[10]

The old Sheremetev gardener at Mikhailovskoe could have told Abbe some stories as well. Like the bizarre tale of Count Pyotr Sheremetev, buried there in 1914. In the spring of 1929 rumors began circulating that Pyotr had been laid to rest with weapons of gold in his coffin. Thieves tried to smash their way into the crypt but failed; to put an end to the rumors, the authorities broke open the crypt and dug up his grave. What they saw upon opening his coffin sent chills down their spines. Placed in a tightly sealed double coffin, Pyotr's body, although fifteen years in the ground, had hardly decayed. All the skin was still there, just dried out and tighter now. Some claimed they had seen the body of a holy man. Having dispelled one rumor, the officials now worried they had inadvertently created a new one. To make certain the crypt did not become a place of pilgrimage, they secretly reburied Pyotr's body in an unmarked spot on the grounds, not bothering to put it back in the coffin.[11]

The eternal rest of a good many Sheremetevs was disturbed during these years. In May 1927, Olga Sheremetev recorded a story Maria Gudovich had told her about the fate of the ancient Sheremetev crypt in Novospassky Monastery's Znamensky Church:

> Today she came from Novospassky where she had met some old woman (I never meet such old women) who talked about how they had opened up the crypts at Novospassky, how they had destroyed the chapel where Sister Dosifeya was buried, how they then dug up the graves and searched the corpses. In the crypt under the Znamensky Church in one of the coffins they even found a gold saber, which they took. The old woman said she saw all this herself and even helped dig, even though they don't let anyone inside its walls. But this is all entirely possible, for I myself saw in 1923 crypts and graves in the Simonov Monastery that had been broken into and dug up. I know that they took tombstones from the Novospassky Monastery for use in the remodeling of the Bolshoi Theater. I know that they rob the dead. This isn't what's interesting; what is interesting is the very romantic legend she talked about, how early in the morning and in the evening candles light themselves and the sound of singing can be heard coming from inside the locked temples. These are the deceased, abandoned and insulted, holding services in the destroyed, crumbling, and forgotten churches, and the prisoners and their guards do not dare enter out of fear.[12]

Alexandra Tolstoy was an inmate at the Novospassky Monastery when this happened. One night she heard the sound of crowbars and spades clanking against marble headstones and tombs as some of the female prisoners dug up the graves. In the morning she went out to see the ground littered with bones and skulls, and women sitting on the profaned grave stones admiring their booty—"gold rings, bracelets, and crosses," many with precious stones. The pillage went on for several nights, and nothing was done to stop it. Only after some of the women went mad, wailing and screaming in the dark and claiming to have seen the ghost of a monk in gray robes in one of the tombs, did they stop.[13]

More Sheremetev graves were desecrated in Nizhny Novgorod. Several generations of Sheremetevs (from the nontitled noble branch of the family) had been buried in a local church that was closed and then vandalized after the revolution. The graves were dug up, the coffins opened, and the bodily remains dumped out, stripped, plundered, and left on the ground. The crypt was turned into a storage room for kerosene, and the church became a cinema.[14]

Of course, the fate of the Sheremetevs' remains was not unique. In 1928, the former prince Pyotr Obolensky went to visit his mother's grave at the Tikhvinskoe Cemetery in Leningrad's Alexander Nevsky Monastery. When he got to the chapel crypt, he saw that the steel doors had been ripped open. Pyotr descended the stairs and found the crypt dirty, dug up, and defiled; people had apparently been living there for a time. The squatters had not been able to get to his mother's grave, though they had managed to dig up that of his aunt. The family crypt of the Baryatinskys at the Marino estate church was ruthlessly destroyed in 1937. The marble sarcophagi were smashed to pieces, and the remains of nineteen Baryatinskys were thrown in a pile and burned in the work yard. The ashes were left to the wind, and the crypt was used to store coal.[15]

Much of the vandalism was spontaneous, although from the late 1920s most of it was officially planned and carried out. The destruction of the Baryatinsky crypt, for example, had been ordered by Moscow. Bricks were needed for a new school floor, and some official decided the best place to get them would be from under the corpses of the Baryatinskys. Across Russia, officials looked to cemeteries for free building material; perhaps as many as forty thousand tons of iron, bronze, granite, and other stones were ripped out of the ground and repurposed. Much of the marble used to decorate the earliest Moscow subway stations in the 1930s came from tombstones. Stripped of their material assets, many cemeteries were then bulldozed, and apartment blocks, workers' clubs, parks, and soccer fields were built over the dead. The obliteration of these old cemeteries and graveyards served both to further erase Russia's tsarist past from the landscape and to show that the Soviet government was indeed making life better, more cheerful.[16]

With the United States and much of the industrialized world mired in the Great Depression, with labor unrest swelling, and with little objective information coming out of the Soviet Union, it is not surprising that some people in the West looked to the rising Communist state with hope. What *is* surprising is that some of them were Russian nobles.

Alexei Ignatiev, born in 1877, had graduated from the Corps des Pages in St. Petersburg and then joined the Chevaliers Gardes. After fighting in the Russo-Japanese War, Ignatiev served in various foreign capitals and was the country's military attaché in Paris when the revolution occurred. As early as November 1917 he sided with the Bolsheviks and helped procure arms for them. He was apparently motivated in part by the murder of his father, Count Alexei Pavlovich Ignatiev, the reactionary governor of Tver Province, killed in 1906 by the Socialist Revolutionaries. Ignatiev had never believed the story of his father's murder, insisting that he had actually been killed by the tsarist secret police because of his father's disgust with Nicholas's political concessions following the Revolution of 1905. Alexei officially began to work for the Soviets in 1925, earning him the revulsion of the White émigré community. After many years in exile, Ignatiev made his first trip back to Russia in 1930. It made a powerful impression on him. On the last night of his visit, Ignatiev stood on Red Square and listened with overflowing emotion as the Kremlin bells rang out the "Internationale." "With pride I felt myself to be a Soviet citizen, an equal among equals, a free man among the free," he confessed. Returned to Paris, he wrote a glowing appraisal of the USSR for the influential *Vu* magazine, which brought even more scorn from the exile community.

"It's funny, and also shameful," he later remarked, "that I have had to hear base lies about Soviet Russia from people of the former 'privileged' class who have abandoned their homeland forever and become traitors." In 1937, at the height of the Great Terror, Molotov tele-grammed Ignatiev asking him to return immediately to Russia to work in the People's Commissariat for Defense. Ignatiev returned, and amazingly, this former nobleman, guards officer, and son of a reaction-ary tsarist official not only survived the Great Terror and Second World War but even outlived Stalin, dying at the age of eighty.[17]

Ignatiev was someone who identified as much with the growing power of the Soviet Union as with its Communist ideology. Not so Dmitry Svyatopolk-Mirsky, another noble returnee. The son of the former tsarist minister of the interior Prince Pyotr Svyatopolk-Mirksy, Dmitry and his brother Alexei had fought with the Whites in the civil war, during which Alexei was killed. Dmitry fled to England, where he became a noted literary scholar and university lecturer. In 1931, he joined the Communist Party of Great Britain and the following year left for the Soviet Union, having been granted a "pardon" by the Soviet government with the help of Gorky. Virginia Woolf saw him days be-fore he left. "I thought as I watched his eyes brighten and fade—soon there'll be a bullet through your head," she wrote. Woolf was wrong, and Mirsky was left alone until the summer of 1937, when he was at-tacked in the press as a "Wrangelite" and "White Guard." Shortly there-after Dmitry was arrested and sentenced to eight years in the camps on "suspicion of espionage." He died of enterocolitis near Magadan in the Far East in June 1939.

The British journalist and writer Malcolm Muggeridge met Mirsky in Moscow in 1932. Privately, he described Mirsky as "very brave," if "a little mad," for returning to Russia; publicly he slurred Mirsky in his novel *Winter in Moscow* in the character of Prince Alexis, describing him thus: "What is he but a man who's managed to be a parasite under three régimes? An Aristocrat under the Tsarism. Professor under the capitalism. Proletarian man-of-letters under the Dictatorship of the Proletariat."[18]

The most famous (or infamous) of all repatriated noblemen was the writer Count Alexei Tolstoy, once described as "the most authorita-tive apologist for the Stalinist regime." A distant relation of Leo Tolstoy's, Alexei was born in 1883, educated in St. Petersburg, and then covered World War I for the Russian press. During the civil war he sided with the Whites, even serving in General Denikin's propaganda section for a period before leaving Russia for Western Europe. Tolstoy was not in exile long before experiencing a political change of heart and returning in 1923. The so-called Comrade Count (also Worker-Peasant Count) established himself as one of the leading men of Soviet letters alongside Gorky. He became chairman of the Soviet Writers' Union in 1936 and was later made a member of the Soviet Academy of Sciences and deputy to the Supreme Soviet. Tolstoy received three Stalin Prizes, including one for his historical novel *Peter the First* in 1941. Under Stalin he lived in grand style in the former Tsarskoe Selo, like "an old-fashioned *barin* out of Turgenev's pages," observed the American journalist Eugene Lyons disdainfully. At his home he was waited on by a servant who had been with the family since before the revolution and who still addressed him as "Your Excellency." He died, unmolested, in Moscow in 1945.[19]

24

POISONOUS SNAKES AND THE AVENGING SWORD: OPERATION FORMER PEOPLE

ate on the afternoon of December 1, 1934, just as he was about to enter his office at the Smolny building in Leningrad, Sergei Kirov, first secretary of the Leningrad Communist Party, was shot in the back of the head at close range. He died instantly. The following day Vladimir Golitsyn wrote in his diary: "Yesterday I heard on the radio that Kirov has been murdered. Our entire family is terrified. We all fear new repressions. God forbid the killer wasn't a prince, count, or some other nobleman. Everyone's been so upset by this senseless trick."[1]

Many observers have long speculated that Stalin had arranged Kirov's murder in order to rid himself of a potential political rival. It now seems most likely, however, that Stalin had nothing to do with the killing and that it was the work of a lone assassin. The gunman, Leonid Nikolaev, the unemployed son of a worker, had a history of emotional problems and had recently been expelled from the party. Angered at the downward spiral his life had taken, he sought revenge for his troubles against his supposed enemies by putting a bullet into the head of the city's boss. Although Vladimir Golitsyn's fear that the murderer was a nobleman proved unwarranted, still, he, like every other former person, had good cause to worry because the Soviet leadership used Kirov's murder as a pretext for a new campaign of repression and terror.[2]

Kirov's assassination was presented to the public as the work of the usual "enemies" who had been targeted since the beginning of Stalin's revolution. Within weeks of the killing the hunt to uncover a supposed underground "Center of Zinovievites" was unleashed, and Stalin signed a resolution exiling 663 former Zinoviev supporters from Leningrad to northern Siberia and Yakutia.[3] The repressive measures also hit non-Russian nationalities living in that part of the country. Ethnic Finns in the Leningrad district and Karelia, for example, were arrested as members of an alleged fifth column. As many as 46,000 people were deported from areas along the Soviet frontier and sent to special labor colonies in western Siberia, Kazakhstan, and Tadzhikistan.[4] In Leningrad itself, however, the main target was former people.

On February 16, 1935, a report marked "top secret" was drafted by the NKVD of the Leningrad district for Genrikh Yagoda, chief of the NKVD, alerting him to the "serious overpopulation of enterprises, institutes of higher learning, and especially administrative offices of the city of Leningrad by members of the defeated bourgeoisie, powerful officials of the former state apparatus, [. . .] the offspring of executed terrorists, saboteurs, spies, and even prominent representatives of the former tsarist aristocracy, former tsarist generals, and their descendants." The report went on to list five groups of enemies, the two largest of which were families of "former big landowners" and "former aristocrats—former princes, barons, counts, and others of the ancient, hereditary nobility."[5] The situation called for action, and on the night of February 27–28, Operation Former People was set in motion to rid Leningrad of every last former person within four weeks. In addition to the typical victims (nobles, tsarist military and police officers, Orthodox clergymen), this time the NKVD made sure to include their children and grandchildren, members of what was called the "counter-revolutionary reserve."[6] Although the Kirov Affair served as the catalyst for the operation, its origins can be traced back to 1933, when plans had been drawn up to purge the city of "socially alien elements."[7] For several years the Leningrad OGPU had already had the city's former people under special observation in light of their "overt hostility," as one police document put it, to the Soviet regime.[8]

Calls for action against former people began appearing in the local press even before the operation was officially launched. On February 8, *Leningradskaia Pravda* printed a letter by one Comrade Yakovlev under the heading "A Nest of Nobles." According to Yakovlev, the apartment building at No. 105/4 Griboedov Canal had been taken over by a gang of former nobles who were "persecuting the workers and tormenting the Communists" who also lived there. The letter named names ("former baron and landowner Osten-Saken, former princess Putyatin") and demanded that the nest be destroyed.[9] Of course, the views expressed in the Soviet press have to be approached with caution and should not be taken as direct, unfiltered expressions of public opinion. Nonetheless, it would be wrong to think there was no popular support for the wide-scale attack on the former people; indeed, there is evidence to suggest that while not universal, such popular sentiment did exist and was cleverly used, though not manufactured, by the authorities for specific purposes.[10]

The Yakovlev letter is significant since it highlights one of the problems the authorities were trying to solve by way of Operation Former People—namely, housing. Following collectivization and the rush of peasants fleeing the countryside for the cities, the housing shortage in many urban centers became critical. One way to alleviate the problem was to empty the cities of undesirables. Between 1933 and 1935, 75,388 Leningraders were exiled, or simply shot, freeing up 9,950 apartments and rooms.[11] Should anyone fail to see the social benefit from such a policy, a Soviet textbook on housing law from 1935 made the point in explicit terms:

> One of the most spectacular demonstrations to the working men of what the Revolution really could mean to them was the moving of people who had been living in the cellars and little shacks out in the poverty-stricken suburbs to the palaces and former mansions of the rich. A worker had only to open his eyes in the morning to realize that something tremendous had happened and to draw the conclusion that as the chief beneficiary he owed allegiance to the cause.[12]

Employment was also a problem, and the newspapers were full of complaints about the injustice of allowing former people—"obvious class enemies," as one writer put it—to remain in their places of work. Not only was it wrong that these people were taking jobs from more deserving workers, as many saw the matter, but they could not be trusted; it was widely believed these former people must be surreptitiously engaged in sabotage.[13] For some Soviet citizens, attacking the old elite quenched their thirst for revenge. In late March the newspaper *The Change* published the letter of a worker from the Red Vyborg factory under the rubric "The Horrid Past." "When they used to beat me," he recalled of his life in tsarist Russia, "I always wondered—will I ever have my revenge on these vermin? The hounds of the revolution settled the score for me. Many of those I have written about are already no longer among the living. As for those still alive, I am certain that the NKVD will 'take care' of them and their friends."[14]

At factories throughout Leningrad meetings were held at which workers called for immediate, merciless action. "The Party organization demanded the purging of the mechanic workshop of all 'former people,'" wrote *Leningradskaia Pravda* about the factory Soviet Star on March 9. "With their resolutions the laborers of the city of Lenin approve the actions of the organs of the NKVD and accept the responsibility of raising their revolutionary vigilance to new heights in order to more actively unmask the enemies of the working class," reported *The Change*. "The honor of living in the great city of Lenin should belong only to workers [. . .] Our horrid past has sunk into oblivion! Never again will these human degenerates—the aristocrats of tsarist Russia—exult over Soviet land. [. . .] We shall clean our great city of any and all counterrevolutionary scum."[15]

Leningradskaia Pravda printed workers' speeches dripping with outrage over the fact that these "age-old exploiters and bloodsuckers" had managed to stay hidden for so long in the "cradle of the proletarian revolution." The workers spoke at length about how the nobles had once dressed in gold and kept pet dogs while they had starved and had spit in their faces and even shot them when they had dared go out on strike. And now, having camouflaged themselves, the old nobles were secretly collaborating with foreign powers to undermine the work of "millions of their former slaves" and stop the advance of socialism. "Hitler's trustworthy allies," one report called them. These people were not even human, but "venomous chameleons, trying to take on a Soviet appearance," "tsarist scum," "poisonous snakes," "parasites," "vermin." Echoing the stories in *The Change*, the workers described in *Leningradskaia Pravda* applauded the efforts of the NKVD and "the Great Leader Comrade Stalin" to clean their city, and they vowed to do their part to sniff out the enemies still hiding at their places of work and in their homes. "The avenging sword of the proletarian dictatorship should know no mercy," proclaimed the workers from the Kirov factory.[16]

Before long former people in Moscow and cities across the country began to fear the witch hunt would reach them.[17] By late February 1935, Olga Sheremetev in Moscow was writing in her diary about the "Petrograd pogrom." On April 1, 1935, the NKVD summoned Olga to appear for questioning at the police headquarters on Petrovka Street. The summons did not surprise her: Pavel Sheremetev had been called in as well the other day. Nonetheless, everyone in her apartment was panicked. Certain she had nothing to fear, Olga took her passport and her work pass and set off to Petrovka. The building was crowded with "old former people of various stripes." From one of the rooms loud voices could be heard every time the door opened; people were coming out in tears, hysterical, having been told they had one day in which to leave Moscow.

Olga waited for about two hours before being called into an interrogation room. She was seated at a table with a green-shaded lamp; across from her sat a man with an upturned collar and a military service cap, his face hidden by the shadows. He started with the usual questions: name, place of work, home address, length of residence in Moscow, parents' names and backgrounds, their dates of birth and death, previous convictions or prison terms. The interrogation was punctuated by long, silent pauses; the interrogator would drum his fingers on the table and appear to be staring at her. Olga stared back, refusing to divert her gaze; to calm her shaking hand, she placed it firmly on the table. Two other women were being interrogated at desks on either side of her. One, an old woman in tears, was desperately trying to convince them that she had never been a noble landowner. When her interrogator got up to leave, the woman fell to pieces and started to scream. Olga sensed her own nerves tightening; a lump had formed in her throat. The questioning turned to Olga's late husband, Boris Sheremetev, arrested in 1918. Then the interrogator got up and left. "I had a feeling everything would be all right," she later wrote, "but the conversations to either side gave me reason for concern. There were tears and categorical orders to leave within two days, and then as some grand gesture of charity an extension of up to ten days was given. Presently, I began to notice how terribly little air there was in this small, smoky room." Eventually, the man returned, handed back her passport, and, with a smile, told her she would be permitted to remain in Moscow and would not be bothered anymore. As she prepared to go, he offered Olga some advice: "You should change your name."

"So that you could then blame me of being afraid of it and thus changing it," she replied.

"If you will," he laughed.

"Of course, my surname does not bring me happiness," she blurted out, surprised at her own directness.

Why did I say that? Regardless, they had let me go. I walked out and those still waiting to be called looked at me with envy.

I went out into the street. The pleasant spring freshness embraced me and I buttoned up my coat when I should have been taking it off, but I had to walk through the streets and people would stare. I walked for a while without thinking, just breathing and enjoying freedom. But when I reached the boulevard I began to feel that I was terribly tired, and I recalled that everyone at home must be worried about me. I climbed into a streetcar and, as I was riding, I kept thinking, what was the point of that interrogation? What is it for, how does it help the state, and what does it cost?[18]

Tatiana Aksakov-Sivers was deemed a "poisonous snake." She was in Leningrad at a friend's apartment with Vladimir Lvov, one of the noble fox-trotters arrested and exiled from Moscow a decade earlier, on the evening of Kirov's murder. Two days later she was stunned to read that 120 "hostages" had already been arrested and shot at the Shpalerka Prison. Soon she heard talk of more arrests. On February 1, Tatiana bumped into an acquaintance on Nevsky Prospect who told her that Vladimir's brothers Yuri and Sergei Lvov (Merinka Gudovich's husband) had been arrested the night before; not long thereafter, Vladimir was also arrested. The NKVD came for Tatiana on February 11 and took her to the Shpalerka for questioning. "Tell me," the interrogator asked, "do you know any princes?" She told him she had known many princes in her life, that there was nothing unusual about this, so what was it exactly, she replied, they were getting at? Unhappy with her answer, they locked her up.

In April, Tatiana, the three Lvov brothers, and many others at the Shpalerka were released for the night and told to return the next day to learn where they were being sent. She and Vladimir Lvov walked out of prison together; after two months inside its walls, the fresh air made her head spin. Between the two of them they had just enough money to split a chocolate bar. When she got home, she found a neighbor who worked for the NKVD had already moved into her room; most of her things had been stolen during a search.[19] The next day she and Vladimir met for lunch—a last meal—at the Hotel Severnaya, filling themselves on soup, chicken and rice, wine, and ice cream before setting off for the Shpalerka. The three Lvovs were to be exiled with twelve others to Kuibyshev for five years; Tatiana to Saratov, for the same period.

Instructions notifying all NKVD agents to be on the lookout for potential acts of terrorism and sabotage against hotels and other prominent buildings by former people were issued during the operation, and the police were put on heightened alert to prevent them from escaping the city. The NKVD found many of its victims by combing existing registration records as well as prerevolutionary city guides and old telephone books. None of those arrested held prominent positions in the city administration, army, or police. Typical of the victims were figures like former Prince B. D. Volkonsky, who worked on the floor of the Leningrad Diary Plant; Baroness V. V. Knoring-Formen, a sanitation worker at Cafeteria No. 89; Prince D. B. Cherkassky, an assistant to the chief accountant at the Aurora candy factory; and Count A. S. Lanskoy, a laborer at the factory Electro-Apparatus. Kirill Frolov was apparently arrested for no other reason than having served as valet to Pyotr Durnovo, minister of the interior under Nicholas II.[20] Regardless, they and the rest were accused of being members of fictitious groups like the Fascist-Terrorist Group of Former Lawyers, the Terrorist Group of Former Noble Officers and Lycée Pupils, and the Terrorist Group of Former Nobles.

The scholar Dmitry Likhachev, freed from Solovki in 1932, was working at the Academy of Sciences in a department full of former people in the winter of 1935. One day Likhachev happened to pass the head of the personnel department in the hall; pausing, she turned to Likhachev: "I am putting together a list of all nobles here. And I have put your name on it." Likhachev was panic-stricken. But I'm not a nobleman, he protested; you must cross my name off the list. (His father had been a "personal noble," a status that did not confer hereditary noble privilege on one's heirs.) It was too late, she told him. It was a long list, she had typed up all the names herself, in alphabetical order, and it would be too much work to redo it. Desperate, Likhachev hired someone with his own money to retype the list without his name. A few weeks later Likhachev arrived one day to find their offices practically empty. He asked one of his colleagues if they all had left for a meeting. "What? Don't you understand," he was told, "they've all been arrested!" Although he had saved himself, nothing seemed the same anymore; even the look of the city appeared altered. "With the exile of the nobility," he recalled years later, "the cultural face of the city changed. The streets changed their appearance. The faces of the passersby became different."[21]

Few were as fortunate as Likhachev. Yelizaveta Grigorevna Golitsyn, the seventy-five-year-old widow of Prince Alexei Lvovich Golitsyn, was arrested in Leningrad along with her daughter and son-in-law. She wrote to Peshkov for help, noting, among other things, that she was a "princess" only by marriage, being "herself more of a proletarian by origin since my father [. . .] was not of noble extraction, but a doctor." On March 14, they were sentenced to five years, exiled to a remote Kazakh village, and left to fend for themselves. Yelizaveta was too frail to work, and her children were too ill. Not long after their arrival, Yelizaveta suffered a stroke. Their friends kept writing to Peshkov begging for help since they were "dying of hunger." Their ultimate fate is unknown.[22] Prince Vladimir Lvovich Golitsyn, who had fought in the Red Army during the civil war, was sentenced to five years in the Karaganda labor camp in Kazakhstan. He served only two years, however, before being arrested a second time (while still in the camps), charged with "counterrevolutionary agitation," and shot. Princess Nadezhda Golitsyn, once a maid of honor at court, had worked for a number of Soviet agencies before being exiled to Turkestan, where, in 1938, she was arrested again and executed at the age of sixty-seven.[23]

As for Tatiana Aksakov-Sivers, she ended up in Saratov with a large group of exiled former people. Their big-city clothing made them stand out as they went door to door looking for rooms, and most had trouble finding work as repressed people. One woman survived by selling small paintings with scenes of Leningrad; another by making and selling women's undergarments through her own small enterprise, which she called the Leningrad Workshop for the Artistic Shaping of the Female Figure. Tatiana scraped together some money by hocking some curtains saved from the old family estate of Popelyova and a portrait miniature by the noted eighteenth-century artist Vladimir Borovikovsky. In the summer of 1937, a new wave of arrests swept over the exiles in Saratov. The NKVD arrested Tatiana in November and sentenced her to eight years in a corrective labor camp. She was packed into a freight car and sent off in the spring of 1938 with no food and nothing but the clothes on her back. Another ex-Leningrader in her car shared her last onion with Tatiana. This woman was later axed to death by a fellow prisoner after she refused to have sex with him. The trip to the camp took two weeks. At stops along the way, Tatiana tossed out through the small cracks in the siding of the car notes addressed to her father and with a few words imploring whoever picked them up to mail them on. Unbelievably, two of these reached him.[24] Tatiana remained in the camps until the summer of 1943.

Operation Former People was a success, and by the end of March 1935 *Leningradskaia Pravda* could report a great outpouring of praise from workers at factories across the city for the NKVD and its efforts to clean the city. WE ARE CLEANING LENIN'S CITY OF THE REMAINS OF THE TSAR'S MEN, OF THE LANDOWNING AND CAPITALIST RIFF-RAFF read the headline on March 22. Indeed, between February 28 and March 27, 1935, more than 39,000 people, 11,072 of them former people, had been expelled from Leningrad.[25] So crowded were the city's railway stations with princes, counts, and the like that a joke was born:

> Dialogue overheard at a railroad ticket window in Leningrad:
> "Comrade Citizen, what do you think you're doing jumping the line?"
> "Well, I'm a princess!"[26]

As in the old days, nobles were being given special treatment, although now of an entirely different sort and for entirely different reasons.

The laughter lasted only so long, however. As late as July of that year, the press was still carrying stories decrying the fact that many former people had somehow managed to escape detection and were still hiding in the city of Lenin.[27]

25

THE GREAT TERROR

The Kirov Affair did not end with Operation Former People. Rather, it opened the door to the darkest chapter in Soviet history, the Great Terror. Having rid Leningrad of "Zinovievites," former people, and other socially alien elements, Stalin and the party leadership expanded the hunt for internal enemies. The international situation was crucial to the origins and logic of the Great Terror. The rise of Hitler's Germany in the west and the imperialist expansionism of Hirohito's Japan in the east were quite rightly seen as serious external threats to the Soviet Union. Stalin, however, was arguably more obsessed with the domestic menace. He and others in the party convinced themselves of the existence of a fifth column comprised of closet anti-Soviet elements waiting to attack from within in coordination with the German and Japanese armies. The Great Terror was conceived as a preemptive strike to destroy any remaining internal enemies once and for all.[1]

The Great Terror is most often associated with the destruction of the Old Bolsheviks and the show trials of 1936–38. Tens of thousands of party members from the state bureaucracy, the NKVD, and the military were purged and arrested. The entire high command of the Red Army was wiped out. Everyone, save Stalin, was suspect; enemies lurked everywhere. "We will destroy every enemy, even if he is an Old Bolshevik," Stalin promised at the height of the terror; "we will destroy his kin, his family. Anyone who by his actions or thoughts encroaches on the unity of the socialist state, we shall destroy relentlessly."[2] In 1935, Yenukidze, the secretary of the Central Executive Committee, was denounced for his links to "former people" and accused of permitting White Guards to infiltrate the Kremlin and nearly assassinate Stalin. He was dismissed, expelled from the party, and shot two years later. The NKVD chief Yagoda also fell under suspicion for his lack of vigilance. At the end of September 1936, Yagoda was suddenly sacked as people's commissar for internal affairs and replaced by his rival, Nikolai Yezhov.

Yezhov, with Stalin's blessing, encouragement, and, most important, guidance, was the ceremonial ringmaster of the Great Terror, the fifteen-month period from August 1937 to November 1938 known in Russian as the *Yezhóvshchina*. It was Yezhov who had attacked Yenukidze and Yagoda. In August 1936, Zinoviev and Kamenev, together with fourteen others of the "United Trotskyite-Zinovievite Center," were tried, convicted, and immediately executed in the first of the Moscow show trials. Yezhov helped organize a second show trial the following year and then, in March 1938, a third, final trial of the "Anti-Soviet Block of Rightists and Trotskyites," after which Bukharin and Yagoda were shot.[3]

Although this side of the Great Terror is well known, its much larger side is not. The vast majority of the victims of the Yezhovshchina were in fact not Communist Party members, but ordinary citizens, mostly the same people who had been targeted as enemies for many years. On July 2, 1937, the Politburo passed a resolution titled On Anti-Soviet Elements. According to the resolution, local officials were to be ordered to register, arrest, and, if necessary, shoot all criminals, a term purposely left vague. On July 20, Yezhov issued Order No. 0047—On an Operation to Repress Former Kulaks, Criminals, and Other Anti-Soviet Elements—setting the date for the commencement of the repressive measures as the first two weeks of August. Quotas were set on the expected numbers of "spies," "traitors," and "counterrevolutionaries" to be arrested. Although these numbers came from the Kremlin, local leaders frequently exceeded the quotas in an effort to demonstrate their zeal and effectiveness; no one wanted to be seen as lacking the necessary vigilance. By the end of November, approximately 766,000 people had been arrested; nearly 385,000 were executed.

The arrests and executions mounted, and the number of victims continued to grow well into 1938. Local party and NKVD officials had proved so enthusiastic and successful that the party leadership in Moscow began to talk about "excesses" and "violations of socialist legality." Stalin decided the repressions had gone far enough, and in November 1938 he forced Yezhov to retire and made him the scapegoat for the terror campaign. He was replaced by the Georgian party boss Lavrenty Beria, who promised a complete reform of the NKVD. On April 10, 1939, Yezhov was arrested. He immediately confessed to being a German spy and having used his position as head of the NKVD to organize a conspiracy to kill Stalin. On the night of February 2, 1940, Yezhov was shot in an execution chamber in the center of Moscow built according to his own design. His corpse was cremated and his ashes were tossed into a mass grave at the Donskoy Cemetery. The Soviet press passed over his death in silence.[4]

We shall likely never know how many people perished in the Great Terror. According to one reliable estimate, the NKVD arrested 1,575,259 people during 1937–38. Of these, 1,344,923 were convicted, and more than half of them—681,692—were shot. This makes for a killing rate of approximately 1,500 people a day between August 1937 and November 1938.[5] The scale of the violence and the fear it instilled in people's hearts are hard to imagine. Few dared speak of such things or even dwell on them at the time.

Among the victims of the Great Terror were two of Vladimir Vladimirovich Golitsyn's three children, Alexander and Olga. In 1936, Alexander had been freed after serving three years in a labor camp but was denied the right to return to Moscow. That August he married a woman by the name of Darya Krotov, the daughter of a repressed peasant, in Yaya, the site of his imprisonment. By the end of 1936, Darya was pregnant, and Alexander began to worry that he was yet again being watched by the NKVD. They talked of fleeing somewhere and settled on a small village called Berikul where they might escape notice. But on the way to the train station, Alexander unexpectedly told Darya that he would not be going with her and that she, and the child she was bearing, would be safer without him. He gave her an address in Moscow as she boarded the train, telling her: "Never say a word about me to anyone. Don't look for me, I will find you myself, if possible. If the baby's a boy, name him Vladimir, if it's a girl, Irina: these are our family names. Always remember what I've told you wherever you may be. If it's absolutely necessary, you have the address. But I ask you, use it only if it's an extreme emergency." That was the last time they saw each other. Alexander sent Darya two short letters after that, but only so she knew he was still alive. He traveled illegally to Moscow to visit his father and then left for the Siberian town of Tomsk. He had long dreamed of becoming an actor and managed to land a job in a local theater.

Alexander was joined in Tomsk by his sister Olga and her husband, Pyotr Urusov, in late September after they had narrowly avoided arrest in Alma-Ata. In the summer of 1937, Pyotr, having completed his three-year term of exile in Petropavlovsk, left with Olga for the Kazakh capital, where his brother Andrei and mother, Natalya, were living. On the night of September 24, NKVD agents came to arrest the brothers, but found only Andrei at home. As soon as they had left, Natalya ran to Pyotr and Olga's apartment to tell them to flee before it was too late. They immediately left for Tomsk to join Alexander. Natalya had saved their lives, although only for a time.

In November, Natalya received word that Andrei had been sentenced to ten years in prison "without the right of correspondence." Like everyone else, she did not realize that this was a lie meant to cover up his execution, which likely took place in Alma-Ata soon after his arrest. Buoyed by the news, Natalya packed up some food and clothes and set off for Siberia in search of her son. In Novosibirsk she found a train loaded with prisoners and convinced herself that Andrei was on it, even though no one could confirm this. Satisfied Andrei was alive, Natalya traveled to Tomsk to be with Pyotr and Olga. Pyotr had found work in the theater with Alexander, and he and Olga felt safe and settled. It was a happy reunion, and mother and children spent three delightful days together full of love and warmth. Then, on the night of December 23, the NKVD came and arrested Pyotr. The bundle Natalya had intended to give to Andrei she now handed to Pyotr. The agents came back on New Year's Eve and took Olga. A month later, on the final day of January 1938, they arrested Alexander.[6]

The NKVD had singled out Tomsk as a center of counterrevolutionary enemies since the early summer of 1937. On June 17, the head of the NKVD for western Siberia wrote Yezhov that he had uncovered a "Monarchist-Kadet-SR organization," working in conjunction with

Japanese agents, that was planning an armed coup. The organization, called the League for Russia's Salvation, the report went on, had been founded by former princes Volkonsky and Dolgoruky and several White generals, including one named Sheremetev. They were being aided by noble émigrés as well as former people within the USSR and had set up a large network of underground cells in Novosibirsk, Tomsk, and other cities. Yezhov forwarded the report on to Stalin.[7] Over the next few months 3,107 people, many of them former people, were arrested in Tomsk as members of the league; 2,801 of them, including the poet Nikolai Klyuev and the philosopher Gustav Shpet, were shot. Overall, 9,505 people were arrested in Tomsk during the Great Terror, and more than three-quarters of them were executed. Needless to say, the charges against them were groundless fabrications.[8]

The absurd nature of the charges and the evidence to prove them can be seen in the case made against Alexander Golitsyn. Accused of being a member of the league, Alexander had supposedly been involved in "counterrevolutionary riotous activity." As proof, the NKVD pointed to his acting, noting that "working on the stage of the Tomsk city theater he acted the roles of heroes in a perverse light and ideologically distorted the inner content of heroes' roles." At first Alexander denied the charges, but then he began to sign whatever papers they put in front of him, most likely after having been tortured. Olga too was broken by her interrogators and confessed to having been engaged in "defeatist agitation and the dissemination of monarchist propaganda." All three of them were shot: Pyotr on January 13, 1938; Olga on March 5; Alexander on July 11.

Alexander's widow, Darya, meanwhile had given birth to a son a year earlier. She kept her promise to Alexander, naming him Vladimir and telling no one about him for two years. Finally, after having no word from Alexander for a long time, she took the "secret address" and wrote a letter to Vladimir Vladimirovich in Moscow, asking whether he knew where Alexander was and enclosing a photograph of little Vladimir. Vladimir Vladimirovich replied that he too had had no word from Alexander or Olga in years, but he offered to raise the boy. Darya thanked him but refused his offer. In hindsight, she likely should have taken the boy to Moscow, for she would be arrested in October 1941. Little Vladimir somehow survived and later settled in Moscow.

Vladimir Vladimirovich lived until 1969 with his sole remaining child, Yelena, and her husband. He died at the age of ninety. He spent the rest of his life trying to learn the whereabouts of his son and daughter, although the authorities never told him the truth. For years the only reply he received was that both Alexander and Olga had been sentenced "without the right of correspondence." In 1974, five years after Vladimir Vladimirovich's death, the Tomsk Office of Civil Registration sent a letter to his old address stating that Alexander had died on January 13, 1944, of sclerosis of the brain. It was not until 1989, fifty years after their murders and twenty years after the death of Vladimir Vladimirovich, that the truth of Alexander's and Olga's deaths was officially acknowledged. As for Natalya Urusov, she too went to her grave never having learned the fate of her sons Andrei and Pyotr.[9]

After two years in Andijan, Vladimir Trubetskoy had grown tired of life in Central Asia. The initial excitement of its natural beauty and cultural exoticism had worn off, and Vladimir had had enough of the town and the area, with its stultifying heat, relentless mosquitoes, and stinging scorpions. Crime was a problem as well. The town had been plagued by a rash of knifings. A waiter in the restaurant where Vladimir played was stabbed in the heart while waiting tables; the assailant was so skilled with a knife no one even noticed the attack. Vladimir's work was monotonous and low-paid. "I have no private life and whether I return home in the day or night it's only to sleep," he wrote in August 1936 to Vladimir Golitsyn back in Dmitrov. "I'm becoming stupid from all these fox-trots, blues, tangos, and Bostons that seem to be slowly turning me into a quiet idiot." Regardless, Vladimir still had more than two years remaining on his sentence. "If we're still alive, then we're thinking of making our way to some nice place on the sea. [. . .] I need the sea, good fishing, hunting, and taverns, taverns that pay well so I can earn enough to feed my family."[10]

His daughter Varya was doing her best to get on with her life. In 1936, she joined the *Osoaviákhim* (Special Detachment of Aviators and Chemists). She took cavalry courses, learned how to shoot and attack with a saber, and began dressing in a Red Army uniform and riding breeches. On January 16, 1937, the Andijan Regional Municipal Soviet of Osoaviakhim issued Varya a certificate on her passing the tests as a "Voroshilov Horseman," noting that she had been given a grade of "Excellent" in "Political Training."[11] Andrei observed that his sister had become a "complete Soviet person"; she even bought a six-volume set of Lenin's writings.[12]

Vladimir sensed the noose tightening around them in the spring of 1937. He sent a letter in May to the local NKVD to say that he knew people were spreading rumors about him and insisting that none of them were true. He was a loyal Soviet citizen, Vladimir wrote, who wished nothing more than to be left alone to work and care for his wife and children. He was not a counterrevolutionary, nor was he a Trotsky-ist, a rumor he found especially ridiculous. "It's absurd to think," Vladi-mir wrote, "that some Jew named Trotsky would want to return to some Russian prince the old estates and wealth of his noble ancestors! I have not yet sunk to that level of moral degradation that I would wish to achieve all this with the price of the destruction of my motherland and the blood and suffering of millions."[13] It is not surprising that reading Vladimir's letter, the NKVD was not about to let him live, for this was not the letter of a scared animal pleading for mercy, but that of a man still unbroken after two decades of repression, a man filled with pride, irony, wit, and humor. For the NKVD, Vladimir's words were a provo-cation. Vladimir no longer cared. A year earlier he had made it clear cowering was pointless. "It makes no difference, for they just look at you like some White Guard bastard," he had remarked.[14]

On July 29, 1937, the NKVD arrested Vladimir and Varya. Andrei came home that evening to find two men in civilian clothes carefully going through the contents of the family's apartment. In a letter from Vladimir Golitsyn they found a Nazi swastika that he had used as a shorthand reference to Hitler's Germany. To the agents, however, this was proof of Trubetskoy's connection to an underground fascist orga-nization. The arrest warrant described Vladimir as a "former Prince—hereditary noble, former guards officer" and charged him with being in contact with counterrevolutionary elements in Western Europe. Varya was accused of having taken part in the plot to kill Kirov. The pressure against the family grew. On August 28, the NKVD arrested Tatya. An-drei and Leonid Yakushev, Tatya's boyfriend, went to look for her at the NKVD's headquarters. From the street they could see her in the win-dow of an interrogation room. An agent noticed them and covered up the window with a newspaper. A short while later Tatya was led out of the building and bundled into a car. She managed to cry out a few frightened words to Andrei and Leonid before the doors shut and the car drove off. She was never seen again. Andrei left Andijan to tell his brother Grisha, then living in a neighboring town, what had happened. "Well, that's it," Grisha said, "that means they'll soon be coming for me." Three days later they did. Upon hearing a group of prisoners were being taken to the railway station, Eli went and found Grisha in the crowd. She, along with many others seeking their loved ones, tried to get close enough to say a few words to him, but the guards drove them back with their dogs.

Eli was crushed by the arrests. She told Andrei that she would never see her husband or her three children again. Andrei tried to convince her otherwise, pointing out that his father had been arrested many times before and had always been released, though in the poisonous climate of 1937 he doubted his own words. One morning Eli awoke to find that a cross had mysteriously appeared on the ceiling over Vladimir's side of the bed. It was a bad omen. She pointed it out to Andrei, saying, "He will never be coming back." Not long thereafter, a policeman came for Vladimir's things. Eli told him there was nothing left except some old boots, trousers, and Vladimir's cello and plastic fife. The man told Eli that Vladimir was soon to be exiled and would need the instruments to earn a bit of money. It was a heartless lie, but Eli was overjoyed at the thought that Vladimir was still alive, and she gave him her husband's things. A few days later, while walking along Andijan's main street, Eli and the children passed a secondhand store; there for sale in the dirty front window lay Vladimir's clothes and musical instruments.

Andrei, a tenth grader, had to continue going to school following the arrest of his father and three siblings. The atmosphere was thick with paranoia and hate. He had to attend meetings at which every pupil was expected to get up and endorse the execution of the country's enemies. Traitors were being hunted and uncovered everywhere. At school someone discovered the face of Trotsky hidden in the campfire depicted on the pins worn by the Pioneer Youth. The next day the pins disappeared. As the country prepared for elections for the Supreme Soviet in December 1937, Andrei proposed placing a red flag on top of the school since it had been selected as one of the polling stations. The principal approved his idea, and Andrei was sent up on the roof with the flag. It was only when he got to the flagpole and looked down that he realized he could see into the inner yard of the NKVD headquarters. It was filled with small cells, and he could not help think-ing that down there sat his father, sisters, and brother. Maybe, he thought, one of the cell doors would open and he would see one of them. (He, like everyone else in the family, did not know that Vladimir and Varya were already dead.) Andrei noticed how his person had been split in two: at school he continued to be a loyal Soviet subject and take an active role in the witch hunt for enemies of the people; at home he put all this aside to dwell on the fate of his family, never believing for a mo-ment that they were guilty of a thing.[15]

Vladimir and his children were questioned throughout the late summer and then sentenced on October 1. He and Varya were sentenced to death for preparing a "terrorist act" against Stalin; Tatya, also charged with plotting to kill Stalin, and Grisha, charged with praising fascism, were given ten years in a work camp.

From prison Tatya wrote two letters to Lavrenty Beria insisting on her innocence. How, she pointed out, could she be arrested as a "for-mer princess" when she was born in 1918, a year after the Bolshevik Revolution? "I am twenty years old. I want to study, to live, to be happy and merry, like all honest girls in the Soviet Union. [. . .] I am a child of October. [. . .] My sole 'guilt' is that I am the daughter of former Prince Trubetskoy. That I am a Trubetskoy. My social origin was apparently a sore point for the investigative organs of the city of Andijan." Like other children of former people arrested in the 1930s, she made certain to include Stalin's own words about how a son does not answer for his father.[16] Tatya was sent to a labor camp in the western Urals and put to work in the forests. She survived for several years, but in early 1943 Tatya became ill, and when it became apparent she would not live, she was freed. There was nothing humanitarian about this, just cold-hearted accounting. The gulag did not like to report deaths, as this undermined its claim to being devoted to rehabilitation; releasing pris-oners at death's door helped whitewash the horror of the camps. A few of her fellow inmates dug a grave and buried Tatya under a birch cross. She was twenty-four years old.[17]

In December 1937, Eli wrote to Stalin pleading for the release of her husband and children. She admitted that there was a good deal of "sabotage" in Uzbekistan and that the authorities had to be vigilant, but she protested their innocence. She wrote that they all "loved" and "respected" Stalin and then dared him to arrest the rest of the family, noting that if her husband and three children truly were "saboteurs," then she and their other children must be as well.[18] But by then it was already too late: Vladimir and Varya had been shot on October 30, 1937. Eli knew nothing of this. It was not until the following year that she received any information about her husband and daughter. The police informed her that Vladimir and Varya had been sentenced to ten years in distant labor camps without the right of correspondence. At the time, victims' loved ones did not know that this was a perverse lie, NKVD code for execution. The Soviet political police did not have the courage to admit to the truth of its actions.

The sentence, not surprisingly, meant families clung to the slender hope that their loved ones were still alive. They put stock in the slightest rumors of sightings of family members by former prisoners. No one wanted to think the worst. Grisha, who finally returned from the camps a broken man in 1947, recalled how prisoners would tell him that they had seen his father in the Kolyma camps, playing in an orchestra. None of it was true, but who could blame them for not wishing it to be so? It was not until Khrushchev's Thaw in the 1950s that the real meaning of this Orwellian language became known. It was then, in 1955, that Grisha was rehabilitated; his father and two sisters would only be rehabilitated three decades later. And it was not until 1991, more than half a century after the executions, that the family finally learned the truth of Vladimir's and Varya's deaths.

As the mother of eight children, Eli had been entitled to yearly state assistance of two thousand rubles beginning in 1936. To receive the money, however, she had to show proof that all her children were alive. When her three children were arrested, the NKVD took their documents, and Eli lost her subsidy. She went to the bank to explain her situation in the hope of receiving the full sum, but the employee spit at her: "We don't give money to such mothers!" Eli's family insisted she leave Andijan, and they scraped together enough money to bring her and the children to the village of Taldom (just outside the one-hundred-kilometer border around Moscow) in 1939 once it became clear there was no more reason to stay.[19]

On May 1, 1937, the first steamship passed through Dmitrov on the newly opened Moscow-Volga Canal. It was a big holiday, and the entire city turned out to celebrate this special May Day. Sergei Golitsyn was there, together with his wife, Klavdia, and their two young children. The sight of the gleaming white *Joseph Stalin* gliding through the canal on this unusually warm spring day filled Sergei with pride, and he considered himself fortunate to have taken part in this Soviet achievement.[20]

Semyon Firin, head of Dmitlag, was not there to mark the occasion. He had been arrested a month earlier along with more than two hundred others from the canal works' administration on charges of espionage and treason. Almost all of them, including Firin, were shot. The arrests in Dmitrov mounted as the year progressed, but amazingly, the Golitsyns were never touched, and the Great Terror passed over them, although it did strike close. Soon after the canal opening Yelena Golitsyn's cousin Dmitry Gudovich was arrested as a member of an underground counterrevolutionary fascist organization. He was taken to the Butyrki and executed on July 2.[21] Sometime that year, Dmitry's brother-in-law Sergei Lvov (Merinka's husband) was also arrested and shot.[22] On August 23, Dmitry's other brother-in-law, Vladimir Obolensky (Varenka's husband), was arrested in Tsaritsyno and then sentenced to death on October 17 as a Finnish spy. Four days later he was driven to a wooded area a few kilometers outside Moscow known as the Butovo Polygon and shot, one of the more than twenty thousand men and women murdered there between August 1937 and October 1938.[23]

To this day, no one knows for certain what happened to Varenka Obolensky. It appears she was arrested on March 3, 1937. According to some in the family, she was shot later that year at the Butovo Polygon, although the most reliable and recent publications do not include her name among the victims; others in the family claim she died of typhus in a Siberian labor camp the following year. According to letters exchanged between family members, it seems many believed Varenka perished in late 1938.[24] Two years later, however, a former camp inmate told Varenka's mother that he had seen her alive in 1939; as late as January 1941, the family was receiving reports of sightings of Varenka in the camps, though these amounted to nothing more than rumors.[25]

Then, in April 1941, Anna Saburov wrote Xenia to say she had received a letter from a certain "lady" who claimed to have watched Varenka die of tuberculosis in the camps with her own eyes. Anna seemed to want to believe this woman's testimony, and she herself had been witness to a sign that she was convinced corroborated the letter.

In late 1940, Anna found two butterflies on her windowsill. At first she thought they were dead, but then, when the weak winter sunlight hit them, they miraculously came to life. Anna fed the butterflies drops of honey, and she managed to keep them alive through the entire winter. She had heard somewhere once that in Japan butterflies were thought to be the souls of departed loved ones, and she could not help thinking that she had been visited by the spirits of Boris and Varenka.[26]

26

WAR: THE END

I n Dmitrov, on the morning of June 22, 1941, Vladimir Golitsyn turned on his Pioneer shortwave radio. He picked up a German broadcast and began to listen. Almost immediately he knew their lives were about to be overturned once again: Germany had invaded the Soviet Union. He looked at Yelena and told her what had happened. Yelena immediately set out for the bank. Food was certain to become scarce, and she went to withdraw their savings and buy as much as she could at the market to fill their shelves. There were 250 rubles in their account. All of it belonged to their son Mishka, who for years had been collecting empty bottles and saving the small return money in the hope of eventually having enough for a bicycle. Mishka's dream would have to wait.

The family had been planning on going fishing that day at their favorite spot on the Yakhroma River, a place they called the meadows. After lunch, Vladimir stood up from the table. "Well," he said to the children, "are you ready? Who knows when we'll be able to go to the meadows again." Accompanying them that day was Yelena's aunt Nadezhda Raevsky. As they walked to the meadows, Mishka overheard Nadezhda and his father talking. "They'll start arresting people again," Vladimir said. "They'll need political hostages." They talked of the Butyrki, where both had spent time. "You know, Vladimir," Nadezhda confessed with a sad grin, "I was calmer in there. You know that they won't come for you anymore, but out here, you wait for them to come every day, or every night, that is." They caught a few perch and bleaks that afternoon and ate them with some roasted potatoes there by the river. It was the family's last fishing trip. The next day Dmitrov mobilized for war. Accompanied by their loved ones and the sounds of the accordion, men marched down the street to the enlistment office. The entire city seemed to be out-of-doors, singing, dancing, and crying.[1]

For the fourth time in forty years Russia was at war.* Each successive war had been more disastrous than the last, and this would be no less true this time, for even though the Soviet Union repulsed Hitler's armies and eventually crushed the enemy, it came at a staggering cost. The Soviet Union bore the brunt of the Nazi war machine. According to historians, for three years roughly 90 percent of Germany's fighting strength was directed against the USSR. As Winston Churchill noted, the Red Army alone "tore the guts" from Hitler's military. Thirty million Soviet men and women were mobilized, and many went off to the front with minimal training and arms. By war's end in May 1945, the country had lost twenty-five million people: about nine million soldiers and sixteen million civilians. The numbers are rough approximations, conservative ones at that. The scorched earth policy of both the Soviet and German militaries left the country in ruins. Perhaps as much as a third of the country's physical wealth (towns, villages, livestock, factories, equipment, etc.) was destroyed.[2]

Vladimir Golitsyn had been right about a new wave of arrests. Indeed, the threat of war had been used as a pretext for years, particularly during the twelve months before the Nazi invasion, when approximately three million Soviet citizens were arrested.[3] On July 18, Vladimir's cousin Kirill Golitsyn was arrested in Moscow and given ten years for anti-Soviet agitation. He served the entire sentence in the camps and was not permitted to return to Moscow until 1955. The NKVD came for Kirill's father the winter following his arrest. His wife told them they were too late; Nikolai had died just the other day. They did not believe her, so she showed them into his study. There he lay on his desk, an icon in his hands, awaiting his coffin. The agents shook the body to be certain he was dead.[4]

---

* Fifth, if one counts the Winter War (1939–40) against Finland.

The NKVD rounded up many remaining former people in the early months of the war. It would be the final act in the Soviet government's campaign against the nobility, begun nearly a quarter of a century before. Now not just counterrevolutionaries and saboteurs, former nobles were construed as followers of Hitler, defeatists, and traitors. On July 2, the former princess Maria Vasilevna Golitsyn and her husband were arrested on charges of espionage and imprisoned in Zlatoust; he died there in prison, she perished in a camp in the Urals two years later. In August, a granddaughter of Prince Lev Lvovich Golitsyn was arrested in the Ukrainian countryside and shot for harboring pro-German sympathies. The following month, Viktor Meyen, Vladimir Golitsyn's brother-in-law, was arrested and sent to a prison camp in Kazakhstan. The evidence against him was his surname, which the NKVD assumed was German; his forefathers were, in fact, Dutch. Viktor survived only one year in the camp.[5]

Vladimir was arrested for reportedly expressing pro-German sympathies on October 22, four months after the outbreak of the war. Around noon two men in civilian arrived at the Golitsyn house and asked to see Vladimir's passport. They presented an order for his arrest and began to search the house. Mishka was stunned at how calmly the adults reacted to what was happening. He was too young to understand that they had been through this many times before and had been readying themselves for it again. Anna prepared lunch, Mikhail continued to work on his translations (or at least pretended to), and Vladimir gathered up the illustrations he had completed and gave them to Yelena with instructions about where to deliver them. The agents searched and searched but found nothing; after a while it seemed they were simply going through the motions.

Yelena wrapped some food in a sack and handed it to her husband. He put on his black sheepskin coat, and they began their goodbyes. Anna made the sign of the cross over her son, then kissed him and whispered a blessing, followed by Mikhail, then Vladimir's wife and daughter, and finally his son Lariusha. Mishka followed his father out the door and down Kropotkinsky Street; it was a cold day, and an unforgiving wind chased the remaining leaves from the trees. Neighbors looked out their windows in frightened silence as they passed. After a few blocks, one of the agents, a man named Koryagin, told Mishka to get on home. He protested, but then Vladimir looked at his son and said, "Go,

Mishka." He hugged Mishka, turned, and walked on. "And I stood there, swallowing my impotent tears and watching," Mishka remembered. He watched them walk until they disappeared from view. Once they were out of sight, Mishka regained himself. He swore he would someday kill Koryagin, not realizing, as he wrote later, "that he was nothing more than a tiny screw in an enormous machine of violence."[6]

Vasily Sheremetev volunteered in the first days of the war. Too young to enlist, he lied about his age and was taken into the home guard and sent to the front as an infantryman. His parents blessed him before he left. During the first few months of the fighting they received the occasional letter from their son, and then in December 1941 Vasily vanished, and they never heard from him again.[7] Although seventy-years old and in poor health, Pavel volunteered as a fire spotter at the monastery. Every night he would go out and patrol for German incendiary bombs. One night twenty bombs landed in the monastery; all of them were doused, thanks in part to Pavel's help.[8] Olga Sheremetev was among those killed during the Moscow air raids when a bomb landed near her apartment in a wing of the Corner House on the night of August 12.[9]

Pavel's nephew Nikolai Sheremetev also remained in Moscow and spent his nights as a fire spotter on the roof of the Vakhtangov Theater, barely escaping with his life on one occasion. Nikolai talked Cecilia into leaving Moscow to stay with his sister Yelena and Vladimir in Dmitrov. In the early autumn of 1941, the entire Vakhtangov theater company was evacuated to Omsk. Yelena, Vladimir, and the rest of the Golitsyns saw Cecilia to the station in Dmitrov. They watched as the train left that evening to take Cecilia to Moscow, her face, streaked by tears, pressing against the glass. Mishka next saw his uncle Nikolai two years later in Moscow. He looked thin and weak. In May 1944, Nikolai died while out hunting with friends. He had apparently been injecting himself with morphine for some time to numb his chronic pancreatic pain. This time he overdosed. They found him dead on the ground near a bog, his rifle in his arms, an empty vial off to his side. Mishka rode alongside his uncle's body in the car from Dmitrov to Moscow. He watched as they cremated his remains. His ashes were interred at the cemetery in the Novodevichy Monastery not far from the tower room of his uncle Pavel and aunt Praskovya. Cecilia was buried alongside him in 1976.[10]

Pavel's sisters, Maria and Anna, found themselves separated and alone in the summer of 1941. Maria was then living in Kuibyshev (Samara), taking care of two young grandchildren, Alexander and Sergei Istomin. The previous year she and the boys had watched in horror as their mother, Merinka Gudovich, drowned in the Volga River in front of them. The heavy current pulled Merinka down below the surface, and she vanished. For days the boys searched the banks for her body. It was not recovered for several weeks.[11] Maria's son Andrei had helped her through this tragedy, but then he volunteered in the summer of 1941. Maria died in Kuibyshev in 1945 before Andrei returned home from the war.

Anna was living in Vladimir, renting a room in the home of a cruel woman who delighted in abusing her. Hard as this was, Anna wrote Xenia in the summer of 1941 that it was for the best that she and Yuri were imprisoned far away, for were they free, Yuri would be sent to the front and Xenia would be forced to spend her days digging trenches.[12] For a brief moment Xenia had expected to be back in Vladimir with her mother by now. A year and a half earlier, in late January 1940, Xenia had been notified that she was to be released from the labor camp in Plesetsk eight years ahead of schedule. Her wish had come true. Xenia could not believe her good fortune; soon she would be reunited with her mother. When she arrived at the local rail stop, however, the officials informed her that her sentence had not been overturned, merely modified: instead of serving the remainder of her time in the camp, she was being sent into internal exile in northern Kazakhstan for five years. She arrived in the remote steppe village of Presnovka with nothing but her torn coat and a small sack of personal items. Abandoned and alone, Xenia went in search of a place to sleep; eventually she found shelter in a simple dugout that she shared with three peasants.[13]

Anna was stunned to learn that Xenia was not coming home to her. She urged Xenia to write to the NKVD chief Beria and plead her case. For the next year Xenia, Anna, and even Pavel wrote to Beria, but with no success.[14] Anna sent her daughter clothing and food that she could ill afford to part with. Xenia begged her to stop, to keep these things for herself. She wrote with pride, for example, how she had bartered her camp skirt for some flour and how she had gotten a job as a street vendor.

Still, she had to admit she was often hungry. "Sometimes I'm able to earn enough for some bread or even some potatoes and milk, but there are days when I've nothing, only boiled water. Nonetheless, I have this inner certainty that this is all just temporary and that everything will be all right. And so my spirits are good, and I'm filled with inner peace."[15]

That winter of 1940–41 tested them both. Anna nearly froze to death in her unheated room. At one point Xenia feared she was on the verge of starvation; she could not even find bread to buy and begged her mother to send anything she could spare. With the arrival of spring, Xenia's spirit revived. She felt certain Yuri would come home to Vladimir any day. Life was looking up again.[16] Anna shared her daughter's hope for the future, even after war broke out. "I am full of confidence that our situation will be reversed and the motherland will be saved," she predicted in October during one of the worst periods of the war when it looked as if Moscow would fall. "This is a difficult moment, and my heart aches for everyone, but it will end with universal joy at the defeat of the Germans, when all nations will together disarm and banish them for good like some madman, and then a bright new era of peace shall begin throughout the world, a 'Golden Age' of sorts and all these nightmares shall be consigned to history. In the meantime, however, we must suffer just a bit more."[17]

Pavel and Praskovya, cold, hungry, and worried about Vasily, suffered through the first winter of war in the Naprudny Tower. By the spring of 1942, they were no longer able to care for themselves and had moved to Tsaritsyno to live with Praskovya's sisters Olga and Yevfimiya and her niece and nephew, Yelizaveta and Nikolai Obolensky (the orphaned children of Vladimir and Varenka Obolensky). They were not there long before Praskovya died of an illness on June 11. Pavel was grief-stricken and chose not to return to their room in the tower. Ever since the revolution and the death of his father in 1918, Pavel had done everything possible to support the family. So many times throughout his life when he had barely enough food and money to keep himself together, he had sacrificed to help a sister, a cousin, a niece or nephew.

On February 16, 1943, Pavel wrote Anna from Tsaritsyno to wish her well on her name day. He apologized for not having written in some time; he had started many letters to her, Pavel explained, but could never finish them. Because he had no money to send her, it pained him too much to write. "I'm sitting here penniless myself, but just as soon as I get some money, I'll immediately send you and Maria a tidy sum. [. . .] I've been ill for a long time now." Four days later, Pavel died. He was seventy-one.[18]

His sisters-in-law did not know how to get Pavel's coffin to the cemetery. No one had a car, and they had no money to hire one; nor were they able to find a horse, so they placed his coffin on a sledge, and Olga and her niece and nephew pulled it themselves through the snowy streets to the cemetery. They wanted Pavel buried alongside Praskovya, but the gravediggers refused, saying the ground was too hard and icy, and so they went off and dug a hole somewhere else and dropped Pavel's coffin into the cold earth.[19]

February 1943 proved to be an especially cruel month for the extended Sheremetev family.

After his arrest in October 1941 Vladimir Golitsyn was taken to the Dmitrov jail across the street from Lariusha's school. Yelena brought him some more food and a warm blanket. He was held there briefly before being moved first to Moscow and then to a labor camp in a former monastery in the small town of Sviyazhsk. Situated on the Volga River, Sviyazhsk had been built by Ivan the Terrible as a fort for his troops during the victorious siege of the Tatar capital of Kazan in 1552. It was later the site for one of the decisive battles of the Russian civil war. It was to Sviyazhsk in August 1918 that Trotsky came in his armored train to rally the Red Army as it retreated in the face of the White advance. Trotsky, who once wrote, "An army cannot be built without repression," imposed discipline with utter ruthlessness. He executed the commander and commissar of a regiment that had abandoned its position and then shot soldiers selected at random from its ranks. "A red-hot iron has been applied to a festering wound," he proclaimed. The retreat was halted, the army reinvigorated, and the next month Kazan fell to the Red Army.[20]

Vladimir had been prohibited from writing or receiving letters, and for ten months he had no word from home. He was extremely worried about what might have become of his loved ones in his absence, especially after hearing rumors that Dmitrov had fallen to the Germans. Finally, in late August 1942, he received a postcard from Yelena saying that they all were fine. He wrote back, telling her how relieved he was to have word from them and to know that they were safe. The past ten months had been hard on Vladimir. "Apparently, I've changed a good deal since my arrest," he confessed to Yelena, "for the men here call me grandfather." (He was all of forty years old.) He was not informed of his sentence—five years in the gulag—until early September, news Vladimir greeted with "indifference"; he had been expecting to get ten years. "I've already been in for one year, so it'll just be one, two, three Easters here, and then I'll be home," he wrote, as much for himself as for his family.[21]

Back home, the family struggled without him. Yelena found work sewing padded jackets and trousers for the army and gathering peat in the nearby bogs for the power station. The children did their part to help, and the hardship brought everyone closer together. Lariusha never forgot the image of his mother sewing late into the night in their unheated house, the old family portraits surrounding her on the walls, a single flame burning in a heavy old candlestick. After the war, the Soviet government gave Yelena a medal "For Labor Prowess." In the first months of the fighting, it looked as if Dmitrov would fall to the Germans. Messerschmitts and Junkers screamed overhead, and the air was filled with the growl of antiaircraft guns; burning villages to the west glowed in the night sky. The town was saved on December 6, when Siberian regiments arrived and pushed the Germans back. As soon as it was safe, Yelena set out for Moscow, traveling much of the way over the ice and snow on foot, to let the rest of the family know they had survived the German attack.[22]

Vladimir's brother, Sergei, was among those defending Moscow. Mobilized in July 1941, he had taken part in the construction of defensive fortifications around the capital during the battle of Moscow that autumn and early winter. Sergei served at Stalingrad the following year and had made it all the way to Berlin with the Red Army by war's end, for which he received numerous medals.[23] He never suffered any repression and went on in the postwar years to fulfill his lifelong wish of becoming a writer.

While one brother fought foreign invaders, the other fought for his life. Hunger had been a major problem for all Soviet citizens during the war; for the prison population it was a problem of life and death. Conditions for gulag prisoners became much worse after the start of the war; work norms increased just as the food rations decreased. "Enemies of the people" were frequently singled out for extra repressive measures. Camp deaths rose rapidly: the years 1942 and 1943 saw the highest mortality rates in the history of the gulag. At least 352,560 prisoners died in 1942, approximately one-quarter of all inmates. Between 1941 and 1946, more than 2 million gulag prisoners perished.[24]

Shortly after arriving at Sviyazhsk, Vladimir came down with pellagra, a common disease in the gulag, caused by a lack of niacin or tryptophan (an essential amino acid). The symptoms include skin lesions, diarrhea, and insomnia; severe cases result in ataxia, dementia, and ultimately death. Vladimir spent most of the last year of his life in the camp's infirmary. Up until the end, he believed he would get better. He drew hope from the fact that he was being kept in ward No. 18 (No. 19 was for the hopeless cases) and from the chance of seeing his family again:

> My dearest wife, will I ever see you again? Do you recall how I studied your face in the final minutes before I left? I felt that we'd not see each other for a long time, but that it would be this long, none of us could have imagined.

> My darling! It's not possible that I'll turn up my toes here and my life beyond these walls is over. Whatever it takes, I'll get out of here—oh, how I wish to love you more!

> Lariushka! Draw more! Try doing portraits. Draw Mama for me. Mishka, you'll no doubt be called up soon. Try to get attached to some technical service and learn mechanics. It'll be of use to you later in life. Yelenka! Don't get married just yet, you can live with me a bit longer and we'll work together. And you, my darling wife, I kiss you 1000 times.

> My dear one, I've been living through my memories. I remember every detail of our daily life as if looking through a magnifying glass. And it's both depressing and sweet. What sentiments! This year has taught us all a lot.

On November 24, 1942, Vladimir's father died.

> My beloved Mama, of course I have awaited the news of Papa's death. But it's so, so sad. When I left you, I parted with him knowing it was forever. But you, my dear old one, live, live for my return. [. . .] Mama, bless your poor son.[25]

Anna did live, hoping for Vladimir's return. She lived for another thirty years, in fact, dying in Moscow at the age of ninety-one, though she never did see her son again.

In the final weeks of 1942, the rations in the camp became even worse. For an entire month the prisoners had to subsist on a diet totally devoid of any fats. Vladimir began to imagine the unspeakable. "We must expect the worst," he wrote to Yelena, "and then if I manage to get out of here, it will be a Miracle! Pellagra is a terrible thing. [. . .] My dearest! We have to see each other once more. We must, but when? I've been making a calendar for 1943 and keep staring at the dates. But perhaps I'm to perish here and my life outside these walls has ended. I'll get out of here somehow. Oh, but how I want to go on loving you."[26]

In early 1943, Yelena received notification that Vladimir was soon to be freed. And then came the devastating letter from Sofia Olsufev. Sofia, a cousin of Vladimir's, had been interned at Sviyazhsk in December. She cared for him in his final weeks. Shortly before his death, Sofia had helped the emaciated Vladimir to bathe, and for a while he felt better but then became weak. She told Yelena of his death in a letter of coded language. "Suddenly, on the morning of February 6, he was sent off from the camp, and so he is now with his father. I can imagine how it grieves you to hear that he has left this place . . . I kiss you all tenderly, and pass along his parting greeting." A month later, Sofia too was dead. In 1956, the Soviet government acknowledged the charges against Vladimir had been baseless, and he was officially rehabilitated.[27]

Vladimir's aunt Eli Trubetskoy was the third family member to die that month. Three of her sons—Andrei, Vladimir, and Sergei—were off at the front, and Eli was living alone with her youngest child, Georgy, aged eight, in a village outside Moscow. Like so many, Eli had been reduced to desperate poverty during the war. At one point she was forced to go from village to village, begging for food; good people showed kindness and would give her a couple of potatoes or carrots and a few slices of bread. Despite her own circumstances, Eli took pity on a war refugee and asked her to come live with her. When the woman found out she was living with a former princess and the wife of an enemy of the people, she began to blackmail her: in exchange for whatever money Eli could scrounge, the woman would keep her mouth shut. In the end, she denounced Eli anyway, telling the NKVD she had heard Eli complain how things had been better under the tsars. Eli was arrested in January 1943; she barely had time to tell an old neighbor woman what was happening and ask her to go find her daughter Irina, then in a tuberculosis sanatorium, and ask her come fetch little Georgy. Eli was taken to the Butyrki in Moscow, where she died of typhus on February 7. Little Georgy was also sick with typhus at the time (their rooms were overrun with lice), but he managed to survive.[28]

While walking along an icy street in January 1942, Anna Saburov slipped and fell. She tried to get up but could not stand. She had broken her leg. She lay there for hours, calling for help, but none of the passersby would stop, mistaking her for a drunk. Eventually, she managed to convince some people to take pity. They picked her up, put her on a sledge, dragged her back to her apartment, and laid her in bed. Someone tried to find a place for her in the hospital, but there was no room. Pavel did what he could for her from Tsaritsyno, and some caring neighbors stopped by every few days to check in on her and bring her food; her landlady would not raise a finger to help.[29]

Xenia became distraught when she heard the news. It grieved her to know her mother was bedridden and she was unable to go to her; she worried Anna would die before her sentence was up.[30] Xenia began writing again to the NKVD, asking permission to go to her mother. She pleaded for mercy, saying that her mother was certain to die if she did not get to her soon. Her letters were ignored. By the autumn of 1942, Xenia had begun to entertain the idea of sneaking away and trying to reach Anna in Vladimir illegally. She had to abandon the idea, however, since she was simply too weak from hunger to make the journey. Some days she had no solid food at all; she was often dizzy and suffered from fainting spells. Finally, in March 1943, Xenia was informed her sentence was up, although because of the disruptions caused by the war, it was not until September that she was able to get a train ticket home.[31]

By the time Xenia reached Vladimir, Anna had been moved to the hospital. She had been saved several months earlier quite by accident when a group of health inspectors turned up at her apartment. The landlady had tried to keep them from entering, but they pushed past her and found Anna. She was immediately taken to the hospital, and a bed was found for her. Out of the fear born from decades of repression, Anna refused to tell them who she was. One of the nurses thought she had seen her face before. Then it came to her. She had cut out the wedding photograph of Alexander Saburov and Anna Sheremetev published in the *Moscow Leaflet* in 1894 and kept it for some reason all these years. She went home and brought the yellowed picture to show to the doctors. No one could believe it at first. Could this be the same person? they wondered. Anna was in dreadful condition, emaciated and weak. For the rest of her life she was unable to walk. No one ever heard her complain, however. She continued to thank God for everything and told anyone who would listen, "So it must be."[32]

After five and a half years apart, mother and daughter were reunited. Xenia took Anna to live with her in a one-room apartment on the edge of town. Anna's doctor visited them there in 1944:

> People who had known the tsars approached the tragic end of their existence. And not one complaint, not one grumble, not one moan. The room had no heat, dinner was rare. They often had no bread. Mother and daughter would go all day without eating. The daughter would spend a few hours at the market trying to sell her things, but no one would buy them, and she would return home when I was there empty-handed. Her mother would console her, saying, "The bad times before the good."[33]

Xenia cared for her mother for the rest of her life. Shortly before her death, Anna, delirious, kept seeing visions of her husband and two sons. "They are coming to me," she would murmur. The day before she died, she gently stroked Xenia's arm and then pointed upward. "Are you leaving?" Xenia asked, and her mother nodded. On May 13, 1949, Anna Saburov, died in bed surrounded by her icons, Xenia at her side. She was seventy-five. Going through her mother's things, Xenia found some uncompleted memoirs. Just to be safe, she burned them. Xenia outlived her mother by thirty-five years, dying in the same one-room apartment in the spring of 1984.[34]

Vasily Sheremetev returned home to Moscow at the end of the war. The details of his war experiences are murky. It seems he had suffered some sort of brain injury during combat and was subsequently taken prisoner by the Germans. According to one source, he managed to escape, joined the Soviet paratroopers, and ended the war in Vienna. He never received the news of his parents' deaths and went straight to the Novodevichy Monastery, only to find their door locked and no one at home. He wrote to his Obolensky aunts in Tsaritsyno, and they told him what had happened to his parents. They were amazed to hear from Vasily. "You can feel my joy, my happiness, my exultation that comes from my having lived to hear from you again, to know that you are alive and well, and that you'll soon be here with us!" Yevfimiya Obolensky wrote him in late June 1945 after receiving his unexpected letter. "Dearest, we embrace you fervently and tenderly for the beloved ones you have lost and for all of us as well. We are full of love and joy at the thought of your soon return to us! In our hearts and minds we are with you forever!"[35]

Vasily was not the only grandson of Count Sergei Dmitrievich Sheremetev to fight in the war. Indeed, amazingly, he was not even the only "Vasily Sheremetev" to fight on the eastern front. His first cousin Vasily Dmitrievich Sheremetev, who had fled southern Russia in 1919 with his family, also saw action there. Like his cousin Vasily Pavlovich, Vasily Dmitrievich fought out of a sense of patriotism and profound love of Russia. Yet the circumstances of their lives largely determined how they understood this love, for Vasily Dmitrievich did not fight alongside his cousin, but against him or, more accurately, against the Red Army, as a member of a French legion under the German army. Vasily Dmitrievich was wounded outside Moscow and nearly froze to death in the snow in the winter of 1941. A Russian peasant woman took him in and saved his life. It is interesting to wonder whether the two Vasilys ever faced each other in combat.

Vasily Dmitrievich considered it his duty to help free Russia from communism. In this he was not alone, but part of the larger so-called Russian Liberation Movement that comprised White émigrés and many Soviet citizens in the German-occupied lands. Their battle against the Soviet Union can been seen as a final echo of the Russian civil war. Russian opposition to the Stalin regime has long been linked to the name of Andrei Vlasov, the grandson of a serf and a lieutenant general in the Red Army, who was captured by the Germans in July 1942. In captivity Vlasov defected and tried to convince the Germans to make use of widespread anti-Soviet sympathy and support his idea for a Russian liberation army. In the Soviet Union, Vlasov's name became synonymous with treason, but Hitler's distrust of Vlasov, and the Russian

Liberation Movement in general, meant his army would never become much more than a grand idea and it played a negligible role in the war. In the spring of 1945, Vlasov was captured by Soviet troops in Austria and taken back to Moscow, where he was convicted of treason and hanged. As for Vasily Dmitrievich, after recovering from his wounds, the Germans sent him to fight in northern Italy. Because he was neither a German nor a Nazi, this was not Vasily's war, and so he deserted and escaped to his family in Rome.[36]

Like his cousin, Vasily Pavlovich was one of the fortunate soldiers to survive the war. He was also fortunate not to be arrested after returning home, as happened to many. Andrei Gudovich was arrested and imprisoned, and it was not until 1959 that he was finally rehabilitated and permitted to move to Moscow. Andrei Trubetskoy had been injured and taken prisoner early in the war. Through the intervention of a relative in Lithuania he was freed and brought back to health. He was determined to return to the fighting and managed to make his way through the German lines first to the Russian partisans and then by war's end to the regular Red Army. Like his brothers Vladimir and Sergei, he came home a decorated war hero, having suffered life-threatening wounds. In 1949, however, after refusing to cooperate with the political police, Andrei was arrested and spent the next six years in the camps laboring in a mine.[37]

Vasily moved back into his parents' room at the Novodevichy Monastery. Relatives soon noticed he was not the same person who had left for the front in the summer of 1941. He was profoundly disturbed by the death of his parents and had been traumatized by the war. Nightmares haunted his sleep. He saw a number of doctors and was in and out of psychiatric hospitals, but nothing seemed to help. He studied art and did a little painting. No matter how he tried, Vasily was unable to adjust to normal life. Some in the family called him Don Quixote, others referred to him as a *yuródovyi*, one of those holy fools common throughout Russian history who combine great piety and faith with poverty and bizarre, unconventional behavior. He suffered a stroke at the age of fifty-seven and spent the last ten years of his life paralyzed and unable to speak.[38]

EPILOGUE

In July 1983, the brothers Mishka and Lariusha (now Mikhail and Illarion, grown men) took a trip to the town of Sviyazhsk. The area had changed since their father, Vladimir, had been brought there in 1941; a dam on the Volga had flooded the land around Sviyazhsk, turning it into a small, steeply sided island reachable only by motorboat from Kazan. The town on the island was still little, no more than a few dozen buildings and houses, a church, and the monastery ringed by a brick wall. A narrow path led along the monastery's outer wall. Before falling away down to the Volga, the ground beyond the path was riven by several large, uneven depressions covered in tall weeds. These were the camp's common graves. They were unmarked, and there was nothing to communicate to the unknowing eye the reason for this odd geographical feature. Here, in one of these graves, lay their father.

The labor camp was gone, and the monastery now housed an insane asylum. Mikhail and Illarion were admitted through the main gate into the courtyard. Before them, enclosed in a large metal net, were dozens of inmates, all shaved bald and dressed alike in work clothes. Many sat in odd poses; others were standing still or walking about the ground, now packed down and devoid of grass from their ceaseless wanderings. To Mikhail, the faces appeared expressionless; he found them terrifying. Yet maybe, he thought, these inmates, unaware of where they were and what had happened to them, were happy in their own way.

As he looked upon them, his mind raced back forty years to a time when the monastery held an entirely different group of prisoners. These men and women had known exactly where they were and what had happened to them, if not always why. He could see before him in the crowd his father: "tall, handsome, but very thin. He was looking through the bars at the church cupolas, at the monastery walls, beyond which flowed the Volga and that near yet distant freedom that he never experienced again."[1]

Vsevolod Azbukin, the man in charge of the restoration work at the monastery, led Mikhail and Illarion about the island. He took the brothers to one of the houses and called the woman living there to come out. She was old and round and had what Mikhail described as a "friendly Russian face." She had been a guard at the camp during the war, and Mikhail was convinced she must have seen their father.

"There were no men then, so they put rifles in our hands," she told them upon learning the reason for their visit. "We were just sixteen-year-old girls, and they ordered us to guard the prisoners."

Mikhail asked, "Do you happen to recall a tall man, an artist with a limp?"

She thought for a minute, and then said: "No, I don't remember. There were so many of them . . ."

There were many indeed. At the beginning of 1941, the NKVD's corrective labor camps, labor colonies, and prisons held almost 2,500,000 prisoners. By the time the war broke out six months later, the number of persons caught up in the numerous divisions of the gulag likely reached 4,000,000. How many of these poor souls perished and were dumped in unmarked graves like Vladimir will never be known.[2]

I met Nikolay Trubetskoy on a clear afternoon in September 2010 outside Moscow's Frunzenskaya subway station, named in honor of the Bolshevik civil war hero Mikhail Frunze. Nikolay, a nephew of Mikhail and Illarion's and a grandson of Vladimir Golitsyn's, had agreed to meet and tell me what he knew about his family's history. We walked upstairs to the TGI Friday's above the station, where we might sit and have some lunch. For the next two hours, over chicken caesar salads and bottles of Perrier and under the relentless blare of Western pop music, we talked about his family, about history, about Russia, and its future.

An energetic, intelligent man in early middle age, Nikolay runs a large logistics company in the oil and gas industry that he built himself after first working as a geologist and then a taxi driver in the difficult early 1990s following the collapse of the Soviet Union. Despite his obvious success, Nikolay is devoid of any self-made-man bravado. He refuses to take too much credit for what he has managed to create, attributing much of what has happened in his life to God's inscrutable influence. But there is something else too. Nikolay knows that in Putin's Russia whatever he builds and whatever capital he manages to amass, be it his business, houses, cars, or money, it can be taken from him as soon as someone with enough power and the right political connections decides he wants it. And he also knows, like every Russian, that should this happen, he is helpless to stop it.

Nevertheless, Nikolay cannot imagine selling his business and leaving Russia for the greater safety and comfort of the West, as many of his partners have tried to convince him to do. For Nikolay his life, and the lives of his family, are too tied to Russia to consider leaving. Material things come and go. His family once possessed large country estates and urban palaces and collections of art. All this was taken from them, and Nikolay has no interest in such things. His decision to remain in Russia is connected to a different form of capital, what he calls the capital of being part of the six-hundred-year-old history of the Trubetskoy family. This is a form of capital, he says, free of vanity, that no one can ever take from him and that he is most proud of; this is the capital—the knowledge of one's family, its role in Russian history, and one's duty to one's ancestors—that he is most adamant on passing about to his children and that keeps him in Russia.

Such an attitude might strike some as irrational, fatalistic, typically Russian. But considering what happened to Nikolay's family, to the nobility, indeed to Russia itself in the last century, it is easy to see where such thinking comes from. To condemn it would prove only an absence of empathy and blind arrogance, for the events described in this book or, more precisely, the causes behind them, lie beyond reason, as much as we might like to think otherwise. Although the larger causes of the revolution can be accounted for, can anyone say why some perished and some survived? Why, for instance, was Count Pavel Sheremetev, the sole surviving male of the family and someone who had taken part in monarchist politics before the revolution, allowed to live and die a free man? Why was Pavel's sister Anna left to die an old woman even though her husband had been imprisoned and shot and all three of her children sent to the gulag, two never to return? Why was Dmitry Gudovich shot in 1938 and his brother Andrei spared? Why did one Prince Golitsyn, Lev, die of typhus while a prisoner of the Reds in Irkutsk in 1920 and another Prince Golitsyn, Alexander, also a prisoner near death from typhus in Irkutsk in 1920, survive, escape Russia, and spend the rest of his life in comfort in Southern California surrounded by his family? Absurd enigmas such as these could be cited over and over. There was a randomness to the violence and repression that speaks to the illogical nature of Russian life in the twentieth century, indeed to the illogical nature of life itself, however much we may wish to think otherwise. There simply is no way to explain why some perished and some survived. It was, and remains, inexplicable. It was chance or, as many Russians would have it, fate.

Of Nikolay's four grandparents, three died behind bars. Vladimir Trubetskoy was shot in Central Asia in 1937, and his wife, Eli, died of typhus in Moscow's Butyrki Prison in 1943, the same year Vladimir Golitsyn perished at Sviyazhsk. Only Nikolay's grandmother Yelena Golitsyn lived a full life, dying of natural causes in 1992, aged eighty-seven. I ask Nikolay whether his grandmother talked much about her life and all that had befallen her family, both the Sheremetevs into whom she had been born and the Golitsyns into whom she had married. Yes, he tells me, she did. What stood out most was the time Yelena told him that three hundred of her relatives had been killed by the Bolsheviks. He once asked her whether she was still angry at their killers and whether she could ever forgive them. I forgave them long ago, she explained to Nikolay, but I will never forget.

NOTE ON SOURCES

NOTES

BIBLIOGRAPHY

ACKNOWLEDGMENTS

INDEX

NOTE ON SOURCES

Former People is the first book in any language to examine the fate of the nobility in the decades following the Russian Revolution, a surprising gap in the historical record that can chiefly be explained by the fact that for most of the past century the subject could not be studied in the country where these events took place. As one of the Soviet Union's many so-called *bélye piátna*, blank spots, the story of the nobility could not be talked about, and so it simply did not exist; it had been blanked out and made to disappear.

It was only in the final years of the Soviet Union under Mikhail Gorbachev that the history of the nobility after 1917 became an acceptable subject of historical inquiry. In the early 1990s, when the dam of official censorship and self-imposed silence was breached, a flood of books, articles, conferences, films, and symposia began to pour forth. Over the past two decades we have learned a great deal of what happened to this class thanks to the work of hundreds of historians, archivists, curators, journalists, and the descendants of noble families who have now published a large amount of documentary material that for decades lay in their desk drawers and cupboards. For the most part, this has been a process of recovery. Something that had been repressed and ignored at long last became part of recorded history. Histories that had been forced into the dark finally came to light. Much of this work has been devoted to the study of particular noble families or clans or to the incorporation of the nobility into local histories that they had either been written out of or depicted in dishonest and propagandistic ways. My goal in writing *Former People* has been to synthesize this vast body of material and thus make the larger history of the nobility clear and intelligible while at the same time highlighting the stories of individual lives so as not to lose sight of the human dimension of this enormous tragedy.

Former People draws on a range of sources—personal correspondence, diaries, memoirs, petitions, laws, fiction, poetry, interviews, genealogies, political tracts, journalism, police reports, biographies, photographs, cartoons, and caricatures. Along with scholarly monographs and a large number of secondary works, I have made use of many primary sources, both published and unpublished. Most of these documents I located in state or public archives, but I was also fortunate to have access to many documents in private family collections.

One of these deserves special mention. I first became acquainted with Father Boris Mikhailov while researching my previous book, *The Pearl*. Now an Orthodox priest in Moscow, Father Boris for many years was a conservator at the Ostankino Estate Museum. For more than a decade he conducted extensive research into the history of the Sheremetevs in various archives, gathered information on the family from its members scattered throughout the world, and conducted interviews with a few surviving Sheremetev descendants in the former Soviet Union, including Xenia Saburov, Andrei Gudovich, and Yelena Golitsyn (née Sheremetev). The archive he managed to assemble (referred to in my notes by the abbreviation "ABM") is an invaluable resource. I am exceedingly grateful to Father Boris for making his archive available to me.

All families tell stories that record who they are and what they have been through. This is especially true of noble families. In researching *Former People* I have met many people who told me stories about their families. These stories, passed down through the generations, are an important source, but like all historical sources, they have their limitations. What is not written down is susceptible to revision with each retelling; what is remembered may be as much what one *wished* had happened—or *how* or *why* it happened—as it is about what in fact *did* happen. Dates are forgotten, names confused, places mistaken. In the case of the Russian nobility, the oral record faced exceptional distortion because of the shattering of families as a result of the revolution and civil war and subsequent waves of emigration as well as the need for silence and, at times, dissembling to survive the repression of the 1920s and 1930s. Whenever possible, I have checked oral testimony (and stories only written down years after the fact) against written documents and particularly against documents contemporary to the period in question.

It would be naive, of course, to think that the written word necessarily has greater purchase on the truth, especially when talking about Soviet history. Documents can and do lie. Soviet officials, for example, repeatedly lied about what had happened to the millions of people arrested and imprisoned in the gulag, writing to the families of many that they were serving their terms when in fact they had been executed. Reconstructing the historical record is never straightforward or easy.

NOTES

ABBREVIATIONS

ABM: Archive of Boris Mikhailov

AVG/M: A. V. Golitsyn, "Memoirs"

AVT/V: A. V. Trubetskoi, "Vospominaniia"

BA: Bakhmeteff Archive

BP: E. A. Bakirov, ed., *Butovskii poligon*

DS: *Dvorianskoe sobranie*

GARF: State Archive of the Russian Federation

HIA: Hoover Institution Archives

IDG: I. D. Golitsyna, *Vospominaniia o Rossii*

KhiG: *Khoziaeva i gosti*

KNA: Kuskovo Scientific Archive

KNG: K. N. Golitsyn, *Vospominaniia*

MVG/M: M. V. Golitsyn, *Mozaika iz moei zhizni*

MVG/MV: M. V. Golitsyn, *Moi vospominaniia*

NIOR RGB: Russian State Library, Scientific Research Division of Manuscripts

OGSh: O. G. Sheremeteva, *Dnevnik i vospominaniia*

OPR: L. Dolzhanskaia and I. Osipova, *Obrecheny po rozhdeniiu*

OR RNB: Russian National Library, Manuscript Division

PG: Alexandre Galitzine, ed., *The Princes Galitzine*

RGADA: Russian State Archive of Ancient Acts

RGALI: Russian State Archive of Literature and Art

RGIA: Russian State Historical Archive

SH: M. I. Smirnov and A. M. Golitsyn, eds., *Sheremetevy*

SVS: A. Alekseeva and M. D. Kovaleva, eds., *Sheremetevy v sud'be Rossii*

TAS: T. Aksakova-Sivers, *Semeinaia khronika*

TsGAMO: Central State Archive of the Moscow Oblast

VMG/D: V. M. Golitsyn, *Dnevnik 1917–1918 godov*

WSHC: Wiltshire and Swindon History Centre

YP/D: E. Pisareva, "Dnevnik (1919–1920)"

YPS/V: E. P. Sheremeteva, "Vospominaniia detstva"

ZU: S. M. Golitsyn, *Zapiski utselevshego*

ZVG: V. M. Golitsyn, "Zapiski khudozhnika"

PROLOGUE

1. OGSh, 78–80; ABM; *DS* 6 (1997): 208–13; Kovaleva, *Staraia Moskva*, 136–40; OR RNB, 585.4614, 4626, 4627, 4628; TAS, 321–22; RGADA, 1287.1.5062; *OPR*, 20–23; YPS/V, 51–52; an excerpt from the memoirs of Y. P. Sheremeteva, published online at moskva.kotoroy.net/histories/31.html. Accessed November 10, 2008.
2. KNA, 27, 1–2; OR RNB, 585.4627, 28–280b; Karnishina, "Vozvrashchaias'."
3. Leggett, *Cheka*, 266–68; Shteinberg, *Ekab Peters*, 28, 255, 266–68; Patterson, "Moscow Chekists"; Peters, "Vospominaniia."
4. Leggett, *Cheka*, 114.
5. *OPR*, 17.
6. Lincoln, *Red Victory*, 134, 136, 146; Afanas'ev, ed., *Istoriia*, 2:523; Tatyana Shvetsova, "Beginning of Terror," The Voice of Russia website, www.ruvr.ru/main.php?lng=eng&q=2445&cid=125&p=08.12.2005, accessed August 15, 2008. See also "Krasnyi terror (Beseda s Petersom)," *Utro Moskvy*, November 4, 1918, 1.
7. Smith, *The Pearl*.
8. A subsequent search did yield one result: Pavel Dzemeshkevich's *Dvorianstvo i*

revoliutsiia (Simferopol, 2004), a short book more revealing for what it says about the nobility's descendants trying to make sense of the past than for any light it casts on the history of the nobility during the revolution.

9. Leggett, *Cheka*, xxxii.
10. *Survival*, 358–60.
11. Marchenko, *Byt*, 268–69.
12. Bashkiroff, *Sickle*, 78–97.
13. Coles and Urusova, *Letters*, 10, 300, 310, 341–44, 376–85.
14. Doyle, *Aristocracy*, 280, 288–90.
15. Ibid., 309.
16. Ibid., 289–90.
17. See *PG*, especially pp. viii–ix.
18. Doyle, *Aristocracy*, 311–40; Raeff, "Russian Nobility," 115; Becker, *Nobility*, 178.
19. Chuikina, *Dvorianskaia pamiat'*, 10, 58, 188–89.
20. Ibid., 190–91.
21. Bertaux, ed., *On Living Through*, 1–22; Figes, *The Whisperers*.
22. Chuikina, *Dvorianskaia pamiat'*, 189.
23. Ibid., 180, 188–89.
24. Among such works, of particular importance for this book have been the many volumes of the series *Khoziaeva i gosti*, the published papers of the annual Golitsyn conference held at the former Golitsyn estate of Bolshie Viazyomy.
25. YPS/V, 51–52; ABM; OGSh, 78–80.
26. YPS/V, 79; ABM; OGSh, 79.
27. OR RNB, 585.4626, 13, 16, 21–210b; 4627, 4, 13, 19; 4268, 4, 9, 13, 19; 4614, 2–3.

1: RUSSIA, 1900

1. Rogger, *Russia*, 102–107, 122; Nove, *Economic History*, 11–19; Falkus, *Industrialization*, 61–74.
2. Solov'ev, *Kruzhok*, 3; McMeekin, *History's Greatest Heist*, xvi–xxii.
3. Rogger, *Russia*, 117–21, 127; Lincoln, *War's Dark Shadow*, 35; Figes, *People's Tragedy*, 88.
4. Rogger, *Russia*, 124–27.
5. See Rogger, *Russia*, chap. 2.
6. See Kolchin, *Unfree Labor*.
7. Rogger, *Russia*, 3–8, 10.
8. Ibid., 52–53; Riasanovsky and Steinberg, *History*, 363–69.
9. Rogger, *Russia*, 16.
10. Ibid., 11.
11. *Once a Grand Duke*, 168–69, 175–76, 186, 223–25, 283.
12. Rogger, *Russia*, 18; Riasanovsky and Steinberg, *History*, 369.
13. *Once a Grand Duke*, 223, 283.
14. Rogger, *Russia*, 20–22, 37–38.

15. Ibid., 2, 51–55, 59–61, 156–68; Emmons, "Russian Nobility," 180–83; Raeff, "Russian Nobility," 116–17; Hamburg, *Politics*.

16. Korelin, *Dvorianstvo*, 42–44, 292–303; Bibin, *Dvorianstvo*, 4; Wirtschafter, *Social Identity*, 21–37. More generally, see Becker, *Nobility*; Grenzer, *Adel*; Hamburg, *Politics*; Manning, *Crisis*.

17. Korelin, *Dvorianstvo*, 22.

18. Emmons, "Russian Nobility," 179.

19. Lieven, "Elites," 227–29, 232–33.

20. Skipworth, *Sofka*, 12–15; Zinovieff, *Red Princess*, 42.

21. Rogger, *Russia*, 88–89; Korelin, *Dvorianstvo*, 123.

22. *The Cherry Orchard*, Act 2, in Chekhov, *Four Plays*.

23. Rogger, *Russia*, 89–94. See also Grenzer, *Adel*, especially pp. 5–6, 99, 209; Becker, *Nobility*, 172–77; Hamburg, *Politics*, 238–39; Lieven, *Aristocracy*, 52–54. For a more negative view of the state of the nobility, see Manning, *Crisis*. On noble landownership, see also Osipova, *Klassovaia bor'ba*, 30–31.

24. Grenzer, *Adel*, 211–12; Lieven, *Aristocracy*, 49–54, 115–16, 133; idem, "Elites," 241–44; Krasko, *Tri veka*, 213.

25. Rogger, *Russia*, 48; Haimson, *Politics*, vii–viii.

26. Number of families: Haimson, *Politics*, vii. Other sources cite some one hundred thousand noble landed estates in 1905. See Barinova, *Vlast'*, 40.

27. Gill, *Peasants*, 2–3, 8, 16–17; Rogger, *Russia*, 71–73, 76, 79; Lincoln, *War's Dark Shadow*, 51, 105.

28. Rogger, *Russia*, 71–72, 76–78, 86, 117–18; Robinson, *Rural Russia*, 64–116. See also Tian-Shanskaia, *Village Life*; Worobec, *Peasant Russia*.

29. Heretz, *Russia on the Eve*, especially chap. 6.

30. "Memoirs of Princess Barbara Dolgoruky," HIA, 61. See also Obolensky, *Bread*, 68.

31. *Russian Sketches*, 177–79.

32. Rogger, *Russia*, 109–11.

33. Fitzpatrick and Slezkine, eds., *In the Shadow*, 169, 243–51.

34. See Lincoln, *War's Dark Shadow*, 103–34.

35. *Speak*, 30.

36. Ibid., 155.

37. Ibid., 30–31, 45–46.

38. See Shtrange, *Russkoe obshchestvo*.

39. Madariaga, *Russia*, 241–55; Alexander, *Emperor*.

40. McConnell, *Russian Philosophe*; Lang, *First Russian Radical*.

41. Raeff, *Origins*; Barinova, *Vlast'*, 129.

42. Rappaport, *Conspirator*, 35.

43. Pomper, *Russian Revolutionary Intelligentsia*, 31–58.

44. Sablin, *Sabliny*, 28–38, 152–53.

45. Pipes, *Unknown Lenin*, 19; Rappaport, *Conspirator*, 11–15 , 111, 198, 212, 247; Pomper, *Lenin's Brother*.

46. *Bagázh*, 84, 85–87.

2: THE SHEREMETEVS

1. *Entsiklopedicheskii slovar' Brokgauz-Efron*, vol. 78, "Sheremetev, Fedor Ivanovich"; *SH*, 1:7–8, 25–26, 37–38.

2. Smith, *The Pearl*.

3. Shchepetov, *Krepostnoe pravo*, 20–21, 26; Krasko, *Tri veka*, 50, 413.

4. Fedorchenko, *Svita*, 2:418–19; *SH*, 2:140; Krasko, *Tri veka*, 415–16; Obolensky, "Semeinye zapiski," 174 (1989): 238–39; ABM.

5. Fedorchenko, *Svita*, 2:418–19; Krasko, *Tri veka*, 416–17; ABM.

6. YPS/V, 3; Grabbe, *Windows*, 60–61; Obolensky, "Semeinye zapiski," 174 (1989): 238–39; Krasko, *Tri veka*, 422; ABM; Iusupov, *Memuary* (1998), 90.

7. *SVS*, 200–01; ABM; Fedorchenko, *Svita*, 2:426–27; Krasko, *Tri veka*, 193; *SH*, 2:134–35, 138–39.

8. Kovaleva, *Staraia Moskva*, 76, 179–96; ABM; Fedorchenko, *Svita*, 2:426–27; *SVS*, 279.

9. Kovaleva, *Staraia Moskva*, 102, 109–14, 129–30; YPS/V, 36; "V. P. Sheremetev v Ostaf'eve," 1990 art exhibition brochure.

10. *SVS*, 204, 311n.; ABM.

11. "Sheremetev, gr. Sergei Dmitrievich," in *Chernaia sotnia*; *SVS*, 200; Kovaleva, *Staraia Moskva*, 4, 168–73.

12. Witte, *Memoirs*, 338, 499n., 679.

13. Kovaleva, *Staraia Moskva*, 70–75, 130–33; Krasko, *Tri veka*, 221; TAS, 65–66; *SVS*, 209, 227–42.

14. Wassiltschikow, *Verschwundenes Russland*, 203–05.

15. *SVS*, 324; Zhuravina, *Dvorianskoe gnezdo*, 141, 152, 173–76; Krasko, *Tri veka*, 344–47; *SII*, 2:144; Nicholas II, *Dnevnik*, 12–23.

16. Krasko, *Tri veka*, 349; *SH*, 2:144–45.

17. *SH*, 2:148–49; ABM; "Nekrolog," *Moskovskie vedomosti*, June 5, 1914; YPS/V, 34–35.

18. YPS/V, 36.

19. Ibid., 15.

20. Skipworth, *Sofka*, 28.

21. Krasko, "Graf"; ABM; *KhiG* 1, pt. 1 (1997): 116; Kovaleva, *Staraia Moskva*, 98–100; Karnishina, "Zhizn'."

22. Krasko, *Tri veka*, 365.

23. RGIA, 1088.2.312, 740b–76; Krasko, *Tri veka*, 364–65.

24. P. Sheremetev, *Zametki*, 9, 37, 40, 53–53, 55, 57, 60–67, 99–100, 109.

25. Iu. B. Solov'ev, *Samoderzhavie*, 18.

26. Ibid., 19; Solov'ev, *Kruzhok*, 31, 40–41, 89, 137–38, 178–79, 210–11, 226–31; V. Obolenskii, *Moia zhizn'*, 177–81, 237, 261–62; Emmons, "Beseda Circle"; Polunov, *Russia*, 208–09; MVG/MV, 262–63, 272–74, 288.

27. Pares, *Memoirs*, 86.

28. ABM.

29. Ibid.

30. TAS, 78–80.

31. Ibid., 78–80; ABM; NIOR RGB, 340.6a.32; *SVS*, 279; Krasko, *Tri veka*, 384.

32. *SVS*, 300–01.

33. Ibid., 302–05; RGIA, 1088.2.627, 80b.

34. *SVS*, 287; ABM.

35. *SVS*, 279–80; Krasko, *Tri veka*, 384; TAS, 78–80; Lieven, *Russia's Rulers*, 9, 14–15, 118–19.

36. ABM; *SH*, 2:151.

37. ABM.

38. Krasko, *Tri veka*, 404–405; ABM; *SH*, 2:151–52.

3: THE GOLITSYNS

1. *PG*, viii–x; KNG, 7–8.

2. *PG*, 31–56; MVG/M, 43.

3. "Moskva i ee zhiteli," 10 (1991): 23, and 11:25–28; ZVG, 4:78; Prishvin, *Dnevniki, 1930–31*, 23–24.

4. "Moskva i ee zhiteli," 10 (1991): 18–23; *PG*, 393.

5. *PG*, 393.

6. *KhiG* 4, pt. 1 (1997): 70.

7. *KhiG* 8, pt. 2 (2002): 171.

8. *KhiG* 4, pt. 1 (1997): 67–69; *KhiG* 5 (1998): 113–14.

9. *KhiG* 5 (1998): 116.

10. *KhiG* 4, pt. 1 (1997): 57–67; *PG*, 393–94.

11. *ZU*, 23–27; S. N. Golitsyna, "Iz vospominaniia," 4:26–29; *KhiG* 6 (1999): 198.

12. *PG*, 422–31; KNG, 25–28.

13. MVG/MV, 31, 90–93; *KhiG* 6 (1999): 191–99.

14. MVG/MV, 196, 199, 262–63, 272–74, 288.

15. MVG/MV, 5–7, 86, 292–94, 321, 329, 338, 340–44; *ZU*, 63–64, 89; Raevskii, *Piat' vekov*, 53.

16. *ZU*, 15; *KhiG* 9 (2002): 109–10; *KhiG* 11, pt. 1 (2004): 134–35; *PG*, 431; V. V. Golitsyn, "Letter."

17. S. N. Golitsyna, "Iz vospominaniia," 35.

18. *PG*, 402, 428; *ZU*, 14–15.

19. See A. E. Trubetskoi, *Rossiia vosprianet*; Schmemann, *Echoes*, 151–52, 156–57.

20. V. S. Trubetskoi, "Zapiski kirasira," in *Rossiia vosprianet*, 482, 487.

21. Trubetskoi, "Zapiski kirasira," 498.

22. *ZU*, 91, 95–96, 102–103.

23. Ibid., 75–76.

24. Ibid., 66–74, 87–88; Raevskii, *Piat' vekov*, 120.

25. *ZU*, 115–16; MVG/MV, 39.

26. *KhiG* 6 (1999): 191–99.

4: THE LAST DANCE

1. King, *Court*, 414–18; Vyrubova, *Memories*, 8.
2. *SH*, 2:141; Alexander Mikhailovich, *Once*, 211.
3. Rogger, *Russia*, 33, 94–95, 107, 114; Lincoln, *War's Dark Shadow*, 224; Riasanovsky and Steinberg, *History*, 378–79.
4. Rogger, *Russia*, 177–80.
5. Ibid., 208–15; Lincoln, *War's Dark Shadow*, 270–303.
6. *Once*, 189, 223. See also *Moia russkaia zhizn'*, 144–45; Elizaveta Isaakova, "A Testimony," BA, 58–59; Wassiltschikow, *Verschwundenes Russland*, 120.
7. *Seed*, 163–74. On anti-Jewish violence, see Klier and Lambroza, eds., *Pogroms*.
8. MVG/MV, 357–71.
9. Krasko, *Tri veka*, 203.
10. *SVS*, 201–202, 216–17.
11. P. S. Sheremetev, *Zametki*, 111; Nicholas II, *Dnevnik*, 205; Kovaleva, *Staraia Moskva*, 98–100; Iu. B. Solov'ev, *Samoderzhavie*, 162, 171; G. A. Hosking and R. T. Manning, "What Was the United Nobility?," in *Politics*, ed. Haimson 144–47; V. Levitskii, "Pravyia partii," in *Obshchestvennoe dvizhenie*, cd. Martov, 366–69; s.v. "Soiuz russkikh liudei," in *Chernaia sotnia* comp. Stepanov; Gurko, *Features*, 386; Rawson, "Union"; "Soiuz russkikh liudei," at www.hrono.info/organ/rossiya /soyuz_ru_ludey.html, accessed April 1, 2009; Kireev, *Dnevnik*, 66–67.
12. Rogger, *Russia*, 23–24, 95; Emmons, "Russian Nobility," 177–78, 210–11; on the noble reaction, see Haimson, ed., *Politics*.
13. Marullo, *Russian Requiem*, 1–4.
14. Ibid., 93–100, 104; Baboreko, *Bunin*, 95–99; Bunin, *Cursed Days*, 5.
15. Marullo, *Russian Requiem*, 180. Recent scholarship supports Bunin's assessment. See Lieven, *Aristocracy*, 224–27.
16. Marullo, *Russian Requiem*, 6–7.
17. Bunin, *Collected Stories*, 18–73.
18. Marullo, *Russian Requiem*, 101; and see Woodward, "The Decline of the Peasantry and Landed Gentry," in *Ivan Bunin*.
19. Figes, *Peasant Russia*, 18–19; and see Barinova, *Vlast'*.
20. Rogger, *Russia*, 95.
21. Anonymous, "An Appreciation," 6.
22. Geifman, *Thou Shalt*, 18–21, 112, 138.
23. Krasko, *Tri veka*, 232–33.
24. Lincoln, *War's Dark Shadow*, 205–206, 271.
25. Geifman, *Thou Shalt*, 50, 55.
26. Lincoln, *War's Dark Shadow*, 347–48.
27. Billington, *Icon*, 500–14; Lincoln, *War's Dark Shadow*, 385–88.
28. Zubov, *Stradnye gody*, 7.
29. Meiendorff, *Through Terror*, 26.
30. Gagarin, *Reminiscences*, 114–16; see also M. Buchanan, *Dissolution*, 72–73; M. Gagarine, *From Stolnoy*, 32–36.

31. *Once*, 254.

32. Rogger, *Russia*, 255–56; Lincoln, *Passage*, 41–50; Lobanov-Rostovsky, *Grinding Mill*, 17.

33. Rogger, *Russia*, 256.

34. B. A. Tatishchev, "Na rubezhe dvukh mirov," Aleksei B. Tatishchev Collection, HIA, 199.

35. *KhiG* 8, pt. 2 (2002): 167–68.

36. Rappaport, *Conspirator*, 259–60; Rogger, *Russia*, 255–56.

37. Schapiro, *Communist Party*, 153, 184.

38. The exact number will never been known. See the discussion in Mawdsley, *Russian Civil War*, 285–87.

39. Lincoln, *Passage*, 89, 145, 255–56; S. Volkov, *Tragediia*, 8.

40. Rogger, *Russia*, 257.

41. V. S. Trubetskoi, *Russian Prince*, xi–xii; idem, *Zapiski kirasira*; Smirnova, ". . . pod pokrov*," 250.

42. *ZU*, 106–107, 126–28; AVG/M, 40–41; *KhiG* 4, pt. 3 (1997): 78–85.

43. RGADA, 1287.1.5955, 174–80; *SH*, 2:139; RGIA, 1088.2.627, 7–10; Karnishina, "Blagotvoritel'naia deiatel'nost."

44. YPS/V, 39–41.

45. Kleinmichel, *Memories*, 217–18; Almedingen, *Tomorrow*, 89; and see M. Gagarin, *From Stolnoy*; M. Gagarin, *Reminiscences*; Carlow, "Memoirs," 22–23.

46. Nabokov, *Speak*, 47.

47. Lincoln, *Passage*, 11, 56, 61, 90–91, 103–104; Riasanovsky and Steinberg, *History*, 392; Rogger, *Russia*, 257–58.

48. Lincoln, *Passage*, 93, 94, 107–10, 147.

49. Ibid., 175.

50. D. S. Sheremetev, *Iz vospominanii*; Nicholas II, *Complete*; Fedorchenko, *Svita*, 2:421; ABM.

51. Lincoln, *Passage*, 194; Rogger, *Russia*, 264–65; Fuller, *Foe*; Krasko, *Tri veka*, 206; SVS, 201–202, 217.

52. Krasko, *Tri veka*, 350–51; "V ianvare i fevrale 1917 g.," 114; Blok, "Poslednye dni," 18; and see Lincoln, *War's Dark Shadow*, 202; Nabokov, *Speak*, 186–88.

53. Barinova, *Vlast'*, 140–41; Alexander Mikhailovich, *Once*, 196–97.

54. Fuller, *Foe*, 262.

55. Podbolotov, "Monarchists."

56. Kir'ianov, *Pravye partii*, 99, 409–10; and see Bibin, *Dvorianstvo*, 220, 263–66.

57. Cockfield, *White Crow*, ix–x.

58. *Grinding Mill*, 167, 193–94.

59. Marullo, *Russian Requiem*, 229; Bunin, *Cursed Days*, 40–41.

60. Lincoln, *Passage*, 215–27.

61. Bashkiroff, *Sickle*, 27.

62. *Grinding Mill*, 193–94; and see Paléologue, *Ambassador's Memoirs*, 3:164.

63. On Rasputin, Varlamov, *Grigorii Rasputin-Novyi*.

64. Lincoln, *Passage*, 311.

65. KNA, 16.1916, 1–2.

66. Pokrovskii, ed., "Politicheskoe polozhenie," 4, 6, 11.

5: THE FALL OF THE ROMANOVS

1. Lincoln, *Passage*, 321–23; Rogger, *Russia*, 266–67.

2. Lincoln, *Passage*, 323–25; Rogger, *Russia*, 266–67; Pipes, *Russian Revolution*, 274–75.

3. Lincoln, *Passage*, 327–31; Rogger, *Russia*, 266–67; Figes, *People's Tragedy*, 311–20.

4. The details are drawn from: RGIA, 1088.2.492, 1–3; 1088.2.307, 34–340b, 97–980b; 1088.2.537; RGADA, 1287.1.5062, 24–35; ABM; Krasko, *Tri veka*, 376–77.

5. RGADA, 1287.1.5062, 310b.

6. Ibid., 32–33.

7. ABM.

8. Pipes, *Russian Revolution*, 280.

9. Lincoln, *Passage*, 331–33; Pipes, *Russian Revolution*, 279–81; Figes, *People's Tragedy*, 320–21.

10. Lincoln, *Passage*, 334–36; Pipes, *Russian Revolution*, 286–87; Figes, *People's Tragedy*, 323–27.

11. Lincoln, *Passage*, 334–36; Figes, *People's Tragedy*, 323–31; Riasanovsky and Steinberg, *History*, 441–43.

12. Figes, *People's Tragedy*, 334–35; Pipes, *Russian Revolution*, 320–23.

13. RGADA, 1287.1.5062, 33–34.

14. Ibid., 34–35; YPS/V, 47–48.

15. YPS/V, 47–48.

16. RGADA, 1287.1.iv.5137, Materialy I–II, 1917; ABM. Family lore has it that after his abdication, Nicholas invited Dmitry to accompany him to Tobolsk, but that his wife refused to let him go, knowing it would mean his certain death. No contemporary sources corroborate the story, nor is there any evidence the two ever saw each other again after Dmitry left headquarters.

17. RGADA, 1287.1.5062, 39; YPS/V, 47–48.

18. Krasko, *Tri veka*, 385–86; ABM; *SH*, 2:151.

19. Accounts of persons who lived through the February Revolution in Petrograd expose the lie of this claim. See, for example, Arbenina (Meiendorff), *Through Terror*, 39–40; Elizaveta Issakova, "A Testimony," BA; Paley, *Memories*, 76–77; Poutiatine, *War*, 51.

20. Grabbe, *Windows*, 131–35; Francis, *Russia*, 62–65. See also Elizaveta Issakova, "A Testimony," BA, 164–65; Robien, *Diary*, 17; M. Buchanan, *Dissolution*, 171–72.

21. Figes, *People's Tragedy*, 321; Chamberlin cites a figure of 1,315 in *Russian Revolution*, 1:85. See also Pipes, *Russian Revolution*, 303–304.

22. Grabbe, *Windows*, 85; Pushkarev, *Vospominaniia*, 52–53, 58; Glenny and Stone, eds., *Other Russia*, 55; Sollohub, *Russian Countess*, 93; Vasil'chikov, "Petrograd, 1918," 128.

23. Figes and Kolonitskii, *Interpreting*, 167–86; Kolonitskii, "Anti-Bourgeois Propaganda"; Smirnova, *Byvshie liudi*, 31–33; Fitzpatrick, *Tear Off*, 3–5.

24. Steinberg, *Voices*, 9, 13, 17–19; Pipes, *Russian Revolution*, 308.

25. Grabbe, *Windows*, 135. It is not clear from Grabbe's book which Countess Sheremetev this was.

26. Ignatieff, *Russian Album*, 115.

27. Sayn-Wittgenstein, *Dnevnik*, 84, 143–46; Rendle, "Symbolic Revolution"; Bashkiroff, *Sickle*, 29–31; Fen, *Remember*, 63.

28. Count E. P. Bennigsen, "Zapiski," BA, 488–89.

29. Mohrenschildt, *Russian Revolution*, 104. For a similar story, see Purishkevich, *Dnevnik*, insert between pp. 64–65.

30. Kleinmichel, *Memories*, 225–38, 258–59; Robien, *Diary*, 19, 54–56, 66–67.

31. Kleinmichel, *Memories*, 70–71; Volkov, *Tragediia*, 11; Wrangel, *Always*, 16; Robien, *Diary*, 55–56; Fel'shtinskii and Cherniavskii, "Krasnyi terror," 9:10–12.

32. Pipes, *Russian Revolution*, 307–17; Lincoln, *Passage*, 337–45.

33. Lincoln, *Passage*, 344; Figes, *People's Tragedy*, 344–49.

34. Igritskii, *1917 god*, 206.

35. Cantacuzène, *Revolutionary Days*, 159, 175–76; Arbenina, *Through Terror*, 42; Pipes, *Russian Revolution*, 322.

36. Rendle, *Defenders*, 52.

37. Dolgorukov, *Velikaia razrukha*, 11, 15; Tarasov-Rodionov, *February*, 92; Poutiatine, *War*, 60; Lobanov-Rostovsky, *Grinding Mill*, 203–204; Coles and Urusova, *Letters*, 270; Paléologue, *Ambassador's Memoirs*, 3:232, 259; Rendle, "Symbolic Revolution."

38. IDG, 57.

39. Issakova, "A Testimony," BA, 164.

40. Krasko, *Tri veka*, 262; RGADA, 1287.1.5062, 39–40.

41. RGADA, 1287.1.5062, 41.

42. RGADA, 1287.1.5062, 38.

43. Krasko, *Tri veka*, 261–62.

44. RGADA, 1287.1.510, 254–550b.

45. Ibid., 260–63.

46. Ibid., 260–690b.

47. RGADA, 1287.1.I.1943, 31–32; 1287.1.5062, 39, 52; YPS/V, 48; Krasko, *Tri veka*, 263, 352, 356.

48. RGADA, 1287.1.5062, 44–45.

49. Paléologue, *Ambassador's Memoirs*, 3:258, 337; Cockfield, *White Crow*, 213–15; Perry and Pleshakov, *Flight*, 148, 154–55, 165–66, 207–209.

50. Chamberlin, *Russian Revolution*, 1:85; Figes, *People's Tragedy*, 345–48; Pipes, *Russian Revolution*, 330–31.

51. *Perelomy*, 39–40. See, for a similar reaction, Rodzianko, *Tattered Banners*, 224.

52. Marie Kastchenko, "A World Destroyed," HIA, 128–29.

53. Menzies, "Certain Vision," 50.

54. *Russian Sketches*, 183–84.

55. ZU, 135–38.

56. MVG/MV, 562–66.

57. *KhiG* 1 (1996): 143.

58. *ZU*, 139.

59. AVG/M, 36–39, 42–44.

60. *ZU*, 15, 142–44; *KhiG* 1 (1996): 143; MVG/MV, 571–72.

61. RGADA, 1287.1.5062, 50, 55.

62. RGADA, 1287.1.5966, 6; 1287.1.6083, 75–76ob.

63. RGADA, 1287.1.6108, 46–46ob; 1287.1.5966, 6.

64. RGADA, 1287.1.6135, 1–3; 1287.1.6115, 28–29.

65. *Ambassador's Memoirs*, 3:256, 281, 339.

66. Ibid., 3:227–29.

67. RGADA, 1287.1.5062, 59; Krasko, *Tri veka*, 421–22.

68. Krasko, *Tri veka*, 421.

69. Barinova, *Vlast'*, 304–306; Rendle, *Defenders*, 1–3, 52–53, 186; Krasko, *Tri veka*, 262–63.

70. OR RNB, 585.4626, 13.

71. RGADA, 1287.1.1555, 160–610b; Krasko, *Tri veka*, 253, 263.

72. RGADA, 1287.1.5062, 64.

6: A COUNTRY OF MUTINOUS SLAVES

1. Lincoln, *Passage*, 361–65; Pipes, *Russian Revolution*, 392–94; Schapiro, *Communist Party*, 162–66.

2. Lincoln, *Passage*, 368. On Lvov, Figes, *People's Tragedy*, 355–56; Pipes, *Russian Revolution*, 300–01.

3. Kerensky, quoted in Lincoln, *Passage*, 371.

4. Figes, *People's Tragedy*, 379–80.

5. Igritskii, *1917 god*, 34–37, 45–49, 86–88.

6. *Novoe vremia*, 14736, p. 3.

7. *Den'*, no. 11, p. 4.

8. *Novoe vremia*, nos. 14744, 14751, 14752, 14753, 14758, 14764; and see Igritskii, "Bor'ba," 85–97.

9. *Novoe vremia*, no. 14767, p. 4–5; and May 4/17, no. 14768, p. 4; May 7/20, no. 14771, p. 4; *Den'*, May 6, 1917, no. 52, p. 4; no. 53, May 7, 1917, p. 3.

10. *Cursed Days*, 80.

11. Igritskii, *1917 god*, 130–33.

12. *Den'*, June 25, 1917, no. 94, p. 5.

13. Ibid., July 25, 1917, no. 118, p. 6; and see Figes, *Peasant Russia*, 55.

14. Sollohub, *Russian Countess*, 115.

15. TAS, 307.

16. *Perelomy*, 40–41.

17. On "strolling players," see *The Other Russia*, 59–63; Igritskii, *1917 god*; "Mart-Mai 1917 g.," 44; "Soiuz zemel'nykh sobstvennikov," 97–121; Gill, *Peasants*, 163–64.

18. "A World Destroyed," HIA, 129–33.

19. "Crossing the Field," 90–92.

20. Baboreko, *Bunin*, 223–25; Marullo, *Russian Requiem*, 238.

21. Marullo, *Russian Requiem*, 238.

22. Ibid., 246–47; *Ustami Bunina*, 163, 168.

23. *ZU*, 146.

24. Ibid., 146–47.

25. Ibid., 147–48; MVG/MV, 581–83.

26. *Revolutionary Days*, 213.

27. "Otryvki iz dnevnika, 1917–1920," BA, 10–11.

28. Robien, *Diary*, 161.

29. Krasko, *Tri veka*, 264, 386; ABM; RGADA, 1287.1.5062, 68.

30. RGADA, 1287.1.510, 271–76, 279–820b.

31. Obolensky, "Semeinye zapiski," 175:177, 179.

32. RGADA, 1287.1.5062, 76; 1287.1.3500, 87–90.

33. Ibid., 1287.1.2843, 71–720b; 1287.1.1490, 44–440b.

34. ABM; RGADA, 1287.1.I.3568; *SH*, 2:153–56.

35. Krasko, *Tri veka*, 422; ABM; *SH*, 2:140.

36. Carlow, "Memoirs," 6; Aleksandrovskii, *Iz perezhitogo*, 103–104.

37. RGADA, 1287.1.5938, 68–680b, 71, 75.

38. *Den'*, April 14, 1917, no. 33, p. 1.

39. Ibid., May 17, 1917, no. 61, p. 4.

40. RGADA, 1287.1.5062, 85–100.

41. *Den'*, October 1, 1917, no. 178, p. 3.

42. *Pravda*, vechernyi vypusk, December 24, 1917, no. 33, p. 2.

43. RGADA, 1287.1.5960, 73–730b.

44. Ibid., 72; YPS/V, 48–49.

45. RGADA, 1287.1.5955, 183–830b, 190–900b, 195–950b.

46. Ibid., 193–94.

47. RGADA, 1287.1.5062, 85–100, 111; 1287.1.3500, 1–30b; 1287.1.2849, 175–760b.

48. YPS/V, 48–54; *SVS*, 318.

49. *Reminiscences*, 1:166–67.

50. Browder and Kerensky, eds., *Russian Provisional Government*, 2:608–609; Rendle, *Defenders*, 84–114; Channon, "The Landowners," in *Society*, ed. Service, 120–46.

51. Compare Pipes, *Russian Revolution*, 419–38; Rabinowitch, *Bolsheviks*, 1–38; Figes, *People's Tragedy*, 423–35.

52. *SVS*, 220–21.

53. RGADA, 1287.1.5062, 68, 79–80.

54. Rendle, *Defenders*, 158–73.

55. VMG/D, 39–40, 50–51, 54–58, 84.

56. Rendle, *Defenders*, 173–80.

57. Ibid., 180–86; Pipes, *Russian Revolution*, 439–67; Riasanovsky and Steinberg, *History*, 445–57.

58. RGADA, 1287.1.5062, 64–66; Wassiltschikow, *Verschwundenes Russland*, 299–314; Osipova, *Klassovaia bor'ba*, 226–28.

59. Igritskii, *1917 god*, 55–59.

60. Wassiltschkow, *Verschwundenes Russland*, 332–33.

61. Igritskii, *1917 god*, 55–59.

62. *Den'*, August 26, 1917, no. 146, p. 4; August 27, 1917, no. 147.

63. RGADA, 1287.1.5062, 112–13.

64. Ibid., 1287.1.1980, 150–500b.

65. Wassiltschikow, *Verschwundenes Russland*, 333; "K istorii provedeniia v zhizn'," 48–49; GARF, 5918.1.5, 122.

66. Osipova, *Klassovia bor'ba*, 227–28; *Zemlia i volia*, August 28, 1917, no. 128, p. 4; October 12, 1917, no. 166, p. 2; *Den'*, September 14, 1917, no. 163, p. 5; September 17, 1919, no. 166, p. 5; *Den'* (under special title *Polnoch'*), November 24, 1917, no. 1, p. 5; Gill, *Peasants*, 142.

67. *Revolutionary Days*, 328.

68. *Den'*, September 30, 1917, no. 177, p. 3; Figes, *People's Tragedy*, 462–63.

69. Ibid., October 13, 1917, no. 188, p. 5.

70. Ibid., October 18, 1917, no. 192, p. 2.

71. Ibid., (published as *Noch*), November 22, 1917, no. 1, p. 6.

72. Figes, *Peasant Russia*, 21–22; Gill, *Peasants*, 157–58.

73. AVG/M, 44–45.

74. VMG/D, 71–72, 77, 89.

75. Sayn-Wittgenstein, *Dnevnik*, 93–95, 149.

7: THE BOLSHEVIK COUP

1. RGADA, 1287.1.5062, 124–25.

2. Figes, *People's Tragedy*, 456–58, 469–78; Rendle, *Defenders*, 199; Robert Service, "The Bolshevik Party," in *Critical Companion*, 234–35.

3. Rendle, *Defenders*, 199; Figes, *People's Tragedy*, 493–95.

4. Figes, *People's Tragedy*, 481–95; Lincoln, *Passage*, 441–53.

5. RGADA, 1287.1.5062, 136–38.

6. Lincoln, *Passage*, 468–70.

7. OGSh, 21.

8. RGADA, 1287.1.5062, 136–38; OGSh, 20–24.

9. OGSh, 24–25.

10. Lincoln, *Passage*, 470–71; RGADA, 1287.1.5062, 139–42.

11. *SVS*, 245; Alekseeva, "Velikii," 25–26.

12. VMG/D, 103–109.

13. AVG/M, 46–47.

14. Appendix II to AVG/M: "Excerpts from the Diaries of Olga and Marina Golitzin and Olga's Poems," 9.

15. Ibid., 5.

16. AVG/M, 48; *PG*, 432.

17. *ZU*, 148–51.

18. VMG/D, 112, 116, 120, 124–25, 133; *ZU*, 152–53.

19. *ZU*, 148–52.

20. Marie Kastchenko, "A World Destroyed," HIA, 138–76.

21. Sayn-Wittgenstein, *Dnevnik*, 102–28; see also TAS, 309–12.

22. TAS, 115.

23. Pipes, *Russian Revolution*, 496–98; Lincoln, *Passage*, 457–58; Figes, *People's Tragedy*, 489–91.

24. Lincoln, *Passage*, 458; Figes, *People's Tragedy*, 492–97; Rabinowitch, *Bolsheviks*, 302–304.

25. Lincoln, *Passage*, 458–61; Pipes, *Russian Revolution*, 499.

26. Ryan, "Revolution," 261.

27. Pipes, *Russian Revolution*, 509.

28. Ibid., 521–24.

29. Rendle, *Defenders*, 54; *Izvestiia*, March 12, 1917, no. 13, p. 4.

30. *Dekrety*, 1:41–42, 71, 132–37; Rendle, *Defenders*, 212.

31. OGSh, 19.

32. Lincoln, *Passage*, 462–63; Pipes, *Russian Revolution*, 526–27.

33. Pipes, *Russian Revolution*, 527–28.

34. Golinkov, *Krakh*, 73.

35. Lincoln, *Passage*, 463–68.

36. OGSh, 27–28.

37. Pipes, *Russian Revolution*, 541–42.

38. OGSh, 27–28.

39. Pipes, *Russian Revolution*, 537–55; Lincoln, *Passage*, 475–79; Figes, *People's Tragedy*, 509–10.

40. Andrew and Gordievsky, *KGB*, 38–41; Lincoln, *Passage*, 474–75.

41. Nabokov, *Speak*, 2, 41–43.

42. "Zapiski M. S. Trubetskoi," in A. B. Tatistcheff Collection, box 4, HIA, 1.

43. VMG/D, 118–19, 121–22, 140, 161; AVG/M, 48–50, and Appendix IV, 15; *KhiG* 9 (2002): 156–62, 203–36; *KhiG* 7 (2000): 368–75.

44. AVG/M, 35, and Appendix II, 7, 9–10; Appendix IV, 2; *ZU*, 80–81, 243–44; VMG/D, 118–19, 121–22, 140, 161; Schmemann, *Echoes*, 155–56, 185; *KhiG* 10, pt. 1 (2003): 203–12.

45. RGADA, 1287.1.5062, 159; 1287.1.5062, 156a.

46. Ibid., 1287.1.5062, 156a.

47. ABM.

48. MVG/M, 65.

49. RGADA, 1287.1.3500, 27–300b.

50. OGSh, 28–31.

51. Sayn-Wittgenstein, *Dnevnik*, 128.

52. RGADA, 1287.1.5062, 172.

53. VMG/D, 116.

8: EXPROPRIATING THE EXPROPRIATORS

1. Mawdsley, *Civil War*, v, 399. Drawing on the work of various experts, Mawdsley estimates between seven and ten million died as a result of the fighting. For more on the number of deaths, see Raleigh, "Russian Civil War," 166. Historians disagree about the day the civil war began, but this book follows the argument put forward by Mawdsley and others that it started with the Bolshevik coup and not, as some claim, the following summer.
2. Mawdsley, *Civil War*, 268–98.
3. Ibid., 4–5.
4. Riasanovsky and Steinberg, *History*, 464.
5. Smirnova, *Byvshie liudi*, 23.
6. *Dekrety*, 6:124; Smirnova, *Byvshie liudi*, 9, 14, 56, 76; Rendle, *Defenders*, 203–204.
7. Nabokov, *Bagazh*, 111.
8. Quoted in Ryan, "Revolution," 270–71.
9. Trifonov, *Likvidatsiia*, 162.
10. Lenin, *Polnoe sobranie*, 34:287–339; 35:156–58.
11. Ibid., 34:195–205.
12. Schapiro, *Communist Party*, 210.
13. Smirnova, *Byvshie liudi*, 73; Applebaum, *Gulag*, 28–29.
14. Zinovieff, *Princess Remembers*, 122–25.
15. Wolksonsky, *Way*, 120–23. See also Robien, *Diary*, 218; WSHC, 1720/1130, Prince Nicholas Galitzine, 6–7.
16. Ivanov, *Byvshie liudi*, 70; Smirnova, *Byvshie liudi*, 57.
17. Figes, *People's Tragedy*, 727.
18. Smirnova, *Byvshie liudi*, 57.
19. Fel'shtinskii, *Krasnyi terror*, 108–10; Fel'shtinskii and Cherniavskii, "Krasnyi terror," 8:14–15; 9:27.
20. Preston, *Before the Curtain*, 92–94.
21. McMeekin, *History's Greatest Heist*, 6–7, 91.
22. Osipova, *Klassovaia bor'ba*, 269; Figes, *Peasant Russia*, 296–97.
23. Figes, *Peasant Russia*, 133–34.
24. Igritskii, *1917 god*, 259–69; Gill, *Peasants*, 154.
25. "K istorii provedeniia v zhizn'," 48–52.
26. McMeekin, *History's Great Heist*, 12–13, 17, 24–25, 35–36, 45, 73–91.
27. Trifonov, *Likvidatsiia*, 117.
28. Dolgorukov, *Velikaia razrukha*, 96; OGSh, 41–42.
29. On consolidation and its effects, see Bertaux, "Transmission," and Chuikina, *Dvorianskaia pamiat'*, 138–40; Zubov, *Stradnye gody*, 80–97; Glenny and Stone, eds., *Other Russia*, 122–24; Shapovalov, *Remembering*, 131–32; Sollohub, *Russian Countess*, 132–34; Reed, *Ten Days*, 354; Kovalevskii, *Dnevniki*, 51–68.
30. Steinberg and Riasanovsky, *History*, 460–66; Raleigh, "Russian Civil War," 157–63; Trifonov, *Likvidatsiia*, 107–108; *Dekrety*, 1:240, 230, 236, 390; 2:136–37.

31. Trifonov, *Likvidatsiia*, 103–105; McMeekin, *History's Greatest Heist*, 12–13, 17, 24–25, 35–36, 45, 73–91.

32. Skariatina, *World*, 229–32. See also M. F. Meiendorff, *Vospominaniia*, 242–43; Meshcherskaya, *Russian Princess*, 11–14.

33. Tatishchev, *Zemli*, 265, 269–70; I. Vasil'chikov, *To, chto mne*, 144; Wassiltschikow, *Verschwundenes Russland*, 335; Robien, *Diary*, 104.

34. McMeekin, *History's Greatest Heist*, 17–21, 46–48, 56–71.

35. IDG, 71–72.

36. GARF, R–5446.5a.737, 2–3; Iusupov, *Memuary*, 1998, 235; Von Meck, *As I*, 179; *Iusupovskii dvorets*, 2:383–84; Clarke, *Lost Fortune*, 106–107, 158–61.

37. Tolstoy, *I Worked*, 56, 149–50; Tatistscheff, "Crossing the Field," 148–50; Zinovieff, *Princess*, 122–25; Horsbrugh-Peter, *Memories*, 101. See also Urusova, *Materinskii plach*, 29; M. F. Meiendorff, *Vospominaniia*, 220; KNG, 155–56; Clarke, *Lost Fortune*, 106–108, 157–61; Williams, *Olga's Story*, 206; Meshcherskaya, *Russian Princess*, 70, 82–83; Shcherbatova, "Dnevnik," 70.

38. Nabokov, *Speak*, 187–88, 244–46.

39. Wassiltschikow, *Verschwundenes Russland*, 345.

40. Welch, *Russian Court*, 133.

41. Von Meck, *As I*, 174–76.

42. Nabokov, *Speak*, 183.

43. Meiendorff, *Through Terror*, 96, 102, 132.

44. Babine, *Civil War*, 75.

45. Skriabina, *Strannitsy*, 79.

46. Trifonov, *Likvidatsiia*, 164; Ivanov, *Byvshie liudi*, 70–71; McMeekin, *History's Greatest Heist*, 49; Sayn-Wittgenstein, *Dnevnik*, 168, 180–82; Von Meck, *As I*, 161–62. See also Gipius, "Iz nebytiia," 90–91; Babine, *Civil War*, 47, 78; E. F. Rodzianko, *Perelomy*, 74–75; Welch, *Russian Court*, 134–35.

47. BP, 4:18.

48. Brovkin, *Behind*, 119–26; OPR, 40; Leggett, *Cheka*, 147–51.

49. Brovkin, *Behind*, 74–75.

50. See, for example, Kovalevskii, *Dnevniki*, 20.

51. Paley, *Memories*, 126, 264; M. Buchanan, *Dissolution*, 265–66.

52. McMeekin, *History's Greatest Heist*, 39.

53. Ibid., 56–71.

54. Coles and Urusova, *Letters*, 326–33.

55. M. Buchanan, *City*, 217–18.

56. Figes and Kolonitskii, *Interpreting*, 186.

57. Robien, *Diary*, 186, 190, 218.

9: THE CORNER HOUSE

1. OGSh, 33–39; RGADA, 1287.1.3500, 54–590b; 64–680b.

2. OR RNB, 585.4627, 3–4, 13, 23; RGADA, 1287.1.3759, 75–750b.; Kraskov, *Tri veka*,

269–79; RGADA, 1287.1.3759, 84; author interview with Yevdokia Sheremetev, March 19, 2009.

3. KNA, 145, 15; 146, 1–3; 148, 1; Zhukov, *Sokhrannye revoliutsiei*, 60, 82–83, 92–93, 172–74; idem, *Stanovlenie*, 165; Konchin, *Revoliutsiei prizvannye*, 88.

4. ABM.

5. Kovaleva, *Staraia Moskva*, 139–40; Krasko, *Tri veka*, 378; OR RNB, 585.4363; ABM; YPS/V, 53; *SH*, 2:147.

6. Krasko, "Graf," 467; idem, "Ob odnom," 93–94; OR RNB, 585.6085, 3–30b; *SH*, 2:147.

7. Kiriushina, "Stranitsy," 184–85; GARF, 2307.8.5, 3; Alekseeva, "Velikii, 25–26; Krasko, "Graf," 467; Wassiltschikow, *Verschwundenes Russland*, 392–93; RGALI, 612.1.2853, 188, 190–92.

8. Lincoln, *Red Victory*, 156–59.

9. Smirnova, *Byvshie liudi*, 67–68.

10. OGSh, 75–76.

11. Lincoln, *Red Victory*, 159–61; Anichkov, *Ekaterinburg*, 155.

12. Figes, *People's Tragedy*, 510.

13. Volkov-Muromtsev, *Iunost'*, 172.

14. ABM.

15. OR RNB, 585.4614, 2–3.

16. ABM; Krasko, *Tri veka*, 267–68; OGSh, 80; YPS/V, 53; RGADA, 1287.1.5919, 24–25; Kovaleva, *Staraia Moskva*, 34–35, 139.

17. ABM.

18. YPS/V, 54.

19. Ibid., 51, 54–55.

20. Ibid., 54–55; Meiendorff, *Through Terror*, 48, 132–33; RGADA, 1287.1.3431, 16–18.

21. YPS/V, 54–55.

22. OR RNB, 585.4628, 110b.

23. For examples of daring escapes, see Korostowetz, *Seed*, 357–79; Paley, *Memories*, 272–73, 302–309; Wolkonsky, *Way*, 144; Belosselsky-Belozersky, *Memoirs*, 65–69; Fitzpatrick and Slezkine, *In the Shadow*, 135–39; Vyrubova, *Memories*, 376–81; Polovtsov, *Glory*, 336–44; Glenny and Stone, *Other Russia*, 120–21; Isaakova, "Testimony," BA, 237; Rodzianko, *Perelomy*, 79–80; Sayn-Wittgenstein, *Dnevnik*, 214–56, 265–70, 290; TAS, 326–28; Wolkonsky, "Diary," 65–66; Ponafidine, *Russia*, 231–301.

24. Meshcherskaya, *Russian Princess*, 9–10.

25. Almedingen, *Tomorrow*, 124.

26. Chuikina, *Dvorianskaia pamiat'*, 18–19, 36.

27. Almedingen, *Tomorrow*, 147. See also Robien, *Diary*, 233, 268; Pethybridge, *Spread*, 170–75.

28. Coles and Urusova, *Letters*, 289.

29. OGSh, 75–76. See also 33–35, 48–51, 56–57, 62–63, 73; RGADA, 1287.1.3500, 60–630b.

30. Bunin, *Cursed Days*, 57.

31. Sayn-Wittgenstein, *Dnevnik*, 175, 179; Coles and Urusova, *Letters*, 360–62.

32. OGSh, 33–35, 58–59, 73.

33. Sayn-Wittgenstein, *Dnevnik*, 175, 179; Kokovtsov, *Iz moego*, 2:428; Sollohub, *Russian Countess*, 99.

34. MVG/M, 65; TAS, 322.

35. YPS/V, 53; ABM; Krasko, *Tri veka*, 383, 393, 403; *SH*, 2:148, 150.

36. *SH*, 3:391–92, 398.

37. RGADA, 1287.1.5062, 81–82; ABM.

38. MVG/M, 64; Krasko, *Tri veka*, 378; author interview with Evdokia Sheremetev, March 14, 2009; ABM.

39. ABM; Reswick, *I Dreamt*, 112, 160–61. On tame Communists, KNG, 219, 232–33.

40. Kaminski, *Konzentrationslager*, 34–36; Afanas'ev, et al., eds., *Istoriia*, 2:523; Applebaum, *Gulag*, 31–32; Leggett, *Cheka*, 176–81; Shapovalov, *Remembering*, 4.

41. GARF, R–1005.1a.148, 141–43, 154, 217–17a; WSHC, 1720/1130, Prince Nicholas Galitzine, 9–10.

42. Letters 39–57 of A. Dolgoruky to his mother in Igor Vinogradoff Collection, box 1, HIA.

43. Benckendorff, *Last Days*, 144; Wolkonsky, *Way*, 110–11; ABM.

44. OPR, 22–23, 150n.1; IDG, 8; ABM; Lincoln, *Red Victory*, 217–26; Mawdsley, *Russian Civil War*, 265, 268–71.

45. ABM; Krasko, *Tri veka*, 386, 406; IDG, 84–85.

10: SPA TOWN HELL

1. ABM; Shkuro, *Zapiski*; Zernov, *Na perelome*, 229–89; Savel'eva, *Kavkazskie Mineral'nye Vody*, 125, 150; GARF, 5819.1.5, 125; Musin-Pushkin, "Kniga," 3:24–25.

2. Kokovtsov, *Iz moego proshlogo*, 2:422–25.

3. V. Urusova, "Moi vospominaniia," 62–64; Kshesinskaia, *Vospominaniia*, 191–203; Shkuro, *Zapiski*, 24–28.

4. Kokovtsov, *Iz moego proshlogo*, 2:428–29, 432–33; Urusova, "Moi vospominaniia," 62–64.

5. Denikin, *Ocherki*, 3:188; Savel'eva, *Kavkazskie Mineral'nye Vody*, 235–36, 242.

6. Ignatieff, *Russian Album*, 133; Luckett, *White Generals*, 184.

7. ABM.

8. P. Uvarova, *Byloe davno*, 201–203.

9. "Zapiski kn. M. S. Trubetskoi," in Aleksei B. Tatishchev Collection, box 4, HIA, 2:1–2; A. A. Tatishchev, *Zemli*, 282; Tatistcheff, "Crossing the Field," 202–29.

10. Savel'eva, *Kavkazskie Mineral'nye Vody*, 124, 135–36, 244–45; Tatistcheff, "Crossing the Field," 204, 209–12; Serge, *Year One*, 214–15, 394–95n.8 and 20, 399n.48; Buldakov, "Revoliutsiia, naselie"; Kriven'kii, *Politicheskie deiateli*; GARF, 5819.1.4, 30b–5; Amfiteatrov-Kadashev, "Stranitsy," 559–60; Acton, ed., *Critical Companion*, 223, 225, 749.

11. *Rod L'vovykh*, 246; Léonida, *Chaque*, 65–66; "Zapiski kn. M. S. Trubetskoi," 2:1–12; GARF, 5819.1.4, 40; Fel'shtinskii and Cherniavskii, "Krasnyi terror," 7:14–15;

Pipes, *Russian Revolution*, 309–14; Tatistcheff, "Crossing the Field," 215–17; Z. N. Yusupov, "Diary," February 7, 8, 10.

12. Fel'shtinskii and Cherniavskii, "Krasnyi Terror," 7:14–15.

13. Ibid., 7:17; L'vova and Bochkareva, *Rod L'vovykh*, 145, 242–60; Coles and Urusova, *Letters*, 274–77, 389–90; GARF, 5819.1.5, 124–25.

14. Fel'shtinskii and Cherniavskii, "Krasnyi terror," 9:19.

15. Ibid., 7:16.

16. Ibid., 7:18–19, 28, 34; Denikin, *Ocherki*, 3:228–29; Savel'eva, *Kavakzskie Mineral'nye Vody*, 78.

17. Fel'shtinskii and Cherniavskii, "Krasnyi terror," 7:21–24; *Akt*.

18. L'vova and Bochkareva, *Rod L'vovykh*, 145, 242–60; Coles and Urusova, *Letters*, 389–90; Zernov, *Na perelome*, 264–70; Fel'shtinskii, *Krasnyi terror*, 34, 35; Fel'shtinskii and Cherniavski, "Krasnyi terror," 7:15–25.

19. L'vova and Bochkareva, *Rod L'vovykh*, 140–47, 257; GARF, 5819.1.125, 126–27.

20. Anonymous, "An Appreciation," 28–36.

21. Serge, *Year One*, 395n.8; Savel'eva, *Kavkazskie Mineral'nye Vody*, 135–36; Buldakov, "Revoliutsiia, nasilie"; Amfiteatrov-Kadashev, "Stranitsy," 559–50. One source states Alexander was shot, not stabbed to death.

22. *Akt*; Fel'shtinskii and Cherniavskii, "Krasnyi terror," 7:25–31; GARF, 5819.1.125, 126–27.

23. GARF, 5819.1.3, 8–80b; 5819.1.5, 126–27; Fel'shtinskii and Cherniavskii, "Krasnyi terror," 7:26.

11: BOGORODITSK

1. VMG/D, 166.

2. Ibid., 182, 201, 206.

3. Ibid., 204, 212, 338.

4. Ibid., 272.

5. Ibid., 229.

6. Ibid., 229, 315–16.

7. Ibid., 352.

8. AVT/V, 1:4–5.

9. *KhiG* 4, pt. 1 (1997): 67–69.

10. ZU, 155–56, 160–61; *KhiG* 1 (1996): 144.

11. ZU, 162–68; VMG/D, 276; KNG, 134–46; AVT/V, 1:2; Rendle, "Family, Kinship," 39–42; idem, "Problems of Becoming," 12–13.

12. A. E. Trubetskoi, "Kak my pytalis' spasti tsarskuiu sem'iu," *DS* 2 (1995): 61–68; S. E. Trubetskoi, *Minuvshee*, 255; VMG/D, 173, 208; Fusso, *Russian Prince*, xii–xiii; Smirnova, ". . . *pod*," 251.

13. S. E. Trubetskoi, *Minuvshee*, 171–73. On the underground, see Kuz'mina, *Kniaz' Shakhovskoi*, 265–66; OPR, 9, 9n.2; Golinkov, *Krakh*, 55–56, 62; Rendle, *Defenders*, 205–206, 228–29; Volkov-Muromtsev, *Iunost'*, 159.

14. *Ocherki russkoi smuty,* 3:74–76.

15. Leggett, *Cheka,* 279–91; *DS* 4 (1996): 364–78; 9 (1999): 272–90; *OPR,* 167–68; Klement'ev, *V bol'shevitskoi moskve.*

16. *OPR,* 9 and 9n.2.

17. *ZU,* 157, 173–75; ZVG, 5:79–80.

18. Mikhail's letter is attached to "Zapiski kn. M. S. Trubetskoi," in A. B. Tatishchev Collection, box 4, HIA.

19. *ZU,* 177–78.

20. Ibid., 179–91; RGADA, 1287.3.90, 32–320b; 1287.3.91, 1; 1287.3.107, 35–380b; KNG, 123–24.

21. *ZU,* 193–94; *KhiG* 4, pt. 1 (1997): 70–71; Muratov, *Rod,* 97.

22. RGADA, 1287.3.100, 225–250b.

23. KNG, 129–30.

24. Ibid., 356–57.

25. RGADA, 1263.3.97, 8–80b, 34–35.

26. Almedingen, *Tomorrow,* 230; S. E. Trubetskoi, *Minuvshee,* 160, 181–83. See also Kovalevskii, *Dnevniki,* 25–27, 44; Meiendorff, *Through Terror,* 96, 102, 132; Britneva, *One Woman's Story,* 87–88; ZVG, 4:87; IDG, 69–70, 85; Alekseev, *Usad'ba andreevskoe,* 59–61; Sollohub, *Russian Countess,* 142–44.

27. *ZU,* 205.

28. "Zapiski kn. M. S. Trubetskoi," in A. B. Tatishchev Collection, box 4, HIA, 28.

29. RGADA, 1263.3.104, 14–150b; AVT/V, 1:4.

30. RGADA, 1263.3.99, 42–430b.

31. Ibid., l. 57–580b.

32. Ibid., 1263.3.95, l. 3–40b.

33. Ibid., 1287.3.100, 180–800b, 187, 1940b, 223.

34. Ibid., 158–590b.

35. *ZU,* 21–17; RGADA, 1263.3.107, 35–380b; 1263.3.106, 46–470b, 75–750b.

36. Leggett, *Cheka,* 96; Rendle, *Defenders,* 223–28; idem, "Officer Corps."

37. Volkov, *Tragediia,* 240, 245, 259–61; Smirnova, *Byvshie liudi,* 254; *Dekrety,* 5:327, 426.

38. *PG,* 73–74, 577–80; Koval', *Kniaz' Vasilii,* 207–208, 275–306; See also Skriabina, *Strannitsy,* 56.

39. Kantor, *Voina*; Butson, *Tsar's Lieutenant.*

40. Figes, *People's Tragedy,* especially pp. 549–50, 644–45, 696–99; Kovalevskii, *Istoriia.* Brusilov was convinced his son had been executed, though it is possible he died of typhus.

41. Figes, *People's Tragedy,* 696n.

42. *ZU,* 221–24; Fusso, *Russian Prince,* xiii; RGADA, 1263.3.95, 36–37; AVT/V, 1:3.

43. KNG, 132–33, 358; *ZU,* 121–23, 154–55, 221–24, 229–40; RGADA, 1263.3.107, 35–380b; 1263.3.104, 25–260b.

44. *ZU,* 221, 239.

45. Rodzianko, *Perelomy,* 48–49, 91. See also Tolstaia-Voeikova, *Russkaia sem'ia.*

46. RGADA, 1263.3.105, 53; 1263.3.107, 35–380b.

47. Ibid., 1263.3.95, 41–420b; 1263.3.104, 109.
48. Ibid., 41–420b.

12: DR. GOLITSYN

1. AVG/M, 48–50.
2. Ibid., 8–9, 50; *KhiG* 10, pt. 1 (2003): 203–12
3. AVG/M, Appendix II:11.
4. AVG/M, 11–18.
5. L'vov, *Vospominaniia*, 295.
6. AVG/M, 22–26.
7. Ibid., 27.
8. AVG/M, App. I:10, 13; VMG/D, 229; Figes, *People's Tragedy*, 650; OGSh, 42.
9. AVG/M, App. I:7; *PG*, 402–03.
10. AVG/M, App. I:8–9; Alexandra, *Last Diary*, 214.
11. AVG/M, 58; "Kniaz' G. E. L'vov," 140–70.
12. Figes, *People's Tragedy*, 650–51.
13. Mawdsley, *Civil War*, 64–68; Lincoln, *Red Victory*, 234–35; Smele, *Civil War*, 25–33.
14. King and Wilson, *Fate*, 10–25, 282–95; Steinberg and Khrustalëv, *Fall*, 277–97; Slater, *Many Deaths*.
15. King and Wilson, *Fate*, 296–315.
16. Ibid., 260–61; Steinberg and Khrustalëv, *Fall*, 301, 322–23; Preston, *Before the Curtain*, 106–107.
17. King and Wilson, *Fate*, 204–11.
18. Anichkov, *Ekaterinburg*, 88, 95, 102.
19. King and Wilson, *Fate*, 218–21, 336–37, 504; Cockfield, *White Crow*, 243–45; Nikolai Mikhailovich, "Pis'mo," 87.
20. OGSh, 56–59, 61; AVG/M, 75–76.
21. *ZU*, 173.
22. VMG/D, 333–34.
23. For one example, see Shcherbatov, *Pravo*, 56.
24. Von Meck, *As I*, 172.
25. AVG/M, 59–65; VMG/D, 281, 287, 298, 300; AVG/M, Appendix I:15, 19; Appendix IV: 1–6, 22–25; RGADA, 1263.3.94, 111–120b.
26. AVG/M, 66–74.
27. Ibid., 74.
28. Mawdsley, *Civil War*, 72, 137–38, 141–42; Lincoln, *Red Victory*, 234, 246.
29. Mawdsley, *Civil War*, 143–50; Smele, *Civil War*, 71–182; Lincoln, *Red Victory*, 235–45.
30. Lincoln, *Red Victory*, 245–46; Mawdsley, *Civil War*, 185.
31. AVG/M, 74–75, 79; L'vov, *Vospominaniia*, 295; Thompson, *Russia*, 64, 77, 79; Figes, *People's Tragedy*, 651–52.
32. AVG/M, Appendix II:17–18.
33. Mawdsley, *Civil War*, 184, 201; Smele, *Civil War*, 215–48, 307–26.

34. Lincoln, *Red Victory*, 250–52.
35. Ibid., 244; Smele, *Civil War*, 277–89.
36. Smele, *Civil War*, 169–81, 439; Lincoln, *Red Victory*, 253–54; Brovkin, *Behind*, 205–206; Mawdsley, *Civil War*, 207.
37. AVG/M, Appendix II:18; Appendix III:2–4.
38. Lincoln, *Red Victory*, 259–65; Mawdsley, *Civil War*, 186–90, 204–207.
39. AVG/M, 81, and Appendix III, 5–6.
40. Smele, *Civil War*, 543–50.
41. AVG/M, 85–86; Lincoln, *Red Victory*, 265–66.
42. Smele, *Civil War*, 587–89; Mawdsley, *Civil War*, 318.
43. AVG/M, 86–92.
44. YP/D, 9, 27; RGADA, 1263.3.107, 28–280b.
45. Smele, *Civil War*, 590–92; Mawdsley, *Civil War*, 318.
46. AVG/M, Appendix III:7.
47. Mawdsley, *Civil War*, 319.
48. YP/D, 1, 3; AVG/M, Appendix III:16; *KhiG* 10, pt. 1 (2003): 203–12.
49. AVG/M, Appendix III:8–10; YP/D, 1, 3.
50. AVG/M, Appendix II:15–16.
51. Ibid., 16–17.
52. Ibid., Appendix III:13–14.
53. Smele, *Civil War*, 549–50; Lincoln, *Red Victory*, 266; Mawdsley, *Civil War*, 319. The sources disagree on the exact date of Kolchak's departure from Omsk; I cite here that given by Smele.
54. Smele, *Civil War*, 584–638, 664–65; Mawdsley, *Civil War*, 319–20; Acton, ed., *Critical Companion*, 715.
55. YP/D, 2–12.
56. Ibid., 13, 24; Mawdsley, *Civil War*, 322. On Semenov, see Khitun, *Dvorianskie pro-siata*, 230–81; Bisher, *White Terror*; Palmer, *Bloody White Baron*; Williams, *Olga's Story*, 156–97.
57. See Fel'shtinskii, *Krasnyi terror*.
58. Smele, *Civil War*, 385n.176.
59. Rodzianko, *Tattered Banners*, 262.
60. Brovkin, *Behind*, 205–206; Welch, *Russian Court*, 101.
61. YP/D, 14–15.
62. Ibid., 15.
63. Ibid., 18.
64. RGADA, 1263.3.107, 28–280b.
65. YP/D, 27; AVG/M, Appendix III:10.
66. See Taskina, ed., *Russkii Kharbin*.
67. YP/D, 21.
68. Ibid., 20; L'vov, *Vospominaniia*, 5.
69. AVG/M, 94–97; YP/D, 25.
70. AVG/M, Barnes epilogue, 66; RGADA, 1263.3.103, 13–130b; 1263.3.94, 109–10; A. V.

Golitsyn's identity card, 6th Irkutskii Svodnyi Evako-gospital' Krasnoi Armii, July 26, 1920, Golitsyn Family Papers, box 3, HIA.

71. T. Galitzine, *Russian Revolution*; PG, 60–61, 243, 259; Anichkov, *Ekaterinburg*, 163, 218; King and Wilson, *Fate*, 342.
72. AVG/M, Appendix IV:22–25; RGADA, 1263.3.94, 111–1120b; Grech, *Venok*, 27–28.
73. RGADA, 1263.3.94, 4–50b.
74. Golitsyn Family Papers, boxes 2 and 3, HIA.

13: EXODUS

1. *Cursed Days*, 10–11.
2. Ibid., 95.
3. Marullo, *Russian Requiem*, 287–88, 294, 339; see also Fen, *Remember*, 101–200.
4. Marullo, *Russian Requiem*, 294, 299.
5. Ibid., 305–306.
6. *Cursed Days*, 139–40.
7. Ibid., 223.
8. Ibid., 107. For more on cocaine, see Zinovieff, *Red Princess*, 124–25.
9. *Cursed Days*, 165.
10. Marullo, *Russian Requiem*, 352. Bunin paraphrases here Joseph's interpretation of the pharaoh's dream in Genesis 4:4.
11. Ibid., 305, 347–50; *Cursed Days*, 214; Z. N. Yusupov, "Diary," January 12, February 23, 24, April 5, 6, 1919; Lincoln, *Red Victory*, 320–24; Figes, *People's Tragedy*, 676–79. On the often exaggerated role of anti-Semitism among the old regime elites at the time, see Rendle, *Defenders*, 7–8, 171–72.
12. Lincoln, *Red Victory*, 317–24. Lincoln writes, likely with exaggeration, that Khmelnitsky's men killed "some two hundred thousand Jews." See also Rogger, *Jewish Policies*; Klier and Lambroza, eds., *Pogroms*.
13. Marullo, *Russian Requiem*, 8–9, 307; *Cursed Days*, 147–49, 159–61, 181–84, 245–46.
14. *Cursed Days*, 243.
15. Ibid., 20–21; Marullo, *Russian Requiem*, 291.
16. Marullo, *Russian Requiem*, 358–59.
17. *Cursed Days*, 23.
18. See Mawdsley, *Civil War*, 377–86.
19. Shcherbatov, *Pravo*, 67.
20. *Always with Honor*, 332–33. The leading Western historian of the war largely concurs with their assessments. Mawdsley, *Civil War*, 386–95. See also Buldakov, "Revoliutsiia, nasilie," 9–10.
21. Z. N. Yusupov, "Diary," February 7, 8, 10, 1919; YPS/V, 43; Krasko, *Tri veka*, 352.
22. Welch, *Russian Court*, 11–17, 27; V. E. Galitzine, "Diary," March 25–April 5, 1919.
23. Krasko, *Tri veka*, 353.
24. Ibid., 176–79; Z. N. Yusupov, "Diary," April 7–8, 20, 1919.

25. Z. N. Yusupov, "Diary," April 13, 1919; Krasko, *Tri veka*, 353.

26. Krasko, *Tri veka*, 357–59; e-mail communication from Kyra Cheremeteff, September 28, 2011.

27. Obolenskii, *Moia zhizn'*, 739–51. The Nabokovs left the Crimea in March 1919, never thinking they would never return. *Speak*, 251, 253.

28. Rodzianko, *Perelomy*, 102–103. Ellipses in original.

29. Lobanov-Rostovsky, *Grinding Mill*, 373–74.

30. ABM; V. E. Galitzine, "Diary," March 3–April 5, 1919.

31. *PG*, 510; Irina Galitzine, *Spirit*.

32. *Always with Honor*, 318, 324; Mawdlsey, *Civil War*, 374.

33. Brovkin, *Behind*, 346–49.

34. Smirnova, *Byvshie liudi*, 82–83.

35. Shcherbatov, *Pravo*, 69–70.

36. Smirnova, *Byvshe liudi*, 82–83; *OPR*, 9, 9–10n.8.

37. *OPR*, 166.

38. Mawdsley, *Civil War*, 322–24.

39. For various estimates, see Rendle, *Defenders*, 213–14; Raymond, *Russian Diaspora*, 7–10; Horsbrugh-Porter, *Memories*, 1; Shoumatoff, *Russian Blood*, 298; Glenny and Stone, eds., *Other Russia*, xx; Raleigh, "Russian Civil War," 166.

40. Engel and Posadskaya-Vanderbeck, *Revolution*, 102.

41. Trifonov, *Likvidatsiia*, 168.

42. *Krasnaia gazeta*, no. 10, January 14, 1922, p. 2.

43. Von Meck, *As I*, 189.

44. Trifonov, *Likvidatsiia*, 395–96.

45. Fitzpatrick, *Tear Off*, 57.

14: SCHOOL OF LIFE

1. Mawdsley, *Civil War*, 399–400; Riasanovsky and Steinberg, *History*, 474–75; Raleigh, "Russian Civil War," 166–67; Ball, "Building," 168–72.

2. Riasanovsky and Steinberg, *History*, 474; Raleigh, "Russian Civil War," 147, 166.

3. Riasanovsky and Steinberg, *History*, 474–75; Lincoln, *Red Victory*, 390, 467–73, 489–511; Figes, *People's Tragedy*, 768; Raleigh, "Russian Civil War," 147–48, 161–62; Ball, "Building," 168, 171.

4. Ball, "Building," 168–71, 179, 181, 182; Riasanovsky and Steinberg, *History*, 474–76.

5. Duranty, *Duranty Reports*, 38, 41.

6. Hullinger, *Reforging*, 204–205.

7. Ibid., 205–208, 214–15.

8. Tolstoy, *I Worked*, 58, 62.

9. Almedingen, *Tomorrow*, 291–92.

10. KNG, 156–59; Fen, *Remember*, 265; Sollohub, *Russian Countess*, 188.

11. KNG, 147–50, 159.

12. ZVG, 4:86–87; *ZU*, 278–79.
13. NIOR RGB, 265.233.37, 710b–73.
14. RGADA, 1263.3.100, 105–1050b; 1263.3.90, 28.
15. ZVG, 4:87.
16. *ZU*, 266–67; Schmemann, *Echoes*, 10–12, 106, 199–204, 190–203, 248; G. N. Trubetskoi, *Gody*, 59–68.
17. RGADA, 1263.3.94, 21–26; 1263.3.100, 500b; 1263.3.103, 11–120b, 14–150b.
18. Golder, *War*, 299.
19. ZVG, 4:86–87; RGADA, 1263.3.104, 19–220b; *PG*, 433–34.
20. Pautenaude, *Big Show*, 197–99; Brooks, "Press," in *Russia*, ed. Fitzpatrick, 244–45.
21. Pautenaude, *Big Show*, 278–79; IDG, 103–28, 149–50.
22. *ZU*, 317–20; A. V. Trubetskoi, *Puti*, 6, 9; Smirnova, ". . . pod," 253–54.
23. *World Can End*, 317–18.
24. *ZU*, 237–38; RGADA, 1263.3.100, 116–170b; 1263.3.103, 7; 1263.3.104, 4–50b.
25. KNG, 150–51.
26. IDG, 101–102.
27. Reswick, *I Dreamt*, 36–38, 42, 160–61.
28. Fen, *Remember*, 255–59, 273–74.
29. Ibid., 290–92; Smith, *The Pearl*.
30. *ZU*, 358; Volkov, *Gorodu*, 404; Schmemann, *Echoes*, 252.
31. Hullinger, *Reforging*, 321–23.
32. RGADA, 1263.3.104, 19–220b.
33. Pautenaude, *Big Show*, 51–52, 278–79, 302–11; Brovkin, *Russia*, 147–49; Reswick, *I Dreamt*, 113–14; Hullinger, *Reforging*, 319–28.
34. *ZU*, 320; *PG*, 430; IDG, 101–102.
35. Leggett, *Cheka*, 291–92; Brooks, "Press," in *Russia*, ed. Fitzpatrick, 244–45; Hullinger, *Reforging*, 144–45.
36. Gorsuch, "Flappers and Foxtrotters," chap. 6 in *Youth*; Starr, *Red*, 90–93; Reswick, *I Dreamt*, 113–14.
37. RGADA, 1263.3.97, 10–17, 65–660b.
38. Ibid., 1263.3.106, 73–740b.

15: NOBLE REMAINS

1. ABM; *KhiG* 13 (2006): 124; *ZU*, 283.
2. *ZU*, 281–83.
3. Ibid., 282–83.
4. OGSh, 109–10.
5. *ZU*, 283.
6. YPS/V, 56.
7. AVT/V, 1:16.

8. *KhiG* 13 (2006): 127.

9. NIOR RGB, 265.233.37, 730b–760b.

10. ABM.

11. TAS, 421.

12. NIOR RGB, 265.233.37, 65–66, 78.

13. *KhiG* 9 (2002): 111; *KhiG* 11, pt. 1 (2004): 135–37.

14. *ZU*, 324; *PG*, 455–56.

15. *ZU*, 281–88; NIOR RGB, 265.233.37, 74–760b.

16. *ZU*, 287–88.

17. YPS/V, 56; ZVG, 2:90.

18. ZVG, 2:91.

19. Ibid., 2:91–92.

20. Ibid., 2:90; *KhiG* 13 (2006): 125–26, 129.

21. ZVG, 2: 91, 93.

22. *KhiG* 1 (1996): 145–46; Muratov, *Rod*, 126; RGADA, 1263.3.104, 19–220b.

23. *ZU*, 241; ZVG, 2:89; *OPR*, 421; Raevskii, *Piat' vekov*, 272; Sofia Golitsyn, undated letter, Golitsyn Family Papers, box 1, folder 1, HIA.

24. NIOR RGB, 265.233. 37, 760b–770b; *KhiG* 13 (2006): 129–30; *ZU*, 307–13.

25. *ZU*, 225–26, 257, 305; *KhiG* 10, pt. 1 (2003): 74–75; AVT/V, 1:6–8.

26. *ZU*, 56–57, 315–17, 347; Smirnova, "... *pod*."

27. *ZU*, 317–20; Fusso, *Russian Prince*, xiii–xiv; A. V. Trubetskoi, *Puti*, 6, 9; AVT/V, 1:8–9; Smirnova, "... *pod*," 245, 253–54; Varlamov, *Prishvin*.

28. Muratov, *Rod*, 124–52; *KhiG* 13 (2006): 128, 130–31; I. V. Golitsyn, "Otets," 89; *OPR*, 421; *ZU*, 342–43, 380–81, 410–11. Trubetskoy's stories have been translated in Fusso, *Russian Prince*.

29. *ZU*, 295–96.

30. Raevskii, *Piat' vekov*, 321–22; *ZU*, 306.

31. ZVG, 4:80.

32. Ibid., 3:89–91; MVG/M, 68. Peter the Great gave the village of Pebalg to Boris Sheremetev, Nikolai's great-great-great-great grandfather, in 1711 for his services in the Great Northern War.

33. Fen, *Remember*, 239–49.

34. Kimerling, "Civil Rights"; Alexopoulos, *Stalin's Outcasts*, 1–6, 97; Pethybridge, *Social Prelude*, 197–99; Fitzpatrick, *Tear Off*, 30–34; idem, *Everyday*, 11; Dobkin, "Lishentsy"; Brovkin, *Russia*, 31–32; Osokina, *Our Daily Bread*, 80.

35. Fitzpatrick, *Tear Off*, 34, 43–45, 50, 54, 59–60; Smirnova, *Byvshie liudi*, 46–48.

36. Sevost'ianov, ed., "*Sovershenno sekretno*," vol. 1, pt. 1, 94–95, 125–26, 195–96.

37. Von Meck, *As I*, 412.

38. Rendle, "Family, Kinship," 14.

39. Solzhenitsyn, *Gulag*, 2:53; Brovkin, *Russia*, 11–13, 16–17, 30–36, 219–22, 198–99; Chuikina, *Dvorianskaia pamiat'*, 46–51; Raleigh, "Russian Civil War," 154; Shearer, *Policing*, 259–60.

40. Brovkin, *Russia*, 184.

41. *KhiG* 13 (2006): 109.

16: THE FOX-TROT AFFAIR

1. Brovkin, *Russia*, 2, 213–15.
2. Smirnova, *Byvshie liudi*, 71, 147, 153–54; Fitzpatrick, *Tear Off*, 36.
3. Andrew and Gordievsky, *KGB*, 85, 94, 97–106; Andrew and Mitrokhin, *Sword*, 33, 34–35, 42; Perry and Pleshakov, *Flight*, 280–92, 296; and, with caution, Nikulin, *Mertvaia zyb'*.
4. *PG*, 64–66, 423–24; KNG, 162–75; *OPR*, 69–71.
5. Troyat, *Gorky*, 62, 65, 76, 100; Dolzhanskaia and Osipova, *"Dorogaia Ekaterina,"* 21–30; *OPR*, 5–6; Mering, "Politicheskii krasnyi krest."
6. Dolzhanskaia and Osipova, *"Dorogaia Ekaterina,"* 30–47; *OPR*, 7.
7. *ZU*, 327–28.
8. *OPR*, 71.
9. *ZU*, 337–38. Uncle Misha was Mikhail Lopukhin, the brother of Sergei's mother, executed by the Bolsheviks.
10. Ibid., 329.
11. KNG, 221–22.
12. Von Meck, *As I*, 245–51.
13. TAS, 423.
14. *ZU*, 330; RGADA, 1287.1.3304, 1–20b; Kovaleva, *Staraia Moskva*, 139–40; S. D. Sheremetev, *Vozdvizhenskii naugol'nyi dom*.
15. YPS/V, 9; ABM; *ZU*, 354–55; Krasko, *Tri veka*, 392; *KhiG* 13 (2006): 126.
16. *SH*, 2:169.
17. *ZU*, 329; MVG/M, 68–69; Elagin, *Ukroshchenie*, 52–53; Kaufman, *Pervaia Turandot*, 35, 309–10.
18. *ZU*, 325–26; ABM; SVS, 20; *OPR*, 23, 405–406, 480–81; *KhiG* 7 (2000): 294–95.
19. KNG, 210–11, 214–16; AVT/V, 1:11–12; Kireev, *Dnevnik*, 406.
20. KNG, 215–16, 243–53; *PG*, 68–70.
21. M. Osorgin, *Zametki*, 617.
22. O. Volkov, *Gorodu*, 404; Schmemann, *Echoes*, 250–53. On mousetraps, Lincoln, *War's Dark Shadow*, 203; Sollohub, *Russian Countess*, 148; *OPR*, 34.
23. *ZU*, 359–60; Schmemann, *Echoes*, 254–58.
24. *ZU*, 365–70; V. M. Golitsyn, "Vyderzhki," 34.
25. *ZU*, 370.
26. Ibid., 371; V. M. Golitsyn, Notes to "Vyderzhki," 35, 36; *PG*, 435–37.
27. *ZU*, 361–62, 371.
28. *PG*, 435–37; *ZU*, 387–88; V. M. Golitsyn, Notes to "Vyderzhki," 48; *OPR*, 241.
29. ZVG, 3:90.
30. *ZU*, 394.
31. KNG, 276.

17: VIRTUE IN RAGS

1. Letter of Alexandra Sipyagin, February 16, 1921, private collection.
2. RGALI, 195.1.5018a, 1.
3. Kiriushina, "Stranitsy," 185.
4. RGALI, 195.1.4983, 1–100.
5. NIOR RGB, 265.233.37, 73–760b.
6. ABM; *SH*, 2:145.
7. *SH*, 2:145; OR RNB, 585. 4614, 40b; ABM.
8. OGSh, 104. Sofia Vasilevna is not identified.
9. ABM.
10. Wassiltschikow, *Verschwundenes Russland*, 203–204; ABM; Karnishina, "Vozvrashchaias," 29.
11. ABM.
12. Ibid.
13. Ibid.; OR RNB, 585.4614.
14. Alekseeva, "Velikii terpelivets," 26; ABM; *SVS*, 245.
15. ZVG, 5:83; Shumikhin, "Konets."
16. Kovaleva, *Staraia Moskva*, 3. My thanks to Mariana Markova for helping with this translation.
17. Koval', *Kniaz' Vasilii*, 231–32.
18. *Moscow Memoirs*, 197.
19. Koval,' *Kniaz' Vasilii*, 231–32.
20. Ibid., 175, 226–72.
21. *OPR*, 71; *ZU*, 398–99.
22. *KhiG* 5 (1998): 114–16; *KhiG* 1 (1996): 150–52; Osokina, *Our Daily Bread*, 72–74.
23. Notes to "Vyderzhki," 40; letter from M. V. Golitsyn to A. V. Golitsyn, Moscow, December 1, 1925, Golitsyn family papers, box 1, folder 2, HIA; *ZU*, 375; ZVG, 4:78.
24. *ZU*, 347; Smirnova, *Byvshie liudi*, 265.
25. Smirnova, *Byvshie liudi*, 184.
26. *ZU*, 354.
27. Ibid., 419–20, 434, 437–49.
28. Ibid., 413.
29. ABM; *OPR*, 23.
30. TAS, 423–24, 454; ABM.
31. ABM.
32. TAS, 453; ABM.

18: THE GREAT BREAK

1. Riasanovsky and Steinberg, *History*, 476–85; Ball, "Building," 184–88; Gladkov, *Cement*, 246–47, 275–76.
2. Brovkin, *Russia*, 219–22; Khlevniuk, *Master*, 1–38; Ball, "Building," 188–91.

3. Riasanovsky and Steinberg, *History*, 484–94; Shearer, "Stalinism," 192–99; Fitzpatrick, *Everyday*, 2, 41–42, 54–57; Viola, *Unknown Gulag*; Werth, *Cannibal Island*; Khlevniuk, *History*, 9, 57, 107, 237; Applebaum, *Gulag*, 4.

4. Fitzpatrick, *Tear Off*, 38–40, 47, 47n34; idem, *Everyday*, 5–12, 19.

5. Smirnova, *Byvshie liudi*, 71, 190.

6. Ivanov, "Byvshie liudi," 71–72; Smirnova, *Byvshie liudi*, 192, 269; Fitzpatrick, *Tear Off*, 49; *Komsomol'skaia Pravda*, no. 266, September 26, 1931, 2; no. 62, March 16, 1933, 1.

7. Smirnova, *Byvshie liudi*, 72, 234–35; *OPR*, 10; Khlevniuk, *History*, 55; Shearer, *Policing*, 57–58, 188, 243, 253.

8. Lyons, *Assignment*, 174–76.

9. *Duranty Reports*, 209–11.

10. Channon, "Tsarist Landowners"; *Komsomol'skaia Pravda*, no. 1, May 24, 1925, 3; no. 13, June 10, 3; no. 14, June 11, 2; no. 24, June 23, 2; Chuikina, *Dvorianskaia pamiat'*, 33–34.

11. Tolstoy, *I Worked*; Croskey, *Legacy*; *OPR*, 153; *Dektrety*, 8:12, 16:70.

19: THE DEATH OF PARNASSUS

1. OGSh, 121–22.

2. ABM; Krasko, *Tri veka*, 380.

3. GARF, 2307.10.218, 31; ABM; Kiriushina, "Stranitsy," 190–93; Krasko, *Tri veka*, 379; *SH*, 2:147.

4. *Komsomol'skaia pravda*, no. 58, March 10, 1929, 1.

5. ABM; *SH*, 2:147; Kiriushina, "Stranitsy," 194.

6. Shumikhin, "Konets."

7. Krasko, *Tri veka*, 380; ABM; Kiriushina, "Stranitsy," 198–201; RGALI, 612.1.2853, 190–92.

8. Krasko, *Tri veka*, 298–332; Mishkevich, *Doktor*, chap. 8.

9. TsGAMO, 66.11.7906, 2.

10. KNA, 29, 1–7; 34; 47, 9; 129; TsGAMO, 66.1.7906, 1–6; 2157.1.522, 15, 93, 94, 99; 4341.1.259, 159–590b; *SVS*, 397.

11. *Okhrana i restavratsiia*, 24; "Russkaia usad'ba," 145, 155; Poliakova, "Usadebnaia kul'tura," 119.

12. Shumikhin, "Konets."

13. Alekseeva, "Velikii terpelivets," 26–27.

14. Hughes, *Sophia*, 242–59.

15. ABM; author interview with Yevdokia Sheremeteva, March 14, 2009.

16. *SH*, 2:147; Krasko, *Tri veka*, 380.

17. ABM; NIOR RGB, 369.367.19, 1–6; 369.367.20, 1–3; 369.367.21, 1–2; 369.224.59, 1–9; 667.7.14, 1–10b, 41–410b; 667.4.5, 40; 369.328.5, 1; Smith, *The Pearl*; Krasko, *Tri veka*, 380.

18. *SVS*, 353; MVG/M, 65; Alekseeva, "Velikii terpelivets," 27.

19. OGSh, 130–31; *SH*, 3:382.
20. *SVS*, 347–52; *SH*, 2:152; RGALI, 195.1.6552a, 6.

20: OUTCASTS

1. *ZU*, 459–63.
2. Ibid., 451–56; *PG*, 423–25; *OPR*, 71; *KhiG* 11, pt. 1 (2004): 138. Not all sources agree on the date of his firing.
3. *ZU*, 390, 459–65, 507.
4. Ibid., 498–501.
5. Ibid., 511–19.
6. Ibid., 470–94; *OPR*, 401.
7. *ZU*, 520–29; Raevskii, *Piat' vekov*, 388.
8. AVT/V, 1:21–22.
9. *Komsomol'skaia pravda*, no. 111, May 15, 1928, 4; Smirnova, ". . . *pod*," 73, 254; Prishvin, *Dnevniki, 1936–37*, 565.
10. *Komsomol'skaia pravda*, no. 113, May 17, 1928, 6. Uppercase letters as in the original.
11. Smirnova, ". . . *pod*," 73–75, 142–43, 180–87; *ZU*, 578–79.
12. Smirnova, ". . . *pod*," 247–49, 258–59; *ZU*, 558; letter of January 19, 1933, Golitsyn Family Papers, box 1, HIA; Rowan-Hamilton, *Under*, 63; Osokina, *Our Daily*, 123–24; idem, *Zoloto*; Fitzpatrick, *Everyday*, 57–58.
13. Smirnova, ". . . *pod*," 258–59; AVT/V, 1:120, 122n.6.
14. AVT/V, 1:52.
15. Prishvin, *Dnevniki, 1930–31*, 68, 71.
16. Varlamov, *Prishvin*, 307, and photo caption between pp. 192–93.
17. AVT/V, 1:13–14, 16, 22–23.
18. *ZU*, 529–39; Schmemann, *Echoes*, 258–66; Likachev, *Vospominaniia*, 153, 200, 262–63; Solzhenitsyn, *Gulag*, 2:44–45; TAS, 480–81; *OPR*, 302.
19. *ZU*, 531–32, 599; Kuz'mina, *Kniaz' Shakhovskoi*, 273, 313, 331–32; *KhiG* 5 (1999): 104–106.

21: THE MOUSE, THE KEROSENE, AND THE MATCH

1. See the articles by N. Fedorov in *BP*, 2:32–42; 8:219–60; 4:12–21. Shalamov, *Vishera*, 37.
2. Khlevniuk, *History*, 102, 114–16.
3. *BP*, 2:32–42; 7:45–52.
4. Von Meck, *As I*, 398–404.
5. Solzhenitsyn, *Gulag*, 2:293–303.
6. ZVG, 3:99; MVG/M, 106.
7. ZVG, 5:84; MVG/M, 105, 110.
8. ZVG, 3:99; MVG/M, 184; *OPR*, 406; ABM.

9. *BP*, 7:53–59.
10. *PG*, 396; *ZU*, 659–60; MVG/M, 24; VMG/D, 355–56.
11. MVG/M, 129, 134; *KhiG* 4, pt. 1 (1997): 97–98; *KhiG* 1 (1996): 147; letter, June 4, 1939, in Golitsyn Family Papers, box 1, HIA.
12. AVG/M: I. M. Barnes epilogue, 67, and M. Dakserhoff and I. M. Barnes, "Natasha Goes to Hollywood"; *PG*, 451–55; Muratov, *Rod*, 87; obituaries for Alexander Golitzen: *Guardian*, August 22, 2005, *New York Times*, August 20, 2005.
13. MVG/M, 87, 138–42.
14. Ibid., 69–72; Kaufman, *Pervaia Turandot*, 115, 219–20, 393; Elagin, *Ukroshchenie*, 48–54, 157, 175, 182; *DS* 2 (1995): 273; ABM; Krasko, *Tri veka*, 394.
15. *KhiG* 11, pt. 1 (2004): 138–39; *KhiG* 1 (1996): 152–53; *ZU*, 689–91; AVT/V, 1:42–43; Taylor, *Stalin's Apologist*, 177–79; ZVG, 3:96; Khlevniuk, *History*, 37–39. On the Urusovs, see Urusova, *Materinskii plach*.
16. AVT/V, 1:40–41.
17. Ashnin, *Delo*; AVT/V, 1:32–43.
18. AVT/V, 2:1–2, 4–9, 11; V. S. Trubetskoi, "Pis'ma."
19. AVT/V, 2:1–5, 16–25, 39–40; V. S. Trubetskoi, "Pis'ma"; Fusso, *Russian Prince*, xv–xviii, 107–43. Prishvin, *Dnevniki, 1938–39*, 264.
20. MVG/M, 112.
21. *ZU*, 683–94, 734–35; *KhiG* 1 (1996): 148–49; letter, March 1934, Golitsyn Family Papers, box 1, HIA; Fusso, *Russian Prince*, 110.
22. *ZU*, 665–66, 687–88; *KhiG* 5 (1998): 107–109.
23. *ZU*, 709–11; MVG/M, 92; ZVG, 5:86.
24. ZVG, 5:79.
25. MVG/M, 111–12.
26. I. V. Golitsyn, "Otets," 89.
27. *ZU*, 712–13; ZVG, 5:83–84; *KhiG* 1 (1996): 153–54.
28. ZVG, 5:79.

22: ANNA'S FORTUNE

1. *KHiG* 7 (2000): 294; *OPR*, 23; ABM.
2. *KHiG* 7 (2000): 294–95.
3. *OPR*, 23; NIOR RGB, 369.328.4, 19–200b; ABM.
4. *OPR*, 23, 405–06; ABM.
5. *SH*, 2:152.
6. NIOR RGB, 667.6.4, 1–7; 667.5.1, 1–7b ob; 667.4.2, 3. The dates of the letters contradict on the precise chronology of their arrests and banishment. I have tried to reconstruct as best as possible the likeliest order of events.
7. NIOR RGB, 667.5.1, 19.
8. Ibid., 667.4.1, 1, 11, 13.
9. Ibid., 667.6.4, 10–110b.
10. Ibid., 667.5.3, 7–180b.

11. Ibid., 667.5.3, 68–680b.

12. Ibid., 667.5.3, 24–29.

13. Ibid., 667.5.3, 63–680b.

14. Ibid., 667.6.9, 22–270b.

15. Ibid., 667.4.3, 1–130b.

16. Ibid., 667.4.2, 29–380b.

17. Ibid., 667.5.3, 610b.

18. Ibid., 667.5.3, 26–350b.

19. Ibid., 38–430b.

20. Ibid., 49–62.

21. Ibid,, 667.4.2, 2, 6, 10, 25; 667.6.9, 1; 369.328.4, 3–50b; *KhiG* 7 (2000): 295–96.

22. ABM; Iudin, *Zamok*, 59–60; NIOR RGB, 667.6.14, 58–580b; 667.7.3; *KhiG* 7 (2000): 296–97; "Dukhom ne ugasavhie," *Rossiiskie vesti* (July 19–26). Accessed online, April 22, 2011.

23. ABM; NIOR RGB, 667.5.4, 27–280b; 667.6.9, 7–10; 667.6.10, 1–2; 667.5.5, 48, 71–730b, 84–870b, 118–180b; 667.6.4, 17.

24. TAS, 502; NIOR RGB, 667.7.14.

25. *KhiG* 7 (2000): 297; NIOR RGB, 667.5.6, 3; 667.6.4, l. 20; Kosik, *Molitva*, 1–24; *OPR*, 481. Sources disagree on when the Saburovs were sent from Ivanovo, though those, chiefly Boris's letters, dating it to September seem the most reliable.

26. NIOR RGB, 667.6.1, 3–40b; ABM; *OPR*, 481.

27. NIOR RGB, 667.5.6, 4–50b.

28. Ibid., 667.6.4, 43–440b.

29. *KhiG* 7 (2000), 297–98; NIOR RGB, 667.6.13, l. 32–320b; 667.4.6, 41.

30. NIOR RGB, 667.5.6, 34–620b; 667.7.10, 1; ABM.

31. NIOR RGB, 667.7.9, 1–20b.

32. Ibid., 667.5.7, 4–440b; 667.5.8, 1–17; *OPR*, 481; *KhiG* 7 (2000): 298–99.

33. Ibid., 667.6.9, 13–160b.

34. Ibid., 667.4.4, 5–60b.

35. Ibid., 19–260b.

36. Kosik, *Molitva*, 274n61.

37. ABM; NIOR RGB, 667.6.13, 49–500b; 667.6.17, 37–370b; *KhiG* 7 (2000): 298–99.

38. NIOR RGB, 667.6.13, 1–80b.

39. Ibid., 13–220b, 270b; 667.6.5, 1–50b; ABM.

40. Ibid., 667.6.12, 1.

41. Ibid., 667.6.13, 21–270b; 667.7.1, 69–690b.

42. Ibid., 667.4.4, 28–290b, 31–360b; 667.6.5, 110b–13.

43. Ibid., 667.6.13, 25–270b, 30–320b, 36–39, 49–500b.

23: HAPPY TIMES

1. Fitzpatrick, *Everyday*, 90; *Komsomol'skaia pravda*, no. 191, August 28, 1935, 4.

2. Fitzpatrick, *Everyday*, 6–7, 93–95; Kamenskii, *Deviatyi vek*, 177–78.

3. Fitzpatrick, *Everyday*, 130–32; idem, *Tear Off*, 40–42; Smirnova, *Byvshie liudi*, 10, 230–37, 267; Chuikina, *Dvorianskaia pamiat'*, 56–58; Alexopoulos, *Stalin's Outcasts*, 181–82; Stalin, *Doklad*, 10.

4. Paley, *Memories*, 195–96, 253–55; Fen, *Remember*, 290–93; Fitzpatrick, *Everyday*, 95–106; Service, *Spies*, 331–32.

5. Ciliberti, *Backstairs*, 44–45, 110, 116; Tzouliadis, *Forsaken*, 142; e-mail communication from Ruzica Popovitch-Krekic, June 4, 2008.

6. KNG, 360–65; Sebag Montefiore, *Court*, 64–66; ZU, 12, 66–67; Volkogonov, *Trotsky*, 213–14.

7. Fitzpatrick, *Everyday*, 105.

8. Rowan-Hamilton, *Under*, 53–44.

9. OGSh, 132–34.

10. Abbe, *I Photograph*, 182–83, 222–33; Tzouliadis, *Forsaken*, 53–54; Iudin, *Zamok*, 60; Kovaleva, *Staraia Moskva*, 76–81, 89–90.

11. OGSh, 122; ABM.

12. OGSh, 109–10.

13. Tolstoy, *I Worked*, 102–103.

14. Iudin, *Zamok*, 208.

15. P. A. Obolensky, "Semeinye zapiski," 176: 186; Shcherbatov, *Pravo*, 40–41.

16. Merridale, *Night*, 173–75.

17. Ignat'ev, *50 let*, 736–38; Ignatieff, *Russian Album*, 17, 80, 97, 145–46, 178; *Bol'shaia sovetskaia entsiklopediia*, s.v. "Ignat'ev, A. A."

18. Muggeridge, *Winter*, 219; idem, *Like It Was*, 24, 50–52, 65, 69, 273; G. Smith, *D. S. Mirsky: A Russian*, xiii, 18–19, 209–10, 224–27, 291–92, 316–18.

19. Terras, *Handbook*, s.v. "Tolstoi, A. N."; Lyons, *Assignment*, 587; Elagin, *Ukroshchenie*, 140 44, 175. On other noble returnees, see Dubinets, *Kniaz'*, Zinovieff, *Red Princess*.

24: POISONOUS SNAKES AND THE AVENGING SWORD: OPERATION FORMER PEOPLE

1. ZVG, 4:87.

2. The most accurate investigation of the killing is Lenoe, *Kirov*.

3. Khlevniuk, *History*, 88; Boterbloem, *Life*, 126–27.

4. Shearer, *Policing*, 215–18.

5. OPR, 298.

6. Ivanov, "Operatsiia," 118; idem, "Bvyshie liudi," 72.

7. Rimmel, "Microcosm," 533.

8. Ivanov, "Byvshie liudi," 71.

9. *Leningradskaia pravda*, no. 33, February 8, 1935, 2; no. 45, February 22, 1935.

10. See Rimmel, "Microcosm," 540–49; Alexopoulos, *Stalin's Outcasts*, 180–81; Sarah Davies, "'Us Against Them': Social Identity in Soviet Russia, 1934–41," in *Stalinism*, ed. Fitzpatrick, 51, 65.

11. Ivanov, "Operatsiia," 121, 126–27; Rimmel, "Microcosm," 530, 534; Boterbloem, *Life*, 126–27.

12. Quoted in Rimmel, "Microcosm," 547–48n.138.

13. *Leningradskaia pravda*, no. 45, February 22, 1935, 3–4; no. 47, February 24, 3; no. 48, February 26, 3; no. 51, March 1, 3; no. 57, March 9, 1935, 3; *Smena*, no. 67, March 22, 2; no. 70, March 26, 3.

14. *Smena*, no. 70, March 26, 1935, 3.

15. *Leningradskaia pravda*, no. 57, March 9, 3; *Smena*, no. 67, March 22, 2; no. 70, March 26, 3.

16. *Leningradskaia pravda*, no. 68, March 22, 1935, 2; no. 69, March 23, 2; no. 70, March 24, 2.

17. *ZU*, 698–99.

18. OGSh, 140–43.

19. TAS, 511–13, 533–41.

20. Ivanov, "Operatsiia," 122–29; idem, "Byvshie liudi," 72–73; Livshin, *Pis'ma*, 261.

21. *Vospominaniia*, 291–92, 299–301.

22. *OPR*, 311, 321–23, 326, 329; Ivanov, "Operatsiia," 129.

23. *PG*, 61–62; *OPR*, 402; Khlevniuk, *History*, 97–98.

24. TAS, 543–45, 563–68, 577, 617–18.

25. Khlevniuk, *History*, 88; Ivanov, "Operatsiia," 118–19, 126–27; idem, "Byvshie liudi," 72.

26. Chuikina, *Dvorianskaia pamiat'*, 172.

27. *Komsomol'skaia pravda*, no. 172, July 28, 1935, 5.

25: THE GREAT TERROR

1. See Khlevniuk, *Master*, intro. and chap. 5; Getty and Naumov, *Road*; Jansen and Petrov, *Stalin's Loyal Executioner*; and McLoughlin and McDermott, *Stalin's Terror*.

2. Jansen and Petrov, *Stalin's Loyal Executioner*, 195.

3. Khlevniuk, *Master*, 194; Getty and Naumov, *Yezhov*.

4. Shearer, "Stalinism," 212–14; Jansen and Petrov, *Stalin's Loyal Executioner*, 139–91; Khlevniuk, *Master*, 180–201.

5. Khlevniuk, *History*, 165–66. Getty and Naumov, *Road*, 591.

6. Urusova, *Materinskii plach*, 351–59, 419–34; *PG*, 66–68; Muratov, *Rod*, 98–99; *KhiG* 11, pt. 1 (2004): 134–35.

7. Khaustov et al., *Stalin*, 332–35.

8. *1936–37gg. Konveier*, 24, 164–66, 269–72, 282–89, 335–36, 341n.1, 401–402.

9. *KHiG* 11, pt. 1 (2004): 134–35, 142; *PG*, 66–67; Muratov, *Rod*, 99; Urusova, *Materinskii plach*.

10. V. S. Trubetskoi, "Pis'ma," 18–20.

11. Fusso, *Russian Prince*, 136–37.

12. A. V. Trubetskoi, *Puti*, 6, 9; AVT/V, 2:40–41.

13. "Sudebnoe delo sem'i Vladimira Sergeevicha Trubetskogo," Golitsyn Family Papers, box 3, pt. 2:19, HIA. [Hereafter cited as "Sudebnoe delo."]
14. Ibid., box 3, pt. 3:3.
15. AVT/V, 2:42–50.
16. "Sudebnoe delo," box 3, pt. 3:14–15; *OPR*, 316, 318, 352.
17. AVT/V, 2:49.
18. "Sudebnoe delo," box 3, pt. 2:1–4; pt. 3:21–23; Fusso, *Russian Prince*, xv.
19. AVT/V, 2:49, 59–64; idem, *Puti*, 6, 9; V. S. Trubetskoi, "Pis'ma"; Fusso, *Russian Prince*, xiv.
20. *ZU*, 740–43.
21. *BP*, 2:40; 4:13–14; 7:51.
22. *OPR*, 23n.2; *SH*, 2:152.
23. *BP*, 3:123; 7:302.
24. NIOR RGB, 667.7.14, 20–21.
25. Ibid., 57–58; 667.4.5, 71–72ob.
26. ABM; *OPR*, 23; e-mail communications with Varvara Pavlinova, November 23–25, 2009; NIOR RGB, 667.4.6, 170b, 22–23.

26: WAR: THE END

1. MVG/M, 93–94, 178, 182–83; *PG*, 82–91.
2. Barber and Harrison, "Patriotic War;" Riasanovsky and Steinberg, *History*, 508–19.
3. Khlevniuk, *History*, 237.
4. KNG, 257–77, 375, 381.
5. *PG*, 58–59, 73–74, 399; *OPR*, 152.
6. MVG/M, 95–96; I. V. Golitsyn, "Otets," 2:89.
7. NIOR RGB, 667.7.14, 63–65ob; 667.7.15, 1–2ob; 667.4.7, 35, 36; 667.6.17, 62ob; *SH*, 2:160; Alekseeva, "Velikii terpelivets," 27–28; ABM; MVG/M, 65.
8. NIOR RGB, 667.4.7, 21–22ob.
9. OGSh, 9, 12–13; TAS, 614–15, 681.
10. MVG/M, 66–68, 72–76, 86; Kaufmann, *Pervaia Turandot*, 246; ABM; *SH*, 2:162.
11. ABM; MVG/M, 132; Krasko, *Tri veka*, 497; *SH*, 2:152; NIOR RGB, 667.4.5, 25–28ob, 33; 667.6.15, 8–9, 16–19ob.
12. NIOR RGB, 667.4.6, 9–11; 667.4.7, 1–7.
13. Ibid., 667.7.4; 667.6.14, 1–2ob, 37.
14. Ibid., 667.4.4, 1–4ob; 667.4.5, 1–4ob; 667.7.3; 667.4.6, 32–41ob; 667.6.8.
15. ABM; *KhiG* 7 (2000): 299–300; NIOR RGB, 667.6.15, 1–7ob.
16. NIOR RGB, 667.4.5, 71–72ob; 667.6.17, 1.
17. Ibid., 667.4.7, 25–25ob.
18. Ibid., 667.4.8, 6, 23–23ob; 667.7.1, 32–32ob; 667.7.14, 79–80; 369.328.5, 1; e-mail communication with Varvara Pavlinova, November 22, 2009.
19. ABM; Alekseeva, "Velikii terpelivets," 28.

20. Lincoln, *Red Victory*, 188–91.

21. Muratov, *Rod*, 128; MVG/M, 99.

22. MVG/M, 65–66, 97–98; *SH*, 2:168; *KhiG* 4, pt. 1, (1997), 100–103; 13 (2006), 130–31.

23. *KhiG* 3 (1996): 157–64; 4 (1999): 302–309; MVG/M, 44.

24. Applebaum, *Gulag*, 374–76.

25. *SVS*, 374–75; MVG/M, 99–100; *PG*, 88.

26. MVG/M, 100.

27. Ibid., 101; Smirnova, ". . . *pod*," 22; *SH*, 2:168.

28. Fusso, *Russian Prince*, xv; "Sudebnoe delo," box 3, 2:1–4; Smirnova, ". . . *pod*," 263–64; A. V. Trubetskoi, *Puti*, 6–9, 191.

29. NIOR RGB, 667.4.8, 5–60b; 44–440b, 53.

30. Ibid., 667.7.1, 25–250b.

31. Ibid., 667.7.1, 32–320b, 39–390b, 48–590b, 77; 667.7.4.

32. Ibid., 667.4.9, 1–80b, 19–320b; ABM.

33. Iudin, *Zamok*, 58–59.

34. ABM; *SH*, 2:150.

35. ABM; Kovaleva, *Staraia Moskva*, 18–19; MVG/M, 65; "V. P. Sheremetev v Ostaf'eve."

36. *SH*, 2:157; Ignatieff, *Russian Album*, 178; author interview with Nikita Chereme-teff, March 8, 2009; e-mail communication with Kyra Cheremeteff, May 17, 2011; Andreyev, *Vlasov*; Fischer, *Soviet Opposition*.

37. ABM; A. V. Trubetskoi, *Puti*, 6–7; Smirnova, ". . . *pod*," 263–66.

38. *SVS*, 21–22, 353–56; *SH*, 2:160; ABM; author interview with Yevdokia Sheremetev, Moscow, March 14, 2009.

EPILOGUE

1. MVG/M, 101–102.

2. Khlevniuk, *History*, 328. For a discussion of the possible numbers killed in the gulag and the impossibility of ever knowing the full truth, see Applebaum, *Gulag*, 515–22. Applebaum "reluctantly" cites one low estimate of those who died in the gulag and special settlements of 2,749,163 for the years 1929–53.

BIBLIOGRAPHY

MANUSCRIPT SOURCES

Chippenham, United Kingdom
Wiltshire and Swindon History Centre

Moscow
Central State Archive of the Moscow Oblast
Kuskovo Scientific Archive
Russian State Archive of Ancient Acts
Russian State Archive of Literature and Art
Russian State Library, Scientific Research Division of Manuscripts
State Archive of the Russian Federation

New York
Bakhmeteff Archive of Russian and East European Culture, Columbia University

St. Petersburg
Russian National Library, Manuscript Division
Russian State Historical Archive

Stanford
Hoover Institution Archive, Stanford University

Personal Collections and Unpublished Sources
Anonymous [Dorothy F.]. "An Appreciation of Ekaterina Galitzine (née Countess Carlowa)." Private collection.

Archive of Father Boris Mikhailov

Carlow, Countess Maria (Merika) von. "Memoirs." Translated by Liza Heseltine. Private collection.

Galitzine, V. E. "Diary (1915–1919)." Private collection.

———. "My Memoirs." Private collection.

Golitsyn, A. V. "Memoirs, with Four Appendices." Private collection.

Golitsyn, V. M. "Vyderzhki iz vospominanii." Private collection.

Golitsyn, V. V. "Letter (undated)." Private collection.

Pisareva, E. P. "Dnevnik (1919–1920)." Private collection.

Shcherbatova, E. P. "Dnevnik." Private collection.

Sheremeteva, E. P. "Vospominaniia detstva." Private collection.

Tatistcheff, Alexis Borisovich. "Crossing the Field. An Autobiography." Private collection.

Trubetskoi, A. V. "Vospominaniia." 2 parts. Private collection.

Trubetskoi, V. S. "Pis'ma ottsa iz Andizhana. 1934–1937 g." Private collection.

Wolkonsky, Marina. "The Diary of a Russian Princess." Private collection.

Yusupov, Zenaida Nikolaevna. "The Diary of Princess Zenaida Nikolaevna Yusupov, January 1–April 25, 1919." Translated by Christine H. Galitzine. Private collection.

NEWSPAPERS

Den'

The Guardian

Komsomol'skaia pravda

Krasnaia gazeta

Leningradskaia pravda

Moskovskie vedomosti

Pravda

Narodnoe slovo

The New York Times

Novoe vremia

Rossiiskie vesti

Smena (The Change)

Trud (Labor)

Utro Moskvy

Vecher

Vecherniaia pochta

Vechernie novosti

Zemlia i volia

PUBLISHED SOURCES

Abbe, James. *I Photograph Russia*. New York, 1934.

Acton, Edward, ed. *Critical Companion to the Russian Revolution, 1914–1921*. Bloomington, Ind., 1997.

Afanas'ev, Iurii, et al., eds. *Istoriia stalinskogo Gulaga: konets 1920-kh-pervaia polovina 1950-kh godov: sobranie dokumentov v semi tomakh*. 7 vols. Moscow, 2004–05.

Aksakova-Sivers, T. *Semeinaia khronika*. Moscow, 2006.

Akt rassledovaniia po delu ob areste i ubiistve zalozhnikov v Piatigorske v Oktiabre 1918 goda. Rostov-na-Donu, 1919.

Aleksandr Mikhailovich. *Once a Grand Duke*. Garden City, N.Y., 1932.

———. *Kniga vospominanii*. Moscow, 1991.

———. *Vospominaniia: dve knigi v odnom tome*. Moscow, 1999.

Aleksandrovskii, B. N. *Iz perezhitogo v chuzhikh kraiakh. Vospominaniia i dumy byvshego emigranta*. Moscow, 1969.

Alekseev, N. *Usad'ba Andreevskoe i eë vladel'tsy: v XVII–nachale XX vv*. Rybinsk, 2005.

Alekseeva, Adel'. *Ostavit' plamen' svoi: povesti i rasskazy*. Moscow, 1986.

———. "Velikii terpelivets." *Slovo*, 1991.

———, and M. D. Kovaleva, eds. *Sheremetevy v sud'be Rossii: vospominaniia, dnevniki, pis'ma*. Moscow, 2001.

Alexander, John T. *Emperor of the Cossacks*. Lawrence, Kan., 1973.

Alexandra, Empress. *The Last Diary of Tsaritsa Alexandra*, ed. V. M. Khrustalëv and V. A. Kozlov. Introd. Robert K. Massie. New Haven, 1997.

Alexopoulos, Golfo. *Stalin's Outcasts. Aliens, Citizens, and the Soviet State, 1926–1936*. Ithaca, N.Y., 2003.

Almedingen, E. *Tomorrow Will Come*. Boston, 1941.

Amfiteatrov-Kadashev, Vladimir. "Stranitsy iz dnevnika," ed. S. V. Shumikhin. *Minuvshee. Istorickeskii al'manakh* 20 (1996).

Andrew, Christopher M., and Oleg Gordievsky. *KGB: The Inside Story of Its Foreign Operations from Lenin to Gorbachev*. New York, 1990.

———, and Vasilii Mitrokhin. *The Sword and the Shield: The Mitrokhin Archive and the Secret History of the KGB*. New York, 1999.

Andreyev, Catherine. *Vlasov and the Russian Liberation Movement. Soviet Reality and Émigré Theories*. Cambridge, U.K., 1987.

Anichkov, V. *Ekaterinburg—Vladivostok (1917–1922)*. Moscow, 1998.

Applebaum, Anne. *Gulag. A History of the Camps*. London, 2003.

Ashnin, F. D., and V. M. Alpatov. *Delo slavistov, 30-e gody*. Moscow, 1994.

Babine, Alexis. *A Russian Civil War Diary: Alexis Babine in Saratov, 1917–1922*, ed. Donald J. Raleigh. Durham, N.C., 1988.

Baboreko, Aleksandr. *Bunin: zhizneopisanie*. Moscow, 2004.

Bakirov, E. A., ed. *Butovskii poligon, 1937–1938 gody: kniga pamiati zhertv politicheskikh repressii*. 8 vols. Moscow, 1997.

Ball, Alan. "Building a New State and Society: NEP, 1921–1928." In *The Cambridge History of Russia*. Vol. 3, ed. Ronald Grigor Suny. Cambridge, U.K., 2006.

Bannikov, A. P. *Russkie kollektsionery i ikh kollektsii*. Moscow, 2008.

Barber, John, and Mark Harrison. "Patriotic War, 1941–1945." In *The Cambridge History of Russia*. Vol. 3, ed. Ronald Grigor Suny. Cambridge, U.K., 2006.

Bariatinskii, Maria. *Moia russkaia zhizn': vospominaniia velikosvetskoi damy, 1870–1918*. Moscow, 2006.

Barinova, E. *Vlast' i pomestnoe dvorianstvo Rossii v nachale XX veka*. Samara, 2002.

———. *Rossiiskoe dvorianstvo v nachale XX veka: ekonomicheskii status i sotsiokul'turnyi oblik*. Moscow, 2008.

Barmine, Alexandre. *One Who Survived: The Life Story of a Russian Under the Soviets*. New York, 1945.

Bashkiroff, Z. *The Sickle and the Harvest*. London, 1960.

Becker, S. *Nobility and Privilege in Late Imperial Russia*. DeKalb, Ill., 1985.

———. "A Conservative Lobby: The United Nobility in 1905–1910." *Kritika* 5, no. 1 (2004).

Benckendorff, Pavel. *Last Days at Tsarskoe Selo: Being the Personal Notes and Memories of Count Paul Benckendorff*. London, 1927.

Berelowitch, Alexis. *Sovetskaia derevnia glazami VChK-OGPU-NKVD, 1918–1939: dokumenty i materialy v 4 tomakh*. Moscow, 1998.

Bertaux, D.; P. Thompson; and A. Rotkirch, eds. *On Living Through Soviet Russia*. London, 2004.

Bertaux., D. "Transmission in Extreme Situations: Russian Families Expropriated by the October Revolution." In *Pathways to Social Class: A Qualitative Approach to Social Mobility*, ed. D. Bertaux and P. Thompson. Oxford, U.K., 1997.

Bibin, M. A. *Dvorianstvo nakanune padeniia tsarizma v Rossii*. Saransk, 2000.

Billington, James. *The Icon and the Axe*. New York, 1966.

Bisher, Jamie. *White Terror: Cossack Warlords of the Trans-Siberian*. London, 2005.

Blok, A. "Poslednye dni starogo rezhima." *Byloe* 15 (1919).

Bogomolov, D. *Leningradskii martirolog: 1937–1938*. St. Petersburg, 1995.

Bol'shaia Sovetskaia entsiklopediia. 51 vols. Moscow, 1949–58.

Bol'shakov, A. M. *Sovetskaia derevnia za 1917–1924 gg*. Leningrad, 1924.

Boterbloem, Kees. *The Life and Times of Andrei Zhdanov, 1896–1948*. Montreal, 2004.

Brooks, Jeffrey. *Thank You, Comrade Stalin!: Soviet Public Culture from Revolution to Cold War*. Princeton, N.J., 2000.

Brovkin, Vladimir. *Behind the Front Lines of the Civil War: Political Parties and Social Movements in Russia, 1918–1922*. Princeton, N.J., 1994.

———. *Russia After Lenin: Politics, Culture and Society, 1921–1929*. London, 1998.

Browder, Robert, and Aleksandr Kerensky, eds. *The Russian Provisional Government, 1917: Documents*. 3 vols. Stanford, Calif., 1961.

Brown, Douglas. *Doomsday 1917: The Destruction of Russia's Ruling Class*. New York, 1976.

Brusilov, Aleksei. *Moi vospominaniia*. Moscow, 2001.

Buchanan, George. *My Mission to Russia and Other Diplomatic Memories*. Boston, 1923.

Buchanan, Meriel. *The City of Trouble*. New York, 1918.

———. *Recollections of Imperial Russia*. New York, 1924.

———. *The Dissolution of an Empire*. New York, 1971.

Buldakov, V. P. "Revoliutsiia, nasilie i arkhaizatsiia massovogo soznaniia v grazh-danskoi voine: provintsial'naia spetsifika." In *Al'manakh "Belaia gvardiia."* 6 *Antibol'shevitskoe povstancheskoe dvizhenie*. Moscow, 2002.

Bunin, Ivan. *Cursed Days: A Diary of Revolution*, tr. Thomas Gaiton Marullo. Chicago, 1998.

———. *Ivan Bunin: Collected Stories*, tr. Graham Hettlinger. Chicago, 2007.

Butenev, M. *Istoriia staroi russkoi dvorianskoi sem'i: khronika sem'i Butenevykh*. Moscow, 2002.

Butson, Thomas. *The Tsar's Lieutenant: The Soviet Marshal*. New York, 1984.

Cantacuzène, Julia. *Revolutionary Days. Recollections of Romanoffs and Bolsheviki, 1914–1917*. Boston, 1919.

Chaadaeva, O. *Pomeshchiki i ikh organizatsii v 1917 godu*. Moscow, 1928.

Chamberlin, William Henry. *The Russian Revolution*. 2 vols. New York, 1965.

Channon, John. "Tsarist Landowners After the Russian Revolution: Former *Pomeshchiki* in Rural Russia During NEP." *Soviet Studies* 39, no. 4 (October 1987).

Chekhov, Anton. *Chekhov. Four Plays*, tr. and with introduction Stephen Mulrine. London, 2005.

Chuikina, Sofia. *Dvorianskaia pamiat': "byvshie" v sovetskom gorode (Leningrad, 1920–30-e gody)*. St. Peterburg, 2006.

Ciliberti, Charles. *Backstairs Mission in Moscow*. New York, 1947.

Clarke, William. *The Lost Fortune of the Tsars*. New York, 1995.

Cockfield, Jamie. *White Crow: The Life and Times of the Grand Duke Nicholas Mikhailovich Romanov: 1859–1919*. Westport, Conn., 2002.

Coles, Amy, and Vera Urusova. *Letters of Life in an Aristocratic Russian Household Before and After the Revolution*, ed. Nicholas Tyrras. Lewiston, N.Y., 2000.

Croskey, Robert. *The Legacy of Tolstoy: Alexandra Tolstoy and the Soviet Regime in the 1920s*. Seattle, 2008.

Crowl, James. *Angels in Stalin's Paradise: Western Reporters in Soviet Russia, 1917 to 1937. A Case Study of Louis Fischer and Walter Duranty*. Washington, D.C., 1982.

Davydov, Aleksandr. *Russian Sketches: Memoirs*. Tenafly, N.J., 1984.

Dekrety sovetskoi vlasti. 18 vols. Moscow, 1957–2009.

Denikin, Anton. *Ocherki russkoi smuty*. 5 vols. Paris, Berlin: 1921–26.

Dobkin, A. "Lishentsy: 1918–1936." In *Zven'ia: istoricheskii al'manakh* 2 (1992).

Dolgorukov, Pavel. *Velikaia razrukha*. Madrid, 1964.

Dolzhanskaia, L., and I. Osipova. *Obracheny po rozhdeniiu—: po dokumentam fondov Politicheskogo Krasnogo Kresta, 1918–1922, Pomoshch' politzakliuchennym, 1922–1937*. St. Petersburg, 2004.

———. *"Dorogaia Ekaterina Pavlovna—": pis'ma zhenshchin i detei, pis'ma v ikh zashchitu, 1920–1936: po dokumentam fondov "Moskovskii politicheskii krasnyi krest", "E. P. Peshkova. Pomoshch' politicheskim zakliuchennym."* St. Petersburg, 2005.

Doyle, William. *Aristocracy and Its Enemies in the Age of Revolution*. New York, 2009.

Dubinets, Elena. *Kniaz' Andrei Volkonskii. Partitura zhizni*. Moscow, 2010.

Duranty, Walter. *Duranty Reports Russia*. New York, 1934.

———. *I Write as I Please*. New York, 1935.

———. *The Kremlin and the People*. New York, 1941.

———. *USSR: The Story of Soviet Russia,* Philadelphia, 1944.

Dvorianskoe sobranie. Nos. 1–10. Moscow, 1994–98.

Dzemeshkevich, P. *Dvorianstvo i revoliutsiia*. Sevastopol, 2004.

Edelman, Robert. *Gentry Politics on the Eve of the Russian Revolution: The Nationalist Party, 1907–1917*. New Brunswick, N.J., 1980.

Elagin, Iurii. *Ukroshchenie iskusstv*. New York, 1952.

Emmons, Terence. "The Beseda Circle, 1899–1905." *Slavic Review* 32, no. 3 (September 1973).

———. "The Russian Landed Gentry and Politics." *Russian Review* 33, no. 3 (July 1974).

———. "The Russian Nobility and Party Politics Before the Revolution." In *The Nobility in Russia and Eastern Europe*, ed. Ivo Banac and Paul Bushkovitch. New Haven, 1983.

Engel, B., and Posadskaya-Vanderbeck, eds. *A Revolution of Their Own: Voices of Women in Soviet History*. Boulder, Colo., 1998.

Entsiklopedicheskii slovar' Brokgauz-Efron. 82 vols. St. Petersburg, 1890.

Falkus, M. E., *The Industrialization of Russia, 1700–1914*. London, 1972.

Fedorchenko, V. *Dvorianskie rody, proslavishie Otechestvo: entsiklopediia dvorianskikh rodov*. Krasnoiarsk-Moscow, 2001.

———. *Svita rossiiskikh imperatorov: entsiklopediia biografii*. 2 vols. Krasnoiarsk-Moscow, 2005.

Fedotoff White, D. *Survival Through War and Revolution in Russia*. Philadelphia, 1939.

Fel'shtinskii, Iurii. *Krasnyi terror v gody Grazhdanskoi voiny: po materialam Osoboi sledstvennoi komissii po rassledovaniiu zlodeianii bol'shevikov*. London, 1992.

———, and G. I. Cherniavskii. "Krasnyi terror v gody grazhdanskoi voiny. Po materialam Osoboi sledstvennoi komissii." *Voprosy istorii* 7–9 (2001).

Fen, Elisaveta. *Remember Russia*. London, 1973.

Figes, Orlando. *Peasant Russia, Civil War: The Volga Countryside in Revolution, 1917–1921*. Oxford, U.K., 1989.

———. *A People's Tragedy: The Russian Revolution, 1891–1924*. London, 1996.

———, and Boris Kolonitskii. *Interpreting the Russian Revolution: The Language and Symbols of 1917*. New Haven, 1999.

Fischer, George. *Soviet Opposition to Stalin: A Case Study in World War II*. Cambridge, Mass., 1952.

Fitzpatrick, Sheila. "Ascribing Class: The Construction of Social Identity in Soviet Russia." *Journal of Modern History* 50, no. 4 (1993).

———. *Tear Off the Masks!: Identity and Imposture in Twentieth-Century Russia*. Princeton, N.J., 2005.

———, ed. *Russia in the Era of NEP: Explorations in Soviet Society and Culture*. Bloomington, Ind., 1991.

————, ed. *Stalinism: New Directions*. New York, 2000.

————, and Yuri Slezkine, eds. *In the Shadow of Revolution: Life Stories of Russian Women from 1917 to the Second World War*. Princeton, N.J., 2000.

Foteeva, E. "Coping with Revolution: The Experiences of Well-to-Do Russian Families." In *On Living Through Soviet Russia*, ed. D. Bertaux, P. Thompson, and A. Rotkirch. London, 2004.

Francis, David R. *Russia from the American Embassy. April 1916–November 1928*. New York, 1922.

Fuller, William C. *The Foe Within: Fantasies of Treason and the End of Imperial Russia*. Ithaca, N.Y., 2006.

Gagarin, Marie. *Reminiscences of Old Russia*. Hartford, Conn., 1951.

Gagarine, Marie. *From Stolnoy to Spartanburg: The Two Worlds of a Former Russian Princess*. Columbia, S.C., 1971.

Galitzine, Alexandre, ed. *The Princes Galitzine: Before 1917—and Afterwards*. Washington, D.C., 2002.

Galitzine, Irina. *Spirit to Survive: The Memoirs of Princess Nicholas Galitzine*. London, 1976.

———— [Irina Golitsyna]. *Vospominaniia o Rossii: 1900–1932*. Moscow, 2005.

Galitzine, Tatiana. *The Russian Revolution: Childhood Recollections*. Princeton, N.J., 1972.

Galitzine, Vera. *Princesse Véra Galitzine: réminiscences d'une émigrée, 1865–1920*. Paris, 1925.

Gavriil, Konstantinovich. *V Mramornom dvortse: iz khronik nashei sem'i*. St. Petersburg, 1993.

Geifman, Anna. *Thou Shalt Kill: Revolutionary Terrorism in Russia, 1894–1917*. Princeton, N.J., 1993.

Gershtein, Emma. *Moscow Memoirs*, tr. and ed. John Crowfoot. London, 2003.

Getty, J. Arch, and Oleg V. Naumov. *Road to Terror: Stalin and the Self-Destruction of the Bolsheviks, 1932–1939*. New Haven, 1999.

————. *Yezhov: The Rise of Stalin's "Iron Fist."* New Haven, 2008.

Gill, Graeme. *Peasants and Government in the Russian Revolution*. New York, 1979.

Gipius, Ziniada. "Iz nebytiia." *Nashe nasledie* 6 (1991).

Gladkov, Fedor. *Cement*, tr. A. S. Arthur and C. Ashleigh. London, 1929.

Glenny, Michael, and Norman Stone, eds. *The Other Russia*. New York, 1990.

Golder, Frank. *War, Revolution, and Peace in Russia: The Passages of Frank Golder, 1914–1927*, comp., ed., and intro. Terrence Emmons and Bertrand Patenaude. Stanford, Calif, 1992.

Golinkov, David. *Krakh vrazheskogo podpol'ia. (Iz istorii bor'by s kontrrevoliutsiei v Sovetskoi Rossii v 1917–1924 gg.)* Moscow, 1971.

Golitsyn, A. D. *Vospominaniia*. Moscow, 2008.

Golitsyn, I. V. "Otets i ego zapiski." *Iunost'* 2 (2003).

Golitsyn, K. N. *Zapiski*. Moscow, 1997.

Golitsyn, Mikhail. *Petrovskoe: ocherk*. St. Petersburg, 1912.

Golitsyn, M. V. *Mozaika moei zhizni*. Moscow, 2008.

Golitsyn, M. V. *Moi vospominaniia, 1873–1917*. Moscow, 2007.

Golitsyn, Sergei V. *Zapiski utselevshego*. Moscow, 2006.

Golitsyn, V. M. *Dnevnik 1917–1918 godov*. Moscow, 2008.

———. "Moskva i ee zhitelei 50-kh godov XIX stoletiia." *Moskovskii zhurnal* 9–11 (1991).

Golitsyn, V. M. "Zapiski khudozhnika Vladimira Mikhailovicha Golitsyna (1922–43)," *Iunost'* 2 (2003).

Golitsyna, N. *Golitsyny (Mikhailovichi)*. Moscow, 2004.

Golitsyna, Sof'ia N. "Iz vospominanii." *Moskovskii zhurnal* 4–5 (1995).

Gorsuch, Anne. *Youth in Revolutionary Russia: Enthusiasts, Bohemians, Delinquents*. Bloomington, Ind., 2000.

Grabbe, Paul. *Windows on the River Neva: A Memoir*. New York, 1977.

Grech, A. N. *Venok usad'bam*. Moscow, 2006.

Grenzer, Andreas. *Adel und Landbesitz im ausgehenden Zarenreich: Der russische Landadel zwischen Selbstbehauptung und Anpassung nach Aufhebung der Leibeigenschaft*. Stuttgart, 1995.

Gurko, V. *Features and Figures of the Past: Government and Opinion in the Reign of Nicholas II*. Stanford, Calif., 1939.

Haimson, L. H. *Russia's Revolutionary Experience, 1905–1917: Two Essays*. New York, 2005.

———, ed. *The Politics of Rural Russia, 1905–1914*. Bloomington, Ind., 1979.

Hall, Coryne. *Little Mother of Russia: A Biography of the Empress Marie Feodorovna (1847–1928)*. New York, 2001.

Hamburg, G. M. *Politics of the Russian Nobility, 1881–1905*. New Brunswick, N.J., 1984.

Hardeman, Hilde. *Coming to Terms with the Soviet Regime*. DeKalb, Ill., 1994.

Heretz, Leonid. *Russia on the Eve of Modernity: Popular Religion and Traditional Culture Under the Last Tsar*. Cambridge, U.K., 2008.

Horsbrugh-Porter, Anna, ed. *Memories of Revolution: Russian Women Remember*. New York, 1993.

Hughes, Lindsey. *Sophia, Regent of Russia: 1657–1704*. New Haven, 1990.

Hullinger, Edwin. *The Reforging of Russia*. London, 1925.

Iakovlev, Ia. *Voina krest'ian s pomeshchikami v 1917 godu (vospominanii krest'ian)*. Moscow, 1926.

Ignat'ev, A. *50 let v stroiu*. Moscow, 1950.

Ignatieff, Michael. *The Russian Album*. New York, 1987.

Igritskii, I. "Bor'ba za zemliu v 1917 g. (Po Kazanskoi gubernii)." *Krasnyi arkhiv* 5 (1936).

———. *1917 god v derevne: vospominaniia krest'ian*. Moscow, 1967.

Iudin, Andrei, and Svetlana Iudina. *Zamok Sheremetevykh: zolotaia mechta dvorianstva*. Nizhnii Novgorod, 2007.

Iusupov, F. *Memuary: v dvukh knigakh*. Moscow, 1998.

Iusupovskii dvorets: Dvorianskie osobniaki. Istoriia roda, usad'by i kollektsii. St. Petersburg, 1999.

Ivanov, V. A. "Operatsiia 'byvshie liudi' v Leningrade (fevral'-mart 1935g.)." *Novyi chasovoi: russkii voenno-istoricheskii zhurnal* 6–7 (1998).

———. "Byvshie liudi." *Rodina* 4 (1999).

Jansen, Marc, and Nikita Petrov. *Stalin's Loyal Executioner. People's Commissar Nikolai Ezhov, 1895–1940*. Stanford, Calif., 2002.

"K istorii provedeniia v zhizn' Leninskogo dekreta o zemle." *Krasnyi arkhiv* 4–5 (1938).

Kamenskii, N. *Deviatyi vek na sluzhbe Rossii—iz istorii roda grafov Kamenskikh*. Moscow, 2004.

Kaminski, Andrzej J. *Konzentrationslager 1896 bis heute: Eine Analyse*. Stuttgart, 1982.

Kantor, Iuliia. *Voina i mir Mikhaila Tukhachevskogo*. Moscow, 2005.

Karnishina, L. M. "Blagotvoritel'naia deiatel'nost' E. P. i S. D. Sheremetevykh." *Ostaf'evskii sbornik* 8 (2002).

———. "Vozvrashchaias' k napechatannomu: Baron Zhosef de Baye." *Ostaf'evskii sbornik* 9 (2004).

———. "Zhizn' i deiatel'nost' P. S. Sheremeteva v dokumentakh i materialakh Rossiiskogo gosudarsvtennogo istoricheskogo arkhiva (Sankt-Peterburg)." *Ostaf'evskii sbornik* 11–12 (2009).

Kaufman, S. *Pervaia Turandot: kniga o zhizni i tvorchestve narodnoi artistki SSSR Tsetselii L'vovny Mansurovoi*. Moscow, 1986.

Khaustov, Vladimir, and Lennart Samuelson. *Stalin, NKVD i repressii 1936–38 gg.* Moscow , 2009.

Khitun, Sergei. *Dvorianskie porosiata*. Sacramento, Calif., 1974.

Khoziaeva i gosti usad'by Viazemy: materialy Golitsynskikh chtenii. Nos. 1–14. Bol'shie Viazemy, 1995–2007.

Kimerling, E. "Civil Rights and Social Policy in Soviet Russia, 1918–1936." *Russian Review* 41, no. 1 (1982).

King, Greg. *The Court of the Last Tsar*. Hoboken, N.J., 2006.

———, and Penny Wilson. *The Fate of the Romanovs*. Hoboken, N.J., 2003.

Kireev, A. A. *Dnevnik, 1905–1910*, ed. K. A. Solov'ev. Moscow, 2010.

Kir'ianov, Iu. *Pravye partii v Rossii, 1911–1917*. Moscow, 2001.

Kiriushina, Z. E. "Stranitsy istorii muzeia-usad'by 'Ostaf'ievo' (1918–1930)." *Ostaf'evskii sbornik* 11–12 (2009).

Kiselev, N. *Sredi peredvizhnikov: Vospominaniia syna khudozhnika*. Leningrad, 1976.

Khlevniuk, Oleg V. *The History of the Gulag: From Collectivization to the Great Terror*, tr. Vadim A. Staklo. New Haven, 2004. Foreword by Robert Conquest.

———. *Master of the House. Stalin and His Inner Circle*. New Haven, 2008.

Kleinmikhel, M. *Memories of a Shipwrecked World, Being the Memoirs of Countess Kleinmichel*. New York, 1923.

Klement'ev, Vasilii. *V bol'shevitskoi Moskve, 1918–1920*. Moscow, 1998.

Klier, John, and Shlomo Lambroza, eds. *Pogroms: Anti-Jewish Violence in Modern Russian History*. Cambridge, U.K., 1992.

"Kniaz' G. E. L'vov v Ekaterinburgskoi tiur'me." *Istoricheskii arkhiv* 2 (2002).

Kokovtsov, V. N. *Iz moego proshlogo. Vospominaniia, 1903–1919 g.g.* Vol. 2. Paris, 1933.

Kolchin, Peter. *Unfree Labor: American Slavery and Russian Serfdom*. Cambridge, Mass., 1987.

Kolonitskii, Boris. "Antibourgeois Propaganda and Anti-Burzhui Consciousness of the February Revolution." *Russian Review* 53, no. 2 (1994).

Konchin, E. *Emissary vosemnadtsatogo goda.* Moscow, 1981.

———. *Revoliutsiei prizvannye: rasskazy o moskovskikh emissarakh.* Moscow, 1988.

Korelin, A. P., ed. *Ob"edinennoe dvorianstvo: S"ezdy upolnomochennykh gubernskikh dvorianskikh obshchestv.* 3 vols. Moscow, 2001.

Korelin, Avenir. *Dvorianstvo v poreformennoi Rossii 1861–1904 gg: Sostav, chislennost', korporativnaia organizatsiia.* Moscow, 1979.

Korostowetz, W. *Seed and Harvest.* London, 1931.

Kosik, O. V. *Molitva vsekh spaset: materialy k zhizneopisaniiu sviatitelia Afanasiia, episkopa Kovrovskogo.* Moscow, 2000.

Koval', L. M. *Kniaz' Vasilii Dmitrievich Golitsyn i Rumiantsevskii muzei.* Moscow, 2007.

Kovaleva, M. D. *Staraia moskva grafa Sergeia Sheremeteva.* Moscow, 2003.

Kovalevskii, N. F. *Istoriia gosudarstva Rossiiskogo. Zhizneopisaniia znamenitykh voennykh deiatelei xviii-nachala xx veka.* Moscow, 1997.

Kovalevskii, Petr. *Dnevniki. 1918–1922.* St. Petersburg, 2001.

Krasko, Alla. "Graf P. S. Sheremetev kak istorik i genealog." In *Kul'turnoe nasledstvie rossiiskoi emigratsii, 1917–1940,* ed. E. P. Chelisheva. Vol. 1. Moscow, 1994.

———. "Ob odnom izdatel'skom prokete grafa P. S. Sheremeteva." In *Knizhnoe delo v Rossii vo vtoroi polovine XIX–nachale XX veka.* Vol. 8. St. Petersburg, 1996.

———. *Tri veka gorodskoi usad'by grafov Sheremetevykh. Liudi i sobytiia.* Moscow, 2009.

Kriven'kii, V. V. *Politicheskie deiateli Rossii 1917. Biograficheskii slovar'.* Moscow, 1993.

Kshesinskaia, Matil'da. *Vospominaniia.* Moscow, 1992.

Kuz'mina, Irina, and Aleksei Lubkov. *Kniaz' Shakhovskoi. Put' russkogo liberala.* Moscow, 2008.

Lagutina, E. I., and S. A. Malyshkin. "Sud'ba arkhiva muzeia-usad'by Ostankino." *Russkaia usad'ba* 1 (1994).

Lang, David M. *The First Russian Radical: Alexander Radishchev (1749–1802).* London, 1959.

Leggett, George. *The Cheka: Lenin's Political Police.* New York, 1987.

Lenin, V. I. *Polnoe sobranie sochinenii.* 2nd ed. 55 vols. Moscow, 1971–75.

Lenoe, Matthew E. *The Kirov Murder and Soviet History.* New Haven, 2010.

Léonida, Grand Duchess of Russia. *Chaque matin est une grâce.* Paris, 2000.

Levitskii, V. "Pravyia partii." In *Obshchestvennoe dvizhenie v Rossii v nachale XX veka.* Vol. 3. St. Petersburg, 1914.

Libedinskaia, Lidiia. *"Zelenaia lampa" i mnogoe drugoe.* Moscow, 2000.

Lieven, Dominic. *Russia's Rulers Under the Old Regime.* New Haven, Conn., 1989.

———. *The Aristocracy in Europe, 1815–1914.* New York, 1993.

———. "The Elites." In *The Cambridge History of Russia.* Vol. 2, ed. Dominic Lieven. Cambridge, U.K., 2006.

Likhachev, Dmitrii. *Vospominaniia.* St. Petersburg, 1995.

———. *Reflections on the Russian Soul: A Memoir.* New York, 2000.

Lincoln, W. Bruce. *In War's Dark Shadow. The Russians Before the Great War.* New York, 1983.

———. *Passage Through Armageddon: The Russians in War and Revolution, 1914–1918.* New York, 1994.

———. *Red Victory. A History of the Russian Civil War, 1918–1921.* New York, 1989.

Lindenmeyr, Adele. "The First Soviet Political Trial: Countess Sofia Panina Before the Petrograd Revolutionary Tribunal." *Russian Review* 60, no. 4 (2001).

Livshin, A. Ia.; I. B. Orlov; and O. V. Khlevniuk, eds. *Pis'ma vo vlast' 1928–1939: Zaiavleniia, zhaloby, donosy, pis'ma v gosudarstvennye struktury i sovetskim vozhdiam.* Moscow, 2002.

Lobanov-Rostovsky, Andrei. *The Grinding Mill: Reminiscences of War and Revolution in Russia, 1913–1920.* New York, 1935.

Luckett, Richard. *The White Generals: An Account of the White Movement and the Russian Civil War.* Edinburgh, 1971.

L'vov, G. E. *Vospominaniia*, comp. N. V. Vyrubov. Moscow, 1998.

L'vova, A. P., and I. A. Bochkareva. *Rod L'vovykh.* Torzhok, 2004.

Lyons, Eugene. *Assignment in Utopia.* New York, 1937.

Madariaga, Isabel de. *Russia in the Age of Catherine the Great.* New Haven, 1981.

Makarov, V., and V. Khristoforov, eds. *Vysylka vmesto rasstrela. Deportatsiia intelligentsii v dokumentakh VChK-GPU, 1921–1923.* Moscow, 2005.

Manning, Roberta. *The Crisis of the Old Order in Russia: Gentry and Government.* Princeton, N.J., 1982.

Marchenko, Nonna. *Byt i nravy pushkinskogo vremeni.* St. Petersburg, 2005.

Marullo, Thomas. *Ivan Bunin: Russian Requiem, 1885–1920: A Portrait from Letters, Diaries, and Fiction.* Chicago, 1993.

"Mart-Mai 1917 g." *Krasnyi arkhiv* 2 (1927)

Martov, L., ed. *Obshchestvennoe dvizhenie v Rossii v nachale XX veka.* Vol. 3. St. Petersburg, 1914.

Mawdsley, Evan. *The Russian Civil War.* Edinburgh, 2008.

Mayer, Arno J. *The Furies: Violence and Terror in the French and Russian Revolutions.* Princeton, N.J., 2000.

McConnell, Allen. *A Russian Philosophe: Alexander Radishchev, 1749–1802.* The Hague, 1964.

McLoughlin, Barry, and Kevin McDermott, eds. *Stalin's Terror: High Politics and Mass Repression in the Soviet Union.* New York, 2003.

McMeekin, Sean. *History's Greatest Heist: The Looting of Russia by the Bolsheviks.* New Haven, 2009.

Meiendorf, M. F. *Vospominaniia.* Valley Cottage, N.Y., 1990.

Menzies, Grant. "A Certain Vision of Truth." *Atlantis Magazine: In the Courts of Memory* (n.d.).

Mering, Berta. "Politicheskii krasnyi krest v Butyrskoi tiur'me." *Novyi zhurnal* 175 (1989).

Merridale, Catherine. *Night of Stone: Death and Memory in Russia.* London, 2000.

Meshcherskaya, Ekaterina. *A Russian Princess Remembers: The Journey from the Tsars to Glasnost.* New York, 1989.

Meyendorff, Stella. *Through Terror to Freedom: The Dramatic Story of an English Woman's Life and Adventures in Russia Before, During & After the Revolution.* London, 1929.

Mikhailov, N. A. *Pavel Korin.* Moscow, 1982.

Mishkevich, G. I. *Doktor zamechatel'nykh nauk: zhizn' i tvorchestvo Iakova Isidorovicha Perel'mana.* Moscow, 1986.

Mohrenschildt, Dmitri von, ed. *The Russian Revolution of 1917: Contemporary Accounts.* New York, 1971.

"Moskva i ee zhiteli 50-kh godov xix stoletiia." *Moskovskii zhurnal* 10–11 (1991).

Muggeridge, Malcolm. *Winter in Moscow.* Boston, 1934.

———. *Like It Was: The Diaries of Malcolm Muggeridge*, sel. and ed. John Bright-Holmes. London, 1981.

Muratov, N. E.; L. Iu. Mukhamedova; E. V. Oleinichenko; and E. Iu. Polishchuk. *Rod. Sem'ia. Otechestvo.* Moscow, 2009.

Musin-Pushkin, Vladimir. "Kniga o schast'e." *Iskusstvo kino* 2–3 (1992).

Muzeu i vlast'. Gosudarstvennaia politika v oblasti muzeinogo dela (XVIII–XX vv). Moscow, 1991.

Nabokov, Nicolas. *Bagázh: Memoirs of a Russian Cosmopolitan.* New York, 1975.

Nabokov, Vladimir. *Speak, Memory: An Autobiography Revisited.* New York, 1966.

Naryshkin-Kurakin, Elizabeth. *Under Three Tsars: The Memoirs of the Lady-in-Waiting, Elizabeth Narishkin-Kurakin*, ed. René Füelöp-Miller, tr. Julia Loesser. New York, 1931.

Nicholas II, Emperor of Russia. *Dnevnik imperatora Nikolaia II.* Berlin, 1923.

———. *The Complete Wartime Correspondence of Tsar Nicholas II and the Empress Alexandra: April 1914–March 1917*, ed. Joseph Fuhrmann. Westport, Conn., 1999.

Nikolai Mikhailovich, Velikii kniaz'. "Pis'mo iz zatocheniia." *Nashe nasledie* 2, no. 25 (1992).

Nikulin, Lev. *Mertvaia zyb'.* Moscow, 1991.

Nove, Alec. *An Economic History of the USSR.* New York, 1984.

Obolensky, Dimitri. *Bread of Exile: A Russian Family.* London, 1999.

Obolensky, Petr Aleksandrovich. "Semeinye zapiski." *Novyi zhurnal* 174–77 (1989).

Obolensky, Serge. *One Man in His Time: The Memoirs of Serge Obolensky.* New York, 1958.

Obolensky, V. *Moia zhizn', moi sovremenniki.* Paris, 1988.

Obshchestvo izuchenie russkoi usad'by. *Russkaia usad'ba: sbornik Obshchestva izucheniia russkoi usad'by.* Moscow-Rybinsk, 1994.

Odom, Anne, and Wendy R. Salmond, eds. *Treasures into Tractors: The Selling of Russia's Cultural Heritage, 1918–1938.* Special issue of *Canadian-American Slavic Studies* 43, nos. 1–4 (2009).

Okhrana i restavratsiia arkhitekturnogo naslediia Rossii. Organizatsionno-pravovye i ekonomicheskie problemy. Moscow, 2000.

Olitskaia, E. *Moi vospominaniia.* [Frankfurt am Main], 1971.

Osipova, Taisiia. *Klassovaia bor'ba v derevne v period podgotovki i provedeniia Velikoi Oktiabr'skoi sotsialisticheskoi revoliutsii*. Moscow, 1974.

Osokina, E. A. *Our Daily Bread: Socialist Distributions and the Art of Survival in Stalin's Russia, 1927–1941*, tr. Kate S. Transchel and Greta Bucher. Armonk, N.Y., 2001.

——. *Zoloto dlia industrializatsii: "TORGSIN."* Moscow, 2009.

Osorgin, Mikhail. *Vremena: avtobiograficheskoe povestvovanie, romany*. Moscow, 1989.

——. *Zametki starogo knigoeda. Vospominaniia*. Moscow, 2007.

P. Korin. *Izbrannye proizvedeniia*. Moscow, 1985.

Paléologue, Maurice. *An Ambassador's Memoirs*. 3 vols. New York, 1924–25.

Paley, Princess. *Memories of Russia, 1916–1919*. London, 1924.

Palmer, James. *The Bloody White Baron: The Extraordinary Story of the Russian Nobleman Who Became the Last Khan of Mongolia*. New York, 2009.

Panin, Dmitrii. *Zapiski sologdina*. Frankfurt am Main, 1973.

Pares, Bernard. *My Russian Memoirs*. London, 1931.

Patenaude, Bertrand. *The Big Show in Bololand: The American Relief Expedition to Soviet Russia in the Famine of 1921*. Stanford, Calif., 2002.

Patterson, Michelle Jane. "Moscow Chekists During the Civil War, 1918–1921." M.A. thesis, Simon Fraser University, 1991.

Payne, Robert. *The Life and Death of Trotsky*. London, 1978.

Perry, John, and Constantine Pleshakov. *The Flight of the Romanovs: A Family Saga*. New York, 1999.

Peters, Ia. "Vospominaniia o rabote v VChK v pervyi god revoliutsii." *Proletarskaia revoliutsiia* 10, no. 33 (1924).

Peters, Tat'iana. *Znakom'tes': kniaz'ia Golitsyny: sbornik istoriko-biografichaskikh ocherkov na osnove neizvestnykh arkhivnykh istochnikov (na frantsuzskom i russkom iazykakh)*. Moscow, 2006.

Pethybridge, Roger. *The Spread of the Russian Revolution: Essays on 1917*. London, 1972.

——. *The Social Prelude to Stalinism*. London, 1974.

——. *One Step Backwards, Two Steps Forward: Soviet Society and Politics in the New Economic Policy*. Oxford, U.K., 1990.

Pipes, Richard, *The Russian Revolution*. New York, 1990.

——, ed. *The Unknown Lenin: From the Secret Archive*. New Haven, 1998.

Podbolotov, S. "Monarchists Against Their Monarch: The Rightists' Criticism of Tsar Nicholas II." *Russian History* 31, nos. 1–2 (2004).

Pokrovskii, M., ed. "Politicheskoe polozhenie Rossii nakanune Fevral'skoi revoliutsii v zhandarskom osveshchenii." *Krasnyi arkhiv* 17 (1926).

Poliakova, M. A. "Usadebnaia kul'tura i sotsial'nye potriaseniia v Rossii v dvadtsatye gody XX veka." In *Russkaia usad'ba na poroge XXI veka. Khmelitskii sbornik*. Vol. 3. Smolensk, 2001.

Polovtsov, P. *Glory and Downfall. Reminiscences of a Russian General Staff Officer*. London, 1935.

Polunov, Alexander. *Russia in the Nineteenth Century: Autocracy, Reform, and Social Change, 1814–1914*, ed. G. Owen and Larissa G. Zakharova, tr. Marshall S. Shatz. Armonk, N.Y., 2005.

Pomper, Philip. *Lenin's Brother: The Origins of the October Revolution*. New York, 2010.

———. *The Russian Revolutionary Intelligentsia*. Arlington Heights, Ill., 1970.

Ponafidine, Emma Cochrane. *Russia—My Home: An Intimate Record of Personal Experiences Before, During, and After the Bolshevist Revolution*. Indianapolis, 1931.

Preston, Thomas. *Before the Curtain*. London, 1950.

Price, M. *My Reminiscences of the Russian Revolution*. London, 1921.

Prishvin, M. M. *Dnevniki, 1914–1917; 1930–1931; 1936–1937; 1938–1939*. St. Petersburg, 2006–10.

———, and V. D. Prishvina. *My s toboi. Dnevnik liubvi*, ed. L. A. Riazanova. Moscow, 1996.

Pushkarev, S. *Vospominaniia istorika: 1905–1945*. Moscow, 1999.

Putiatina, Ol'ga. *War and Revolution: Excerpts from the Letters and Diaries of the Countess Olga Poutiatine*, tr. and ed. George Alexander Lensen. Tallahassee, Fla., 1971.

Rabinowitch, Alexander. *The Bolsheviks Come to Power: The Revolution of 1917 in Petrograd*. New York, 1976.

Raeff, Marc. *Origins of the Russian Intelligentsia: The Eighteenth-Century Nobility*. New York, 1966.

———. "The Russian Nobility in the Eighteenth and Nineteenth Centuries: Trends and Comparisons." In *The Nobility in Russia and Eastern Europe*, ed. Ivo Banac and Paul Bushkovitch. New Haven, 1983.

Raevskii, Sergei. *Piat' vekov Raevskikh*. Moscow, 2005.

Raleigh, Donald J. "The Russian Civil War 1917–1922." In *The Cambridge History of Russia*. Vol. 3, ed. Ronald Grigor Suny. Cambridge, U.K., 2006.

Rappaport, Helen. *Conspirator: Lenin in Exile*. New York, 2009.

Rawson, Don. "The Union of the Russian People, 1905–1907: A Study of the Radical Right." Ph.D. dissertation. University of Washington, 1971.

Raymond, Boris. *The Russian Diaspora, 1917–1941*. Lanham, Md., 2000.

Reed, John. *Ten Days that Shook the World*. New York, 1935.

Rendle, Matthew. "Identity, Conflict and Compromise: The Russian Nobility, 1917–1924." Ph.D. dissertation. University of Exeter, 2003.

———. "Family, Kinship and Revolution: The Russian Nobility, 1917–1923." *Family and Community History* 8 (2005).

———. "The Symbolic Revolution: The Russian Nobility and February 1917." *Revolutionary Russia* 18, no. 1 (2005).

———. "Conservatism and Revolution: The All-Russian Union of Landowners, 1916–18." *Slavonic and East European Review* 84, no. 3 (July 2006).

———. "The Officer Corps, Professionalism, and Democracy in the Russian Revolution." *Historical Journal* 51 (2008).

———. "The Problems of 'Becoming Soviet': Former Nobles in Soviet Society, 1917–41." *European History Quarterly* 38, no. 1 (2008).

———. *Defenders of the Motherland: The Tsarist Elite in Revolutionary Russia*. Oxford, U.K., 2009.

Reswick, William. *I Dreamt Revolution*. Chicago, 1952.

Riasanovsky, Nicholas V., and Mark D. Steinberg. *A History of Russia*, 7th ed. New York, 2005.

Rimmel, L. A. "A Microcosm of Terror, or Class Warfare in Leningrad: The March 1935 Exile of 'Alien Elements.'" *Jahrbücher für Geschichte Osteuropas* 48, no. 4 (2000).

Robien, Louis. *The Diary of a Diplomat in Russia, 1917–1918*. New York, 1970.

Robinson, G. T. *Rural Russia Under the Old Regime*. Berkeley–Los Angeles, 1960.

Rodzianko, Aleksandr. *Vospominaniia o Sievero-Zapadnoi armii*. Berlin, 1920.

Rodzianko, E. F. *Perelomy zhizni*. Valley Cottage, N.Y., 1991.

Rodzianko, Paul. *Tattered Banners: An Autobiography*. London, 1939.

Rogger, Hans. *Russia in the Age of Modernisation and Revolution, 1881–1917*. New York, 1983.

———. *Jewish Policies and Right-Wing Politics in Imperial Russia*. Berkeley, Calif., 1986.

Roosevelt, Priscilla. *Life on the Russian Country Estate: A Social and Cultural History*. New Haven, 1995.

Rowan-Hamilton, Norah. *Under the Red Star*. London, 1930.

Rudnev, Sergei. *Pri vechernikh ogniakh: vospominaniia*. Newtonville, Mass., 1978.

"Russkaia usad'ba i ee sud'by. Kruglyi stol." *Otechestvennaia istoriia* 5 (2002).

Russkaia usad'ba XVIII-nachala XX vekov: problemy izucheniia, restavratsii i muzeefikatsii. Iaroslavl', 2007.

Ryan, James. "'Revolution Is War': The Development of the Thought of V. I. Lenin on Violence, 1899–1907." *Slavonic and East European Review* 89, no. 2 (April 2011).

Sablina, V. V., comp. *Sabliny: gody, sobytiia, liudi*. St. Petersburg, 2007.

Savel'eva, V. V., comp. *Kavkazskie Mineral'nye Vody*. Moscow, 1987.

Sayn-Wittgenstein [Sain-Vitgenshtein], E. *Dnevnik, 1914–1918*. Paris, 1986.

———. *Als unsere Welt unterging: Tagebuch der Prinzessin Katherina Sayn-Wittgenstein aus den Tagen der Russischen Revolution*. Berlin, 1984.

Schakovskoy, Zinaïda. *The Privilege Was Mine. A Russian Princess Returns to the Soviet Union*. London, 1959.

Schapiro, Leonard. *The Communist Party of the Soviet Union*. New York, 1971.

Schmemann, Serge. *Echoes of a Native Land*. New York, 1997.

Sebag Montefiore, Simon. *Stalin: The Court of the Red Tsar*. New York, 2004.

Serge, Victor. *Year One of the Russian Revolution*, tr. and ed. Peter Sedgwick. New York, 1972.

Service, Robert, ed. *Society and Politics in the Russian Revolution*. Basingstoke, U.K., 1992.

———. *Spies and Commissars. Bolshevik Russia and the West*. London, 2011.

———. *Trotsky: A Biography*. London, 2009.

Sevost'ianov, Grigorii, ed. *"Sovershenno sekretno": Lubianka—Stalinu o polozhenii v strane (1922–1934 gg)*. 8 vols. Moscow, 2001–08.

Shalamov, Varlam. *Vishera: antiroman*. Moscow, 1989.

Shapovalov, Veronica. *Remembering the Darkness: Women in Soviet Prisons*. Lanham, Md., 2001.

Shchepetov, K. N. *Krepostnoe pravo v votchinakh Sheremetevykh*. Moscow, 1947.

Shcherbatov, Aleksei. *Pravo na proshloe*. Moscow, 2005.

Shchulepnikova, E. I. "Gibel' arkhivov i bibliotek pomeshchech'ikh usadeb v 1917–1920 godakh." *Russkaia usad'ba* 1 (1994).

Shearer, David R. "Stalinism, 1928–1940." In *The Cambridge History of Russia*. Vol. 3, ed. Ronald Grigor Suny. Cambridge, U.K., 2006.

———. *Policing Stalin's Socialism: Repression and Social Order in the Soviet Union, 1924–1953*. New Haven, 2009.

Sheremetev, D. S. *Iz vospominanii o gosudare Imperatore Nikolae II*. Brussels, 1936.

Sheremetev, Pavel. *Zametki: 1900–1905*. Moscow, 1905.

Sheremetev, S. D. *Vozdvizhenskii naugol'nyi dom sto let nazad*. 2 pts. Moscow, 1899–1902.

———. *Domashniaia starina*. Moscow, 1900.

———. *Moskovskiia vospominaniia*. Moscow, 1901.

———. "Otryvki iz 'dnevnikov'," ed. L. I. Shokhin. *Rossiiskii arkhiv* 6 (1995); 1 (1996).

———. *Memuary grafa S. D. Sheremeteva*. Moscow, 2001.

Sheremeteva, O. G. *Dnevnik i Vospominaniia*, ed. G. I. Vzdornov. Moscow, 2005.

Shipov, Dmitrii. *Vospominaniia i dumy o perezhitom*. Moscow, 1918.

Shkuro, Andrei. *Zapiski belogo partizana*. Buenos Aires, 1961.

———. *Tragediia kazachestva*. Moscow, 1994.

Shoumatoff, Alex. *Russian Blood: A Family Chronicle*. New York, 1982.

Shteinberg, V. A. *Ekab Peters*. Moscow, 1989.

Shtrange, M. M. *Russkoe obshchestvo i frantzuzskaia revoliutsiia, 1789–1794 gg.* Moscow, 1956.

Shumikhin, Sergei. "Konets 'Russkogo Parnasa.'" *Politicheskii zhurnal* 34 (85) (October 17, 2005). Accessed at: http://www.politjournal.ru/index.php?action=Articles&dirid=50&tek=4326&issue=124 on March 17, 2011.

Siljak, Ana. *Angel of Vengeance: The "Girl Assassin," the Governor of St. Petersburg, and Russia's Revolutionary World*. New York, 2008.

Skariatina, Irina. *A World Can End*. New York, 1931.

———. *First to Go Back. An Aristocrat in Soviet Russia*. Indianapolis, 1933.

Skipwirth, Sofka [née Princess Sophy Dolgorouky]. *Sofka: The Autobiography of a Princess*. London, 1968.

Slater, Wendy. *The Many Deaths of Tsar Nicholas II. Relics, Remains, and the Romanovs*. New York, 2007.

Smele, Jonathan D. *Civil War in Siberia. The Anti-Bolshevik Government of Admiral Kolchak, 1918–1920*. Cambridge, U.K., 1996.

Smirnov, M. I., and A. M. Golitsyn, eds. *Sheremetevy. Sbornik materialov*. 3 pts. Moscow, 2000.

Smirnova, T. M. *"Byvshie liudi" Sovetskoi Rossii: strategii vyzhivaniia i puti integratsii, 1917–1936 gody*. Moscow, 2003.

Smirnova, T. V. ". . . *pod pokrov Prepodobnogo*": *ocherki o nekotorykh izvestnykh sem'iakh, zhivshikh v Sergievom Posade v 1920-e gody*. Sergiev Posad, 2007.

Smith, Douglas. *The Pearl: A True Tale of Forbidden Love in Catherine the Great's Russia*. New Haven, 2008.

Smith, Gerald. *D. S. Mirsky to Dorothy Galton: Forty Letters from Moscow (1932–1937)*. Oxford, U.K. 1996.

———. *D. S. Mirsky: A Russian-English Life, 1890–1939*. New York, 2000.

"Soiuz zemel'nykh sobstvennikov v 1917 g." *Krasnyi arkhiv* 2 (1927).

Sollohub, Edith. *The Russian Countess: Escaping Revolutionary Russia*. Exeter, U.K., 2009.

Solov'ev, Iu. B. *Samoderzhavie i dvorianstvo v 1902–1907 gg*. Leningrad, 1981.

Solov'ev, K. A. *Kruzhok "Beseda": V poiskakh novoi politicheskoi real'nosti, 1899–1905*. Moscow, 2009.

Solzhenitsyn, Alexander. *The Gulag Archipelago, 1918–1956. An Experiment in Literary Investigation*, tr. Thomas P. Whitney. 3 vols. London, 1974–78.

St. Just, Maria [Mary Britnev]. *One Woman's Story*. London, 1934.

Stalin, Joseph. *Doklad o proekte Konstitutsii SSSR. Doklad na chrezvychainom VIII Vsesoiuznom s"ezde sovetov 25 noiabria 1936 g*. Leningrad, 1951.

Starodubtseva, Marina. *Krugovorot: vremena i sud'by*. N.p. [Russia], 1997.

Starr, S. Frederick. *Red and Hot: The Fate of Jazz in the Soviet Union, 1917–1980*. New York, 1983.

Steinberg, Mark D., *Voices of Revolution, 1917*. New Haven, 2001.

———, and Vladimir M. Khrustalëv. *The Fall of the Romanovs. Political Dreams and Personal Struggles in a Time of Revolution*. New Haven, 1995.

Stepanov, A. P., and A. A. Ivanov, comps. *Chernaia sotnia: istoricheskaia entsiklopediia*. Moscow, 2008.

Tarasov-Rodionov, A. *February, 1917*. New York, 1931.

Taskina, E. P., comp. *Russkii Kharbin*. Moscow, 1998.

Tatishchev, A. *Zemli i liudi: v gushche pereselencheskogo dvizheniia, 1906–1921*. Moscow, 2001.

Taylor, S. J. *Stalin's Apologist: Walter Duranty, The* New York Times's *Man in Moscow*. New York, 1990.

Terras, Victor. *A Handbook of Russian Literature*. New Haven, 1985.

Thompson, John M. *Russia, Bolshevism, and the Versailles Peace*. Princeton, N.J., 1966.

Tian-Shanskaia, Olga Semyonovna. *Village Life in Late Tsarist Russia*, ed. David L. Ransel. Bloomington, 1993.

Tolstaia-Voeikova, Ol'ga. *Russkaia sem'ia v vodovorote "velikogo pereloma": pis'ma O. A. Tolstoi-Voeikovoi, 1927–1929 gg*. St. Petersburg, 2005.

Tolstoy, Alexandra. *I Worked for the Soviet*. New Haven, 1934.

———. *Out of the Past*. New York, 1981.

Trenin, B. P., comp. *1936–1937 gg. Konveier NKVD. Iz khroniki 'bol'shogo terror' na tomskoi zemle. Sbornik dokumentov i materialov*. Tomsk, 2004.

Trifonov, I. *Klassy i klassovaia bor'ba v SSSR v nachale NEPa, 1921–1923 gg*. Leningrad, 1964.

———. *Likvidatsiia ekspluatorskikh klassov v SSSR*. Moscow, 1975.

Troyat, Henri. *Gorky*, tr. Lowell Blair. London, 1991.

Trubetskaia, Ol'ga. *Kniaz' S. N. Trubetskoi. Vospominaniia sestry*. New York, 1953.

Trubetskoi, A. E. *Rossiia vosprianet*. Moscow, 1996.

Trubetskoi, A. V. *Puti neispovedimy (vospominaniia, 1939–1955 gg)*. Moscow, 1997.

Trubetskoi, E. N. *Iz proshlago: s 12 portretami i illiustratsiami*. Vienna, [192?].

Trubetskoi, G. N. *Gody smut i nadezhd, 1917–1919*. Montreal, 1981.

Trubetskoi, S. E. *Minuvshee*. Paris, 1989.

Trubetskoi, V. S. *Zapiski kirasira*. Moscow, 1991.

———. *A Russian Prince in the Soviet State: Hunting Stories, Letters from Exile, and Military Memoirs*, tr. and ed. Susanne Fusso. Evanston, Ill., 2006.

Tzouliadis, Tim. *The Forsaken: An American Tragedy in Stalin's Russia*. New York, 2008.

Urusova, N. V. *Materinskii plach sviatoi Rusi*. Moscow, 2006.

Urusova, V. "Moi vospominaniia o voine Velikoi i voine grazhdanskoi." *Nashe nasledie* 38 (1996).

Uvarova, Praskov'ia. *Byloe, davno proshedshie schastlivye dni*. Moscow, 2005.

"V ianvare i fevrale 1917 g. Iz donesenii sekretnykh agentov A D Protopov." *Byloe* 13 (July 1918).

"V. P. Sheremetev v Ostaf'eve." Brochure to an Exhibition of the Works of V. P. Sheremetev. Ostafievo, 1990.

Varlamov, Aleksei. *Prishvin*. Moscow, 2003.

———. *Grigory Rasputin-Novyi*. Moscow, 2007.

Vasil'chikov, Boris. *Vospominaniia*. Moscow, 2003.

Vasil'chikov, Illarion. *To, chto mne vspomnilos'—: vospominaniia kniazia Ilariona Sergeevicha Vasil'chikova: iz arkhiva sem'i Vasilchikovykh*. Moscow, 2002.

Vasil'chikov, L. "Petrograd, 1918." *Nashe nasledie* 66 (2003).

Vasilii Sheremtev. Zhivopis. Grafika. Teatral'noe-dekoratsionnoe iskusstvo. Katalog vystavki. Moscow, 1983.

Vida, Lynne. *The Unknown Gulag: The Lost World of Stalin's Special Settlements*. New York, 2007.

Vishnevskii, A. *Perekhvachennye pis'ma: roman-kollazh*. Moscow, 2001.

Volkogonov, Dmitri. *Trotsky: The Eternal Enemy*. London, 1996.

Volkonsky, Sergei. *My Reminiscences*. 2 vols. London, 1925.

Volkov, Oleg. *Vek nadezhd i krushenii*. Moscow, 1989.

———. *Gorodu i miru: povest', pis'ma*. Moscow, 2001.

Volkov, S. *Tragediia russkogo ofitsera*. Moscow, 1999.

Volkov-Muromtsev, N. *Iunost' ot Viaz'my do Feodosii, 1902–1920*. Paris, 1983.

Von Meck, Galina. *As I Remember Them*. London, 1973.

Vyrubova, Anna. *Memories of the Russian Court*. New York, 1923.

Wassiltschikow, Lydia. *Verschwundenes Russland: Die Memoiren der Fürstin Lydia Wassiltschikow, 1886–1919*. Vienna, 1980.

Welch, Frances. *The Russian Court at Sea: The Voyage of the HMS* Marlborough, *April 1919*. London, 2011.

Werth, Nicolas. *Cannibal Island: Death in a Siberian Gulag*. Princeton, N.J., 2007.

White, Stephen, ed. *New Directions in Soviet History*. Cambridge, U.K., 1992.

Williams, Stephanie. *Olga's Story*. London, 2006.

Wirtschafter, Elise. *Social Identity in Imperial Russia*. DeKalb, Ill., 1997.

Witte, Sergei. *The Memoirs of Count Witte*, tr. and ed. Sidney Harcave. Armonk, N.Y., 1990.

Wolkonsky, Peter [S. A. Volkonskaia]. *The Way of Bitterness*. London, 1931.

Woodward, James B. *Ivan Bunin. A Study of His Fiction*. Chapel Hill, N.C., 1980.

Worobec, Christine D. *Peasant Russia. Family and Community in the Post-Emancipation Period*. Princeton, N.J., 1991.

Wrangel, Baron Peter N. *Always with Honour*. New York, 1957.

Zernov, Nicolas. *Na perelome. Tri pokoleniia odnoi sem'i*. Paris, 1970.

———. *Na perelome: tri pokoleniia odnoi moskovskoi sem'i: semeinaia khronika Zernovykh (1812–1921)*. Moscow, 2001.

Zhukov, Iu. N. *Sokhranennye revoliutsii: Okhrana pamiatnikov istorii i kul'utry v Moskve v 1917–1921 godakh*. Moscow, 1985.

———. *Stanovlenie i deiatel'nost' sovetskikh organov okhrany pamiatnikov istorii i kul'tury, 1917–1920 gg*. Moscow, 1989.

Zhuravina, T. *Dvorianskoe gnezdo: Sankt-Peterburg, Angliiskaia naberezhnaia, 10*. St. Petersburg, 2002.

Zinovieff, Elizabeth. *A Princess Remembers: A Russian Life, 1892–1982: Veta Zinovieff: A Personal Reminiscence*. [London], 1997.

Zinovieff, Sofka. *Red Princess: A Revolutionary Life*. London, 2007.

Zubov, V. *Stradnye gody Rossii: Vospominaniia o revoliutsii (1917–1925)*. Munich, 1968.

ACKNOWLEDGMENTS

The idea for this book came over dinner. In the winter of 2005 I was invited to the Connecticut home of Nikita and Maïko Cheremeteff. At the time I was writing a book on Nikita's ancestor Count Nikolai Cheremeteff (Sheremetev) and was keen to meet a direct descendant of my subject. Although Nikita had no long-lost documents or startling family secrets to share, I will never forget the wonderful evening I spent with my hosts: the relaxed conversation, the good food, and the genuinely warm hospitality. Within an hour I felt as if I had known them for years. During dinner Nikita paused briefly and then held up a piece of silverware, something vaguely resembling a small pâté knife. "Douglas," he said to me with a slight grin, "this is all that remains of the Cheremeteff fortune." And then he laughed. The moment lodged in my brain. I remember thinking: What must that have been like for his family, to belong to a distinguished, powerful, and wealthy clan and then suddenly, in the course of a few months, lose everything and be in danger for one's life? Such a sudden and dramatic reversal of fortune seemed difficult to imagine. It must have been horrific to have experienced, yet it seemed to promise a fascinating subject to explore. Soon I knew I had the idea for my next book. I am extremely grateful to Nikita and to Maïko, who passed away in the summer of 2010, for their help and friendship over the years.

I have been fortunate in the course of my work on *Former People* to encounter similar generosity among the diaspora of the Russian nobility.

Whether in Russia, France, England, or the United States, I have been repeatedly astonished by the enthusiasm that has greeted my research. My requests for information were granted in nearly every instance, and I have been moved by so many people's readiness to share with me for this book their most intimate family documents and photographs. Kyra Cheremeteff has been an enormous help. She has made crucial introductions, answered countless questions, read the book in manuscript, offering valuable suggestions and supplying additional information, and has given unflagging support. Catherine Cheremeteff Davison, Nikita's sister, invited me to her home and permitted me to read from her extensive personal library. Nicholas Cheremeteff, Kyra's brother, kindly introduced me to several key people in Moscow. Prascovia Cheremeteff-de Mazières of Rabat, Morocco, graciously wrote to me the details of her family's experiences following the revolution and has been an informative correspondent on all things pertaining to the Sheremetevs and the nobility. I would like to recognize Mrs. Mary Jordan, Roger van Hanwehr, Paul Rodzianko, and Countess Nicholas Bobrinskoy for their comments and suggestions. Larissa Scherbatow kindly sent me a copy of her late husband's book (*Pravo na proshloe*) and his sister's unpublished diary. George Golitzin of California sent me a number of family documents that proved vital in reconstructing the experiences of Alexander and Lyubov Golitsyn and their children. I am extremely grateful to him. The late Peter Tatistcheff kindly permitted me to quote from his father's unpublished memoir, "Crossing the Field." I would also like to thank Eugene and Helen Troubetzkoy, Andrew Kotchoubey, and Sergei Lobanov-Rostovsky for their comments about my research.

In England, I have benefited greatly from the assistance of the descendants of Prince Nikolai Emanuelovich Galitzine. Alexander "Konky" Galitzine shared his knowledge of the family and introduced me to relatives who could be of further help. His brother George Galitzine spent hours showing me his extensive collection of family photographs, some of which he permitted me to use in my book, and he put me in touch with his cousin Liza Heseltine, who generously allowed me to cite her translation of her grandmother's memoirs. Katya Galitzine invited me to her Cotswold home, where I spent a fascinating and fruitful day reading through her family archive. Katya's mother, Jean

Galitzine, opened her home to me as well and allowed me to examine her rich collection of Russian materials. Sonya and Philip Goodman gave me a delightful lunch and shared many fascinating family stories. Alexandre and Christine Galitzine of St. Pierre-lès-Nemours, France, were incredibly helpful. They provided photographs for the book, introduced me to other members of the Golitsyn family, and patiently answered my seemingly infinite questions. They opened their beautiful home to me and my family for lunch and informative talk about Russia and their family. Christine, an expert in Russian art and culture, allowed me to quote from her translation of Princess Zenaida Yusupov's diary, and I have made extensive use of her translations published in the magisterial *Princes Galitzine* (2002), the definitive work on the Golitsyns that she, Alexandre, and several other members of the family labored on for many years.

In Russia, I cannot thank enough Andrei and Tania Golitsyn. They took the time to meet with me on several occasions and did everything possible to help, supplying me with books, offering family documents and photographs, arranging introductions, and critiquing my book in manuscript. I owe them a large debt. Ivan Golitsyn welcomed me to his studio to talk about his family and to show me the items in his personal collection; he has always been ready to answer my many questions. Nikolay Trubetskoy agreed to meet and tell me what he knew of his families' past and, unknown to us both at the time, gave me the ending to my book. His brother Mikhail Trubetskoy provided many family photographs and the unpublished letters of his grandfather and an unpublished portion of his father's memoirs, materials that proved to be of great use. Yevdokia Sheremetev, the sole grandchild of Count Pavel Sheremetev, allowed me to visit her on several occasions and told me much about her family. I also wish to acknowledge the generous assistance of Alexandra Olsufiev, Elizabeth Apraxine, Konstantin and Marianna Smirnov, Mikhail Katin-Yartsev, Yekaterina Lansere, and the Pavlinovs—Varvara, Nikolai, and Sergei.

Mikhail Vladimirovich Golitsyn and his wife, Tamara Pavlovna, deserve special acknowledgment. Although surrounded by boxes in anticipation of a big move to a new apartment in Moscow, they invited me to lunch at short notice and welcomed me with a well-laid table. We talked for several hours—and drank perhaps a few too many vodka toasts—and I left feeling amazed by their youthful spirit, despite their advanced age, and by their sense of optimism, despite the hardships they have faced in their lives. It was a day I shall never forget.

Father Boris Mikhailov helped me immensely with both my previous book and now with *Former People*. For years he gathered information on the Sheremetev family while working as a curator at the Ostankino Estate Museum. He had himself intended to write a book on the fate of the family after 1917 but then gave this up to become an Orthodox priest after the collapse of the Soviet Union. When I called him while on a visit to Moscow in 2009 and mentioned the topic of my new book, he asked if we might meet because he had something he wanted to give me. I was shocked when he showed up carrying two large bags full of his research. He handed it to me and asked me to make good use of it, saying he was glad to know the years he had spent gathering the information had not been wasted. I am humbled by his generous gift.

It is a pleasure to thank the many friends and colleagues who have provided assistance during the course of my research and writing: Nikita Sokolov, Tatiana Safronova, Alexander Bobosov, Aleksei Kovalchuk, Elena Campbell, Ekaterina Pravilova, Igor Khristoforov, Bob Edelman, Mark Steinberg, William Husband, Steve A. Smith, Seymour Becker, Richard Robbins, Golfo Alexopoulos, Glennys Young, Michael Biggins, Anatol Shmelev, Carol Leadenham, Catriona Kelly, Sofia Chuikina, Richard Davies, Sean McMeekin, Susanne Fusso, Ruzica Popovitch-Krekic, Stephanie Lock and Gary Hawkey at iocolor, Eric Lohr, Steve Hanson, April Bodman, Ronald Vroon, Frances Welch, John Bowlt, Randy Steiger and the team at Conflare, Tatiana Enikeeva, Ludmila Syagaeva, Olga Novikova, Galina Kalinina, Olga Solomodenko, Mikhail Loukianov, Marina Kovaleva, Lena Marassinova, Alla Krasko, Maxim Smirnov, Tatiana Chvanova-Leto, Varvara Rakina, Tatiana Smirnova, Tanya Chebotarev, Svetlana Dolgova, Marina Sidorova, Boris Dodonov, Galina Korolyova, Marina Chertilina, Iskender Nurbekov, and Gerold Vzdornov.

For help gathering material I am grateful to Veronika Egorova, Yulia Galper, Dmitry and Arina Belozerov, Yury Nikiforov, and especially Natalya Bolotina, Yelena Matveeva, Yelena Mikhailova, and Mariana Markova. David Cain produced beautiful maps and family trees for the book and was a pleasure to work with. Several colleagues read various drafts of the book and gave me excellent advice on how to improve it: Arch Getty, Lisa Kirschenbaum, Willard Sunderland, Geoffrey Hosking, Priscilla Roosevelt, and Peter Pozefsky.

I am grateful to a number of archives, museums, and libraries and their staffs: the Bakhmeteff Archive at Columbia University; the London Library; the British Library; the University of Washington Libraries; the Russian State Library; the Russian National Library; the Russian State Historical Archive; the Russian State Archive of Literature and Art; the Central State Archive of the Moscow Oblast; the Literary Museum of Moscow; the Kuskovo Estate Museum, the Russian State Archive of Ancient Acts; the State Archive of the Russian Federation; the Russian State Archive of Documentary Films and Photographs; the Hoover Institution Archives; and the Wiltshire and Swindon History Centre.

I benefited from the opportunity to present some of the material in *Former People* at Columbia and Oxford universities. At Columbia, I am especially grateful to Timothy Frye, director of the Harriman Institute, and to Alla Rachkov and Masha Udensiva-Brenner. Cynthia Whittaker, Richard Wortman, and Hilde Hoogenboom attended my talk and offered insightful comments on my research. At Oxford, I would like to thank Andrei and Irina Zorin for their assistance and friendship. Andrew Kahn, also of Oxford University, has been a marvelous source of information and the perfect guide to all things Russian (and English) for a long time.

I would like to thank Melissa Chinchillo, Christy Fletcher, and the employees of Fletcher and Company for their hard work and commitment over the years. I have been exceedingly fortunate to have had Eric Chinski as my editor and am grateful to him for all his encouragement, insight, and enthusiasm. I would like to thank Jonathan Galassi and everyone I have worked with at FSG, especially Eugenie Cha, Gabriella Doob, Jeff Seroy, Kathy Daneman, Katie Freeman, Abby Kagan, Marion Duvert, and Devon Mazzone. Georgina Morley, my U.K. editor at Macmillan, has not only been wonderful to work with but a welcoming friend. I wrote this book at a window overlooking the house where nearly two hundred years ago Thomas Carlyle wrote his famous history of the French Revolution. A historian could hardly ask for better company, although this is just what I was fortunate to receive from so many wonderful friends (too many to name) in London.

While working on this book, I have been constantly reminded of the importance of family. I wish to thank my loving parents, Bill and Annette Smith, Michael and Merdice Ellis, Allyson and Todd Aldrich, Graham Smith, Angela Ellis, Emma Bankhead, Emily and Robert Aldrich, Tara and Elana Smith, and especially Emma and Andrew—my children—to whom *Former People* is dedicated. As always, my greatest debt is to my wife, Stephanie, for her patience, wisdom, and love.

INDEX